ENVIRONMENTAL INTEGRATION IN THE EU'S EXTERNAL RELATIONS

The book examines the integration of environmental protection requirements into EU external relations focusing on unilateral, bilateral and inter-regional instruments, which have been less explored than the multilateral dimension of EU environmental policy. The book also explores for the first time the complex interplay and mutual influences between EU environmental integration initiatives and environmental multilateralism. On the one hand it identifies the legal and other instruments used by the EU to support the implementation of multilateral environmental agreements in third countries (particularly developing ones). On the other hand, it singles out the legal and other tools employed by the EU as a means to build partnerships with third countries in order to influence ongoing multilateral negotiations concerning the environment and sustainable development, or to contribute to the development of new international environmental norms in the absence of such multilateral negotiations. Ultimately, the book traces the significant evolution of, and complex interaction between, the various tools deployed by the EU to integrate environmental concerns in its external relations, with a view to identifying emerging challenges and future directions.

Volume 29 in the series Modern Studies in European Law

Modern Studies in European Law

Recent titles in this series:

Unfair Contract Terms in European Law: A Study in Comparative and EC Law
Paolisa Nebbia

Energy Security: The External Legal Relations of the European Union with Major Oil and Gas Supplying Countries *Sanam S Haghighi*

EU Criminal Law *Valsamis Mitsilegas*

Effective Judicial Protection and the Environmental Impact Assessment Directive in Ireland *Áine Ryall*

Network-Based Governance in EC Law: The Example of EC Competition and EC Communications Law *Maartje de Visser*

Legitimacy in EU Cartel Control *Ingeborg Simonsson*

Mixed Agreements Revisited: The EU and its Member States in the World
Edited by Christophe Hillion and Panos Koutrakos

Reflexive Governance: Redefining the Public Interest in a Pluralistic World
Edited by Olivier De Schutter and Jacques Lenoble

The Impact of EU Law on Minority Rights *Tawhida Ahmed*

Direct Investment, National Champions and EU Treaty Freedoms: From Maastricht to Lisbon *Frank S Benyon*

The Cyprus Issue: The Four Freedoms in a Member State under Siege *Nikos Skoutaris*

The European Union and Global Emergencies: A Law and Policy Analysis
Edited by Antonis Antoniadis, Robert Schütze and Eleanor Spaventa

Public Liability in EU Law: *Brasserie, Bergaderm* and Beyond *Pekka Aalto*

Professional Services in the EU Internal Market: Quality Regulation and Self-Regulation *Tinne Heremans*

Environmental Integration in the EU's External Relations: Beyond Multilateral Dimensions *Gracia Marín Durán and Elisa Morgera*

For the complete list of titles in this series, see
'Modern Studies in European Law' link at
www.hartpub.co.uk/books/series.asp

Environmental Integration in the EU's External Relations

Beyond Multilateral Dimensions

Gracia Marín Durán
and
Elisa Morgera

·HART·
PUBLISHING

OXFORD AND PORTLAND, OREGON
2012

Published in the United Kingdom by Hart Publishing Ltd
16C Worcester Place, Oxford, OX1 2JW
Telephone: +44 (0)1865 517530
Fax: +44 (0)1865 510710
E-mail: mail@hartpub.co.uk
Website: http://www.hartpub.co.uk

Published in North America (US and Canada) by
Hart Publishing
c/o International Specialized Book Services
920 NE 58th Avenue, Suite 300
Portland, OR 97213-3786
USA
Tel: +1 503 287 3093 or toll-free: (1) 800 944 6190
Fax: +1 503 280 8832
E-mail: orders@isbs.com
Website: http://www.isbs.com

British Library Cataloguing in Publication Data
Data Available

ISBN: 978-1-84946-187-0

Typeset by Hope Services, Abingdon
Printed and bound in Great Britain by
CPI Group (UK) Ltd, Croyden CR0 4YY

A Firenze, Pretoria ed Edimburgo

Acknowledgements

This book is the product of a long journey of reflection, which we enthusiastically planned as doctoral students at the European University Institute (EUI) in Florence in 2006 and finally completed at the Edinburgh University School of Law in June 2011, with a crucial stepping-stone at Long Street in Pretoria in 2010. There are certainly many individuals that have inspired and supported us towards the completion of this endeavour, and we remain deeply indebted to each of them individually. In particular, we would like to express our immense gratitude to Prof Bruno de Witte, Prof Marise Cremona and Prof Francesco Francioni at the EUI, for their intellectual guidance and unfailing support throughout the years. In addition, a special debt of gratitude is due to Prof Douglas Brodie, Prof Lesley McAra, Prof Niamh Nic Shuibhne, Dr Rachael Craufurd Smith, and our friends at the Edinburgh University School of Law. Our heartfelt thanks also go to Dr Kati Kulovesi and Dr Annalisa Savaresi, for stimulating exchanges of ideas on critical parts of this book.

Our warm thanks are owed to several other academics for their hospitality and fruitful discussions on our preliminary findings, including: Prof Alessandro Fodella and Prof Antonino Alí, at the Università degli studi di Trento; Prof Anita Rønne and Prof Peter Pagh at the University of Copenhagen; Dr Jacques Hartmann and his colleagues at the Ministry of Foreign Affairs of Denmark; Prof Maxi Schoeman and her colleagues at the University of Pretoria; Fabiano de Andrade Corrêa, Mery Ciacci and the other members of the EUI Working Groups on Environmental Law and on EU External Relations; and Dr Paul James Cardwell and Prof Duncan French at the University of Sheffield. A more mature version of the manuscript greatly benefited from the feedback offered by the participants in the workshop 'The Environmental Dimension of EU External Relations after Lisbon' (Edinburgh, 4–5 February 2011).

Gracia is profoundly grateful to several officials from the European Union who allowed her to benefit tremendously from their expertise into the complex but fascinating field of EU external relations, while she was working at the EU Delegation to South Africa (February 2009–December 2010) and in contacts thereafter. Elisa sincerely thanks the officials from the European Commission (DG Environment and DG Clima), who generously shared their time and expertise with her during a series of research missions to Brussels in July-August 2010: Andrea Vettori, Julius Langendorff, Matthias Buck, Rok Zvelc, Paolo Caridi, Magnus Gislev, Hans Stielstra, Lars Müller, Jürgen Lefevere, Irina Lazzerini, Andrew Murphy and Flip Van Helden. Equally, Elisa greatly benefitted, during these missions, from meeting with Dr Alessandro Fusacchia, Pawel Swiderek, Kate Dooley (FERN), Jean-Philippe Palasi (Conservation International-Europe) and Bruna Campos (Birdlife International). We of course remain solely responsible for any errors and omissions in this book.

We further gratefully acknowledge the financial support provided by the Edinburgh University School of Law for our research project and the Christie Law Fellowship 2009–2010 awarded to Elisa, as well as the funding offered by the Europa Institute and the Scottish Centre for International Law of the University of Edinburgh for convening the February 2011 workshop. We are also grateful to Dr Kasey McCall-Smith, Dr Massimo Fichera and Dr Phoebe Hung for their research assistance.

We are, in addition, very grateful to Richard Hart, Rachel Turner, Melanie Hamill, Tom Adams, and their teams at Hart Publishing for their patience, commitment and hard work as the book was finalised.

Last but not least, our ever-lasting gratitude to our families and friends for their vital comfort and love throughout this journey, and for understanding our temporary absences.

Gracia Marín Durán
Elisa Morgera

Table of Contents

Acknowledgements vii
List of Abbreviations xiii
List of Tables xvii
Table of Cases xix
Table of Legislation xxiii

Introduction 1

1. The EU Legal and Policy Framework 5
1. Introduction 5
2. The EU as an International Actor in the Environmental Field 5
3. EU External Competence on Environmental Matters 9
3.1 Emergence and evolution 9
3.2 Substantive scope of EU external environmental competence 13
3.3 Shared nature of EU external environmental competence 17
3.4 Instruments and decision-making procedures 20
3.5 The multilateral dimension of EU environmental action 21
4. The Environmental Integration Requirement 25
4.1 Emergence and evolution 25
4.2 Analysis of Article 11 TFEU 28
4.2.1 Textual analysis 28
4.2.2 Implications 32
4.2.3 Contextual analysis 34
5. Environmental Integration in EU External Relations 43
5.1 Overview of environmental priorities and external policy tools 43
5.2 Environmental integration and EU external trade policy 46
5.3 Environmental integration and EU cooperation policies 52
6. Conclusions 54

2. Environmental Integration in Bilateral/Inter-regional Agreements 56
1. Introduction 56
2. Types of Agreements 57
2.1 Association agreements 57
2.2 Other general agreements 61
3. Environmental Integration in Association as Prelude to EU Membership 64
3.1 Enlargement and its environmental dimension 64
3.2 Stabilisation and association process 67

3.3 General approach to the environment 68
3.4 Environmental cooperation clauses 68
3.5 Environmental integration clauses 69
3.6 Trade and environment 72
3.7 Institutional aspects 73

4. Environmental Integration in Association as Substitute to EU Membership 75

4.1 EU relations with its MENA neighbours 75
4.2 General approach to the environment 77
4.3 Environmental cooperation clauses 78
4.4 Environmental integration clauses 79
4.5 Trade and environment 80
4.6 Institutional aspects 81

5. Environmental Integration in Association as a Development Tool 82

5.1 EU relations with the ACP group 82
5.2 Environmental dimension of the Cotonou Agreement 84

5.2.1 General approach to the environment 85
5.2.2 Environmental cooperation clauses 87
5.2.3 Environmental integration clauses 89
5.2.4 Trade and environment 92
5.2.5 Institutional aspects 94

5.3 Environmental dimension of the CARIFORUM EPA 95

5.3.1 General approach to the environment 97
5.3.2 Trade and environment chapter 98
5.3.3 Environmental integration clauses 104
5.3.4 Institutional aspects 106

6. Association as an Instrument of Inter-regional Cooperation 109

6.1 EU relations with Chile and South Africa 109
6.2 General approach to the environment 110
6.3 Environmental cooperation clauses 111
6.4 Environmental integration clauses 112
6.5 Trade and environment 114
6.6 Institutional aspects 115

7. Other Agreements 117

7.1 2010 Agreements with South Korea 117

7.1.1 Environmental cooperation clauses 118
7.1.2 Environmental integration clauses 120
7.1.3 Trade and environment 121
7.1.4 Institutional aspects 127

7.2 Partnership and cooperation agreements with CIS countries 130

7.2.1 Environmental cooperation clauses 131

7.2.2 Environmental integration clauses 132

8. Assessment and Conclusions 133
   - 8.1 Differentiated emphasis on the environment 134
   - 8.2 Different cooperation priorities and scope of integration 136
   - 8.3 A differentiated approach to trade and environment nexus 138
   - 8.4 Institutional differentiation 139
   - 8.5 Questions arising in relation to implementation 142

3. Environmental Integration in the Generalised System of Preferences 144

1. Introduction 144
2. Origins and History of the EU GSP 145
3. Environmental Integration in the Old EU GSP (2001–05) 148
   - 3.1 General structure and legislative background 148
   - 3.2 Special-incentive arrangement for the protection of the environment 151
   - 3.3 Temporary withdrawal of GSP preferences 153
4. Environmental Integration in the Current GSP (2005–11) 155
   - 4.1 General structure and legislative background 155
   - 4.2 Special-incentive arrangement for sustainable development and good governance 159
   - 4.3 Temporary withdrawal of GSP preferences 168
5. Assessment and Conclusions 169

4. Environmental Integration in External Assistance 173

1. Introduction 173
2. EU External Assistance: Instruments and Actors 174
3. Environmental Integration through Thematic Instruments 177
   - 3.1 Thematic instruments 2000–06 178
   - 3.2 Thematic programme 2007–13 180
     - 3.2.1 Environment under the Development Cooperation Instrument 180
     - 3.2.2 ENRTP Strategy 185
   - 3.3 Assessment 189
4. Environmental Integration through Geographic Instruments 191
   - 4.1 Instrument for Pre-Accession Assistance 191
   - 4.2 European Neighbourhood and Partnership Instrument 193
   - 4.3 Development Cooperation Instrument 195
   - 4.4 European Development Fund 197
   - 4.5 Instrument for Cooperation with High-Income Countries (ICI) 200
   - 4.6 Assessment 201
5. Conclusions and Future Prospects 203

5. Environmental Integration in Institutionalised Dialogues 207
1. Introduction 207
2. Types and Objectives of Institutionalised Dialogues 208
3. An Overview of Practice 211
3.1 The EU-ACP dialogue 211
3.2 EU-Africa dialogue 213
3.3 The Euro-Med dialogues 216
3.4 Dialogues with Latin America and the Caribbean 218
3.5 Dialogues with Asian countries 222
3.6 Regulatory dialogues with developed countries 225
3.6.1 EU-US dialogue 225
3.6.2 EU-Canada dialogue 227
3.6.3 EU-Japan dialogue 227
4. Thematic Dialogues: The Case of the Global Climate Change Alliance 229
5. Assessment and Conclusions 230

6. Environmental Integration through Sustainability Impact Assessments 234
1. Introduction 234
2. An Introduction to SIAs 235
2.1 Procedural aspects of the SIA exercise 239
3. An Overview of SIA Practice 242
4. Assessment and Conclusions 249

7. Supporting Environmental Multilateralism 254
1. Introduction 254
2. Supporting the Implementation of *Existing* MEAs 255
2.1 The international climate change regime 258
2.2 Biodiversity-related conventions 261
3. Building Alliances for *Ongoing* Multilateral Environmental Negotiations 265
3.1 Ongoing climate change negotiations 267
3.2 Biofuels 269
4. Consensus Building in the *Absence* of Multilateral Environmental Negotiations 271
4.1 Sustainable forest management 272
4.2 Corporate environmental accountability 277
5. Assessment and Conclusions 280

Conclusions 285

Bibliography 289
Index 303

List of Abbreviations

AA	Association Agreement
ACP	African, Caribbean and Pacific Group of States
ASEAN	Association of South-East Asian Nations
ASEM	Asia-Europe meeting
AU	African Union
CARIFORUM	Caribbean Forum
CAP	Common Agricultural Policy
CBD	Convention on Biological Diversity
CCP	Common Commercial Policy
CCS	Carbon Capture and Storage
CDM	Clean Development Mechanism
CIS	Commonwealth of Independent States
CITES	Convention on International Trade in Endangered Species of Wild Fauna and Flora
CMS	Convention on the Conservation of Migratory Species of Wild Animals
COP	Conference of the Parties
CSP	Country Strategy Papers
CSR	Corporate Social Responsibility
CTE	WTO Committee on Trade and Environment
DCI	Development Cooperation Instrument
DG	Directorate-General (European Commission)
EC	European Community
EBA	'Everything But Arms'
ECA	European Court of Auditors
ECJ	European Court of Justice
EDF	European Development Fund
EEA	European Economic Area
EEC	European Economic Community
EIAs	Environmental Impact Assessments
EIS	Environmental Information Systems
EMAS	Environmental Management and Audit Scheme
EMP	Euro-Mediterranean Partnership
ENP	European Neighbourhood Policy
ENPI	European Neighbourhood and Partnership Instrument
ENRTP	Environment and Sustainable Management of Natural Resources Thematic Programme
EPA	Economic Partnership Agreement

ETS	Emission Trading Scheme
EU	European Union
FA	Framework Agreement
FAO	Food and Agriculture Organization of the United Nations
FDI	Foreign Direct Investment
FLEGT	Forest Law Enforcement, Governance and Trade
FTA	Free Trade Agreement
GATS	General Agreement on Trade in Services
GATT	General Agreement on Tariffs and Trade
GCC	Cooperation Council of the Arab States of the Gulf
GCCA	Global Climate Change Alliance
GDP	Gross Domestic Product
GNI	Gross National Income
GSP	Generalised System of Preferences
IAs	Impact Assessments
ICTSD	International Center for Trade and Sustainable Development
ILO	International Labour Organisation
IPA	Instrument for Pre-Accession
ITPGR	International Treaty on Plant Genetic Resources for Food and Agriculture
ITTO	International Tropical Timber Organisation
JPA	EU-ACP Joint Parliamentary Assembly
LAC	Latin America and the Caribbean
LDC	Least-Developed Country
MDG	Millennium Development Goal
MEA	Multilateral Environmental Agreement
MENA	Mediterranean and North African countries
MERCOSUR	Mercado Común del Sur (Southern Common Market)
MIFF	Multiannual Indicative Financial Framework
MIP	Multiannual Indicative Programmes
MIPD	Multi-Annual Indicative Planning Document
MFN	Most-Favoured Nation
MOP	Meeting of the Parties
NGO	Non-Governmental Organisation
NIEO	New International Economic Order
OCTs	Overseas Countries and Territories
ODA	Official Development Assistance
OECD	Organisation for Economic Co-operation and Development
PCA	Partnership and Cooperation Agreement
POPs	Persistent Organic Pollutants
PPM	Process and Production Method
REDD	Reducing Emissions from Deforestation and Degradation
REIO	Regional Economic Integration Organisation
RSP	Regional Strategy Papers

SADC	Southern African Development Community
SACU	Southern African Customs Union
SAICM	Strategic Approach to International Chemicals Management
SAA	Stabilisation and Association Agreement
SDS	Sustainable Development Strategy
SEA	Single European Act
SEAs	Strategic Environmental Assessments
SIA	Sustainability Impact Assessment
SIDS	Small Island Developing States
SMAP	Short and Medium Term Environmental Action Programme
TEC	Treaty establishing the European Community
TEEB	The Economics of Ecosytems and Biodiversity
TFEU	Treaty on the Functioning of the European Union
TEU	Treaty on the European Union
UfM	Union for the Mediterranean
TRIPS	Trade-Related Intellectual Property Rights
UN	United Nations
UNCCD	United Nations Convention to Combat Desertification
UNCTAD	United Nations Conference on Trade and Development
UNCLOS	United Nations Convention on the Law of the Sea
UNFCCC	United Nations Framework Convention on Climate Change
UNDP	United Nations Development Programme
UNECE	United Nations Economic Commission for Europe
UNEP	United Nations Environment Programme
UNGA	United Nations General Assembly
UNITAR	United Nations Institute for Training and Research
VPA	Voluntary Partnership Agreement (FLEGT)
WIPO	World Intellectual Property Organisation
WSSD	World Summit on Sustainable Development
WTO	World Trade Organisation
WWF	World Wild Fund for Nature

List of Tables

Table 1. *Environmental Integration in Bilateral and Inter-regional Agreements*
Table 2. *List of Countries Qualifying for 'GSP-plus'*
Table 3. *EU Environment Thematic Funding (2000–13)*
Table 4. *EU Environment Funding under Geographic Instruments (2007–13)*
Table 5. *Timing of Sustainability Impact Assessments*
Table 6. *MEAs and EU Environmental Priorities*

Table of Cases

EU Cases

AETR *see* Commission v Council (Case 22/70)
ARCO Chemie Nederland Ltd v Minister Van Volkshuisvesting (Joined Cases C–418/97 and C–419/97) [2000] ECR I–4475 31
Artegodan GmbH v Commission (Joined Cases T–74, 76, 83, 85, 132, 137 and 141/00) [2002] ECR II–4945 .... 29, 30
Bellio F.lli Srl v Preffettura di Treviso (Case C–286/02) [2004] ECR I–3465 24
Bettati v Safety Hi–Tech (Case C–341/95) [1998] ECR I–4355 32–33
Cartagena Protocol, Article 300(6) EC (Opinion 2/00) [2001] ECR I–9713 32
Chernobyl I *see* Greece v Council (Case C–62/88)
Commission v Belgium (Case C–2/90) [1992] ECR I–4431 16
Commission v Council (Case C–22/70) [1971] ECR 263 10
Commission v Council (Case C–155/91) [1993] ECR I–939 32
Commission v Council (re Rotterdam Convention) (Case C–94/03) [2006] ECR I–1 32
Commission v Parliament and Council (Case C–178/03) [2006] ECR I–107 32
Commission v France (Etang de Berre) (Case C–239/03) [2004] ECR I–9325 19
Commission v Germany (re International Dairy Agreement) (Case C–61/94) [1996] ECR I–3989 24
Commission v Germany (re Inland Waterways Agreement) (Case C–433/03) [2005] ECR I–6985 19
Commission v Ireland (Case C–459/03) [2006] ECR I–4635 9
Commission v Luxembourg (re Inland Waterways Agreement) (Case C–266/03) [2005] ECR I–4805 19
Commission v Sweden (re POPs Convention) (Case C–246/07) [2010] ECR I-3317 19
Demirel v Stadt Schwäbisch Gmünd (Case 12/86) [1987] ECR 3719 .... 60, 61
Deutsche Shell AG v Hauptzollamt Hamburg-Harburg (Case C–188/91) [1993] ECR I–363 61
Draft Agreement establishing a Laying-up Fund for Inland Waterway Vessels (Opinion 1/76) [1977] ECR 741 10–11
Etablissements Armand Mondiet v Société Armement Islai (Case C–405/92) [1993] ECR I–6133 .... 14, 29, 32
Fornasar and others (Case C–318/98) [2000] ECR I–4785 31
Greece v Commission (Case 30/88) [1989] ECR 3711 61
Greece v Council (Case C–62/88) [1990] ECR I–1527 .... 29, 32
Haegeman v Belgium (Case C–181/73) [1974] ECR 449 24

IATA and ELFAA v Department of Transport (Case C–344/04) [2006] ECR I–403 24
International Fruit Company NV et al v Producktschap voor Groenten en Fruit (Joined Cases 21–24/72) [1972] ECR I–1219 24
Kramer (Cornelis) and others (Joined Cases 3, 4 and 6/76) [1976] ECR 1279....14
Lesoochranárske zoskupenie (re Aarhus Convention) (Case C–240/09), judgment 8 March 2011 24
Lirussi and Bizzaro (Joined Cases C–175/98 and C–177/98) [1999] ECR I–6881 31
Ministère de l'Économie, des Finances et de l'Industrie v GEMO SA (Case C–126/01) [2003] ECR I–13769 30
Missouri v Holland 252 US 416 (1920) 8
Mondiet *see* Etablissements Armand Mondiet v Société Armement Islai (Case C–405/92)
National Farmers Union *see* Queen and Ministry of Agriculture, Fisheries and Food, Commissioners of Customs & Excise ex parte National Farmers Union (Case C–157/96)
Opel Austria GmbH v Council (Case T–115/94) [1997] ECR II–39 24
Parliament v Council (re Lomé IV) (Case 316/91) [1994] ECR I–625....19
Portugal v Council (Case C–268/94) [1996] ECR I–06177 52
Portugal v Council (Case C–149/96) [1999] ECR I–8395 24
Preussen-Elektra AG v Schleswag AG (Case C–379/98) [2001] ECR I–2099 30
Queen v Minister of Agriculture, Fisheries and Food and Secretary of State for Health, ex parte Fedesa and others (Case C –331/88) [1990] ECR I–4023 32
Queen v Secretary of State for Environment, Transport and the Regions, ex parte First Corporate Shipping Ltd (Case C–371/98) [2000] ECR– I 9235 36
Queen v Secretary of State, Minister of Agriculture, Fisheries and Food, ex parte HA Standley and others and DGD Metson and others (Case C–293/97) [1999] ECR I–2603 16–17
Queen and Ministry of Agriculture, Fisheries and Food, Commissioners of Customs & Excise, ex parte National Farmers Union (Case C–157/96) [1998] ECR I–2211 ....16, 29
Queen (on the application of International Association of Independent Tanker Owners (Intertanko) and others) v Secretary of State for Transport (Case C–308/06) [2008] ECR I–4057 25
Queen (on the application of Mayer Parry Recycling Ltd) v The Environment Agency and Secretary of State for Environment, Transport and the Regions (Case C–444/00) [2003] ECR I–6163 30
Racke GmbH & Co v Hauptzollant Mainz (Case C–162/96) [1998] ECR I–3655 24
Republik *Österreich* v Martin Huber (Case C–336/00) [2002] ECR I–7699 32

Safety High-Tech v S & T Srl (Case C–284/95) [1998] ECR I–4301 .... 15, 32–33, 100
Sevince v Staatssecretaris van Justitie (Case C–192/89) [1990] ECR I–3461........61
Standley *see* Queen v Secretary of State, Minister of Agriculture, Fisheries and Food, ex parte HA Standley and others and DGD Metson and others (Case C–293/97)
Sydhavnens Sten & Grus (Case C–209/98) [2000] ECR I–3743............................16
United Kingdom v Commission (Case C–180/96) [1998] ECR I–2265 33
Upjohn v The Licensing Authority (Case C–120/97) [1999] ECR I–223 33
Waste Directive *see* Commission v Council (Case C–155/91)

GATT/WTO Cases:

European Communities-Conditions for the Granting of Tariff Preferences to Developing Countries, Panel Report (adopted 20 April 2004 as modified by Appellate Body Report) WT/ DS246/R...156–58, 165
European Communities-Conditions for the Granting of Tariff Preferences to Developing Countries, Appellate Body Report (adopted 20 April 2004) WT/DS246/AB/R 156,
United States–Import Prohibition on Certain Shrimp and Shrimp Products, Appellate Body Report (adopted 6 November 1998) WT/DS58/AB/R...........115
United States–Restrictions on Imports of Tuna (Mexico), GATT Panel Report (3 September 1991, unadopted) BISD 39S/155..115
United States–Tuna (Canada), GATT Panel Report (adopted 22 February 1982) BISD 29S/91..115

Table of Legislation

International Treaties

International Agreement Creating the Office International des Epizooties, 25 January 1924, www.oie.int/about-us/key-texts/basic-texts/ 94
International Labour Organisation Convention 29 on Forced Labour, 28 June 1930, ILO/C29 ....149, 160
General Agreement on Trade and Tariffs (GATT) 1947 ....7, 145
art I:1 146
art XIV.......................115, 124
(a) 115
(b).......................115
art XX 102, 115, 124, 125, 138, 141, 150, 153
(b).......................49, 102, 124
(g) 49, 102, 124
art XXIV 46
International Labour Organisation Convention 87 on Freedom of Association and Protection of the Right to Organise 9 July 1948, ILO/C87.......................149, 160
Convention on the Prevention and Punishment of the Crime of Genocide, 9 December 1948, 78 UNTS 277 160
International Labour Organisation Convention 98 on the Right to Organise and Collective Bargaining 1 July 1949, ILO /C98.......................149, 160
International Labour Organisation Convention 100 on Equal Remuneration 29 June 1951, ILO/C100 ....149, 160
International Labour Organisation Convention 105 on the Abolition of Forced Labour, 25 June 1957, ILO /C105.......................149, 160
International Labour Organisation Convention 111 on Discrimination (Employment and Occupation) 25 June 1958, ILO/C111.......................149, 160
Single Convention on Narcotic Drugs, 30 March 1961, 520 UNTS 151 160
International Convention on the Elimination of All Forms of Racial Discrimination, 7 March 1966, 660 UNTS 195.......................160
International Convention on the Conservation of Atlantic Tuna, 14 May 1966, 673 UNTS 63.......................154
International Covenant on Civil and Political Rights, 26 December 1966, 999 UNTS 171.......................160
International Covenant on Economic, Social and Cultural Rights, 16 December 1966, 993 UNTS 3.......................160
Convention on Wetlands of International Importance, 2 February 1971, 996 UNTS 245.......................41, 161, 262, 280

Convention on Psychotropic Substances, 21 February 1971, 1019 UNTS 175...160
Convention on International Trade in Endangered Species of Wild Fauna and Flora, 3 March 1973, 993 UNTS 243 .... 23, 41, 100, 104, 119, 123, 125, 160, 161, 163, 168, 169, 170, 172, 215, 262, 264, 273, 280
International Labour Organisation Convention 138 on Minimum Age for Admission to Employment 26 June 1973, ILO/C138 .... 149, 160
International Convention on the Suppression and Punishment of the Crime of Apartheid, 30 November 1973, 1015 UNTS 243 160
Convention on the Protection of the Marine Environment of the Baltic Sea Area, 22 March 1974, 1507 UNTS 167 23
Barcelona Convention for the Protection of the Mediterranean Sea against Pollution, 16 February 1976, 1102 UNTS 44 .... 24, 78, 141, 194, 216, 255
Convention on Future Multilateral Cooperation in the Northwest Atlantic Fisheries, 24 October 1978, 1135 UNTS 369 154
Convention on the Conservation of Migratory Species of Wild Animals, 23 June 1979, 1651 UNTS 333 .... 11, 23, 161, 262
Convention on the Conservation of European Wildlife and Natural Habitats, 19 September 1979, 1284 UNTS 290 11
Convention on Long-range Transboundary Air Pollution, 13 November 1979, 1302 UNTS 217 .... 11, 23
Convention on the Elimination of All Forms of Discrimination against Women, 18 December 1979, 1249 UNTS 13 160
Convention on the Conservation of Antarctic Marine Living Resources, 20 May 1980, 1329 UNTS 47 11
Convention on Future Multilateral Cooperation in the North-East Atlantic Fisheries, 18 November 1980, 1285 UNTS 129 154
Convention for the Conservation of Salmon in the North Atlantic Ocean, 2 March 1982, 1338 UNTS 33 154
UN Convention on the Law of the Sea, 10 December 1982, 1833 UNTS 3 .... 22, 25, 42
Convention against Torture and other Cruel, Inhuman or Degrading Treatment or Punishment, 10 December 1984, 1465 UNTS 85 160
Vienna Convention for the Protection of the Ozone Layer, 22 March 1985, 1513 UNTS 293 .... 22, 41, 161
Montreal Protocol on Substances that Deplete the Ozone Layer, 16 September 1987, 1522 UNTS 3 .... 22, 41, 100, 123, 160, 161, 163, 170, 280
  art 5 171
  art 7 163
  art 9 171
  art 10(1)–(3) 171
UN Convention against Illicit Traffic in Narcotic Drugs and Psychotropic Substances, 20 December 1988, 1582 UNTS 95 160

Basel Convention on the Control of Transboundary Movements of Hazardous Wastes and their Disposal, 22 March 1989, 1673 UNTS 57 .... 22, 42, 93, 100, 123, 131, 160, 161, 163, 170, 172, 188, 198, 256

art 10(3)–(4) 171

art 13(3) 163

Convention on the Rights of the Child, 20 November 1989, 1577 UNTS 3 160

Convention on Environmental Impact Assessment in a Transboundary Context, 25 February 1991, 1989 UNTS 309 .... 24, 131, 255

Convention on the Protection of the Alps, 7 November 1991 1917 UNTS 135 23

UN Framework Convention on Climate Change, 9 May 1992, 1771 UNTS 107 .... 22, 42, 44, 119, 161, 196, 198, 212, 214, 220, 257, 264

art 2 119

art 3(5) 172

art 4(2) 163

(3)–(4) 172

art 12 163

Annex I 120

Kyoto Protocol, 11 December 1997, 2303 UNTS 148 .... 22, 42, 69, 100, 120, 123, 160, 161, 163, 169, 170, 221, 259, 267

art 6 120

art 7.2 163

art 10 161

art 12 120

art 17 120

Annex B 120

Convention on Biological Diversity, 5 June 1992, 1760 UNTS 79 .... 23, 42, 44, 45, 94, 100, 105, 123, 126, 160, 161, 163, 168, 170, 196, 198, 215, 219, 228, 257, 259, 262–64, 266, 269, 271

art 8(j) 105, 126, 263

art 12 171

art 17 171

art 20(2) 171

(4) 171, 204

art 21 172

art 26 163

art 39 172

Cartagena Protocol on Biosafety, 29 January 2000, 2226 UNTS 208 .... 23, 42, 44, 100, 123, 160, 163, 167, 170, 172, 262

art 20(1)(b) 171

art 22(2) 171

art 28(2) 172

art 33 163

art 34 163
Nagoya Protocol on Access and Benefit-Sharing, 29 October 2010, UNEP/CBD/COP/DEC/X/1 .... 126, 215, 263, 264, 265, 266
Convention on the Protection and Use of Transboundary Watercourses and International Lakes, 17 March 1992, 1936 UNTS 269 23
Convention on the Transboundary Effects of Industrial Accidents, 17 March 1992, 2105 UNTS 457 24
Convention for the Protection of the Marine Environment of the North-East Atlantic, 22 September 1992, 2354 UNTS 67 23
Agreement to Promote Compliance with International Conservation and Management Measures by Fishing Vessels on the High Seas, 24 November 1993, 2221 UNTS 91 42
General Agreement on Trade in Services, 15 April 1994
art XIV(b) 49
WTO Agreement on Agriculture, 15 April 1994
Annex 2 48
WTO Agreement on Sanitary and Phytosanitary Measures, 15 April 1994 94
WTO Agreement on Trade-Related Aspects of Intellectual Property Rights, 15 April 1994 .... 48, 105
art 27.2 49
art 27.3 49
Convention on Cooperation for the Protection and Sustainable Use of the Danube River, 29 June 1994, [1997] OJ L342/19 23
Agreement relating to the Implementation of Part XI of the United Nations Convention on the Law of Sea of 10 December 1982, 28 July 1994, 1836 UNTS 3 22
UN Convention to Combat Desertification in Countries Experiencing Serious Drought and/or Desertification, Particularly in Africa, 14 October 1994, 1954 UNTS 3 .... 22, 42, 44, 196, 198, 257, 264
Agreement for the Implementation of the Provisions of the United Nations Convention on the Law of the Sea relating to the Conservation and Management of Straddling Fish Stocks and Highly Migratory Fish Stocks, 4 August 1995, 2167 UNTS 3 .... 22, 42, 104, 137, 283–84
International Plant Protection Convention, 17 November 1997, 2367 UNTS 223 94
Convention on Access to Information, Public Participation in Decision-Making and Access to Justice in Environmental Matters, 25 June 1998, 2161 UNTS 447 .... 24, 253, 255
Rotterdam Convention on the Prior Informed Consent for Certain Hazardous Chemicals and Pesticides, 10 September 1998, 2244 UNTS 337 .... 22, 42, 44, 100, 123, 161, 187, 189, 198, 256
Convention on the Protection of the Rhine, 12 April 1999 [2000] OJ L289/31 23

International Labour Organisation Convention 182 on the Prohibition and Immediate Action for the Elimination of the Worst Forms of Child Labour, 17 June 1999, ILO/C182 .... 149, 160
Stockholm Convention on Persistent Organic Pollutants, 22 May 2001, 2256 UNTS 119..22, 42, 44, 100, 123, 160, 161, 163, 167, 170, 187, 189, 198, 256
art 4(7) 171
art 11(2)(c) 171
art 12(5) 171
art 13 172
(5) 171
art 14 171
art 15 163
International Treaty on Plant Genetic Resources for Food and Agriculture, 3 November 2001, 2400 UNTS 303 .... 23, 42, 161, 262
UN Convention against Corruption, 31 October 2003, 2349 UNTS 41 160
Agreement on Port State Measures to Prevent, Deter and Eliminate Illegal, Unreported and Unregulated Fishing, 22 November 2009 (2009) FAO Doc C2009/REP 104

EU Treaties

Treaty establishing the European Economic Community, Bulletin EC 1972, No 10 .... 8, 9, 11, 57
pt IV 82
title II ch 3 46
art 9 46
Single European Act 1986 [1987] OJ L169/1 .... 9, 10, 11, 13, 17, 25
title VII 11
art 130r(2) 26, 29
(5) 11
Treaty on European Union (Treaty of Maastricht)1992 [1992] OJ C191/1 .... 11–12, 26
art 2 12
art 3(k) 12
art 130r 26
(2) 26
Treaty of Amsterdam 1997 [1997] OJ C340/1 .... 12, 26
art 2 12
art 3c 12
art 130s(a) 12
(b) 12
Treaty of Nice 2001 [2001] OJ C80/1 47

Treaty establishing the European Community (consolidated text) [2006] OJ C321E/1 ... 12
art 2 ... 35
art 3(2) ... 27
art 6 ... 30, 32, 47
art 131 ... 46
art 133(1) ... 46
(2) ... 47
(4) ... 47
art 177(1) ... 52
(2) ... 52
art 203(2) ... 210
art 300(3) ... 47, 61
art 310 ... 60
Treaty of Lisbon *see* Treaty on European Union and Treaty on the Functioning of the European Union
Treaty on European Union (consolidated text) [2010] OJ C83/13
recital 9 ... 35
art 1 ... 21, 27
art 2 ... 64
art 3 ... 35
(3) ... 15, 35
(5) ... 2, 12, 35, 42, 55
art 4(3) ... 19
art 5(2) ... 7
(3) ... 8, 15
(4) ... 8, 14
art 6(1) ... 27, 64
art 8 ... 76
art 15(5)–(6) ... 211
(6) ... 211
art 16(6) ... 43
(9) ... 210
art 18(2) ... 211
(4) ... 211
art 21 ... 25
(1) ... 35, 208
(2) ... 2, 42, 47, 52, 53, 55
(d) ... 13, 42, 52, 147, 208
(f) ... 13, 35, 42, 52, 208
(g) ... 42
(h) ... 208, 254
(3) ... 43
art 23 ... 13

art 47 ... 7
art 49 ... 64, 65, 66
Treaty on the Functioning of the European Union (consolidated text) [2010] OJ C83/47
pt V title III ... 52
art 3 ... 47
arts 3–6 ... 27, 30
art 4(2)(e) ... 17
(3) ... 17
(4) ... 54
art 7 ... 27, 28, 43
arts 7–13 ... 27
art 8 ... 27, 29
art 9 ... 27, 29
art 10 ... 27, 29
art 11 ... 1, 3, 5, 13, 19, 25, 28–43, 47, 52–55, 56, 144, 147, 173, 174, 182, 249, 285–86
art 12 ... 27
art 13 ... 27, 29
art 36 ... 73, 81, 114, 138, 141, 150
art 114 ... 10
(3) ... 10
art 167(4) ... 28
art 191 ... 13–14, 29, 30, 31, 32, 33, 55
(1) ... 13–14, 17, 88, 181
(2) ... 13, 15, 17, 29, 100
(3) ... 17, 29
(4) ... 8, 17, 18, 20, 28
art 192 ... 14, 20, 28
(1) ... 20
(2) ... 20
art 193 ... 18, 19
art 194(1) ... 27
art 207 ... 62, 144
(1) ... 47
(2) ... 47, 156
(3) ... 47
art 208(1) ... 52, 54
(2) ... 54, 181
art 209(1) ... 52, 53, 174
(2) ... 18, 52
art 212 ... 53, 200
(2) ... 53, 174
art 216(2) ... 24, 61

art 217 ... 58, 60
art 218 ... 20
(6)(v) ... 47
art 228 ... 288
art 263 ... 32, 33
arts 286–87 ... 177
art 294 ... 20
art 296 ... 33
art 312 ... 174
arts 318–19 ... 177
art 352 ... 10, 62
Charter of Fundamental Rights of the European Union [2010] OJ C83/389 ... 27
art 37 ... 15, 27
art 44 ... 288

EU Agreements

Agreement creating an Association between the European Economic Community and Turkey [1964] OJ L217/3687 ... 58
Convention of Yaoundé I between the European Economic Community and its Member States and the Associated African and Malgache Countries [1964] OJ L93/1431 ... 82
Convention of Yaoundé II between the European Economic Community and its Member States and the Associated African and Malgache Countries [1970] OJ L 282/2 ... 82
First Lomé Convention between the European Economic Community and the African, Caribbean and Pacific States [1976] OJ L25/2 ... 82
Framework Agreement for commercial and economic cooperation between the European Communities and Canada [1976] OJ L260/2 ... 209, 227
Cooperation Agreement between the European Economic Community and Indonesia, Malaysia, the Philippines, Singapore and Thailand (member countries of ASEAN) [1980] OJ L144/2 ... 63, 222
Second Lomé Convention between the European Economic Community and the African, Caribbean and Pacific States [1980] OJ L347/1 ... 82
Agreement on Trade and Economic Cooperation between the European Economic Community and the People's Republic of China [1985] OJ L250/2 ... 209
Third Lomé Convention between the European Economic Community and the African, Caribbean and Pacific States [1986] OJ L86/3 ... 82
Cooperation Agreement between the European Economic Community, of the one part, and the countries parties to the Charter of the Cooperation Council for the Arab States of the Gulf (the State of the United Arab Emirates, the State of Bahrain, the Kingdom of Saudi Arabia, the Sultanate

of Oman, the State of Qatar and the State of Kuwait), of the other part [1989] OJ L54/3 64
Agreement between the European Economic Community and the European Atomic Energy Community and the Union of Soviet Socialist Republics on trade and commercial and economic cooperation [1990] OJ L68/3 130
Fourth Lomé Convention between the European Economic Community and the African, Caribbean and Pacific States [1991] OJ L229/3 ....82–83, 92–93, 95, 110
art 174 93
Agreement on the European Economic Area (EEA) [1994] OJ L1/3 58
Cooperation Agreement between the European Community and the Republic of India on partnership and development [1994] OJ L223/24 63
Framework Agreement for Cooperation between the European Economic Community and the Federative Republic of Brazil [1995] OJ L262/54 219
Interregional Framework Cooperation Agreement between the European Community and its Member States, of the one part, and the Southern Common Market and its Party States, of the other part [1996] OJ L69/4 63
Euro–Mediterranean Interim Association Agreement on Trade and Cooperation between the European Community, of the one part, and the Palestine Liberation Organization (PLO) for the benefit of the Palestinian Authority of the West Bank and the Gaza Strip, of the other part [1997] OJ L187/3 ....59, 77–81
titles I–II 77
title II 80
title III 77
title VI 81
art 1 77
art 2 77
art 24 81
art 35(2) 79
art 36(4) 79
art 37 77
art 41 77
art 44 79
art 48 80
art 50 78
art 55 78
art 61 77
Agreement on Partnership and Cooperation between the European Communities and their Member States, of one part, and the Russian Federation, of the other part [1997] OJ L327/3 ....62, 130–133, 255
art 1 ....130, 131
art 2 130

art 55(2)....131
art 56(2)....132
art 57....133
art 61....133
art 64....132
art 65(2)....133
art 68....133
art 69(1)....131
(2)....131
(3)....131, 132
art 84....133
Cooperation Agreement between the European Community and the Lao People's Democratic Republic [1997] OJ L334/15....63
Partnership and Cooperation Agreement between the European Communities and their Member States, of the one part, and Ukraine, of the other part [1998] OJ L49/3....62, 255
art 1....130
art 2....130
Cooperation Agreement between the European Community and the Republic of Yemen [1998] OJ L72/18....64
Euro–Mediterranean Agreement establishing an Association between the European Communities and their Member States, of the one part, and the Republic of Tunisia, of the other part [1998] OJ L97/2....59, 77–81
title I....77
title II....80
titles II–IV....77
title III....80
title V....77
title VIII....81
art 1....77
art 2....77
art 28....81
art 42(2)....79
art 43(4)....79
art 44....77
art 45....78
art 48....78
art 52....77
art 75....77
Framework Agreement on Cooperation between the European Economic Community and the Cartagena Agreement and its member countries, namely the Republic of Bolivia, the Republic of Colombia, the Republic of Ecuador, the Republic of Peru and the Republic of Venezuela [1998] OJ L127/11....63

Agreement amending the fourth ACP–EC Convention of Lomé [1998] OJ L156/3 82
Partnership and Cooperation Agreement between the European Communities and their Member States, of the one part, and the Republic of Moldova, of the other part [1998] OJ L181/3 ....62, 130–33, 255
art 1 ....130, 131
art 2 130
art 50(2) 131
art 51(2) 132
art 52 133
art 56 133
art 59 132
art 60(2) 133
art 61(1) 131
(2) 131
(3) 131, 132
Framework Cooperation Agreement between the European Economic Community and the Republics of Costa Rica, El Salvador, Guatemala, Honduras, Nicaragua and Panama [1999] OJ L63/39 63
Inter-regional Framework Cooperation Agreement between the European Community and its Member States, of the one part, and the Southern Common Market and its Party States, of the other part [1999] OJ L112/66 ....219, 244, 245
Partnership and Cooperation Agreement between the European Communities and their Member States, of the one part, and the Republic of Kazakhstan, of the other part [1999] OJ L196/3 ....62, 130–33, 255
preamble 130
art 1 130
art 2 130
art 44(2) 132
art 45 133
art 49 133
art 52 132
art 53 133
art 54(1) 131
(2) 131
(3) 131
art 61 132
art 70 ....133, 256
Partnership and Cooperation Agreement establishing a partnership between the European Communities and their Member States, of the one part, and the Kyrgyz Republic, of the other part [1999] OJ L196/48 ....62, 131–33, 255
preamble 130

art 1 ... 130
art 2 ... 130
art 45(2) ... 132
art 46 ... 133
art 50 ... 133
art 53 ... 132
art 54 ... 133
art 55(1) ... 131
(2) ... 131
(3) ... 131
art 61 ... 132
Partnership and Cooperation Agreement between the European Communities and their Member States, of the one part, and Georgia, of the other part [1999] OJ L205/3 ... 62, 130–33, 255
art 1 ... 130, 131
art 2 ... 130
art 43(2) ... 131
art 45(2) ... 132
art 47 ... 133
art 48 ... 133
art 52 ... 133
art 55 ... 132
art 56 ... 133
art 57(1) ... 131
(2) ... 131, 272
(3) ... 131, 132
art 72 ... 133
Partnership and Cooperation Agreement establishing a partnership between the European
Communities and their Member States, of the one part, and the Republic of Uzbekistan, of the other part [1999] OJ L229/3 ... 63, 130–33, 255
preamble ... 130
art 1 ... 130
art 2 ... 130
art 43(2) ... 132
art 45 ... 133
art 49 ... 133
art 52 ... 132
art 53 ... 133
art 54(1) ... 131
(2) ... 131
(3) ... 131
art 60 ... 132
art 69 ... 133

Partnership and Cooperation Agreement between the European Communities and their Member States, of the one part, and the Republic of Armenia, of the other part [1999] OJ L239/3 ....62, 130–33, 255
art 1 ....130, 131
art 2 130
art 44(2) 132
art 46 133
art 53 132
art 54 133
art 55(1) 131
(2) 131, 262
(3) 131, 132
art 69 133
Partnership and Cooperation Agreement between the European Communities and their Member States, of the one part, and the Republic of Azerbaijan, of the other part [1999] OJ L246/3 ....62, 130–33, 255
art 1 ....130, 131
art 2 130
art 43(2) 131
art 44(2) 132
art 46 133
art 47 133
art 51 133
art 54 132
art 55 133
art 56(1) 131
(2) 131
(3) 131, 132
art 72 133
Cooperation Agreement between the European Community and the Kingdom of Cambodia [1999] OJ L269/18 63
Agreement on Trade, Development and Cooperation between the European Community and its Member States, of the one part, and the Republic of South Africa, of the other part [1999] OJ L311/3 ....60, 109–16, 135, 213, 256
preamble para 4 110
title I 110
title II 110
title III 110
title IV 110
title V 110
title VI 110, 112
title VII 110
art 1(c) 110
art 3 116

art 27 ... 115
art 51(b) ... 113, 277
art 57 ... 260
(1) ... 113
art 58 ... 113
art 59 ... 114
art 60(1) ... 114
art 61 ... 113
art 65 ... 111
(2) ... 111
art 66(3) ... 111
art 84 ... 262, 272
(1) ... 112
(2) ... 112
(2)–(3) ... 112
(3) ... 112
art 93(1) ... 111
art 97 ... 116
art 104 ... 116
Euro–Mediterranean Agreement establishing an Association between the European Community and its Member States, of the one part, and the Kingdom of Morocco, of the other part [2000] OJ L70/2 ... 59, 77–81
title I ... 77
title II ... 80
titles II–IV ... 77
title IV ... 80
title V ... 77
title VIII ... 81
art 1 ... 77
art 2 ... 77
art 28 ... 81
art 42(2) ... 79
art 43(4) ... 79
art 44 ... 77
art 45 ... 78
art 48 ... 78
art 52 ... 77
art 57 ... 80
art 75 ... 77
Joint Declaration on art 90 ... 81
Euro–Mediterranean Agreement establishing an Association between the European Community and its Member States, of the one part, and the State of Israel, of the other part [2000] OJ L147/3 ... 59, 77–81
title I ... 77

title II 80
titles II–IV 77
title III 80
title VI 77
title IX 81
art 1 77
art 2 77
art 27 81
art 42(2) 79
art 43 77
art 46 79
art 50 78
(2) 78
art 51 80
art 55 77
Economic Partnership, Political Coordination and Cooperation Agreement between the European Community and its Member States, of the one part, and the United Mexican States, of the other part [2000] OJ L276/45 ....63, 219, 221
(Cotonou) Partnership Agreement between the Members of the African, Caribbean and Pacific Group of States of the one part and the European Community and its Member States of the other [2000] OJ L317/3 ....59, 82–98, 103, 110, 111, 124, 135, 137, 140, 142, 144, 197, 199, 211, 263
preamble para 12 ....84, 85
para 13bis 84, 85
part I title I 85
title II 85
part III title I 85, 87, 96
title II 85, 92, 96
ch 5 93
part IV 85, 197
title I 96
art 1 ....84, 87, 260
(2) 83
(3) 86
(4) 86
art 2 ....83, 84
art 4 84
art 6 ....84, 260
(1)(b) 213
art 8 87
(3) 86
(4)–(5) 84

art 9(2)–(3) 84
art 10....84
art 11....84, 88, 260
(3)....86
art 12....84
art 15(2)....94
(d)....95
(3)....94, 212
art 16....95
art 17....95
art 19....84
art 20(1)(e)....89
(2) 86, 87, 88
(3) 83
art 23(e)....90
(f)....90
(m)....90
art 23a....89
art 28(2)(c)....90
art 29(3)(a)–(b) 91
art 30(1)(b) 90
art 32....87, 272
(1) 87, 256, 262
(2) 87
art 32bis....84, 88, 136, 260, 276
arts 34–37 92
art 34(4)....92
art 36(1)....92
art 37....92
art 38....95
art 39....94
art 42....90
art 46(2)....94, 263
art 48(2)....94
art 49....93
(1)....93
(2)....93
(3)....93
art 53(1)....89
art 58....84
art 72(2)....91
art 83....95
art 95(3)....84
art 96....95

art 97 95
art 98 95
Annex I 197
Annexes I–IV 85, 197
Annex IV art 2 ....84, 197
art 4(2) 197
art 8 197
(3)(a) 84
art 10(2) 197
art 12a(2)(a) 84
art 15 197
art 17 197
Annex VI Protocol 3 82
Joint Declaration on art 49 93
Framework Agreement for Trade and Cooperation between the European Community and its Member States, on the one hand, and the Republic of Korea, on the other hand [2001] OJ L90/46 117
Cooperation Agreement between the European Community and the People's Republic of Bangladesh on partnership and development [2001] OJ L118/48 63
Euro–Mediterranean Agreement establishing an Association between the European Community and its Member States, of the one part, and the Hashemite Kingdom of Jordan, of the other part [2002] OJ L129/3 ....59, 77–81
title I 77
title II 80
titles II–IV 77
title III 80
title V 77
title VIII 81
art 1 77
art 2 77
art 27 81
art 59(2) 79
art 60(4) 79
art 61 77
art 62 78
art 65 78
(2) 78
art 69 77
art 71 79
art 74 ....80, 260
art 75 80
art 86 77

Agreement establishing an Association between the European Community and its Member States, of the one part, and the Republic of Chile, on the other part [2002] OJ L352/3 .... 59, 109–16, 140, 143, 242–43, 251, 277
part II 109
part III 109
title I 111
part IV 109, 114
title VIII 116
art 1 109
(2) 110
arts 3–5 116
art 6 116
art 9 116
art 10 116
art 11 116
art 16 114
(1)(b) 111
(2) 111
art 22(1) 113
art 24(1) 112
(2)(a) 113
art 25 113
art 28 111
(1) 111
(2) 112
art 44(4)(h) 114
art 49(3)(b) 114
art 52(3) 116
art 53 .... 111, 116
art 84 112
art 91(1) 115
(b) 115
(e) 115
art 135(1) 115
(b) 115
(d) 115
art 188 116
Stabilisation and Association Agreement between the European Communities and their Member States, of the one part, and the former Yugoslav Republic of Macedonia, of the other part [2004] OJ L84/13 .... 58, 67–74
title II 68
title III 68
title IV 72

titles IV–V 68
title V 72
title VII 68
title VIII 68, 70
title X 73
art 1(2) 67
art 2 67
art 3 68
art 41 73
art 61 73
art 63 67
art 78(1) 72
art 80(2) 70
(3) 74
art 85(1) 72
art 98 71
art 99 71
art 100 70
art 103 ....69, 262
(4) 72
art 104 68
art 118 74
Euro–Mediterranean Agreement establishing an Association between the European Communities and their Member States, of the one part, and the Arab Republic of Egypt, of the other part [2004] OJ L304/39 ....59, 77–81
title I 77
title II 80
titles II–IV 77
title III 80
title V 77
title VIII 81
art 1 77
art 2 77
art 26 81
art 39(2) 79
art 40(4) 79
art 41 77
art 44 78
(2) 78
art 48 77
art 53 80
art 54 80
art 60 78
art 73 77

Cooperation Agreement between the European Community and the Islamic Republic of Pakistan on partnership and development [2004] OJ L378/23.....63
Stabilisation and Association Agreement between the European Communities and their Member States, of the one part, and the Republic of Croatia, of the other part [2005] OJ L26/3.....58, 67–74
title II.....68
title III.....68
title IV.....72
titles IV–V.....68
title V.....72
title VII.....68
title VIII.....68, 70
title X.....73
art 1(2).....67
art 2.....67
art 3.....68
arts 3–4.....68
art 42.....73
art 62.....73
art 69.....67
art 80(1).....72
art 81(2).....70
(3).....74
art 86(1).....72
art 92.....70
art 100(1).....71
art 101.....71
art 102.....72
art 103.....69, 256, 262, 272
art 106.....68
art 120.....74
Protocol 6 art 2(2).....71
art 7.....71
art 15.....71
Joint Declaration on art 120.....74
Euro–Mediterranean Agreement establishing an Association between the European Community and its Member States, of the one part, and the People's Democratic Republic of Algeria, of the other part [2005] OJ L265/2.....59, 77–81
title I.....77
title II.....80
titles II–IV.....77
title III.....80
title V.....77
title IX.....81

art 1 77
art 2 77
art 27 81
art 47(2) 79
art 48(4) 79
art 49 77
art 50 78
art 52 78
(2) 78, 262
art 56 77
art 58 79
art 61 80
art 62 80
art 79 77
art 86 80
Joint Declaration on art 104 81
Euro–Mediterranean Agreement establishing an Association between the European Community and its Member States, of the one part, and the Republic of Lebanon, of the other part [2006] OJ L143/2 .....59, 77–81
title I 77
title II 80
titles II–IV 77
title III 80
title V 77
title VIII 81
art 1 77
art 2 77
art 27 81
art 40(3) 79
art 41(3) 79
art 42 77
art 45 78
(2) 78
art 49 77
art 51 79
art 54 80
art 55 80
art 61 80
art 71 77
Joint Declaration on art 86 81
Economic Partnership Agreement between the CARIFORUM States, of the one part, and the European Community and its Member States, of the other [2008] OJ L289/3 .....94–108, 120–24, 127–29, 134, 139, 140, 243, 248, 249, 263

preamble 98
part I 97
part II 97
title I 97
title II ch 2 108
title IV ch 4 98
art 1 98
art 2 96
art 3(1) 97
(2)(a) 97
(3) 98
art 4 98
art 7 103
(3) 97
art 37(1) 104
(4) 104
(5) 104
art 43(2)(c) 105
(f) 105
art 72 .... 101, 108, 123, 278
art 73 .... 101, 108
art 115 105
art 116 105
art 117(2)(b) 106
(d) 106
art 138(1) 106
(2) 106
art 150(1) 105, 127, 263
(3) 105
(5) 105, 263
art 183(2) 102
(3) 99
(4) 99
(5) 99
art 184(1) 100
(3) 102
art 185 99
art 186 102
art 187 102
art 188(1) 101
(2) 101
art 189(1) 106
(2) 106
(3) 106

(4) 107
(5)–(6) 107
art 190....103
art 204(6)....107
art 205....107
art 207(4)....107
arts 210–12....107
art 213(2)....108
art 224....102
art 229....106
art 230(3)(a)(vi)....106
art 232(1)....107
art 241(1)....96
Stabilisation and Association Agreement between the European Communities and their Member States, of the one part, and the Republic of Serbia, of the other part, 29 April 2008, www.ec.europa.eu/enlargement/pdf/serbia/key_document/saa_en.pdf....58, 67–74
title II....68
title III....68
title IV....72
titles IV–V....68
title V....72
title VII....68
title VIII....68, 70
title X....73
art 1(2)....67
art 2....67
art 5....68
art 61(2)....73
art 72....67
art 86....72
art 88(2)....70
(3)....74
art 94....72
art 97....70
art 98....70
art 108....71
art 109....71, 260
arts 109–10....72
art 111....68, 69, 259, 260
art 115....68
art 129....74
Protocol 4 art 2(2)....71
art 7....71

art 15 ... 71

Stabilisation and Association Agreement between the European Communities and their Member States, of the one part, and the Republic of Bosnia and Herzegovina, 16 June 2008, www.delbih.ec.europa.eu/files/docs/publications/en/SAP_eng.pdf ... 58, 67–74

title II ... 68

title III ... 68

title IV ... 72

titles IV–V ... 68

title V ... 72

title VII ... 68

title VIII ... 68, 70

title X ... 73

art 1(2) ... 67

art 2 ... 67

art 5 ... 68

arts 5–6 ... 68

art 43 ... 73

art 59(2) ... 73

art 63 ... 73

art 70 ... 67

art 84 ... 72

art 86(2) ... 70

(3) ... 74

art 92 ... 72

art 95 ... 70

art 96 ... 70

art 106 ... 71

art 107 ... 71

art 108 ... 68, 259

art 112 ... 68

art 125(4) ... 74

Protocol 3 art 2(2) ... 71

art 7 ... 71

art 15 ... 71

Protocol 6 ... 74

Stabilisation and Association Agreement between the European Communities and their Member States, of the one part, and the Republic of Albania, of the other part [2009] OJ L107/166 ... 58, 67–74

title II ... 68

title III ... 68

title IV ... 72

titles IV–V ... 68

title V ... 72

title VII 68
title VIII 68, 70
title X 73
art 1(2) 67
art 2 67
art 3 68
art 42 73
art 59(2) 73
art 70 67
art 85 72
art 86(2) 70
(3) 74
art 92 ....72, 277
art 95 70
art 96 70
art 106 71
art 107 71
art 108 69
art 112 68
art 126 74
Protocol 5 art 2(2) 71
art 7 71
art 15 71
Joint Declaration on art 136 74
Stabilisation and Association Agreement between the European Communities and their Member States, of the one part, and the Republic of Montenegro, of the other part [2010] OJ L108/3 ....58, 67–74
title II 68
title III 68
title IV 72
titles IV–V 68
title V 72
title VII 68
title VIII 68, 70
title X 73
art 1(2) 67
art 2 67
art 5 68
art 45 73
art 61(2) 73
art 65 73
art 72 67
art 86 72
art 88(2) 70

(3) 74
art 94....72
art 97....70
art 98....70
art 108....71
art 109....71
arts 109–10....72
art 111....68, 69, 259
art 115....68
art 129....74
Protocol 4 art 2(2)....71
art 7....71
art 15....71
Protocol 7....74
Voluntary Partnership Agreement between the European Community and the Republic of Ghana on FLEGT in timber products into the Community [2010] OJ L70/3
art 15....273
Annex II....274
Framework Agreement between the European Union and its Member States, on the one part, and the Republic of Korea, on the other part, 10 May 2010, www.eeas.europa.eu/korea_south/docs/framework_agreement_final_en.pdf....63, 117–29, 137, 201
preamble para 15....118
para 16....118
title II....118
title V....118, 119
title VI....118
title VII....118
art 1(1)....127
(3)....118
art 2....119
(d)....118
art 16....260
art 17(1)(a)....120
(c)....120
(d)....120
art 18(1)....121
(2)(b)....121
(c)....121
(e)....121
art 23....119, 262
(1)....119
(2)(a)–(h)....119

(i) 119
(3) 119
art 24 ....119, 136, 260
(1) 119
(a)–(g) 120
(2) 119
art 25(f) 120
(g) 120
(i) 120
art 26 120
art 43(4) 127
art 44 127
art 45 127
(2) 119
art 46 127
Joint Declaration concerning arts 45 and 46 127
Free Trade Agreement between the European Union and its Member States, of the one part, and
the Republic of Korea, of the other part, 6 October 2010, www.trade.ec.europa.eu/doclib/press/index.cfm?id=443&serie=273&langId=en 63, 117–29, 134, 139, 201, 244
preamble para 11 118
chap 13 121
art 1 118
(g) 118
(h) 118
art 2.15(1) 124
art 13.1(1) 121, 122
(2) 122
(3) 122
art 13.2(2) 124
art 13.3 122
art 13.5(1) 125
(1)–(2) 122
(3) 125, 136, 268
art 13.6 278
(2) 121
art 13.7 122
art 13.8 124
art 13.9 124
art 13.10 ....128, 253
art 13.11 ....125, 136, 262
art 13.12(2) 128
(4) 128

(5) 128
art 13.13....128
art 13.14....129
(2) 129
art 13.15....129
art 13.16....128
art 15.1(2)....128
Annex 13....125, 136
Agreement establishing an Association between the EU and its Member States, on the one hand, and Central America on the other, 22 March 2011, www.trade.ec.europa.eu/ doclib/press/index.cfm?id=689....59, 86–108, 120, 134, 139, 244, 256
part I title II....94
title VI....91
part III title V....88
part IV title II....98
title III....98
title VIII....98
art 1(2)....86
art 2(b)....86
(c)....86
(g)....86
art 11....95
art 12(a)–(b)....86
art 13(3)....86
art 20....87, 271, 276
art 25(e)....86
art 45(3)....89
art 50(3)....89, 136
(d)....88
(4)....89
art 59....91, 247
art 63....103, 136, 260, 278
(3)(b)....88
art 64(1)....91, 277
art 65(2)(c)....91, 264
(d)....88
art 66....92
art 67(2)(c)–(d)....92
art 68(2)(d)....92
art 77(1)....98
art 126....102
art 132....102
art 203(1)(b)–(c)....102

art 284(1)....99
(4)....108
art 285(1)....100
(2)....100, 262
art 287(2)....100, 262
(3)–(4)....100
(4)....123
(5)....102
art 288....104, 278
art 289....104, 246, 275
art 290....104
art 291(2)–(3)....101
(4)....101
art 292....104
art 298....108
art 294....108
art 295....108
arts 296–301....108
art 301(3)....108
Free Trade Agreement between the EU and its Member States, on one side, and Colombia and Peru, on the other, 23 and 24 March 2011, www.trade.ec.europa.eu/doclib/press/index.cfm?id=691....63, 121–29, 134, 139, 244, 245, 256
title IX....121
art 63....268
art 178....125
art 267(1)....122
(2)....123
(b)....262
(5)....125
art 268....122
art 270(2)....123, 262
(3)....123
(4)....125
art 271....125, 278
art 272....262
(1)....126
(2)–(5)....127
art 273....126, 246, 263, 275
art 274....126, 247
art 275....126, 136, 260
art 277....123
(3)....124
(4)....124

art 278 ... 126
art 279 ... 128, 253
art 280 ... 128
(6) ... 128
art 281 ... 128
art 282 ... 128
art 283 ... 129
art 284 ... 129
art 285 ... 129
(4) ... 129
art 286 ... 125, 276

EU Legislation

Decisions

Council Decision (EC) 2002/979 on the signature and provisional application of certain provisions of an Agreement establishing an association between the European Community and its Member States, of the one part, and the Republic of Chile, of the other part [2002] OJ L352/3 ... 242
preamble paras 1–2 ... 242
Council Decision (EC) 2002/628 concerning the conclusion, on behalf of the European Community, of the Cartagena Protocol on Biosafety [2002] OJ L201/48 ... 19
Annex B ... 19
European Parliament and Council Decision (EC) 1600/2002 laying down the Sixth Environmental Action Programme [2002] OJ L242/1 ... 44–45
art 1(4) ... 44
art 3(5) ... 45
art 6 ... 44
art 7 ... 44
art 8 ... 44
art 9(2)(j) ... 44
Commission Decision (EC) 2005/924 on the list of the beneficiary countries which qualify for the special incentive arrangement for sustainable development and good governance, provided for by art 26(e) of Council Regulation (EC) No 980/2005 [2005] OJ L337/50 ... 166
Council Decision (EC) 2007/249 amending Decision 2001/822/EC on the association of the overseas countries and territories with the European Community [2007] L109/33 ... 197
Commission Decision (EC) 2008/938 on the list of the beneficiary countries which qualify for the special incentive arrangement for sustainable development and good governance provided for in Council Regulation (EC) No 732/2008 [2008] OJ L334/90 ... 166

European Council Decision (EU) 2009/881 on the exercise of the Presidency of the Council [2009] OJ L315/50 210
Commission Decision (EU) 2010/318 on the beneficiary countries which qualify for the special incentive arrangement for sustainable development and good governance for the period from 1 July 2010 to 31 December 2011 as provided in Council Regulation (EC) No 732/2008 [2010] OJ L142/10....166

Directives

Council Directive 92/3/Euratom on the supervision and control of shipments of radioactive waste between Member States and into and out of the Community [1992] OJ L35/24....93
Council Directive 92/43/EC on the conservation of natural habitats and of wild fauna and flora [1992] OJ L206/7....35, 261
European Parliament and Council Directive 2009/28/EC on the promotion of the use of energy from renewable sources [2009] OJ L140/16....246, 260, 270–71, 287
preamble para 74....270
art 17(7)....270
art 18(4)....270
art 23(2)....270
European Parliament and Council Directive 2009/29/EC amending Directive (EC) 2003/87 so as to improve and extend the greenhouse gas emission allowance trading scheme of the Community [2009] OJ L140/63....259
art 9(1)....260
art 10(3)....259
art 25(1)(a)....259
European Parliament and Council Directive 2009/31/EC on the geological storage of carbon dioxide [2009] OJ L140/114....268, 271
preamble para 7....225, 268
European Parliament and Council Directive (EC) 2009/147/EC on the conservation of wild birds [2010] OJ L20/7....261

Regulations

Council Regulation (EC) 338/97 on the protection of species of wild fauna and flora by regulating trade therein [1997] L61/1....23, 261
Council Regulation (EC) 552/97 temporarily withdrawing access to generalised tariff preferences from the Union of Myanmar [1997] OJ L85/8....155
Commission Regulation (EC) 1649/2000 granting the Republic of Moldova the benefit of the special incentive arrangements concerning labour rights [2000] OJ L189/13....152
European Parliament and Council Regulation (EC) 2493/2000 on measures to promote the full integration of the environmental dimension

in the development process of developing countries [2000] L288/1 .... 36, 148, 153, 177–78, 190, 208
preamble para 3 178
para 4 178
para 11 178
art 1(1) 178
(3) 178
art 2 .... 36, 178
(4) 178
art 3(1) 178
art 7 178
European Parliament and Council Regulation (EC) 2494/2000 on measures to promote the conservation and sustainable management of tropical forests and other forests in developing countries [2000] OJ L288/6 .... 153, 177–80, 189–90, 272
preamble para 5 178
para 6 178
para 7 178
art 1 178
art 3 179
art 8 179
Council Regulation (EC) 2501/2001 applying a scheme of generalised tariff preferences for the period from 1 January 2002 to 31 December 2004 [2001] OJ L346/1 147–54
preamble para 5 .... 147, 149
art 3 149
art 7 149
art 8(3) 152
art 9 149
art 10 150
art 12 148
arts 14–20 149
art 21(1) 152
(2) 151, 162
arts 22–23 152
art 25 150
(2) 150
(3) 150
art 26 153
(1)(a) 153
(b) 153
(c) 153
(d) 153
(e) 153

(g) 154
(h) 153
(3) 152
Annex I 148
Commission Regulation (EC) 2342/2003 granting the Democratic Socialist Republic of Sri Lanka benefit from the special arrangement for the protection of labour rights [2003] OJ L346/34 152
Council Regulation (EC) 980/2005 applying a scheme of generalised tariff preferences [2005] OJ L169/1 156
preamble para 2 157
para 7 165
para 8 166
art 9(1) 160
art 10(1)(a) 162
Annex I col E 166
Council Regulation (EC) 2173/2005 on the establishment of a FLEGT licensing scheme for imports of timber into the European Community [2005] OJ L347/1 .....104, 246, 273
Council Regulation (EC) 1085/2006 establishing an Instrument for Pre–Accession Assistance [2006] OJ L210/82 .....191–92, 203–4
preamble para 13 192
art 1 191
art 2 192
art 4 192
art 6 192
art 7 192
art 8 192
art 9 192
(2) 192
art 10 192
art 11 192
art 12 192
art 14 192
art 26 191
Annex I 191
Annex II 191
European Parliament and Council Regulation (EC) 1638/2006 laying down general provisions establishing a European Neighbourhood and Partnership Instrument [2006] OJ L310/1 .....191, 193–95, 203, 204
preamble para 4 193
para 5 193
para 7 231
art 1(1) 193
art 2(2)(b) 194

(e)....................193
(g)....................193
(h)....................194
(m)....................194
(o)....................193
(t)....................194
(x)....................194
(y)....................193
art 3(1)....................193, 231
art 4....................231
(1)....................194
art 5(1)....................193
art 6(1)(a)(ii)....................194
art 9....................194
art 12(1)....................194
art 29....................193
(b)....................194
Annex....................193
European Parliament and Council Regulation (EC) 1905/2006 establishing a financing instrument for development cooperation [2006] OJ L378/41....................175–76, 180–85, 188, 191, 194–96, 203, 204
preamble para 13....................182
para 15....................182
Title I....................175
Title II....................175
Title III....................175
art 1(1)....................182
art 2(1)....................181
(2)....................181, 260, 264
art 3(3)....................182, 195
(8)(e)....................196
art 5(2)(a)....................196
(j)....................196
(n)....................196
(o)....................196
(p)....................196
(q)....................196
(r)....................196
(s)....................196
(t)....................196
art 6(e)....................196, 272
art 7(e)....................196, 272
art 8(f)....................196
art 11(2)....................181

art 12 ... 181
art 13 ... 181
(1) ... 182
(2) ... 185
(a) ... 183
(b) ... 183
(c) ... 183
(e) ... 183
art 14 ... 181
(1)(a)(ii) ... 183
art 15 ... 181
(2)(b)(ii) ... 183
(e) ... 183
art 16 ... 181
art 17 ... 181
art 18(1) ... 176
arts 18–19 ... 196
art 19(3) ... 176
(4) ... 176
art 20 ... 176
art 21 ... 183
art 22 ... 176, 183
(4) ... 184
art 24(1) ... 182
art 31(11) ... 185
art 33 ... 185
art 34 ... 185
art 38 ... 175
(4) ... 184
Annex I ... 181, 182, 195
Annex IV ... 175, 181, 183, 189, 195
European Parliament and Council Regulation (EC) 1907/2006 concerning the Registration, Evaluation, Authorisation and Restriction of Chemicals [2006] OJ L396/1 ... 223, 247, 256
Council Regulation (EC) 1934/2006 establishing a financial instrument for cooperation with industrialized and other high-income countries and territories [2006] OJ L405/41 ... 200–1, 203
art 1 ... 200
art 2(1) ... 200
art 3(3) ... 200, 231
art 4 ... 201, 260
art 5(2) ... 201
arts 5–6 ... 201
art 16 ... 200

Annex....200
Commission Regulation (EC) 951/2007 laying down implementing rules for cross–border cooperation programmes financed under Regulation (EC) 1638/2006 [2007] OJ L210/10
art 5(2)(d) 194
Council Regulation (EC) 55/2008 introducing autonomous trade preferences for the Republic of Moldova [2008] OJ L20/1 166
Council Regulation (EC) 732/2008 applying a scheme of generalised tariff preferences for the period from 1 January 2009 to 31 December 2011 [2008] OJ L211/1 .... 156, 159, 162, 164–66, 168
preamble para 7 159
para 19....159
para 23....168
art 6....156
art 7....159
art 8(1)(a)....159, 162
(2)....165
art 9(1)(a)....162
(2)....162
art 10(1)....162
(2)....164
(3)....164
(4)....164
arts 11–12 156
art 13....156
art 15(1)....168
(a) 168
(e) 168
(2)....164
Annex I 156, 165
col A 159
col D....159
col C 159
Annex II....156
Annex III 160
European Parliament and Council Regulation (EC)1221/2009 on the voluntary participation by organisations in a Community eco-management and audit scheme [2009] OJ L342/1 247
art 2(7)....279
art 11(1)....279
Annex I para 2(b)(vii) 279
(v)....279
European Parliament and Council Regulation (EC) 66/2010 on the EU Eco-label [2010] OJ L27/1

art 2 279
art 3(2) 279
art 6(3)(e) 279
art 9(c) 279
European Parliament and Council Regulation (EU) 995/2010 laying down the obligations of operators who place timber and timber products on the market [2010] OJ L295/23
art 3 274
art 4 274

Introduction

'Environmental protection requirements must be integrated into the definition and implementation of the Union's policies and activities, in particular with a view to promoting sustainable development.'
(Article 11 TFEU)[1]

THE ENVIRONMENTAL INTEGRATION requirement enshrined in Article 11 TFEU – one of the oldest integration clauses in European Union (EU)[2] primary law – has captured scholarly interest over the past decades. It has been treated as one of the most important aspects of EU environmental law in leading textbooks,[3] but also as the core subject of specialist studies. Legal scholars have enriched our understanding of the content and legal effects of Article 11 TFEU,[4] as well as offered an examination of its articulation in the context of the EU agricultural, competition, energy and transport policies.[5] Political scientists[6] have contributed to the analysis of Article 11 TFEU, by looking into environmental policy integration both within various EU sectoral policies and in the practice of some of the Member States. Against this background, what are the additional perspectives on environmental integration that this book seeks to offer?

[1] Unless otherwise specified, throughout this book reference will be made to the consolidated versions of the Treaty on the Functioning of the European Union (TFEU) and the Treaty on the European Union (TEU) [2010] OJ C83/1, jointly referred to as the Treaty of Lisbon. Given that most of the EU measures analysed in this book were adopted during the pre-Lisbon period, complementary reference will be made where relevant to the consolidated version of the preceding Treaty establishing the European Community (TEC) [2006] OJ C 321E/1.

[2] For simplification purposes, throughout this book the term 'European Union' (EU) will be generally used, as the EU has superseded the old European Community (EC) since the entry into force of the Lisbon Treaty. In purely legalistic terms, it should be clarified that most of the measures examined in this book were adopted by the EC during the pre-Lisbon period, although this distinction had become increasingly fictitious in practice and largely irrelevant in non-legal literature.

[3] See eg, JH Jans and HHB Vedder, *European Environmental Law* (Groningen, Europa Law Publishing, 2008) 16–23; L Kramer, *EC Environmental Law* (London, Sweet & Maxwell, 2007) ch 11.

[4] N Dohndt, *Integration of Environmental Protection into Other EC Policies – Legal Theory and Practice* (Groningen, Europa Law Publishing, 2003); M Wasmeier, 'The Integration of Environmental Protection as a General Rule for Interpreting Community Law' (2001) 38(1) *Common Market Law Review* 159; M Hession and R Macrory, 'The Legal Duty of Environmental Integration: Commitment and Obligation or Enforceable Rights?' in T O'Riordan and H Voisey (eds), *The Transition to Sustainability: The Politics of Agenda 21 in Europe* (London, Earthscan, 1998). Note that these, and other pre-Lisbon studies, dealt with former versions of article 11 TFEU.

[5] Dohndt, above n 4; R Macrory (ed), *Reflections on 30 Years of EU Environmental Law: A High Level of Protection?* (Groningen, Europa Law Publishing, 2005) chs 9–10; S Kingston, 'Integrating Environmental Protection and EU Competition Law: Why Competition Isn't Special' (2010) 16(6) *European Law Journal* 780.

[6] A Lenschow (ed), *Environmental Policy Integration – Greening Sectoral Policies in Europe* (London, Earthscan Publications, 2002).

Most of the existing academic literature has focused on the integration of environmental protection requirements into the *internal* policies of the EU, while in this study attention is instead directed towards the *external* relations of the Union, encompassing both its external policies (on which this book concentrates) and the external dimension of internal policies (such as agricultural, energy and transport policies). The shift in focus appears particularly timely in light of the entry into force of the Treaty of Lisbon on 1 December 2009. Not only has the Lisbon Treaty underscored the growing importance of the EU role as a global player (notably, through a series of institutional innovations aimed at increasing the visibility and effectiveness of the EU external action), but it has also established environmental protection and sustainable development among the key objectives of the Union's external relations. Notably, these include an explicit commitment to facilitate the development of 'international measures to preserve and improve the quality of the environment and the sustainable management of natural resources'.[7] The EU has, moreover, pledged at the international level to pursue an integrated approach to policy- and law-making in the economic, social and environmental fields, through its endorsement of the 1992 Rio Declaration on Environment and Development[8] and of the 2002 Declaration of the World Summit on Sustainable Development.[9] Global progress made in this regard will be reviewed at the upcoming UN Conference on Sustainable Development (Rio de Janeiro, June 2012), which also addresses on the emerging notion of 'green economy'[10] and likely provide renewed impetus for the EU's own environmental integration initiatives.

Like any other international actor, the EU can advance environmental protection objectives through participation in *multilateral* environmental processes, but also on the basis of *bilateral or inter-regional*[11] engagements. Emphasis in this book is primarily placed on the latter, less explored, avenue that is becoming an increasingly important factor in the shaping of global environmental governance, running in parallel to multilateral processes. As will be seen, the EU has, over the years, put in place a sophisticated network of instruments to define and implement its relations with individiual third countries or regions, other than through multilateral processes. Such external relations tools can be unilaterally adopted by the EU or bilaterially/inter-regionally agreed with third parties. In addition, these tools can be legal or non-legal in nature; even in the latter case, we found that they

[7] Articles 3(5) and 21(2) TEU.

[8] 'Rio Declaration on Environment and Development' (12 August 1992) UN Doc A/CONF.151/26 vol 1, Annex 1.

[9] 'Political Declaration of the World Summit on Sustainable Development' (4 September 2002) UN Doc A/CONF.199/20, Resolution 1.

[10] UN General Assembly, 'Implementation of Agenda 21, the Programme for Further Implementation of Agenda 21 and the Outcomes of the World Summit on Sustainable Development' (2010) UN Doc A/RES/64/236.

[11] Throughout this book, the term 'inter-regional' is used to refer to the relations of the EU (as a region) and a group of third countries (that usually form part themselves of a regional organisation), rather than with an individual third country for which the term 'bilateral' is used instead.

can contribute significantly to the development and implementation of legal norms. That being said, this book will also draw attention to the complex interplay and mutual influences between these EU environmental integration initiatives and environmental multilateralism.

As this book is the first attempt to verify the significance of Article 11 TFEU in the context of EU external relations, it is important to indicate from the outset the limits of the scope of our enquiry. While an important number of EU external relations tools are explored, our analysis is by no means exhaustive but aims at providing a solid basis for future academic research in this domain. Similarly, underlying aspects of EU law and international environmental law could only be treated with the degree of depth necessary to inform our analysis, while we attempted to make the book accessible both to EU external relations and environmental experts. In addition, this book confines itself to a *legal* appraisal of the degree and manner in which environmental protection requirements have been integrated into EU external relations, focusing on unilateral, bilateral and inter-regional tools, whilst assessing interactions with multilateral environmental regimes and processes.[12] Consequently, it does not purport to evaluate the impacts of the EU measures examined on the third countries or regions concerned, but may lay the ground for future empirical research in this direction.

The book will start by tracing the legal and policy contours of the environmental integration requirement, offering a detailed textual and contextual analysis of Article 11 TFEU, as well as of the constitutional foundations of the EU's environmental policy to which this requirement is inherently linked. While Article 11 TFEU is clearly construed as an obligation of environmental integration into all EU policies and activities (both internal and external), the EU political institutions enjoy a wide margin of discretion as to the degree and the modalities in complying with this requirement (Chapter One).

Building on this premise, the book turns to an analysis of practice in integrating environmental protection concerns into EU relations with third countries or regions, with each of the core five chapters examining a different instrument. A substantial part of the analysis is first devoted to a comparison of EU *bilateral and inter-regional agreements*, as treaties are the most defining legal expression of foreign policy-making, and also an instrument of external relations that has been negotiated with, and agreed upon by, the third country or region concerned. Chapter Two thus exposes the reader to the environmental dimension of these agreements, as well as to the variety of provisions that have been used to pursue environmental integration in EU bilateral and inter-regional relations. A considerable (although, by no means, exhaustive) array of case studies has been carefully selected from a geographic perspective (to provide a balanced representation, encompassing EU relations with several individual countries or regions in Africa, Asia, Eastern Europe and Latin America), as well as from a historical standpoint (to allow for a delineation of the evolution of practice).

12 The law and policy developments throughout this book are reflected as they were on 30 June 2011.

The two subsequent chapters explore, in turn, the extent to which environmental concerns have been integrated through tools that are, for the most part, *unilaterally* adopted by the EU, but which closely interact with its bilateral and inter-regional agreements. To this end, Chapter Three concentrates on the Generalised System of Preferences, which is a tool of EU external trade policy and regulates its trade relations with a number of developing countries. Chapter Four considers several instruments that underpin EU financial and technical assistance to third countries or regions, and that are adopted within the framework of other purely external policies of the Union such as enlargement and development policies. The analysis therefore does not extend to scrutinising environmental integration through unilateral measures of EU internal policies (such as agriculture, fisheries and energy policies), albeit these also have an important external environmental dimension.

Other *less legalised* tools used by the EU to pursue environmental integration in its relations with third countries or regions have also been identified. On the one hand, various dialogues have been institutionalised between the EU and third parties on a bilateral or inter-regional basis, within the framework of an existing agreement but also outside such a formal structure. While diverging in form, scope and objectives, these institutionalised dialogues affect environmental cooperation between the EU and the third parties concerned (Chapter Five). The other non-legalised instrument is the unilateral undertaking by the EU to carry out systematic prior assessments of the socio-economic and environmental impacts of an envisaged agreement that has a trade component. The EU practice related to these so-called sustainability impact assessments will be overviewed, followed by an evalution of its relevance in ensuring environmental integration through other EU external relations tools (Chapter Six).

Drawing on the tool-by-tool analysis just outlined, Chapter Seven unveils the complex and evolving interactions of the EU's external environmental action at the unilateral, bilateral and inter-regional levels with multilateral environmental treaties and processes. A dynamic typology will be drawn to illustrate how EU external relations tools have been used as a means to: favour the implementation of existing MEAs in third parties (particularly developing countries); build alliances at the bilateral/inter-regional level with a view to influencing ongoing multilateral environmental negotiations; or contribute to the development of new international environmental norms in the absence of multilateral negotiations. The book concludes by offering some normative reflections regarding the credibility and legitimacy of environmental integration in the EU's external relations beyond multilateral dimensions.

1

The EU Legal and Policy Framework

1. INTRODUCTION[1]

THE AIM OF this chapter is to trace the broad legal and policy contours of the environmental integration requirement enshrined in Article 11 TFEU. The chapter begins by introducing the reader to the special character of the EU as an international environmental actor from the perspective of both public international law and EU constitutional law (section 1). It will then examine the constitutional features of the EU's environmental policy, to which Article 11 TFEU is inherently linked. The granting of external competence to the EU on environmental matters will first be looked at from a historical perspective, before turning to an examination of its substantive scope and nature, as well as to the instruments available to the EU to articulate and implement the external dimension of its environmental policy (section 2).

The analysis is then directed to the core subject of this study: Article 11 TFEU (section 3). The environmental integration requirement will be explored in detail, to fully explain its legal relevance as a lens for the examination of EU external measures in subsequent chapters of this book. The emergence and evolution of this provision in EU primary law will be discussed first. This will be followed by a textual and contextual interpretation of Article 11 TFEU to determine its legal significance. The consequences that may be derived under EU law from 'environmental integration failures'[2] will also be considered.

Finally, the chapter will offer an overview of the EU's approach to environmental integration in the specific area of external relations, with a view to identifying the key environmental priorities and instruments that characterise EU environmental integration efforts in this particular field.

2. THE EU AS AN INTERNATIONAL ACTOR IN THE ENVIRONMENTAL FIELD

The EU has increasingly sought to assert itself as a prominent player in global environmental governance, by gradually developing an environmental policy

[1] The authors are extremely grateful to Professor Bruno de Witte for his timely and rigorous feedback on this chapter. As usual, any errors or omissions are entirely our own.

[2] This term is proposed by N Dhondt, *Integration of Environmental Protection into Other EC Policies: Legal Theory and Practice* (Groningen, Europa Law Publishing, 2003), 190.

with a marked external dimension and by being proactively engaged in the shaping and application of international environmental law. This includes, most notably, its participation in over 40 Multilateral Environmental Agreements (MEAs), but also in other environmental processes at regional and bilateral levels.[3] The EU has a clear potential to act as a powerful negotiating block in MEAs and other international environmental processes, speaking not only on behalf of its 27 Member States but often also of other associated countries.[4] However, whether due to lack of formal capacity or political will, the EU has not always been able to speak with a 'single voice' in international fora and coordination challenges still exist between its external action and that of its Member States. Nonetheless, the growing importance and weight of the EU in international environmental processes goes largely undisputed, particularly in light of the fact that the EU and its Member States represent the largest provider of official development aid and contributions to UN budgets.[5]

The emergence and consolidation of the EU as a global environmental actor has required, inter alia, important changes in both the EU founding Treaties and in public international law. Like other international entities, the EU needs to fulfil three necessary conditions to be an international environmental actor, whether at the multilateral or other levels: international legal personality; external recognition; and the necessary competence (and autonomy vis-a-vis its Member States) to undertake binding commitments.

The second condition is dependent upon the willingness of other international actors to recognise the Union as a negotiating partner and as a future party to the international agreement in question. Such external recognition of the EU has required some adaptation in the process of international law-making and enforcement, given that the EU is not a 'traditional actor' in public international law: it is neither a sovereign state, nor an international organisation. As opposed to the EU, international organisations usually have limited capacity to act and only rarely conclude international treaties.[6] The unique and complex nature of the Union as an international actor generated uncertainty among negotiating part-

[3] See s 3.5 below.

[4] For instance, at the UN World Summit the EU spoke on behalf of 36 countries, see E Morgera and G Marín Durán, 'The UN 2005 World Summit, the Environment and the EU: Priorities, Promises and Prospects' (2006) 15(1) *Review of Community and International Environmental Law* 11, 11.

[5] According to official data, the EU and its Member States collectively are the world's largest provider of official development assistance (ODA), providing 56 per cent of global ODA. See, Commission, 'Communication on a twelve-point EU action plan in support of the Millennium Development Goals' COM (2010) 159 final, 5 (Communication Action Plan MDGs 2010). The EU and its Member States are also the single largest financial contributor to the UN system: the 27 EU Member States fund 38 per cent of the UN's regular budget, more than two-fifths of UN peacekeeping operations, and about one-half of all UN member States' contributions to UN funds and programmes; while the European Commission alone contributes more than $1.35 bn in support of UN external assistance programmes and projects (source: EU Delegation to the United Nations: www.europa-eu-un.org/Arts/Artslist_s88_en.htm).

[6] B de Witte, 'The Emergence of a European System of Public International Law: the EU and its Member States as Strange Subjects' in J Wouters, A Nollkaemper and E de Wet (eds), *The Europeanisation of International Law* (The Hague, TMC Asser Press, 2008), 39.

ners and made the path towards external recognition rather rocky in the 1970s and 1980s.[7] At present, the EU is widely recognised as a party to international agreements, albeit still a complex one to many of its counterparts.[8]

In the vast majority of MEAs, the EU's participation has been accommodated, as a 'regional economic integration organisation' (REIO), through the so-called REIO clauses.[9] Beyond the institutional structures created by MEAs, the EU is also a full member of the UN Food and Agriculture Organisation (FAO) and of the World Trade Organisation (WTO), which are also of relevance to global environmental governance. The 1991 accession of the then European Community (EC) to the FAO was enabled through the insertion of an 'REIO-clause' into the FAO Constitution,[10] while the case of the WTO was very different given that the Community was already a contracting party to its predecessor, the 1947 General Agreement on Trade and Tariffs (GATT).[11] Full member status represents, however, a rather exceptional case for the EU, which otherwise has only observer status (such as in the UN General Assembly,[12] the UN Environment Programme and the Global Environment Facility),[13] and in other instances (such as the Commission on Sustainable Development and UN environmental summits) 'speaking rights'.[14]

The first and third conditions of the EU's status as an international actor are, instead, primarily determined by the EU's own constitutional order. The EU is explicitly granted international legal personality by its founding Treaties, and thus clearly possesses the capacity to act in the international system from an EU law perspective.[15] However, the condition of substantive competence deserves more attention, due to the EU's very existence as a constitutional system based upon the principle of conferral (or *compétences d'attribution*), that is, the EU 'shall only act within the limits of the competences conferred upon it by the Member States in the Treaties to attain the objectives set out therein'.[16] This principle, together with

[7] T Delreux, *The EU as an International Environmental Negotiator* (Surrey, Ashgate, 2011), 15.

[8] See s 3.3 below.

[9] See generally L Kramer, 'Regional Economic International Organisations: The European Union as an Example' in J Brunnée, D Bodansky and E Hey (eds), *The Oxford Handbook of International Environmental Law* (Oxford, Oxford University Press, 2007).

[10] Constitution of the Food and Agriculture Organisation of the United Nations, 16 October 1945, entered into force for the EC on 26 November 1991, in FAO, *Basic Texts* vol I (Rome, FAO, 2010), art II.

[11] General Agreement on Trade and Tariffs (GATT) in WTO Secretariat, *The Legal Texts – The Results of the Uruguay Round of Multilateral Trade Negotiations* (Cambridge, Cambridge University Press, 1999).

[12] See also the post-Lisbon recognition of the modalities of EU representation by General Assembly 'Participation of the European Union in the work of the United Nations' (2011) UN Doc A/RES/65/276.

[13] P Eeckhout, *External Relations of the European Union: Legal and Constitutional Foundations* (Oxford, Oxford University Press, 2004), 199–205.

[14] J Vogler, 'The European Union as an Actor in International Environmental Politics' (1999) 8(3) *Environmental Politics* 25, 32–34.

[15] Art 47 TEU reads: 'The Union shall have legal personality'. Before the Lisbon Treaty, only the European Community was explicitly granted legal personality (former Art 281 TEC). See also, Delreux, above n 7, 15 arguing the EC also met the criteria for international legal personality from a public international law perspective.

[16] Art 5(2) TEU further stating that: 'Competences not conferred upon the Union in the Treaties remain with the Member States'.

those of subsidiarity and proportionality,[17] govern the exercise of EU competences and the vertical division of powers between the Union and the Member States, both internally and externally. In essence, the principle of conferral poses two inter-linked constitutional limits on the adoption of any EU legislative act, including those pertaining to the conclusion and/or implementation of an international agreement: the existence of substantive powers and the choice of an appropriate legal basis.[18]

At least from a legal perspective, this constitutional principle may be singled out as the most distinctive characteristic of the EU as an international actor: its action on the international scene may be internally constrained either by lack of competence, or where competence exists, by the objectives it must pursue and the extent to which it can act in an autonomous manner from its Member States.[19] The original Treaty of Rome[20] only contained two provisions granting express external competences[21] to the then European Economic Community (EEC), and the broadening of such competences has been a particularly sensitive issue for the EU Member States, which generally perceive treaty-making powers as being a core element of their national sovereignty. These constitutional and political features help to explain why there is a greater degree of legalisation and judicialisation of EU foreign relations when compared with those of sovereign States,[22] and also why more often than not, the EU acts on the international scene jointly with its Member States.

As far as environmental matters are concerned, there is no ambiguity that the EU has been expressly empowered to act externally and to undertake international commitments on the basis of Article 191(4) TFEU, which reads: 'Within their respective spheres of competence, the Union and the Member States shall cooper-

[17] Art 5(3) and (4) TEU, respectively (see below nn 68 and 69).

[18] The choice of the appropriate legal basis is of constitutional significance, as it has important implications for intra-EU policy-making, as well as for the delimitation of powers between the EU and its Member States and has generated substantial case law (including cases involving environmental and 'trade-and-environment' measures). An examination of this case law is beyond the scope of this study: see generally P Koutrakos, 'Legal Basis and Delimitation of Competence in EU External Relations' in M Cremona and B de Witte (eds), *EU Foreign Relations Law: Constitutional Fundamentals* (Oxford, Hart, 2008).

[19] The type of constraints posed by the principle of conferred powers would, for instance, not arise in the case of the United States where the Constitution grants the federal government exclusive and substantially unrestricted powers for 'the conduct of foreign relations' (art I (8) and (9) and Amendment X). The US Supreme Court has interpreted this constitutional provision rather extensively, even beyond the principle of parallelism developed by the ECJ. Most significantly, in *Missouri v Holland* 252 U.S. 416 (1920), the US Supreme Court held that the US federal government may conclude international agreements even on matters on which it cannot adopt internal legislation according to domestic rules. See further, G Marín Durán, *Development-based Differentiation in the European Community's External Trade Policy – Selected Issues under Community and International Trade Law* (Doctoral thesis, European University Institute, 2007), 51–55.

[20] Treaty establishing the European Economic Community, Bulletin EC 1972, No 10 (EEC Treaty).

[21] Namely, the common commercial policy (see s 5.2 below) and associations (see Ch 2, s 2.1).

[22] B de Witte, 'Too Much Constitutional Law?' in Cremona and de Witte (eds), above n 18, 7–12 pointing to a situation of 'constitutional overabundance' in the area of EU external relations and partly attributing this to the existence of abundant and complicated case law.

ate with third countries and with the competent international organisations. The arrangements for Union cooperation may be the subject of agreements between the Union and the third parties concerned'.[23] These express treaty-making powers have furthermore been interpreted broadly by the European Court of Justice (ECJ), as enabling the EU to participate in an agreement even if (some of) the specific matters covered by the agreement are not yet, or only very partially, the subject of EU internal legislation.[24] Yet, by virtue of the principle of conferral, a question remains as to whether EU primary law imposes nonetheless limits on the exercise of such external environmental competence, depending on the objectives the EU must pursue in its external environmental action, as well as on the degree of autonomy it enjoys vis-a-vis the Member States. Before addressing these questions, the next section will first look at the attribution of EU environmental competence (in a broader sense) from a historical perspective.

3. EU EXTERNAL COMPETENCE ON ENVIRONMENTAL MATTERS

3.1 Emergence and evolution

The original Treaty of Rome did not vest in the European Economic Community any express competence on environmental matters (whether internal or external), and contained only meagre provisions conferring upon it the power to conclude international agreements, notably in the field of external trade and association agreements. It quickly became apparent that such limited express conferral of internal and external powers did not offer a sufficient legal basis for the growing needs of the Community to act in the field of the environment, including on the international scene.

With the convening of the first global summit on environmental protection, the 1972 Stockholm Conference on the Human Environment,[25] the Community joined other international actors in recognising environmental protection as an issue requiring urgent action.[26] The same year, a Summit of Heads of State of the Member States requested the drawing up of an action programme for a Community environmental policy, even in the absence of an express basis for the articulation of such a policy in the Treaty of Rome.

[23] This express external competence for environmental matters was granted by the Single European Act of 1986 (below n 35) and has remained unchanged since then (see s 3.1 below).

[24] Case C-459/03 *Commission v Ireland* [2006] ECR I-4635, para 94 in particular.

[25] Declaration of the United Nations Conference on the Human Environment (16 June 1972) UN Doc. A/Conf.48/14/rev.1.

[26] I van Homeyer, 'The Evolution of EU Environmental Governance' in J Scott (ed), *Environmental Protection, European Law and Governance* (Oxford, Oxford University Press, 2009), 4; P Sands, *Principles of International Environmental Law* 2nd edn (Cambridge, Cambridge University Press, 2003), 741; D McGillivray and J Holder, 'Locating EC Environmental Law' (2001) 2 *Yearbook of European Environmental Law* 139, 144, all arguing that this influence explains the 'anthropocentric' approach of EU environmental law.

The following year the First Programme of Action of the European Communities on the Environment (1973–76) was adopted:[27] it was a policy declaration setting broad-ranging environmental objectives for the Community that already embodied some external dimension. Notably, its chapter on 'Community action and joint action by Member States in international organizations' stated that the Community 'must *continue* the *very active cooperation* it has established in [the environmental] field with most of the international bodies' (emphasis added), both because proposed international measures, even where non binding, could affect international trade, the functioning of the common market or other areas within the (exclusive) competence of the Community, and because the comparison with the activities of third countries participating in international organisations would benefit the Community by shedding new light on its own activities.[28]

Environmental legislation was then enacted in an 'incidental' fashion in the 1970s and early 1980s on the basis of the 'approximation of laws' provision, which provided for legislative action to approximate national laws that directly affected 'the functioning of the common market', but did not back then explicitly refer to environmental protection.[29] In addition, to remedy this lacuna, the Council often also invoked the 'flexibility clause,'[30] which allows more generally the adoption of legislative measures necessary for attaining the objectives of the Treaty where no other more specific legal basis is provided for.[31]

In parallel to these political and legislative developments, the ECJ laid down the 'classic authorities' of the doctrine on implied treaty-making powers in its breakthrough *AETR* judgment[32] and *Opinion 1/76*.[33] In an attempt to summarise rather complex case law, the Court essentially established two independent conditions for the existence of *implied* external competences: (i) where this competence is explicitly provided for within an internal legislative act (existence *à la AETR*); (ii) even prior to the adoption of secondary legislation, by implication from the simple existence of internal powers (that is, the principle of parallelism), insofar as participation by the Community in an envisaged international agreement is

[27] Council of the European Communities and Representatives of the Governments of the Member States meeting in the Council, 'Declaration on the Programme of Action for the European Communities on the Environment' [1973] OJ C112/1 (First Environmental Action Programme).

[28] Ibid, 11 and 47–48.

[29] Former art 100a EEC Treaty, later art 95 TEC, now art 114 TFEU. Since the Single European Act (below n 35), environmental (alongside health and consumer) protection mainstreaming has been explicitly included in this provision as an obligation on the Commission when proposing harmonisation measures. Following various Treaty amendments, the current wording in art 114(3) TFEU is: 'The Commission, in its proposals envisaged in paragraph 1 concerning health, safety, environmental protection and consumer protection, will take as a base a high level of protection, taking account in particular of any new development based on scientific facts. Within their respective powers, the European Parliament and the Council will also seek to achieve this objective.'

[30] Art 352 TFEU (former art 235 EEC Treaty, later art 308 TEC).

[31] For an overview of this early environmental legislation, see J Jans and H Vedder, *European Environmental Law* 3rd edn (Groningen, Europa Law Publishing, 2008), 4–5; J Holder and M Lee, *Environmental Protection: Law and Policy* (Cambridge, Cambridge University Press, 2007), 157–58.

[32] Case C-22/70 *Commission v Council* (AETR) [1971] ECR 263.

[33] *Opinion 1/76 on the Draft Agreement establishing a Laying-up Fund for Inland Waterway Vessels* [1977] ECR 741.

necessary for the achievement of the objectives contemplated within the Treaty provision conferring the internal competence (existence *à la Opinion 1/76*).[34] This judicially-made doctrine of implied treaty-making powers allowed for broader leeway in international environmental law-making by the EEC, including its participation in four multilateral environmental agreements, before the entry into force of the Single European Act (SEA) of 1986:[35] a global one, the Convention on the Conservation of Migratory Species,[36] and three regional ones.[37]

Introducing and developing a doctrine of implied treaty-making powers within a constitutional system based upon the principle of conferral was undoubtedly a major legal (and political) challenge for the ECJ, and a clear sign to the Member States that the Treaty of Rome did not reflect the growing needs for the European Economic Community to act internationally. The SEA, the first treaty substantively amending the Treaty of Rome, introduced among other provisions a new title on the environment,[38] which included an explicit competence in the area of external environmental relations.[39] The new title also laid down a set of objectives and principles to underpin EEC action in the environmental field, which equally determined the material scope of the Community internal and external environmental competence. In procedural terms, the exercise of these new powers by the Community was subject to unanimous decision-making by the Council in consultation with the European Parliament. Significantly, the new environmental title also included an obligation for environmental protection requirements to be a component of the other Community policies.

Following the convening of the 1992 United Nations Conference on Environment and Development in Rio de Janeiro,[40] the Maastricht Treaty[41] for the first time placed the environment among the core objectives of the renamed European Community, which included the promotion throughout its territory of a 'harmonious and balanced development of economic activities' and 'sustainable and

[34] The Court has generally asserted the existence of implied powers and this has been largely accepted by the EU political institutions. What has often been the crucial ground for legal battles between the Council and Commission is not so much the question of existence of implied powers but rather of their nature, and particularly the extent to which implied external powers may also become exclusive. On this case law, see generally A Dashwood and C Hillion, *The General Law of EC External Relations* (London, Sweet and Maxwell, 2000), chs 1 and 8; Eeckhout, above n 13, ch 3.

[35] Single European Act [1987] OJ L169/1 (SEA).

[36] Convention on the Conservation of Migratory Species of Wild Animals, 23 June 1979, 1651 UNTS 333 entered into force for the EU on 1 November 1983.

[37] Convention on the Conservation of European Wildlife and Natural Habitats, 19 September 1979, 1284 UNTS 290, entered into force for the EU on 1 September 1982 (Berne Convention); Convention on the Conservation of Antarctic Marine Living Resources, 20 May 1980, entered into force for the EU on 21 May 1982, 1329 UNTS 47; UNECE Convention on Long-range Transboundary Air Pollution, 13 November 1979, 1302 UNTS 217 entered into force for the EU on 16 March 1983. Throughout this book, it is referred to as CMS. See discussion in Sands, above n 26, 742; Jans and Vedder, above n 31, 58–60.

[38] Title VII SEA.

[39] Art 130r(5) SEA.

[40] 'Rio Declaration on Environment and Development' (12 August 1992) UN.Doc A/CONF.151/26 vol 1, Annex I (Rio Declaration).

[41] Treaty on the European Union [1992] OJ C191/1 (Treaty of Maastricht).

non-inflationary growth respecting the environment'.[42] Similarly, a 'policy in the sphere of environment' was recognised as one of the central activities of the EC.[43] While the Maastricht Treaty did not use the expression 'sustainable development', which had been endorsed at the Rio Summit, the weaker expressions relating to balanced development and sustainable growth were still considered to be of great political importance.[44] In addition, the Maastricht Treaty significantly amended the substantive provisions on EC environmental policy, by adding reference to the precautionary principle – also a principle of international environmental law[45] – and the objective of 'promoting international measures to deal with regional or worldwide environmental problems'.[46]

The Amsterdam Treaty of 1997[47] fine-tuned the inclusion of environmental protection and sustainable development in the key clauses of the EC Treaty. It reformulated reference to the 'harmonious, balanced and *sustainable* development of economic activities' (emphasis added),[48] which seems more in line with the internationally-accepted notion of 'sustainable development', and added a 'high level of protection and improvement of the quality of the environment'[49] to the core tasks of the Community. It also upgraded the requirement for environmental mainstreaming to a general principle of EU law, rather than a provision within the environmental title.[50] Finally, the Amsterdam Treaty established co-decision as the general procedure for environmental decision-making, thus ensuring a veto power for the European Parliament in this policy field.[51] This procedure has remained relevant for environmental policy-making at present, although it has been renamed 'ordinary legislative procedure' by the Lisbon Treaty.[52]

Possibly the most significant environmental feature of the Lisbon Treaty,[53] for present purposes, is the emphasis placed on the external dimension of the EU environmental policy. The Lisbon Treaty has first introduced an express link between sustainable development and EU external relations, by clarifying that 'in its relations with the wider world, the Union 'shall contribute to . . . the sustainable development of the Earth',[54] as one of the general objectives of the Union. Furthermore, a more explicit link with environmental protection is found in the new common set of non-prioritised objectives for the EU's external action, which

[42] Art 2 Treaty of Maastricht.
[43] Art 3(k) Treaty of Maastricht.
[44] See Jans and Vedder, above n 31, 7.
[45] Sands, above n 26, 266–79.
[46] Art 130r Treaty of Maastricht. See further s 3.2 below.
[47] Treaty of Amsterdam [1997] OJ C340/1 (Treaty of Amsterdam).
[48] Art 2 Treaty of Amsterdam.
[49] Ibid.
[50] Art 3c Treaty of Amsterdam, see s 4 below for further discussion.
[51] Art 130(s) (a) and (b) Treaty of Amsterdam. See Jans and Vedder, above n 31, 8–9.
[52] See s 3.4 below.
[53] See further M Lee, 'The Environmental Implications of the Lisbon Treaty' (2008) 10(2) *Environmental Law Review* 131; H Vedder, 'The Treaty of Lisbon and European Environmental Policy' (2010) 22(2) *Journal of Environmental Law* 285.
[54] Art 3(5) TEU.

require the Union to 'define and pursue common policies and actions, and work for a high degree of cooperation in all fields of international relations' in order to, inter alia, 'foster the sustainable economic, social and environmental development of developing countries' and to 'help to develop international measures to preserve and improve the quality of the environment and the sustainable management of global natural resources, in order to ensure sustainable development'.[55] With regards to the environment title, the Lisbon Treaty singles out climate change as the global environmental issue on which the EU must promote action at the international level:[56] this reflects the political priority attached to this specific environmental problem by the EU since the early 2000s.[57]

3.2 Substantive scope of EU external environmental competence

The key purpose of this section is to assess whether there are any limits in EU primary law on the content of the EU's external environmental action. Pursuant to the principle of conferral, the substantive scope of the EU environmental competence (whether internal or external) is determined by the objectives and principles enshrined in Articles 191(1) and (2) TFEU, respectively.[58] As will be seen, an analysis of these foundational objectives and principles is also of significance for understanding the meaning of 'environmental protection requirements' in Article 11 TFEU.

The TFEU sets out three general objectives for EU action in the field of the environment, whether internally or externally, which have remained unchanged since the SEA, namely: 'preserving, protecting and improving the quality of the environment'; 'protecting human health'; and 'ensuring the prudent and rational utilisation of natural resources'.[59] In addition, a fourth objective is prescribed for the external dimension of EU environmental policy, which was inserted by the Maastricht Treaty and revised by the Lisbon Treaty: 'promoting measures at international level to deal with regional or worldwide environmental problems, and in particular combating climate change'.[60]

In light of this broad Treaty-based definition of objectives, it is almost impossible to clearly define the substantive boundaries of EU environmental policy. The TFEU in fact does not seek to (unduly) restrict the substantive scope of EU environmental competence, but leaves the EU legislator a wide margin of

[55] Art 21(2)(d) and (f) TEU. Note that these objectives are also applicable to the EU common foreign and security policy (art 23 TEU).

[56] Art 191(1) TFEU.

[57] The EU elevated climate change as a priority too in its overall agenda on sustainable development and international cooperation, building upon the UN-driven inclusion of climate change among key threats to global security. See Morgera and Marín Durán, above n 4, 16.

[58] It is worth noting that the wording of art 191 TFEU is clearly mandatory: 'the Union policy on the environment shall contribute to the pursuit of the following objectives'.

[59] Art 191(1) TFEU.

[60] Art 191(1) TFEU, the emphasis on climate change was added by the Lisbon Treaty (see s 3.1 above).

appreciation in deciding what action and measures, if any, are necessary to achieve the environmental objectives stipulated in Article 191 TFEU.[61] This seems a desirable approach, given the need for flexibility and adaptation in formulating a policy that can address different environmental issues and adjust to new developments and specific circumstances. In addition, it has been argued that this broad definition of objectives allows for the adoption of a wide range of measures that result directly or indirectly in an improvement of the environment, such as conservation, restoration, repressive, precautionary, preventive and eminently procedural environmental measures.[62] As the term 'environment' is nowhere defined in the TFEU, a flexible interpretation has also been favoured, including both natural and man-made environment, with the exclusion of animals born in captivity.[63] The substantive content of the EU environmental policy (both internal and external) is therefore gradually defined by the EU political institutions[64] as they adopt measures in pursuance of the broadly-framed Treaty objectives, whether unilaterally or by concluding international agreements. These measures form part of the EU environmental '*acquis*',[65] which is subject to continuous evolution.

As to the territorial scope of EU environmental competence, reference to 'regional and worldwide environmental problems' in Article 191(1) TFEU indicates that the EU can also take measures targeting the environment beyond its borders, in the same way in which its Member States can do so, within the limits imposed by international law on the extraterritorial application of domestic environmental law.[66] This interpretation is arguably supported by the ECJ case law in the context of the common fisheries policy, where the Court held that the EU has competence over fishing in the high seas insofar as its Member States have similar authority under public international law.[67]

While there are no clear substantive limits to the exercise of EU environmental competence, this is still subject to the general principles of subsidiarity and proportionality. Under the proportionality principle, 'the content and form of Union action shall not exceed what is necessary to achieve the objectives of the Treaties'.[68] In addition, as for any other type of non-exclusive EU competence, the principle of subsidiarity requires that EU action be taken only if the objectives of the proposed action cannot be sufficiently achieved by the Member States but,

[61] See in particular wording of Art 192 TFEU discussed in s 3.4 below.

[62] Jans and Vedder, above n 31, 26–35.

[63] Dhondt, above n 2, 75.

[64] See s 3.4 below on instruments and decision-making procedures.

[65] The EU *acquis* (French term for 'that which has been agreed') refers to the body of common rights and obligations that binds all the EU Member States and comprises: the content, principles and political objectives of the Treaties; legislation adopted in the application of the Treaties; the case law of the ECJ; international agreements concluded by the EU.

[66] Jans and Vedder, above n 31, 31–36; see also L Bartels, 'Art XX of the GATT and the Problem of Extraterritorial Jurisdiction' (2002) 6(2) *Journal of World Trade* 353.

[67] Jans and Vedder, above n 31, 35, on the basis of Joint Cases 3, 4 and 6/76 *Cornelis Kramer and Others* [1976] ECR 1279; and Case C-405/92 *Etablissements Armand Mondiet v Société Armement Islais* (Mondiet) [1993] ECR I-6133.

[68] Art 5(4) TEU.

by reason of the scale or effects of the proposed action, are better achieved at EU level.[69]

Article 191(2) TFEU further lays down a set of principles that are specifically applicable to the exercise of EU environmental competence (both internal and external) as guide for law-making and for interpretation. These principles are: high level of environmental protection; precaution; prevention; rectification at source; and the polluter pays.

The principle of 'high level' of environmental protection is considered 'the most important substantive principle of European environmental policy'[70] given its inclusion among the general objectives of the EU.[71] Nonetheless, the principle is not defined by the Treaties and is made subject to consideration of the 'diversity of situations in the various regions of the Union.'[72] While it cannot be understood as allowing the EU to adopt the lowest common denominator among the Member States' standards of environmental protection,[73] the Court of Justice clarified that such a level of protection does not necessarily have to be the highest that is technically possible.[74] Overall, it can be concluded that the principle reflects a moving target – the idea of continuous improvement of environmental protection standards across the Member States.[75]

The precautionary principle, also a principle of international environmental law,[76] has been interpreted by scholars as allowing action by the EU institutions or Member States if there is a 'strong suspicion that a certain activity may have environmental harmful consequences' but insufficient scientific evidence exists to 'incontrovertibly show the causal connection'.[77] To implement the principle, the Commission clarified that a risk assessment is necessary,[78] that should be as complete as possible given the particular circumstances of the individual case, with a view to establishing precautionary measures that are 'proportional to the chosen level of protection, non-discriminatory in their application, consistent with similar measures already taken, based on an examination of the potential benefits and costs of action or lack of action, and subject to review in the light of new scientific data'.[79]

The prevention principle, also a principle of international environmental law,[80] calls for action to be taken to protect the environment at an early stage, with a

[69] Art 5(3) TEU. Initially, this principle was specifically applicable to environmental policy and later became a general principle of EU law. See D Chalmers, G Davies and G Monti, *European Union Law* 2nd edn (Cambridge, Cambridge University Press, 2010), 363–66.

[70] Jans and Vedder, above n 31, 36.

[71] Art 3(3) TEU. Note that the EU Charter of Fundamental Rights (EU Charter) [2010] OJ C83/389 also uses this expression with regard to environmental integration (art 37).

[72] Art 191(2) TFEU.

[73] L Kramer, *EC Environmental Law* 6th edn (London, Sweet & Maxwell, 2006), 12–13.

[74] Case C-284/95 *Safety High-Tech v S. & T. Srl* (Safety High-Tech) [1998] ECR I-4301; see Jans and Vedder, above n 31, 36–37.

[75] L Kramer, *EC Environmental Law*, above n 73, 12.

[76] Rio Declaration, principle 15. See Sands, above n 26, 266–78.

[77] Jans and Vedder, above n 31, 37.

[78] Commission, 'Communication on the precautionary principle' COM (2000) 1.

[79] Jans and Vedder, above n 31, 38.

[80] Sands, above n 26, 246–48.

view to preventing damage from occurring rather than repairing it.[81] The main difference with the precautionary principle lies in the availability of scientific evidence on the existence of a risk, although such a distinction may be difficult to be drawn in practice. The ECJ, for instance, relied on the prevention principle, as well as that of high level of protection, to review an export ban on British beef adopted in the context of the common agricultural policy because of a possible, rather than certain, risk related to bovine spongiform encephalopathy commonly known as mad-cow disease.[82] Guidance on the application of the prevention principle can be found in the Third Environmental Action Programme, which stressed the need to improve information for decision-makers and the public (for instance through monitoring and surveying requirements), to introduce procedures supporting prompt and informed decision-making on the environment such as environmental impact assessments, and to monitor implementation of adopted measures to ensure their adaptation in light of new circumstances or knowledge.[83]

The rectification at source principle entails that environmental damage should, as a priority, be rectified at its source.[84] The principle has had particular resonance in the area of waste management. Notably, the ECJ has interpreted this principle as requiring local authorities to take measures necessary to ensure the reception, processing and removal of its own waste so that waste can be disposed of as close as possible to its place of production. On this basis the Court considered justified trade-restrictive measures that discriminated against waste produced in different areas.[85] In another case, the Court specified that the principle could serve to justify restrictions on waste exports only when the waste in question was harmful to the environment.[86]

The polluter pays principle, another principle of international environmental law,[87] posits that the costs of the measure to deal with pollution should be borne by those causing the pollution, through the imposition of environmental charges, environmental standards or environmental liability. In addition, the principle has been interpreted so that generally environmental protection should not a priori rely on the granting of state aid or policies placing the burden on society, and that requirements should not target persons or undertakings for the elimination of pollution that they did not contribute to produce.[88] In the *Standley* case, for

[81] Jans and Vedder, above n 31, 40–42.

[82] Case C-157/96 *The Queen and Ministry of Agriculture, Fisheries and Food, Commissioners of Customs & Excise ex parte National Farmers Union et al* (National Farmers Union) [1998] ECR I-2211, para 64, although it has been convincingly argued that the precautionary principle rather than the prevention principle was relevant in this case given that the risk was a possibility rather than a certainty: see Dhondt, above n 2, 151.

[83] Resolution of the Council of the European Communities and of the Representatives of the Governments of the Member States, meeting within the Council, on the continuation and implementation of a European Community policy and action programme on the environment (1982–1986) [1983] OJ C46/1, (Third Environmental Action Programme), 6–7.

[84] Jans and Vedder, above n 31, 42–43.

[85] Case C-2/90 *Commission v Belgium* [1992] ECR I-4431.

[86] Case C-209/98 *Sydhavnens Sten & Grus* [2000] ECR I-3743; see Jans and Vedder, above n 31, 43.

[87] Rio Declaration, principle 16.

[88] Jans and Vedder, above n 31, 43–45.

instance, the ECJ indicated that farmers are not obliged to bear all the costs of pollution by nitrates, but only those caused by their activities.[89]

Finally, Article 191(3) TFEU lists a number of criteria that the EU legislator 'shall take into account' when 'preparing' its policy on the environment, including: available scientific and technical data; environmental conditions in the various regions of the EU; potential benefits and costs of action or lack of action; and the economic and social development of the EU as a whole and the balanced development of its regions. It has been argued that the objectives and principles of Article 191(1) and (2) TFEU are hierarchically superior to the criteria listed in Article 191(3) TFEU.[90] Thus, for instance, the first criteria requiring the EU legislator to base its actions on 'available scientific and technical data' should be read in the light of the precautionary principle, so that provisional or indicative scientific data would be deemed an acceptable basis for legislative action, albeit complete lack or inadequacy of supporting data may be cause for annulment. The second and fourth criteria, in turn, allow for possible differentiation in environmental policy based on the quality of the environment or the economic and social development in a given region. The third criterion, instead, calls for an assessment of potential costs and benefits of action for the EU, its Member States and private operators.[91]

3.3 Shared nature of EU external environmental competence

While the TFEU clearly grants the EU treaty-making powers in the field of the environment, and leaves significant leeway to the EU legislator to articulate the substance of its external environmental action, it states equally clearly that EU external environment competence is shared with the Member States: 'Within their respective spheres of competence, the Union and the Member States shall cooperate with third countries and international organisations'.[92] Furthermore, agreements between the Union and the third parties concerned 'shall be without prejudice to Member States' competence to negotiate in international bodies and to conclude international agreements.'[93]

The terms of Article 191(4) TFEU, which was first introduced by the SEA, may be understood as a reaction from the Member States to the classical 'pre-emption' doctrine established by the Court in the 1970s, as a corollary of the principle of primacy of EU law and the general duty of cooperation.[94] Pursuant to this judicial

[89] Case C-293/97 *The Queen v Secretary of State, Minister of Agriculture, Fisheries and Food ex parte H.A. Standley and Others and D.G.D. Metson and Others* (Standley) [1999] ECR I-2603. See L Kramer, 'Environmental Justice in the European Court of Justice' in J Ebbesson and P Okowa (eds), *Environmental Law and Justice in Context* (Cambridge, Cambridge University Press, 2009), 202.

[90] Holder and Lee, above n 31, 153.

[91] All these arguments have been put forward by Jans and Vedder, above n 31, 47–50.

[92] Art 191(4) TFEU.

[93] Ibid. See also art 4(2)(e) TFEU.

[94] Art 4(3) TEU (former art 10 TEC) reads: 'The Member States shall take any appropriate measure, general or particular, to ensure fulfilment of the obligations arising out of the Treaties or resulting from the acts of the institutions of the Union. The Member States shall facilitate the achievement of the Union's tasks and refrain from any measure which could jeopardise the attainment of the Union's objectives.'

doctrine, the Member States are precluded from acting externally when the EU has adopted common rules in a policy field. Article 191(4) TFEU, and similar provisions found in the case of other EU external competences,[95] thus seeks to exclude the potential pre-emptive effect of EU external environmental competence. In light of more recent case law,[96] however, pre-emption appears to be limited to cases where EU rules aim to achieve a substantial degree of harmonisation in the areas covered by the envisaged agreement, to prevent the Member States from undertaking international obligations that would affect those EU rules. If, instead, the EU adopts minimum standards internally, thus allowing the Member States to adopt more stringent measures (which is often the case in the environmental sphere), they retain in principle the possibility of undertaking more stringent international obligations.[97]

As a result, the precise division of environmental treaty-making powers between the EU and the Member States is difficult to determine in the abstract, as EU environmental legislation is subject to continuous evolution.[98] The practice of the EU and the Member States to deal with the intricacies of shared competence has often been that of concluding 'mixed agreements',[99] an imaginative legal tool that allows for their joint participation in international treaties. This is the case of most agreements discussed in this book, namely MEAs, associations and other bilateral/inter-regional agreements.[100] In many instances, however, the joint participation of the EU and the Member States in these agreements may be more attributed to a political choice of the Member States (which generally perceive treaty-making powers as a core expression of their national sovereignty) than to a lack of sufficient competence on the part of the EU.[101] For agreements covering environmental matters, the Member States may also wish to become contracting parties because of their (conditional) right, under Article 193 TFEU,

[95] See for instance, art 209(2) TFEU containing a similar provision in the context of development cooperation agreements.

[96] Among the vast literature on the division of treaty-making powers between the EU and the Member States, see M Cremona, 'External Relations and External Competence: The Emergence of an Integrated Policy' in P Craig and G de Burca (eds), *The Evolution of EU Law* (Oxford, Oxford University Press, 1999); J Klabbers, 'Restraints Imposed on the Treaty-Making Powers of the Member States Deriving from EU Law: A Framework for Analysis' in E Canizzaro (ed), *The European Union as an Actor in International Relations* (The Hague, Kluwer, 2002).

[97] Jans and Vedder, above n 31, 62–63. See also art 193 TFEU, which states that in the case the EU adopts minimum protection requirements, these 'shall not prevent any Member State from maintaining or introducing more stringent protective measures. Such measures must be compatible with the Treaties. They shall be notified to the Commission'. This right, however, may be limited in the context of a mixed agreement (see below n 102).

[98] Jans and Vedder, above n 31, 61–64.

[99] Note that 'mixed agreements' are not explicitly recognised in the TFEU and no specific procedure is thus found for their conclusion.

[100] Practice with regards to MEAs is briefly discussed in s 3.5 below, while a detailed examination of the other agreements can be found in Ch 2.

[101] While mixity is often equated with the existence of shared competences, this is something of a misconception. From a purely legal perspective, a given agreement covering matters for which both the EU and the Member States are competent may be concluded by the EU alone.

to introduce more stringent environmental protection measures than an EU minimum standards measure.[102]

The practice of 'mixed agreements', however, entails significant internal challenges for the EU and the Member States in terms of ensuring proper coordination throughout the negotiation, conclusion and implementation phases.[103] This challenge has been to some extent addressed by the duty of sincere cooperation enshrined in Article 4(3) TEU,[104] which the Court has interpreted as entailing enforceable substantive and procedural obligations with a view to protecting the unity in the international representation of the EU.[105] 'Mixed agreements' pose, furthermore, important challenges for third parties, which are left with the unenviable task of working out whether the EU or the Member States are responsible for each matter covered by the agreement.[106] While this complexity does generate confusion and at times mistrust from third parties, and thus risks undermining the EU's credibility and effectiveness as an international (environmental) actor, the present book will not deal with these matters that mainly concern the 'vertical coherence' between the EU's external (environmental) action and that of the Member States.[107] Our focus is, instead, on Article 11 TFEU whose function, as

[102] A Dashwood, 'Mixity in the Era of the Treaty of Lisbon' in C Hillion and P Koutrakos (eds), *Mixed Agreements Revisited: the EU and its Member States in the World* (Oxford, Hart, 2010), 364. However, in Case C-246/07 *Commission v Sweden (re POPs Convention)* [2010] ECR I-3317, the Court held that Sweden could not rely on art 193 TFEU to unilaterally propose a more stringent protective measure in the context of an MEA, as this could have legal 'consequences for the Union' which is also a party to the MEA (paras 92–102) and undermine the unity of the Union's external representation as a party to the MEA and its negotiating power in that forum (para 104). On this decision, see M Cremona, 'Coherence and EU External Environmental Policy' in E Morgera (ed), *The External Environmental Policy of the European Union: EU and International Law Perspectives* (Cambridge, Cambridge University Press, forthcoming 2012).

[103] For a comprehensive analysis of the EU as an environmental negotiator in the context of mixed agreements, see Delreux, above n 7, particularly 13–27.

[104] Above n 94.

[105] Case C-266/03 *Commission v Luxembourg (re Inland Waterways Agreement)* [2005] ECR I-4805, para 60 and Case C-433/03 *Commission v Germany (re Inland Waterways Agreement)* [2005] ECR I-6985, para 66; Case *Commission v Sweden,* above n 102, para 104. See C Hillion, 'Mixity and Coherence in the EU External Relations: the Significance of the Duty of Cooperation' in Hillion and Koutralkos, above n 102.

[106] De Witte, above n 22, 14. In some cases, third parties insist that a 'Declaration of Competences' be attached to the agreement by the EU and the Member States, specifying the allocation of competences and responsibilities between them. These declarations, however, usually do not clarify much and often mention that the 'Union's competence is, by its nature, subject to continuous development'. See, for instance, P Koutrakos, *EU International Relations Law* (Oxford, Hart, 2006), 165–75, and by way of example, the Declaration on the Cartagena Protocol on Biosafety (Annex B to Council Decision (EC) 2002/628 concerning the conclusion, on behalf of the European Community, of the Cartagena Protocol on Biosafety [2002] OJ L201/48). For mixed agreements not containing such a declaration, the Court has held that both the EU and the Member States are collectively responsible for fulfilling the obligations owed to the third party: Case C-316/91 *Parliament v Council (re Lomé IV)* [1994] ECR I-625, paras 24–35; and Case 239/03 *Commission v France (Etang de Berre)* [2004] ECR I-9325, paras 29–30.

[107] On 'mixed agreements' see most recently, Hillion and Koutrakos, above n 102; and also M Björklund, 'Responsibility of the EC and the Member States for Mixed Agreements – Should Non-Member Parties Care?' (2001) 70(3) *Nordic Journal of International Law* 373; NA Neuwahl, 'Shared Powers or Combined Incompetence? More on Mixity' (1996) 33(4) *Common Market Law Review* 667; A Rosas, 'The European Union and Mixed Agreements' in Dashwood and Hillion, above n 34.

will be seen, is to ensure a certain 'horizontal coherence' (or complementarity)[108] between the EU's external environmental policy and other policy dimensions of its relations with third countries and regions.

3.4 Instruments and decision-making procedures

Having examined the substantive scope and nature of EU external environmental competence, this section turns to the instruments available to the EU for exercising such competence. As was indicated above, Article 191(4) TFEU empowers the EU to enter into international agreements in the area of environmental protection even if specific matters covered by the agreements are not yet, or only very partially, the subject of internal rules at EU level.[109] In addition, Article 192 TFEU grants the EU legislator a more general power to 'decide what action is to be taken by the Union in order to achieve' the environmental policy objectives established in the Treaty.

In terms of decision-making, autonomous measures (including those that may have an extraterritorial application) are generally adopted by the Council and the European Parliament following the 'ordinary legislative procedure'.[110] However, decision-making on a number of specific matters is still subject to unanimity in the Council, namely: provisions primarily of a fiscal nature; measures affecting town and country planning, quantitative management of water resources or affecting, directly or indirectly, the availability of those resources, and land use with the exception of waste management; and measures significantly affecting a Member State's choice between different energy sources and the general structure of its energy supply.[111] These are areas in which the Member States wish to retain a higher degree of control (that is, veto power) because of their politically sensitive nature or concerns about the preservation of national sovereignty.[112]

The conclusion of agreements with third countries and international organisations based on Article 191(4) TFEU[113] is undertaken in accordance with the general procedure laid down in Article 218 TFEU. The Council, usually based on a recommendation from the Commission, will authorise the opening of negotiations. The Commission usually acts as the negotiator for the EU side, on the basis of directives set by the Council and often in consultations with a committee of national representatives set up jointly with the Member States for this purpose.

[108] This distinction between 'vertical' and 'horizontal' coherence is often made in the context of EU external relations, see for instance Cremona, above n 102; C Gebhard, 'Coherence' in C Hill and M Smith (eds), *International Relations and the EU* 2nd edn (Oxford, Oxford University Press, 2011).

[109] Above n 24.

[110] Art 192(1) TFEU and art 294 TFEU on the 'ordinary legislative procedure'.

[111] Art 192(2) TFEU.

[112] Holder and Lee, above n 31, 154; McGillivray and Holder, above n 26, 145.

[113] Note that the conclusion of agreements based on other legal bases may be subject to a slightly different procedure, even if these may also cover environmental matters (see for instance, association agreements in Ch 2, s 2.1).

The Council, after obtaining the consent of the European Parliament, will then take a decision authorising the signing of the agreement and another decision on the conclusion of the agreement on behalf of the EU, which is equivalent to an 'authorisation to ratify' the agreement. The Council generally acts by qualified-majority voting throughout this procedure, except in cases where unanimous decision-making is required internally (for example, if the agreement covers the specific environmental matters indicated above). In the case of 'mixed agreements', the Member States will also take part in the negotiation process, as well as concluding and ratifying the agreement in question in accordance with each Member State's constitutional requirements.

Thus, recalling the discussion at the beginning of this chapter,[114] the EU Member States have to some extent limited their autonomy as international environmental actors, having pooled their sovereignty within the institutional structure of the EU to enhance their joint capacity for effective international environmental action. At the same time, they retain partial but direct influence on the content of EU external environmental policy-making through their participation in the Council, as well as the ability to co-negotiate international environmental treaties alongside the EU.[115]

3.5 The multilateral dimension of EU environmental action

The main purpose of this book is to assess the degree to which environmental integration has occurred in the EU's external action at the unilateral, bilateral and inter-regional levels. This section, however, sketches the multilateral dimension of the EU's external action, by providing an overview of MEAs to which the EU[116] is a party. This is to serve as a backdrop for gauging the linkages that the EU has built between these different dimensions of its external environmental action, which will be discussed in subsequent chapters.[117] The legal status of MEAs and other bilateral/inter-regional agreements in the EU legal order will also be examined briefly.

As indicated above, the EU is a party to several global MEAs.[118] With regard to climate change and the protection of the atmosphere, the EU is a party to the:

[114] Above s 2.

[115] De Witte, above n 6, 49.

[116] Note that these agreements were formally concluded by the EC, not by the EU. However, following the entry into force of the Lisbon Treaty, the EU has replaced and succeeded the EC (art 1 TEU). While these agreements form part of the EU *acquis*, and the EU has confirmed to the relevant international agreements secretariats that the EU has 'replaced and succeeded the EC' following the Lisbon Treaty, this has not been immediately accepted by all third countries. See C Spence and A Vavilov, 'Summary of the First Session of the Preparatory Committee for the 2012 United Nations Conference on Sustainable Development' (2010) 27(1) *Earth Negotiations Bulletin* 10 (all Earth Negotiations Bulletins cited in this book can be found at www.iisd.ca/).

[117] See, in particular, Chs 2, 3, 4 and 7.

[118] See Commission, 'Multilateral Environmental Agreements to which the EC is a Contracting Party or a Signatory' (as of 2006) at www.ec.europa.eu/environment/international_issues/pdf/agreements_en.pdf. On MEAs, see generally, P Birnie, A Boyle and C Redgwell, *International Law and the Environment* 3rd edn (Oxford, Oxford University Press, 2009) and Sands, above n 26.

- UN Framework Convention on Climate Change (UNFCCC)[119] and its Kyoto Protocol,[120] and
- Convention for the Protection of the Ozone Layer (Ozone Convention)[121] and its Montreal Protocol.[122]

It is also party to major agreements on hazardous substances:

- the Basel Convention on the Control of Transboundary Movements of Hazardous Wastes and their Disposal (Basel Convention),[123]
- the Stockholm Convention on Persistent Organic Pollutants (POPs Convention)[124] and
- the Rotterdam Convention on the Prior Informed Consent Procedure for Certain Hazardous Chemicals and Pesticides in International Trade (Rotterdam Convention).[125]

The EU is also a party to the UN Convention on the Law of the Sea (UNCLOS),[126] with its implementing agreements on fish stocks[127] and seabed mining,[128] and the Convention to Combat Desertification (UNCCD).[129]

The EU is, in addition, a party to several biodiversity-related conventions, namely:

[119] United Nations Framework Convention on Climate Change, 9 May 1992, 1771 UNTS 107, entered into force for the EU on 21 March 1994. Throughout this book, it is referred to as UNFCCC.

[120] Kyoto Protocol to the United Nations Framework Convention on Climate Change, 11 December 1997, 2303 UNTS 148, entered into force for the EU on 16 February 2005. Throughout this book, it is referred to as the Kyoto Protocol.

[121] Vienna Convention for the Protection of the Ozone Layer, 22 March 1985, 1513 UNTS 293, entered into force for the EU on 22 September 1988. Throughout this book, it is referred to as the Ozone Convention

[122] Montreal Protocol on Substances that Deplete the Ozone Layer, 16 September 1987, 1522 UNTS 3, entered into force for the EU on 1 January 1989. Throughout this book, it is referred to as the Montreal Protocol.

[123] Basel Convention on the Control of Transboundary Movements of Hazardous Wastes and their Disposal, 22 March 1989, 1673 UNTS 57, entered into force for the EU on 5 May 1992. Throughout this book, it is referred to as the Basel Convention.

[124] Stockholm Convention on Persistent Organic Pollutants, 22 May 2001, 2256 UNTS 119, entered into force for the EU on 17 May 2004. Throughout this book, it is referred to as the POPs Convention.

[125] Rotterdam Convention on Prior Informed Consent for Certain Hazardous Chemicals and Pesticides, 10 September 1998, 2244 UNTS 337, entered into force for the EU on 24 February 2004. Throughout this book, it is referred to as the Rotterdam Convention.

[126] United Nations Convention on the Law of the Sea, 10 December 1982, 1833 UNTS 3, entered into force for the EU on 16 November 1994.

[127] Agreement for the Implementation of the Provisions of the United Nations Convention on the Law of the Sea relating to the Conservation and Management of Straddling Fish Stocks and Highly Migratory Fish Stocks, 4 August 1995, 2167 UNTS 3, entered into force for the EU on 11 December 2001. Throughout this book, it is referred to as the UN Fish Stocks Agreement.

[128] Agreement relating to the Implementation of Part XI of the United Nations Convention on the Law of Sea of 10 December 1982, 28 July 1994, 1836 UNTS 3, entered into force for the EU on 28 July 1996.

[129] Convention to Combat Desertification in Countries Experiencing Serious Drought and/or Desertification, Particularly in Africa, 14 October 1994, 1954 UNTS 3, entered into force for the EU on 26 December 1996. Throughout this book it is referred to as UNCCD.

- the Convention on the Conservation of Migratory Species of Wild Animals;[130]
- the Convention on Biological Diversity[131] and its Cartagena Protocol on Biosafety,[132] and
- the International Treaty on Plant Genetic Resources for Food and Agriculture.[133]

The most notable case of an MEA to which the EU is not a party is the Convention on International Trade in Endangered Species of Wild Fauna and Flora (CITES),[134] because this Convention does not allow membership from REIOs, and its Gaborone Amendment (adopted in 1983) that would permit REIO membership to CITES has not yet entered into force.[135] Meanwhile, the EU has adopted unilateral and more stringent domestic legislation on trade in endangered species.[136]

In addition, it should be noted that the EU is party to several multilateral environmental instruments adopted at the regional level,[137] such as regional seas conventions[138] and river basin conventions.[139] Particularly relevant for present purposes are the environmental conventions adopted under the aegis of the UN Economic Commission for Europe (UNECE), which are significant in the EU's relations with Eastern European and Central Asian countries.[140] These include:

- UNECE Convention on Long-range Transboundary Air Pollution;[141]
- UNECE Water Convention;[142]

[130] Above n 36.

[131] Convention on Biological Diversity, 5 June 1992, 1760 UNTS 79, entered into force for the EU on 29 December 1993. Throughout this book, it is referred to as CBD.

[132] Cartagena Protocol on Biosafety, 29 January 2000, 2226 UNTS 208, entered into force for the EU on 11 November 2003. Throughout this book, it is referred to as the Biosafety Protocol.

[133] International Treaty on Plant Genetic Resources for Food and Agriculture, 3 November 2001, 2400 UNTS 303, entered into force for the EU on 29 June 2004. Throughout this book, it is referred to as ITPGR.

[134] Convention on International Trade in Endangered Species of Wild Fauna and Flora, 3 March 1973, 993 UNTS 243. Throughout this book, it is referred to as CITES.

[135] See CITES, 'Gaborone Amendment' at www.cites.org/eng/disc/gaborone.shtml.

[136] Council Regulation (EC) 338/97 on the protection of species of wild fauna and flora by regulating trade therein, [1997] L61/1, as amended by Commission Regulation (EC) 1332/2005 [2005] OJ L21/1.

[137] As well as the conventions cited above n 36, Convention on the Protection of the Alps, 7 November 1991 1917 UNTS 135, entered into force for the EU on 14 April 1998.

[138] Convention for the Protection of the Marine Environment of the North-East Atlantic, 22 September 1992, 2354 UNTS 67, entered into force for the EU on 25 March 1998; Convention on the Protection of the Marine Environment of the Baltic Sea Area, 22 March 1974, 1507 UNTS 168, entered into force for the EU on 17 January 2000.

[139] Convention on the Protection of the Rhine, 12 April 1999, entered into force for the EU on 1 January 2003 [2000] OJ L289/31; Convention on Cooperation for the Protection and Sustainable Use of the Danube River 29 June 1994, entered into force for the EU on 22 October 1998 [1997] OJ L342/19.

[140] See Ch 2, s 6.2.

[141] Convention on Long-range Transboundary Air Pollution, 13 November 1979, 1302 UNTS 217, entered into force for the EU on 16 March 1983.

[142] Convention on the Protection and Use of Transboundary Watercourses and International Lakes, 17 March 1992, 1936 UNTS 269, entered into force for the EU on 6 October 1996.

- UNECE Convention on Environmental Impact Assessment in a Transboundary Context (Espoo Convention);[143]
- UNECE Aarhus Convention on Access to Environmental Information, Public Participation in Environmental Decision-making and Access to Justice (Aarhus Convention);[144] and
- UNECE Convention on Transboundary Effects of Industrial Accidents.[145]

Another critical group of regional environmental agreements includes the Barcelona Convention for the Protection of the Mediterranean Sea against Pollution and its protocols, which are particularly significant in the cooperation of the EU with Mediterranean countries.[146]

MEAs, as well as other international agreements concluded by the EU, formally enjoy a high status within its internal legal order as they 'are binding upon the institutions of the Union and on its Member States'[147] also as a matter of EU law. The ECJ has generally taken an extensive interpretation of this provision, applying it also to general principles of international law and customary international law.[148] It has further held that international agreements to which the EU is a party 'form an integral part'[149] of its legal system, and are also capable of constituting a basis for reviewing the legality of EU legislative acts, over which the agreements take precedence.[150] Yet, EU primary law has primacy – at least for the ECJ – over the obligations contained in international agreements concluded by the EU (or by its Member States).[151] More recent case law however may signal a shift in the

143 Convention on Environmental Impact Assessment in a Transboundary Context, 25 February 1991, 1989 UNTS 309, entered into force for the EU on 10 September 1997. Throughout this book, this is referred to as the Espoo Convention.

144 Convention on Access to Information, Public Participation in Decision-Making and Access to Justice in Environmental Matters, 25 June 1998, 2161 UNTS 447, entered into force for the EU on 30 October 2001. Throughout this book, this is referred to as the Aarhus Convention.

145 Convention on the Transboundary Effects of Industrial Accidents, 17 March 1992, 2105 UNTS 457, entered into force for the EU on 19 April 2000.

146 Convention for the Protection of the Mediterranean Sea against Pollution (with annex and Protocols for the prevention of pollution of the Mediterranean Sea by dumping from ships and aircraft and Protocol concerning co-operation in combating pollution of the Mediterranean Sea by oil and other harmful substances in cases of emergency), 16 February 1976, 1102 UNTS 44, entered into force for the EU on 15 April 1978; and amended in 1995 (as Convention for the Protection of the Marine Environment and the Coastal Region of the Mediterranean, 10 June 1995, entered into force for the EU on 9 July 2004). See Ch 2, s 4.

147 Art 216 (2) TFEU (former art 300(7) TEC).

148 Case T-115/94 *Opel Austria GmbH v Council* [1997] ECR II-39; Case C-162/96 *RackeGmbH & Co v Hauptzollant Mainz* [1998] ECR I-3655.

149 Note that this case law was mainly developed in relation to former art 300(7) TEC and the 'Community legal order', but this has been confirmed as settled case law in Case C-240/09 *Lesoochranárske zoskupenie (re Aarhus Convention)*, judgment 8 March 2011, paras 29–30.

150 Joined Cases C-21-24/72 *International Fruit Company NV et al v Producktschap voor Groenten en Fruit* [1972] ECR I-1219, paras 5–6; Case 181/73 *Haegeman v Belgium* [1974] ECR 449, paras 2–6; Case C-61/94 *Commission v Germany (re International Dairy Agreement)* [1996] ECR I-3989, para 52; Case C-286/02 *Bellio F.lli Srl Preffettura di Treviso* (Case C-286/02) [2004] ECR I-3465, para 33; Case C-344/04 *IATA and ELFAA v Department of Transport* [2006] ECR I-403, para 5.

151 Case C-149/96 *Portugal v Council* [1999] ECR I-8395, para 22. See further, Eeckhout, above n 13, ch 9; C Kaddous, 'Effects of International Agreements in the EU Legal Order' in Cremona and de Witte (eds), above n 18; C Tietje, 'The Legal Status of International Law in the European Legal Order: The

Court's approach to the status of international agreements within the EU legal order. Notably, the Court refused to test the legality of EU secondary law against the UN Convention on the Law of the Sea, because the 'nature and broad logic' of the Convention prevented its use as a benchmark for assessing legality.[152]

4. THE ENVIRONMENTAL INTEGRATION REQUIREMENT

As advanced earlier, the requirement of environmental integration is most prominently enshrined in Article 11 TFEU as a general principle of EU law. While this is not the only mainstreaming requirement in EU primary law – but forms part of a series of other Treaty integration clauses progressively introduced as part of the Union's broader policy coherence efforts – it is one of the oldest of such clauses, which has led to several legislative, policy and institutional experimentations at EU level. This section will first trace the evolution of the environmental integration requirement, particularly through an examination of the successive Treaty amendments since the SEA. It will then proceed to explore the legal significance and implications of this requirement, on the basis of both a textual analysis of Article 11 TFEU and a contextual analysis with reference to the notion of 'sustainable development' to which environmental integration is closely tied in EU law and policy practice, as well as to other Treaty provisions that underscore the environmental dimension of the EU's external action (notably, Article 21 TEU). Attention will then be directed to the EU's approach to environmental integration in the specific area of external relations, with a view to identifying the key environmental priorities and instruments that characterise EU environmental integration efforts in this area.

4.1 Emergence and evolution

The requirement of environmental integration dates back to the very beginnings of EEC activity in the field of environmental protection.[153] Before its formal recognition by the SEA, it was already mentioned in the First Environmental Action Programme[154] in 1973, which categorised it as a 'principle of Community environmental policy' and phrased it as follows: 'effects on the environment should be taken into account at the earliest possible stage in all the technical planning and decision-making processes' because the environment 'must be considered an

Case of International Treaties and Non-binding International Instruments' in Wouters et al, above n 6. On the case law pertaining to the direct applicability of EU international agreements, see Ch 2, s 2.1.

[152] Case C-308/06 *The Queen on the application of International Association of Independent Tanker Owners (Intertanko) and Others v Secretary of State for Transport* [2008] ECR I-4057, para 65; see comments by Chalmers et al, above n 69, 655–56.

[153] L Kramer, 'The Genesis of EC Environmental Principles' in R Macrory (ed), *Principles of European Environmental Law* (Groningen, Europa Law Publishing, 2004), 33–35.

[154] First Environmental Action Programme, 11.

essential factor in the organization and promotion of human progress'.[155] The Action Programme also referred to it as an 'action' ensuring that ecological factors be integrated in devising and implementing common policies, in particular.[156] These references were inspired by Principle 13 of the Stockholm Declaration on the Human Environment,[157] and further developed in the Council's resolution on the Third Environmental Action Programme in 1983, which qualified integration as a priority for future action, linking it with the prevention principle.[158]

As indicated earlier, the first inclusion of the environmental integration requirement into EU primary law was in 1987 through the addition of a title on environment by the SEA, which stipulated that: 'environmental protection requirements shall be a component of the Community's other policies'.[159] The requirement was later reinforced by the Maastricht Treaty as follows: 'environmental protection requirements must be integrated into the definition and implementation of other Community's policies.'[160] The Amsterdam Treaty significantly upgraded the status of the requirement in EU law, by removing it from the environment title and placing it among the general principles of EU law. It further introduced an express link between environmental integration and sustainable development: 'environmental protection requirements must be integrated into the definition and implementation of the Community policies and activities referred to in Article 3, in particular with a view to promoting sustainable development'.[161] This formulation made it clear that the integration requirement constituted the bridge between environmental policy and all other (listed) policies and activities undertaken at (then) Community level, and equally applied to all of them whether internal or external in nature.[162] It should be noted that the link to sustainable development had already been emphasised by the Fifth Environmental Action Programme of 1993, whose preparation was influenced by the 1992 Rio Conference on Environment and Development.[163]

With the Lisbon Treaty, environmental integration is still included among the general principles of EU law and framed in clearly mandatory terms, albeit re-formulated as follows: 'Environmental protection requirements must be

[155] Ibid, 6.

[156] Ibid, 7. See comments by Dhondt, above n 2, 18.

[157] Stockholm Declaration, principle 13 reads: 'In order to achieve a more rational management of resources and thus to improve the environment, States should adopt an integrated and coordinated approach to their development planning so as to ensure that development is compatible with the need to protect and improve environment for the benefit of their population'. Dhondt, above n 2, 18.

[158] Third Environmental Action Programme, 5. See discussion in Dhondt, above n 2, 18–19.

[159] Art 130r(2) SEA.

[160] Art 130r Treaty of Maastricht.

[161] Art 130r(2) Treaty of Maastricht.

[162] Kramer, *EC Environmental Law*, above n 73, 21.

[163] Resolution of the Council and the Representatives of the Governments of the Member States, meeting within the Council, on a Community programme of policy and action in relation to the environment and sustainable Development', which contains 'Towards sustainability: A European programme of policy and action in relation to the environment and sustainable development' [1993] OJ C138/1 (Fifth Environmental Action Programme); see Dhondt, above n 2, 22; Rio Declaration, Principle 4 reads: 'In order to achieve sustainable development, environmental protection shall constitute an integral part of the development process and cannot be considered in isolation from it'.

integrated into the definition and implementation of the Union policies and activities, in particular with a view to promoting sustainable development'. The change in wording not only accounts for the fact that the EU has, since the entry into force of the Lisbon Treaty, replaced and succeeded the European Community,[164] but also links its scope of application to 'Union policies and activities' (without further specification).[165]

In addition, the Lisbon Treaty provided for the inclusion of three additional levels of environmental integration.[166] By recognising the legally binding character of the EU Charter of Fundamental Rights, which is of the same legal value as the Treaties,[167] the Lisbon Treaty has strengthened the Charter's environmental provision, which, albeit not framed in rights-based language, restates the commitment to environmental integration.[168] Furthermore, as a result of the Lisbon Treaty, two new provisions further support environmental integration: one requires integrating animal welfare requirements in certain policy areas,[169] and the other requires regard to the need to preserve the environment in the context of EU energy policy, which is aimed, inter alia, at promoting energy efficiency and energy saving and the development of new and renewable forms of energy.[170]

However, following the Lisbon amendments, environmental integration is no longer among the *few* mainstreaming requirements enjoying the status of general principle of EU law.[171] New Articles 7 to 13 TFEU include a general integration principle,[172] as well as specific integration clauses on gender equality,[173] employment and social and human health protection,[174] non-discrimination[175] and consumer protection,[176] in addition to the above-mentioned environmental and animal welfare integration requirements. While it can be argued that this change

[164] Art 1 TEU.

[165] The older specification of ('listed in Article 3') has not been incorporated in the current formulation, through a link, for instance, to arts 3–6 TFEU listing the various areas of EU competence.

[166] Vedder, 'The Treaty of Lisbon', above n 53, 289.

[167] Art 6(1) TEU.

[168] EU Charter, art 37.

[169] Namely, in the areas of agriculture, fisheries, transport, internal market, research and technological development and space policies (art 13 TFEU).

[170] Art 194(1) TFEU.

[171] Before the Lisbon Treaty, the only other integration clause to occupy such a prominent position was art 3(2) TEC on gender equality mainstreaming. Note also that the relevant TFEU heading is now titled 'provisions of general application'.

[172] Art 7 TFEU reads: 'The Union shall ensure consistency between its policies and activities, taking all of its objectives into account and in accordance with the principle of conferral of powers'.

[173] Art 8 TFEU reads: 'In all its activities, the Union shall aim to eliminate inequalities, and to promote equality, between men and women'.

[174] Art 9 TFEU reads: 'In defining and implementing its policies and activities, the Union shall take into account requirements linked to the promotion of a high level of employment, the guarantee of adequate social protection, the fight against social exclusion, and a high level of education, training and protection of human health'.

[175] Art 10 TFEU reads: 'In defining and implementing its policies and activities, the Union shall aim to combat discrimination based on sex, racial or ethnic origin, religion or belief, disability, age or sexual orientation'.

[176] Art 12 TFEU reads: 'Consumer protection requirements shall be taken into account in defining and implementing other Union policies and activities'.

may have decreased the visibility[177] and special status in EU law of the environmental integration requirement,[178] it remains true that the wording of Article 11 TFEU is the most forceful among the mainstreaming clauses.[179] Nonetheless, there is no hierarchy among these requirements, as confirmed by Article 7 TFEU requiring the Union to ensure consistency between *all* its policies and activities.[180]

4.2 Analysis of Article 11 TFEU

The policy rationale behind the environmental integration requirement lies in the realisation that progress in the environmental field by itself is not sufficient and may be countered by developments in other policy fields that disregard environmental protection requirements.[181] To put this in EU law terms, the very essence of Article 11 TFEU resides in the fact that Treaty provisions other than the environmental legal bases[182] may be used by the EU legislator to adopt measures which may (negatively) affect the environment. In broad terms, the environmental integration requirement calls therefore for a 'continuous greening' of Union policies and activities.[183] Yet, what exactly is meant by the integration of environmental protection requirements into other Union policies and activities, and to what extent should such an environmental mainstreaming take place in practice, legally speaking? Is Article 11 TFEU intended to be a mere procedural rule requiring the EU legislator to consider the environmental dimension of other Union policies and activities, or does it demand a substantive integration of environmental concerns? And how much discretion is left to the EU legislator in assessing and balancing environmental and other (at times) conflicting policy objectives?

The legal significance and reach of Article 11 TFEU is to be inferred first on the basis of a careful analysis of its wording, and in particular: the notion of 'environmental protection requirements'; the verb 'must be integrated'; and the reference to both the 'definition' and the 'implementation' of the 'Union policies and activities'. A textual analysis of Article 11 TFEU thus follows along these lines, before turning to an assessment of its legal implications.

4.2.1 Textual analysis

The substance of the 'environmental protection requirements' that are the object of the integration obligation in Article 11 TFEU is to be inferred from (albeit not

177 M Lee, *EU Environmental Law: Challenges, Change and Decision-Making* (Oxford, Hart Publishing, 2005), 134; Vedder, 'The Treaty of Lisbon', above n 53, 3.

178 Ibid, 3; Dhondt, above n 2, 85.

179 Below s 4.2.1. Note also that not all mainstreaming clauses have been upgraded by the Lisbon Treaty to the status of general principle of EU Law (see eg art 167(4) TFEU, former art 151(4) TEC).

180 Vedder, 'The Treaty of Lisbon', above n 53, 3.

181 Holder and Lee, above n 31, 164.

182 Namely, arts 191(4) and 192 TFEU (see s 3.4 above).

183 Kramer, *EC Environmental Law*, above n 73, 21.

explicitly limited to) the objectives, principles and criteria of the EU environmental policy.[184] We have already noted that the broad formulation of Article 191 TFEU allows for including all conceivable environmental issues within the remit of EU environmental competence: this means that the object of the environmental integration requirement can similarly be interpreted in a non-restrictive manner. A more precise indication is to be found on a case-by-case basis in EU legislation, which represents the EU political choice as to the specific environmental issues that need to be tackled in pursuance of the Treaty environmental objectives. It should also be underscored that the post-Lisbon formulation of the EU environmental policy objectives, read in conjunction with Article 11 TFEU, places special emphasis on mainstreaming climate change in EU action, particularly when the EU acts at the international level.[185] In addition, the environmental integration requirement should be read in light of the environmental principles enshrined in Article 191(2) TFEU. The ECJ, for instance, has seized various opportunities to apply the precautionary principle outside the environmental sphere in the area of the protection of public health,[186] and the prevention and high level of protection principles in the area of agriculture.[187] Finally, the substance of the environmental protection requirements may also be guided by the policy criteria listed in Article 191(3) TFEU. Because of the comparatively weaker language of this provision, however, such criteria may exert less influence in determining the content of the environmental protection requirements to be integrated, than the objectives and principles of EU environmental policy.[188]

As to its legal strength, Article 11 TFEU is clearly framed in mandatory terms ('must be integrated'), and ECJ case law[189] also points to an interpretation of this provision as imposing a legal obligation.[190] In addition, it is the only integration clause that uses the term 'must' as opposed to 'shall aim at'[191] or 'shall take into account'[192] found in other mainstreaming clauses, which would appear to limit more significantly the margin of institutional discretion.[193] Article 11 TFEU seems

184 Jans and Vedder, above n 31, 17.

185 E Morgera, 'Relevance Beyond Borders: Recent Developments in the EU' (2010) 40(5) *Environmental Policy and Law* 234, 234–36.

186 Jans and Vedder, above n 31, 21, on the basis of Joined Cases-T-74, 76, 83, 85, 132, 137 and 141/00 *Artegodan GmbH a.o. v Commission* [2002] ECR II-4945.

187 Case *National Farmers' Union*, above n 82.

188 Jans and Vedder, above n 31, 20–21.

189 Note that jurisprudence on the environmental integration requirement precedes the entry into force of the Lisbon Treaty, and no cases have dealt with the current art 11 TFEU at the time of writing.

190 Case C-62/88 *Greece v Council* [1990] ECR I-1527, para 20 (referring to former art 130r(2) SEA, above n 159): 'That provision, which reflects the principle whereby *all* Community measures *must satisfy* the requirements of environmental protection, implies that a Community measure cannot be part of Community action on environmental matters merely because it takes account of those requirements' (emphasis added). The Court repeated this interpretation in the *Mondiet* case, above n 67, para 27.

191 Which is used in art 8 TFEU (gender equality) and art 10 TFEU (non-discrimination).

192 Which is used in art 9 TFEU (employment and social protection) and art 12 TFEU (consumer protection). Art 13 TFEU on animal welfare uses also a weaker term ('pay full regard').

193 Dhondt, above n 2, 101–03; E Psychogiopoulou, *The Integration of Cultural Considerations in EU Law and Policies* (Doctoral thesis, European University Institute, 2006), 68–73, offering a comparative analysis of the legal strength of the environmental integration requirement.

therefore to be construed as a legal obligation demanding substantive integration of environmental protection requirements, and not solely as a policy guideline or procedural requirement that could be easily satisfied by the EU legislator through a superficial examination of the environmental implications of the measure envisaged. This obligation on the EU legislator can be seen both in negative terms (not to impair the achievement of the objectives, principles and criteria in Article 191 TFEU) and positive terms (to actively support these objectives, principles and criteria). Furthermore, given its status of general principle of EU law,[194] Article 11 TFEU is crucial to the interpretation of EU law as a whole.[195] That is, when interpreting EU (primary and secondary) law, the ECJ may only opt for an interpretation whose effects are positive or neutral on the environmental interests involved. By the same token, an interpretation favouring other competing policy goals over environmental integration is a priori inconsistent with the Treaty and would need to be justified on the basis of Treaty exceptions or other overriding reasons. In the pre-Lisbon period at least, the environmental integration principle has had concrete effects as a source of interpretation in the jurisprudence of the ECJ.[196]

Regarding its scope of application, the environmental integration requirement extends to all 'policies' of the EU, internal and external ones, both at the stage of 'definition' (which includes every stage of the EU legislative processes – definition of policy objectives, development of proposals and adoption of policies and legislation, as well as their review); and at the stage of 'implementation' (which includes the adoption of further implementing acts, adoption of decisions outside the legislative process, and enforcement).[197] The requirement also applies to a more operational level, that of EU 'activities'; this implies that areas of EU action that are not formally defined as 'policies' in the Treaty[198] are also subject to the requirement. This includes, for instance, competition rules and the internal market freedoms that are not properly labelled as 'policies', but also more 'ad hoc actions'.

These references to 'Union policies and activities', coupled with the lack of additional addressees, has led commentators to believe that the environmental integration requirement only binds the EU institutions, particularly the

[194] See S Kingston, 'Integrating Environmental Protection and EU Competition Law: Why Competition Isn't Special' (2010) 16(6) *European Law Journal* 780, 787, noting that the integration principle's status as a general principle of EU law can also be seen as flowing from the national constitutional traditions (often cited by the ECJ as a source of general principles) with many Member States according constitutional status to the goal of environmental protection.

[195] Former art 6 TEC was used as a tool in interpreting Treaty provisions as well as secondary law in, eg: Opinion of AG Jacobs in Case C-379/98 *Preussen-Elektra AG v Schleswag AG* [2001] ECR I-2099, paras 231–32; Joined Cases T-74/00 etc, *Artegodan and Others v Commission* [2002] ECR II-4945, paras 183–84; Opinion of AG Jacobs in Case C-126/01 *Ministère de l'Économie, des Finances et de l'Industrie v GEMO SA* [2003] ECR I-13769, paras 65–67; Opinion of AG Alber in Case C-444/00 *The Queen on the application of Mayer Parry Recycling Ltd v The Environment Agency and Secretary of State for Environment, Transport and the Regions* [2003] ECR I-6163, para 124.

[196] See further F Jacobs, 'The Role of the European Court of Justice in the Protection of the Environment' (2006) 18(2) *Journal of Environmental Law* 185; M Wasmeier, 'The Integration of Environmental Protection as a General Rule for Interpreting Community Law' (2001) 38(1) *Common Market Law Review* 159.

[197] Dhondt, above n 2, 45–53.

[198] In Arts 3–6 TFEU.

Commission, the Council and the European Parliament for their legislative functions.[199] The reference to 'implementation' indicates that also acts of other EU institutions, such as agencies or other bodies to which the Council has delegated powers to apply primary or secondary EU law, may be covered.[200] Nonetheless, Article 11 TFEU has also implications for the EU Member States. Most directly, the Member States are under an obligation to transpose into national law EU secondary legislation reflecting or implementing the environmental integration requirement.[201] In addition, Article 11 TFEU can be interpreted, in a combined reading with the duty of sincere cooperation,[202] as imposing a passive obligation on the Member States 'to refrain from action that might frustrate the future achievement and observance of the [EU] environmental objectives and principles', even outside concrete EU secondary legislation.[203]

The main purpose of Article 11 TFEU is therefore to put environmental objectives, principles and criteria 'at the forefront of other policy areas', 'lifting them to the same level' as the original objectives of such policies.[204] It encompasses two levels of integration. First, environmental integration functions as a requirement for EU legislative action, as well as an interpretative tool of EU primary and secondary law, outside the environmental field (external integration).[205] It requires that the environmental objectives, principles and criteria are 'applied' in other EU policy areas in the same way as they must be applied in its environmental policy: that is, other policy areas 'must pursue' the environmental objectives, 'aim at' or 'be based on' the environmental principles, and 'take account of' the environmental criteria.[206] Second, the requirement also entails that EU environmental law itself is interpreted broadly, in light of the objectives, principles and criteria enshrined in Article 191 TFEU, even when they are not explicitly incorporated in a specific piece of secondary environmental legislation (internal integration). In several cases on EU waste legislation, for instance, the Court of Justice clarified that environmental obligations contained in a directive should be interpreted broadly in light of the environmental objectives and principles of Article 191 TFEU.[207]

By requiring the systematic pursuance of environmental objectives, principles and criteria in all EU policies and activities, the environmental integration requirement has an 'amplifying effect' on EU environmental policy.[208] While

199 Dhondt, above n 2, 30–32.

200 Ibid, 49.

201 Such EU legislation (if directly effective) may also be relied upon by individuals to challenge national law before a national court (Dhondt, above n 2, 34). For a discussion of direct effect in EU environmental law, see Jans and Vedder, above n 31, 168–96.

202 Above n 94.

203 Dhondt, above n 2, 35–37.

204 Ibid, 94.

205 Jans and Vedder, above n 31, 17.

206 Dhondt, above n 2, 84.

207 Ibid, 179 on the basis of joined cases C-175/98 and C-177/98 *Lirussi and Bizzaro* [1999] ECR I-6881; joined cases C-418/97 and C-419/97 *ARCO Chemie Nederland Ltd v Minister Van Volkshuisvesting* [2000] ECR I-4475; and Case C-318/98 *Fornasar and Others* [2000] ECR I-4785.

208 E Morgera, 'European Environmental Law' in S Alam et al (eds), *Routledge Handbook of International Environmental Law* (London, Routledge, forthcoming 2012).

Article 11 TFEU does not prescribe a clear precedence of environmental protection requirements over other EU policy objectives, it imposes a general obligation on the EU institutions to carry out, at the least, an integrated and balanced assessment of all the relevant environmental aspects when defining and implementing Union policies and activities.[209] The precise outcome of this assessment is, however, largely a matter of political evaluation, as will be shown next.

4.2.2 Implications

Having examined the legal strength and reach of Article 11 TFEU, this section turns to an assessment of its implications. From a legal perspective, it is plain that Article 11 TFEU is construed as a legal obligation, and has been used as a source of interpretation of EU law. What is less clear is the extent to which it gives rise to an enforceable obligation. In other words, to what extent may an EU act be annulled on the basis that it does not – or not sufficiently – integrate environmental protection requirements?[210]

The degree of the legal enforceability of Article 11 TFEU is not easily inferred from the ECJ case law, partly because the Court has often dealt with the role of this provision in the choice of the appropriate legal basis of EU acts,[211] rather than with its implications for the normative content of such acts. Certainly, Article 11 TFEU has been relied upon by the Court to review the legality of EU acts,[212] and it would seem evident that any piece of EU legislation that leads to environmental degradation breaches a clear Treaty obligation and may therefore be subject to annulment by the Court. Such a breach, however, may be difficult to prove in practice because of the broad discretion that is generally left to the EU political institutions in implementing and striking a balance between the various policy objectives and principles in the Treaties, with the exercise of judicial review usually being restricted to verifying that the competent institution did not clearly exceed the bounds of its discretion or misuse its powers.[213] This judicial approach

[209] Jans and Vedder, above n 31, 17.

[210] An action for annulment can be brought pursuant to art 263 TFEU: 'The Court of Justice of the European Union shall review the legality of legislative acts, of acts of the Council, of the Commission and of the European Central Bank, other than recommendations and opinions, and of acts of the European Parliament and of the European Council intended to produce legal effects *vis-à-vis* third parties. It shall also review the legality of acts of bodies, offices or agencies of the Union intended to produce legal effects *vis-à-vis* third parties'.

[211] Note that the relevant case law relates to former art 6 TEC: Case C-62/88 *Greece v Council* (Chernobyl I) [1990] ECR I-1527; Case 155/91, *Commission v Council* (Waste Directive) [1993] ECR I-939; *Opinion 2/00 pursuant to Article 300(6) EC, Cartagena Protocol* [2001] ECR I-9713; Case C-336/00 *Republik Österreich v Martin Huber* [2002] ECR I-7699; Case C-94/03 *Commission v Council (re Rotterdam Convention)* [2006] ECR I-1; Case C-178/03 *Commission v Parliament and Council* [2006] ECR I-107. For an overview of this case law, see Cremona, above n 102; Dhondt, above n 2, 169–75; Marín Durán, above n 19, 254–61.

[212] Most obvious in Case *Safety Hi-Tech*, above n 74; and Case C-341/95 *Bettati v Safety Hi-Tech* (Bettati) [1998] ECR I-4355. See Dhondt, above n 2, 144–64 for an overview of ECJ case law applying former art 6 EC (now art 11 TFEU) and art 174 EC (now art 191 TFEU) in judicial review cases.

[213] See eg Cases C-331/88 *The Queen v Minister of Agriculture, Fisheries and Food and Secretary of State for Health, ex parte: Fedesa and others* [1990] ECR I-4023, para 8, Case *Mondiet*, above n 67, para

applies, of course, to the objectives, principles and criteria of EU environmental policy (Article 191 TFEU), which are the object of the environmental integration obligation in Article 11 TFEU.[214] For instance, in disputes over the lawfulness of an ozone depletion regulation,[215] the ECJ confirmed the wide discretionary powers of the EU institutions with respect to the Treaty-based environmental objectives and principles, and justified it on the need for a margin of institutional appreciation in making complex assessments of and balancing between these objectives, principles and criteria. As a result, the Court only addressed the question of whether the institution concerned committed a 'manifest error of appraisal' regarding the conditions for the application of these Treaty objectives, principles and criteria.

It is therefore hard to imagine a situation where Article 11 TFEU could, in practice, be the successful basis of a legal challenge of an EU measure which does not (or not sufficiently) integrate environmental protection requirements. Against this background, scholars have generally underscored the procedural relevance of the environmental integration requirement,[216] whereby a 'manifest error of appraisal' could be found if the motivation that EU institutions have to provide for each legal act[217] would not demonstrate that the institution chose a policy that facilitated or encouraged environmental protection, or where this has not been possible, the least environmentally damaging way of achieving a policy-specific objective.[218] The absence of reasons or inadequate reasons concerning environmental integration would per se, as an infringement of an essential procedural requirement,[219] constitute a ground for annulment of an EU act.[220]

Aside from these legal implications, the environmental integration requirement visibly influenced the style of policy-making at EU level.[221] In 1998, a high-level policy process was launched by the European Council (the Cardiff process), requiring each EU institution to participate in an environmental integration joint action. Sectoral Council formations were to integrate environmental considerations into

32, C-180/96 *United Kingdom v Commission* [1998] ECR I-2265, para 60; and C-120/97 *Upjohn v The Licensing Authority* [1999] ECR I-223, para 34. Psychogiopoulou, above n 193, 74–80.

[214] See s 4.2.1 above.

[215] Case *Bettati*, above n 212, especially paras 32–35; Case *Safety Hi-Tech*, above n 74, especially paras 34–37; Opinion of AG Léger in *Bettati* case.

[216] McGillivray and Holder, above n 26, 154. See also M Hession and R Macrory, 'The Legal Duty of Environmental Integration: Commitment and Obligation or Enforceable Rights?' in T O'Riordan and H Voisey (eds), *The Transition to Sustainability: The Politics of Agenda 21 in Europe* (London, Earthscan, 1998), 100–12.

[217] Art 296 TFEU provides: 'Legal acts shall state the reasons on which they are based and shall refer to any proposals, initiatives, recommendations, requests or opinions required by the Treaties'.

[218] Dhondt, above n 2, 91–92.

[219] Art 263 TFEU provides that the ECJ shall have jurisdiction in 'actions brought by a Member State, the European Parliament, the Council or the Commission on grounds of lack of competence, *infringement of an essential procedural requirement*, infringement of the Treaties or of any rule of law relating to their application, or misuse of powers' (emphasis added).

[220] Dhondt, above n 2, 175–77. For a different view, see Cremona, above n 102, 8 stating that on the basis of the Court's legal basis case law, 'it is difficult even to argue that all legal acts should include a reference in their reasoning' to these environmental objectives.

[221] McGillivray and Holder, above n 26, 154.

their respective activities by reviewing existing policies to assess whether environmental concerns were properly integrated, develop strategies for action in key areas, and identify priority actions as well as mechanisms for monitoring implementation. The Commission undertook to carry out detailed environmental impact assessments of new proposals, as well as to review existing policies in light of environmental integration, while the European Parliament was to review its own organisational arrangements and set priorities for environmental integration. The European Council was expected to review progress made by all institutions.[222] A stocktaking exercise of the Cardiff process in 2004, however, already noted the need to 'revitalise' the process, thus implicitly acknowledging its limited impact.[223] In 2005 the European Environment Agency noted that the Cardiff process had failed, mainly due to a shift in political priorities through the mid-term review of the Lisbon Strategy,[224] as well as unclear roles and responsibilities at EU level and inconsistent leadership.[225] While the Cardiff process as such is now considered defunct,[226] the practice of carrying out environmental impact assessments has continued, although it has turned into 'impact assessments' as an integrated approach to assess the potential impacts of new legislation or policy proposals in economic, social and environmental fields, involving also consultations with stakeholders. This has been crystallised in an inter-institutional 'Common Approach' by the Commission, the Council and the European Parliament,[227] thus demanding impact assessments not only of Commission proposals but also of substantive amendments by the Council and Parliament.

4.2.3 Contextual analysis

4.2.3.1 Environmental integration and sustainable development

As previously noted, Article 11 TFEU stipulates that environmental integration is ultimately aimed at promoting sustainable development. The notion of sustainable development is primarily an international construct, and was in fact first con-

[222] Commission, 'Communication on partnership for integration: a strategy for integrating environment into EU policies' COM (1998) 333 final.

[223] Commission, 'Working Document on integrating environmental considerations into other policy areas – A stocktaking of the Cardiff process' COM (2004) 394 final.

[224] European Council, 'Presidency Conclusions' Lisbon 23–24 March 2000, providing an action plan to make Europe 'the most competitive and dynamic knowledge-based economy in the world capable of sustainable economic growth with more and better jobs and greater social cohesion' by 2010.

[225] European Environment Agency, Technical Report No 2/2005 on environmental policy integration in Europe: state of play and an evaluation framework', cited by N van der Grijp and T Etty, 'Incorporating Climate Change into EU Development Cooperation Policy' in J Gupta and N van der Grijp (eds), *Mainstreaming Climate Change in Development Cooperation* (Cambridge, Cambridge University Press, 2010), 204.

[226] Kramer, *EC Environmental Law*, above n 73, 395.

[227] European Parliament, Council and Commission, 'Inter-institutional Common Approach to Impact Assessment' (November 2005): www.ec.europa.eu/governance/impact/ia_in_other/docs/ii_common_approach_to_ia_en.pdf.

ceived in the area of international environmental law.[228] In order to better understand the significance of Article 11 TFEU, it is therefore necessary to explore briefly what sustainable development means in the context of EU law, as well as under international law.

Since the Amsterdam Treaty, the international principle of sustainable development has been part of the 'raison d'être' of the EU, given its inclusion among the foundational objectives of both the EU's internal and external action as a whole:[229] it has thus not been restricted to the development of EU environmental law.[230] Arguably, when comparing the current formulation with former Article 2 TEC referring to the 'sustainable development of economic activities', Article 3 TEU (as amended by the Lisbon Treaty) reinforces the cross-cutting nature of this objective by stating that the EU 'shall work for the sustainable development of Europe',[231] without being confined to its economic activities.[232] In addition, sustainable development is referred to as a 'principle' in the preamble of the TEU and is specifically linked to, inter alia, environmental protection,[233] but somewhat surprisingly is not mentioned in the TFEU provisions on EU environmental policy.[234] Notably, 'sustainable development' is not found in Article 21(1) TEU, which defines the Union's foundational principles and values in the context of its external action as: 'democracy, the rule of law, the universality and indivisibility of human rights and fundamental freedoms, respect for human dignity, the principles of equality and solidarity, and respect for the principles of the United Nations Charter and international law.'[235]

The EU Treaties lack a precise definition of sustainable development – just as of other objectives or principles contained therein. The ECJ itself has not (as yet) engaged in defining the legal implications of sustainable development as an objective in EU primary law. For instance, in a case concerning the EU Habitats Directive,[236] Advocate General Léger contended that 'sustainable development

[228] What is traditionally considered the first definition of sustainable development is that proposed by the World Commission on Environment and Development, *Our Common Future* (Oxford, Oxford University Press, 1987) (Brundtland Report), ch 2, para 1: 'development that meets the needs of the present without compromising the ability of future generations to meet their own needs'.

[229] Arts 3(3) and (5), and 21(2)(f) TEU.

[230] McGillivray and Holder, above n 26, 148.

[231] Art 3(3) TEU.

[232] Vedder, 'The Treaty of Lisbon', above n 53, 2.

[233] TEU preambular recital 9, which reads 'determined to promote economic and social progress for their peoples, taking into account the principle of sustainable development and within the context of the accomplishment of the internal market and of reinforced cohesion and environmental protection, and to implement policies ensuring that advances in economic integration are accompanied by parallel progress in other fields'. See also, European Council, 'Presidency Conclusions' Brussels, 16–17 June 2005 adopting the 'Guiding Principles of Sustainable Development' (Brussels Council Conclusions 2005).

[234] See comments by L Kramer, 'Sustainable Development in the EC' in H Bugge and C Voight (eds), *Sustainable Development in International and National Law* (Groningen, Europa Law Publishing, 2008), 378–79.

[235] Art 21(1) TEU, preceded by: 'The Union's action on the international scene shall be guided by the principles which have inspired its own creation, development and enlargement, and which it seeks to advance in the wider world'.

[236] Council Directive (EC) 92/43 on the conservation of natural habitats and of wild fauna and flora [1992] OJ L206/7.

does not mean that environmental interests should prevail necessarily and systematically over other interests defended in the context of other policies pursued by the Community. On the contrary, it emphasises the necessary balance between various interests which sometime clash, but which must be reconciled.'[237] The Court itself, however, did not elaborate on this part of the Advocate General's Opinion. This jurisprudential approach has been aptly attributed to the identification of sustainable development as a source of inspiration for EU policy formation rather than as an enforceable obligation,[238] whereby the definition of sustainable development, as well as of the adequate means of action, is primarily a political question and thus a matter for legislative discretion.

At the level of EU secondary law, the notion of sustainable development has been defined in a few instruments in different ways, thus highlighting that the concept plays out differently in different contexts.[239] One of the most illuminating definitions that can be found in hard law,[240] notably in a piece of legislation that is particularly relevant for present purposes, is in a regulation on environmental integration in development cooperation.[241] There, sustainable development is framed as 'the improvement of the standard of living and welfare of the relevant populations within the limits of the capacity of the ecosystems by maintaining natural assets and their biological diversity for the benefit of present and future generations'.[242] Notwithstanding this clear link between sustainable development and the carrying capacity of the earth, in most instances the connection between sustainable development and environmental protection is unclear in EU law: some authors argue that sustainable development rather provides a 'continued link with economic priorities'[243] and is actually rarely used in the context of environmental protection.[244]

Conversely, policy documents produced by the EU include a plethora of references and guidance on sustainable development. The Fifth Environmental Action Programme[245] quoted the definition of the 1987 Brundtland Report: 'development that meets the needs of the present without compromising the ability of future generations to meet their own needs'.[246] In the lead up to the 2002 World Summit on

[237] AG Léger Opinion in Case C-371/98 *R v. Secretary of State for Environment, Transport and the Regions, ex parte First Corporate Shipping Ltd* [2000] ECR-I 9235, para 54.

[238] McGillivray and Holder, above n 26, 151. On the role of objectives, principles and values in the specific area of EU external relations law, see M Cremona, 'A Constitutional Basis for an Effective External Action' (2006) *EUI Law Working Paper* 2006/30 (with reference to the draft Constitutional Treaty, but still of significance for the Lisbon Treaty).

[239] McGillivray and Holder, above n 26, 150.

[240] Lee, *EU Environmental Law*, above n 177, 32.

[241] Regulation (EC) 2493/2000 of the European Parliament and of the Council of 7 November 2000 on measures to promote the full integration of the environmental dimension in the development process of developing countries, [2000] L288/1.

[242] Ibid, art 2.

[243] McGillivray and Holder, above n 26, 149.

[244] Kramer, 'Sustainable Development', above n 234, 378–79.

[245] Above n 163; see comments by Kramer, 'Sustainable Development', above n 234, 388.

[246] Brundtland Report, ch 2, para 1.

Sustainable Development (WSSD),[247] the EU adopted its own Sustainable Development Strategy (SDS) at the highest political level,[248] with a view to adding an environmental dimension to the Lisbon Strategy (aimed to make the EU the world's most dynamic and competitive knowledge-based economy by 2010),[249] and to establish a new approach to policy-making.[250] Reiterating the Brundtland Report definition of sustainable development,[251] the SDS aimed at providing a 'long-term positive vision,' which recognises that 'economic growth, social cohesion and environmental protection must go hand in hand'[252] and ensures 'all policies have sustainable development as their core concern'.[253] Yet, particular emphasis was placed on environmental integration in the agriculture, fisheries, transport and public health policies, as well as on targeting a number of environmental priorities for sustainability (including climate change, biodiversity loss, desertification and waste).[254] With regard to the new approach to policy-making, the European Council stressed in particular: improved internal policy coordination between different sectors within EU institutions; impact assessments to be carried out by the Commission for analysing the economic, social and environmental consequences of all its major policy proposals; and wide stakeholder consultation.[255] The external dimension of the SDS was elaborated a year later, and set several key objectives and areas of action to underpin the EU's contribution to the global challenge of sustainable development[256] – without however offering a more specific definition of this term.[257]

The adoption of the SDS marked the beginning of a policy process that has continued to the present day, with ongoing monitoring and periodic reviews. In this context, the European Council endorsed in 2005 a set of Principles for Sustainable Development,[258] to serve as a guide for decision-making in all EU

247 Below n 280.

248 The SDS was proposed by the Commission in May 2001 and adopted by the European Council in June 2001: Commission, 'Communication on a sustainable Europe for a better world: a European Union strategy for sustainable development' COM (2001) 264 final (Communication SDS 2001); European Council, 'Presidency Conclusions' Göteborg 15–16 June 2001 (Göteborg Council Conclusions).

249 Above n 224. Note that following the global economic crisis, the Commission has put forward a new economic strategy: Commission, 'Communication on Europe 2020. A strategy for smart, sustainable and inclusive growth' COM (2010) 2020 (Communication Europe 2020), which is discussed at s 5.1 below.

250 Göteborg Council Conclusions, 4.

251 Communication SDS 2001, 2; Göteborg Council Conclusions, 4.

252 Communication SDS 2001, 2.

253 Ibid, 6.

254 Communication SDS 2001, 4 and 6; Göteborg Council Conclusions, 6–8.

255 Göteborg Council Conclusions, 4–6.

256 Commission, 'Communication – Towards a global partnership for sustainable development' COM (2002) 82 final (Communication Global SD 2002); European Council, 'Presidency Conclusions' Barcelona, 15–16 March 2002, 6. This Global Partnership covers economic, social, environmental and financial aspects of sustainable development, as well as the coherence of EU policies and better governance at all levels. Aspects of most relevance to environmental integration are discussed at s 5.1 below.

257 Communication Global SD 2002, 3 stating: 'To be sustainable, development must strike a balance between the economic, social and environmental objectives of society, in order to maximise well-being in the present, without compromising the ability of future generations to meet their needs'.

258 Brussels Council Conclusions 2005, Annex I; and preceding Commission, 'Communication on draft declaration on guiding principles for sustainable development' COM (2005) 218 final.

policies and actions, which notably include 'policy integration'[259] – albeit clearly not limited to environmental integration – and principles of EU environmental law (precaution and polluter pays),[260] alongside 'the promotion and protection of fundamental rights', 'intra and inter-generational equity', 'open and democratic society', 'involvement of citizens, business and social partners', policy coherence and governance, and 'use of best available knowledge'.[261] The definitional parameters of sustainable development are (overly) extended in light of these principles, and remain very broadly framed. Sustainable development is said to be 'about safeguarding the earth's capacity to support life in all its diversity', and to be 'based on respect for fundamental rights, principles of democracy and rule of law'. In addition, sustainable development is aimed at 'the continuous improvement of the quality of life on earth of both current and future generations', together with the promotion of a 'dynamic economy with full employment' and a 'high level of education, health protection, social and territorial cohesion and environmental protection in a peaceful and secure world, respecting cultural diversity'.[262]

This all-encompassing notion of sustainable development is reflected in the renewed SDS adopted in 2006,[263] following the 2004 EU enlargement. The renewed strategy sets out overall objectives and concrete actions for the period 2006–10 for seven key priority challenges, some of which have a predominantly environmental dimension.[264] Of particular significance to this study, in endorsing the renewed SDS, the European Council gave a clear political mandate to integrate environmental concerns in EU bilateral and inter-regional agreements: 'the Commission and Member States will increase efforts to make globalisation work for sustainable development by stepping up efforts to see that international trade and investment are used as a tool to achieve genuine global sustainable development. In this context, the EU should be working together with its trading partners to improve environmental and social standards and should use the full potential of trade or cooperation agreements at regional or bilateral level to this end'.[265]

[259] Brussels Council Conclusions 2005, 30 defining the integration principle as: 'Promote integration of economic, social and environmental considerations so that they are coherent and mutually reinforce each other by making full use of instruments for better regulation, such as balanced impact assessment and stakeholder consultations'.

[260] See s 3.2 above.

[261] Brussels Council Conclusions 2005, 29–30.

[262] Ibid, 29.

[263] European Council, 'Review of the EU sustainable development strategy (EU SDS) – Renewed strategy' Brussels 15–16 June 2006 (Brussels Council Conclusions 2006); see also the preceding Commission, 'Communication on the 2005 review of the EU sustainable development strategy: initial stocktaking and future orientations' COM (2005) 37 final.

[264] Brussels Council Conclusions 2006, 7–21.These are: climate change and clean energy; sustainable transport; sustainable production and consumption; conservation and management of natural resources; public health; social inclusion, demography and migration; global poverty and sustainable development challenges.

[265] Brussels Council Conclusions 2006, 21.

A review of the SDS was launched in 2009 towards the preparation of a new strategy to be in place until 2020,[266] once again in parallel with an international process leading to a UN Summit assessing sustainable development twenty years after the Rio Conference on Environment and Development (so-called 'Rio+20').[267] In that process, the international community is focusing on the incipient notion of the 'green economy', which places environmental protection centrestage as a business and employment opportunity that can contribute to overcoming the global economic crisis, rather than as a limitation on economic growth. The EU intends to contribute to this international debate with its own vision on 'green growth', which according to the proposed 2020 SDS, indicates a shift towards a low-carbon and resource-efficient economy, based on eco-innovation and smart investment.[268] The external dimension of the proposed new SDS, however, has (as yet) received little attention,[269] although interestingly the Commission suggests that the concept of the green economy 'applies in particular to developing countries' and should be implemented through the economic valuation of natural resources, sustainable consumption and production, market-based mechanisms and greater private sector involvement.[270]

Overall, the EU has interpreted the goal of sustainable development flexibly and adapted it to different contexts and new developments. This renders it difficult to identify the exact implications of the link between environmental integration and sustainable development in Article 11 TFEU, beyond the general proposition that environmental integration is a means for the realisation of that broader objective. Kramer has criticised the EU's 'inflationary use' of sustainable development as a separate concept from environmental protection, and the lack of systematic attempts to assess the ability of self-proclaimed sustainable development measures to comply with environmental protection requirements.[271] Lee, on the other hand, has underscored the potential of sustainable development to stimulate debate in the EU, privileging participatory processes into the EU political institutions'

[266] Commission, 'Communication on mainstreaming sustainable development into EU policies: 2009 review of the European Union strategy for sustainable development' COM (2009) 400 final (Communication SDS 2009); European Council, '2009 review of the EU sustainable development strategy – Presidency report' Brussels 1 December 2009 (Presidency SDS Report).

[267] The UN Conference on Sustainable Development, convened by the UN General Assembly in Rio de Janeiro in June 2012 to mark the twentieth anniversary of the 1992 Rio Conference on Environment and Development (see UN General Assembly, 'Implementation of Agenda 21, the Programme for Further Implementation of Agenda 21 and the Outcomes of the World Summit on Sustainable Development' (2009) UN Doc A/RES/64/236, paras 20–29), will have as one of its two main themes the green economy.

[268] Presidency SDS Report, 7: 'An eco-efficient economy will contribute to achieving the key objectives and the overall aim of the SDS. It represents new business opportunities and will, given adequate framework conditions, boost EU competitiveness and stimulate significant employment growth, and should therefore also be an essential element of a new EU 2020 strategy'. See also Council, 'Conclusions on towards sustainability: eco-efficient economy in the context of the post-2010 Lisbon strategy and EU sustainable development strategy' 21 October 2009.

[269] Presidency SDS Report, 17–18.

[270] Commission, 'Communication on Rio+20: towards the green economy and better governance' COM (2011) 363 final (Communication Rio+20), 5.

[271] Kramer, 'Sustainable Development', above n 234, 391–93.

balancing of different interests.[272] Against this background, this book will examine how the linkage between environmental integration and sustainable development in Article 11 TFEU has been articulated in the specific context of the EU's external action at unilateral, bilateral and inter-regional levels. In doing so, it will pay particular attention to the extent to which the EU has related, and indeed anchored, its external policy initiatives to developments in public international law concerning environmental integration and sustainable development. To this end, it is necessary first to provide a brief account of the definitional parameters of sustainable development in public international law.

Sustainable development is not a monolithic, well-defined notion in international law and policy-making, where it has mainly been articulated through soft law instruments. Since the endorsement of the Brundtland Report by the UN General Assembly in 1987,[273] sustainable development has considerably broadened the conceptual boundaries of 'development' over time, shifting away from the view that had prevailed since the end of the Second World War that essentially equated development with the furtherance of national economic growth and thus justified a trade-off between economic and non-economic values in the interest of fostering such growth.[274] While not denying the importance of economic development, the contemporary notion of sustainable development requires something more than the traditional goals of industrialisation and export-led economic growth, but what exactly that is cannot be easily asserted.[275] The 1992 Rio Declaration, placed the human person 'at the centre of concerns for sustainable development',[276] and stated that the 'right to development must be fulfilled so as to equitably meet developmental and environmental needs of present and future generations'.[277] It further provided that 'environmental protection shall constitute an integral part of the development process and cannot be considered in isolation from it'.[278] On this basis, four elements of sustainable development have been

[272] Lee, *EU Environmental Law*, above n 177, 45–47.

[273] UN General Assembly, 'Report of the World Commission on Environment and Development' (1987) UN Doc A/RES/42/187.

[274] This view was in line with the dominant economic theories of modernisation, which were strongly challenged during the 1970s by dependency theories. For an exposition of these different theories, see G Marín Durán, above n 19, 9–11 and references therein.

[275] This is not the place to exhaustively account for the normative evolution of the concept of development in public international law. See further, P Alston and M Robinson (eds), *Human Rights and Development: Towards Mutual Reinforcement* (Oxford, Oxford University Press, 2005); V Barral, *Le Développement Durable en Droit International: essai sur les incidences juridiques d'un concept évolutif.* (Doctoral thesis, European University Institute, 2007); A Boyle and D Freestone (eds), *International Law and Sustainable Development. Past Achievements and Future Challenges* (Oxford, Oxford University Press, 1999); M-C Cordonier-Segger and K Ashfaq, *Sustainable Development Law: Principles, Practices and Prospects* (Oxford, Oxford University Press, 2004).

[276] Rio Declaration, Principle 1, which adds that human beings 'are entitled to a healthy and productive life in harmony with nature'. This builds upon the 1986 UN Declaration on the Right to Development (UN General Assembly, 'Declaration on the Right to Development' (1986) UN Doc A/RES/41/128) which first proclaimed that the human person, rather than economic growth itself, should be the central subject of the development process.

[277] Rio Declaration, Principle 2.

[278] Ibid, Principle 3.

identified in the literature: environmental integration, inter-generational equity, intra-generational equity and sustainable use.[279]

At the 2002 World Summit on Sustainable Development, attention was focused on the three 'interdependent and mutually reinforcing pillars of sustainable development: economic development, social development and environmental protection at the local, national, regional and global levels'.[280] Environmental protection, together with economic and social issues (including human rights protection),[281] were considered inter-dependent constituent elements of sustainable development, thus demanding the integration (in a non-hierarchical manner) of these three dimensions in decision-making at all levels. 'Good governance' practices, in turn, were seen as a necessary process in the exercise of public authority and the management of public resources (including ODA) to advance the international sustainable development agenda.[282] The WSSD then significantly expanded the notion of 'sustainable development', recognising reciprocal influences between environmental protection and poverty eradication, health and human rights, as well as governance-related matters, underscoring the urgent need to address them in a coherent fashion. In doing so, however, this approach has brought about a risk of 'squeezing out environmental protection' from sustainable development, as it facilitates preference for shorter and medium-term measures to the benefit of social and economic development, while environmental concerns that have a long-term dimension and do not relate to specified constituencies become more difficult to protect in the balancing exercise.[283] This is the very reason why an environmental integration requirement is still needed.

Whilst recognising the multidimensionality of sustainable development, this book deals only with its environmental protection component, and the extent to which environmental integration into EU external relations has followed international environmental standards and approaches. In this regard, it should be noted that the Johannesburg Plan of Implementation highlights key MEAs in relation to the environmental pillar of sustainable development, including:

- the Convention on International Trade in Endangered Species of Wild Fauna and Flora;
- the Ramsar Convention on Wetlands of International Importance;[284]
- the Vienna Convention for the Protection of the Ozone Layer and its Montreal Protocol on Substances that Deplete the Ozone Layer;

[279] Sands, above n 26, 253.

[280] 'Political Declaration of the World Summit on Sustainable Development' (4 September 2002) UN Doc A/CONF.199/20, Resolution 1 (WSSD Declaration) para 5.

[281] On the social development component of sustainable development, see Chs I ('Poverty Eradication') and VI ('Health and Sustainable Development') in 'Plan of Implementation of the World Summit on Sustainable Development' (4 September 2002) UN Doc A/CONF.199/20, Resolution 2.

[282] Ibid, in particular paras 138 and 141.

[283] Lee, *EU Environmental Law*, above n 177, 35. See also, A Ross-Robertson, 'Is the Environment Getting Squeezed Out of Sustainable Development?' (2003, Sum) *Public Law* 249.

[284] Ramsar Convention on Wetlands of International Importance, 2 February 1971, 996 UNTS 245.

- the Basel Convention on the Control of Transboundary Movements of Hazardous Wastes and their Disposal;
- the Convention on Biological Diversity and its Cartagena Protocol on Biosafety;
- the UN Framework Convention on Climate Change and its Kyoto Protocol;
- the UN Convention on the Law of the Sea, and related agreements;[285]
- the Convention to Combat Desertification;
- the International Treaty on Plant Genetic Resources for Food and Agriculture;
- the Rotterdam Convention on Prior Informed Consent Procedures for Hazardous Chemicals and Pesticides in International Trade; and
- the Stockholm Convention on Persistent Organic Pollutants.

4.2.3.2 Environmental integration and coherence in EU external relations

As noted above, Article 11 TFEU is the primary provision of 'horizontal coherence' (or complementarity) between EU environmental policy and other Union policies and activities. It should therefore be placed within the context of other more general provisions in the EU Treaties dealing with policy coherence in EU law. In the field of EU external relations, two types of provisions have this function: (i) a set of common objectives; and (ii) an institutional (and inter-institutional) obligation to ensure consistency.

First of all, Article 11 TFEU needs to be read alongside Article 3(5) TEU ('common provisions') and Article 21(2) TEU ('general provisions on the Union's external action'), which contain the objectives and principles underpinning EU external policy-making. Article 3(5) TEU provides that 'in its relations with the wider world' the EU 'shall contribute to peace, security, *the sustainable development of the Earth*, solidarity and mutual respect among peoples, free and fair trade, eradication of poverty and the protection of human rights, in particular the rights of the child, as well as to *the strict observance and the development of international law*, including respect for the principles of the United Nations Charter' (emphasis added).

Article 21(2) TEU establishes, in greater detail, a single set of objectives, values and principles for all EU external action. The list of non-prioritised objectives includes pledges to: 'help to develop international measures to preserve and improve the quality of the environment and the sustainable management of global natural resources, in order to ensure sustainable development';[286] 'foster the sustainable economic, social and *environmental* development of developing countries, with the primary aim of eradicating poverty' (emphasis added);[287] and 'assist populations, countries and regions confronting natural or man-made disasters'.[288] These environmental and sustainable development objectives are to

[285] Namely, the 1982 Fish Stocks Agreement, above n 127, and the 1993 Agreement to Promote Compliance with International Conservation and Management Measures by Fishing Vessels on the High Seas, 24 November 1993, 2221 UNTS 91.

[286] Art 21(2)(f) TEU.

[287] Art 21(2)(d) TEU.

[288] Art 21(2)(g) TEU.

be pursued in all fields of EU external action (that is, common foreign and security policy, development, trade and cooperation policies), as well as in the external aspects of its other policies (for example, agricultural, fisheries, transport and energy policies, as well environmental policy itself),[289] thus reinforcing the application of the environmental integration requirement to the EU's external action. The EU is furthermore called upon to promote 'multilateral solutions to common problems' as well as 'an international system based on stronger multilateral cooperation and good global governance', which can be read as including the development of international environmental law and governance.

While a set of common values and objectives guiding foreign policy-making can also be found in other contemporary European constitutions,[290] the second dimension of 'horizontal coherence' is quite unique to EU constitutional law: namely, a formal requirement for the EU legislator to ensure consistency[291] in policy-making. As noted earlier, a general formulation of this consistency requirement is found in Article 7 TFEU, which mandates the Union 'to ensure consistency between its policies and activities' (both external and internal), taking all of its objectives into account. The demand for consistency is further reiterated in the common provisions on the EU's external action, where the Council and the Commission are entrusted with the primary responsibility of ensuring coherence between the different areas of the EU's external action, as well as between these and its other policies.[292] Thus, in a similar vein to Article 11 TFEU, these consistency provisions require a shift away from the sectoral decision-making model traditionally followed by the EU institutions,[293] and instead, support more systematically the integration of, inter alia, the sensitiveness of environmental matters into all Union policies and activities.

5. ENVIRONMENTAL INTEGRATION IN EU EXTERNAL RELATIONS

5.1 Overview of environmental priorities and external policy tools

In order to prepare the ground for the analysis of EU external measures in subsequent chapters, this section provides an overview of EU policy documents dealing with environmental integration in the specific area of external relations, with a

[289] Art 21(3) TEU.

[290] De Witte, 'Too Much Constitutional Law?', above n 22, 9–11.

[291] Note that while for present purposes the concepts of 'coherence' and 'consistency' will be used interchangeably, a distinction between these two terms is often made in legal scholarship on EU external relations. See, for instance, C Hillion, 'Tous pour un, un pour tous! Coherence in the External Relations of the European Union' in M Cremona (ed), *Developments in EU External Relations Law* (Oxford, Oxford University Press, 2009), 12–16.

[292] Art 21(3) TEU; see also art 26(2) TEU.

[293] For instance, through the different Council configurations (art 16(6) TEU) and the different Directorates-General of the Commission. See generally, H Wallace, W Wallace and MA Pollack, *Policy-Making in the European Union* 6th edn (Oxford, Oxford University Press, 2010).

view to identifying the key environmental priorities and instruments that characterise the EU's approach to environmental integration in this area.

Among the environmental themes prioritised by the EU in its external action, it should be stressed from the outset that the fight against *climate change* has undoubtedly taken the lion's share, as could be anticipated from the prominent attention it receives in the TFEU.[294] In the Europe 2020 Strategy on smart, *sustainable* and inclusive growth, which was endorsed in 2010 as the successor to the Lisbon Strategy,[295] the concept of a more resource-efficient, greener and more competitive economy is clearly dominated by climate change policy considerations. It entails shifting towards a low-carbon economy, increasing the use of renewable energies, decarbonising the transport sector and promoting energy efficiency, with the international dimension of the strategy mostly focusing on continuing efforts in the multilateral climate change negotiations.[296] The green pillar of the Europe 2020 Strategy is likely to influence the ongoing review of the EU Sustainable Development Strategy, which is expected to continue to provide, in parallel to Europe 2020, the overarching sustainable development framework for all Union policies and strategies. It can thus be expected that the new SDS will equally be marked by an increased focus on climate change and energy issues (particularly in the transport sector) in support of the shift to a green economy.[297]

Aside from climate change, the EU has also highlighted other environmental challenges to be tackled through its external action: the protection of *biodiversity*, including reference to benefit-sharing from the use of genetic resources (the third objective of the CBD), sustainable forest management, and genetically modified organisms (through the implementation of the Cartagena Protocol on Biosafety in third countries);[298] *environment and health* issues, such as the safe management chemicals (based on the Rotterdam Convention and the POPs Convention)[299] and water;[300] and the *sustainable use of natural resources*, including waste management.[301] It should also be noted that the EU seeks to promote better policy coherence between the international regimes on climate change and on biodiversity.[302] While *desertification* was mentioned as one of the international priorities of the

[294] See s 3.2 and n 60 above.

[295] Communication Europe 2020; endorsed by the European Council, 'Conclusions' Brussels 17 June 2010, 1.

[296] Morgera, 'Relevance Beyond Borders', above n 185, 243.

[297] Communication SDS 2009, 4–5 and 14.

[298] Decision (EC) 1600/2002 of 22 the European Parliament and of the Council laying down the Sixth Environmental Action Programme [2002] OJ L242/1 (Sixth Environmental Action Programme), arts 1(4) and 6. Biodiversity is seen as a 'strategy' to move towards the green economy. Key areas to be addressed at Rio+20 in this respect include: sustainable forest management and marine biodiversity in areas beyond national jurisdiction. See Communication Rio+20, 5 and 11–12.

[299] Sixth Environmental Action Programme, arts 1(4) and 7; Communication Rio+20, 12 where the Commission advocates for a new international framework convention on all chemicals and hazardous substances.

[300] Sixth Environmental Action Programme, arts 1(4) and 7; Communication Rio+20, 11 where it is specifically suggested that an international partnership on water could build on the EU bilateral 'Water Initiative' (www.euwi.net/).

[301] Sixth Environmental Action Programme, art 1(4) and 8.

[302] Ibid, art 9(2)(j).

EU as early as in the Third Environmental Action Programme,[303] it has not played a prominent role in EU external relations, possibly because the relevant international convention has not 'demonstrated the potential of action at the global level'.[304]

Another cross-cutting theme that is particularly relevant from an environmental integration perspective is the EU corporate social responsibility (CSR) agenda, which the Commission sees as 'an opportunity for enterprises to combine economic, social and environmental objectives' with a view to contributing to 'enhance Europe's capacity for sustainable development'.[305] While CRS usually involves the setting up of voluntary initiatives to improve the environmental performance of companies,[306] the Commission has also referred more generally to the need for greater involvement of the private sector through market-based mechanisms, eco-innovation and innovative financing for the implementation of MEAs.[307] In the framework of the Europe 2020 Strategy, the EU has also made a (still rather undefined) move towards a new policy on business and human rights, and on company disclosure of environmental, social, employment-related, and governance information.[308]

Turning to external policy tools, the EU has been emphasising environmental integration into development policy since the mid-1980s, somewhat surprisingly perhaps as this preceded the inclusion of an explicit legal basis on development cooperation in the Treaties.[309] Since 2002, and particularly as part of the external dimension of the SDS, the EU external trade policy is receiving increasing attention as a tool for environmental integration. This does not come as a surprise in light of the EU's growing economic weight on the global stage, as well of what

[303] Third Environmental Action Programme, 16.

[304] This can be deduced by reverse reasoning from Communication Rio+20, 3, where the Commission refers to the achieved potential of the other two Rio Conventions (the CBD and UNFCCC). The Commission suggests later in the Communication launching a global economic valuation of the costs and benefits of improving land quality, probably with a view to raising the profile and facilitating the mainstreaming of the UNCCD (Communication Rio+20, 12).

[305] Communication SDS 2009, 3.

[306] Sixth Environmental Action Programme, art 3(5).

[307] Communication Rio+20, 5 and 8.

[308] Commission, 'Communication on an integrated industrial policy for the globalisation era: putting competitiveness and sustainability at centre stage' COM (2010) 614, 23 which builds on the succinct reference to a 'renewed' CSR strategy in Communication Europe 2020, 17.

[309] Council and Representatives of the Governments of the Member States of the European Communities, meeting within the Council, 'Resolution on the link between the environment and development' [1984] OJ C272/1, stating that 'the inclusion of ecological criteria must be an integral part of the development policy strategy' and that 'the Community must consider environmental protection as an integral part of its development cooperation policy,' while noting that 'environmental problems can provide a focus for greater collaboration and solidarity with developing countries to the benefit not only of those countries but also of Member States'. See also Resolution of the Council of the European Communities and the Representatives of the Governments of the Member States, meeting within the Council, on the continuation and implementation of a European Community policy and action programme on the environment (1987–1992) [1987] OJ C328/1, which included development cooperation policies among the priority areas in which to ensure environmental integration; and SP Johnson and G Corcelle, *The Environmental Policy of the European Communities* (London, Kluwer Law International, 1995), 459–63.

Cremona has elegantly described as the interplay between its international role as a 'market player' and as a 'rule generator'[310]: the EU uses its market size and economic power to 'export' its own regulatory norms, including environmental standards, as well as to influence multilateral rule-setting within the WTO and in other fora, including the Doha Round negotiations on trade and environment. Given their significance for our purposes, a closer examination of these two EU external policies is undertaken below. Environmental integration has also been hinted at in other EU internal policies that may have an external dimension, particularly the agricultural, fisheries, transport, energy and industrial policies.[311] This aspect will not, however, be covered extensively in this book.[312]

5.2 Environmental integration and EU external trade policy

The common commercial policy (CCP) is the oldest among the EU's external policies, introduced by the original Treaty of Rome as the necessary external dimension of establishing the EEC as a customs union.[313] From the start, the Community actively sought to promote and defend its trade interests through a network of autonomous and contractual measures,[314] and as a result the CCP is also amongst the most developed EU policies. Overall, the impact and effectiveness of the CCP go largely undisputed and it has been often considered a successful means to assert the EU's identity on the international scene.[315] Against this background, one may have expected the CCP also to be amongst the most clearly defined policies in EU primary law. On the contrary, until the Lisbon amendments, the Treaty provisions on the CCP were strikingly silent regarding its objectives and principles, particularly if compared with those on EU environmental policy.[316] Before the Lisbon Treaty, the only clear constitutional requirement for the conduct and formulation of the CCP was that it be based on 'uniform principles',[317] coupled with an aspirational commitment to trade liberalisation.[318]

[310] M Cremona, 'The Union as a Global Actor: Roles, Models and Identity' (2004) 41(2) *Common Market Law Review* 566, 557.

[311] Communication Global SD 2002, 14–15.

[312] Only marginally in the examination of bilateral/inter-regional agreements, as part of the 'environmental integration clauses', see further Ch 2.

[313] Art 9 and ch 3, title II EEC Treaty provided for the adoption of a common external tariff and the development of a common commercial policy. These provisions have to be placed in the context of the founding Member States' pre-existing commitments under the GATT of 1947 and in particular the requirements for the formation of customs unions under art XXIV GATT.

[314] See generally, Eeckhout, above n 13, ch 10; S Inama, and E Vermulst, *Customs and Trade Law of the European Community* (London, Kluwer, 1999); T Lyons, *EC Customs Law* (Oxford, Oxford University Press, 2001).

[315] M Cremona, 'The Common Commercial Policy' in C Saunders and G Triggs (eds), *Trade and Cooperation with the European Union in the New Millennium* (London, Kluwer, 2002), 43.

[316] Above s 3.2.

[317] Former art 133(1) TEC.

[318] Former art 131 TEC stated: 'By establishing a customs union between themselves Member States *aim to contribute*, in the common interest, to the harmonious development of world trade, the progressive abolition of restrictions on international trade and the lowering of customs barriers' (emphasis

Nonetheless, the CCP was clearly amongst the 'Community policies' to which the environmental integration requirement (old Article 6 TEC) applied, and in fact various trade measures (including trade restrictions) were adopted for environmental protection purposes.[319]

With the Lisbon Treaty, the interplay between the EU's external trade and environmental policies has been recognised more explicitly. The CCP is not only still subject to the environmental integration requirement (Article 11 TFEU), but also to the common set of objectives for the EU's external action which, as we have seen, contains several environmental protection goals.[320] Article 207 TFEU reiterates the need for the CCP to be conducted 'in the context of the principles and objectives of the Union's external action'[321] and requires that trade agreements be 'compatible with the internal Union policies and rules'.[322] It should be noted that another important change introduced by the Lisbon Treaty has been to strengthen the role of the European Parliament in the formulation of the CCP. While the European Parliament had been, until the Lisbon amendments, formally excluded from the decision-making process in CCP matters,[323] its consent is now required for both the adoption of autonomous measures (such as the generalised system of preferences) and the conclusion of international agreements covering trade matters.[324]

Apart from these Treaty-based linkages, the EU has been actively involved in international discussions on the relationship between trade and environment that have followed the Rio commitment to make trade and environmental policies 'mutually supportive',[325] and which have taken place primarily within the WTO Committee on Trade and Environment (CTE) that was established at the conclusion of the Uruguay Round of multilateral trade negotiations in April

added). As a result, the constitutional features of the CCP were mostly developed through numerous legal disputes before the ECJ from 1970s to 1990s. The 2001 Treaty of Nice was the first to substantively amend the provisions of the CCP, albeit these amendments did not concern its foundational objectives. On the evolution of the CCP, see M Cremona, 'The External Dimension of the Single Market. Building on Foundations' in C Barnard and J Scott (eds), *The Law of the Single European Market: Unpacking the Premises* (Oxford, Hart, 2002); Marín Durán, *Development-based Differentiation,* above n 19, 22–50. On the Nice amendments, see M Cremona, 'A Policy of Bits and Pieces? The Common Commercial Policy after Nice' (2001) 4 *Cambridge Yearbook of European Legal Studies* 61; CW Hermann, 'Common Commercial Policy after Nice: Sisyphus Would Have Done a Better Job' (2002) 39(1) *Common Market Law Review* 7.

319 For an overview with reference to relevant ECJ case law, see Eeckhout, above n 13, 39–48.

320 Art 21(2) TEU, see s 4.2.3.2 above.

321 Art 207(1) TFEU.

322 Art 207(3) TFEU. Note that the Lisbon Treaty lists the CCP among the areas of exclusive EU competence (art 3 TFEU) and its scope now encompasses foreign direct investment in addition to trade in goods and services as well as commercial aspects of intellectual property.

323 Former art 133(2) and (4) TEC for CCP autonomous measures; and former art 300(3) TEC (where even consultation of the European Parliament was excluded for pure CCP agreements).

324 Art 207(2) TFEU (for the adoption of EU regulations in accordance with the ordinary legislative procedure) and art 218(6)(v) TFEU (for the conclusion of international agreements).

325 Rio Declaration, Principle 12: 'States should cooperate to promote a supportive and open international economic system that would lead to economic growth and sustainable development in all countries, to better address the problems of environmental degradation'; see also 'Agenda 21' (12 August 1992) UN Doc A/CONF.151/26/Rev.1 vol 1, Annex II, ch 2.

1994.[326] Only a year after the CTE formally began its work, the Commission put forward its first Communication on Trade and Environment in 1996, notably stating that an active participation of the EU in these international discussions was 'essential' and called for by the environmental integration requirement.[327] The EU was also a central proponent of the inclusion of environmental issues into the agenda of the ongoing round of multilateral trade negotiations launched at the Doha Ministerial Conference in 2001,[328] which has brought the relationship between trade and the environment into the spotlight. While this book will not contribute to this widely-documented political and academic debate,[329] it is still necessary to identify the key regulatory links between trade and environment in order to enquire whether (and how) these have been addressed in the EU's bilateral and inter-regional agreements examined in the next chapter. Broadly speaking, the trade and environment nexus can be looked at from three regulatory angles:

The use of trade measures for environmental protection purposes: these measures can be based on domestic standards of environmental protection or taken to implement specific trade obligations under MEAs, and may have an impact (partly or totally) outside the jurisdiction of the regulating state.[330] They generally take the form of import/export bans, tariffs, taxes and other fiscal charges, but can also encompass government procurement and domestic support measures.[331] By their very nature, these measures can often restrict or distort trade and thus run

[326] WTO Ministerial Decision on Trade and Environment, adopted in Marrakesh on 17 April 1994 in WTO Secretariat, above n 11. The CTE was given the broad mandate of identifying 'the relationship between trade and environmental measures in order to promote sustainable development' and of making 'appropriate recommendations on whether any modifications of the provisions of the multilateral trading system are required, compatible with the open, equitable and non-discriminatory nature of the system'.

[327] Commission, 'Communication on trade and environment' COM (1996) 54 final, 9 (Communication Trade and Environment).

[328] Doha Ministerial Declaration (WT/MIN(01)/DEC/1, 14 November 2001) (Doha Declaration). Paragraph 31 contains the trade and environment issues of the Doha 'negotiating' mandate, namely: (i) the relationship between existing WTO rules and specific trade obligations set out in MEAs; (ii) observer status of MEA Secretariats in the WTO and procedures for regular information exchange; (iii) trade liberalisation of environmental goods and services. The Doha Declaration also includes other 'non-negotiating' trade and environment issues to be considered by the CTE, such as the effect of environmental measures on market access, the relationship between the WTO Trade-related Intellectual Property Rights (TRIPS) Agreement (in WTO Secretariat, above n 11) and the CBD, eco-labelling, technical assistance and capacity-building, and environmental review (paras 32, 33 and 51).

[329] See generally, A Najam, M Halle and R Meléndez-Ortiz (eds), *Trade and Environment – A Resource Book* (Geneva, ICTSD, 2007); J Wiers, *Trade and Environment in the EC and the WTO – A Legal Analysis* (Groningen, Europa Law Publishing, 2002).

[330] For an overview of specific trade obligations under MEAs, see UNCTAD, *Trade and Environment Review* (Geneva, UNCTAD, 2003), 13–39; WTO Secretariat, 'Matrix on Trade Measures Pursuant to Selected Multilateral Environmental Agreements' (WT/CTE/W/160/Rev.5, 15 June 2011). According to the WTO Secretariat, 20 out of the 250 MEAs currently in force contain implementation provisions that can affect trade.

[331] eg, the environmental support programmes that fall within 'green box' (Annex 2) of the WTO Agreement on Agriculture in WTO Secretariat, above n 11.

against basic trade disciplines, such as the principle of non-discrimination or the prohibition of quantitative restrictions. This tension is usually addressed through 'exception clauses' in trade liberalisation agreements, including in the WTO,[332] which recognise a *right* for Parties to adopt trade measures aimed at protecting the environment under certain conditions. One of the key aspects of the Doha trade and environment mandate is in fact to consider whether WTO rules would need to be revised in order to *permit* WTO members to implement their specific trade obligations under MEAs.[333] It should be noted, however, that the majority of developing countries remain wary of these measures being used as tools of 'disguised protectionism'. Another, more positive, aspect of this first dimension of the trade and environment nexus relates to the use of trade liberalising measures (for example, reduction of tariffs) to encourage trade in certain goods and services that are considered beneficial from an environmental standpoint, which is also part of the Doha negotiating mandate.[334]

The (potential) effects of environmental measures on market access: This second dimension of the trade and environment nexus stems from the fact that standards, priorities and objectives of environmental protection tend to differ across countries, given that these need to reflect the environmental and developmental context to which they apply, as stipulated in Principle 11 of the Rio Declaration.[335] In many instances, high environmental standards or related product requirements (for example, eco-labelling) in developed-country markets – no matter how legitimate from an environmental policy viewpoint – can hinder exports from less developed countries that are simply not in a developmental position to meet them. In addition, developing-country WTO members are generally wary of 'green protectionism', whereby high environmental standards are used as an excuse for protectionism rather than for legitimate policy objectives. This dimension of the trade and environment nexus is usually addressed through *cooperation* measures, such as technical assistance and capacity building, in order to enable developing-country exporters to meet higher standards of environmental protection. This is an issue that is receiving particular attention within the work of CTE, albeit it is not part of the Doha negotiating mandate.[336]

The (potential) impact of environmental standards on international competitiveness: While also deriving from differences in national environmental regulations, this third dimension of the trade and environment nexus is instead concerned with

[332] eg, art XX(b) and (g) GATT; art XIV(b) GATS; arts 27.2 and 27.3 TRIPS.

[333] Doha Declaration, para 31(i), which however states that: 'The negotiations shall be limited in scope to the applicability of such existing WTO rules as among parties to the MEA in question. The negotiations shall not prejudice the WTO rights of any Member that is not a party to the MEA in question'.

[334] Doha Declaration, para 31(iii).

[335] Rio Declaration, Principle 11: 'Environmental standards, management objectives and priorities should reflect the environmental and development context to which they apply'.

[336] Doha Declaration, para 32(i). Among the measures being discussed in the CTE are: transparency, notification, early warning, consultation, impact assessment, technical assistance and capacity building.

the potential effect that such regulatory differences can have on the international competitiveness of traded goods and services. It is a key issue primarily for developed countries, which fear the prospect of a 'race to the bottom' in environmental regulation, whereby (developing) countries try to encourage trade and investment by lowering or not enforcing domestic environmental standards.[337] Such weakening of environmental regimes is perceived as creating an 'unfair competitive advantage', particularly if the costs of reduced environmental regulation are partly or fully externalised outside the territory of the de-regulating State. Countries with more stringent environmental laws may therefore seek to address this matter in their bilateral/regional trade agreements (the United States being the most prominent example), through the inclusion of provisions that prevent regulatory competition in the environmental domain and ensure a 'level playing field' between the Parties as regards environmental standards. Such provisions can take the form of a *prohibition* to lower existing domestic environmental standards (through changes in law or lack of enforcement), and/or an *obligation* (whether in mandatory or 'best-endeavour' terms) to enhance or harmonise standards of environmental protection. However, and importantly, this dimension of the trade and environment nexus is not part of the Doha agenda. In line with the principle of common but differentiated responsibility,[338] it is generally recognised that each WTO member has the right to set its own standards of environmental protection at the level it considers appropriate, and it would be arguably beyond the WTO mandate (not being an environmental agency) to require otherwise.

Until recently, the EU had largely confined its efforts in shaping the trade and environment regulatory nexus to the multilateral level, where it has been an active *demandeur* as regards the clarification of the relationship between WTO rules and specific trade obligations set out in MEAs. It has also supported the liberalisation of trade in environmental goods and services (particularly those that it views as beneficial in tackling climate change), whilst also pressing for the recognition of eco-labelling in WTO agreements.[339] However, a shift in the EU's approach is starting to be noticed following the endorsement of the renewed SDS in June 2006, where the European Council gave a clear mandate for the integration of environmental (and social) concerns in bilateral and inter-regional trade and cooperation agreements.[340] In the particular case of trade agreements, a new strategy named 'Global Europe –

[337] This is based on the 'pollution haven' argument that, under free trade, firms will migrate to countries where environmental regulations are less stringent as using cheaper but environment-costly process and production methods (PPMs) will give them a competitive edge.

[338] Rio Declaration, Principle 7: 'States shall cooperate in a spirit of global partnership to conserve, protect and restore the health and integrity of the Earth's ecosystem. In view of the different contributions to global environmental degradation, States have common but differentiated responsibilities'; and Principle 11 (above n 335).

[339] Proposals submitted by the EU in this regard can be found at www.wto.org/english/tratop_e/envir_e/envir_negotiations_e.htm.

[340] See s 4.2.3.1 and n 265 above.

Competing in the World' was also adopted in November 2006,[341] which announced the launch of negotiations on new 'competitiveness-driven' Free Trade Agreements (FTAs) that would include, inter alia, the incorporation of 'cooperative provisions in areas related to labour standards and environmental protection'.[342]

The Global Europe Strategy is thus indicative of a change in the EU's approach to the trade and environment nexus in two particular respects. First, unlike the 1996 Communication on Trade and Environment, the Global Strategy is not based on a thorough assessment of the trade and environment linkages,[343] but rather motivated by the desire to put EU external trade and investment policies 'at the service' of its broader competitiveness and economic reform agenda as presented in the renewed Lisbon Strategy.[344] In order words, the integration of environmental matters in these new FTAs appears to be primarily concerned with the third dimension of the trade and environment nexus seen above. Second, in the 1996 Communication, the focus of EU action was on the multilateral trading system and on how WTO rules should be adapted to accommodate environmental protection concerns (including the implementation of specific trade obligations under MEAs),[345] while this multilateral dimension is largely absent in the Global Europe Strategy. The EU does reaffirm that concluding the Doha Round negotiations remains its 'first priority',[346] but the emphasis in the Global Europe Strategy is clearly placed on how the new FTAs can serve EU competitiveness interests in the meantime, including with regards to the trade and environment nexus. While the EU has often argued that its multilateral and bilateral approaches are 'mutually supportive', and now maintains that its new FTAs would also serve as a 'stepping stone' (and not a 'stumbling block') to progress at the multilateral level, this rhetoric has not gone unquestioned.[347]

[341] Commission, 'Working paper on global Europe – competing in the world. A contribution to the EU's growth and job strategy SEC (2006) 1230, endorsed by the Council, 'Conclusions on Global Europe – competing in the world' (14799/06) 13 November 2006 (Global Europe Strategy).

[342] Global Europe Strategy, 12.

[343] Communication Trade and Environment, part 2 (analysing the key issues in the trade and environment debate) and part 3 (considering the interests of developing countries in these issues). Cf with scant references to the environment in the Global Europe Strategy, at 5, 7, and 12.

[344] See above n 224, which was re-launched by the Commission on 2 February 2005. See also, Commission 'Press Release – New strategy puts EU trade policy at the service of European competitiveness and economic reform' 4 October 2006.

[345] Communication Trade and Environment, part 4 (detailing issues that arise in the context of environmental protection and the multilateral trading system, including dispute settlement) and part 5 (on the way forward within the CTE and other multilateral bodies).

[346] Global Europe Strategy, 2. See also more recent Communication Rio+20, 9 where the 'mutual supportiveness between trade and sustainable development' is said 'to include' actions through the multilateral trading system.

[347] See generally, M Cremona, 'Rhetoric and Reticence: EU External Commercial Policy in a Multilateral Context' (2001) 38(2) *Common Market Law Review* 359. On the proclaimed 'mutual supportiveness' of its multilateral and regional approaches to the trade and environment nexus, see G Marín Durán, 'The EU Role in Shaping the Trade & Environment Regulatory Nexus: Multilateral and Regional Approaches' in S Blockmans, B van Vooren and J Wouters (eds), *The Legal Dimension of Global Governance – What Role for the EU?* (Oxford, Oxford University Press, forthcoming 2012).

5.3 Environmental integration and EU cooperation policies

The European Union (then European Community) was first granted express competence for development cooperation by the Maastricht Treaty,[348] being empowered to adopt autonomous measures, as well as to conclude agreements with third countries and international organisations.[349] The substantive scope of this competence was broadly defined by the objectives of fostering 'the sustainable economic and social development of developing countries', the 'smooth and gradual integration of developing countries into the world economy' and 'the campaign against poverty in the developing countries',[350] thereby leaving significant room for institutional discretion in determining the content and priorities of Community action in the field of development cooperation.[351] While the sustainability objective did not explicitly contain an environmental dimension, EC development policy was clearly subject to the environmental integration requirement (old Article 6 TEC), and in fact a number of environment-specific funding regulations were adopted during this pre-Lisbon period.[352]

The Lisbon Treaty has further extended the substantive scope of this EU competence, which is now to be conducted within the overall framework of the principles and objectives of the Union's external action[353] – namely, those enshrined in Article 21(2) TEU.[354] This new provision has in fact upgraded the three objectives that were previously specific to EC development policy, making them now applicable to the whole of the EU's external action, albeit with a notable textual change to introduce an explicit environmental dimension in the sustainability objective.[355] At the same time, Article 21(2) TEU requires EU development policy to support all other objectives of the Union's external action, including that of helping to 'develop international measures to preserve and improve the quality of the environment and the sustainable management of global natural resources, in order to ensure sustainable development'.[356] This Lisbon amendment can thus be seen as reinforcing the environmental integration requirement in Article 11 TFEU, which remains clearly applicable to EU development policy.

As to the geographical scope of EU development policy, this seems to be limited to cooperation with 'developing countries' (a term not defined in the Treaty), in

[348] Former title XX TEC, now title III, part V TFEU.

[349] Former art 179(1) TEC, now art 209(1) TFEU (for autonomous measures) and former art 181 TEC, now art 209(2) TFEU (for international agreements).

[350] Former art 177(1) TEC. Community action in the field of development cooperation was also required to contribute to the 'general objective of developing and consolidating democracy and the rule of law, and that of respecting human rights and fundamental freedoms' (former art 177(2) TEC).

[351] See Case-268/94 *Portugal v Council* [1996] ECR I-06177, where the Court favoured a broad interpretation of these Treaty objectives. For a critical analysis, see G Marín Durán, above n 19, 271–78.

[352] See further Ch 4, s 3.1.

[353] Art 208(1) TFEU.

[354] See s 4.2.3.2 above.

[355] Art 21(2)(d) now reads: 'foster the sustainable economic, social and *environmental* development of developing countries' (emphasis added); cf with former art 177(1) TEC (above n 350).

[356] Art 21(2)(f) TEU.

light of the existence of a separate legal basis for 'economic, financial and technical cooperation with third countries'[357] (other than developing ones). For our purposes, it is sufficient to note that this additional basis for EU cooperation is equally subject to the common set of principles and objectives of the Union's external action in Article 21(2) TEU and the environmental integration requirement in Article 11 TFEU. It should also be noted that EU cooperation policies with both developing and developed countries are subject to the ordinary legislative procedure, and thus formulated and implemented through co-decision between the Council and the Parliament.[358]

In addition to these Treaty-based linkages, the need to integrate environmental concerns into the EU's development and economic cooperation with third countries has been further recognised at policy level. In May 2001, the Council endorsed the Commission's proposed strategy on environmental integration in EU development and cooperation activities,[359] which emphasised that 'poor environmental quality undermines the developing countries' efforts to alleviate poverty and it will further jeopardise future prospects for sustainable economic and social development',[360] thus running against the EU's development policy objectives. The strategy highlighted potential synergies between poverty eradication, sustainable development and the environment, and called for environmental mainstreaming into all six thematic priorities for Community assistance.[361] More significantly, in the 'European Consensus on Development'[362] – a high-level policy document jointly adopted by all the main EU institutional actors and the EU Member States in December 2005 – environmental sustainability is recognised as an objective in itself and as a cross-cutting issue to be mainstreamed in all Community (now EU) activities.[363] In particular, an undertaking is made to support the efforts by partner countries (governments and civil society) to incorporate environmental considerations into development, including by supporting their capacity to implement MEAs.[364]

[357] Art 212 TFEU (former art 181(a) TEC, added by the Treaty of Nice [2001] OJ C80/1).

[358] Art 209(1) TFEU for cooperation with developing countries and art 212(2) TFEU for cooperation with other countries.

[359] Commission, 'Working paper on integrating the environment into economic and development cooperation' SEC (2001) 609 (WP Environmental Integration into Cooperation); endorsed by the Council, 'Conclusions on strategy for the integration of environmental considerations into development policy to promote sustainable development' 31 May 2001, 14. Note that this followed the Commission, 'Communication on the European Community's development policy' COM (2000) 212 final, recognising links between environmental protection and the overarching goal of poverty reduction.

[360] WP Environmental Integration into Cooperation, 4.

[361] Namely: trade and development; regional integration and cooperation; support to macroeconomic policies linked to social sector programmes; transport; sustainable rural development and food security; and institutional capacity building, good governance and the rule of law. See WP Environmental Integration into Cooperation, 12–18.

[362] Council, Representatives of the Governments of the Member States meeting in the Council, European Parliament and Commission, 'Joint Statement on the European Development Policy: The European Consensus' [2006] OJ C46/1 (European Consensus on Development) still in effect as the highest-level policy statement to guide EU development policy-making at the time of writing.

[363] European Consensus on Development, paras 101 and 105.

[364] Ibid, paras 38 and 75.

At the international level, environmental integration into cooperation policies is less controversial than the trade and environment nexus mentioned above. In fact, a particularly important aspect of the principle of common but differentiated responsibility is international assistance, including financial aid and technology transfer, in recognition of the fact that developed countries have historically played the greatest role in creating most global environmental problems, and have also greater capacity to address them.[365] In a similar vein, 'environmental sustainability' is one of the eight Millennium Development Goals (MDGs) universally endorsed as the development blueprint.[366] The achievement of the MDGs has, inter alia, revived commitments by donors (including the EU) to reach the long-standing UN target for ODA of 0.7 per cent GNI by 2015.[367] In this context, it should be underscored that the EU (and the Member States)[368] are explicitly required 'to comply with the commitments and take account of the objectives they have approved in the context of the United Nations and other competent international organisations'[369] when conducting their development policies. This can be read as including the commitments made at the Rio Summit, the WSSD as well as in relation to the MDGs.[370]

6. CONCLUSIONS

Article 11 TFEU obliges the EU political institutions to integrate environmental protection requirements into all Union policies and activities. While not prescribing a clear priority for environmental protection to the detriment of other EU

[365] Rio Declaration, Principle 7: 'The developed countries acknowledge the responsibility that they bear in the international pursuit to sustainable development in view of the pressures their societies place on the global environment and of the technologies and financial resources they command'. See generally, L Rajamani, *Differential Treatment in International Environmental Law* (Oxford, Oxford University Press, 2006).

[366] The MDGs were developed by the UN, following consultations among international agencies, as a set of interconnected and mutually reinforcing development goals, accompanied by targets and benchmarks based on the time-bound commitments contained in UN General Assembly, 'United Nations Millennium Declaration' (2000) UN Doc A/RES/55/2. The MDGs were then intergovernmentally approved at the 2005 UN Summit: UN General Assembly, 'World Summit Outcome' (2005) UN Doc A/RES/60/1, para 17. The other seven MDGs are to: eradicate extreme poverty and hunger; achieve universal primary education; promote gender equality and empower women; reduce the mortality rate of children; improve maternal health; combat HIV/AIDS, malaria and other diseases; and develop a global partnership for development. For more information, visit www.un.org/millenniumgoals/.

[367] This international aid target was first pledged in the UN General Assembly in 1970 and was then reiterated in 2002: 'Monterrey Consensus of the International Conference on Financing for Development' (22 August 2002) UN Doc A/CONF.198/11, para 42.

[368] Note that EU development competence is complementary (a special type of shared competence) to that of the Member States (arts 4(4) and 208(1) TFEU).

[369] Art 208(2) TFEU.

[370] On EU contribution to the MDGs, see Commission, 'Communication on policy coherence for development – accelerating progress towards attaining the millennium development goals' COM (2005) 134 final; more recently Communication Action Plan MDGs 2010, 5 stating that, in 2009, the EU ODA level had slightly decreased and amounted to €49bn, corresponding to 0.42% of EU GNI. This meant that the EU was behind schedule to meet the intermediate collective target of 0.56% GNI by 2010, as a step towards reaching the UN target of 0.7% GNI by 2015.

policy objectives, Article 11 TFEU requires that, at a minimum, an integrated and balanced assessment of relevant environmental concerns takes place in EU decision-making processes. The substantive scope of such an environmental integration exercise is conceived in very broad terms in light of the environmental objectives, principles and criteria enshrined in Article 191 TFEU, albeit an emphasis on climate change is manifest in both EU primary law and policy documents. The environmental integration requirement is also purposely linked, both in EU primary and policy documents, to the broader objective of sustainable development, and can thus be expected to figure as a means to achieving this objective in both EU internal and external measures. In the particular field of EU external relations, environmental integration is further supported by a more general requirement for 'horizontal coherence' in the EU's external action, which has an important environmental dimension (Articles 3(5) and 21(2) TEU). Yet, the precise extent to which environmental concerns are effectively integrated into EU policies and activities, including external ones, is largely a matter of legislative and executive discretion, with which the EU judiciary is unlikely to interfere. In other words, the practical value of these Treaty-based mainstreaming requirements and objectives rests upon concrete action by the EU political institutions.

Based on this premise, the reminder of this book will enquire into the degree(s) to which the EU political institutions have in effect integrated environmental protection requirements into the Union's external relations, by examining a number of key external policy instruments: (i) bilateral and inter-regional agreements (which regulate EU relations with third parties generally, including in terms of economic and trade cooperation); (ii) the generalised system of preferences (which is an unilateral measure of the CCP); (iii) EU funding regulations (which include environment-specific, as well as more general tools); (iv) bilateral and inter-regional institutionalised dialogues (which are conducted within the context of an existing agreement, but also outside this formal framework); and finally (v) sustainability impact assessments.

2

Environmental Integration in Bilateral/Inter-regional Agreements

1. INTRODUCTION

THIS CHAPTER WILL identify, classify and compare environmental provisions in associations and other bilateral or inter-regional agreements concluded by the EU with third countries or regions, with a view to assessing the extent to which environmental requirements have been integrated into the *definition* of the EU's external relations, as required by Article 11 TFEU.[1] In doing so, the chapter will expose the reader to the environmental dimension of these agreements, as well as to the variety of provisions that have been used to pursue environmental integration in the EU's bilateral and inter-regional external relations.

The chapter will start by providing a brief introduction to the types of agreements concluded by the EU with third countries or regions based on a combination of underlying Treaty provisions and practice. The core section of the chapter will then provide a comparative analysis of the different categories of EU agreements, underscoring differences and similarities in their *environmental cooperation clauses* (dealing solely with the environment) and *environmental integration clauses* (mandating or encouraging the incorporation of environmental concerns into other cooperation areas). It should be clarified that both of these sets of provisions are relevant (and necessary) from an environmental integration standpoint. Environmental cooperation clauses are easily singled out within a given agreement and have the function of integrating environmental concerns into the EU's external relations as a whole, while environmental integration clauses serve the integration exercise at the more microscopic level of individual EU policies covered by a given agreement and are usually spread throughout its text.

Ultimately, the key finding of this chapter is that environmental protection requirements have been generally integrated in the EU's bilateral and inter-regional external relations but in a differentiated manner. The chapter thus concludes by recapitulating, contextualising and assessing the key aspects of such a

[1] This chapter is based on an earlier analysis by the authors: G Marín Durán and E Morgera, 'Towards Environmental Integration in EC External Relations? A Comparative Analysis of Selected Association Agreements' (2006) 6 *Yearbook of European Environmental Law* 179.

differentiated approach to environmental integration with regard to: (a) legal wording and environmental standards used; (b) the choice of priority issues for environmental cooperation; (c) the selection of cooperation areas in which environmental integration is ensured; and (d) the trade and environment nexus. Yet, the analysis of more recent agreements concluded against the backdrop of the 2006 Global Europe Strategy[2] seems to indicate a shift in EU practice towards a more systematic approach to environmental integration. Finally, some emerging questions of implementation will be highlighted, to be addressed in subsequent chapters of the book.

2. TYPES OF AGREEMENTS

Since its foundation, and with the widening of its external competences, the EU has concluded a significant number of agreements with third countries or regions, as well as with international organisations. These have been of a general nature (for example, associations, partnerships and other cooperation agreements) covering a wide range of areas, or have dealt only with specific subject matters (for example, fisheries and transport).[3] As will be seen, environmental cooperation and environmental integration clauses are included in most EU agreements of a general nature, although to different extents. This section will introduce the various types of agreements, with a view to providing a background for the analysis of their environment-related clauses that is the core of this chapter.

2.1 Association agreements

Associations present a number of distinctive legal and political features when compared to other bilateral and inter-regional agreements concluded by the EU and are often proclaimed by the EU to be the most advanced form of contractual relations in which it can engage with a third party.

The power to conclude 'agreements establishing an association' with third countries and international organisations was among the few express external competences granted to the EU (then European Economic Community) by the original Treaty of Rome.[4] Even though EU external competences have been

[2] Commission, 'Working paper on global Europe – competing in the world. A contribution to the EU's growth and job strategy SEC (2006) 1230, endorsed by the Council, 'Conclusions on Global Europe – competing in the world' (14799/06) 13 November 2006 (Global Europe Strategy). See Ch 1, s 5.2.

[3] The Commission provides a useful database on agreements concluded by the EU (including a short description of the agreement and its key legal features, such as date of signature/entry into force, OJ reference, type of EU competences, and legal bases in EU Treaties) at www.ec.europa.eu/world/agreements/default.home.do. The Council of the EU also offers a database that includes agreements concluded by the Member States only at www.consilum.europa.eu/showPage.aspx?id=252.

[4] The other express external competence in the Treaty of Rome was the common commercial policy, see Ch 1, s 5.2.

considerably expanded through successive treaty revisions, associations have maintained a distinctive position in the EU Treaties (Article 217 TFEU)[5] vis-a-vis other agreements concluded by the EU. However, there is as yet no positive Treaty-based definition of the principal objectives and substantive scope of an association, besides the formal requirement that it involves reciprocal rights and obligations, common action and special procedures.

This vague Treaty definition has permitted the EU to conclude, since the 1960s, association agreements with a large number of countries at varying levels of development and geographical locations, and with very different ultimate purposes. From their signatories to the objectives, principles and substantive scope of these agreements, the long-standing practice of 'associating' third countries with the EU has been determined overall by political choices and priorities, not law.

At present, four broad categories of association agreements may be distinguished:[6]

1. *Association as a prelude to EU membership*: these are agreements with neighbouring countries that are considered by the EU as 'candidates' or 'potential candidates' for membership. This is currently the case of the Ankara Agreement with Turkey[7] and of the Association and Stabilisation Agreements with five South-Eastern European countries (Albania,[8] Bosnia and Herzegovina,[9] Croatia,[10] the former Yugoslav Republic of Macedonia,[11] Montenegro[12] and Serbia).[13]
2. *Association as a substitute for EU membership*: these are agreements with neighbouring countries that either do not wish to join the EU or are not considered as potential candidates by the EU itself. The Agreement with Norway[14] is an

[5] Former art 310 TEC.

[6] This categorisation is partly based on that made in D Hanf and P Dengler, 'Accords d'Association' (2004) 1 College of Europe Research Paper in Law 9; MF Christophe-Tchakaloff (ed), *Le Concept d'Association dans les Accords passés par la Communauté: essai de clarification* (Brussels, Bruylant, 1999).

[7] Agreement creating an Association between the European Economic Community and Turkey [1964] OJ L217/3687. See generally, NA Neuwahl, 'The EU-Turkey Customs Union: a Balance but No Equilibrium' (1999) 4(1) *European Foreign Affairs Review* 37; S Peers, 'Living in Sin: Legal Integration under the EC-Turkey Customs Union' (1996) 13(3) *European Journal of International Law* 411.

[8] Stabilisation and Association Agreement between the European Communities and their Member States, of the one part, and the Republic of Albania, of the other part [2009] OJ L107/166 (Albania AA).

[9] Stabilisation and Association Agreement between the European Communities and their Member States, of the one part, and the Republic of Bosnia and Herzegovina, of the other part, signed on 16 June 2008, not yet in force, full text at www.delbih.ec.europa.eu/files/docs/publications/en/SAP_eng.pdf (Bosnia AA).

[10] Stabilisation and Association Agreement between the European Communities and their Member States, of the one part, and the Republic of Croatia, of the other part [2005] OJ L26/3 (Croatia AA).

[11] Stabilisation and Association Agreement between the European Communities and their Member States, of the one part, and the former Yugoslav Republic of Macedonia, of the other part [2004] OJ L84/13 (Macedonia AA).

[12] Stabilisation and Association Agreement between the European Communities and their Member States, of the one part, and the Republic of Montenegro, of the other part [2010] OJ L108/3 (Montenegro AA).

[13] Stabilisation and Association Agreement between the European Communities and their Member States, of the one part, and the Republic of Serbia, of the other part, signed on 29 April 2008, not yet in force, full text at www.ec.europa.eu/enlargement/pdf/serbia/key_document/saa_en.pdf (Serbia AA).

[14] Agreement on the European Economic Area (EEA) [1994] OJ L1/3, amended by the EEA Enlargement Agreement [2004] OJ L 130/3 and the EEA Supplement No 23 [2004] OJ L130/1. The

example of the former while agreements with the countries participating in the Euro-Mediterranean Partnership are examples of the latter. Euro-Mediterranean Association Agreements have been concluded with: Algeria[15], Egypt[16] Israel,[17] Jordan,[18] Lebanon,[19] Morocco,[20] Tunisia[21] and as an interim Agreement with Palestine.[22]

3. *Association as a development tool*: these are agreements with developing and least-developed countries, most of which were former colonies of the EU Member States. The most emblematic example is the Cotonou Partnership Agreement[23] with 78 African, Caribbean and Pacific (ACP) States. A more recent example is the Association Agreement initialled with Central American countries on 22 March 2011.[24]
4. *Association as an instrument for inter-regional cooperation*: these are agreements with more advanced developing countries (or 'emerging economies') from geographically distant regions, such as the Associations with Chile[25] and

other two states participating in the EEA are Iceland and Liechtenstein. Negotiations on Iceland's accession to the EU were open on 17 June 2010.

[15] Euro-Mediterranean Agreement establishing an Association between the European Community and its Member States, of the one part, and the People's Democratic Republic of Algeria, of the other part [2005] OJ L265/2 (Algeria AA).

[16] Euro-Mediterranean Agreement establishing an Association between the European Community and its Member States, of the one part, and the Arab Republic of Egypt, of the other part [2004] OJ L304/39 (Egypt AA).

[17] Euro-Mediterranean Agreement establishing an Association between the European Community and its Member States, of the one part, and the State of Israel, of the other part [2000] OJ L147/3 (Israel AA).

[18] Euro-Mediterranean Agreement establishing an Association between the European Community and its Member States, of the one part, and the Hashemite Kingdom of Jordan, of the other part [2002] OJ L129/3 (Jordan AA).

[19] Euro-Mediterranean Agreement establishing an Association between the European Community and its Member States, of the one part, and the Republic of Lebanon, of the other part [2006] OJ L143/2 (Lebanon AA).

[20] Euro-Mediterranean Agreement establishing an Association between the European Community and its Member States, of the one part, and the Kingdom of Morocco, of the other part [2000] OJ L70/2 (Morocco AA).

[21] Euro-Mediterranean Agreement establishing an Association between the European Community and its Member States, of the one part, and the Republic of Tunisia, of the other part [1998] OJ L97/2 (Tunisia AA).

[22] Euro-Mediterranean Interim Association Agreement on Trade and Cooperation between the European Community, of the one part, and the Palestine Liberation Organization (PLO) for the benefit of the Palestinian Authority of the West Bank and the Gaza Strip, of the other part [1997] OJ L187/3 (Palestine AA).

[23] The Partnership Agreement between the Members of the African, Caribbean and Pacific Group of States of the one part and the European Community and its Member States of the other [2000] OJ L317/3 (Cotonou Agreement).

[24] Agreement establishing an Association between the EU and its Member States, on the one hand, and Central America on the other, initialled on 22 March 2011, full text available at www.trade.ec.europa.eu/doclib/press/index.cfm?id=689 (Central America AA). The Central American countries concerned are: Costa Rica, El Salvador, Guatemala, Honduras, Nicaragua and Panama. The agreement needs to undergo the formal process of translation, signature and ratification before it can enter into force.

[25] Agreement establishing an Association between the European Community and its Member States, of the one part, and the Republic of Chile, on the other part [2002] OJ L352/3 (Chile AA).

South Africa.[26] An association agreement with MERCOSUR is currently under negotiation.[27]

Although the precise content and ultimate objectives of association agreements vary from case to case, some common characteristics in their overall structure make them an ideal case study in the context of environmental integration in EU external relations. First, given that Article 217 TFEU contains no substantive limitations on their scope and content, associations may, in principle, cover all 'Union policies and activities'. They generally encompass three main domains of cooperation: the traditional areas of trade and financial/technical assistance; cooperation in a vast number of specific policy areas (for instance, environmental protection, energy, transport, agriculture, social and cultural matters); and political dialogue on cooperation in issues such as security and immigration. It should be noted that the European Court of Justice seems to see no obstacle to the use of Article 217 TFEU as an all-encompassing legal basis upon which all Union policies and activities may be integrated, having held that such provision 'must necessarily empower the Community [now EU] to guarantee commitments towards non-member countries in all the fields covered by the Treaty.'[28] Being the single most comprehensive and multi-purpose instrument for contractual relations between the EU and third countries, associations are potentially the ideal cooperation framework for integrating environmental protection in the definition of all EU external policies.[29]

The second peculiarity common to most association agreements is the establishment of a highly sophisticated institutional structure for their implementation, including political and quasi-judicial organs. Among them, the Association Council, composed of representatives from the European Commission, the EU Member States and the third party concerned, has the paramount responsibility of implementing the different policy objectives contemplated in the agreement

[26] Agreement on Trade, Development and Cooperation between the European Community and its Member States, of the one part, and the Republic of South Africa, of the other part [1999] OJ L311/3 (South Africa AA). Note that, notwithstanding its name, the agreement was concluded on the basis of former art 310 TEC.

[27] MERCOSUR is the acronym for 'Mercado Común del Sur' (Southern Common Market), which designates the process of regional integration among the countries of Argentina, Brazil, Paraguay and Uruguay. Negotiations for an inter-regional association agreement between the EU and MERCOSUR were first launched in 1999 but suspended in October 2004. The negotiations were formally relaunched at the EU-MERCOSUR Summit in Madrid on 17 May 2010. Among the few academic contributions on this matter, see G Müller-Brandeck-Bocquet, 'Perspective for a New Regionalism: Relations between the EU and Mercosur' (2000) 5(4) *European Foreign Affairs Review* 561; S Santander, 'EU-Mercosur Inter-regionalism: Facing up to the South American Crisis and the Emerging Free Trade Area of the Americas' (2002) 7(4) *European Foreign Affairs Review* 491.

[28] Case 12/86 *Demirel v Stadt Schwäbisch Gmünd* (Demirel) [1987] ECR 3719, para 9.

[29] Furthermore, the generalised practice of concluding associations as 'mixed agreements' (ie, agreements to which both the EU and the Member States are contracting parties) also avoids problems of external competence constraints on the part of the EU.

and has, to this effect, the power to adopt, by consensus, legally binding decisions upon all contracting parties.[30]

A third specificity of associations relates to their 'special status' within the EU legal order. In terms of the decision-making process, the conclusion of association agreements involves all three EU political institutions as they are negotiated by the Commission and approved by both the Council and the European Parliament.[31] Furthermore, the ECJ has upheld the special legal status of associations as 'special, privileged links with a non-member country which must, at least to a certain extent, take part in the Community [now EU] system'.[32] In fact, it was in the context of the Association with Turkey that the Court developed a two-stage test for determining whether individual provisions contained in EU agreements could have 'direct effects' within the internal legal order of the Union.[33] In addition, the Court has extended the applicability of the requirement found in Article 216(2) TFEU[34] that EU agreements are binding upon the Union institutions and the Member States to the decisions adopted by the Association Council.[35]

2.2 Other general agreements

While association agreements enjoy a privileged status in both political and legal terms, they are not the only instruments for contractual relations between the EU and third countries or regions. Over the past three decades, the EU has in fact developed a vast network of other general agreements covering most regions and countries in the world (with noticeable exceptions of industrialised countries, such as the United States and Japan).[36] As their name suggests, these agreements

[30] For a more detailed account of the substantive nature and institutional structure of association agreements, as well as their 'special status' within the EU legal order, see Hanf and Dengler, above n 6; Christophe-Tchakaloff, above n 6.

[31] Under former art 300(3) TEC, associations were among the few EU agreements subject to democratic control as the assent of the European Parliament was mandatory for their conclusion. This requirement now applies to all 'agreements covering fields to which either the ordinary legislative procedure applies, or the special legislative procedure where the consent by the European Parliament is required' (art 218(6)(a)(v) TFEU).

[32] Case *Demirel*, above n 28, para 9.

[33] Ibid, para 14. This test would be satisfied when a provision in an agreement contains 'a clear and precise obligation which is not subject, in its implementation or effects, to the adoption of any subsequent measure,' considered in the context of the agreement's 'wording and the purpose and nature of the agreement itself'. Accordingly, environment-related provisions are unlikely to satisfy this test as these do not always lay down a 'clear and precise obligation' and in most instances do require the adoption of subsequent measures.

[34] Former art 300(7) TEC.

[35] Case 30/88 *Greece v Commission* [1989] ECR 3711, para 13; Case C-192/89 *Sevince v Staatssecretaris van Justitie* [1990] ECR I-3461, paras 8–15; Case 188/91 *Deutsche Shell AG v Hauptzollamt Hamburg-Harburg* [1993] ECR I-363, para 17.

[36] EU relations with these countries are conducted through 'soft law' measures, rather than formal agreements: the 1998 Transatlantic Economic Partnership with the US and the 2001 Action Plan with Japan. Note, however, that the EU and Japan agreed in May 2011 to launch negotiations for a comprehensive agreement. See further Ch 5, s 3.6.

generally seek to establish a legal and institutional framework for political and economic cooperation or at most a partnership, rather an association, with the EU. Unlike associations, such partnerships or cooperation agreements have no specific legal basis in the EU Treaties and thus, in accordance with the constitutional principle of conferred powers,[37] need to be concluded on multiple legal bases depending on the subject matter covered.[38] Yet, in terms of substantive content and institutional setup, these agreements may not differ very significantly from associations. In fact, as will be seen, a particular partnership or cooperation agreement may even contain stronger environmental integration commitments than an association. In most cases, the type of agreement that the EU concludes with a given third country or region is determined by political considerations, not law.[39]

Among the partnership or cooperation agreements in force (or recently concluded) at the time of writing, the following may be highlighted:

- In Eastern Europe/Central Asia: Partnership and Cooperation Agreements (PCAs) concluded with former Soviet Union countries[40] (Armenia,[41] Azerbaijan,[42] Georgia,[43] Kazakhstan,[44] Kyrgyz Republic,[45] Moldova,[46] Russia,[47] Ukraine[48]

[37] See Ch 1, s 2.

[38] During the pre-Maastricht era, in light of limited express external competences, agreements were often concluded on the basis of both (former) art 133 TEC (now art 207 TFEU) and the so-called 'flexibility clause' (former art 308 TEC, now art 352 TFEU), that allows the adoption of measures necessary for attaining the objectives of the Treaty where no other specific legal basis is provided. With the broadening of express external competences in the post-Maastricht era, agreements have tended to be concluded on the specific Treaty bases dealing with the areas covered, albeit not in all cases. See S Peers, 'EC Frameworks of International Relations: Cooperation, Partnership and Association' in A Dashwood and C Hillion (eds), *The General Law of the EC External Relations* (London, Sweet and Maxwell, 2000), 160–65.

[39] On this point, see Peers, 'EC Frameworks', above n 38, 175; see also P Koutrakos, *EU International Relations Law* (Oxford, Hart, 2006), 359.

[40] C Hillion, 'Partnership and Cooperation Agreements between the European Union and the New Independent States of the Ex-Soviet Union' (1998) 3(3) *European Foreign Affairs Review* 399; B Berdiyev, 'The EU and Former Soviet Central Asia: An Analysis of the Partnership and Cooperation Agreements' (2003) 22 *Yearbook of Environmental Law* 463.

[41] Partnership and Cooperation Agreement between the European Communities and their Member States, of the one part, and the Republic of Armenia, of the other part [1999] OJ L239/3 (Armenia PCA).

[42] Partnership and Cooperation Agreement between the European Communities and their Member States, of the one part, and the Republic of Azerbaijan, of the other part [1999] OJ L246/3 (Azerbaijan PCA).

[43] Partnership and Cooperation Agreement between the European Communities and their Member States, of the one part, and Georgia, of the other part [1999] OJ L205/3 (Georgia PCA).

[44] Partnership and Cooperation Agreement between the European Communities and their Member States, of the one part, and the Republic of Kazakhstan, of the other part [1999] OJ L196/3 (Kazakhstan PCA).

[45] Partnership and Cooperation Agreement establishing a partnership between the European Communities and their Member States, of the one part, and the Kyrgyz Republic, of the other part [1999] OJ L196/48 (Kyrgyzstan PCA).

[46] Partnership and Cooperation Agreement between the European Communities and their Member States, of the one part, and the Republic of Moldova, of the other part [1998] OJ L181/3 (Moldova PCA).

[47] Agreement on Partnership and Cooperation between the European Communities and their Member States, of one part, and the Russian Federation, of the other part [1997] OJ L327/3 (Russia PCA).

[48] Partnership and Cooperation Agreement between the European Communities and their Member States, of the one part, and Ukraine, of the other part [1998] OJ L49/3 (Ukraine PCA).

and Uzbekistan)[49] that are part of the Commonwealth of Independent States (CIS).

- In Latin America: Economic Partnership, Political Coordination and Cooperation Agreement with Mexico;[50] Framework Cooperation Agreement with the Andean Community;[51] Framework Cooperation Agreement with Central American countries;[52] Inter-regional Framework Cooperation Agreement with MERCOSUR.[53]
- In Asia: Inter-regional Cooperation Agreement with the Association of South-East Asian Nations (ASEAN);[54] Cooperation Agreements with Bangladesh,[55] Pakistan,[56] Cambodia,[57] India,[58] and Lao People's Democratic Republic;[59] and the Framework Agreement[60] and Free Trade Agreement[61] with South Korea.

[49] Partnership and Cooperation Agreement establishing a partnership between the European Communities and their Member States, of the one part, and the Republic of Uzbekistan, of the other part [1999] OJ L229/3 (Uzbekistan PCA).

[50] Economic Partnership, Political Coordination and Cooperation Agreement between the European Community and its Member States, of the one part, and the United Mexican States, of the other part [2000] OJ L276/45. This is an example of a high degree of similarity in terms of objectives and substantive scope with an association agreement (that with Chile).

[51] Framework Agreement on Cooperation between the European Economic Community and the Cartagena Agreement and its member countries, namely the Republic of Bolivia, the Republic of Colombia, the Republic of Ecuador, the Republic of Peru and the Republic of Venezuela [1998] OJ L127/11. A more comprehensive Political Dialogue and Cooperation Agreement was signed on 15 December 2003, but has not entered into force. A Free Trade Agreement between the EU and its Member States, on one side, and Colombia and Peru, on the other was initialled on 23 and 24 March 2011, full text available at www.trade.ec.europa.eu/doclib/press/index.cfm?id=691 (COPE FTA).

[52] Framework Cooperation Agreement between the European Economic Community and the Republics of Costa Rica, El Salvador, Guatemala, Honduras, Nicaragua and Panama [1999] OJ L63/39. A more comprehensive Political Dialogue and Cooperation Agreement was signed on 15 December 2003, but did not enter into force. An association agreement has been recently initialled with these countries, see above n 24.

[53] Interregional Framework Cooperation Agreement between the European Community and its Member States, of the one part, and the Southern Common Market and its Party States, of the other part [1996] OJ L69/4. Negotiations on an EU-MERCOSUR Association Agreement are ongoing, see above n 27.

[54] Cooperation Agreement between the European Economic Community and Indonesia, Malaysia, the Philippines, Singapore and Thailand (member countries of ASEAN) [1980] OJ L144/2. More comprehensive PCAs were signed with Indonesia in 2009 and with the Philippines in 2010.

[55] Cooperation Agreement between the European Community and the People's Republic of Bangladesh on partnership and development [2001] OJ L118/48.

[56] Cooperation Agreement between the European Community and the Islamic Republic of Pakistan on partnership and development [2004] OJ L378/23.

[57] Cooperation Agreement between the European Community and the Kingdom of Cambodia [1999] OJ L269/18.

[58] Cooperation Agreement between the European Community and the Republic of India on partnership and development [1994] OJ L223/24.

[59] Cooperation Agreement between the European Community and the Lao People's Democratic Republic [1997] OJ L334/15.

[60] Framework Agreement between the European Union and its Member States, on the one part, and the Republic of Korea, on the other part, signed on 10 May 2010, not yet in force, full text available at www.eeas.europa.eu/korea_south/docs/framework_agreement_final_en.pdf (South Korea FA).

[61] Free Trade Agreement between the European Union and its Member States, of the one part, and the Republic of Korea, of the other part, signed on 6 October 2010, not yet in force, full text available at www.trade.ec.europa.eu/doclib/press/index.cfm?id=443&serie=273&langId=en (South Korea FTA).

- In the Gulf region: Cooperation Agreement with the Gulf Cooperation Council[62] (Bahrain, Kuwait, Oman, Qatar, Saudi Arabia and the United Arab Emirates); and Cooperation Agreement with Yemen.[63]

This book does not enquire exhaustively into environmental integration in all types of EU agreements but primarily concentrates on associations. In the following sections, association agreements with candidate and potential candidate countries will be analysed first, followed by the Euro-Med Association Agreements, the Cotonou Partnership Agreement and the Economic Partnerships Agreements concluded under its umbrella, and then the association agreements for inter-regional cooperation. In the final section of this chapter a number of other bilateral agreements will also be examined in order to establish comparisons with these associations. For each agreement, environmental cooperation clauses will first be examined, then those mandating or encouraging environmental integration in other cooperation areas (environmental integration clauses). Trade cooperation will be dealt with separately from other areas in an attempt to identify the key tenets of the EU's approach to the integration of trade and environmental policies at the bilateral/inter-regional levels. Special attention will also be paid, where particularly relevant, to monitoring and dispute settlement mechanisms.

3. ENVIRONMENTAL INTEGRATION IN ASSOCIATION AS PRELUDE TO EU MEMBERSHIP

3.1 Enlargement and its environmental dimension

Before analysing the environment-related provisions in association agreements as a prelude to EU membership, this section briefly introduces the process of EU enlargement and highlights its environmental dimensions. Accession of new Member States to the European Union is formally governed by Article 49 TEU, according to which a state that wishes to become a member of the Union must satisfy two key conditions: it shall be a 'European state', and respect the common values of the Member States and undertake to promote them. These values are human dignity, liberty, democracy, the rule of law and respect for human rights including those of minorities.[64] In procedural terms, the aspiring state must address its accession application to the Council as well as notifying the European Parliament and the national parliaments of its application. Decisions on accession are unanimously taken by the Council after consulting the Commission and

[62] Cooperation Agreement between the European Economic Community, of the one part, and the countries parties to the Charter of the Cooperation Council for the Arab States of the Gulf (the State of the United Arab Emirates, the State of Bahrain, the Kingdom of Saudi Arabia, the Sultanate of Oman, the State of Qatar and the State of Kuwait), of the other part [1989] OJ L54/3.

[63] Cooperation Agreement between the European Community and the Republic of Yemen [1998] OJ L72/18.

[64] Arts 2 and 6(1) TEU.

receiving assent by qualified majority of the European Parliament. The conditions and date of accession, any transition periods required and the necessary adjustments to the EU Treaties are agreed in the form of an Accession Treaty between the 'acceding state'[65] and the Member States, which is submitted to a process of national ratification.

In practice, however, accession to the EU is far from automatic but is preceded by a pre-accession period (of varying length) that involves different stages from the initial 'applicant state' status to the final 'acceding state' status. During this pre-accession phase, aspiring new Member States shall demonstrate 'a necessary degree of compliance' – in the EU's eyes – with a broader set of membership conditions than those explicitly provided for in Article 49 TEU. These so-called 'Copenhagen criteria', established by the Copenhagen European Council in 1993 and strengthened by the Madrid European Council in 1995,[66] comprise:

- Political conditions: stability of institutions guaranteeing democracy, respect for the rule of law, human rights and minority rights;
- Economic conditions: existence of a functioning market economy and the capacity to cope with the competitive pressures and market forces within the Union;
- Acceptance of the *acquis communautaire*: transposition of EU law into national law, its effective implementation and enforcement through appropriate administrative and judicial structures, and the ability to take on the obligations of membership.

The pre-accession strategy provides the framework for structured dialogue between the EU institutions and the applicant countries and relies on various specific instruments, including as a first step a bilateral association agreement that envisages as its ultimate objective full EU membership of the associated country. Before accession negotiations are formally launched, an extensive 'screening' exercise of the EU *acquis* is jointly undertaken by the European Commission and the authorities of the country concerned in order to determine the latter's position vis-a-vis the requirements of EU membership. On this basis, the Commission delivers an opinion to the Council covering all aspects of the accession criteria, on whether to open accession negotiations and on whether to grant the country concerned 'candidate' or 'potential candidate' status.

Accession negotiations are essentially aimed at agreeing on how and when the (potential) candidate country will align its national legislation and procedures with the EU *acquis*.[67] These are conducted on the basis of an 'Accession

[65] Once the Accession Treaty is signed, the candidate country becomes an 'acceding state' and is entitled to interim privileges, such as commenting on draft EU proposals, communications, recommendations or initiatives, and enjoying 'active observer status' in EU bodies and agencies. Once the ratification process is complete the Treaty enters into force on its scheduled date and the acceding state becomes a Member State.

[66] European Council, 'Conclusions of the Presidency' Copenhagen, 22 June 1993; European Council, 'Conclusions of the Presidency' Madrid, 16 December 1995.

[67] Such negotiations take place between the EU Member States and candidate countries at the level of ministers and ambassadors, and also cover financial arrangements (such as the new Member's

Partnership' set out by the EU which specifies the priority reforms that the candidate country must undertake in order to join the EU and the benchmarks to measure progress. In response, the candidate country draws up a national programme and action plan for the adoption of the EU *acquis*, detailing the measures, timetables and costs associated with the fulfilment of the EU accession requirements. The European Commission plays a critical role in assessing and monitoring (potential) candidate countries' relative progress towards the adoption and implementation of the EU *acquis*, and keeps the Council and the European Parliament informed (through regular reports and strategy papers) throughout the process until eventual accession.[68] Thus, while formally based on dialogue and negotiations, the enlargement process is in practice a unidirectional evaluation by the EU of other countries' performance in meeting a set of existing EU rules and procedures that are in fact not negotiable.[69]

The process of enlargement has several environmental dimensions. At the bilateral level, the prospect, or promise, of EU membership has an enormous influence on the national environmental laws in candidate countries. During the pre-accession phase, these countries need to align their existing environmental laws with EU standards which involves not only a review of legislation but also of administrative and judicial capacity to ensure effective implementation and enforcement. The EU provides financial and technical assistance to the candidate countries,[70] based on national programmes for the adoption of the *acquis*, including its environmental components.[71] On the international scene, a larger EU is, politically and economically, a more important international actor with arguably more prominence in multilateral environmental negotiations. In this regard, it should be noted that candidate countries (and even aspiring ones) tend to support the EU negotiating positions in multilateral arenas, further contributing to the international weight of the EU.[72]

contribution to the revenue of the EU budget and the expected volume of transfers to that Member State within the overall expenditure from the EU budget) as well as possible transitional arrangements.

[68] Once negotiations on all the chapters of the EU *acquis* are concluded the detailed terms and conditions are incorporated into a draft Accession Treaty, which lists all transitional arrangements and deadlines, as well as details of financial arrangements and any safeguard clauses. If the Treaty wins the support of the Council and the European Parliament it is signed by the candidate country and the representatives of all the Member States and then submitted for national ratifications, in accordance with art 49 TEU.

[69] On EU enlargement, see generally M Cremona, 'Enlargement: A Successful Instrument of Foreign Policy?' in T Tridimas and P Nebbia (eds), *European Union Law for the Twenty-First Century* (Oxford, Hart Publishing, 2004); M Cremona (ed), The *Enlargement of the European Union* (Oxford, Oxford University Press, 2003).

[70] Since 2007, EU pre-accession assistance (to both candidates and potential candidates) is channelled through the Instrument for pre-Accession Assistance, see further Ch 4, s 4.1.

[71] K Inglis, 'Enlargement and the Environment Acquis' (2004) 13(2) *Review of Community and International Environmental Law* 135; M Soveroski, 'EC Enlargement and the Development of European Environmental Policy: Parallel Histories, Divergent Paths?' (2004) 13(2) *Review of Community and International Environmental Law* 127.

[72] For instance, at the UN World Summit the EU spoke on behalf of 36 countries, see E Morgera and G Marín Durán, 'The UN 2005 World Summit, the Environment and the EU: Priorities, Promises and Prospects' (2006) 15(1) *Review of Community and International Environmental Law* 11, 11.

At the time of writing, there are nine countries on the road to EU membership,[73] the vast majority of which are part of the stabilisation and association process to be discussed below.

3.2 Stabilisation and association process

The stabilisation and association process was launched at the Zagreb Summit in November 2000 as a framework for the renewal of closer relations between the Union and the five countries of South-Eastern Europe to foster regional cooperation and security.[74] These countries have the prospect of joining the EU, with Croatia and the former Yugoslav Republic of Macedonia enjoying 'candidate' status, while Albania, Bosnia and Herzegovina, Montenegro and Serbia are still 'potential candidates'. As part of the pre-accession strategy, Stabilisation and Association Agreements (SAAs) have been concluded with all six countries to assist their efforts to fulfil the Copenhagen criteria, including the adoption and effective implementation of the EU environmental *acquis*.[75]

In addition, the Stabilisation and Association Agreements[76] are also aimed at: providing an appropriate framework for bilateral political relations; supporting the associated country's efforts in the transition to a market economy and the progressive development of a free trade area with the EU; supporting the associated country's efforts in developing economic and international cooperation; and fostering regional cooperation in all areas covered by the agreement.[77] Among the general principles underpinning the association, the respect for democratic principles, human rights, international law and the rule of law as well as the principles of an open market economy, are stated as essential elements of the agreement, forming the basis of the Parties' domestic and external policies.[78] Furthermore, the associated country's commitment to regional cooperation and good neighbourly

[73] Namely five 'candidate countries' (Croatia, Iceland, the Former Yugoslav Republic of Macedonia, Montenegro and Turkey) and four 'potential candidate countries' (Albania, Bosnia and Herzegovina, Kosovo as defined by UN Security Council Resolution 1244, and Serbia).

[74] Commission, 'Communication on the stabilisation and association process with Bosnia and Herzegovina, Croatia, Federal Republic of Yugoslavia, former Yugoslav Republic of Macedonia and Albania' COM (99) 235 final.

[75] On the approximation of associated countries' legislation to EU law see Albania AA, art 70; Bosnia AA, art 70; Croatia AA, art 69; Macedonia AA, art 68; Montenegro AA, art 72; Serbia AA, art 72. For an overview of the environmental components of the *acquis*, see E Morgera and G Marín Durán, 'Enlargement and EU Development Policy: An Environmental Perspective' (2004) 13(2) *Review of Community and International Environmental Law* 152, 152–55.

[76] For a general assessment of these agreements, see M Cremona, 'Creating the New Europe: The Stability Pact for South-Eastern Europe in the Context of EU-SEE Relations' (2000) 2 *Cambridge Yearbook of European Legal Studies* 464; D Phinnemore, 'Stabilisation and Association Agreements: Europe Agreements for the Western Balkans' (2003) 8(1) *European Foreign Affairs Review* 77; C Pippan, 'The Rocky Road to Europe: The EU's Stabilisation and Association Process for the Western Balkans and the Principle of Conditionality' (2004) 9(2) *European Foreign Affairs Review* 219.

[77] Albania AA, art 1(2); Bosnia AA, art 1(2); Croatia AA, art 1(2); Macedonia AA, art 1(2); Montenegro AA, art 1(2); Serbia AA, art 1(2).

[78] Albania AA, art 2; Bosnia AA, art 2; Croatia AA, art 2; Macedonia AA, art 2; Montenegro AA, art 2; Serbia AA, art 2.

relations is presented as a 'key factor' in achieving the ultimate objective of full EU membership.[79] Accordingly, the agreements lay down detailed provisions on high-level political dialogue, regional cooperation and cooperation in justice and home affairs,[80] on the progressive establishment of a free trade area in goods and the liberalisation of the movement of services, capital and workers, [81] as well as on cooperation in a wide range of specific policy areas.

3.3 General approach to the environment

In general terms, Stabilisation and Association Agreements are characterised by a high degree of consistency in content and legal wording of their environmental cooperation and environmental integration clauses, which are essentially placed in the operative text of the agreement under the 'cooperation policies' title.[82] No specific reference to environmental protection is found in the preamble or objectives of the agreements but a commitment of the Parties to the principle of sustainable development is stated in the preamble of the Agreements with Bosnia, Montenegro and Serbia. Given their role in the pre-accession process, all agreements rely heavily on approximation to EU environmental and other laws, and EU cooperation and assistance is clearly tied to the fulfilment of this and other Copenhagen criteria.[83] These agreements also make explicit references to key MEAs to which the EU is a party.

3.4 Environmental cooperation clauses

Two formulations can be found for the clause on environmental cooperation, both however are drafted in clearly legally binding terms ('shall develop'). In the case of Montenegro, Serbia and Bosnia, Parties are mandated to develop and strengthen their cooperation in the environmental field with the vital task of 'halting further degradation and start improving the environmental situation with the aim of sustainable development.'[84] These articles further require Parties to establish cooperation with the aim of 'strengthening administrative structures and procedures to ensure strategic planning of environment issues and coordination between relevant actors and shall focus on the alignment of the partner country legislation to the [Union] *acquis*.'[85] The alternative formulation can be found in

[79] Albania AA, art 3; Bosnia AA, arts 5–6; Croatia AA, arts 3–4; Macedonia AA, art 3; Montenegro AA, art 5; Serbia AA, art 5.

[80] Titles II, III and title VII for all SAAs.

[81] Titles IV–V for all SAAs.

[82] Title VIII for all SAAs.

[83] See provisions on financial cooperation: Albania AA, arts 3 and 112; Bosnia, AA, arts 5 and 112; Croatia AA, arts 3 and 106; Macedonia AA, arts 3 and 104; Montenegro AA, arts 5 and 115; Serbia AA, arts 5 and 115.

[84] Montenegro AA, art 111; Serbia AA, art 111; Bosnia AA, art 108.

[85] Ibid.

the Agreements with Albania, Croatia and Macedonia, where Parties are more succinctly required to 'develop and strengthen their cooperation in the vital task of combating environmental degradation, with the view to promoting environmental sustainability.'[86]

The clauses on environmental cooperation then single out specific priorities, with the exception of the Agreement with Albania, where the only specification is the that cooperation 'shall mainly focus on priority areas related to the [Union] *acquis* in the field of environment.'[87] Otherwise, two groups of priorities can be distinguished. On the one hand, in the Agreements with Bosnia, Montenegro and Serbia, cooperation 'could also centre' on the development of strategies to: significantly reduce local, regional and trans-boundary air and water pollution; to establish a framework for efficient, clean, sustainable and renewable production and consumption of energy; and to execute environmental impact assessments (EIAs) and strategic environmental assessments (SEAs). Furthermore, special attention shall be paid to the ratification and the implementation of the Kyoto Protocol.[88] On the other hand, the priorities that are common to the Agreements with Croatia and Macedonia have a more marked international dimension. They include a general reference to the 'international conventions in the area of environment to which the [Union] is a party,' 'cooperation at regional and international level,' development of strategies with regard to global and climate issues, the conservation of biodiversity, as well as 'waste reduction, recycling and safe disposal, and the implementation of the Basel Convention.' Other common priorities for environmental cooperation in the Association Agreements with Croatia and Macedonia include: air and water pollution, energy, chemicals, agriculture, town and country planning; the protection of the flora and fauna, including forests; environmental assessments (EIAs and SEAs); and natural disasters.[89] The Agreement with Croatia also includes among these priorities transboundary watercourses, industrial plants and economic incentives.

3.5 Environmental integration clauses

All the Stabilisation and Association Agreements include the same formulation calling for environmental integration across all cooperation areas, through a mix of mandatory and soft law language:

> Policies and other measures shall be designed to bring about sustainable[90] economic and social development of [the associated country]. These policies should ensure that

[86] Albania AA, art 108; Croatia AA, art 103; Macedonia AA, art 103.
[87] Albania AA, art 108.
[88] Bosnia AA, art 108; Montenegro AA, art 111; Serbia AA, art 111.
[89] Croatia AA, art 103; Macedonia AA, art 103.
[90] The term 'sustainable' is missing in the relevant articles of the agreements with Croatia and Macedonia.

> environmental considerations are also fully incorporated from the outset and that they are linked to the requirements of harmonious social development.[91]

This cross-cutting provision is particularly significant for those areas in which no specific environmental integration clause is found in the agreements, as is the case in tourism and investment. It should be noted, however, that this provision applies only to the listed 'cooperation policies',[92] and does not to extend to trade relations between the EU and the associated countries that are regulated by other parts of the agreement.[93] In addition, more specific provisions provide for environmental integration in the areas of agriculture, fisheries, transport, energy, criminal activities and industrial development, with certain variations depending on the agreement.

With regards to environmental integration in the *agriculture* sector, clauses refer generally to cooperation in agriculture with a view to aligning the associated countries' legislation with that of the EU:[94] this type of provision, if implemented, will support environmental integration only to the extent to which EU legislation on agriculture is itself supporting environmental integration.[95] The majority of the Stabilisation and Association Agreements also make explicit provision, in mandatory terms, for improving water management and rural development, as well as developing the forestry sector in the context of agricultural cooperation.[96]

In the area of *fisheries*, the majority of the Stabilisation and Association Agreements use the same wording in making reference to the EU's own legislation (which, similarly to the case of agriculture, is significant to the extent to which the EU's own rules on fisheries ensure environmental integration),[97] specifically pointing to relevant international conservation obligations that have become part of the EU legal system:

> The Parties shall explore the possibility of identifying mutually beneficial areas of common interest in the fisheries sector. Cooperation shall take due account of priority areas related to the [Union] acquis in the field of fisheries, including the respect of international obligations concerning international and regional fisheries organisation rules of management and conservation of fishery resources.[98]

As to the *transport* sector, similar legally binding wording in the majority of the Stabilisation and Association Agreements calls implicitly for approximation to

[91] Albania AA, art 86(2); Bosnia AA, art 86(2); Croatia AA, art 81(2); Macedonia AA, art 80(2); Montenegro AA, art 88(2); Serbia AA, art 88(2).

[92] Under title VIII in all SAAs.

[93] See s 3.6 below.

[94] Albania AA, art 95; Bosnia AA, art 95; Montenegro AA, art 97; Serbia AA, art 97.

[95] For an assessment see N Dhondt, *Integration of Environmental Protection into Other EC Policies – Legal Theory and Practice* (Groningen, Europa Law Publishing, 2003), 199–289.

[96] Croatia AA, art 92; Macedonia AA, art 100; Montenegro AA, art 97; Serbia AA, art 97.

[97] For an assessment see W Howarth, 'The Interpretation of "Precaution" in the European Community Common Fisheries Policy' (2008) 20(2) *Journal of Environmental Law* 213; C Coffey, 'Integrating Environment into the Common Fisheries Policy' (2000) *Institute for European Environmental Policy*.

[98] Albania AA, art 96; Bosnia AA, art 96; Montenegro AA, art 98; Serbia AA, art 98. Note that the Agreement with Macedonia makes a succinct reference to fisheries under the article on cooperation in agriculture (Macedonia AA, art 100).

EU law – so, once again, actual environmental integration depends on the extent to which the EU's own transport law ensures it.[99] It also contains an explicit clause on environmental integration: 'Parties shall develop and step up the cooperation in order to enable the [associated country] to . . . develop a transport system compatible and aligned with the [Union] system and improving protection of the environment in transport.'[100]

A more elaborate provision can be found in the Agreements with Croatia and Macedonia where Parties are required to develop and step up cooperation in order to enable the associated country to improve the protection of the environment in the transport sector and reduce harmful effects and pollution, as well as prioritising cooperation in the social and environmental aspects of transport road.[101] Going a step further, the Agreements with Croatia, Serbia, Albania, Montenegro and Bosnia include a whole protocol on transport which elaborates on land transport, integrating environmental concerns in three instances. First, legally binding language is used to indicate that the cooperation is aimed at developing a land transport system that meets environmental needs.[102] Second, the Parties also agree to adopt mutually coordinated measures necessary for the development and promotion of rail and combined transport as a means of ensuring that 'in the future a major proportion of their bilateral and transit transport through the associated country is performed under more environmentally friendly conditions.'[103] The third instance is a best-endeavour provision completely devoted to the environment, according to which the Parties 'shall endeavour' to introduce standards on gaseous and particulate emissions and noise levels for heavy goods vehicles to ensure a high level of environmental protection.[104]

With regards to the *energy* sector, the same wording for general cooperation has been used in all the Stabilisation and Association Agreements with legally binding language related to the energy *acquis* but soft-law language on specific areas for environmental integration in the energy sector:

> Cooperation shall focus on priority areas related to the [Union] acquis in the field of energy. It shall be based on the Energy Community Treaty, and it shall be developed with a view to the gradual integration of [the associated country] into Europe's energy markets . . . Cooperation may include in particular: . . . (b) the promotion of energy saving, energy efficiency, renewable energy and studying the environmental impact of energy production and consumption.[105]

Thus, similarly to the transport sector, this formulation provides both for approximation to EU energy law – the degree of environmental integration within the EU

[99] For an assessment see Dhondt, above n 95, 293–378.

[100] Albania AA, art 106; Bosnia AA, art 106; Montenegro AA, art 108; Serbia AA, art 108.

[101] Croatia AA, art 100(1); Macedonia AA, art 98.

[102] Croatia AA, Protocol 6, art 2(2).

[103] Ibid, art 7.

[104] Ibid, art 15. The same articles 2(2), 7 and 15 can be found in: Serbia AA, Protocol 4; Bosnia AA, Protocol 3; Albania AA, Protocol 5; and Montenegro AA, Protocol 4.

[105] Albania AA, art 107; Bosnia AA, art 107; Croatia AA, art 101; Montenegro AA, art 109; Serbia AA, art 109; Macedonia AA, art 99.

in this sector being determinant of the impacts on (potential) candidate countries[106] – as well as (possibly) specific environmental integration objectives that include an application of environmental impact assessment in the energy sector. In addition, the Agreements with Croatia, Macedonia, Montenegro and Serbia open the way to addressing environmental concerns in relation to nuclear energy, albeit in a non-mandatory manner. Cooperation in the field of nuclear safety and safeguards 'could cover': (i) upgrading the laws and regulations of the Parties on radiation protection, nuclear safety and nuclear materials accountancy and control as well as strengthening the supervisory authorities and their resources; (ii) encouraging the promotion of agreements between the EU Member States, or European Atomic Energy Community, and the associated country on early notification and exchange of information in cases of nuclear accidents and on emergency preparedness and on nuclear safety issues in general; and (iii) nuclear third party liability.[107]

Provisions on cooperation on *criminal matters* provide an interesting example of environmental integration: all the Stabilisation and Association Agreements include the same wording mandating collaboration on combating and preventing criminal and illegal activities, organised or otherwise, including illegal transactions on products such as industrial waste and radioactive material.[108]

Furthermore, environmental integration in the area of *industrial development* seeks to advance corporate environmental accountability in associated countries. All the Stabilisation and Association Agreements include an identical formulation mandating cooperation to promote the modernisation and restructuring of industry and individual sectors, covering industrial cooperation between economic operators, with the objective of strengthening the private sector under conditions ensuring that the environment is protected.[109]

3.6 Trade and environment

Economic integration is a central pillar of the EU's relations with the Western Balkan countries under the Stabilisation and Association Agreements. These agreements are all aimed at the gradual establishment of a reciprocal free trade area in goods.[110] In view of the possible integration of the associated countries into the EU single market, the agreements go beyond trade liberalisation in goods and contain provisions on the other fundamental freedoms in EU law (that is, the free movement of workers, of services supplier and the right of establishment).[111]

[106] Dhondt, above n 95, 381–449.

[107] Croatia AA, art 102; Macedonia AA, art 103(4); Montenegro AA, arts 109–110; Serbia AA, arts 109–110.

[108] Albania AA, art 85; Bosnia AA, art 84; Croatia AA, art 80(1); Montenegro AA, art 86; Serbia AA, Art 86; Macedonia, AA, art 78(1).

[109] Albania AA, art 92; Bosnia AA, art 92; Croatia AA, art 86(1); Montenegro AA, art 94; Serbia AA, art 94; Macedonia AA, art 85(1).

[110] Title IV in all SAAs.

[111] Title V in all SAAs.

As was noted in the previous chapter,[112] linkages between trade and environment in free trade agreements are typically addressed through 'exception clauses', which recognise the right of the Parties to use trade restrictive measures for environmental protection purposes. A general exception clause, modelled on Article 36 TFEU,[113] is found in all Stabilisation and Association Agreements. Prohibitions or restrictions on the movement of goods and services may be imposed by the Parties to protect 'the life and health of humans, animals and plants', and more generally if justified on grounds of 'public policy'.[114]

The agreements, however, do not elaborate extensively on the other regulatory dimensions of the trade and environment nexus. Only the Agreements with Albania, Bosnia, Montenegro and Serbia contain an identical provision in relation to the supply of international maritime transport services, which requires the Parties to 'respect international and European obligations in the fields of safety, security and environmental standards'.[115] The absence of more clauses linking trade liberalisation and environmental regulation can be explained by the fact that the risk of regulatory competition and 'race to the bottom' in environmental standards is fairly minimal in the context of these agreements as the associated countries are under a general obligation to align their domestic environmental laws with the EU *acquis*, and this process is being supported by EU technical and financial assistance. Accordingly, at the end of applicable transitional periods, standards of environmental protection should be harmonised with the EU's, preventing regulatory competition among the Parties.

3.7 Institutional aspects

The monitoring of environmental commitments takes place at two levels within the context of Stabilisation and Association Agreements. First, the general institutional provisions[116] established in the agreements are in principle applicable to environmental clauses. Under such provisions, the Stabilisation and Association Council has the primary responsibility for supervising the application and implementation of the whole agreement. The Stabilisation and Association Council is

[112] See Ch 1, s 5.2.

[113] Former art 30 TEC, which reads: 'The provisions of Articles 34 and 35 shall not preclude prohibitions or restrictions on imports, exports or goods in transit justified on grounds of public morality, public policy or public security; the protection of health and life of humans, animals or plants; the protection of national treasures possessing artistic, historic or archaeological value; or the protection of industrial and commercial property. Such prohibitions or restrictions shall not, however, constitute a means of arbitrary discrimination or a disguised restriction on trade between Member States.'

[114] Albania AA, art 42 (goods) and art 63 (services); Bosnia AA, art 43 (goods) and art 63 (services); Croatia AA, art 42 (goods) and art 62 (services); Macedonia AA, art 41 (goods) and art 61 (services); Montenegro AA, art 45 (goods) and art 65 (services).

[115] Albania AA, art 59(2); Bosnia AA, art 59(2); Montenegro AA, art 61(2); and Serbia AA, art 61(2).

[116] Title X in all SAAs.

composed of members of the Council and the European Commission on the EU side and of members of the government of the associated country. The Council has the power to adopt decisions to implement the provisions of the agreement where this is explicitly provided for. Such decisions are binding on all Parties, which must take all necessary measures to implement them. In the case of environmental cooperation and integration clauses, however, such decision-making power of the Council is largely limited to 'defining priorities'.[117] The Council is assisted by a Stabilisation and Association Committee (of a similar composition) in the performance of its duties, and may also create sub-bodies or committees to deal with the implementation of specific issues in the agreement, including the environment.

In addition, as we have seen,[118] special procedures apply to the monitoring of the approximation of the associated country's legislation to the EU *acquis*, which forms the core of most environmental cooperation and integration clauses in these associations. While this process is formally based on dialogue and negotiations, it is ultimately the EU that assesses the 'merits' of each associated country in complying with the environmental and other components of the *acquis* and that takes the final decision on its eventual readiness to become a member of the Union.

Any dispute relating to the application or interpretation of the agreement needs to be referred by the complaining Party to the Stabilisation and Association Council for consultations, with a view to settling the dispute by means of a binding decision. All Stabilisation and Association Agreements also foresee, 'in cases of special urgency', the adoption of unilateral 'appropriate measures' without prior consultation against an infringing Party,[119] but this is unlikely to be applicable to environment-related provisions that are largely conceived in cooperative terms. Indeed, most agreements contain joint declarations on the interpretation of this extreme remedy, which specify that it applies to 'material breaches' consisting of a 'repudiation of the Agreement not sanctioned by general rules of international law' or violations of the 'essential elements' clause.[120] Only the Agreements with Bosnia and Montenegro contain an additional Protocol that provides for the initiation of formal arbitration proceedings after consultations in the Council fail to reach an acceptable solution, but this is largely limited to trade and trade-related cooperation disputes.[121]

[117] Albania AA, art 86(3); Bosnia AA, art 86(3); Croatia AA, art 81(3); Macedonia AA, art 80(3); Montenegro AA, art 88(3); Serbia AA, art 88(3).

[118] Above s 3.1.

[119] Albania AA, art 126; Bosnia AA, art 125(4); Croatia AA, art 120; Macedonia AA, art 118; Montenegro AA, art 129; Serbia AA, art 129.

[120] Albania AA, Joint Declaration on art 136; Croatia AA, Joint Declaration on art 120. On EU practice in this regard, see below n 286.

[121] Bosnia AA, Protocol 6; Montenegro AA, Protocol 7 (in both cases disputes over trade restrictive measures undertaken pursuant to the 'general exception clauses').

4. ENVIRONMENTAL INTEGRATION IN ASSOCIATION AS SUBSTITUTE TO EU MEMBERSHIP

4.1 EU relations with its MENA neighbours

Within this category of association can be found the Euro-Mediterranean Agreements, which represent a 'second-best' special relationship between the EU and third countries – short of fully-fledged membership. These bilateral agreements were concluded within the broader framework of the 1995 Barcelona Declaration,[122] signed by the EU, its (at the time) 15 Member States and 12 Mediterranean and North African (MENA) partners, namely: Algeria, Cyprus, Egypt, Israel, Jordan, Lebanon, Malta, Morocco, Syria, Tunisia, Turkey and the Palestine Authority. The Barcelona process sought to significantly upgrade Euro-Mediterranean relations from the cooperation agreements in place since the 1970s by formally launching a triple inter-regional Euro-Mediterranean Partnership (EMP) with the ambitious goals of: (i) creating a 'common area of peace and stability' (underpinned by sustainable development, rule of law, democracy and human rights); (ii) creating an 'area of shared prosperity' (mainly by envisaging the establishment of an integrated Euro-Mediterranean free trade area by 2010); and (iii) promoting understanding and intercultural dialogue and facilitating exchanges among their peoples and civil societies. The Barcelona Declaration also indicates that the environment is one of the priorities of economic cooperation.[123]

Over the years, the Barcelona-driven EMP came under serious reform pressure. While there is certainly disagreement as to what exactly constitute the most serious flaws of the EMP, there is little doubt that it has not lived up to its original ambition as progress in each of the Partnership's broad areas has been either modest or nonexistent.[124] An attempt was made in 2008 to re-launch and broaden the Partnership as the 'Union for the Mediterranean' (UfM) – now encompassing the EU, its 27 Member States and 16 Southern Mediterranean, African and Middle Eastern partners[125] – with the initiation of new regional and sub-regional projects and the establishment of a functional Secretariat. Of relevance from an environmental perspective, the UfM agenda includes: the de-pollution of the Mediterranean sea (including coastal and marine protected areas); a joint civil protection programme on prevention, preparation and response to natural and

[122] Euro-Mediterranean Conference, 'Barcelona Declaration' Barcelona, 27–28 November 1995.

[123] Ibid, 5.

[124] See, among others, S Hakura, 'The Euro-Mediterranean Policy: The Implications of the Barcelona Declarations' (1997) 34(2) *Common Market Law Review* 337, 338–46; E Philippart, 'The Euro-Mediterranean Partnership: A Critical Evaluation of an Ambitious Scheme' (2003) 8(2) *European Foreign Affairs Review* 201, 201–05.

[125] Namely: Albania, Algeria, Bosnia and Herzegovina, Croatia, Egypt, Israel, Jordan, Lebanon, Mauritania, Monaco, Montenegro, Morocco, the Palestinian Authority, Syria, Tunisia and Turkey. Note that Cyprus and Malta acceded to the EU in 2004.

man-made disasters; and a Mediterranean solar energy plan that explores opportunities for developing alternative energy sources in the region.[126]

It should also be noted that nine of the original 12 MENA countries[127] have also been included (together with Libya and six other Eastern European neighbours of the enlarged EU-27)[128] by the EU into the European Neighbourhood Policy (ENP), launched in March 2003 by the Commission (more precisely, by DG Enlargement),[129] and formally endorsed by the Council and the European Council in June 2003.[130] The ENP envisages the forging of a privileged relationship with the countries concerned ('founded on values of the Union' and including a 'significant measure of economic and political integration', comprehending enhanced cooperation in all EU's policies and a 'share in the internal market'), while formally ruling out any prospects of full EU membership. Significantly, the ENP has now been sanctioned by the Lisbon Treaty, which introduced a new legal basis (Article 8 TEU) for concluding agreements with the countries concerned.[131]

No such ENP-specific agreement has been concluded at the time of writing[132] and EU relations with its Mediterranean neighbours continue to be regulated by the Barcelona-driven associations that will be analysed in the subsequent sections.[133] In line with the general objectives of the Barcelona process, such agreements institutionalised a wide-ranging cooperation encompassing political, security, immigration, economic, socio-cultural, environmental and humanitarian matters. In particular, their objectives are: to provide a framework for the

[126] For more information on the UfM, visit www.eeas.europa.eu/euromed/index_en.htm.

[127] Given that Cyprus and Malta were in the process of acceding to the EU and Turkey became a candidate country for EU membership in 1999.

[128] Namely: Armenia, Azerbaijan, Belarus, Georgia, Moldova and Ukraine.

[129] Commission, 'Communication on wider Europe-neighbourhood: a new framework for relations with our Eastern and Southern Neighbours' COM (2003) 104 final; and Commission, 'Strategy paper on European neighbourhood policy' COM (2004) 373 final.

[130] Council, 'Council Conclusions on Wider Europe-New Neighbourhood' (16 June 2003); European Council, 'Presidency Conclusions' Thessaloniki, 19 and 20 June 2003, 13.

[131] Art 8 TEU reads:

1. The Union shall develop a special relationship with neighbouring countries, aiming to establish an area of prosperity and good neighbourliness, founded on the values of the Union and characterised by close and peaceful relations based on cooperation.
2. For the purposes of paragraph 1, the Union may conclude specific agreements with the countries concerned. These agreements may contain reciprocal rights and obligations as well as the possibility of undertaking activities jointly. Their implementation shall be the subject of periodic consultation.

See among others, R Del Sarto and T Schumacher, 'From EMP to ENP: What's at Stake with the European Neighbourhood Policy Towards the Southern Mediterranean?' (2005) 10(1) *European Foreign Affairs Review* 17; C Hillion, 'The EU's Neighbourhood Policy towards Eastern Europe' in A Dashwood and M Maresceau, *Law and Practice of EU External Relations* (Cambridge, Cambridge University Press, 2008); S Pardo and L Zemer, 'Towards a New Euro-Mediterranean Neighbourhood Space' (2005) 10(1) *European Foreign Affairs Review* 39.

[132] To date, the ENP has mainly been implemented through bilateral action plans (a benchmarking instrument 'borrowed' from the EU pre-accession strategy setting out an agenda for political and economic reforms in the short-to-medium term) with 12 of the 16 countries concerned.

[133] Note that the signature of the EU-Syria Association Agreement has been pending since October 2009 (and thus will not form part of this study) and that there is (as yet) no agreement between Libya and the EU.

development of close political ties; to establish the conditions for the gradual liberalisation of trade; to promote the expansion of economic, financial, social and cultural relations; and to encourage regional integration among MENA countries.[134] Accordingly, these agreements lay down detailed provisions for: political dialogue in security issues and in regional and international cooperation;[135] the progressive establishment of a free trade area and trade-related cooperation;[136] and economic cooperation in a wide number of other areas.[137] Respect for the democratic principles and fundamental human rights are set as constituting 'essential elements' of these agreements.[138]

4.2 General approach to the environment

As will be seen, the Euro-Mediterranean Agreements are characterised by a mix of mandatory, best-endeavour and soft law language in their environmental cooperation and environmental integration clauses, which are mainly found in the operative part of the agreements under their 'economic cooperation' title.[139] In line with this cooperative approach, the main modalities for implementing environmental clauses are: regular dialogue; EU funding; technical, administrative and regulatory assistance; information exchanges; transfer of expertise and training; and joint ventures.[140] There are quite a number of variations in their environment-related content and a notable absence of references to MEAs.

One important difference across the agreements is the approach taken to the approximation of laws, with half of them (Agreements with Algeria, Morocco, Palestine and Tunisia)[141] stating the alignment of the associated country's legislation to EU law as one of the objectives of cooperation. Regulatory convergence with EU standards, including on environmental protection, can thus also be expected to occur outside the enlargement process and be, for instance, an element of 'conditionality' of EU technical and financial assistance also to non-candidate countries (albeit, not in such strict terms as in the context of the pre-accession strategy seen earlier). The other four Euro-Mediterranean Associations only contain a 'best-endeavour' clause for the Parties to approximate 'their respective laws in order to facilitate the implementation of the Agreement'.[142]

[134] Art 1 in all Euro-Mediterranean AAs.

[135] Title I in all Euro-Mediterranean AAs, except the Palestine AA which contains no such provision.

[136] Titles II–IV in all Euro-Mediterranean AAs, except the Palestine AA (titles I–II).

[137] Title V in all Euro-Mediterranean AAs, except Israel AA (title VI) and Palestine AA (title III).

[138] Art 2 in all Euro-Mediterranean AAs.

[139] Algeria AA, title V; Egypt AA, title V; Israel AA, title VI; Jordan AA, title V; Lebanon AA, title V; Morocco AA, title V; Palestine AA, title III; Tunisia AA, title V.

[140] Algeria AA, arts 49 and 79; Egypt AA, arts 41 and 73; Israel AA, art 43 (and no specific provision on EU financial assistance); Jordan AA, arts 61 and 86; Lebanon AA, arts 42 and 71; Morocco AA, arts 44 and 75; Palestine AA, arts 37 and 61 (the latter listing the environment as one of the priority areas for EU funding to the Palestine Authority); Tunisia AA, arts 44 and 75. EU financial assistance to the Euro-Med countries is channelled through a geographic instrument (the European Neighbourhood and Partnership Instrument) as well as various EU thematic instruments, see further Ch 4, ss 3.2.2 and 3.2.

[141] Algeria AA, art 56; Morocco AA, art 52; Palestine AA, art 41; Tunisia AA, art 52.

[142] Egypt AA, art 48; Israel AA, art 55; Jordan AA, art 69; Lebanon, art 49.

4.3 Environmental cooperation clauses

All the Euro-Mediterranean Agreements have similar general provisions, drafted in best-endeavour language ('shall encourage'), on environmental cooperation aimed at preventing deterioration of the environment, controlling pollution and ensuring the rational use of natural resources, with a view to ensuring sustainable development.[143]

Priorities for environmental cooperation present several commonalities. All the Euro-Mediterranean Agreements prioritise work on soil and water quality; the consequences of development, particularly industrial development (especially safety of installations and waste); and monitoring and preventing marine pollution.[144] The latter reference may be understood as an implicit reference to the Barcelona (regional sea) Convention system.[145] A few agreements also place specific emphasis on environmental assessment[146] by mandating that cooperation be fostered by the use of advanced tools of environmental management, environmental monitoring methods and surveillance, including the use of environmental information systems (EIS) and EIAs. A good portion of these agreements also draws attention to desertification, salinisation, environmental education and awareness.[147] On the other hand, it is notable that only the Agreement with Algeria includes among the priorities for environmental cooperation biodiversity.[148] Environmental management of coastal and sensitive areas, and the impact of agriculture on water quality and soil can also be found among the cooperation priorities of the Agreements with Algeria, Egypt, Israel, Lebanon and Palestine.[149] A reference to the appropriate use of energy and water resource management can also be found in some instances.[150]

Finally, a general clause on regional cooperation requires focusing on activities with regional impacts or involving third countries in relation to environmental issues for the vast majority of the Euro-Mediterranean Agreements.[151] Once again, this provision can be understood as cooperation in the framework of the Barcelona Convention system.

[143] Algeria AA, art 52; Egypt AA, art 44; Israel AA, art 50; Jordan AA, art 65; Lebanon AA, art 45; Morocco AA, art 48; Palestine AA, art 50; Tunisia AA, art 48.

[144] Algeria AA, art 52; Egypt AA, art 44; Israel AA, art 50; Jordan AA, art 65; Lebanon AA, art 45; Morocco AA, art 48; Palestine AA, art 50; Tunisia AA, art 48.

[145] The Barcelona Convention parties include: Algeria, Egypt, Israel, Lebanon, Lybia, Morocco, Syria and Tunisia, see www.ecolex.org.

[146] Israel AA, art 50(2); Jordan AA, art 65; Lebanon AA, art 45; Palestine AA, art 50.

[147] Algeria AA, art 52(2); Egypt AA, art 44(2); Israel AA, art 50(2); Jordan AA, art 65(2); Lebanon AA, art 45(2); and Palestine AA, art 50 (without education).

[148] Algeria AA, art 52(2).

[149] Algeria AA, art 52(2); Egypt AA, art 44(2); Israel AA, art 50(2); Lebanon AA, art 45(2); Palestine AA, art 50.

[150] Egypt AA, art 44(2); Jordan AA, art 65(2); and Palestine AA, art 50.

[151] Algeria AA, art 50; Egypt AA, art 60; Jordan AA, art 62; Morocco AA, art 45; Palestine AA, art 55; Tunisia AA, art 45.

4.4 Environmental integration clauses

All Euro-Mediterranean Agreements provide that 'the objective of economic cooperation shall be to support [the associated country]'s own efforts to achieve sustainable economic and social development',[152] and contain a cross-cutting obligation on environmental integration in all areas of cooperation. There are, however, two formulations requiring environmental integration with decreasing mandatory force:

> Preservation of the environment and ecological balances shall constitute a central component of the various fields of economic cooperation.[153]
>
> [or]
>
> Conservation of the environment and ecological balance shall be taken into account in the implementation of the various sectors of economic cooperation to which it is relevant.[154]

These cross-cutting provisions are particularly relevant for those areas in which no specific environmental integration clause is found in the agreements, as is the case for transport and investment. It should be underscored, however, that this provision applies only to the areas listed under the 'Economic Cooperation' Title, and does not extend to trade relations between the EU and the Euro-Med countries that are regulated by other parts of the agreement.[155]

Explicit references to environmental integration can be found in provisions on agriculture, fisheries, tourism, energy, criminal matters and, in one isolated case, mining. Furthermore, there is no requirement for environmental integration in the provision dealing with industrial development, although the latter is listed among the priority areas for environmental cooperation.

In the area of *agriculture and fisheries*, there are significant variations in formulation. A requirement for environmental integration can be found in a few agreements in exhortatory terms: 'cooperation should focus on environmentally friendly agriculture and rural development'.[156] Forestry, agricultural water resources, fishing and aquaculture are singled out only in the Agreement with Lebanon[157] while fishing alone appears in two other agreements.[158] The Agreement with Algeria also includes the evaluation and rational management of natural resources.[159]

152 Algeria AA, art 47(2); Egypt AA, art 39(2); Jordan AA, art 59(2); Lebanon AA, art 40(3); Morocco AA, art 42(2); Palestine AA, art 35(2); Tunisia AA, art 42(2).

153 Algeria AA, art 48(4); Lebanon AA, art 41(3); Morocco AA, art 43(4); Tunisia AA, art 43(4).

154 Egypt AA, art 40(4); Israel AA, art 42(2); Jordan AA, art 60(4); Palestine AA, art 36(4).

155 See s 4.5 below.

156 Algeria AA, art 58; Israel AA, art 46; Jordan AA, art 71; Lebanon AA, art 51; Palestine AA, art 44.

157 Lebanon AA, art 51, which provides: 'to develop the forestry sector, especially in the fields of reafforestation, forest fire prevention, forest pasture and combating desertification.'

158 Algeria AA, art 58; Palestine AA, art 44.

159 Algeria AA, art 58.

As opposed to the silence on *tourism* of the Stabilisation and Association Agreements,[160] the Agreements with Egypt, Jordan and Lebanon contain mandatory language on environmental integration in this sector: 'cooperation shall aim to ensure that the interaction between tourism and the environment is suitably maintained'.[161] The Agreement with Algeria makes in turn a weaker reference to 'promoting exchanges of experiences with a view to the smooth and sustainable development of tourism'.[162]

With regards to *energy*, the same mandatory wording for environmental integration can be found in most Euro-Mediterranean Agreements: 'the priority areas of cooperation shall be: the promotion of renewable energies and indigenous energy resources; and the promotion of energy-saving and energy efficiency'.[163] There appear to be no references to the environmental impacts of energy production, which were instead included in the Stabilisation and Association Agreements.[164] Only the Agreement with Israel links energy cooperation with climate change:

> The Parties consider that global warming and the depletion of fossil fuel sources are a serious threat to mankind. The Parties shall therefore cooperate with a view to developing sources of renewable energy, to ensure the use of fuels with the purpose of limiting pollution of the environment and promoting energy conservation.[165]

Similarly to the Stabilisation and Association Agreements,[166] the Agreements with Lebanon and Algeria integrate certain environmental concerns in the cooperation in criminal matters with regards to illegal transactions in industrial waste and radioactive materials.[167]

4.5 Trade and environment

Trade liberalisation and trade-related cooperation are key elements of the Euro-Mediterranean Associations, as these were concluded as building-blocks for achieving the long-term (elusive) goal of creating an integrated Euro-Mediterranean free trade area foreseen in the Barcelona Declaration. All the agreements provide for the gradual establishment of a reciprocal free trade area in goods (in most cases, with special arrangements and exclusions for agriculture and fisheries products)[168] and lay down the basis for a possible future liberalisation of trade in services and commercial presence.[169] They do not, however, sub-

[160] See s 3.5 above.
[161] Egypt AA, art 54; Jordan AA, art 75; Lebanon AA, art 55.
[162] Algeria AA, art 62.
[163] Algeria AA, art 61; Egypt AA, art 53; Jordan AA, art 74; Lebanon AA, art 54; Morocco AA, art 57; Palestine AA, art 48.
[164] Above s 3.5.
[165] Israel AA, art 51.
[166] Above s 3.5.
[167] Algeria AA, art 86; Lebanon AA, art 61.
[168] Title II in all Euro-Mediterranean Agreements.
[169] Title III in all Euro-Mediterranean Agreements, except that with Palestine.

stantively address the trade and environment nexus, other than through general 'exception clauses'.

As in the case of Stabilisation and Association Agreements,[170] exception clauses are here also modelled on Article 36 TFEU, enabling Parties to impose, under certain conditions, prohibitions or restrictions on the movement of goods to protect 'the life and health of humans, animals and plants', or that are more broadly justified on grounds of 'public policy'.[171] The latter may, arguably, outweigh the lack of an express reference to environmental protection as such.[172]

4.6 Institutional aspects

Euro-Mediterranean Associations do not establish special procedures for monitoring the implementation of environmental commitments, nor for resolving environment-related disputes. Thus, the general institutional provisions[173] apply, whereby the Association Council (composed of members of the Council and the European Commission on the EU side and members of the government of the associated country) may make 'appropriate recommendations' by consensus on environmental matters and the Association Committee (of a similar composition to the Council) may take implementation decisions by consensus that are binding upon the Parties. The Association Council also has the power to set up sub-bodies or working groups to deal with the implementation of specific issues in the agreement, including the environment.

Environment-related disputes should also be settled according to the general procedure, which provides for consultations in the Association Council and, where these fail to lead to a mutually satisfactory solution, for an arbitration panel to be established whose decision (by majority voting) is binding upon the Parties. No provision is made for temporary remedies in cases of non-compliance. As in the case of Stabilisation and Association Agreements, the adoption of unilateral 'appropriate measures' without prior consultation against an infringing Party is limited to 'cases of special urgency' and thus is unlikely to be applicable to environment-related provisions that are largely conceived in cooperative terms.[174]

[170] Above s 3.6.

[171] Algeria AA, art 27; Egypt AA, art 26; Israel AA, art 27; Jordan AA, art 27; Lebanon AA, art 27; Morocco AA, art 28; Palestine AA, art 24; Tunisia AA, art 28.

[172] A Cosbey et al, 'The Rush to Regionalism: Sustainable Development and Regional/Bilateral Approaches to Trade and Investment Liberalisation' (International Institute for Sustainable Development, 2005) 12.

[173] Algeria AA, title IX; Egypt AA, title VIII; Israel AA, title IX; Jordan AA, title VIII; Lebanon AA, title VIII; Morocco AA, title VIII; Palestine AA, title VI (with less elaborated provisions); Tunisia AA, title VIII.

[174] Joint declarations in some Euro-Mediterranean Agreements specify that this extreme remedy is available for 'material breaches' consisting of a 'repudiation of the Agreement not sanctioned by general rules of international law' or violations of the 'essential elements' clause. See, for instance, Algeria AA, Joint Declaration on Article 104; Lebanon AA, Joint Declaration on Article 86; Morocco AA, Joint Declaration on Article 90.

5. ENVIRONMENTAL INTEGRATION IN ASSOCIATION AS A DEVELOPMENT TOOL

5.1 EU relations with the ACP group

Relations between the European Union and the 78 African, Caribbean and Pacific group of States[175] are presently governed by the Cotonou Partnership Agreement, which represents the world's largest economic and political framework for North-South cooperation. Concluded in June 2000 and in force since April 2004 for a 20-year period, the Cotonou Agreement marks the latest, but significantly novel, stepping-stone in a cooperation process spanning several decades between the EU and the ACP group. While its immediate predecessor is the Lomé IV Convention, signed in December 1989 and revised in November 1995,[176] the very origins of this long-standing contractual cooperation are to be traced back to the Yaoundé I and Yaoundé II Conventions[177] concluded during the 1960s between the six founding Members of the European Economic Community and several African States which had been for the most part under French and Belgian dominion during the colonial era.[178] Concluded on the basis of shared colonial legacy and the develop-

[175] The ACP group was formally institutionalised by the 1975 Georgetown Agreement and currently has 79 Member States. Whereas Cuba is a member of the ACP group it is not a party to the Cotonou Agreement. The participation of South Africa in the Cotonou Agreement is subject to the qualifications set out in Protocol 3 in Annex VI, including the non-application of its trade and development finance cooperation provisions. EU-South Africa trade and economic cooperation is governed by their pre-existing bilateral agreement, the South Africa AA (see s 6 below), and EU development assistance to South Africa is channelled through the Development Cooperation Instrument (see Ch 4, s 4.3) and not the European Development Fund (EDF) as for the rest of the Cotonou signatories.

[176] Fourth Lomé Convention between the European Economic Community and the African, Caribbean and Pacific States [1991] OJ L229/3 (Lomé IV); Agreement amending the fourth ACP-EC Convention of Lomé [1998] OJ L156/3 (Lomé IV-bis Convention).

[177] Convention of Yaoundé I between the European Economic Community and its Member States and the Associated African and Malgache Countries [1964] OJ L93/1431 (Yaoundé I); Convention of Yaoundé II between the European Economic Community and its Member States and the Associated African and Malgache Countries [1970] OJ L 282/2 (Yaoundé II).

[178] The African and Malgache States in question had been 'associated' to the then European Economic Community under Part IV of the Rome Treaty before their accession to independence in the early 1960s. Thus, the Youndé I Convention constituted the first 'negotiated' association between the Community and these countries. The geographical coverage and substantive scope of this relationship were broadened with the conclusion of the First Lomé Convention between the European Economic Community and the African, Caribbean and Pacific States [1976] OJ L25/2 (Lomé I), adding 21 Commonwealth countries and another six African countries to the original 19 Yaoundé II signatories. Lomé I was subsequently renewed and revised by: the Second Lomé Convention between the European Economic Community and the African, Caribbean and Pacific States [1980] OJ L347/1; the Third Lomé Convention between the European Economic Community and the African, Caribbean and Pacific States [1986] OJ L86/3; and Lomé IV (n 176 above). For an historical account of the EU-ACP relations from Youndé I to Lomé IV, see JA McMahon, *The Development Cooperation of the EC* (London, Kluwer, 1998), ch 2. For a comprehensive assessment of the various Lomé Conventions, see the series of articles by KR Simmonds: 'The Lomé Convention and the New International Economic Order' (1976) 13(3) *Common Market Law Review* 315; 'The Second Lomé Convention: the Innovative Features' (1980) 17(3) *Common Market Law Review* 99; 'The Third Lomé Convention' (1985) 22(3) *Common Market Law Review* 389; 'The Fourth Lomé Convention' (1991) 28(3) *Common Market Law Review* 521.

ment constraints of ACP States,[179] this series of agreements has constituted to date the only association[180] between the EU and the world's poorest countries with no realistic prospects of becoming full members of the Union.[181] Indeed, the Cotonou Agreement and its Lomé predecessors are often seen as representing the very symbol of EU development cooperation policy.

The Cotonou Partnership is a comprehensive framework agreement consisting of general objectives, principles and options for future EU-ACP relations, with many of the implementation rules being shifted to the various Annexes and Protocols and subject to renegotiation at shorter intervals than the total 20-year duration of the agreement.[182] The road from Lomé IV to Cotonou was, however, rocky and implied profound changes in terms of objectives, principles and instruments. The perceived need for transformation in the long-standing EU-ACP relationship was fuelled by an accumulation of factors which were legal and non-legal in nature as well as external and internal to the EU. An extensive examination of these multiple and complex factors is beyond the scope of the present study.[183]

The key novel aspects of the Cotonou Agreement vis-a-vis Lomé IV are: (i) new principles of differentiation, regionalisation and participation of non-state actors in the design and implementation of development strategies;[184] (ii) a broader vision of development (adding a clear-cut emphasis on 'reducing and eventually eradicating poverty, consistent with the objective of sustainable development and the gradual integration of the ACP countries in the world economy');[185] (iii) a reinforced political dimension (with express provisions on political dialogue to address issues such as human rights, democratic principles, the rule of law, good

[179] Forty-two out of the 48 countries classified by the UN as least-developed countries belong to the ACP group and many ACP countries also fall within the UN-based categories of 'small island developing States' and 'land-locked States'. Similarly, an important number of ACP countries are found within the UNDP category of 'low human development' in terms of the 2010 Human Development Index, see UNDP, *Human Development Report 2010* (November 2010) at www.hdr.undp.org/en/reports/global/hdr2010/chapters/en/.

[180] While labelled a 'partnership agreement', Cotonou was concluded as an association agreement, like its Lomé predecessors. For an in-depth analysis of the Cotonou Agreement, see O Babarinde and G Faber (eds), *The European Union and Developing Countries: the Cotonou Agreement* (Dordrecht, Martinus Nijhoff, 2005).

[181] The only noticeable exception is the 2010 Association with Central American countries (see below n 200).

[182] The legal nature of the Cotonou Agreement as a framework agreement explains why its text is composed of only 100 articles while Lomé IV contained 369 articles. In addition to the various Annexes and Protocols, a 'Compendium on Cooperation Strategies' has also been approved by the EU-ACP Council of Ministers, as provided for in art 20(3).

[183] For the EU assessment of these multiple factors calling for change, see Commission, 'Green Paper on the relations between the European Union and the ACP countries on the eve of the 21st century – challenges and options for a new partnership' COM (1996) 570 final, 1 – 36. Among the abundant academic literature, see K Arts and AK Dickson (eds), *EU Development Cooperation. From Model to Symbol?* (Manchester, Manchester University Press, 2004), chs 2–7; O Babarinde and G Faber, 'From Lomé to Cotonou: Business as Usual?' (2004) 9(1) *European Foreign Affairs Review* 27, 28–35; JA McMahon, 'Negotiating at a Time of Turbulent Transition: The Future of Lomé' (1999) 36(3) *Common Market Law Review* 599; B Martenzuck, 'From Lomé to Cotonou: The ACP-EC Partnership Agreement in a Legal Perspective' (2000) 5(4) *European Foreign Affairs Review* 461.

[184] Cotonou Agreement, art 2.

[185] Ibid, art 1(2).

governance, peace and security);[186] (iv) a new framework for trade cooperation (including the negotiation of Economic Partnership Agreements);[187] and (v) a reformed framework for financial cooperation.[188] In addition, the Cotonou Agreement qualifies the principle of equality of the partners and of ownership of ACP development strategies by laying down respect for human rights, democratic principles, the rule of law and good governance as 'essential' or 'fundamental' elements of the agreement.[189]

Since its entry into force, the agreement has been revised on two occasions,[190] first in 2005 and then in 2010.[191] From an environmental perspective, the most significant changes introduced through these revisions are a stronger commitment to meet the Millennium Development Goals[192] and an explicit reference to the fight against climate change.[193] The role of ACP national parliaments and local authorities, of ACP regional organisations and the African Union (AU), and of non-state actors has also been strengthened in the context of the partnership[194] with the inclusion of clauses on prior consultations in the preparation of country strategy papers,[195] regional strategy papers[196] and intra-ACP strategy papers – all comprising an analysis of the environmental country context[197] – as well as on involvement in the implementation of cooperation projects and programmes in areas of their concern.[198] Finally, more forceful language has been introduced for the EU to enhance coherence between its development cooperation and other policies that affect the ACP States, including through regular dialogue with the ACP Secretariat.[199]

5.2 Environmental dimension of the Cotonou Agreement

The following sections will primarily analyse the environment-related provisions of the Cotonou Agreement. Where relevant, comparisons will be made with the more recent Association Agreement with Central American countries which can

[186] Cotonou Agreement, art 8(4)–(5).
[187] See s 5.3 below.
[188] This essentially implies a rationalisation of the EDF resources into two channels: a grant facility and an investment facility. On the EDF, see further Ch 4, s 4.4.
[189] Cotonou Agreement, art 9(2)–(3). Different suspension procedures apply to 'essential' and 'fundamental' elements of Cotonou (see below n 286).
[190] Ibid, art 95(3) stipulates that the agreement may be revised every five years.
[191] Second Revision of the Cotonou Partnership Agreement – Agreed Consolidated Text (11 March 2010) at www.ec.europa.eu/development/icenter/repository/second_revision_cotonou_agreement_20100311.pdf (Cotonou Agreement-2010 revision).
[192] On the MDGs, see Ch 1, s 5.3.
[193] Cotonou Agreement-2010 revision, preamble paras 12 and 13 bis and arts 1, 19 and 32bis.
[194] Ibid, arts 2, 4, 6, 10 and 11. Note that a Joint Declaration on Article 6 specifies that 'environmental movements' are among the non-Sate actors of the EU-ACP Partnership.
[195] Ibid, Annex IV, art 2.
[196] Ibid, Annex IV, art 8(3)(a).
[197] Ibid, Annex IV, art 12a(2)(a).
[198] Ibid, arts 4 and 58.
[199] Ibid, art 12.

also be considered as falling within this category of association as a development tool.[200]

5.2.1 General approach to the environment

The Cotonou Agreement should be singled out for its approach to environmental protection as a thematic and cross-cutting issue. Environmental concerns are integrated into the preamble and body of the agreement: its objectives;[201] its political pillar;[202] and in its cooperation strategies, both under the title on 'development strategies'[203] and that on 'economic and trade cooperation'.[204] In light of the divergences in development levels, EU financial and technical assistance to the ACP States is one of the key modalities for implementing the Cotonou Agreement, including its environmental clauses. In fact, the Cotonou Agreement has unusually detailed provisions on development finance cooperation,[205] establishing the overall EU financial commitments for projects and programmes in the ACP States as well as the conditions and procedures applicable to such financing.[206]

While initially the preamble to the Cotonou Agreement only contained references to sustainable development, more forceful language on the MDGs and climate change was added by the second revision of the agreement. The EU and ACP States thus acknowledge the need to make a 'concerted effort to accelerate progress towards attaining' all MDGs: this implicitly contributes to environmental integration, as MDG-7 focuses on environmental sustainability.[207] In addition, the Parties recognise 'the serious global environmental challenge' posed by climate change and the threats posed by climate-related phenomena to the livelihoods and sustainable development of the most vulnerable populations in developing countries, particularly least-developed countries (LDCs) and small island developing states (SIDS).[208]

200 This Association involves countries (El Salvador, Guatemala, Honduras, Nicaragua) that fall within the UNDP category of 'medium human development' in terms of the 2010 Human Development Index (above n 179), as do some of the ACP countries.

201 Cotonou Agreement, part I, title 1.

202 Ibid, part I, title II.

203 Ibid, part III, title I.

204 Ibid, part III, title II.

205 Cotonou Agreement, part IV and Annexes I–IV.

206 This can be also explained by the peculiarity of the EDF as a financial instrument outside the EU budget, see further Ch 4, s 4.4.

207 MDG-7 (ensure environmental sustainability) includes the following targets to: integrate the principles of sustainable development into country policies and programmes and reserve the loss of environmental resources; reduce the loss of biodiversity, achieving by 2010 a significant reduction in biodiversity loss; halve by 2015 the proportion of population without sustainable access to safe drinking water and basic sanitation; and achieve by 2020 a significant improvement in the lives of at least 100 million slum dwellers (www.un.org/millenniumgoals/environ.shtml).

208 Cotonou Agreement-2010 revision, preamble paras 12 and 13bis. This is in line with recognition at UN level of the importance of environmental sustainability and more recently of effective responses to climate change to ensure the attainment of all the other MDGs (UNGA, 'Keeping the Promise: United to Achieve the Millennium Development Goals' (2010) UN Doc A/RES/65/1). See E Morgera, 'Environmental Dimension of the MDGs: Progress Made?' (2010) 40(6) *Environmental Policy and Law* 269.

The agreement's central objectives of poverty reduction, sustainable development and gradual integration of ACP countries into the world economy must be pursued through an integrated approach that takes into account 'at the same time' the political, economic, social, cultural and environmental aspects of development[209] and through the application, at every level of the partnership, of the principle of sustainable management of natural resources and the environment.[210] Environmental sustainability is further included among the thematic or cross-cutting issues of the agreement to be taken into systematic account for mainstreaming into all areas of EU-ACP cooperation: economic development, social and human development, and regional and international cooperation.[211] The environment, as well as cultural heritage, is also included among the areas covered by the high-level political dialogue among the Parties.[212] In addition, peace-building policies, conflict prevention and resolution activities are mandated to include support for mediation, negotiation and reconciliation efforts for effective regional management of shared and scarce natural resources.[213]

The Association with Central America also adopts a cross-cutting approach to environmental integration, albeit not to the same extent seen in the Cotonou Agreement. The Association includes the environment among the 'cross-cutting issues' to be taken into account in cooperation activities;[214] but not necessarily into 'all areas of cooperation' as required by the Cotonou Agreement. In addition, it is 'sustainable development' (rather than the 'sustainable management of natural resources and the environment' found in the Cotonou Agreement) that figures as a 'guiding principle' for the implementation of the Association with Central America, taking into account the MDGs.[215] The overall objectives of this association do nonetheless include the maintenance (and preferably the development) of the level of environmental standards through the effective implementation of MEAs to which Parties are party at the time of entry into force of their association,[216] in addition to the broader aim of achieving more sustainable and equitable social and economic development.[217] In the provisions on high-level political dialogue, emphasis is placed on both sustainable development (set as one of the objectives and principles of the political partnership, and coupled with a commitment to 'promote and protect it on the world stage in such a way that it contributes to the strengthening of multilateralism')[218] and on the environment itself, with a provision specifically dedicated to dialogue in this area, unlike in the

209 Cotonou Agreement, art 1(3).

210 Ibid, art 1(4).

211 Ibid, art 20(2).

212 Ibid, art 8(3).

213 Ibid, art 11(3).

214 Central America AA, art 25(e).

215 Ibid, art 1(2).

216 Ibid, arts 2(g) and 13(3), confirming that the political dialogue will cover effective implementation of MEAs.

217 Ibid, art 2(c).

218 Ibid, art 2(b). See also art 12(a)–(b), which makes express reference to the framework of the United Nations.

Cotonou Agreement. This clause embodies an obligation for the EU and Central American countries to promote dialogue on local and global environmental issues, recognising the principle of common but differentiated responsibility, and focusing on the fight against climate change, biodiversity conservation, sustainable forest management including reducing emissions from deforestation and degradation (REDD),[219] the protection of water and marine resources, renewable energy and – quite unusually – the reform of environmental governance.[220]

5.2.2 *Environmental cooperation clauses*

The central provision of the Cotonou Agreement expressly devoted to 'environment and sustainable development', namely Article 32, is found in the 'development strategies' title as one of the 'thematic and cross-cutting issues',[221] and is clearly eligible for EU financial support.[222] This provision states the key aims of the cooperation on environmental protection and sustainable utilisation and management of natural resources, namely: (i) mainstreaming environmental sustainability into all aspects of development cooperation; (ii) capacity building for all environmental stakeholders; (iii) taking account of transport and disposal of hazardous waste; and (iv) supporting specific measures and schemes aimed at addressing critical sustainable management issues, including those related to current and future, regional and international commitments concerning mineral and natural resources.[223]

An indicative list of critical sustainable management issues encompasses: tropical forests; water resources and biodiversity; fragile ecosystems; renewable energy; desertification and deforestation; urban environment; and sustainable tourism.[224] Within this framework, and in line with the differentiation principle, account will also be taken of the vulnerability of SIDS, LDCs and land-locked countries to climate-related threats, including the worsening of drought and desertification problems.[225]

As previously mentioned, the second revision of the Cotonou Agreement added unprecedented text on climate change. Climate change is first singled out among the objectives of the partnership, as an issue that should be integrated at every level of the partnership,[226] to be specifically addressed by the political dialogue[227] and be considered a cross-cutting theme to be mainstreamed in all areas of cooperation, as

[219] REDD is an item on the agenda of the multilateral negotiations on a post-2012 climate change regime (more recently, the agenda item is referred to as REDD-plus, to include also 'conservation of forest-carbon stocks, sustainable management of forests, and enhancement of forest-carbon stocks'). It will be discussed in Ch 7, s 4.1.

[220] Ibid, art 20.

[221] Cotonou Agreement, part III, title I.

[222] Ibid, art 20(2).

[223] Ibid, art 32(1).

[224] Ibid.

[225] Ibid, art 32(2).

[226] Cotonou Agreement-2010 revision, art 1.

[227] Ibid, art 8.

well as being eligible for EU funding.[228] Climate change is also included in the list of security threats that need to be taken into account in the partnership, as the Parties acknowledge that 'without development and poverty reduction there will be no sustainable peace and security and that without peace and security there can be no sustainable development'.[229]

A whole new article is devoted to climate change cooperation. The article starts with Parties' recognition of climate change as a threat to the achievement of the MDGs requiring adequate, predictable and timely financial support. Mandatory language calls for cooperation to strengthen and support mitigation and adaptation policies and programmes, including through institutional development and capacity-building, and to enhance the capacity of ACP States in the development of and participation in the global carbon market. Mandatory language also singles out as specific cooperation activities: integrating climate change into development strategies and poverty reduction efforts; raising the political profile of climate change in development cooperation through appropriate policy dialogue; assisting ACP States' adaptation in relevant sectors (such as agriculture, water and infrastructure) including through the transfer and adoption of environmentally-sound technologies; promoting disaster risk reduction; providing financial and technical support for mitigation action of ACP States where this benefits poverty reduction and sustainable development objectives, including REDD and reducing emissions in the agricultural sector; improving weather and climate information and forecasting and early warning systems; and, finally, promoting renewable energy and low-carbon technologies that enhance sustainable development.[230] These provisions are in line with the political priority attached by the EU[231] to combating climate change, which has been sanctioned at the constitutional level by the Treaty of Lisbon.[232]

While the Association Agreement with Central America also singles out climate change among global environmental issues to be addressed through bilateral cooperation, it does so without devoting a single article to it and generally provides a more balanced approach to cooperation across various MEAs. So, on the one hand, it calls for joint initiatives for climate change mitigation and adaptation, including: the strengthening of carbon market mechanisms; trade-related cooperation to contribute to the implementation of the current and future international climate change regime; and cooperation in the field of energy to promote the application of the Clean Development Mechanism (CDM).[233] On the other hand, it places more emphasis on the implementation and enforcement of other MEAs, pointing to illegal trade in that regard.[234] The priorities of environmental cooperation, which are identified with legally binding language, thus include: the

[228] Ibid, art 20(2).
[229] Ibid, art 11.
[230] Ibid, art 32bis.
[231] Morgera and Marín Durán, above n 75, 16.
[232] Art 191(1) TFEU, see Ch 1, s 3.2.
[233] Central America AA, arts 50(3)(d), 63(3)(b) and 65(2)(d).
[234] Ibid, part III title V.

protection and sustainable management of ecosystems, including forests and fisheries; the fight against pollution, including sound management of waste and chemicals; and global issues, such as climate change, biodiversity, desertification, deforestation, the depletion of the ozone layer and biosafety[235] – the last two issues were not explicitly referred to in the Cotonou Agreement. In addition, the measures to carry out environmental cooperation are spelt out in much more detail than in the Cotonou Agreement, albeit in soft language. They include, inter alia: capacity building and institutional strengthening; technology transfer; integration of environmental considerations in land-use management; promotion of sustainable production and consumption patterns; assisting in the implementation and enforcement of MEAs to which the Parties are party; and strengthening environmental management, monitoring and control systems.[236] It should also be noted that the agreement includes an unusual provision on indigenous peoples and other ethnic groups, according to which cooperation is required to ensure the effective participation of these groups in the sustainable management and use of land and natural resources, and in environmental protection.[237]

5.2.3 *Environmental integration clauses*

As far as other areas of cooperation are concerned, an integrated approach to environmental issues is reiterated and specific environmental aims are set out in the Cotonou Agreement. These include the promotion of: environmental sustainability, regeneration and best practices, and the preservation of the natural resource base.[238] It should be noted, however, that such environmental aims are listed only after economic, social, cultural and institutional goals. Therefore, the integration approach in the Cotonou Agreement does not only or primarily apply to environmental concerns, but actually includes a whole range of issues, without indication of any priority among them. Presumably, it is the responsibility of the political bodies established under the agreement[239] to undertake a genuine balancing exercise and integrate the various (and at times conflicting) cross-cutting themes and objectives of the Cotonou Agreement in the decision-making and implementation process.

Before the 2010 revision of the Cotonou Agreement, limited references to environmental sustainability could be found in the provisions on *fisheries agreements and marine transport*. Parties 'expressed their willingness' to negotiate fisheries agreements aimed at guaranteeing 'sustainable' and mutually satisfactory conditions for fishing activities in ACP States.[240] With regard to marine transport, the Parties 'acknowledge the importance' of cost-effective and efficient maritime

235 Ibid, art 50(3).
236 Ibid, art 50(4).
237 Ibid, art 45(3).
238 Cotonou Agreement, art 20(1)(e).
239 See s 5.2.5 below.
240 Cotonou Agreement, art 53(1).

transport services in a safe and 'clean' marine environment as the main mode of transportation facilitating international trade.[241]

With the 2010 revision, a new reference to sustainable development of aquaculture and fisheries has been introduced in the Cotonou Agreement, including both inland fisheries and marine resources within the exclusive economic zones of ACP States.[242] This is coupled with a whole new article on fisheries, which requires cooperation to aim at further developing these sectors in ACP countries to increase the associated social and economic benefits in a sustainable manner in light of the contribution of these sectors to employment creation, revenue generation, food security, livelihoods of rural and coastal communities and poverty reduction. The article identifies in detail the cooperation activities to be undertaken to this end, including: development and implementation of national and regional sustainable aquaculture and fisheries development strategies and management plans; mainstreaming of aquaculture and fisheries into national and regional development strategies; and the development of joint ventures for investment in the sector.[243] Notably, the new provision anticipates a high-level consultation, including at ministerial meetings, upon joint agreement with a view to developing, improving or strengthening ACP-EU development cooperation in this sector. It also requires that any fisheries agreements that may be negotiated between the EU and ACP States pay due consideration to consistency with development strategies in this area.[244]

With the 2010 revision, more detailed and legally-binding language has also been inserted to ensure environmental integration in the *agriculture sector*, with new references to integrated water resource management principles, ensuring equitable and sustainable distribution of shared water resources between different users[245] as well as development and implementation of specific climate change adaptation strategies addressing the impacts of erosion.[246]

Furthermore, the Cotonou Agreement required that *regional cooperation* supports the fields of environment, waste resource management and energy to address specifically common problems and take advantage of economies of scale.[247] A new sub-provision added by the 2010 revision calls for promoting the management of sustainable development challenges with transnational dimensions through coordination and harmonisation of regional and sub-regional policies.[248] The sustainable management of natural resources (including water

[241] Ibid, art 42.

[242] Cotonou Agreement-2010 revision, art 23(f).

[243] Ibid, art 23a.

[244] Fisheries has been a particularly controversial aspect of the EU-ACP relations under both Lomé and Cotonou and now within the EPA negotiations, see L Campling, 'Fisheries Aspects of the EU-ACP Interim Economic Partnership Agreements: Trade and Sustainable Development Implications' (2008) *ICTSD Issue Paper No 6*.

[245] Cotonou Agreement-2010 revision, art 23(e).

[246] Ibid, art 23(m).

[247] Cotonou Agreement, art 30(1)(b).

[248] Cotonou Agreement-2010 revision, art 28(2)(c).

and energy) and climate change have also been incorporated as specific areas for cooperation in the context of regional economic integration.[249]

Finally, the revised version of the Cotonou Agreement hints at environmental integration in the chapter on *humanitarian, emergency and post-emergency assistance* by acknowledging the fact that situations of crisis may also result from extraordinary circumstances having comparable effects related to climate change, environmental degradation, access to energy and natural resources or extreme poverty[250] which can be read in conjunction with cross-references to disaster prevention in this chapter and in the new article devoted to climate change seen earlier.[251]

Unlike the Cotonou Agreement, the Association Agreement with Central America does not contain a cross-cutting provision calling for environmental integration across all areas of cooperation, but only specific clauses covering several cooperation fields under the 'economic and trade development' title.[252] Soft language provides that technical cooperation assistance on *fisheries and aquaculture* which (unlike the Cotonou Agreement) focuses on technical rather than policy aspects of sustainable fisheries by aiming at: promoting sustainable exploitation and management; data collection to gather the best available scientific information for resource assessment and management; and monitoring, control and surveillance. It also makes explicit reference to international issues and approaches, namely the fight against illegal, unregulated and unreported fishing; and reinforcing cooperation with international and regional organisations, to ensure 'better understanding of the added value of international legal instruments in achieving a proper management of marine resources'.[253] On *industrial cooperation*, mandatory language requires Parties to promote the modernisation and restructuring of Central American industry with the objective of strengthening the private sector under conditions promoting environmental protection.[254] Such wording has been seen in other associations (but not in the Cotonou Agreement)[255] reflecting the EU's attempts to advance on corporate environmental accountability. The provision on environmental integration in the *energy* sector is particularly detailed, albeit couched in voluntary terms: it indicates that cooperation 'may' include the 'promotion of energy saving, energy efficiency, renewable energy and assessing the environmental impacts of energy production and consumption, *in particular its effects on biodiversity, forestry and land use change*' (emphasis added on the unprecedented formulation).[256] Furthermore, the agreement provides for environmental integration in the *mining* sector through exchange of information

[249] Ibid, Art 29(3)(a)–(b).
[250] Ibid, Art 72(2).
[251] See s 5.2.2 above.
[252] Central America AA, part III, title VI.
[253] Ibid, art 59.
[254] Ibid, art 64(1).
[255] See s 3.5 above for a similar clause in the SAAs.
[256] Central America AA, art 65(2)(c).

and experts and technology transfer;[257] in the cooperation on 'fair and sustainable *tourism*,' both by integrating environmental considerations in the development of the sector and involving local communities in ecotourism;[258] and in *transport* cooperation, through the improvement of pollution prevention standards, including cooperation in appropriate international fora to ensure better enforcement of international standards.[259]

5.2.4 *Trade and environment*

One of the most interesting and novel features of the Cotonou Agreement is that environmental concerns have been explicitly and extensively integrated in the area of 'trade and economic cooperation'.[260] It should be clarified, however, that the trade provisions of the Cotonou Agreement are only applicable for a transitory period (which should have ended on 31 December 2007) until new WTO-compatible trading arrangements – the so-called Economic Partnership Agreements (EPAs)[261] – are in place between the EU and the ACP States. As a framework agreement, the Cotonou Partnership thus lays down the objectives, principles, modalities and procedures for the negotiation of these new trade agreements.[262] During this transitory period (still lasting for most ACP countries), the Lomé IV preferential and non-reciprocal trade regime[263] has been (partially)

257 Ibid, art 66.

258 Ibid, art 67(2)(c)–(d).

259 Ibid, art 68(2)(d).

260 Cotonou Agreement, part III, title II.

261 Following the successive legal challenges to the Lomé trade regime in the GATT/WTO, the EU and the ACP States agreed (in arts 34(4) and 36(1) of the Cotonou Agreement) to conclude new WTO-compatible trading arrangements by 31 December 2007 (as established in the two WTO political waivers, secured at the launch of Doha Development Round, for the provisional and partial extension of the Lomé trade regime under the Cotonou Agreement). One should note that the 2000 version of the Cotonou Agreement (art 37) contemplated at least three possible options for WTO-compatible EU-ACP preferential trade relations including, but not limited to, the conclusion of EPAs aimed at the progressive establishment of a reciprocal free trade area in goods (and possibly services). EPA negotiations were ultimately launched with the vast majority of ACP countries (split into seven regional groups) from 2003 and the Cotonou Agreement revised accordingly in 2010 (Cotonou Agreement-2010 revision, arts 36 and 37). On the complex and long-standing GATT/WTO disputes over the Lomé trade regime, see F Breuss, S Griller and E Vranes (eds), *The Banana Dispute. An Economic and Legal Analysis* (New York, Springer, 2003); JA McMahon, 'The Long-Standing Banana Saga – Towards an Acceptable Solution' (2005) 11(6) *International Trade Law and Regulation* 181; F Smith, 'Renegotiating Lomé: the Impact of the World Trade Organisation on the European Community's Development Policy after the Bananas Conflict' (2000) 25(3) *European Law Review* 247. On the difficulties of making the EU-ACP trade relations WTO-compliant, see A Abass, 'The Cotonou Regime and WTO Law' (2004) 10(4) *European Law Journal* 439; MG Desta, 'EC-ACP Economic Partnership Agreements and WTO Compatibility: An experiment in North-South Inter-Regional Agreements?' (2006) 43(5) *Common Market Law Review* 1343; J Huber, 'The Past, Present and Future of the ACP-EC Trade Regime and the WTO' (2000) 11(2) *European Journal of International Law* 427; F Matambalya and S Wolf, 'The Cotonou Agreement and the Challenges of Making the EU-ACP Trade Regime WTO Compatible' (2001) 35(1) *Journal of World Trade* 123.

262 Cotonou Agreement, arts 34–37.

263 Under the Lomé IV trade regime, the EU extended generous trade preferences to the ACP countries on a non-reciprocal basis: duty-free access for industrial and agricultural products (except for agricultural commodities covered by the EU Common Agricultural Policy, CAP), preferential treatment for certain CAP-covered commodities under specific Protocols, and duty exemptions for fishery

maintained in order to facilitate the gradual transition of the ACP to the new trading environment and thus should also be considered here.

In the Lomé IV Convention, the trade and environment nexus is essentially addressed through an exception clause[264] modelled on Article 36 TFEU, similar to that seen in the other associations.[265] This is complemented by an unprecedented provision in the Cotonou Agreement (Article 49) that further elaborates the relationship between trade and environment and expressly provides for cooperation between the EU and the ACP countries on the basis of positive actions. This provision is entitled 'trade and environment' and found in the chapter on 'trade-related areas'.[266] It first reaffirms the commitment of the Parties 'to promoting the development of international trade in such a way as to ensure sustainable and sound management of the environment in accordance with international conventions and undertakings in this area'.[267] Respective levels of development and special needs of individual ACP countries 'should' be taken into account in the design and implementation of environmental measures, including those dealing with climate change.[268] Reaffirming the commitment to the Rio Principles[269] and the objective of reinforcing the mutual supportiveness of trade and environment, the agreement further provides for enhanced cooperation between the Parties in relation to: the design of coherent national, regional and international policies; the reinforcement of quality controls of goods and services related to the environment; and the improvement of environmentally friendly production methods in relevant sectors.[270] In a Joint Declaration on Article 49 annexed to the Cotonou Agreement, the Parties undertake to 'make every effort' to sign and ratify as quickly as possible the Basel Convention and its 1995 ban amendment.[271] The 2010 revision of the Cotonou Agreement added that the Parties 'agree that environmental measures should not be used for protectionist purposes',[272] a rather soft commitment although this is a key concern for ACP countries in particular.

products. On this regime, see OA Babarinde, *The Lomé Conventions and Development* (Aldershot, Ashgate Publishing, 1994); E Grilli, *The European Community and Developing Countries* (Cambridge, Cambridge University Press, 1993), ch 4; AK Dickson, 'The Demise of the Lomé Protocols: Revising European Development Policy' (2000) 5 *European Foreign Affairs Review* 197.

264 Lomé IV-bis Convention, art 174.

265 See ss 3.6 and 4.5 above.

266 Cotonou Agreement, part III, title II, ch 5.

267 Ibid, art 49(1).

268 Ibid, and Cotonou Agreement-2010 revision, art 49(1) which added the specification of climate change-related measures.

269 'Rio Declaration on Environment and Development' (12 August 1992) UN Doc A/CONF.151/26 vol 1, Annex I (Rio Declaration).

270 Cotonou Agreement, art 49(2).

271 Ibid, Joint Declaration on art 49(2) trade and environment. Decision III/1 Amendment to the Basel Convention on the Control of Transboundary Movements of Hazardous Wastes and their Disposal, 28 November 1995, not yet in force, UN Doc UNEP/CHW.3/35. In the same Declaration, the Parties confirm the applicability of Council Directive (Euratom) 3/92 on the supervision and control of shipments of radioactive waste between Member States and into and out of the Community [1992] OJ L35/24, which stipulates that the competent authorities of the EU Member States shall not authorise shipments of radioactive waste to ACP Parties of Cotonou.

272 Cotonou Agreement-2010 revision, art 49(3).

In addition to this specific provision, environmental issues are also integrated into other trade-related areas. With respect to the protection of intellectual property rights, the Cotonou Agreement stresses the importance of adhering to the CBD. [273] In reaffirming their commitments under the WTO Sanitary and Phytosanitary Agreement,[274] the Parties also agree on prior consultation and coordination concerning the Codex Alimentarius,[275] the International Office of Epizooties,[276] and the International Plant Protection Convention,[277] with a view to furthering their common interests.[278] Finally, the Parties undertake to cooperate in international fora, and in particular the WTO, to further their common interests on all aspects included in the 'trade and economic cooperation' title of the Cotonou Agreement, including the aforementioned linkages between trade and environment.[279]

5.2.5 Institutional aspects

As in other EU associations discussed above,[280] the general institutional provisions of the Cotonou Agreement apply to the environment-related clauses. These include, first of all, the Council of Ministers (composed of members of the Council and the Commission on the EU side, and members of the government on the ACP side) that has the primary responsibility for implementing the agreement by: conducting high-level political dialogue (including on environmental issues); adopting by consensus binding decisions or policy guidelines/recommendations as necessary for implementing the development strategies part of the agreement (where the key environmental clauses are placed); and examining and resolving any issue that is liable to impede the effective and efficient implementation of the agreement.[281] In line with the principle of participation underpinning the Cotonou Agreement, the Council of Ministers is required to conduct regular dialogue with social and economic stakeholders and other actors of civil society in the ACP and in the EU.[282]

[273] Cotonou Agreement, art 46(2).

[274] Agreement on Sanitary and Phytosanitary Measures in WTO Secretariat, *The Legal Texts – The Results of the Uruguay Round of Multilateral Trade Negotiations* (Cambridge, Cambridge University Press, 1999).

[275] Statutes of the Codex Alimentarius Commission in FAO/World Health Organization (WHO), *Codex Alimetarius Commission: Procedural Manual* (Rome, FAO/WHO, 2010) 4.

[276] International Agreement Creating the Office International des Epizooties, 25 January 1924, in World Organization for Animal Health, *Basic Texts*, at www.oie.int/about-us/key-texts/basic-texts/.

[277] International Plant Protection Convention, 17 November 1997, 2367 UNTS 223.

[278] Cotonou Agreement, art 48(2).

[279] Ibid, art 39. Note that the trade and environment provisions of the Association with Central America will be compared with those found in the EU-CARIFORUM EPA (see s 5.3.2 below), as both of these agreements (unlike Cotonou) fully establish a preferential trade regime between the EU and the third countries concerned.

[280] See ss 3.7 and 4.6 above.

[281] Cotonou Agreement, art 15(2).

[282] Ibid, art 15(3). On the strengthening of the role of non-state actors by subsequent revisions of Cotonou, see s 5.1 above. Note that the AA with Central America (Part I Title II) contains similar

The Council is assisted by the Committee of Ambassadors (made up of each EU Member State permanent representative to the EU, a Commission representative and a head of mission for each ACP State to the EU), which is responsible for monitoring the implementation of the agreement and the progress made towards the achievement of its objectives.[283] A Joint Ministerial Trade Committee is also established to deal with trade and trade-related issues (including trade and environment linkages) of common concern to all ACP States, and in particular in the context of the EPA and multilateral negotiations.[284]

Environment-related disputes should also be addressed through the general procedure for the settlement of disputes, which provides for consultations in the Ministerial Council and, if no mutually satisfactory solution is reached, for an arbitration panel to be established whose decision (to be taken within three months by majority voting) is binding upon the Parties. The Parties are required to take the measures necessary to carry out the arbitrators' ruling, although no provision is made for temporary remedies in cases of non-compliance.[285] Unilateral 'appropriate measures' against an infringing Party (including suspension) are explicitly limited to violations of the 'essential' and 'fundamental' elements of the agreement.[286]

5.3 Environmental dimension of the CARIFORUM EPA

Although the Cotonou Agreement seems groundbreaking when compared to other EU associations examined, it remains to be seen whether and how these original commitments, in terms of the trade and environment nexus, would be lived up to in the final EPAs. The conclusion of EPAs between the EU and the ACP countries has been, arguably, the single most contentious issue emerging from the Cotonou Agreement:[287] at the time of writing and over three years after

institutional provisions, including with regard to the involvement of civil society through regular dialogue (art 11).

[283] Cotonou Agreement, art 16.

[284] Ibid, art 38. Another key institution established under Cotonou is the Joint Parliamentary Assembly (art 17) which – despite its advisory status – has played an active role, including in relation to environmental cooperation, see discussion in Ch 5, s 3.1. A Joint Development Finance Committee was also set up to deal specifically with the implementation of financial and technical assistance (art 83), see further Ch 4, s 4.4.

[285] Cotonou Agreement, arts 15(2)(d) and 98.

[286] Ibid, arts 96 and 97, respectively. It is interesting to note that on the basis of a comparative analysis of suspension clauses on grounds of violations of 'essential' or 'fundamental' elements across EU associations, Bartels found that they have (as yet) been limited to the Lomé IV Convention and the Cotonou Agreement and that it is the very poorest ACP countries that have been targeted, usually in response to military coups. The measures employed by the EU have been generally limited to the suspension or redirection of financial aid and other cooperation matters, but not extended to trade sanctions. On one occasion only the EU also suspended its obligation to impose no restrictions on payments between residents of the EU and Zimbabwe in order to allow for the freezing of funds of certain members of that country's government. See L Bartels, *Human Rights Conditionality in the EU's International Agreements* (Oxford, Oxford University Press, 2005), 35–40.

[287] The conclusion of EPAs was the option clearly favoured by the EU as the basis for future ACP-EU

the deadline for concluding negotiations,[288] only one final EPA has been signed with the CARIFORUM States in October 2008,[289] while negotiations are still dragging on with the other six regional groups of ACP States.[290] This study will thus focus on the CARIFORUM EPA, to verify in particular whether the Cotonou Agreement's novel focus on the mutual supportiveness between trade and environment has resulted in substantive provisions complementing the typical exceptions clauses that were seen in previous EU agreements.[291] This agreement is furthermore likely to be the benchmark against which other regional EPAs (if concluded) would be measured, including in relation to trade and environment clauses.

The agreement with the CARIFORUM States also provides some initial guidance as to the precise relationship between the EPAs and the Cotonou Agreement, which is likely to be replicated in other final EPAs (if concluded). While both agreements must be implemented in a 'complementary and mutually reinforcing manner', a certain hierarchy is established: the EPA replaces and, in case of conflict, prevails over the Cotonou Agreement provisions on 'trade and economic cooperation' matters.[292] However, it is important to bear in mind that the development cooperation and finance provisions of the Cotonou Agreement[293]

trade relations and the EU (at least DG Trade) continues to maintain that EPAs are the trade instrument for development *par excellence*. However, the EU position has not gone unchallenged and debates over the developmental implications of these agreements have become increasingly polarised in academic and other circles. See, eg, S Bilal and F Rampa, 'Alternative(s) EPAs. Possible Scenarios for the Future ACP Trade Relations with the EU' (2006) ECDPM Policy Management Report 11 (February 2006); E de Vos, 'The Cotonou Agreement: A Case of Forced Regional Integration?' in G Kreijen et al (eds), *State, Sovereignty and International Governance* (Oxford, Oxford University Press, 2002); R Perez, 'Are Economic Partnership Agreements a First-Best Option for the ACP countries?' (2006) 40(6) *Journal of World Trade* 999; LA Winters, 'Post-Lomé Trading Arrangements: the Multilateral Alternative' in J von Hagen and M Widgren (eds), *Regionalism in Europe. Geometries and Strategies after 2000* (London, Kluwer, 2001). The International Center for Trade and Sustainable Development (ICTSD) publishes monthly 'Trade Negotiations Insights' analysing trade and economic matters of concern to the ACP countries, including key issues and updates in the EPA negotiations at www.ictsd.org/news/tni/.

[288] 31 December 2007, as established in the two WTO political waivers and provided for in Cotonou (see above n 261).

[289] Economic Partnership Agreement between the CARIFORUM States, of the one part, and the European Community and its Member States, of the other [2008] OJ L289/3 (CARIFORUM EPA). The CARIFORUM States include all the 14 members of the Caribbean Community (CARICOM, namely Antigua and Barbuda, the Bahamas, Barbados, Belize, Dominica, Grenada, Guyana, Haiti, Jamaica, Saint Lucia, Saint Vincent and the Grenadines, Saint Kitts and Nevis, Surinam, and Trinidad and Tobago) plus the Dominican Republic. The agreement has been provisionally applied by all parties since 29 December 2008, except for Haiti which only signed the agreement in December 2009 and for which ratification is still pending.

[290] For the purpose of conducting EPA negotiations, the ACP group is currently split into seven regional groupings, namely: CARIFORUM; Central Africa; Eastern and Southern Africa; East African Community; Pacific; Southern African Development Community; and West Africa.

[291] See ss 3.6 and 4.5 above. An examination of other interim EPAs and of negotiating texts will not be entered into this study as their precise language is subject to change until the negotiating process is concluded. An overview of their environment-related provisions is offered by B Chaytor, 'Environmental Issues in Economic Partnership Agreements: Implications for Developing Countries' *ICTSD Issue Paper* 1 (September 2009).

[292] Cotonou Agreement, title II, part III is referred to in CARIFORUM EPA, arts 2 and 241(1).

[293] Cotonou Agreement, title I, parts III and IV.

remain applicable to the CARIFORUM EPA Parties. In other words, while the CARIFORUM EPA is essentially aimed at regulating trade and trade-related matters between the EU and the CARIFORUM States, and can also provide for specific cooperation activities (including EPA-implementation assistance and/or environment-related issues), these will be implemented through the Cotonou Agreement's rules and procedures.[294] In terms of political dialogue, this can be conducted depending on the subject matter at both EU-CARIFORUM level through the EPA institutional structures,[295] and at EU-ACP level (including the CARIFORUM States) through the Cotonou Agreement institutional framework.

5.3.1 General approach to the environment

The bulk of the CARIFORUM EPA deals with 'trade and trade-related matters',[296] and implies a radical overhaul in the EU's trade relations with countries from the ACP group by introducing reciprocity for the first time in decades of partnership.[297] The EPA provides not only for the establishment of a free trade area in goods (albeit on an asymmetric and progressive basis)[298] but also lays down reciprocal commitments on the liberalisation of trade in services (following a positive list approach and also on an asymmetric basis) and on the opening to foreign direct investment (FDI). Notwithstanding its focus on trade, the agreement treats the environment as a 'trade-related matter' and contains a specific chapter devoted to it, which is unprecedented in EU practice.

Within the context of the EPA itself, the novel trade and environment chapter can be explained by the fact that this agreement, as opposed to the others previously examined, builds upon the Cotonou Agreement's overriding objective of sustainable development and its thematic and cross-cutting approach to the environment. In fact, in Part I of the CARIFORUM EPA entitled 'trade partnership for sustainable development', a core provision reaffirms that sustainable development is 'to be applied and integrated at every level of [the Parties'] economic partnership'.[299] Furthermore, the Parties understand this as a commitment to ensure that the application of the agreement takes 'fully into account the human, cultural, economic, social, health and environmental best interests of their respective populations and future generations',[300] and agree to work cooperatively

[294] CARIFORUM EPA, art 7(3). Namely, the EDF as well as the EU thematic instruments (see Ch 4, ss 3.2.2 and 4.4).

[295] See s 5.3.4 below.

[296] CARIFORUM EPA, Part II.

[297] Except for South Africa, with which the EU concluded the a bilateral agreement in 1999 aimed, inter alia, at establishing a free trade area in goods, see s 6 below.

[298] CARIFORUM EPA, Part II, Title I. According to the EU, since 1 January 2008 all CARIFORUM products (other than rice and sugar) benefit from duty-and-quota free access to the EU market while CARIFORUM tariff elimination commitments cover less than 100% (approximately 87%) of EU exports and are spread over a 25-year transition period. Duties and quotas on rice and sugar were also removed by the end of 2009, but a transitional safeguard mechanism remains in place for sugar until 2015. See Commission, 'Factsheet CARIFORUM-EC EPA: Trade in Goods' (October 2008).

[299] CARIFORUM EPA, art 3 (1).

[300] Ibid, art 3(2)(a).

towards the realisation of human-centred sustainable development.[301] Additional references to sustainable development can be found in the preamble (underscoring the need to promote economic and social progress for people in a manner consistent with sustainable development by protecting the environment in line with the 2002 WSSD Declaration),[302] among the objectives of the agreement (establishing links with poverty reduction and the MDGs), and in the regional integration provisions (requiring account of the respective levels of development, needs, geographical realities and sustainable development strategies).[303]

Aside from the central attention paid to sustainable development within the Cotonou Agreement framework, it should also be noted that the CARIFORUM EPA was negotiated and concluded against the backdrop of the Global Europe Strategy endorsed by the EU in 2006, which calls for more detailed trade and environment provisions in new free trade agreements considered by the EU.[304] This is also the case of the Association Agreement with Central America, whose trade and sustainable development chapter[305] will be referred to, where relevant, by way of comparison with the CARIFORUM EPA. The Association with Central America provides for the progressive establishment of a free trade area covering both goods and services[306] between the EU and the six Central American countries concerned which, at present, still access the EU market on a preferential and non-reciprocal basis under the generalised system of preferences, and more specifically its GSP-plus arrangement.[307]

5.3.2 Trade and environment chapter

The CARIFORUM EPA contains a whole chapter devoted to trade and environment within the 'trade-related issues' title[308] also dealing with competition, intellectual property, public procurement, labour aspects and personal data protection. After reaffirming the Cotonou Agreement principles, the chapter approaches the trade and environment nexus in a number of innovative ways.

[301] Ibid, art 3(3).

[302] 'Political Declaration of the World Summit on Sustainable Development' (4 September 2002) UN Doc A/CONF.199/20, Resolution 1 (WSSD Declaration).

[303] CARIFORUM EPA, preamble and arts 1 and 4.

[304] Albeit, the ACP countries are not explicitly mentioned among the priority trading partners with which the EU will seek to conclude such new-generation FTAs. The trade and environment provisions of the CARIFORUM EPA may nonetheless have been influenced by this EU policy strategy and present similarities with those found in the FTA with South Korea (see s 7.1.3 below), which does figure among the priority FTA partners for the EU: see Global Europe Strategy, 11.

[305] Central America AA, part IV title VIII.

[306] Ibid, art 77(1), title II (part IV) on the progressive establishment of a free trade area in goods and title III (part IV) on the progressive establishment of a free trade area in services.

[307] The GSP-plus arrangement requires, inter alia, that beneficiary countries ratify and implement seven MEAs, see discussion in Ch 3, s 4.2. Presumably, these Central American countries will continue to benefit from the 'GSP-plus' until their association agreement with the EU enters into force and the free trade area is fully implemented.

[308] CARIFORUM EPA, part II, title IV, ch 4.

First, the chapter reiterates the general commitment, found in the 1992 Rio Declaration[309] and the WTO Agreement (among other international instruments), to ensure *mutual supportiveness* between trade and environment: the Parties 'reaffirm their commitment to promoting the development of international trade in such a way as to ensure sustainable and sound management of the environment, in accordance with their undertakings in this area including the international conventions to which they are party and with due regard to their respective level of development'.[310] In addition, specific emphasis is placed on the facilitation of trade in environmental goods and services – also an EU priority in the Doha Round of multilateral trade negotiations.[311] An indicative list of the products concerned includes: environmental technologies, renewable and energy-efficient goods and services and eco-labelled goods.[312]

Second, the chapter deals with *standards of environmental protection* and contains provisions linking domestic environmental performance with MEAs, albeit without using bold mandatory language. The Parties undertake to 'conserve, protect and improve the environment, including through multilateral and regional environmental agreements to which they are parties'.[313] This should be read in conjunction with a subsequent provision, titled 'regional integration and use of international environmental standards',[314] according to which Parties 'recognise the importance of' (rather than committing to) establishing effective strategies and measures at the regional level in order to promote the development of international trade in an environmentally sustainable and sound manner. Parties further agree that, in the absence of relevant environmental standards in national or regional legislation, they 'shall seek to adopt and implement' the relevant international standards, guidelines or recommendations, qualifying this commitment by the phrase 'where practical and appropriate'.[315] Thus, while the EPA clearly embraces international environmental standards as the benchmark for assessing domestic environmental performance, it does not specify the MEAs or soft-law instruments in question. It has also been reported that CARIFORUM States rejected the EU proposal to use certain regional environmental standards (already applied in the EU) as benchmarks out of concern that these exceeded international standards.[316]

The chapter further seeks to support a 'high level' of environmental protection under domestic laws, while allowing the Parties to set their own minimum

[309] Above n 269.

[310] CARIFORUM EPA, art 183(4). Similar language is found in the Central America AA, art 284(1), making explicit reference to 'Agenda 21' (12 August 1992) UN Doc A/CONF.151/26/Rev.1 (vol 1), Annex II; and WSSD, 'Plan of Implementation' (4 September 2002) UN Doc A/CONF.199/20, Resolution 2.

[311] See Ch 1, s 5.2.

[312] CARIFORUM EPA, art 183(5). While non-exhaustive, this list seems to indicate that the scope of environmental goods and services under the CARIFORUM EPA is confined to industrial goods.

[313] Ibid, art 183(3).

[314] Ibid, art 185.

[315] Ibid.

[316] Chaytor, above n 291, 8.

standards: the sovereign right of Parties to regulate is recognised, but they 'shall seek to ensure' that their own environmental and public health laws and policies provide for and encourage high levels of environmental and public health protection and 'shall strive' to continue to improve those laws and policies.[317] The language may be inspired by the EU's own objective of achieving a 'high level' of environmental protection,[318] which has been interpreted as not necessarily implying the highest possible level of protection.[319] It has been argued that such a standard does not have a precise international reference,[320] and cannot be interpreted in light of EU law.[321]

In comparison, the Association with Central America makes a clearer linkage between domestic environmental performance and international environmental standards, which is supported by a specific reference to a closed list of MEAs. While a sovereign right to regulate[322] is equally recognised, each Party shall 'strive to ensure' that its laws and policies provide for a 'high level'[323] of environmental protection, which is here defined as 'consistent'[324] with the following MEAs: the Montreal Protocol; the Basel Convention, the POPs Convention, CITES, the CBD and its Biosafety Protocol, and the Kyoto Protocol.[325] Significantly, this closed list of MEAs also encompasses any 'protocols, amendments, annexes and adjustments' to these agreements that have been ratified by the Parties.[326] The Parties further undertake to ratify (by the date of the entry into force of their association)[327] the Gaborone Amendment to CITES[328] (which would amend CITES so as to allow membership by REIO, thereby enabling the EU to become a party to the Convention) and the Rotterdam Convention.[329]

Third, the trade and environment chapter of CARIFORUM EPA requires the Parties to *uphold levels of protection*, using significantly strict wording. Subject to their sovereign right to regulate, they commit:

> not to encourage trade or foreign direct investment to enhance or maintain a competitive edge by:
>
> (a) lowering the level of protection provided by domestic environmental and public health legislation

[317] CARIFORUM EPA, art 184(1).

[318] Art 191(2) TFEU. See Ch 1, s 3.2.

[319] Case C-284/95 *Safety Hi-Tech Srl. v S. & T. Srl* [1998] ECR I-4301; see also J Jans and H Vedder, *European Environmental Law* 3rd edn (Groningen, Europa Law, 2008), 36–37.

[320] Chaytor, above n 291, 8.

[321] A Rosas, 'The European Court of Justice and Public International Law' in J Wouters et al (eds), *The Europeanization of International Law* (The Hague, TMC Asser Press, 2008), 82.

[322] Central America AA, art 285(1) reads: 'The Parties reaffirm the respect for their respective Constitutions and for their rights there under to regulate in order to set their own sustainable development priorities, to establish their own levels of domestic environmental and social protection, and to adopt or modify accordingly their relevant laws and policies.'

[323] Ibid, art 285(2).

[324] Ibid, qualifying this by the terms 'appropriate to its social, environmental and economic conditions'.

[325] All fully cited in Ch 1, s 3.5.

[326] Central America AA, art 287(2), n 43.

[327] Ibid, art 287(3)–(4).

[328] Fully cited in Ch 1, s 3.5.

[329] Ibid, art 287(3)–(4).

(b) derogating from, or failing to apply, such legislation[330]

[and]

not to adopt or apply regional or national trade or investment-related legislation or other related administrative measures in a way which has the effect of frustrating measures intended to benefit, protect or conserve the environment or natural resources or to protect public health.[331]

Moreover, the undertaking to uphold protection levels is reinforced in the separate investment chapter, where Parties are more forcefully required to ensure that FDI is not encouraged by lowering domestic environmental legislation and standards or by relaxing laws aimed at protecting and promoting cultural diversity.[332] A provision titled 'behaviour of investors' goes into further detail on enforcement and mandates the Parties, 'within their own respective territories',[333] to take 'such measures as may be necessary' in order to ensure that, inter alia, 'investors do not manage or operate their investments in a manner that circumvents international environmental or labour obligations arising from agreements' to which the EU and the CARIFORUM states are Parties.[334] As will be seen below,[335] these provisions in the investment chapter are fully subject to the general dispute settlement procedures and represent the only environment-related commitments that, if not observed, could theoretically lead to the suspension of trade concessions under the agreement.

By way of comparison, the Association with Central America also contains legally binding provisions to uphold levels of environmental protection, albeit these are more limited in scope. As under the CARIFORUM EPA, the Association with Central America forbids the Parties 'to derogate [from] or waive', as well as 'to fail to effectively enforce', their respective environmental legislation in a manner affecting trade or as an encouragement for FDI.[336] Yet, it does not address the other side of the coin, namely the prohibition found in the CARIFOUM EPA on the adoption or application of trade or investment-related legislation in way that has the effect of frustrating environmental protection measures. In addition, the provisions on investment in the Association with Central America do not seek to regulate the behaviour of investors themselves in observing international environmental standards, as does the CARIFORUM EPA. Furthermore, the Association with Central America is more precise in clarifying that a Party may not undertake law enforcement activities in the territory of another Party with regards to environmental (and labour) matters.[337]

330 CARIFORUM EPA, art 188(1).

331 Ibid, art 188(2).

332 Ibid, art 73.

333 This specification seems to exclude home state regulation, whereby the EU would adopt legal measures to regulate extra-territorially the activities of its private investors in the CARIFORUM States.

334 CARIFORUM EPA, art 72.

335 See s 5.3.4 below.

336 Central America AA, art 291(2)–(3).

337 Ibid, art 291(4).

Fourth, the trade and environment chapter of the CARIFORUM EPA also provides for *special and differential treatment* of the CARIFORUM States, in line with the Cotonou Agreement's principle of differentiation.[338] In this regard, the Parties agree to take into account the special needs and requirements of CARIFORUM States in the design and implementation of measures aimed at protecting the environment and public health that affect trade between them. This should be read in conjunction with the recognition of the importance, when preparing and implementing these measures, of taking account of scientific and technical information, the precautionary principle, and relevant international standards, guidelines or recommendations.[339] Furthermore, a requirement for transparency is put in place when developing, introducing and implementing any measures aimed at protecting the environment and public health that affect trade between the Parties. This includes: due notice, appropriate and timely communication, mutual consultation as well as public consultation of non-state actors (including the private sector).[340]

Fifth, the chapter provides for a specific *environmental exception clause*, modelled on Article XX(b) and (g) GATT, albeit broader in scope. The right of Parties to adopt (or maintain) measures 'necessary to protect human, animal or plant life or health' (as in Article XX(b) GATT) and/or 'related to the conversation of natural resources or the protection of the environment' (broader than Article XX(g) GATT) is recognised, subject to the requirement that such measures are not applied in a manner that would constitute a means of arbitrary or unjustifiable discrimination or a disguised restriction on trade between them (as under Article XX-chapeau GATT).[341] The Association with Central America instead fully incorporates the provisions of Article XX GATT as a general exception clause.[342] In addition, the agreement explicitly requires measures undertaken to implement or enforce the listed MEAs to meet the conditions of Article XX-chapeau.[343]

Finally, the trade and environment chapter of the CARIFORUM EPA provides for *cooperation in relation to trade and environmental issues*. The Parties agree to

338 Explicitly made applicable to the 'trade and environment' chapter of the CARIFORUM EPA (art 183(2)).

339 CARIFORUM EPA, art 186.

340 Ibid, art 187. Note that the AA with Central America does not provide for special and differential treatment in the context of the trade and sustainable chapter, although it does for other trade-related matters (such as technical standards, arts 126 and 132).

341 CARIFORUM EPA, art 184(3). In a rather confusing fashion, the general exception provisions (art 224) somehow restrict the Parties' right to use trade measures for environmental purposes by replicating the wording of art XX(g) GATT. Pursuant to this general provision, such measures need to be 'related to the conversation of exhaustible natural resources' (with no mention of environmental protection in general) and to be made effective in conjunction with restrictions on domestic production or consumption of goods, domestic supply and consumption of services, and on domestic investors. It is thus unclear whether a trade measure for environmental purposes other than the conservation of exhaustible natural resources could be justified under this general provision. An argument could be made however that the more specific environmental exception clause would prevail over the general exception clause.

342 Central America AA, art 203(1)(b)–(c).

343 Ibid, art 287(5).

cooperate on the following areas: technical assistance and capacity building, in particular to the public sector, in the implementation and enforcement of MEAs, including with respect to trade-related aspects; facilitation of trade between the Parties in natural resources (including timber and wood products from legal and sustainable sources); technical assistance to producers in meeting EU product and other standards; assistance to producers to develop and/or improve production of goods and services, which the Parties consider to be beneficial to the environment; promotion and facilitation of private and public voluntary market-based schemes (including relevant labelling and accreditation schemes); and promotion and facilitation of public awareness and education programmes in respect of environmental goods and services in order to foster trade in such products between the Parties.[344] Such cooperation is to be undertaken within the framework of the Cotonou Agreement's financing instrument (the European Development Fund) and procedures and thus, although not explicitly mentioned, one would expect it to take the form mainly of EU assistance to the CARIFORUM States. That being said, the EU has generally resisted undertaking bold commitments on financial and technical assistance as part of the EPA negotiations, and the CARIFORUM EPA in fact addresses the matter in very general terms: 'Commensurate with their respective roles and responsibilities, [the Parties] shall take all necessary measures to ensure the effective mobilisation, provision and utilisation of resources aimed at facilitating development cooperation activities under this Agreement.'[345]

A similar cooperative approach is found in the Association with Central America, where Parties agree to target financial assistance, capacity-building and training towards: supporting the development of incentives to foster environmental protection through legal and sustainable trade and corporate social responsibility; promoting trade-related cooperation mechanisms to help implement the current *and* future international climate change regime; promoting trade in products derived from sustainably managed natural resources (including wildlife, fisheries and timber); and strengthening institutional frameworks for the implementation and enforcement of MEAs and environmental laws as well as for combating illegal trade with environmental relevance.[346] This agreement further elaborates on positive trade measures to support sustainable development. A best-endeavour obligation is laid down for Parties to: consider the elimination or reduction of obstacles to trade that would benefit sustainable development (taking into account the interactions between environmental measures and market access); facilitate and promote trade and FDI in environmental technologies and services, renewable energy and energy efficiency (including by addressing related non-tariff barriers); facilitate and promote trade in products responding to sustainability considerations (such as eco-labelling, organic production and corporate social responsibility standards); and fostering appropriate economic

344 CARIFORUM EPA, art 190.

345 Ibid, art 7.

346 Central America AA, art 63.

returns from the conservation and sustainable use of the environment, such as ecotourism.[347] The Parties also commit to promote sustainable trade in forest, with explicit references to CITES and the EU FLEGT[348] initiative,[349] and fish products,[350] which is notable in referring to global (rather than regional) treaties on sustainable fisheries. Finally, it should be noted that the Association with Central America also includes a clause on the precautionary approach.[351]

5.3.3 *Environmental integration clauses*

The EU-CARIFORUM EPA follows the Cotonou Agreement's approach to environmental protection and the sustainable management of natural resources as thematic and cross-cutting issues. In addition to trade, the agreement also provides for environmental integration in the areas of agriculture, fisheries, intellectual property, tourism and energy sectors, albeit using relatively soft language when compared to the trade provisions seen in the previous section.

Environmental integration in *agriculture and fisheries* is addressed jointly. The CARIFORUM EPA 'should' contribute to increasing the competitiveness of production, processing and trade in agricultural and fishery products in both traditional and non-traditional sectors between the Parties, consistent with the sustainable management of natural resources.[352] In this context, the Parties recognise that ensuring food security and enhancing livelihoods of rural and fishing communities are critical elements for the eradication of poverty and the pursuit of sustainable development, as well as the need to avoid major disruption of markets for agricultural, food and fish products in CARIFORUM States.[353] In doing so, they commit to take full account of the diversity of the economic, social and environmental characteristics and needs and development strategies of the CARIFORUM States.[354] This should be read in conjunction with a provision identifying as an area for agricultural cooperation compliance with and adoption of quality standards relating to food production and marketing, including standards relating to environmentally and socially sound agricultural practices and organic

[347] Ibid, art 288.

[348] Regulation (EC) 2173/2005 on the establishment of a FLEGT licensing scheme for imports of timber into the European Community [2005] OJ L347/1. See discussion in Ch 7, s 4.1.

[349] Central America AA, art 289.

[350] Ibid, art 290, which refers to the UN Fish Stocks Agreement, international and regional cooperation on illegal, unreported and unregulated fishing, and the Agreement on Port State Measures to Prevent, Deter and Eliminate Illegal, Unreported and Unregulated Fishing, 22 November 2009 (2009) FAO Doc C2009/REP.

[351] Ibid, art 292, titled 'scientific information', which reads: 'The Parties recognise the importance, when preparing and implementing measures aimed at protecting the environment or health and safety at work, of taking account of scientific and technical information, and relevant international standards, guidelines or recommendations, while acknowledging that when there are threats of serious or irreversible damage, the lack of full scientific certainty should not be used as reason for postponing protective measures.'

[352] CARIFORUM EPA, art 37(1).

[353] Ibid, art 37(4).

[354] Ibid, art 37(5).

and non-genetically modified foods; and building or strengthening the scientific and technical human and institutional capability at regional level for sustainable trade in fisheries products, including aquaculture.[355]

Within the chapter dealing with *innovation and intellectual property*, a provision is specifically devoted to genetic resources, traditional knowledge and folklore. It embodies the Parties' commitment, 'subject to their domestic legislation', 'to respect, preserve and maintain knowledge, innovations and practices of indigenous and local communities embodying traditional lifestyles relevant for the conservation and sustainable use of biological diversity' and to 'promote their wider application with the involvement and approval of the holders of such knowledge, innovations and practices and encourage the equitable sharing of the benefits arising from the utilisation of such knowledge, innovations and practices'[356] – basically inserting the language from the CBD[357] on traditional knowledge into the inter-regional agreement. The Parties also 'agree' that the patent provisions of the CARIFORUM EPA and the CBD 'shall be implemented in a mutually supportive way.'[358] They further 'agree' to regularly exchange views and cooperate in relevant multilateral discussions in the World Intellectual Property Organisation (WIPO) (on issues dealt with in the framework of the WIPO Intergovernmental Committee on Intellectual Property and Genetic Resources, Traditional Knowledge and Folklore) as well in the WTO (on issues related to the relationship between the TRIPS Agreement[359] and the CBD).[360]

With regards to the *tourism* sector, the Parties undertake to encourage the participation of CARIFORUM services suppliers in international, regional, subregional, bilateral and private financing programmes to support the sustainable development of tourism.[361] In addition, they are required to encourage compliance with environmental and quality standards applicable to tourism services 'in a reasonable and objective manner' ('without constituting unnecessary barriers to trade'), and endeavour to facilitate the participation of CARIFORUM States in relevant international organisations setting environmental and quality standards applicable to tourism services.[362] The creation of mechanisms for the effective participation of CARIFORUM States in international standard-setting bodies is also among the cooperation priorities in this sector, together with the

355 Ibid, art 43(2)(c) and (f).

356 Ibid, art 150(1).

357 CBD, art 8(j), which reads: 'Each Contracting Party shall, as far as possible and as appropriate . . . Subject to its national legislation, respect, preserve and maintain knowledge, innovations and practices of indigenous and local communities embodying traditional lifestyles relevant for the conservation and sustainable use of biological diversity and promote their wider application with the approval and involvement of the holders of such knowledge, innovations and practices and encourage the equitable sharing of the benefits arising from the utilization of such knowledge, innovations and practices.'

358 CARIFORUM EPA, art 150(3).

359 Agreement on Trade-Related Aspects of Intellectual Property Rights in WTO Secretariat, above n 274.

360 CARIFORUM EPA, art 150(5).

361 Ibid, art 115.

362 Ibid, art 116.

development of programmes to achieve and ensure equivalency between national/regional and international standards for sustainable tourism.[363]

In the *energy* sector, the CARIFORUM EPA provides for cooperation on eco-innovation (that is, innovation that benefits the environment in all sectors of their economy), energy efficiency and renewable energy with a view to achieving sustainable development and in order to help maximise any positive, and prevent any negative, environmental impacts resulting from the agreement.[364] More specifically, cooperation should take the form of, inter alia: projects related to environmentally-friendly products, technologies, production processes, services, management and business methods, including those related to appropriate water-saving applications and the CDM; and promotion of eco-innovation networks.[365]

5.3.4 Institutional aspects

As with other agreements,[366] the CARIFORUM EPA establishes a general institutional framework that is applicable to environmental clauses. The Joint EU-CARIFORUM Council (composed of members of the Council and the Commission on the EU side as well as of members of the government of the CARIFORUM States) has the primary responsibility for implementing the agreement. To this effect, the Joint Council is granted the power to adopt binding decisions as well as to make recommendations on all matters covered by the agreement.[367] The Joint Council is assisted by the EU-CARIFORUM Trade and Development Committee (composed of representatives of the Parties normally at senior officials level), which is in charge of monitoring the implementation and proper application of the agreement. Significantly, one of the specific functions of the Committee is to monitor and assess the impact of the agreement's implementation on the sustainable development of the Parties.[368]

In addition, the EU-CARIFORUM EPA creates a number of monitoring mechanisms specifically applicable to environmental matters. For instance, the Parties may consult the EU-CARIFORUM Consultative Committee (whose composition is to be decided by the Joint Council) on any issue pertaining to the trade and environment chapter, which may make recommendations on disseminating and sharing best practices.[369] This is complemented by the opportunity for the Parties to seek advice from the relevant international bodies on best practice, the use of effective policy tools for addressing trade-related environmental challenges, and the identification of any obstacles that may prevent the effective implementation of environmental standards under relevant MEAs.[370] The Consultative Committee

[363] Ibid, art 117(2)(b) and (d).
[364] Ibid, art 138(1).
[365] Ibid, art 138(2).
[366] See ss 3.7, 4.6 and 5.2.5 above.
[367] CARIFORUM EPA, art 229.
[368] Ibid, arts 189(1) and 230(3)(a)(vi).
[369] Ibid, art 189(2).
[370] Ibid, art 189(3).

is also entrusted with the task of promoting dialogue and cooperation between representatives of civil society organisations (including the academic community, and social and economic partners) on all economic, social and environmental aspects of the relations (that is, not only the trade and environment chapter) between the EU and CARIFORUM States.[371]

As to the settlement of environment-related disputes, the CARIFORUM EPA differs from other EU agreements seen earlier in that it establishes a specific consultation procedure for all matters covered by the trade and environment chapter, which needs to be exhausted before recourse to the general dispute settlement procedure. The specific procedure allows for consultations on matters concerning the interpretation and application of the trade and environment chapter between the Parties. As a general rule, these consultations should not take longer than three months, unless advice is sought on the matter from competent international bodies in which case the consultation period can last a maximum of six months.[372] Where the dispute has not been satisfactorily resolved through these initial consultations, any Party may request that a Committee of Experts be convened to examine the matter in question and present a report to the Parties (and the EU-CARIFORUM Consultative Committee). Interestingly, such a Committee must comprise at least three members with specific expertise in environmental issues and the chairperson shall not be a national of the Parties.[373] The general dispute settlement procedures can only be invoked if the matter is not satisfactorily resolved within nine months of the initiation of this specific consultative process.[374]

Under the general dispute settlement procedures, the Parties may seek to resolve the dispute through third-party mediation[375] and/or through arbitration proceedings. If the dispute concerns a matter falling within the trade and environment chapter of the agreement, the arbitration panel shall comprise at least two members (out of three) with specific expertise in environmental issues.[376] Parties are required to take any necessary measures to comply with the arbitration panel ruling 'within a reasonable period of time', and the Party found in breach must notify any measures taken to this effect for review.[377] If it fails to do so, or if the notified measure(s) fails to comply with the panel ruling, it must present an offer of financial compensation to the complaining Party. If no agreement on compensation is reached, the complaining Party is entitled to adopt 'appropriate measures' which usually involve fines but the suspension of trade concessions is also possible. However, and importantly, trade sanctions are explicitly ruled out

[371] Ibid, art 232(1).

[372] Ibid, art 189(4).

[373] Ibid, art 189(5)–(6).

[374] Ibid, art 204(6).

[375] Ibid, art 205. Note that recourse to mediation is not mandatory prior to requesting the establishment of an arbitration panel.

[376] Ibid, art 207(4).

[377] Ibid, arts 210–212.

for disputes concerning the trade and environment chapter.[378] Yet, the specific provisions on investment and environment (including the obligation upon Parties to ensure that investors do not circumvent international environmental obligations)[379] could, theoretically, be enforced through trade sanctions.[380]

In a similar vein, the Association with Central America creates an institutional mechanism to deal exclusively with its trade and sustainable development chapter, including a specialised Board on Trade and Sustainable Development to oversee the implementation[381] and a specific dispute settlement procedure (including consultations within the Board and the establishment of a Panel of Experts), also allowing for advice to be sought from competent international organisations in the resolution of disputes.[382] Yet, and significantly different from the CARIFORUM EPA, there is no strict obligation of compliance with the Panel's recommendations,[383] and no sanction is available to enforce the provisions of the trade and sustainable development chapter of the Association with Central America. In addition, this Association provides for a commitment to jointly review, monitor and assess the sustainability of the cooperation,[384] and formalises dialogue with civil society through a bi-regional forum to enable exchanges with a balanced range of environmental, social and economic stakeholders on the sustainable development aspects of the trade relations between the EU and Central American countries.[385]

Thus, while significantly expanding the trade and environment nexus, both of these agreements still favour a cooperative and consultation-based approach to the integration of environmental concerns into trade policy. This is a welcome step, given the inherent limitations of enforcing environmental standards through negative trade measures, particularly when different levels of development (and thus of economic strength) are involved. As previously discussed,[386] developing countries in particular continue to be wary of the idea that negative trade instruments may be used to enforce environmental obligations.

[378] Ibid, art 213(2). Note that trade sanctions are also ruled out in the case of disputes concerning the trade and 'social aspects' of the agreement.

[379] Ibid, arts 72 and 73 (see s 5.3.2 above).

[380] Given that these provisions are situated in another chapter of the CARIFORUM EPA (part II, title II, ch 2) that is fully subject to the general dispute settlement procedure. See further, L Bartels, 'Comments on CARFORUM-EU Economic Partnership Agreement' (Comments to the European Commission, 13 February 2008), 3 at www.trade.ec.europa.eu/doclib/docs/2008/february/tradoc_138072.pdf.

[381] Central America AA, art 294.

[382] Ibid, arts 296–301. Note that recourse to the general dispute settlement procedures is explicitly excluded for matters falling within the trade and sustainable development title (art 284(4)).

[383] Ibid, art 301(3) reads: 'The Party to which the recommendations are addressed shall inform the Board on Trade and Sustainable Development as regards its intentions concerning the report and recommendations of the Panel of Experts including, where appropriate, by presenting an action plan.'

[384] Ibid, art 293, titled 'sustainability review', also referred to in art 63(f) on exchanging views on the development of methodologies and indicators for the sustainability review as part of the cooperation and technical assistance on trade and sustainable development.

[385] Ibid, art 295.

[386] See Ch 1, s 5.2 for an overview of developing countries' positions in relation to the trade and environment nexus.

6. ASSOCIATION AS AN INSTRUMENT OF INTER-REGIONAL COOPERATION

6.1 EU relations with Chile and South Africa

At the time of writing, the EU has only extended the fourth type of association to two geographically distant countries: Chile and South Africa.[387] Whereas there are differences in development levels between these two associated countries and the EU, these cannot be compared with the development gap existing between the EU and the vast majority of the ACP countries.[388] The agreements with Chile and South Africa thus represent a couple of interesting case-studies of associations as a tool for inter-regional cooperation, rather than as a development tool.

The origins of the EU's relations with Chile can be traced back to the signature of the framework cooperation agreements in 1993 and 1996, which officially restored bilateral relations following the end of Pinochet's dictatorship and re-establishment of democracy in Chile. These were replaced by a more ambitious association agreement, signed on 18 November 2002 and in force since 1 March 2005.[389] This association is structured in three main chapters: political relations; trade relations; and cooperation in other policy fields. As in other EU associations, respect for democratic principles, human rights and the rule of law are defined as essential elements of the agreement, while the promotion of sustainable economic and social development, and the equitable distribution of the benefits of the agreement are guiding principles for its implementation.[390] The Parties undertake to strengthen and deepen their political relations through a regular high-level political dialogue, and ('as far as possible') to coordinate positions and undertake joint initiatives in international fora.[391] The trade chapter provides for the progressive establishment of a free trade area covering both goods and services, and for the liberalisation of investment, current payments and capital movements.[392] The Parties also agree to establish close cooperation in a wide array of areas, including industry, agriculture, energy, transport, environment, science and technology, culture and education, public administration and inter-institutional cooperation, social cooperation, immigration, illicit drugs and organised crime.[393]

In a similar vein, EU-South African relations have flourished since 1994 following the end of apartheid and the establishment of a multi-racial democracy in South

[387] A third inter-regional association agreement has been under negotiation with MERCOSUR since 1999, see above n 27.

[388] In the UNDP Human Development Report 2010 (above n 179), Chile is classified as a 'high human development' country. While South Africa still belongs to the group of countries ranked by UNDP as 'medium human development', it still performs better than most of the other ACP countries.

[389] Chile AA, above n 25.

[390] Ibid, art 1.

[391] Ibid, part II.

[392] Ibid, part IV.

[393] Ibid, part III.

Africa, with the Trade, Development and Cooperation Agreement concluded on 11 October 1999 (and fully in force since 1 May 2004) and both sides entering into a Strategic Partnership in May 2007.[394] One of the key aims of the Agreement with South Africa is thus to support this country's own transition process as well as regional integration efforts in Southern Africa more broadly,[395] together with providing an appropriate framework for closer political relations and dialogue between the Parties, for the progressive creation of a free trade area in goods (and possible extension to services), and for cooperation in a wide range of areas. Respect for democratic principles, human rights and the rule of law are also set as essential elements of this association agreement. A bilateral high-level political dialogue is established, to complement what then existed within the framework of Lomé IV, and now of the Cotonou Agreement,[396] at an ACP-wide level.[397] This is accompanied by substantive provisions on 'trade and trade-related matters',[398] one title on 'economic cooperation'[399] (covering, inter alia, industry, investment, energy, transport, agriculture and fisheries) and another on 'cooperation in other areas'[400] (where environment is found alongside science and technology, social issues and fight against drugs), as well as provisions dealing with development assistance.[401]

6.2 General approach to the environment

Both associations adopt a cooperative approach to the environment, with key environmental clauses mainly found under the cooperation part of their operative text, but there are great variations in legal force and content. Only the Association Agreement with Chile contains a preambular statement recognising the need to promote economic and social progress for the Parties' peoples, taking into account the principle of sustainable development and environmental protection requirements.[402] In addition, the promotion of 'sustainable economic and social development' is common to both agreements' overall objectives and principles,[403] while only the agreement with Chile further specifies that the promotion of social development 'should go hand in hand with' economic

[394] South Africa AA, above n 26.

[395] Namely, the Southern African Customs Union (SACU) and the Southern African Development Community (SADC).

[396] Note that the EU bilateral agreement with South Africa was concluded one year earlier than the Cotonou Agreement and that South Africa is a party to both agreements.

[397] South Africa AA, title I.

[398] Ibid, titles II and III.

[399] Ibid, title IV.

[400] Ibid, title VI.

[401] Ibid, title V 'development cooperation' and title VII 'financial aspects of cooperation'. EU development assistance to South Africa is channelled through the Development Cooperation Instrument as well as the EU thematic instruments, see further, Ch 4, ss 3.2 and 4.3.

[402] South Africa AA, preamble para 4.

[403] Chile AA, art 1(2); South Africa AA, art 1(c). Although in the latter, it is included as a complementary objective of regional integration: 'to promote regional cooperation and economic integration in the Southern African region to contribute to its harmonious and sustainable social and economic development.'

development and the protection of the environment,[404] as a general objective of bilateral cooperation,[405] which is worded in a way that falls short of imposing a clear legal requirement. As will be seen, the Agreement with Chile is, however, characterised by comparatively weaker legal language and more timid provisions on environmental cooperation.

The Association with Chile is also very vague in relation to implementation modalities of the agreement's cooperation provisions (including environmental clauses), simply stating that 'the Parties reaffirm the importance of economic, financial and technical cooperation, as a means of contributing towards implementing the objectives and principles' of the agreement,[406] without making explicit indications of EU assistance to Chile.[407] However, the Agreement with South Africa, as with most other EU associations examined, does specify bilateral policy dialogues and EU financial and technical assistance to South Africa[408] among the implementation tools for its cooperation clauses. It further requires focusing development cooperation programmes on the basic needs of the previously disadvantaged communities and reflect the gender and environmental dimensions of development.[409]

6.3 Environmental cooperation clauses

The key provision on environmental cooperation in the Agreement with Chile is Article 28, which is placed in the context of 'economic cooperation'.[410] It provides that the aim of cooperation in the field of the environment is to 'encourage' conservation and improvement of the environment, prevention of contamination and degradation of natural resources and ecosystems, and their rational use 'in the interests of sustainable development'.[411] Interestingly, this provision also emphasises the particular relevance in environmental cooperation of the relationship between poverty and the environment, the environmental impact of economic activities, and land-use management – along the lines of the Association with Central America.[412] Projects to reinforce Chile's environmental structures and policies, exchanges of information, technology and experience particularly in

404 Chile AA, art 16(1)(b).

405 In the South Africa AA, 'harmonious sustainable and economic development' is also restated as an objective of development cooperation (art 65(2)).

406 Chile AA, art 16(2).

407 See also Chile AA, art 53 entitled 'resources' that reads: 'With the aim of contributing to fulfilling the cooperation objectives established in this Agreement, the Parties commit themselves to providing, within the limits of their capacities and through their own channels, the appropriate resources, including financial resources.'

408 South Africa AA, arts 65(1) and 93(1), the latter reading: 'In order to achieve the objectives of this Agreement, South Africa shall benefit from financial and technical assistance from the Community' (albeit the overall amount of EU resources available is not specified as in the Cotonou Agreement).

409 South Africa AA, art 66(3).

410 Chile AA, title I, part III (Cooperation).

411 Chile AA, art 28(1).

412 See s 5.2.2 above.

relation to environmental standard-setting, training and education, technical assistance and joint research programmes are also highlighted.[413]

The Agreement with South Africa contains a significantly more elaborate and lengthy provision on environmental cooperation – Article 84 placed under the 'cooperation in other areas' title.[414] It states that Parties undertake to cooperate to 'pursue sustainable development through the rational use of non-renewable natural resources and the sustainable use of renewable natural resources, thus promoting protection of the environment, prevention of its deterioration and the control of pollution'.[415] Using softer legal language, the Parties will also 'aim to' improve the quality of the environment and work together to combat global environmental problems. Dialogue will be used for the identification of environmental priorities, and the Parties will give special consideration to the development of capacity in environmental management, while the impact of past South African policies on the state of the environment will be reviewed and addressed where possible.[416]

Significantly, the Agreement with South Africa calls attention to specific global environmental problems, singling out global environmental issues such as: biodiversity; marine pollution; management of international river basins; management of waste, including hazardous and nuclear waste; management of dangerous chemicals; desertification; and climate change.[417] It includes a long list of other matters for environmental cooperation including: urban development and land use for agricultural and non-agricultural purposes; the sustainable management of forestry resources; water quality control; control of pollution from industrial and other sources; and water demand management.[418]

6.4 Environmental integration clauses

The two associations agreements integrate environmental concerns in other areas of cooperation, albeit not always in the same sectors. Environmental integration in the agriculture and energy sectors is common to both agreements. The Agreement with South Africa also provides for environmental integration clauses in the tourism and transport sectors, while that with Chile provides for an environmental integration clause in social cooperation.

With regards to *agriculture*, the Agreement with Chile provides that cooperation is designed 'to support and stimulate agricultural policy measures in order to promote and consolidate the Parties' efforts towards sustainable agriculture, and agricultural and rural development'.[419] In addition, cooperation will focus on capacity building, infrastructure and technology transfer, addressing, inter alia, specific projects aimed at supporting sanitary, phytosanitary, environmental and

[413] Chile AA, art 28(2).
[414] South Africa AA, title VI.
[415] Ibid, art 84(1).
[416] Ibid, art 84(2).
[417] Ibid, art 84(2)–(3).
[418] Ibid, art 84(3).
[419] Chile AA, art 24(1).

food quality measures, taking into account the legislation in force for both Parties, in compliance with WTO rules and other competent international organisations.[420] In the Agreement with South Africa, the article on agricultural cooperation only makes a succinct reference to 'sustainable rural development'.[421] The Agreement with Chile also foresees the possibility of concluding bilateral (and/or multilateral agreements) covering fisheries on the high seas.[422]

On environmental integration in the *energy* sector, the Agreement with Chile mandates consolidation of economic relations in key sectors such as hydroelectricity, oil and gas, renewable energy, energy-saving technology and rural electrification.[423] The Agreement with South Africa sets more ambitious aims for energy cooperation, namely to: improve the access of South Africans to affordable, reliable and sustainable sources of energy; reorganise and modernise the energy producing, distributing and consuming subsectors so that appropriate services are provided on optimum terms of economic efficiency, social development and environmental acceptability; support cooperation between countries in the Southern African region to exploit locally available energy resources in an efficient and environmentally friendly manner; develop new and renewable forms of energy and support infrastructure especially for rural energy power supply; improve the rational use of energy notably by the promotion of energy systems' efficiency; and promote transfer and use of environmentally friendly technologies.[424]

The Agreement with South Africa contains several provisions supporting *corporate environmental accountability*. It states that cooperation aims, inter alia, to support policies which ensure that mining activities take place with due consideration for the environment and sustainable development, taking into account the specific circumstances in the country and nature of mining.[425] More general mandatory language further calls for cooperation to focus on, inter alia, backing the efforts of South Africa's public and private sectors to restructure and modernise industry 'under conditions ensuring environmental protection, sustainable development and economic empowerment.'[426] While the Agreement with Chile does not contain any similar provision, the Parties, in a joint declaration, 'remind their multinational enterprises of their recommendation to observe the OECD Guidelines for Multinational Enterprises, wherever they operate.'[427] Notably, the OECD Guidelines include several standards on corporate environmental accountability.[428]

420 Chile AA, art 24(2)(a).
421 South Africa AA, art 61.
422 Chile AA, art 25.
423 Ibid, art 22(1).
424 South Africa AA, art 57(1).
425 Ibid, art 58.
426 Ibid, art 51(b).
427 Chile AA, Joint Declaration concerning Guidelines to Investors. Organization for Economic Co-operation and Development (OECD), 'The OECD Guidelines for Multinational Enterprises: Text, Commentary and Clarifications' OECD Doc DAFFE/IME/WPG(2000)15/FINAL (2001) (OECD Guidelines).
428 E Morgera, *Corporate Accountability in International Environmental Law* (Oxford, Oxford University Press, 2009) ch 5.

The Agreement with South Africa also provides for environmental integration in the *tourism* and *transport* sectors. In the latter, one of the key aims of cooperation is to support the development of intermodal networks and transport systems that are 'economically viable and environmentally sustainable' as well as regional efforts to create a sustainable transport network.[429] As to tourism, Parties are required to cooperate with the aim of strengthening the development of a competitive industry, seeking to establish a strategic alliance involving public, private and community interests in order to ensure the sustainable development of tourism.[430]

In line with its general stance that the promotion of social development should go hand in hand with economic development and the protection of the environment,[431] the Agreement with Chile provides for environmental integration in the area of *social cooperation*. In this area, cooperation should prioritise measures aimed, inter alia, at promoting programmes of land management, with special attention to areas with higher social and environmental vulnerability.[432]

Finally, the regional dimension of environmental cooperation is recognised in various provisions of the Agreement with South Africa, reflecting the fact that this country participates in a number of regional integration processes within Southern Africa.[433] Nonetheless, the Agreement with Chile also provides for the development of regional cooperation on the environment with a view to developing an active and reciprocal cooperation between the Parties and MERCOSUR.[434]

6.5 Trade and environment

Trade liberalisation and trade-related cooperation are key elements of both associations, given that they both seek to establish a free trade area between the EU and the associated country concerned, albeit the Agreement with Chile is more comprehensive covering not only goods but also services and establishment.[435] Neither, however, deals substantively with the trade and environment nexus, other than through general 'exception clauses.'

As in other association agreements,[436] the Agreement with South Africa recognises the right of the Parties to use trade measures for environmental protection purposes, through a general exception clause modelled on Article 36 TFEU. Prohibitions or restrictions on the movement of goods may be imposed by the Parties, inter alia, to protect 'the life and health of humans, animals and plants', and more generally if justified on grounds of 'public policy'. Such prohibitions or

[429] South Africa AA, art 59.

[430] Ibid, art 60(1).

[431] Chile AA, art 16.

[432] Ibid, art 44(4)(h).

[433] Namely, SACU and SADC (above n 394).

[434] Chile AA, art 49(3)(b).

[435] The Chile AA (part IV), in fact, contains one of the most detailed and far-reaching trade chapters found (as yet) in EU agreements with non-candidate countries, where there is a move from a 'potential' to an actual liberalisation of trade in services and establishment.

[436] See ss 3.6 and 4.5 above.

restrictions must not, however, constitute 'a means of arbitrary or unjustifiable discrimination where the same conditions prevail' or a 'disguised restriction on trade between the Parties'.[437]

The Agreement with Chile, instead, relies on a GATT-type general exceptions clause for goods (and GATS-type clause for services), whereby Parties may deviate from their trade commitments in order to, inter alia, undertake measures 'necessary to protect human, animal and plant life and health', and/or 'relating to the conservation of exhaustible natural resources'.[438] This is subject to the requirement that, as under Article XX-chapeau GATT, such measures 'are not applied in a manner that would constitute a means of arbitrary or unjustifiable discrimination where the same conditions prevail' or 'a disguised restriction on trade between the Parties'.[439] It has rightly been observed that the lack of an express reference to the environment may give rise to controversies similar to those already encountered in the WTO dispute settlement proceedings.[440]

6.6 Institutional aspects

None of the associations for inter-regional cooperation establishes special procedures for monitoring the implementation of environmental commitments, nor for resolving environment-related disputes. The general institutional and dispute settlement provisions are thus applicable in both cases to environment-related clauses.

As in other EU associations,[441] the agreements with Chile and South Africa establish joint institutions, albeit the latter's institutional framework is less sophisticated.[442] In the case of Chile, the Association Council (composed of members of the Council and the Commission on the EU side, and members of the Chilean government, at ministerial level) is entrusted with the supervision of the agreement's overall implementation and may make 'appropriate recommendations' by

[437] South Africa AA, art 27.

[438] Chile AA, arts 91(1)(b) and (e) and 135(1)(b) and (d) for services and establishment, which integrates environmental concerns more broadly than art XIV GATS by also including 'measures relating to the conservation of natural exhaustible resources if such measures are applied in conjunction with restrictions on domestic supply or consumption of services and on domestic investments' as a ground for exception in addition to those 'necessary to protect human, animal or plant life or health' (art XIV(b) GATS) and 'necessary to protect public morals' (art XIV(a) GATS).

[439] Chile AA, art 91(1) for goods and art 135(1) for services and establishment.

[440] Cosbey et al, above n 172, 11. The cases in point are: *United States-Tuna (Canada)*, GATT Panel Report (adopted 22 February 1982) BISD 29S/91; *United States-Restrictions on Imports of Tuna (Mexico)*, GATT Panel Report (3 September 1991, unadopted) BISD 39S/155; *US-Import Prohibition on Certain Shrimp and Shrimp Products*, Appellate Body Report (adopted 6 November 1998) WT/DS58/AB/R. In particular, the general exception clause in the Association with Chile lacks the interpretative flexibility, which may be provided in this respect by an Article 36 TFEU-type clause allowing for measures justified on grounds of 'public policy'.

[441] See ss 3.7, 4.6 and 5.2.5 above.

[442] This can partly be explained by the fact that South Africa also participates in the Cotonou-based institutional structures.

consensus on environmental matters.[443] It is assisted by the Association Committee (of a similar composition to the Council, but at senior officials level), which meets on an annual basis to review the implementation of the agreement and reports to the Council on the application and fulfilment of the cooperation aspects of the agreement (which includes environmental clauses). The Committee may also make recommendations to the Parties on long-term strategic cooperation objectives and on specific priorities for EU financial and technical assistance.[444] The Agreement with South Africa, instead, establishes a Joint Cooperation Council (whose composition is not defined), which is solely responsible for ensuring the proper functioning and implementation of the agreement and has the power to take by consensus binding decisions on the Parties on all matters covered by the agreement.[445] The Agreement with Chile also provides for public participation through regular dialogues to be promoted by the Parties with stakeholders (including social and economic organisations, non-governmental organisations (NGOs) and the academic community), in order to keep them 'informed of the implementation of the agreement and gather their suggestions for its improvement'.[446]

The general dispute settlement procedure is also applicable to environment-related disputes under both agreements. In essence, these provide for initial consultations (in the Association Committee in the case of Chile and in the Cooperation Council for South Africa) and, where these fail to settle the dispute, for an arbitration panel to be established. The panel's ruling (by majority voting) is binding upon the Parties, which must take all necessary measures to comply with it.[447] Only the agreement with Chile specifies temporary remedies in cases of non-compliance, which can include the suspension of benefits granted under the agreement by the complaining Party under certain conditions.[448] Yet, it is hard to foresee a situation where such sanctions could be applied in practice in the context of environment-related provisions that are largely conceived in cooperative terms and, for the most part, not worded as fully enforceable obligations on the part of the Parties.

[443] Chile AA, arts 3–5 and 52(3) dealing specifically with the Council's tasks on cooperation matters.

[444] Ibid, arts 6 and 53 dealing specifically with the Committee's tasks on cooperation matters. The Chile AA institutional framework also includes an Association Parliamentary Committee with an advisory role (art 9) and a Joint Consultative Committee to promote dialogue on all cooperation issues in the agreement between civil society organisations from both Parties (art 10). EU financial and technical assistance to Chile is channelled through both the Development Cooperation Instrument and thematic instruments, see further Ch 4, ss 3.2 and 4.3.

[445] South Africa AA, art 97.

[446] Chile AA, art 11.

[447] Ibid, part IV, title VIII; South Africa AA, art 104, the former being more detailed and far-reaching.

[448] Chile AA, art 188. As it is general practice under EU associations, the Agreement with South Africa (art 3) limits the adoption of unilateral 'appropriate measures' against an infringing Party (including suspension) to violations of the 'essential elements clause'.

7. OTHER AGREEMENTS

As noted earlier in this chapter,[449] a plethora of other bilateral and inter-regional agreements has been concluded by the EU including environmental cooperation and integration clauses comparable in many respects with those found in association agreements. While a detailed examination of these additional agreements is not possible here, the next sections will concentrate on two selected groups of agreements, to allow for an in-depth analysis and comparison with association agreements. First, two agreements concluded by the EU with South Korea in 2010 will be analysed, as they represent not only a case-study of EU relations with a country from Asia (a region that is not yet covered by any association agreement) but also because they are indicative of a shift in EU practice following the adoption of the 2006 Global Europe Strategy. In fact, the agreements with South Korea, and particularly the free trade agreement, represent the first concrete instance of a new and more expansive approach to the trade and environment nexus, which the EU wishes to replicate in its future FTA negotiations.[450] Where relevant, the trade and environment provisions of the FTA with South Korea will be compared with those of the FTA with Colombia and Peru (COPE),[451] which was initialled in March 2011, and is equally representative of the new trend in addressing the trade and environment nexus, although with some legal differences. Second, the Partnership and Cooperation Agreements (PCAs) concluded by the EU with CIS countries will be briefly discussed, highlighting their largely homogenous clauses related to the environment. As some CIS countries[452] participate in the EU's Neighbourhood Policy,[453] their PCAs present an interesting case-study for comparison with the Euro-Mediterranean association agreements analysed above.[454]

7.1 2010 Agreements with South Korea

EU-South Korea political and economic relations have evolved significantly since their first Framework Agreement on Trade and Cooperation concluded in 1996,[455] and particularly after South Korea was designated a priority partner in the EU's Global Europe Strategy. This is mostly demonstrated by the signing of two

[449] See s 2.2 above.

[450] Global Europe Strategy, 11. The priority trading partners with which the EU will seek to conclude such new-generation FTAs are, in addition to South Korea: the Association of South-East Asian Nations (comprising: Brunei Darussalam, Cambodia, Indonesia, Lao PDR, Malaysia, Myanmar (Burma), Philippines, Singapore, Thailand and Vietnam); the Gulf Cooperation Council countries (Bahrain, Kuwait, Oman, Qatar, Saudi Arabia and United Arab Emirates); India; MERCOSUR; and Russia.

[451] Above n 51.

[452] Namely: Armenia, Azerbaijan, Belarus, Georgia, Moldova and Ukraine.

[453] Above nn 129–31.

[454] See s 4 above.

[455] Framework Agreement for Trade and Cooperation between the European Community and its Member States, on the one hand, and the Republic of Korea, on the other hand [2001] OJ L90/46.

agreements in 2010: a Framework Agreement (FA) and an FTA.[456] The former provides the basis and institutional framework for strengthening political dialogue and economic cooperation across a wide range of issues, ranging from the non-proliferation of weapons of mass destruction and the fight against terrorism[457] to sustainable development (with a particular emphasis on climate change),[458] education and culture,[459] justice and security matters.[460] The FTA with South Korea is, as stated by the EU itself, 'groundbreaking': it is the first such trade deal to be concluded by the EU with an Asian country, containing the most comprehensive trade provisions outside the enlargement context.[461] The agreement has the ambitious goal of establishing a free trade area covering goods, services and investment and lays down far-reaching trade-related rules.[462]

Environmental concerns are integrated into both agreements from the outset, with preambular language reaffirming the Parties' commitment to 'promote sustainable development in its economic, social and environmental dimensions',[463] to 'ensure a high level of environmental protection',[464] and to 'strengthen the development and enforcement of labour and environmental laws and policies'.[465] In the FA, environmental protection forms part of the basis for bilateral cooperation, whereby the Parties reiterate their commitment 'to cooperate to address global environmental challenges, and in particular climate change',[466] and is also listed as one of the central aims of the agreement.[467] Under the FTA, sustainable development is recognised as an 'overarching objective', and the Parties commit 'to the development of international trade in such a way as to contribute to the objective of sustainable development and strive to ensure that this objective is integrated and reflected at every level'[468] of their trade relationship. Parties further undertake 'to promote foreign direct investment without lowering or reducing environmental [and other] standards'[469] as part of the overall objectives of the FTA.

7.1.1 Environmental cooperation clauses

The FA with South Korea contains two key provisions on environmental cooperation, both situated in the title dealing with 'cooperation in the area of sustainable

456 South Korea FA, above n 60; South Korea FTA, above n 61.
457 South Korea FA, title II.
458 Ibid, title V.
459 Ibid, title VI.
460 Ibid, title VII.
461 The agreement consists of 15 chapters, three protocols, several annexes and appendixes and four understandings.
462 South Korea FTA, art 1.
463 South Korea FA, preamble para 15.
464 Ibid, preamble, para 16.
465 South Korea FTA, preamble para 11.
466 South Korea FA, art 1(3).
467 Ibid, art 2(d)
468 South Korea FTA, art 1(g).
469 Ibid, art 1(h).

development':[470] one of general scope, entitled 'environment and natural resources'[471] and one specifically addressing climate change, recognised as a 'common global threat'.[472] Regular dialogue at policy and technical levels and the mutual exchange of information, expertise and best practices (including where possible through participation in each other's relevant programmes) are set as the principal modalities for implementation.[473]

Under the general provision, the Parties 'agree on the need to conserve, and manage in a sustainable manner, natural resources and biological diversity as a basis for the development of current and future generations.'[474] This is complemented by another, qualified statement that the 'outcome of the World Summit on the Sustainable Development and the implementation of relevant multilateral environmental agreements shall be taken into account, as relevant.'[475] Using similarly soft-law wording, Parties identify a list of priority environmental issues on which they 'shall endeavour to strengthen their cooperation', including in a regional context, including: climate change and energy efficiency; environmental awareness; participation and implementation of MEAs (emphasising those dealing with biodiversity and biosafety, and specifically mentioning CITES); promotion of environmental technologies, products and services (including environmental management systems and eco-labelling); prevention of illegal transboundary movement of hazardous substances, hazardous wastes and other forms of waste; costal and marine environment (conservation, pollution and degradation control); soil and land management; and local participation in environmental protection.[476]

Turning to the more specific provision on climate change, the Parties 'recognise the need to cut emissions in order to stabilise greenhouse gas concentrations at a level that would prevent dangerous anthropogenic interference with the climate system'[477] – that is, the overall objective of the international climate change regime.[478] They further undertake to enhance bilateral cooperation in this field (without prejudice to discussions in other fora, such as the UNFCCC), aimed in particular at: pursuing a rapid transition to low-carbon societies through nationally appropriate mitigation and adaptation actions; advocating an efficient use of resources (through, inter alia, widespread use of best available and economically viable low-carbon technologies and standards for mitigation and adaptation); exchanging information and expertise regarding the benefits of trading schemes

[470] South Korea FA, title V.

[471] Ibid, art 23.

[472] Ibid, art 24.

[473] Ibid, arts 2, 23(2)(i), 24(2) and 45(2).

[474] Ibid, art 23(1).

[475] Ibid, art 23(3).

[476] Ibid, art 23(2)(a)–(h).

[477] Ibid, art 24(1).

[478] UNFCCC, art 2, first sentence, reads: 'The ultimate objective of this Convention and any related legal instruments . . . is to achieve, in accordance with the relevant provisions of the Convention, stabilization of greenhouse gas concentrations in the atmosphere at a level that would prevent dangerous anthropogenic interference with the climate system.'

and the monitoring of greenhouse gases' effects; enhancing public and private sector financing instruments (including market mechanisms and public-private partnerships); collaborating on low-carbon technology research, development, diffusion, deployment and transfer; and supporting (where appropriate) mitigation and adaptation actions of developing countries, including through the Flexible Mechanisms of the Kyoto Protocol.[479]

7.1.2 Environmental integration clauses

Environmental concerns have been integrated into four cooperation areas under the FA with South Korea: agriculture, fisheries, energy and transport. Unlike in most of the other EU agreements examined, there is no cross-cutting clause on environmental integration, which is significant in the absence of specific environmental integration clauses in other cooperation areas, such as tourism and security.

In the field of *agriculture, rural development and forestry*, the Parties undertake to exchange information and develop cooperation on, inter alia: the integration of environmental requirements into agriculture policy; sustainable forest management to prevent deforestation and encourage the creation of new woodland ('including due regard to the interests of developing countries where timber is sourced'); and more generally on the links between these three policy fields and the environment.[480] In the area of *fisheries*, they are required to 'encourage marine and fisheries cooperation, at bilateral and multilateral levels, particularly with a view to promoting sustainable and responsible marine and fisheries development and management.'[481]

Best-endeavour language is utilised for the integration of environmental concerns into the *energy* sector, where Parties 'shall endeavour' to enhance cooperation (including through information exchanges and joint studies) 'with a view to', inter alia: developing new sustainable, innovative and renewable forms of energy (including biofuels and biomass, wind and solar energy as well as hydropower generation); promoting energy efficiency in production, transportation, distribution and end-use of energy; and fostering the transfer of technology aimed at sustainable energy production and energy efficiency.[482]

While also framed in best-endeavour terms, the clause on environmental integration in the field of *transport* is more detailed. Environmental protection figures

[479] South Korea FA, art 24(1)(a)–(g). The Flexible Mechanisms were introduced in the international climate change regime to provide cost-effective ways to comply with the time-bound and quantified emission reduction obligations of the Kyoto Protocol. The Flexible Mechanisms include the Joint Implementation, the international emissions trading and the CDM: see arts 6, 17 and 12 respectively of the Kyoto Protocol. The CDM is also mentioned in other bilateral or inter-regional agreements analysed in this chapter (namely, the Central America AA and the CARIFORUM EPA, above nn 233 and 364), as it is the only Flexible Mechanism involving developing country parties to the Kyoto Protocol. Note that South Korea is not included in the UNFCCC Annex I or the Kyoto Protocol Annex B, and has therefore no specific emission reduction commitments under the international climate change regime.

[480] South Korea FA, art 25(f), (g) and (i).

[481] Ibid, art 26.

[482] Ibid, art 17(1)(a), (c) and (d).

among the objectives of bilateral cooperation in this field,[483] with a requirement to promote, inter alia, regulatory convergence on the environmental aspects of transport policy, the reduction of greenhouse emissions in the transport sector and the implementation of pollution prevention standards (notably as regards maritime transport and aviation) 'in line with the relevant international conventions applicable to both Parties, including cooperation in the appropriate international fora aimed at ensuring better enforcement of international regulations.'[484]

7.1.3 *Trade and environment*

Environmental concerns have been decisively integrated into the EU-Korea FTA, where a whole chapter is devoted to 'trade and sustainable development',[485] and deals, inter alia, with trade and environment regulatory linkages.[486] This chapter addresses the trade and environmental nexus along the lines of the provisions of the EU-CARIFORUM EPA seen earlier,[487] albeit with some legal and institutional differences. To further highlight these differences, relevant provisions will be compared with those in the trade and sustainable development chapter of the FTA with COPE,[488] which includes instead a closed list of MEAs as was seen in the context of the Association with Central America.[489] This comparative exercise will illustrate the extent to which there is an incipient systematic approach to the trade and environment nexus in the post-Global Europe agreements, regardless of whether these involve developing countries or more advanced economies (notably, South Korea).[490]

The FTA with South Korea begins by reaffirming, in best-endeavour language, the Parties' commitment to ensure the *mutual supportiveness* between trade and sustainable development (and not specifically between 'trade and environment' as in the CARIFORUM EPA): 'the Parties reaffirm their commitments to promoting the development of international trade in such a way as to contribute to the objective of sustainable development' and to 'strive to ensure that this objective is integrated and reflected at every level of their trade relationship'.[491] This is to be achieved through, inter alia, the promotion (including by addressing non-tariff barriers) of trade and investment in environmental goods and services (such as environmental technologies, sustainable renewable energy, energy efficient products and services and eco-labelled goods),[492] as under the CARIFORUM EPA. The EU and South Korea also 'underline the benefit of cooperation on trade-related

483 Ibid, art 18(1).
484 Ibid, art 18 (2)(b), (c) and (e).
485 South Korea FTA, chapter 13.
486 Chapter 13 of the South Korea FTA also addresses trade and labour issues.
487 See s 5.3.2 above.
488 COPE FTA, Title IX.
489 See s 5.3.2 above.
490 South Korea, unlike the other countries, is ranked (number 12) within the 'very high human development' group in terms of the Human Development Index (see above n 179).
491 South Korea FTA, art 13.1(1).
492 Ibid, art 13.6(2).

social and environmental issues as part of a global approach to trade and sustainable development', and commit to undertake a number of cooperative activities (discussed below).[493] Several international instruments, including Agenda 21[494] and the WSSD Plan of Implementation,[495] are identified as providing the context of this chapter.[496] The FTA with COPE makes reference to these, as well as to the Rio Declaration,[497] the MDGs and WSSD Declaration[498] as the international backdrop of its sustainable and development chapter. There Parties also undertake to promote the mutual supportiveness between trade and sustainable development,[499] using similar language to that used in the FTA with Korea, and commit to carry out a number of cooperative activities (discussed below).

Regarding *standards of environmental protection*, the FTA with South Korea makes clear from the outset that it is not the intention of the Parties to harmonise such standards, but 'to strengthen their trade relations and cooperation in ways that promote sustainable development.'[500] The agreement, however, contains provisions linking domestic environmental performance with MEAs in more concrete terms than the CARIFORUM EPA. While recognising their respective sovereign right to regulate, the EU and South Korea 'shall seek to ensure' that their domestic laws and policies provide for a 'high level' of environmental protection – which is here framed, unlike in the CARIFORUM EPA, as 'consistent with the internationally recognised standards' – and 'shall strive to continue to improve those policies and laws.'[501] This should be read in conjunction with another provision explicitly devoted to MEAs, under which the Parties 'reaffirm their commitments to the effective implementation in their laws and practices of the multilateral environmental agreements to which they are party.'[502] Thus, the FTA with South Korea embraces international environmental standards as the benchmark for assessing domestic environmental performance but fails to specify the MEAs in question, like the CARIFORUM EPA.

In contrast, the FTA with COPE links more specifically domestic environment performance with an almost identical closed list of MEAs that is found in the Association with Central America. While a sovereign right to regulate[503] is also recognised under the FTA with COPE, each Party shall 'strive to ensure' that its laws and policies provide for a 'high level'[504] of environmental protection, which

[493] Ibid, art 13.1(2).
[494] Above n 310.
[495] Ibid.
[496] South Korea FTA, art 13.1(1).
[497] Above n 269.
[498] Above n 302.
[499] COPE FTA, art 267(1). The Parties also reiterate their commitment to address global environmental challenges 'in accordance with the principle of common but differentiated responsibilities' (art 267(4)).
[500] South Korea FTA, art 13.1(3).
[501] South Korea FTA, art 13.3.
[502] Ibid, art 13.5(1)–(2).
[503] COPE FTA, art 268.
[504] Ibid.

is here defined as 'consistent' with the following MEAs: the Montreal Protocol, the Basel Convention, the POPs Convention, CITES, the CBD and its Biosafety Protocol, the Kyoto Protocol, and the Rotterdam Convention.[505] This almost complete[506] matching in provisions between the FTA with COPE and the Association with Central America can be partly explained by the fact that all these countries are, until these agreements come into force, accessing the EU market under the terms of the 'GSP-plus', which requires the ratification and effective implementation of all the listed MEAs, with the exception of the Rotterdam Convention.[507] The FTA with COPE, however, presents a variation to the closed list when compared with the Association with Central America, as it expressly provides for an institutional mechanism to enable amendments of the list.[508]

As under the CARIFORUM EPA, a bold commitment to *uphold levels of protection* is also laid down in the FTA with South Korea, although it is narrower in scope:

> A Party shall not fail to effectively enforce its environmental and labour laws, through a sustained or recurring course of action or inaction, in a manner affecting trade or investment between the Parties.
>
> A Party shall not weaken or reduce the environmental or labour protections afforded in its laws to encourage trade or investment, by waiving or otherwise derogating from, or offering to waive or otherwise derogate from, its laws, regulations or standards, in a manner affecting trade or investment between the Parties.[509]

It should be noted that no additional provision on this matter is found in the investment chapter of the FTA with Korea, unlike in the CARIFORUM EPA where Parties are also under an obligation to ensure that investors do not manage or operate their investments in a manner that circumvents international environmental obligations.[510] This is also the case in the FTA with COPE, where there is only one provision on upholding the level of environmental protection,[511] similar to those found in the Korea FTA and in the Association with Central America. Just like the latter agreement, the FTA with COPE clarifies that that a Party may

505 Ibid, art 270(2). Note that strengthening compliance with this MEAs also figures among the objectives of the trade and sustainable title (art 267(2)).

506 The only difference is that in the Association with Central America the Rotterdam Convention is not included in the list but in a separate provision in which Parties undertake to ratify the Convention (Central America AA, art 287(4)).

507 See Ch 3, s 4.2.

508 COPE FTA, art 270(3), by the Parties based on a recommendation of the Trade Committee following a proposal from the Subcommittee on Trade and Sustainable Development.

509 South Korea FTA, art 13.7. The comparable provision in the EU-CARIFORUM EPA also addresses the 'other side of the coin', by further prohibiting the adoption or application of 'regional or national trade or investment-related legislation or other related administrative measures in a way which has the effect of frustrating measures intended to benefit, protect or conserve the environment or natural resources' (see s 5.3.2 above).

510 CARIFORUM EPA, art 72 (see s 5.3.2 above).

511 COPE FTA, art 277, prohibiting the Parties from waiving (or otherwise derogating) from domestic environmental laws in order to 'encourage trade and investment', and/or from failing to effectively enforce such laws (through a sustained or recurring course of action or inaction) in a manner 'affecting trade and investment' between them.

not undertake law enforcement activities in the territory of another Party.[512] The FTA with COPE further recognises the right of each Party to a 'reasonable discretion with regard to the decision on resource allocation relating to investigation, control and enforcement of domestic environmental . . . regulations and standards'.[513]

The FTA with South Korea also deals with *the design and implementation of measures* aimed at protecting the environment, albeit in soft-law terms. First, the Parties 'recognise the importance' of taking account of scientific and technical information, and relevant international standards, guidelines or recommendations, when preparing and implementing such environmental measures.[514] In addition, the Parties 'agree to' develop, introduce and implement any environmental measures that affects trade between them in a transparent manner, with due notice and public consultation, and with appropriate and timely communication to and consultation of non-state actors, including the private sector.[515] Given the different development context when compared to the CARIFORUM EPA, special and differential treatment is not made applicable to the design and implementation of environmental measures affecting trade between the EU and South Korea.

Unlike the CARIFORUM EPA, the FTA with South Korea does not contain a specific environmental exception clause, but fully incorporates the general exception clause from the GATT.[516] Thus, the right of the Parties to adopt (or maintain) measures 'necessary to protect human, animal, or plant life or health' (Article XX(b) GATT), and/or 'related to the conservation of exhaustible natural resources' (Article XX(g) GATT) is recognised, subject to the requirement that such measures are not applied in a manner that would constitute a means of arbitrary or unjustifiable discrimination or a disguised restriction on trade between them (Article XX-chapeau GATT). The agreement further stresses that environmental standards 'should not be used' for protectionist trade purposes, and in even softer terms, the Parties 'note that their comparative advantage should in no way be called into question'.[517] Notwithstanding the soft-law language used, this recognition is important, particularly for developing countries, and it should be recalled that it was absent in the CARIFORUM EPA.[518] The FTA with COPE contains a more general provision (albeit in mandatory language) that environmental measures (including those undertaken to implement MEAs) 'shall not' be applied

[512] COPE FTA, art 277(4).

[513] Ibid, art 277(3).

[514] South Korea FTA, art 13.8.

[515] Ibid, art 13.9.

[516] South Korea FTA, art 2.15(1). In the context of trade in services and investment, the FTA with South Korea (Chapter 7, art 7.50) replicates the general exception clause found in the association with Chile, integrating environmental concerns more broadly than art XIV GATS by also including 'measures relating to the conservation of natural exhaustible resources if such measures are applied in conjunction with restrictions on domestic supply or consumption of services and on domestic investments' as a ground for exception.

[517] Ibid, art 13.2(2).

[518] Albeit a similar formulation is found in the Cotonou Agreement (see s 5.2.4 above).

in a manner which would constitute 'a means of arbitrary or unjustifiable discrimination' or a 'disguised restriction' on trade between the Parties,[519] but does not address the question of 'comparative advantage'.

Finally, the FTA with South Korea provides for *cooperation in relation to trade and environmental issues.* Parties commit to initiate cooperative activities, such as to: promote the ratification of MEAs that have an impact on trade; cooperate on their trade-related aspects (including customs) and exchange views on the relationship between these agreements and international trade rules; exchange views on the positive and negative impacts of their FTA on sustainable development (including sustainability impact assessments carried out by the Parties); and exchange views on the trade impact of their environmental regulations, norms and standards. In addition, Parties commit to cooperate on trade-related aspects of a series of global environmental issues, namely: the current *and future* international climate change regime (including issues relating to global carbon markets, ways to address adverse effects of trade on climate, as well as means to promote low-carbon technologies and energy efficiency); biodiversity (including in relation to biofuels); sustainable fishing practices; and deforestation (including by addressing problems regarding illegal logging).[520] The agreement further emphasises cooperation in international fora (in particular in the context of the UN Environment Programme, MEAs and the WTO): 'the Parties commit to consulting and cooperating as appropriate with respect to negotiations on trade-related environmental issues of mutual interest'.[521]

The FTA with COPE is more detailed in elaborating cooperation on trade and environment issues. First, like other agreements, the FTA with COPE identifies possible cooperation activities, including: the evaluation of the impacts of the FTA on the environment; the monitoring and effective implementation of MEAs, including trade-related aspects; activities related to climate change adaptation and mitigation, including REDD; and exchange of information and experiences related to the promotion of corporate social responsibility.[522] In addition, it provides for positive trade measures to support sustainable development, along the lines of the Association with Central America. Pursuant to the general provision on 'trade favouring sustainable development',[523] parties: 'shall strive' to facilitate and promote trade and FDI in environmental goods and services; 'agree to promote' best business practices related to corporate social responsibility; and 'recognise' that flexible, voluntary and incentive-based mechanisms can contribute to coherence between trade practices and the objectives of sustainable development. A specific provision deals with sustainable trade in forest products, that not only refers to CITES but (unlike the Association with Central America) also

[519] COPE FTA, arts 267(5) and 270(4). This FTA also lacks a specific environmental exception clause and just incorporates the wording of art XX GATT (art 178).

[520] South Korea FTA, art 13.11 and Annex 13. On cooperation on the future climate change regime, see explicit reference to the Bali Action Plan in art 13.5(3).

[521] Ibid, art 13.5(1).

[522] COPE FTA, art 286.

[523] Ibid, art 271.

to transparency and public participation, independent supervision and certification without an explicit mention of the EU FLEGT initiative.[524] Sustainable trade in fish products also receives specific attention, and reference is made to cooperation with regional fisheries management organisations rather than also to global instruments[525] (which was the case in the Association with Central America). Similarly to the Association with Central America, the FTA with COPE includes a provision on the precautionary approach.[526]

Finally, it is significant that only the FTA with COPE contains provisions exclusively devoted to climate change and biodiversity within the sustainable and development chapter. The provision on climate change makes reference to the international climate change regime and emphasises adaptation, coupled with commitments to: promote the sustainable use of natural resources; promote trade and investment measures facilitating technology transfer for adaptation and mitigation; facilitate the removal of trade and investment barriers to climate-related goods, services and technologies; and promote measures for energy efficiency and renewable energy.[527] A uniquely wide-ranging provision is dedicated to biological diversity, which is considered 'a key element for the achievement of sustainable development'.[528] In the provision, Parties 'recognise' their commitments towards: the creation of protected area systems, in light of applicable international goals; joint promotion of programmes to foster economic returns from the conservation and sustainable use of biodiversity; the protection, respect and maintenance of traditional knowledge and the encouragement of benefit-sharing. The latter part of the provision goes beyond the letter of CBD,[529] by requiring the 'prior informed consent' of the holders of traditional knowledge (indigenous and local communities), thereby using language that is more in line with relevant human rights instruments but remains controversial in the CBD context.[530] Only the

[524] Ibid, art 273.

[525] Ibid, art 274.

[526] Ibid, art 278, titled 'scientific information', which reads: 'The Parties recognize the importance, when preparing and implementing measures aimed at protecting . . . the environment which affect trade between the Parties, of taking into account scientific and technical information and relevant international standards, guidelines and recommendations, while acknowledging that, where there are threats of serious or irreversible damage, lack of full scientific certainty should not be used as a reason for postponing protective measures.'

[527] Ibid, art 275.

[528] Ibid, art 272(1).

[529] CBD art 8(j), above n 357.

[530] Note that reference to 'prior informed consent' under the CBD can be found in the Programme of Work on Article 8(j), where general principle 4 refers to 'prior informed consent or prior informed approval from the holders of such knowledge, innovations and practices' (see CBD, Decision V/16, *Article 8(j) and related provisions* (2000) UN Doc UNEP/CBD/COP/5/23). Nonetheless, evidence of CBD Parties' inability to unequivocally incorporate 'prior informed consent' can be found in the text of the Nagoya Protocol on Access to Genetic Resources and the Fair and Equitable Sharing of Benefits Arising from their Utilization to the Convention on Biological Diversity (2010) UN Doc UNEP/CBD/COP/DEC/X/1 (throughout this book, Nagoya Protocol on Access and Benefit-Sharing), where reference is made throughout to 'prior informed consent or the approval and involvement of indigenous and local communities.' For a discussion, see E Morgera and E Tsioumani, 'Yesterday, Today and Tomorrow: Looking Afresh at the Convention on Biological Diversity' (forthcoming) 21 *Yearbook of International Environmental Law.*

CARIFORUM EPA included a provision on cooperation related to traditional knowledge, but without reference to 'prior informed consent.'[531] The FTA with COPE also includes an unusual commitment, couched in best-endeavour language, to ensure access and benefit-sharing related to genetic resources.[532]

7.1.4 Institutional aspects

Both agreements with South Korea contain institutional provisions that are applicable to their respective provisions (including environment-related clauses), and which are set to form part of a common institutional framework.[533]

The FA, for its part, establishes a general Joint Committee (consisting of representatives of the Council and the Commission on the EU side and of members of the South Korean government on the other) that is entrusted with facilitating the implementation and further the general aims of the agreement, as well as to ensure coherence with other specific agreements concluded by the Parties (such as the FTA). The Committee is mandated to: ensure the proper operation of the FA and set priorities in relation to its aims; monitor the development of the Parties' relationship and make suggestions on future actions; request information and consider reports from bodies established under other specific agreements; and dispute-avoidance and resolution.[534] Implementation of the agreement is thus to be carried out through dialogue and consensus, and is the primary responsibility of the Parties, which are under an obligation to take any general or specific measure required to fulfil their obligations under the agreement and to comply with its objectives.[535]

Any dispute arising within the context of the FA should first be addressed through consultations (with the possibility of mediation if the Parties agree) in the Joint Committee, and where these fail to lead to a settlement of the dispute, through arbitration leading to a final decision (by majority voting) that is binding upon the Parties. No provision is made for temporary remedies in cases of non-compliance.[536] As in the case of most other EU agreements, the adoption of unilateral 'appropriate measures' without prior consultation against an infringing Party is limited to 'cases of special urgency' and thus is unlikely to be applicable to environment-related provisions that are essentially conceived in cooperative terms.[537]

531 CARIFORUM EPA, art 150(1) in s 5.3.3 above.
532 COPE FTA, art 272(2)–(5).
533 South Korea FA, art 43(4).
534 Ibid, art 44.
535 Ibid, art 45.
536 South Korea FA, arts 45 and 46.
537 In fact, a 'Joint Declaration concerning Articles 45 and 46' in the South Korea FA specifies that 'cases of special urgency' refer to a 'material breach' of the agreement by one of the Parties, consisting in either a repudiation of the agreement not sanctioned by general rules of international law or a 'particularly serious and substantial' violation of the 'essential elements' clause (art 1(1)).

The FTA with Korea, in turn, provides for a more detailed institutional mechanism to deal specifically with its trade and sustainable development chapter, in line with the recent EU practice already discussed in the context of the CARIFORUM EPA and the Association with Central America.[538] A specialised Committee on Trade and Sustainable Development (exact composition to be determined, but likely to involve also environmental experts from both sides at senior official level)[539] is established to oversee the implementation of the trade and sustainable development chapter, including the identification of cooperative activities foreseen therein.[540] This is comparable to the Sub-committee on Trade and Sustainable Development established by the FTA with COPE, although the latter provides more details as to its functions, including: identifying specific actions and areas of cooperation, verifying the effective implementation of the cooperation, and assessing the impacts of the implementation of the FTA on the environment; while promoting transparency and public participation by considering inputs from the public and making its decisions and reports available to the public.[541]

Under the FTA with South Korea, each Party is also required to set up a Domestic Advisory Group on sustainable development (comprising members from 'independent' civil society organisations in a balanced representation of environment, labour and business organisations as well as other stakeholders) with the task of advising on the chapter's implementation.[542] Both the FTA with South Korea and that with COPE foresee a mechanism for conducting dialogue with these stakeholders (an annual Civil Society Forum), which may submit opinions to the Parties regarding the sustainable development aspects of their trade relations.[543] In addition, the FTA with South Korea includes a commitment to reviewing, monitoring and assessing the impacts of the implementation of the FTA on sustainable development through their respective participatory processes as well as through instruments set up under the agreement, with specific reference to sustainability impact assessments.[544]

Any dispute between the EU and South Korea concerning the trade and sustainable development chapter of the FTA should be resolved solely through the specific dispute settlement procedure provided therein,[545] which resembles (but is

538 See s 5.3.4 above.

539 Given that this is created as a specialised committee to assist the general Trade Committee, composed of representatives from the EU Commission and South Korea responsible for trade matters. South Korea FTA, art 15.1(2).

540 Ibid, art 13.12(2).

541 COPE FTA, art 280, particularly 280(6).

542 South Korea FTA, art 13.12(4) and (5). A more general commitment to ensure domestic consultations with environmental and sustainable development committees can be found in the COPE FTA, art 281.

543 South Korea FTA, art 13.13; COPE FTA, art 282.

544 South Korea FTA, art 13.10. Note that COPE FTA, art 279 provides for a more general commitment to review, monitor and assess the impacts of the FTA implementation on the environment through Parties' respective domestic and participatory processes.

545 South Korea FTA, art 13.16.

not identical to) that found in the CARIFORUM EPA.[546] Parties are first required to seek a mutually satisfactory resolution of the matter through consultations (including within the Committee on Trade and Sustainable Development). As a general rule, these consultations should not take longer than three months, and the Parties 'may' seek advice from Domestic Advisory Groups as well as from competent international bodies.[547] Significantly, Parties 'shall ensure' that the resolution arrived at 'reflects the activities of . . . relevant multilateral environmental organisations or bodies so as to promote greater cooperation and coherence between the work of the Parties and these organisations'[548] – a specification not made in the CARIFORUM EPA, Association with Central America or in the FTA with COPE.[549] Where these initial governmental consultations do not lead to a satisfactory resolution, any Party may request that a Panel of Experts be convened to examine the matter in question and present a report to the Parties within three months (as a general rule). Interestingly, all 15 members of the Panel are required to have expertise on sustainable development issues, be fully independent and not take instructions from either the Parties or the organisations represented in the Domestic Advisory Groups (that is, civil society and other stakeholders). At least five of the Panel's members must be non-nationals of either Party. In its deliberations, the Panel 'should seek advice' from the Domestic Advisory Groups as well as from competent international organisations. There is, however, no strict obligation of compliance with the Panel's report: 'Parties shall make their best efforts to accommodate the advice or recommendations of the Panel of Experts', although the implementation of such recommendations is to be monitored by the Committee on Trade and Sustainable Development.[550]

This is also the case of the FTA with COPE, which lays down a similar dispute settlement procedure to deal specifically with disputes arising in the context of its trade and sustainable development chapter, including inter-Party consultations[551] and the establishment of a Group of Experts,[552] whose recommendations are not strictly binding upon the Parties.[553] Thus, unlike under the CARIFORUM EPA, no kind of sanction is available under the other three post-Global Europe agreements examined (FTA with South Korea, Association with Central America, and FTA with COPE) to enforce their respective trade and environment provisions.

546 See s 5.3.4 above.

547 South Korea FTA, art 13.14.

548 Ibid, art 13.14 (2).

549 As to the latter, see COPE FTA, art 283.

550 South Korea FTA, art 13.15.

551 COPE FTA, art 283.

552 Ibid, arts 284 and 285.

553 Ibid, art 285(4) reads: 'The Party to the procedure concerned shall inform the Subcommittee on Trade and Sustainable Development of its intentions as regards the recommendations of the Group of Experts, including the presentation of an action plan to implement the recommendations. The Subcommittee on Trade and Sustainable Development shall monitor the implementation of the measures that such Party has determined.'

7.2 Partnership and cooperation agreements with CIS countries

EU relations with the Eastern European and Central Asian countries that are members of the Commonwealth of Independent States are presently regulated by bilateral PCAs,[554] which were concluded during the mid-1990s to replace the 1989 Trade and Cooperation Agreement with the former Soviet Union,[555] and to provide these countries with a framework for the development of 'close' political and economic relations with the EU but as an alternative to accession. All PCAs define the objectives of the partnership in broadly similar terms, including: to provide an appropriate framework for the development of political relations; to promote trade and investment; to provide a basis for cooperation in various fields (ranging from environment, energy and transport to social, cultural, and immigration matters), and to support the partners' efforts to consolidate its transition to democracy and to a market economy.[556] As in other EU agreements, respect for human rights and democratic principles are set as 'essential elements' of the PCAs.[557] They also create an institutional structure, which is similar to that seen under other general agreements, comprising of a Cooperation Council, a Cooperation Committee and a Parliamentary Cooperation Committee, which are responsible for conducting political dialogue and ensuring a smooth application of the agreement.[558] Yet, unlike other agreements examined, the PCAs do not establish a free trade area between the EU and the countries concerned. As a result, these countries currently access the EU market under the generalised system of preferences, and a few of them under the 'GSP-plus' arrangement.[559] Nonetheless, the EU relations with some CIS countries[560] may be upgraded through new agreements negotiated in the context of the European Neighbourhood Policy, which are likely to provide for, inter alia, the establishment of a free trade and the (partial) integration of these countries into the EU market.[561]

The following sections offer an overview of the environmental cooperation and integration provisions of the PCAs. In this regard, Parties to most PCAs express the desire of 'establishing close cooperation in the area of environment protection taking into account the interdependence existing between the Parties in this field',[562] and include among their overall aims an explicit linkage between the

[554] Above nn 41–49.

[555] Agreement between the European Economic Community and the European Atomic Energy Community and the Union of Soviet Socialist Republics on trade and commercial and economic cooperation [1990] OJ L68/3.

[556] Art 1 in all PCAs.

[557] Art 2 in all PCAs.

[558] See Koutrakos, above n 39, 363–65.

[559] Namely: Armenia, Azerbaijan (since January 2009) and Republic of Moldova (from December 2005 to December 2008). See further Ch 4, s 4.2.

[560] Namely: Armenia, Azerbaijan, Belarus, Georgia, Moldova and Ukraine.

[561] On the ENP, see s 4.1 and nn 129–31 above.

[562] Kazakhstan PCA, preamble; Kyrgyzstan PCA, preamble; and Uzbekistan PCA, preamble.

promotion of bilateral economic relations and the fostering of their sustainable economic development.[563]

7.2.1 Environmental cooperation clauses

All the PCAs with CIS countries feature the same, detailed article on environmental cooperation requiring parties to develop and strengthen their cooperation on environment and human health[564] and listing several specific areas for cooperation in mandatory terms. The list includes references to MEAs, such as implementation of the Basel Convention and of the Espoo Convention, as well as several other global issues that are covered by prominent MEAs, such as the 'conservation of biodiversity, protected areas and sustainable use and management of biological resources', and 'global climate change'. Other common priorities include: effective monitoring of pollution levels and environmental assessment; information systems on the state of the environment; combating local, regional and transboundary air and water pollution; ecological restoration; sustainable, efficient and environmentally effective production and use of energy; ecological safety of industrial plants; classification and safe handling of chemicals; water quality; the environmental impact of agriculture, soil erosion, and chemical pollution; the protection and renewal of forests; land-use planning, including construction and urban planning; use of economic and fiscal instruments; environmental education and awareness; technical assistance concerning rehabilitation of zones affected by radioactivity and addressing related health and social problems.[565]

The PCAs with CIS countries also spell out the means through which environmental cooperation should be undertaken, making reference to: environmental impact studies; disaster planning and other emergency situations; exchange of information and experts, including information and experts dealing with the transfer of clean technologies and the safe and environmentally sound use of biotechnologies; joint research activities; environmental training; and environmental monitoring. Significantly, in the same clause reference is also made to the approximation of laws towards EU standards, institutional strengthening, and cooperation within the framework of the European Environment Agency,[566] which could

[563] Armenia PCA, art 1; Azerbaijan PCA, art 1; Georgia PCA, art 1; Moldova PCA, art 1; Russia PCA, art 1.

[564] Armenia PCA, art 55(1); Azerbaijan PCA, art 56(1); Georgia PCA, art 57(1); Kazakhstan PCA, art 54(1); Kyrgyzstan PCA, art 55(1); Moldova PCA, art 61(1); Russia PCA, art 69(1); Uzbekistan PCA, art 54(1).

[565] Armenia PCA, art 55(2); Azerbaijan PCA, art 56(2); Georgia PCA, art 57(2); Kazakhstan PCA, art 54(2); Kyrgyzstan PCA, art 55(2); Moldova PCA, art 61(2); Russia PCA, art 69(2); Uzbekistan PCA, art 54(2).

[566] Armenia PCA, art 55(3); Azerbaijan PCA, art 56(3); Georgia PCA, art 57(3); Kazakhstan PCA, art 54(3); Kyrgyzstan PCA, art 55(3); Moldova PCA, art 61(3); Russia PCA, art 69(3); Uzbekistan PCA, art 54(3). Note also a more general provision on 'legislative cooperation' that can be found in most agreements with CIS countries, requiring approximation of laws in the areas of protection of health and life of humans, animals and plants, the environment, the exploitation and utilisation of natural resources, consumer protection, technical rules and standards, nuclear laws and regulations and transport (Azerbaijan PCA, art 43(2); Georgia PCA, art 43(2); Moldova PCA, art 50(2); and Russia PCA, art 55(2)).

be compared to those of associations with candidate countries and of some Euro-Mediterranean associations.[567] It should also be stressed that the list of means to pursue environmental cooperation explicitly includes provisions for alliance-building in multilateral fora, by making reference to 'cooperation at regional level and at international level' and the 'development of strategies, particularly with regard to global and climatic issues and also in view of achieving sustainable development.'[568]

7.2.2 Environmental integration clauses

The PCAs with CIS countries include environmental integration clauses in the areas of social and economic cooperation, agriculture, energy, mining, industrial development, construction, and organised crime. A common provision on *social cooperation* specifically concerning health and safety, requires cooperation between parties on the prevention of major accident hazards and the management of toxic chemicals.[569] A similar function is also played by general clauses on economic cooperation in the PCAs with CIS countries, according to which economic cooperation is to be 'guided by the requirements of sustainability and harmonious social development' and 'fully incorporate environmental considerations'.[570] This general clause is particularly significant for areas of economic cooperation (such as transport or tourism) where no specific environmental integration clause is found.

The vast majority of agreements with CIS countries require that *agricultural cooperation* be pursued 'in conditions that ensure the protection of the environment, taking into account the necessity to improve security of food supply as well as the development of agribusiness, the processing and distribution of agricultural products.'[571] The same provision also requires the gradual approximation of standards to EU technical regulations concerning industrial and agricultural food products including sanitary and phytosanitary standards. The Agreement with the Russian Federation is, however, weaker in requiring simply agricultural cooperation 'in conditions which ensure that the environment is respected' through, inter alia, 'improvement of agricultural land-use planning' and achieving 'compatibility between their sanitary and phytosanitary standards'.[572]

The Agreements with the Russian Federation and Moldova employ mandatory language referring to the improvement of *energy* supply, including security of supply, in an economic and environmentally sound manner, promotion of energy saving and energy efficiency, and the assessment of environmental impacts of

[567] See ss 3.3 and 4.2 above.

[568] Armenia PCA, art 55(3); Azerbaijan PCA, art 56(3); Georgia PCA, art 57(3); Moldova PCA, art 61(3); Russia PCA, art 69(3).

[569] Kazakhstan PCA, art 61; Kyrgyzstan PCA, art 61; Uzbekistan PCA, art 60.

[570] Armenia PCA, art 44(2); Azerbaijan PCA, art 44(2); Georgia PCA, art 45(2); Kazakhstan PCA, art 44(2); Kyrgyzstan PCA, art 45(2); Moldova PCA, art 51(2); Russia PCA, art 56(2); Uzbekistan PCA, art 43(2).

[571] Armenia PCA, art 53; Azerbaijan PCA, art 54; Georgia PCA, art 55; Moldova PCA, art 59; Kazakhstan PCA, art 52; Kyrgyzstan PCA, art 53; Uzbekistan PCA, art 52.

[572] Russia PCA, art 64.

energy production, supply and consumption, in order to prevent or minimise the environmental damage resulting from these activities.[573] On the other hand, the agreements with other CIS countries make reference to the 'promotion of energy saving and energy efficiency and implementation of the Energy Charter Protocol on energy efficiency and related environmental aspects'.[574] This can be explained by the fact that the Russian Federation is not a party to the Protocol, and Moldova became one a few years after the conclusion of the PCA with the EU.[575] The Agreement with Uzbekistan is the only one among those with CIS countries that explicitly refers to the development of hydro-electric and other renewable energy resources.[576]

Some of the agreements with CIS countries include the same provision on cooperation in increasing investment and trade in *mining* and raw materials, which mandates a focus on, inter alia, the adoption and implementation of environmental legislation.[577] With regard to *industrial development*, mandatory language provides for cooperation to aim at promoting, inter alia, environmental protection in most PCAs,[578] with the exception of the Agreement with the Russian Federation that instead requires industrial development cooperation to aim at promoting efforts in both the public and private sector, to restructure and modernise the sector, 'under conditions ensuring environment protection and sustainable development'.[579] Some PCAs also include a provision on *construction*, which requires cooperation in modernising and restructuring the construction sector in the partner country in line with the principles of a market economy and 'duly taking into account related health, safety and environmental aspects.'[580]

Finally, clauses integrating certain environmental concerns in cooperation on combating *organised crime* can also be found in most agreements with CIS countries, where Parties are mandated to establish cooperation aimed at preventing illegal transactions of industrial waste.[581]

8. ASSESSMENT AND CONCLUSIONS

Environmental concerns have generally been integrated into the *definition* of EU external relations through agreements with third countries or regions: an

573 Moldova PCA, art 60(2); Russia PCA, art 65(2).

574 Armenia PCA, art 54; Azerbaijan PCA, art 55; Georgia PCA, art 56; Kazakhstan PCA, art 53; Kyrgyzstan PCA, art 54; Uzbekistan PCA, art 53; see also their respective preambles.

575 ECOLEX on membership at www.ecolex.org.

576 Uzbekistan PCA, art 53.

577 Azerbaijan PCA, art 51; Georgia PCA, art 52; Kazakhstan PCA, art 49; Kyrgyzstan PCA, art 50; Moldova PCA, art 56; Russia PCA, art 61; Uzbekistan PCA, art 49.

578 Armenia PCA, art 46; Azerbaijan PCA, art 46; Georgia PCA, art 47; Kazakhstan PCA, art 45; Kyrgyzstan PCA, art 46; Moldava PCA, art 52; Uzbekistan PCA, art 45.

579 Russia PCA, art 57.

580 Azerbaijan PCA, art 47; Georgia PCA, art 48; Russia PCA, art 68.

581 Armenia PCA, art 69; Azerbaijan PCA, art 72; Georgia PCA, art 72; Kazakhstan PCA, art 70; Russia PCA, art 84; Uzbekistan PCA, art 69.

approach based on cooperation and consultations has been favoured to that end. However, there has been no uniform practice in such an integration effort. Differentiation thus exists in relation to: (i) the degree of attention paid to the environment and the legal strength with which environmental requirements are formulated; (ii) the choice of standards underpinning environmental cooperation; (iii) the selection of priorities for environmental cooperation; (iv) the specific cooperation areas in which environmental concerns are integrated; (v) the approach to the trade and environment nexus; and finally (vi) the underlying institutional mechanisms. Yet, the agreements concluded after the endorsement of the Global Europe Strategy[582] reflect a more systematic approach to environmental integration. The key manifestations of these two approaches to environmental integration are discussed in each of the above-listed areas of differentiation in the following sub-sections, with a view to highlighting emerging questions of implementation that will be addressed in subsequent chapters of this book.

8.1 Differentiated emphasis on the environment

While environmental clauses can be found in all EU bilateral and inter-regional agreements examined, a gradually weaker prioritisation of the environment can be clearly detected, which is generally accompanied by a decreasing degree of strength in the legal wording used to formulate environmental commitments. At the outset, some degree of differentiation comes as no surprise, as the relative emphasis placed on environmental cooperation, and the legal wording and normative basis used to articulate it, are deemed to be dictated (at least to some extent) by the broader political and economic relationship that the EU has with the third country or region in question.

At the upper end of the spectrum are the Association and Stabilisation Agreements (concluded as a prelude to EU membership) and the Cotonou Agreement (concluded as a development tool), placing a comparatively stronger focus on environmental protection that is usually translated into legally-binding commitments. In the middle, are the Euro-Mediterranean Associations (concluded as a substitute to EU membership), which show a more varied emphasis on environmental protection together with a hybrid of mandatory and best-endeavours environmental clauses. These appear to be less ambitious in their wording and substance than the Partnership and Cooperation Agreements with CIS countries, which are characterised by legally binding language and detailed content (with the exception of the Agreement with the Russian Federation),[583] confirming the proposition advanced earlier in this chapter that an association, as the closest form of contractual relationship with the EU, does not necessarily

[582] Namely, the CARIFORUM EPA, the Association with Central America and the FTAs with South Korea and COPE.

[583] This can be explained in light of the EU and CIS membership in regional environmental agreements concluded under the UN Economic Commission for Europe.

bring about stronger commitments for environmental integration. At the lower end of the spectrum, are the associations as an instrument for inter-regional cooperation, which are characterised by a more generic approach to the environment often formulated in soft-law terms, although the Agreement with South Africa – perhaps due to the influence of the Cotonou Agreement negotiated in parallel – contains more detailed provisions and systematically underscores the regional dimension of environmental cooperation. The agreements with South Korea are more difficult to place within this spectrum: while their degree of focus and legal language could be generally compared (in form, not necessarily substance) to the Agreement with South Africa, they also contain groundbreaking trade and environment provisions.

In addition, a lack of uniform practice can be noted in relation to the environmental standards used across these agreements. Associations as a prelude to EU membership do (naturally) heavily rely on the EU *acquis* – which also includes international environmental standards binding upon the Union. It is understandable that the EU will actively use these agreements to export the EU *acquis* (including its environmental component) to candidate (and potential candidate) countries, and that it will do so through strict legally-binding provisions. Yet, it is less clear why exporting the EU environmental *acquis* is also being attempted in the Euro-Mediterranean context – an association ostensibly based on partnership and joint ownership, not candidacy – or even in the case of the Partnership and Cooperation Agreements with CIS countries. It is even less clear why a differentiated approach is being pursued to the approximation of laws between the EU and its MENA neighbours, if the long-term objective seems to remain economic integration at the Euro-Mediterranean level that would arguably be best served by a progressive harmonisation of environmental (and other) standards. Aside from policy coherence considerations, it should also be underscored that reliance on the EU *acquis* as the normative basis for environmental cooperation is not itself unproblematic. It will inevitably build upon the EU's own successes in environmental protection, as well as replicate its shortcomings. It also represents an important challenge for third countries that (albeit supported by EU assistance) are called upon to comply with an externally-determined and constantly-evolving set of rules.

Relying on international environmental standards, rather than on EU standards, is instead the approach of the Cotonou Agreement, which can be singled out as the agreement providing for most systematic references to MEAs across its array of cooperation activities. The post-Global Europe agreements have followed this trend, where a more systematic approach can be detected in using international environmental standards as the benchmark for assessing domestic environmental performance, with increased emphasis on questions related to implementation and enforcement. This appears to be a more appropriate course of action to legitimise the EU's efforts to promote environmental protection outside its borders and avoid criticisms on grounds of 'extra-territoriality' and 'neo-colonialism'. On the other hand, international environmental standards have hardly penetrated the associations with the Euro-Mediterranean countries, Chile and South Africa. Achieving consistency in referring to MEAs across EU associations and other agreements is thus critical in avoiding a double-standard approach to environmental integration in the EU's external relations.

In all cases, whether harmonisation of environmental standards is sought through an approximation to the EU *acquis*, or through bilateral/inter-regional commitments on MEA implementation, both need to be coupled with the necessary institutional and technical capacity-building assistance to ensure an even level of compliance among the Parties.

8.2 Different cooperation priorities and scope of integration

Differentiation has also manifested itself with regard to both the specific priorities for environmental cooperation, as well as the scope of environmental integration into other areas covered by the various agreements. Once again, some degree of differentiation at this level is to be expected, as it is reflective of the different environmental needs of the various EU partners involved. However, differentiation is certainly also a reflection of varying bargaining powers and dependency on EU assistance, as well as a product of the EU's own environmental priorities and broader interests towards a given country or region.

The content of environmental cooperation clauses does tend to vary significantly across the agreements, even within the same category of association. In all cases, these are generally drafted as open-ended clauses, allowing for ongoing re-assessment of cooperation priorities at the implementation stage through policy dialogue. Nonetheless, a number of global environmental issues have frequently been singled out, such as climate change, biodiversity, waste and chemicals management, and to a lesser extent also water, forests and environmental assessments.[584] Climate change, in particular, has gradually emerged not only as the key cooperation priority common to most agreements, but also as a distinct and ambitious area of environmental cooperation: most post-Global Europe agreements have either devoted a whole provision to climate change cooperation[585] or provided significantly detailed language on climate change in the context of cooperation on trade and sustainable development.[586] The insertion of these types of clauses is likely to become common practice in future agreements concluded by the EU (or as existing ones are reviewed), given the political priority attached to climate change by the EU.[587]

With regard to the scope of environmental integration, differentiation is first observed in the uneven presence of a cross-cutting clause requiring environmental concerns to be integrated across all areas of cooperation, and which is only

[584] See generally Ch 7.

[585] Cotonou Agreement-2010 revision, art 32bis; COPE FTA, art 275; and South Korea FA, art 24.

[586] Central America AA, arts 50(3) and 63; South Korea FTA, arts 13.5(3), 13.11 and Annex 13.

[587] See Ch 7, ss 2.1 and 3.1 for further discussion.

found in three categories of associations (the Stabilisation and Association Agreements, the Euro-Mediterranean Agreements and the Cotonou Agreement). In addition, the specific cooperation areas in which environmental concerns are explicitly integrated vary, but some are recurrent in most agreements. Energy is the area in which the agreements examined are most systematic in requiring environmental integration, generally using mandatory language and emphasising renewable energy and energy efficiency. Clauses providing for environmental integration in the agriculture sector are common but tend to be quite general. The only notable exception is that of association agreements as a prelude to EU membership, where environmental integration in the agriculture sector is based on approximation to EU law, which has not been considered very successful in that respect. The inclusion of clauses on environmental integration in industrial development and mining is also uneven, but significant in bringing forward the international agenda of the EU on corporate environmental accountability.[588] Only occasionally have environmental concerns been explicitly integrated into the transport and tourism sectors, and generally in soft law terms, although both have clear and important environmental implications. The increased emphasis on climate change cooperation, however, may well lead to a stronger focus on environmental integration into transport cooperation in future agreements.[589]

Environmental integration in the EU's external action in the area of fisheries is more complicated. The EU's bilateral and inter-regional agreements have frequently included provisions to this end, and in more recent cases explicit references to regional and/or international processes or instruments to ensure sustainability. However, it should be recalled that the EU negotiates independently and on a bilateral basis the so-called Fisheries Partnership Agreements, which have been criticised for the lack of actual environmental integration,[590] thus undermining the usefulness of the more general agreements between the EU and the third countries concerned. This may point to a possible trend by the EU to deal with certain critical natural resources (such as fisheries and timber products)[591] on a bilateral level that is separate from more general agreements, where the EU may find itself in a stronger negotiating position, albeit to the potential detriment of the policy coherence of its external action.[592]

[588] See Ch 7, s 4.2 for further discussion.

[589] Possibly following the example of the South Korea FA (s 7.1.2 above).

[590] J Vogler and C Bretherton, 'The European Union as a Sustainable Development Actor: the Case of External Fisheries Policy' (2008) 30(3) *Journal of European Integration* 401. These agreements, concluded as part of the EU common fisheries policy, seek to ensure access by EU fishing fleets to fisheries resources in the exclusive economic zone of partner countries.

[591] On timber products and sustainable forest management, the EU has initiated specialised bilateral negotiations under the FLEGT initiative, which will be discussed in Ch 7, s 4.1.

[592] Chaytor, above n 291, 5–6.

8.3 A differentiated approach to trade and environment nexus

Another important aspect of differentiation pertains to the trade and environment regulatory nexus, and is mainly due to a recent shift in EU practice towards a more elaborate and mutual supportiveness-focused approach. Traditionally, the only direct linkage between trade and environment found in EU agreements was in the general exception clause, usually modelled on Article 36 TFEU (except for the Association with Chile) that is considered more flexible than Article XX GATT in allowing Parties to pursue environmental protection objectives through trade measures. Yet, a change in approach is clearly observed in the Cotonou Agreement, and even more markedly in the post-Global Europe agreements that include a trade and sustainable development chapter, where the trade and environment nexus is not only seen through the lens of trade restrictions (exception clauses), but is further elaborated through positive commitments on 'mutual supportiveness' and 'high levels of protection' as well as cooperative measures. The EU intends, furthermore, to make these extended trade and environment provisions a recurrent practice in its future FTA negotiations.[593]

This move takes the EU's stance on integrating environmental concerns into trade policy within bilateral and regional agreements closer to US practice,[594] and beyond the current multilateral trade and environment agenda. In fact, the EU agreements are not primarily concerned with clarifying the relationship between WTO rules and specific trade obligations set out in MEAs, which is one of the key issues being discussed in the WTO Trade and Environment Committee in order to determine what WTO members can and cannot do to implement these international environmental obligations.[595] The post-Global Europe agreements are aimed instead at establishing what Parties should do in terms of promoting a 'high level' of environmental protection, and in particular what Parties should not do in terms of lowering environmental standards as a means to promote trade and investment – that is, the competitiveness dimension of the trade and environment nexus.[596] Albeit using best-endeavours language, these agreements seek to

[593] See the recent Commission, 'Communication on Trade, Growth and World Affairs – Trade Policy as a Coherent Component of the EU's 2020 Strategy' COM (2010) 612, 8 (emphasising the implementation of trade and sustainable development chapters in current agreements) and 9 (reiterating the ambition to include these chapters in future FTAs).

[594] Although the EU has (to date) distanced itself from the US approach to subject the enforcement of environmental clauses in FTAs to the same dispute-settlement procedures as for the trade provisions. For a comparative analysis, see Chaytor, above n 291, 15–24. It appears that the stronger enforcement mechanisms in the US FTAs are not implemented practice but rather used as a deterrent: see C George, 'Regional Trade Agreements and the Environment: Monitoring Implementation and Assessing Impacts: Report on the OECD Workshop' (2011) *OECD Trade and Environment Working Papers 2011/02*, 7; and S Jinnah, 'Strategic Linkages: The Evolving Role of Trade Agreements in Global Environmental Governance' (2011) 20(2) *Journal of Environment and Development* 191, 209.

[595] The North American Free Trade Agreement, for instance, contains a specific clause (art 104) that would exempt MEA-related measures from the agreement's trade disciplines. See Chaytor, above n 291, 27.

[596] See Ch 1, s 5.2, and in particular the discussion on the third dimension of the trade and environment that is not part of the multilateral trade and environment agenda.

anchor domestic environmental performance upon international environmental standards, either through an open-ended reference to the MEAs to which Parties are party (FTA with South Korea, and to a lesser extent CARIFORUM EPA), or through a closed list of specific MEAs (Association with Central America and FTA with COPE).

References to international standards or high levels of protection in relation to domestic environmental laws may be challenging particularly for developing countries, such as the ACP, which may find that they are called upon to enforce through their agreements with the EU higher environmental standards than they have the human, technical and financial capacity to implement. The fact that the CARIFORUM EPA recognises and addresses this, through its provisions on cooperation and capacity building (including with regard to MEA ratification and implementation), is undoubtedly a welcome step. But it remains to be seen whether, and how, this important cooperative element of the trade and environment nexus is given meaningful effect in practice. In fact, it has been argued that the CARIFORUM EPA was in this respect a 'missed opportunity' to elaborate on the substance of provisions that could be used as a demonstration of positively promoting mutual supportiveness of trade and environment.[597] The Agreements with Central America and COPE are more ambitious in this regard, providing also for a number of positive trade and trade-related measures to support sustainable development.

8.4 Institutional differentiation

A final element of differentiation concerns the institutional framework established under the various agreements. Interestingly, this institutional differentiation has gone hand in hand with the evolution in the trade and environment nexus seen above. Generally speaking, the agreements concluded by the EU do not entrust a particular institution with environmental issues, nor do they provide for specific procedures to settle environment-related disputes between the Parties. The general institutional provisions instead apply to environmental clauses. It is the joint body responsible for implementing and overseeing the whole agreement – typically an Association/Cooperation Council/Committee – that may also monitor progress on environmental clauses and make recommendations for improvement (and in some cases take binding decisions), as well as settle any environment-related dispute arising between the Parties. In line with the cooperative approach favoured in EU agreements, the Parties should seek to implement environmental provisions by consensus and to resolve disputes through consultations. Even if the possibility of arbitration exists, full enforceability through sanctions is generally excluded for environmental clauses. Very few

[597] Chaytor, above n 291, 7.

agreements (for example, the Association with Chile and the Cotonou Agreement) provide for public participation in these processes.

The post-Global Europe agreements – the agreements in which the trade and environment nexus is most comprehensive – offer important institutional innovations, which are specifically linked to the trade and sustainable development chapter in these agreements. They establish a specialised Committee (or Sub-committee) to oversee the implementation of such a chapter, as well as special procedures for settling trade and environment disputes, requiring the involvement of environmental experts and also allowing for advice to be sought from MEA Secretariats. As with other EU agreements, they tend to favour decision-making by consensus and dispute settlement through consultations (though arbitration is also available). These agreements, in addition, seek to allow for public participation more systematically, including specific procedural guarantees or adjustments to the institutional structure.

The EU has therefore maintained, even in more recent agreements, an essentially cooperative approach to environmental integration, whereby compliance with MEAs is being more systematically supported as part of the trade and sustainable development chapter (through best-endeavours commitments, cooperation measures, and specific institutional mechanisms), but not as a fully-enforceable legal obligation. This mirrors the general approach of international environmental law towards compliance (that is, collaborative, non-confrontational and focused on assistance and problem-solving). This new EU approach to environmental integration in its bilateral and inter-regional agreements is also significantly different from that followed by the EU to integrate human rights considerations into such agreements, the so-called 'essential elements clauses', which are usually made applicable to the agreement as a whole, framed in strict mandatory terms, and may be enforced through the suspension of concessions.[598] The only exception (as yet) is the CARIFORUM EPA, whose investment and environment clauses are potentially enforceable through sanctions – a development that requires careful consideration before similar provisions make their way into other EPAs, or other agreements between the EU and developing countries.

[598] See Bartels, above n 286, for a comprehensive analysis of these clauses and of EU practice.

Table 1. *Environmental Integration in Bilateral and Inter-regional Agreements*

Type of Agreement	Environmental Integration
SAAs (Prelude to EU membership)	• Strong overall attention to environment • Generally mandatory language • Heavy reliance on EU *acquis* • Similar cooperation priorities • Cross-cutting clause on environmental integration (specific clauses on agriculture, fisheries, transport, energy, industry and criminal matters) • Only general exception clause (art 36 TFEU) • No specific institutional mechanism, but special arrangements for approximation to EU *acquis*
Euro-Med Associations (Substitute for EU membership)	• Weaker overall attention to environment • Mixed legal force • Approximation to EU *acquis* (4/8), no reference to MEAs • Variations in priorities for environmental cooperation • Cross-cutting clause on environmental integration (specific clauses for agriculture, fisheries, energy, criminal matters, regional cooperation) • Emphasis on regional environmental issues (Barcelona Convention) • Only general exception clause (art 36 TFEU) • No specific institutional mechanism
Cotonou Agreement (Development tool)	• Strong overall attention to environment • Mandatory language • Systemic references to MEAs • Innovative provision on climate change • Strong cross-cutting approach to environmental integration (specific clauses for agriculture, fisheries, marine transport, humanitarian assistance) • Extended trade and environment linkages • No specific institutional mechanism, but emphasis on public participation
Associations Chile/ South Africa (Inter-regional cooperation)	• Weaker overall attention to environment • Generally soft legal language • No reference to MEAs, albeit South Africa AA underscores global environmental issues • Variations in priorities for cooperation • No cross-cutting environmental integration clause (specific provisions for agriculture and energy in both) • General exception clauses (art XX GATT/art 36 TFEU) • No specific institutional mechanism, but emphasis on public participation

Table 1. *Environmental Integration in Bilateral and Inter-regional Agreements*

Type of Agreement	Environmental Integration
'Post-Global Europe' Agreements • CARIFORUM EPA • Agreements with South Korea • Central America AA • COPE FTA	• Innovative provisions on trade, investment and environment (positive commitments, cooperation and capacity building) • Detailed provisions on climate change • Specific integration clauses for energy, tourism and research • International standards as benchmark for domestic environmental performance (generic references to MEAs/closed list of selected MEAs) • Specific monitoring and dispute settlement mechanisms (public participation, consultations and no full enforceability)

8.5 Questions arising in relation to implementation

Some commentators have criticised the environmental provisions in EU agreements for their open-ended nature, often avoiding details as regard the procedures and timeframes for implementation.[599] In fact, most of the clauses simply provide an indication of the general aims and possible key areas for cooperation, but concrete cooperation activities are to be developed through regular dialogue between the Parties, on the basis of mutual interests and needs, and of the capability to meet those needs. The agreements thus fail to establish clear benchmarks and indicators of success in implementing environmental clauses, as well as precise monitoring and evaluation procedures, which for instance would specify the frequency and the actors involved in reviewing progress or to ensure implementation is proceeding according to the intention of the Parties.[600] Furthermore, the EU has generally been reluctant to undertake contractual commitments on its financial and technical assistance to third countries and regions, and when it has exceptionally done so as in the Cotonou Agreement, funding allocations among the various cooperation activities remain unspecified. This is particularly regrettable (though not a practice that is exclusive to the EU) as the provisions aimed at improving environmental protection levels or supporting compliance with MEAs found in the EU's bilateral and inter-regional agreements can become a real burden for partner countries that do not have the necessary technical and institutional capacity to implement and enforce higher environmental standards (such as, but not limited to, the case of most ACP public and private actors). These provisions risk therefore not being implemented properly, if at all, unless backed up by well-targeted and appropriate assistance.

Environmental integration in the EU's bilateral and inter-regional agreements thus also needs to be verified in the context of other external tools. It has in fact been

[599] Chaytor, above n 293, 34–35.
[600] Ibid.

reported that formal differences in the wording of environmental clauses in these agreements do not necessarily have an impact on their actual implementation, which instead rests with the provision of funding and the continued momentum provided by policy dialogue between the Parties.[601] Subsequent chapters of this book will turn to three EU external relations tools that are of relevance to environmental clauses under most agreements examined: EU financial and technical assistance; bilateral/regional policy dialogue; and sustainability impact assessments. First, an enquiry will be conducted into the extent to which EU funding instruments actually match the priorities for environmental cooperation jointly established in the agreements or through policy dialogues.[602] The EU practice of institutionalising 'dialogues' with associated and partner countries will then be assessed, with a view to determining its legal significance for environmental integration.[603] In addition, EU practice in carrying out sustainability impact assessments will be examined, with a view to determining whether these have any impact on the negotiation and implementation of the relevant agreements and whether they can serve as an instrument for stakeholder involvement and consultation.[604]

[601] T Greven, A Leopold and E Molinari, 'An analysis of the Relative Effectiveness of Social and Environmental Norms in Free Trade Agreements' (2009 Study, European Parliament), 25–26, based on a comparison between the wording and implementation of the EU-Mexico and EU-Chile agreements.

[602] Ch 4.

[603] Ch 5.

[604] Ch 6.

3

Environmental Integration in the Generalised System of Preferences

1. INTRODUCTION

WHILE INTERNATIONAL AGREEMENTS, such as the associations examined in the previous chapter, are the most defining legal feature of the EU's external relations, these relations are also articulated and implemented through measures unilaterally adopted by the Union. In this chapter, the analysis of environmental integration is directed towards one of these unilateral measures: the Generalised System of Preferences (GSP). The GSP offers an interesting case-study to explore environmental integration in the definition and implementation of EU external policies mandated by Article 11 TFEU. As an instrument of the common commercial policy,[1] this measure governs the terms of access to the EU market for an important number of countries (and territories). Due to its 'generalised' character, the GSP is formally open to all countries recognised as developing and least-developed by the EU, which at present number 176.[2] Yet, it should be clarified from the outset that the actual number of GSP beneficiary countries is much smaller in light of the existing FTAs and other preferential trade arrangements between the EU and some of these developing countries or regions, which grant more favourable terms of access to the EU market than the GSP. For the purpose of illustration, the Cotonou Agreement and the Euro-Mediterranean Associations alone reduce the number of actual beneficiaries of the GSP by almost a quarter. Nonetheless, the GSP provides an interesting basis for examining the EU's unilateral approach to the trade and environment regulatory nexus, and to compare it with that seen in the context of EU bilateral or inter-regional agreements.

This chapter begins with a brief introduction to the EU GSP programme in order to place the measure within its broader historical and legal context, both

[1] Adopted on the basis of art 207 TFEU (former art 133 TEC).

[2] The term 'developing country' has resisted definition in public international law. In the absence of a precise definition, countries are generally recognised as 'developing' according to a principle of self-selection, but other countries are under no clear obligation to accept such a decision. GSP providers, such as the EU and the US, have not followed the method of self-selection but instead use a series of unilaterally-determined criteria for identifying developing countries that can benefit from their preference schemes.

internally and externally. In order to trace the evolutionary process of environmental integration into the GSP, the chapter will first concentrate on the 'old' GSP, which was in place from 2001 to mid-2005 and was the first to contain an arrangement specifically dealing with environmental matters (GSP Environment). The chapter then turns to the current GSP scheme which has been in place since July 2005 and introduced a novel arrangement to integrate, inter alia, environmental concerns (commonly known as 'GSP-plus'). While the analysis will focus primarily on environmental integration at the stage of the definition of EU policy through a detailed examination of the substantive and procedural provisions of the two GSP regulations in question, attention will also be paid to EU practice in implementing this measure of its external trade policy. A key finding of this chapter is that the GSP provides further evidence of an evolution in the approach of the EU to environmental integration, initially limited to one global environmental issue (deforestation) and progressively shifting towards a more systematic approach by integrating a selected number of multilateral environmental agreements. The chapter concludes by offering some reflections on this evolution from an international law perspective.

2. ORIGINS AND HISTORY OF THE EU GSP

The GSP is primarily an international construct, the origins of which lie in the first and second sessions of United Nations Conference on Trade and Development (UNCTAD) in the 1960s.[3] In essence, the GSP is a mechanism to improve market access conditions for developing and least-developed countries through preferential tariff treatment which is granted by developed countries on a voluntary and non-reciprocal basis. To date, it remains the most concrete application of the principle of differential and more favourable treatment of developing countries in international trade law. As such, the GSP retains considerable political

[3] UNCTAD, 'Final Act of the First United Nations Conference on Trade and Development' (1964) UN Doc E/CONF.46/141, Principle 8 of Recommendation A.I.1; UNCTAD, 'Resolution of the Second Session of UNCTAD on the Expansion and Diversification of Exports of Manufacturers and Semi-Manufacturers of Developing Countries. Resolution 21(II)' (1968) UN Doc TD/97 (UNCTAD Resolution 21(II)). Established in 1964, UNCTAD offered an alternative institutional forum exclusively dedicated to trade and development issues and in which developing countries were able to exercise more influence in the decision-making process than within the old GATT. From this forum, and under the stewardship of Argentinean economist Raúl Prebisch, developing countries began to advance their quest for the establishment of a New International Economic Order (NIEO). In particular, they sought to overhaul the GATT ethos of formal equal treatment in trade liberalisation enshrined in the twin principles of non-discrimination and reciprocity in trade concessions, on the ground that it overlooked the wide disparities in development levels among the GATT Contracting Parties. The recognition of a special status of developing countries, coupled with the articulation of a general principle of special and more favourable treatment, in international trade law were argued as being necessary for achieving 'substantial equality' among GATT Contracting Parties. On the NIEO and its ramifications for the GATT/WTO regimes, see generally G Abi-Saab, 'Le Droit au Dévelopment' (1988) XLIV *Annuaire Suisse de Droit International* 9; SR Chowdhury, EMG Denters and P de Wart (eds), *The Right to Development in International Law* (Dordrecht, Martinus Nijhoff, 1992); B Taxil, *L'OMC et les Pays en Dévelopment* (Paris, Monchrestien, 1998), chs 1–2.

significance in North-South trade relations independently of its disputed importance in assisting the development process of preference-beneficiaries.[4]

As providing tariff preferences only to some WTO members would ordinarily contravene the most-favoured-nation (MFN) obligation in Article 1 GATT[5] (one of the fundamental pillars of the multilateral trading system), the establishment of GSP schemes required an explicit authorisation under GATT/WTO law, which is found in the so-called GATT Enabling Clause.[6] Recognising the disparities in development levels among WTO members, this provision permits – but does not require – developed WTO members to accord, inter alia,[7] preferential tariff treatment to products originating in developing and least-developed countries on a 'generalised, non-reciprocal and non-discriminatory'[8] basis, in an attempt to increase their export earnings and promote their industrialisation and (economic) development.[9] Yet, and partly because of the non-mandatory character of the Enabling Clause, the use and implementation of GSP preferences have long engendered legal, political and economic contentions, including that which forms the focus of this chapter: the use of such preferences for environmental purposes.[10]

The EU stood out as the first developed GATT Contracting Party to establish a GSP programme in 1971.[11] In line with the original purpose of the GSP as an instrument to support industrialisation and export-led economic growth in developing and least-developed countries, the initial focus of the Union's scheme

[4] The most comprehensive academic analysis of GSP programmes is offered by JC Sánchez Arnau, *The Generalised System of Preferences and the World Trade Organisation* (London, Cameron, 2002). Among the critical views, see C Ozden and E Reinhardt, 'The Perversity of Preferences: the Generalised System of Preferences and Developing Countries Trade Policies, 1976–2000' (2003) *World Bank Policy Research Paper Series* No 2955; AO Sykes, 'A Preference for Development: the Law and Economics of the GSP' (2005) 4(1) *World Trade Review* 41. UNCTAD-based assessments of GSP schemes can be found at www.unctad.org/Templates/Page.asp?intItemID=3601&lang=1.

[5] GATT art I:1 reads: 'With respect to customs duties . . . any advantage, favour, privilege, or immunity granted by any Member to any product originating in or destined for any other country shall be accorded immediately and unconditionally to the like product originating in or destined for the territories of all other Members.'

[6] GATT Contracting Parties, 'Differential and More Favourable Treatment, Reciprocity and Fuller Participation of Developing Countries' (Decision of 28 November 1979) L/4903, BISD 26S/203 (GATT Enabling Clause), para 2(a). This should be read in conjunction with the preceding 10-year waiver which details the purpose and nature of the GSP, GATT Contracting Parties, 'General System of Preferences' (Decision of 25 June 1971) BISD 18S/24 (GATT GSP Decision).

[7] It also permits other forms of differential treatment, including: preferential non-tariff measures, preferential arrangements among developing countries themselves, and more favourable treatment of least-developed countries, see GATT Enabling Clause, para 2(b)–(d).

[8] GATT GSP Decision, preamble para 3; reiterating the wording of UNCTAD Resolution 21(II).

[9] Ibid, para 1 of preamble; reiterating the wording of UNCTAD Resolution 21(II).

[10] See generally D Bodansky, 'What is So Bad about Unilateral Actions to Protect the Environment?' (2000) 11(2) *European Journal of International Law* 339; and also WTO dispute discussed in s 4.1 below.

[11] Technically speaking, the first country to offer a GSP scheme was the Soviet Union in 1965 and the first GATT Contracting Party was Australia in 1966 authorised by a specific waiver. L Bartels, 'The Trade and Development Policy of the European Union' (2007) 18(4) *European Journal of International Law* 715, 739. At the time of writing, 13 national GSP schemes have been notified to the UNCTAD Secretariat: www.unctad.org/Templates/Page.asp?intItemID=2309&lang=1.

was on manufactured and semi-manufactured products.[12] Between 1971 and 1994, the EU GSP scheme was reviewed on an annual basis, and on some occasions, amended by fresh legislation adopted separately for industrial, agricultural, coal and steel, and textile products. These successive unilateral changes involved product coverage, depth of tariff cuts, quotas, ceilings and beneficiaries, particularly for agricultural products.[13] Between 1995 and 2001, the EU undertook a more ambitious revision of the GSP which brought important changes to the nature and structure of this measure.[14] Of direct relevance to this study was the introduction of 'special-incentives mechanisms', pointing to the emergence of a policy of 'positive' trade conditionality linked to, inter alia, environmental protection requirements.[15]

This move towards environment-related conditionality in the EU GSP must be placed within the broader developments that occurred in both EU and international law since the GSP was first articulated within UNCTAD in the late 1960s. Internally, as we saw in chapter one, by the early 1990s the EU had acquired an explicit external competence for both environmental and development policies, which are linked by the environmental integration requirement (Article 11 TFEU), as well as by the Treaty-based objective of fostering the 'sustainable economic and social development of developing countries'.[16] In fact, the preambular language of the old GSP Regulation acknowledged that the Treaty of Maastricht had 'lent a fresh impetus to Community development policy as an aspect of the Union's external policy, by setting as a priority objective the sustainable economic and social development of developing countries'.[17] The EU had furthermore

[12] As these only compromised a very small proportion of total EU imports from developing countries (around 7%), the original scheme also included a limited number of processed agricultural products which was gradually increased over the following decades. Bartels, above n 11, 740.

[13] While the 1971–94 EU GSP was considered far more generous in terms of the total volume of preferential imports allowed into the EU market in relation to that of other preferences-giving countries, the still limited product coverage, its excessively restrictive rules of origin, its quantitative restrictions and its complex administration hampered its full utilisation by developing-country exporters. For a more comprehensive account of the pre-1995 EU GSP scheme, see S Inama and E Vermulst, *Customs and Trade Law of the European Community* (London, Kluwer, 1999), 48–49 and 87–88; S Peers, 'The Reform of the European Community's General System of Preferences. A Missed Opportunity' (1995) 29(6) *Journal of World Trade* 79.

[14] The various amendments were integrated into a single regulation for all covered agricultural and industrial products: Council Regulation (EC) 2501/2001 applying a scheme of generalised tariff preferences for the period from 1 Jan. 2002 to 31 Dec. 2004 [2001] OJ L346/1 (old GSP Regulation).

[15] Other important changes included the introduction of the principle of tariff modulation (dividing products into four categories of 'sensitivity' depending on the production situation of a given product in the EU market) and of an open policy of graduation (entailing the unilateral withdrawal of GSP treatment, either in full or in respect to a specific sector, from a given developing country that meets certain economic criteria established by the EU). See Commission, 'Communication on integration of the developing countries into the international trading system: role of the GSP 1995–2004' COM (94) 212 final, 5–9 (GSP Communication 1994).

[16] Formerly art 177(1) TEC, as part of the specific objectives of EU development policy, now art 21(2)(d) TEU as one of the objectives of the EU's external action as a whole, which reads: 'foster the sustainable economic, social and *environmental* development of developing countries' (emphasis added). See Ch 1, ss 4.2 and 5.3.

[17] Old GSP Regulation, preamble para 5.

adopted legislation aimed at ensuring that environmental protection was central to its emerging development policy *acquis*.[18]

These developments within the EU were preceded by an evolution in the normative definition of development at the international level, away from the vision that had prevailed for three decades after the end of the Second World War and that had underpinned the drafting of the legal texts on the GSP in the late 1960s and 1970s. Since the 1980s, the definitional parameters of development have been considerably broadened over time and are no longer confined to the furtherance of national economic growth. In particular, development has been increasingly framed as 'sustainable development',[19] a concept that was first conceived in the area of international environmental law and is understood to support environmental integration.[20] With this evolving notion of sustainable development, the prevailing trade-off between economic growth and other societal values, including environmental protection, has been progressively questioned. In this context, it is interesting to note that at its eighth conference in 1993 UNCTAD recommended the mainstreaming of sustainable development into policies aimed at fostering the growth of developing countries,[21] though (as of yet) this has not led to a fundamental rethinking of the role of the GSP itself within UNCTAD.

3. ENVIRONMENTAL INTEGRATION IN THE OLD EU GSP (2001–05)

3.1 General structure and legislative background

Before turning to a detailed examination of environmental integration in the old GSP scheme, this section briefly overviews the overall structure and legislative background of this measure as a backdrop for gauging the rationale and operation of the arrangement specifically dealing with the environment (GSP Environment). The old GSP contained five distinct arrangements, each offering different preferences in terms of product coverage and tariff margins in relation to MFN-based duties. There was, first, a general arrangement, the General GSP, open to any developing country recognised by the EU as a 'nominal beneficiary'[22] and providing basic tariff

[18] Regulation (EC) 2493/2000 of the European Parliament and of the Council on measures to promote the full integration of the environmental dimension in the development process of developing countries [2000] OJ L288/1. On the incremental creation of an EU 'development policy *acquis*' see E Morgera and G Marín Durán, 'Enlargement and EU Development Policy: An Environmental Perspective' (2004) 13(2) *Review of European Community and International Environmental Law* 152, 152–54.

[19] On this conceptual evolution, see Ch 1, s 4.2.3.1.

[20] P Sands, *Principles of International Environmental Law* 2nd edn (Cambridge, Cambridge University Press, 2003), 253.

[21] UNCTAD, 'Proceedings of the United Nations Conference on Trade and Development, 8th Session' (1993) UN Doc TD/364/Rev.I, paras 38 and 63.

[22] Old GSP Regulation, art 12 and Annex I, listing a total of 178 'nominal' beneficiaries. These countries and territories (except LDCs) were subject to a graduation mechanism, if the following cumulative criteria were met during three consecutive years: 'being classified as a high-income country by the World Bank' and 'the country's development index, as defined in Annex II, is higher than –1' (old GSP

preferences on roughly 7000 products, the breadth of which varied depending on the product-sensitivity in the EU market.[23] Second, there was a special arrangement granting the most favourable GSP treatment (duty-and-quota free to the EU market for virtually all products)[24] to all countries classified as least-developed countries by the UN General Assembly, known as the 'Everything But Arms Initiative' (EBA initiative).[25] Third, and of most relevance here, there were three special-incentive mechanisms, which accorded *additional* tariff preferences to those received under the General GSP, and were *conditional* upon compliance with different sets of non-economic criteria – environment, labour and drug-related:

- The special-incentive arrangement for the protection of the environment: known as the GSP Environment, its details are examined below.
- The special-incentive arrangement for the protection of labour rights: known as the GSP Labour, it extended additional tariff margins for all products classified as 'sensitive' under the General GSP to any nominal beneficiary that demonstrated its national legislation incorporated 'the substance of the standards laid down in eight conventions of the International Labour Organisation (ILO)'[26] following a similar procedure to that found in the GSP Environment.[27]

Regulation, art 3). If countries failed to meet these same criteria during three consecutive years after having been removed, they were re-inserted into the EU GSP scheme.

[23] Old GSP Regulation, art 7. According to EU data, the roughly 3250 products classified as 'non-sensitive' (mainly manufactured goods, except for their agricultural component) enjoyed duty-free access to the EU market while the 3750 goods classified as 'sensitive' (mainly agricultural and textile products) only received a flat-rate reduction of 3.5% points on MFN-based ad valorem duties and a relative reduction of 30% on MFN-based specific duties (with some exceptions for textiles and clothing). Commission, 'Brochure on the European Union's Generalised System of Preferences' (February 2004) (EU GSP Brochure 2004), 5. All EU documents related to the GSP mentioned in this chapter can be found at www.trade.ec.europa.eu/doclib/cfm/doclib_section.cfm?sec=160&langId=en.

[24] Old GSP Regulation, art 9. Arms and ammunition are excluded from the scope of the EBA initiative. In addition, three agricultural products considered 'highly sensitive' in the EU market (namely, fresh bananas, rice and sugar) were not subject to immediate full liberalisation, but remaining duties and quotas were set to be gradually eliminated by 2009. On the merits and shortcomings of this initiative, see S Inama, 'Market Access for LDCs. Issues to be Addressed' (2002) 36(1) *Journal of World Trade* 85, 95 and 99–100; P Bretton, 'Integrating the Least Developed Countries into the World Trading System: The Current Impact of the European Preferences under the "Everything But Arms Initiative"' (2003) 37(3) *Journal of World Trade* 623, 631–45; M Gasiorek et al, 'Mid-term Evaluation of the EU's Generalised System of Preferences. Final Report' (*CARIS*, 26 May 2010) ss 2.3 and 2.4.

[25] Old GSP Regulation, preamble para 5. The UN official list of LDCs and defining criteria may be found at www.unohrlls.org/en/ldc/related/62/.

[26] Old GSP Regulation, arts 14–20 laying down the substantive and procedural rules applicable to the 'GSP Labour'. The ILO Conventions in question were the core eight: Convention C29 on Forced Labour, 28 June 1930, ILO/C29; Convention C105 on the Abolition of Forced Labour, 25 June 1957, ILO/C105; Convention C 87 on Freedom of Association and Protection of the Right to Organise, 9 July 1948, ILO/C87; Convention 98 on the Right to Organise and Collective Bargaining, 1 July 1949, ILO/C98; Convention 100 on Equal Remuneration, 29 June 1951, ILO/C100; Convention 111 on Discrimination (Employment and Occupation) 25 June 1958, ILO/C111; Convention 138 on Minimum Age for Admission to Employment, 26 June 1973, ILO/C138; Convention 182 on the Prohibition and Immediate Action for the Elimination of the Worst Forms of Child Labour, 17 June 1999, ILO/C182.

[27] For a more comprehensive analysis, see A Cole, 'Labour Standards in the Generalised System of Preferences: the European Communities/India GSP Dispute' (2004) 25(1) *Michigan Journal of International Law* 179, 193–96. On the US GSP Labour, see L Compa and J Vogt, 'Labor Rights in the Generalized System of Preferences: A 20-Year Review' (2001) 22(2–3) *Comparative Labor Law and Policy Journal* 199.

- The special-incentive arrangement to combat drug production and trafficking: known as the GSP Drugs, this was the second-best preferential treatment available under the old GSP (after the EBA initiative), but operated in a more obscure fashion in substantive and procedural terms than the other two special-incentive mechanisms. It provided duty-free access for important industrial goods classified as 'sensitive' under the General GSP (for example, textiles and clothing) as well as preferential tariff margins on agricultural products that were excluded from the general arrangement to a closed group, pre-selected by the EU, of 12 developing countries that were presumably undertaking effective programmes to combat illicit drugs production and trafficking.[28]

A 1994 Communication from the Commission to the Council and European Parliament on the role of the EU GSP provides the legislative background to environmental integration in the old GSP. The Commission justified the introduction of the GSP Environment (and GSP Labour) into the old scheme on the following grounds: 'the special incentives should be positive inducements and logical components of development policy in that they reflect the idea of social progress and protection of the environment as aspects of, rather than preconditions for, sustainable development'.[29] In line with this statement, the GSP Environment would be used to promote 'products and production methods internationally recognised as consistent with the objectives set out in international conventions on the environment', and additional preferential margins would be granted under the arrangement to 'offset the extra costs of bringing the industries concerned in line with these standards'.[30]

Thus, environmental integration within the old GSP was primarily construed through an incentive-based approach: additional tariff preferences were granted in return for adherence to certain environmental conditions. This positive approach significantly differs from that adopted to the trade and environment nexus under most of the EU's bilateral/inter-regional agreements, which was traditionally limited to 'exception clauses' (modelled on Article 36 TFEU or Article XX GATT) that authorise (under certain conditions) the adoption of trade restrictive measures when certain standards of environmental protection are not met.[31] In the GSP context, instead, environmental concerns are primarily to be

[28] Old GSP Regulation, arts 10 and 25. The beneficiaries concerned were 11 Latin American countries (Bolivia, Colombia, Costa Rica, Ecuador, El Salvador, Guatemala, Honduras, Nicaragua, Panama, Peru and Venezuela) and Pakistan (added in 2002). The old GSP Regulation (art 25(2)) also requested the Commission to evaluate each beneficiary country's social development (in particular the respect and promotion of the standards laid down in the ILO Conventions referred to in the ILO Declaration on Fundamental Principles and Rights at Work) and environmental policy (in particular the sustainable management of tropical forest), and to take into account the 'findings of the relevant international organisations and agencies' (art 25(3)). This evaluation was however 'without prejudice' to the continuation of their beneficiary status of the GSP Drugs until 2004 and its extension thereafter (art 25(3)).

[29] GSP Communication 1994, 10.

[30] Ibid, 12.

[31] See Ch 2, ss 3.6, 4.5 and 6.5. Except for the more recent post-Global Europe agreements, whose trade and sustainable development chapters are much broader and also provide for cooperative measures (Ch 2, ss 5.3.2 and 7.1.3).

integrated through trade liberalising measures (that is, additional tariff preferences) that reward compliance with certain environmental standards, rather than just penalising non-compliance with such standards. Nonetheless, as will be seen below, the old GSP also contained provisions on the (temporary) withdrawal of trade preferences, which included one ground that is of environmental relevance (sustainable fishery practices).

This difference in approaches to the use of trade measures for environmental (and other) purposes – trade incentives versus trade sanctions – is often distinguished in the literature as 'positive' and 'negative' conditionality,[32] even though the term 'conditionality' itself carries a negative connotation particularly in the case of the GSP. GSP-conditionality is highly controversial because its very operation is based upon an unbalanced and one-directional relationship between developed and developing countries: only the former have the economic strength to attach conditions to the granting of trade preferences upon which the latter remain heavily dependent. As a result, the conditioning of GSP preferences has repeatedly been criticised on 'neo-colonialist' grounds (whereby economically powerful States alone are capable of imposing 'their values and interests' upon economically weaker ones) and also more recently as an instrument of 'disguised protectionism' (where, for instance, environmental standards are imposed as a result of fears of increased competition from more-advanced developing countries rather than a genuine concern about environmental protection). While these concerns are certainly not misplaced, it will be illustrated below that 'positive' and 'negative' conditionality do have different implications on (at least some of) these contentious issues.

3.2 Special-incentive arrangement for the protection of the environment

Under the GSP Environment, the EU extended *additional* tariff preferences a priori to any beneficiary of its old GSP that was capable of proving that it effectively applied national legislation 'incorporating the substance' of internationally acknowledged standards and guidelines concerning the sustainable management of tropical forests[33] and in particular those elaborated by the International Tropical Timber Organization (ITTO).[34] In quantitative terms, the additional trade benefits offered under this arrangement consisted of a flat-rate reduction of 8 percentage points on MFN-based ad valorem duties and an additional reduction of 30 per cent on the basic preferential duties applied under the General GSP.

[32] A well-elaborated framework for approaching the different forms of conditionality from a legal perspective is offered in E Fierro Sedano, *The EU's Approach to Human Rights Conditionality in Practice* (The Hague, Kluwer, 2003), ch 3.

[33] Old GSP Regulation, art 21(2).

[34] It should be noted that express reference to the ITTO is only found in the GSP Communication 1994 (at 12) but not in the actual old GSP Regulation. In addition, it can be highlighted that the GSP Communication foresaw the possible expansion of the GSP Environment to other international agreements, such as on the ozone layer, climate change and biodiversity.

However, these preferential margins were confined to tropical forest products (around 50 tariff lines).[35]

In addition, the GSP Environment contained detailed procedures concerning the submission and assessment of requests, as well as the granting and eventual withdrawal of the additional trade benefits. In order to take advantage of this arrangement, interested developing countries had to submit a written request to the Commission, including comprehensive evidence of compliance with the applicable environmental criteria. Once received, a notice was published in the Official Journal of the European Communities (Official Journal) inviting any interested natural or legal person to make appropriate observations. The responsibility for examining these requests fell upon the Commission which reserved the right to verify the information provided by the requesting country through a variety of means. Within a maximum period of one year from the date of receipt, a final decision was to be adopted by the Commission in cooperation with the 'GSP Committee', which was also subject to publication in the Official Journal. The requesting country had to be involved throughout the evaluation process, it had to be notified of the final decision, and in cases of denial it had the right to request a reasoned explanation to the Commission.[36] Once applications were deemed successful, the recipient country undertook to maintain the relevant national legislation in force and had the responsibility for the necessary administrative cooperation. Failure to do so would result in the withdrawal of the additional trade benefits conferred.[37]

The GSP Environment in practice was very limited as only one GSP beneficiary, China, applied for its benefits.[38] This under-utilisation of the GSP Environment can be partly explained by its limited scope as an incentive mechanism in both substantive and geographical terms. While the arrangement was formally open to any of the 178 nominal beneficiaries of the old GSP, de facto it could only act as a real incentive with respect to those developing countries accessing the EU market under the terms of the General GSP, given that all other three arrangements (EBA initiative, GSP Drugs and GSP Labour) offered more favourable terms of market access than the GSP Environment. In addition, although the granting of the GSP Environment was not restricted to countries that are members of the ITTO

[35] Old GSP Regulation, arts 8(3) and 21(1). See also, EU GSP Brochure 2004, 7.

[36] Old GSP Regulation, arts 22–23.

[37] Ibid, art 26(3).

[38] Commission, 'Notice regarding the request submitted by the People's Republic of China in order to benefit from the special-incentive arrangement for the protection of the environment' [2002] OJ C143/6. The authors were unable to find the reasons for the presumed refusal of this request. Note that the 'GSP Labour' itself was not tremendously appealing either with only four applications for inclusion submitted, two of which were approved by the EU: Commission, 'Notice regarding the request by the Republic of Moldova to take advantage of the special incentive arrangement concerning labour rights' [1999] OJ C176/13, and Commission Regulation (EC) 1649/2000 granting the Republic of Moldova the benefit of the special incentive arrangements concerning labour rights [2000] OJ L189/13; Commission, 'Notice regarding the request submitted by the Democratic Socialist Republic of Sri Lanka in order to benefit from the special arrangement concerning labour rights' [2002] OJ C95/14, and Commission Regulation (EC) 2342/2003 granting the Democratic Socialist Republic of Sri Lanka benefit from the special arrangement for the protection of labour rights [2003] OJ L346/34.

(whose membership was limited to countries producing and consuming tropical timber products),[39] the factual limitation remained that only countries with tropical forests in their territories could apply for the additional trade preferences available under the arrangement.

This focus on tropical forests in the GSP Environment mirrored the approach of EU environment-related funding to developing countries during the same period in which a larger financial envelope was devoted to the Tropical Forests Regulation[40] than to the broader Environment Regulation.[41] Nonetheless, the 1994 Commission Communication underpinning the introduction of the GSP Environment had already anticipated that the scope of the arrangement would be broadened 'as and when international standards or criteria were introduced pursuant to international conventions on the environment or Agenda 21'.[42] As will be seen, the approach to environmental integration was indeed expanded considerably under the current GSP scheme.

3.3 Temporary withdrawal of GSP preferences

Whereas the EU generally favoured a positive approach to environmental integration in the old GSP, minor signs of negative conditionality were also present. By virtue of Article 26 of the old GSP Regulation, the trade benefits granted to a particular country under any of the five GSP arrangements indicated above could be temporarily and unilaterally withdrawn, in whole or in part, on various grounds. This provision thus reproduced, within the GSP context, the approach found in the 'exception clauses' of the EU's bilateral/inter-regional agreements and in Article XX GATT on the basis of which trade restrictions may be justified (under certain conditions) on non-commercial policy grounds, such as the protection of human, animal and plant life or the conservation of (exhaustible) natural resources.[43] Among the grounds for suspending GSP status[44] was the 'infringement of objectives of the

[39] Of the current 59 members (counting the EU and its Member States as one), the vast majority are developing countries, visit www.itto.int/itto_members/.

[40] Regulation (EC) 2494/2000 of the European Parliament and of the Council on measures to promote the conservation and sustainable management of tropical forests and other forests in developing countries [2000] OJ L288/6, with an indicative financial envelope of €249 million for the period 2000–2006 (see Ch 4, s 3.1).

[41] Regulation (EC) 2493/2000, above n 18, with an indicative financial envelope of €93m for the period 2000–06 (see Ch 4, s 3.1).

[42] GSP Communication 1994, 12. 'Agenda 21' (13 June 1992) UN Doc A/CONF.151/26/Rev.1(vol 1).

[43] It does not necessarily follow that all the criteria for 'negative' conditionality under the old GSP scheme were compatible with WTO law, an issue that ultimately depends on the unclear relationship between art XX GATT and the GATT Enabling Clause.

[44] The other grounds for suspending GSP preferences were: practice of any form of slavery or forced labour (art 26(1)(a)); serious and systemic violations of core labour standards (art 26(1)(b)); exports of goods made by prison labour (art 26(1)(c)); shortcomings in customs controls on export or transit of drugs or failure to comply with international conventions on money laundering (art 26(1)(d)); fraud or systemic failure to comply with rules of origin or to provide the necessary administrative cooperation (art 26(1)(e)); unfair trading practices (art 26(1)(h)).

international conventions, such as NAFO,[45] NEAFC,[46] ICCAT,[47] NASCO[48] concerning the conservation and management of fishery resources'.[49] While these regional fisheries management conventions (with a limited membership) are not environmental treaties properly speaking, the sustainable management of fish stocks is an issue of great environmental relevance[50] and an area in which EU external action has been controversial.[51]

These two manifestations of environmental integration in the old GSP scheme serve to illustrate the difference between the 'positive' and 'negative' approach to the use of unilateral trade measures for environmental purposes, which essentially boils down to whether such actions are cooperative or punitive in nature. To further exemplify this point, the implications of using the 'carrot' of additional trade preferences to encourage the observance of the ITTO standards concerning the sustainable management of tropical forests through the GSP Environment, and those of using the 'stick' of trade sanctions to punish infringements of the objectives of regional fisheries management conventions, are critically different from normative and policy viewpoints. In addition to the normative arguments raised against the use of trade sanctions more generally,[52] it should be underlined that the GSP Environment remained essentially voluntary in nature or at least more consensual than the unilateral withdrawal of GSP preferences by the EU. That is, EU decisions on the granting of the GSP Environment are made in response to a request for inclusion by interested countries (such as China), whereas GSP preferences may be withdrawn on the EU's sole initiative with no engagement of the

[45] Convention on Future Multilateral Cooperation in the Northwest Atlantic Fisheries, 24 October 1978, 1135 UNTS 369 (NAFO). Out of the 12 Contracting Parties (counting the EU and its Member States as one) only one is a developing country (Cuba), see www.nafo.int/about/frames/con-index.html.

[46] Convention on Future Multilateral Cooperation in the Northeast Atlantic Fisheries, 18 November 1980, 1285 UNTS 129 (NEAFC). Of the five Contracting Parties (counting EU and its Member States as one) none is a developing country, see www.neafc.org.

[47] International Convention on the Conservation of Atlantic Tuna, 14 May 1966, 673 UNTS 63 (ICCAT). Most Contracting Parties are developing countries, visit www.iccat.es/en/contracting.htm.

[48] Convention for the Conservation of Salmon in the North Atlantic Ocean, 2 March 1982, 1338 UNTS 33 (NASCO). Of the seven Contracting Parties (counting the EU and its Member States as one) none is a developing country, visit www.nasco.int/about.html.

[49] Old GSP Regulation, art 26(g).

[50] Note that these are included in the UN Environment Programme (UNEP), 'Register of International Treaties and Other Agreements in the field of the Environment' (2005) UN Doc UNEP/Env.Law/2005/3. The environmental dimension of the regional fisheries management arrangements has been increasingly addressed by the UN General Assembly: 'Sustainable Fisheries' (2007) UN Doc A/RES/61/105, paras 70 and 80; and 'Sustainable Fisheries' (2009) UN Doc A/RES/64/72, paras 51 and 84.

[51] See, among others, J Vogler and C Bretherton, 'The European Union as a Sustainable Development Actor: the Case of External Fisheries Policy' (2008) 30(3) *Journal of European Integration* 401. This includes the so-called 'Fisheries Partnership Agreements' whereby the EU seeks to obtain access to fisheries resources in the exclusive economic zones of the third countries concerned for EU fishing fleets.

[52] See generally, B Jansen, 'The Limits of Unilateralism from an European Perspective' (2000) 11(2) *European Journal of International Law* 309; P Sands, 'Unilateralism, Values and International Law' (2000) 11(2) *European Journal of International Law* 291.

affected third country. Furthermore, the operation of the GSP Environment is strictly tied to 'internationally acknowledged standards and guidelines' including by the beneficiary countries, whereas GSP preferences may also be withdrawn on the basis of regional fisheries management conventions to which the EU, but not necessarily the affected third country, is a Party.[53] From a more practical perspective it can be argued that through the operation of the GSP Environment the EU partially absorbs the costs incurred by the beneficiary countries (or/and their industries) in conforming with the specified environmental standards, as recognised by the Commission in its 1994 Communication.[54]

Nonetheless, the EU appears to see the withdrawal of GSP preferences as 'an exceptional measure applied only in cases of clearly unacceptable practices'[55] and made scant recourse to GSP-linked trade sanctions under the old GSP. The only noticeable exception was the withdrawal of all GSP preferences from Myanmar in 1997 on forced labour grounds – a decision taken following a manifest refusal of the country to cooperate with the EU during the investigations.[56] It is interesting to note that EU approach and practice to 'negative' GSP-conditionality contrasts with that of the United States – the other major GSP donor – which, in addition to packing its GSP programme with all sorts of mandatory and discretionary eligibility conditions,[57] has also been far more assertive than the EU in imposing such conditions in practice.[58]

4. ENVIRONMENTAL INTEGRATION IN THE CURRENT GSP (2005–11)

4.1 General structure and legislative background

In 2005, the EU GSP programme underwent a far-reaching reform which, among other things, simplified its overall structure by reducing the number of preferential arrangements from the existing five to three. The crux of this structural change was the merger of the old special-incentive arrangements (that is, GSP Labour, GSP Environment and GSP Drugs) into one single arrangement for 'sustainable development and good governance,' re-named in EU jargon as the 'GSP-plus'.

[53] See above nn 45–48.

[54] See s 3.1 and n 30 above.

[55] EU GSP Brochure 2004, 18.

[56] Regulation (EC) 552/97 temporarily withdrawing access to generalised tariff preferences from the Union of Myanmar [1997] OJ L85/8, still in force at the time of writing. For a more detailed account, see B Brandtner and A Rosas, 'Trade Preferences and Human Rights' in P Alston (ed), *The EU and Human Rights* (Oxford, Oxford University Press, 1999), 713–18.

[57] These are not environment-related but include: 'Communism'; failure to provide adequate protection to US investors; granting sanctuary from prosecution to any individual or group that has committed an act of international terrorism; violation of internationally-recognised labour rights; and failure to give effective protection to US intellectual property rights. See UNCTAD, 'Generalised System of Preferences. Handbook of the Scheme of the United States of America' (2010) UN Doc UNCTAD/ITCD/TSB/Misc.58/Rev.2, 9.

[58] On US active use of 'negative' conditionality, see G Shaffer, *Defending Interests: Public-Private Partnerships in the WTO Litigation* (Washington DC, Brooking Institution Press, 2003), 54–55.

The reformed scheme, which entered into force on 1 July 2005,[59] was first reviewed in 2008 but no major changes were introduced to the GSP-plus, which is of most relevance to this study. The current EU GSP,[60] in place until 31 December 2011, consists of three preferential arrangements: the General GSP,[61] the EBA initiative,[62] and the GSP-plus – the latter being analysed in detail in the next section. It should also be noted that the European Commission has recently put forward two proposals to the Council and the European Parliament,[63] whereby the current GSP will be extended until 31 December 2013 and then replaced by a reformed system as of 1 January 2014.[64]

In its Communication to the Council and the European Parliament of July 2004,[65] the Commission laid down the rationales and general guidelines behind the 2005 reform of the EU GSP. One of the factors triggering the reform process was external in nature, namely a challenge by India to the GSP Drugs before the WTO dispute settlement bodies in 2003. Known as the India-EU GSP case,[66] this WTO dispute was charged with political sensitivity – not least because it was the first instance in which WTO judicial bodies were asked to adjudicate on the WTO-compatibility of the contentious issue of GSP-conditionality,[67] and has

[59] Regulation (EC) 980/2005, [2005] OJ L169/1. Note that only the provisions pertaining to the GSP-plus entered into force on 1 July 2005, the remainder of this Regulation entered into force on 1 January 2006.

[60] Regulation (EC) 732/2008 of 22 July 2008 applying a scheme of generalised tariff preferences for the period from 1 January 2009 to 31 December 2011 and amending Regulations (EC) 552/97, (EC) 1933/2006 and Commission Regulations (EC) 1100/2006 and (EC) 964/2007 [2008] OJ L211/1 (current GSP Regulation).

[61] Current GSP Regulation, art 6. The General GSP offers tariff cuts on roughly 6350 products (listed in Annex II) with those classified as 'non-sensitive' (mainly manufactured goods, except for their agricultural component) enjoying duty-free access to the EU market while goods classified as 'sensitive' (mainly agricultural and textile products) only receiving a flat-rate reduction of 3.5% points on MFN-based ad valorem duties and a relative reduction of 30% on MFN-based specific duties (with some exceptions for textiles and clothing). The total 176 countries and territories (except LDCs) listed as 'nominal' beneficiaries (Annex I) are subject to a reinforced graduation mechanism (art 13). See UNCTAD, 'Generalised System of Preferences. Handbook on the Scheme of the European Community' (2008) UN Doc UNCTAD/ITCD/TSB/Misc.25/Rev.3, 3–8, (UNCTAD EU GSP Handbook).

[62] Current GSP Regulation, arts 11–12. The EBA initiative has been maintained and since 1 October 2009 has offered unrestricted duty-free access to LDCs for all products (7200 tariff lines), except arms and ammunition (HS Ch 93). See Commission, 'Press Release EBA -End of transitional quotas for sugar and rice' 1 October 2009; UNCTAD EU GSP Handbook, 9–11.

[63] Note that, in accordance with the post-Lisbon decision-making provisions on the common commercial policy, this proposed GSP Regulation is the first to be jointly adopted by the Council and the Parliament following the ordinary legislative procedure (art 207(2) TFEU).

[64] Commission, 'Proposal for a regulation of the European Parliament and Council. Applying a scheme of generalised tariff preferences' COM (2011) 241 final (Proposed GSP Regulation 2014).

[65] Commission, 'Communication on developing countries, international trade and sustainable development: the function of the Community's system of preferences (GSP) for the ten-year period from 2006–2015' COM (2004) 416 final (Communication on GSP reform 2004).

[66] *European Communities–Conditions for the Granting of Tariff Preferences to Developing Countries*, Panel Report (adopted 20 April 2004 as modified by Appellate Body Report) WT/ DS246/R; *European Communities–Conditions for the Granting of Tariff Preferences to Developing Countries*, Appellate Body Report (adopted 20 April 2004) WT/DS246/AB/R (AB Report *EC–Tariff Preferences*).

[67] See s 3.1 above.

been exhaustively discussed in the literature.[68] Ultimately, the GSP Drugs was deemed inconsistent with WTO law and thus a review of the old GSP was required as a result.[69] Beyond this particular issue, this WTO ruling is important, at least from a WTO law perspective, because it imposes certain substantive and procedural constraints on the integration of environmental concerns into the GSP.

In an attempt to summarise a rather complex jurisprudence, the WTO Appellate Body held that in light of the non-discrimination requirement in the GATT Enabling Clause,[70] GSP donors may only differentiate in the tariff treatment accorded to beneficiaries of their schemes (including through special incentive mechanisms) under the following five conditions: (i) a specific intent requirement (tariff differentiation shall be aimed at positively responding to the 'special development, financial and trade needs' of the GSP beneficiaries it addresses); (ii) an objectiveness requirement (the existence of the 'special development, financial and trade needs' to which the tariff differentiation is intended to respond must be based upon objective criteria, such as broad-based recognition in the WTO Agreement, or in multilateral instruments adopted by international organisations); (iii) an effectiveness requirement (the nature of the 'special needs' at issue must be such that it can be effectively addressed through tariff preferences); (iv) a de jure non-discrimination requirement (identical tariff treatment must be made available to all GSP beneficiaries who share those 'special needs'); (v) a de facto non-discrimination requirement (the conditions attached to these special arrangements shall not impose 'unjustifiable burdens' upon other GSP beneficiaries).[71]

On this basis, the Appellate Body found that the GSP Drugs was inconsistent with WTO law as the EU had failed to demonstrate that it was making available identical tariff treatment to all GSP beneficiaries facing a similar drug problem (thus not fulfilling the de jure non-discrimination requirement), given that it had

[68] See generally, Y Apea and G Shaffer, 'Institutional Choice in the GSP Case: Who Decides the Conditions for Trade Preferences? The Law and Politics of Rights' (2005) 39(6) *Journal of World Trade* 977; J Harrison, 'Incentives for Development: The EC's Generalised System of Preferences, India's WTO Challenge and Proposals for Reform' (2005) 42(6) *Common Market Law Review* 1663; S Charnovitz et al, 'Internet Round: The Appellate Body's Decision' (2004) 3(2) *World Trade Review* 239; JH Mathis, 'Benign Discrimination and the Generalised System of Preferences (GSP)' (2004) 31(4) *Legal Issues of Economic Integration* 289.

[69] Regulation (EC) 980/2005, above n 59, preamble para 2, acknowledging this WTO ruling.

[70] GATT Enabling Clause, para 2a, which describes the GSP as a 'mutually acceptable system of generalized, non-reciprocal and non-discriminatory preferences beneficial to the developing countries,' by reference to the 1971 GATT GSP Decision (above n 6). A substantial part of this case law dealt with the much-debated legal status of the GATT Enabling Clause and in particular its relationship to art I GATT. See generally L Bartels, 'The WTO Enabling Clause and Positive Conditionality in the European Community's GSP Program' (2003) 6(2) *Journal of International Economic Law* 513; R Howse, 'Back to the Court after Shrimp/Turtle: India's Challenge to Labour and Environmental Linkages in the EC Generalised System of Preferences' in E Benvenisti and M Hirsch (eds), *The Impact of International Law on International Cooperation. Theoretical Perspectives* (Cambridge, Cambridge University Press, 2004) 264–72.

[71] AB Report *EC-Tariff Preferences*, paras 148–73. The Appellate Body developed this framework on WTO-consistent needs-based differentiation within the GSP on the basis of para 3(a)–(c) of the GATT Enabling Clause.

pre-selected a closed number of beneficiaries without clear substantive and procedural criteria.[72] Aside from this specific finding, it should be noted that the Appellate Body's ruling clearly favoured the use of trade incentives – 'positive response' – over the use of trade sanctions when countries wish to integrate environmental concerns into their GSP schemes. Significantly, the Appellate Body also made clear that it restrains such a use of GSP preferences to the promotion of internationally-recognised (and not unilaterally-determined) 'special needs'.[73]

The introduction of the GSP-plus is not, however, to be misinterpreted as a direct product of this WTO decision[74] but rather as a concerted attempt by the EU to devise a new single incentive mechanism that incorporates 'the integral nature of the concept of sustainable development',[75] while meeting the Appellate Body's requirements. Unlike previous reforms,[76] this time the EU seeks to justify its policy choice on grounds that

> it is universally recognised that sustainable development involves a variety of aspects, such as respect of fundamental human and labour rights, good governance and environmental protection. Interrelationship among these elements has been expressed, in particular, in multiple international conventions and instruments such as the UN Declaration on the Right to Development of 1986,[77] the Rio Declaration on Environment and Development of 1992,[78] the ILO Declaration on Fundamental Principles and Rights at Work of 1998,[79] the UN Millennium Declaration of 2000[80] and the Johannesburg Declaration on Sustainable Development of 2002[81].[82]

[72] AB Report *EC-Tariff Preferences*, paras 177–89. Given this peculiarity of the GSP Drugs, the Appellate Body did not need to elaborate any further on the other requirements in addition to the de jure non-discrimination one.

[73] On the broader implications of this WTO decision, see L Bartels, 'The Appellate Body Ruling on EC – Tariff Preferences to Developing Countries and its Implications for Conditionality in GSP Programmes' in T Cottier, J Pauwelyn and E Bürgi (eds), *Human Rights and International Trade* (Oxford, Oxford University Press, 2005); R Howse, 'India's WTO Challenge to Drug Enforcement in the European Community Generalised System of Preferences. A Little Known Case with Major Repercussion for "Political" Conditionality in US Trade Policy' (2003) 42(2) *Chicago Journal of International Law* 385.

[74] From a strictly legal perspective, the EU could have complied with the Appellate Body's ruling simply by substantively and procedurally adjusting the GSP Drugs or even by withdrawing it altogether.

[75] Commission, 'Proposal for a Council Regulation applying a Scheme of Generalised Tariff Preferences' COM (2004) 699 final (Commission GSP proposal 2004) Explanatory Memorandum, 3.

[76] See s 3.1 above.

[77] UNGA, 'Declaration on the Right to Development' (1986) UN Doc A/RES/41/128.

[78] 'Rio Declaration on Environment and Development' (12 August 1992) UN Doc A/CONF.151/26 vol I Annex I (Rio Declaration).

[79] ILO, Declaration on Fundamental Principles and Rights at Work (Geneva, 1998) at www.unhcr.org/refworld/docid/425bbdf72.html.

[80] UNGA, 'United Nations Millennium Declaration' (2000) UN Doc A/RES/55/2.

[81] 'Political Declaration of the World Summit on Sustainable Development' (4 September 2002) UN Doc A/CONF.199/20, Resolution 1, Annex (WSSD Declaration).

[82] Commission GSP Proposal 2004, 3 (footnotes not included in the original text).

4.2 Special-incentive arrangement for sustainable development and good governance

The 'special-incentive arrangement for sustainable development and good governance' (or GSP-plus) is aimed at promoting 'sustainable development and good governance' in 'vulnerable countries' through the provision of *additional* tariff preferences vis-a-vis those received under the General GSP. In essence, whereas product coverage is roughly the same for both arrangements,[83] the GSP-plus extends preferential margins on products listed as 'sensitive' under the General GSP,[84] which may enter the EU market mostly on a duty-free basis (with few exceptions).[85] Given the scope of the additional trade benefits offered under the GSP-plus, it can be argued that this new arrangement may only act as an incentive to the (approximately) 80 current beneficiaries[86] of the General GSP, but not to the 50 LDCs[87] benefiting from the EBA initiative. While LDCs are not formally excluded, these countries already enjoy more favourable treatment under the EBA initiative without the need to meet the eligibility criteria set out in the GSP-plus. As will be shown below, the substantive criteria for eligibility of the GSP-plus goes beyond a simple merger of the conditions existing under the three older special-incentive arrangements (GSP Labour, GSP Environment and GSP Drugs). In addition, some procedural ambiguities regarding EU practice to date in the granting of GSP-plus benefits will be discussed.

In line with the preambular objective of establishing a comprehensive special-incentive mechanism that aims to reflect the internationally recognised 'integral nature of the concept of sustainable development',[88] the granting of GSP-plus additional preferences is made conditional upon the ratification and effective implementation[89] of 27 international conventions by 31 December

[83] According to EU data, the 'General GSP' currently covers 6244 goods and the 'GSP-plus' 6336 goods. See Commission, 'More Benefits from Preferential Trade Tariffs for Countries Most in Need: Reform of the EU Generalised System of Preferences' (MEMO/11/284, 2011), 6.

[84] See above n 61.

[85] Current GSP Regulation, art 7. As a general rule there is a total suspension of all duties, except eligible products whose duty is composed of both ad valorem and specific duties for which only the former is suspended. It is also important to note that, unlike the old GSP Environment and GSP Labour, the current GSP-plus treatment is not available to graduated products (listed in Annex I, Column C).

[86] Ibid, preamble para 19 and Annex I, column A. This figure is estimated by excluding from the 176 countries and territories listed as 'nominal' beneficiaries of the EU GSP the 50 LDCs (EBA initiative) and countries that have a more preferential trade agreement with the EU.

[87] Ibid, Annex I, column D, indicating the least developed countries and territories currently included in the EBA initiative.

[88] Ibid, preamble para 7, stating: 'The special incentive arrangement for sustainable development and good governance is based on the integral concept of sustainable development, as recognised by international conventions and instruments such as the 1986 UN Declaration on the Right to Development, the 1992 Rio Declaration on Environment and Development, the 1998 ILO Declaration on Fundamental Principles and Rights at Work, the 2000 UN Millennium Declaration and the 2002 Johannesburg Declaration on Sustainable Development'.

[89] Ibid, art 8(1)(a).

2008,[90] namely: 16 core UN/ILO conventions on the protection of human and labour rights,[91] as well as, seven multilateral environmental agreements and four other international treaties identified by the EU as relating to 'good governance'.[92] The environmental component of the new GSP-plus thus offers a much broader spectrum for linking unilateral trade incentives to environmental protection than the old GSP Environment. As opposed to the narrow focus on tropical forests, the scope of the GSP-plus extends to seven multilateral agreements covering the key environmental issues of biodiversity, climate change and atmosphere, hazardous waste and chemicals. These MEAs are:

1. Montreal Protocol on Substance that Deplete the Ozone Layer (Montreal Protocol)
2. Basel Convention on the Control of Transboundary Movements of Hazardous Wastes and their Disposal (Basel Convention)
3. Stockholm Convention on Persistent Organic Pollutants (POPs Convention)
4. Convention on International Trade in Endangered Species (CITES)
5. Convention on Biological Diversity (CBD)
6. Cartagena Protocol on Biosafety (Biosafety Protocol)
7. Kyoto Protocol to the UN Framework Convention on Climate Change (Kyoto Protocol)[93]

While the GSP-plus endorses a more comprehensive approach to environmental integration, some degree of selectivity can nonetheless be noticed in the choice of

[90] When the 'GSP-plus' was first introduced in 2005 (Regulation (EC) 980/2005, above n 59, art 9(1)), there was some flexibility in meeting this eligibility criteria, with countries being required to ratify and effectively implement all 16 core UN/ILO conventions relating to the protection of human and labour rights as well as at least seven of the 11 treaties in the fields of environmental protection and 'good governance', while committing to ratify and effectively implement all 27 conventions by 31 December 2008.

[91] Current GSP Regulation, Annex III. These are: International Covenant on Civil and Political Rights, 26 December 1966, 999 UNTS 171; International Covenant on Economic, Social and Cultural Rights, 16 December 1966, 993 UNTS 3; International Convention on the Elimination of All Forms of Racial Discrimination, 7 March 1966, 660 UNTS 195; Convention on the Elimination of All Forms of Discrimination against Women, 18 December 1979, 1249 UNTS 13; Convention against Torture and other Cruel, Inhuman or Degrading Treatment or Punishment, 10 December 1984, 1465 UNTS 85; Convention on the Rights of the Child, 20 November 1989, 1577 UNTS 3; Convention on the Prevention and Punishment of the Crime of Genocide, 9 December 1948, 78 UNTS 277; ILO Convention 138 on Minimum Age, above n 26; ILO Convention 182 on the Worst Forms of Child Labour, above n 26; ILO Convention C105 on the Abolition of Forced Labour, above n 26; ILO Convention C29 on Forced Labour, above n 26; ILO Convention 100 on Equal Remuneration, above n 26; ILO Convention 111 on Discrimination (Employment and Occupation), above n 26; Convention 87 on Freedom of Association and Protection of the Right to Organize, above n 26; ILO Convention 98 on the Right to Organise and Collective Bargaining, above n 26; International Convention on the Suppression and Punishment of the Crime of Apartheid, 30 November 1973, 1015 UNTS 243.

[92] Current GSP Regulation, Annex III. These are: UN Single Convention on Narcotic Drugs, 30 March 1961, 520 UNTS 151; UN Convention on Psychotropic Substances, 21 February 1971, 1019 UNTS 175; UN Convention against Illicit Traffic in Narcotic Drugs and Psychotropic Substances, 20 December 1988, 1582 UNTS 95; UN Convention against Corruption, 31 October 2003, 2349 UNTS 41.

[93] Current GSP Regulation, Annex III; see also Ch 1, s 3.5 on EU's own ratification of these MEAs (fully cited).

MEAs set as eligibility criteria. For instance, it may appear odd that the EU does not also require the ratification and implementation of the UNFCCC as an environmental condition to become a GSP-plus beneficiary, given that this agreement, rather than the Kyoto Protocol,[94] sets out the key commitments of developing countries under the international climate change regime and the two instruments are usually read together.[95] In fact, in its recently proposed new GSP Regulation, the Commission has incorporated the UNFCCC as part of the environmental component of a future GSP-plus.[96] It remains unclear, however, why this proposed new GSP regulation does not incorporate the Ozone Convention, which is similarly read in conjunction with its Montreal Protocol.[97] It can be speculated with a certain degree of confidence, however, that the decision to include the UNFCCC relates to the uncertain fate of the Kyoto Protocol post-2012.[98] Furthermore, it is unclear why no reference is made to the Rasmar Convention on Wetlands of International Importance or to the Rotterdam Convention on Prior Informed Consent, which were also singled out by the World Summit on Sustainable Development.[99] The latter discrepancies seem to contrast with the international efforts to ensure a coordinated implementation of the biodiversity-related conventions[100] and of the chemicals conventions.[101]

In substantive terms, when compared to the old GSP Environment, the GSP-plus also has the potential of reducing the margin of discretion enjoyed by EU institutions (and particularly the European Commission) when deciding about the eligibility of requesting countries. The granting of the arrangement's benefits is tied to, inter alia, the 'ratification and effective implementation' of a clear set of international environmental agreements, significantly departing from the more easily subjectivised requirement of applying national legislation 'incorporating the substance of internationally acknowledged standards and guidelines concerning the sustainable management of tropical forests' (including the ITTO

[94] Art 10 of the Kyoto Protocol specifically states that it does not introduce any new commitments for developing countries but reaffirms those under the UNFCCC. See M McKenzie, 'Climate Change and the Generalised System of Preferences' (2008) 11(3) *Journal of International Economic Law* 679, 689.

[95] 'Plan of Implementation of the World Summit on Sustainable Development' (4 September 2002) UN Doc A/CONF.199/20, Resolution 2 Annex, para 39 (WSSD Plan of Implementation).

[96] Proposed GSP Regulation 2014, Annex VIII. The International Convention on the Suspension and Punishment of the Crime of Apartheid would also be dropped from the list, so the total number of international conventions would remain 27.

[97] WSSD Plan of Implementation, para 39(c).

[98] We are thankful to Dr Kati Kulevosi for a useful exchange of ideas on this issue. For a more detailed discussion of the linkages between multilateral negotiations on climate change and the EU approach to this global issue in its bilateral and inter-regional relations, see Ch 7 (ss 2.1 and 3.1).

[99] WSSD Plan of Implementation, paras 23(a) and 32(e).

[100] These include: the CBD; Ramsar Convention; CITES; CMS; and ITGPR. See the website of the Liaison Group at www.cbd.int/blg/.

[101] These include the Basel Convention, the POPs Convention and the Rotterdam Convention, which have held joint meetings of their respective Conference of the Parties (the first simultaneous extraordinary meeting of the Conferences of the Parties to the Basel, Rotterdam and POPs Conventions was held on 22–24 February 2010 in Nusa Dua, Bali, Indonesia).

standards) found in the old GSP Environment.[102] Conversely, as will be detailed below, the procedure for requesting inclusion into the GSP-plus presents both improvements and drawbacks when compared to that found under the GSP Environment.

Under the current GSP Regulation, interested ('vulnerable') countries should provide the Commission with comprehensive written information concerning their ratification of all 27 international conventions, their national legislation and measures undertaken to effectively implement the provisions of these conventions, and a commitment to accept and fully comply with the monitoring and review mechanisms envisaged in the relevant conventions.[103] Surprisingly, unprecedented deadlines were established for submitting such applications: 31 October 2008 (to be granted the GPS-plus as from 1 January 2009) or 30 April 2010 (to be granted the GSP-plus as from 1 July 2010).[104] It is not clear why the potential benefits of the GSP-plus have been procedurally constrained in this manner without allowing, for instance, an interested country to apply for inclusion during the remaining time period (a year and eight months) during which the current GSP Regulation is in place (30 April 2010–31 December 2011).[105] In addition, requests for inclusion are no longer subject to a publication requirement in the Official Journal, as was the case under the GSP Environment, rendering the whole decision-making process for granting the GSP-plus more difficult to trace and less transparent to the public.

After the Commission receives any such request, it should proceed with its examination 'taking account of the findings of the relevant international organisations and agencies'.[106] The setting of the evaluations by the relevant international bodies as benchmarks for deciding on GSP-plus eligibility is surely a procedural improvement vis-a-vis the GSP Environment, as this constitutes a priori more objective and desirable grounds upon which to judge other countries' performance in honouring their international commitments. However, the practical significance of this procedural improvement will ultimately depend upon the actual availability of such internationally-based assessments, and indeed on the actual existence of monitoring mechanisms under each of the 27 listed conventions.

[102] Current GSP Regulation, art 8(1)(a), with old GSP Regulation, art 21(2).

[103] Current GSP Regulation, art 9(2). See also Commission, 'Information notice on submission of requests under art 9.1(a)(ii) of Regulation (EC) 732/2008 of 22 July 2008 to be granted the special incentive arrangement as from 1 July 2010' (17 November 2009).

[104] Current GSP Regulation, art 9(1)(a). This was also the case under Regulation (EC) 980/2005, above n 59, art 10(1)(a), albeit there was only one deadline to apply (31 October 2005) and unsuccessful applicants were obliged to wait three years before being able to reapply.

[105] See, however, Proposed GSP Regulation 2014, art 10, where the Commission has proposed to remove this restriction and allow countries to apply any time for inclusion in the GSP-plus.

[106] Current GSP Regulation, art 10(1). The Commission may also ask the requesting country any questions that it considers relevant and may verify the information received with the requesting country or any other relevant sources. Note that a similar legal nexus between EU decision-making and the assessments of international supervisory bodies was already found in the old GSP Drugs, see above n 28.

In the case of MEA implementation, the European Commission can, in principle, take into account the findings and recommendations of the compliance mechanisms that have been established under five out of seven of the listed agreements: the Basel Convention,[107] the Montreal Protocol,[108] the Biosafety Protocol,[109] the Kyoto Protocol,[110] and CITES.[111] A compliance mechanism is currently being negotiated under the POPs Convention.[112] The CBD, instead, has no compliance mechanism as such and its Parties have not manifested the intention to create one.[113] Both because some of the listed MEAs do not have compliance mechanisms and because some of the existing compliance mechanisms are not actively used to assess the compliance of specific parties,[114] the Commission would also need to rely on the information provided by countries' self-reporting exercises to the respective Conferences of the Parties (COP) of the MEAs[115] and on the relevant decisions taken by those bodies – which, however, for the most part, provide for general recommendations on reporting rather than specific comments on individual parties' compliance. Availability of timely and conclusive international assessments on countries' implementation performance under the various MEAs (and indeed,

[107] Basel COP Decisions VI/12, 'Establishment of a mechanism for promoting implementation and compliance' and VI/13, 'Interim procedure for electing the members of the committee for administering the mechanism for promoting implementation and compliance' (2003) UN Doc UNEP/CHW.6/40.

[108] UNEP, 'Report of the Implementation Committee for the Montreal Protocol, Twentieth Meeting' (1998) UN Doc NEP/OzL.Pro./ImpCom20/4, paras 24–33.

[109] Biosafety Protocol, art 34 and COP/MOP Decision BS-I/7, 'Establishment of Procedures and Mechanisms on Compliance under the Cartagena Protocol on Biosafety' (2004) UN Doc UNEP/CBD/BS/COP-MOP/1/15.

[110] Kyoto Protocol COP/MOP, Decision 27/CMP.1 'Procedures and Mechanisms relating to Compliance under the Kyoto Protocol' (2006) UN Doc FCCC/KP/CMP/2005/8/Add.3.

[111] CITES has developed a set of procedures over time which monitor compliance with the convention, including the Review of Significant Trade and the National Legislation Project. See S Biniaz, 'Remarks about the CITES Compliance Regime' in U Beyerlin, PT Stoll and R Wolfrum (eds), *Ensuring Compliance with Multilateral Environmental Agreements* (Dordrecht, Martinus Nijhoff, 2006).

[112] In April 2011 the Conference of the Parties to the POPs Convention decided to continue consideration of draft procedures and institutional mechanisms on non-compliance. See M Ashton et al, 'Summary of the fifth meeting of the Conference of the Parties to the Stockholm Convention on Persistent Organic Pollutants: 25–29 April 2011' (2011) 15(182) *Earth Negotiations Bulletin*, 12–13.

[113] Note, however, that the CBD Conference of the Parties decided in 2010 to consider the possible reinforcement of its monitoring of parties' compliance, albeit without necessarily pointing to the need to establish a fully-fledged compliance mechanism. See CBD Decisions X/2, 'The Strategic Plan for Biodiversity 2011–2020 and the Aichi Biodiversity Targets' (2010) UN Doc UNEP/CBD/COP/10/27, paras 14–15. For a discussion, see E Morgera and E Tsioumani, 'Yesterday, Today and Tomorrow: Looking Afresh at the Convention on Biological Diversity' (forthcoming) 21 *Yearbook of International Environmental Law*.

[114] This is the case of the Basel Convention and the Biosafety Protocol, see A Fodella, 'Mechanisms for Promoting Implementation and Compliance with the 1989 Basel Convention on the Transboundary Movement of Hazardous Wastes and their Disposal' in T Treves et al (eds), *Non-compliance Procedures and Mechanisms and the Effectiveness of International Environmental Agreements* (The Hague, TMC Asser Press, 2009), 46 and C Ragni, 'Procedures and Mechanisms on Compliance under the 2000 Cartagena Protocol on Biosafety to the 1992 Convention on Biological Diversity' in T Treves et al (eds), *Non-compliance Procedures and Mechanisms and the Effectiveness of International Environmental Agreements* (The Hague, TMC Asser Press, 2009), 109.

[115] CBD, art 26; Basel Convention, art 13(3); Biosafety Protocol, art 33; CITES, art 8(7); Montreal Protocol, art 7; POPs Convention, art 15; Kyoto Protocol art 7.2; UNFCCC arts 4.2 and 12.

under the other 20 listed conventions) cannot therefore be taken for granted each time the Commission takes a decision on the granting of the GSP-plus.

Following the examination of requests, the Commission takes a final decision on the granting of the GSP-plus in close coordination with the 'GSP Committee'.[116] Interestingly again, the current GSP Regulation also sets a specific deadline for making such a decision: by 15 December 2008 (for requests received by 31 October 2008) or by 15 June 2010 (for requests received by 30 April 2010).[117] The Commission is further required to publish a notice in the Official Journal listing the 'vulnerable' countries qualifying for GSP-plus additional benefits. In cases of unsuccessful applications, the country concerned may request a reasoned explanation from the Commission.[118] As in the case of the GSP Environment, a suspension clause is also found in the current GSP Regulation whereby the GSP-plus additional preferences may be suspended if the national legislation of a beneficiary country 'no longer incorporates' the listed 27 conventions or if that legislation is 'not effectively implemented'.[119]

Unlike for its initial granting, decisions on (possible) suspension of the GSP-plus are not, regrettably, anchored to the assessments of any international review mechanisms, at least de jure.[120] There appear to be no compelling grounds for such a differentiation other than a desire by the EU (and the Commission in particular) to retain greater room for manoeuvre in relation to suspension. This also raises questions on the extent to which the European Commission continues to cooperate with, and rely on the assessments of, international supervisory bodies in monitoring continued compliance by GSP-plus beneficiaries.[121] In this regard, a significant improvement is proposed in the new GSP regulation through the introduction of a specific procedure for monitoring performance under the GSP-plus. The Commission would be required, as of the date of the granting of the arrangement, to keep under review the status of ratification of the 27 listed conventions by the GSP-plus beneficiaries and to monitor their effective imple-

[116] Current GSP Regulation, art 10(2).

[117] Ibid, art 10(3).

[118] Ibid, art 10(4).

[119] Ibid, art 15(2). Note that the rationale of this suspension clause is arguably different from 'negative' conditionality: if one accepts that a given developing country is entitled to *additional* preferences because of its special burdens in honouring its commitments under the listed international conventions, one should equally accept that such preferences are withdrawn whenever the competent international monitoring bodies denounce serious breaches on the part of a given GSP-plus beneficiary.

[120] Ibid, art 15(2) provides that the GSP-plus additional benefits 'may be withdrawn temporarily, in respect of all or of certain products included in this arrangement and originating in a beneficiary country, *in particular* if the national legislation no longer incorporates . . . [the 27 international conventions listed in Annex III] . . . or if that legislation is not effectively implemented' (emphasis added), without any reference to the 'findings of the relevant international organizations and bodies' found in the provisions governing the granting of the arrangement (see above n 106). The term 'in particular' presumably refers to the fact that suspension can also take place if a beneficiary country no longer meets the 'vulnerable country' criteria (see below n 125), independently of whether its national legislation continues to incorporate the relevant international conventions and is effectively implemented.

[121] In practice, however, the Commission claims to have relied 'heavily' on reports by relevant UN bodies when conducting its human rights investigations in respect to El Salvador and Sri Lanka (see below n 133).

mentation by 'examining the conclusions and recommendations of the relevant monitoring bodies.'[122] The proposed new GSP regulation further strengthens the requirement upon GSP-plus beneficiaries to 'accept without reservation the reporting requirements imposed by each convention' and to 'give a binding undertaking to accept regular monitoring and review of its implementation record in accordance with the provisions of the conventions.'[123] Failure to do so would lead to a suspension of GSP-plus benefits.[124]

Notwithstanding the provisions examined above, the EU retains a large degree of discretion in allocating the GSP-plus additional preferences through the operation of the self-defined criterion of 'vulnerable country'. It should be stressed that the GSP-plus, as opposed to the old GSP Environment, is not a priori open to any GSP beneficiary willing to, and capable of, ratifying and implementing the listed 27 international conventions but only to those which are considered by the EU as 'vulnerable'.[125] In practical terms, this cumulative criterion of 'vulnerability' restricts the GSP-plus eligibility to countries with an extremely low share of GSP-covered exports to the EU market (that is, one per cent), de facto excluding (around) 20 out of the 80 potential applicants.[126] This self-defined and largely arbitrary criterion[127] has thus constrained – at least to some extent – the potential of the 'GSP-plus' as an incentive mechanism to promote 'sustainable development and good governance': while any developing country seeking the arrangement's benefits has it (arguably) in its power to ratify and implement the listed international conventions, it cannot be legitimately expected also to keep its share of GSP-covered exports to the EU market below the one per cent threshold so as to meet the 'vulnerability' criterion.

Turning to an analysis of available EU policy practice, the GSP-plus was first granted on 1 July 2005, on a provisional and rather obscure basis,[128] to 14 developing

[122] Proposed GSP Regulation 2014, art 13(1).

[123] Ibid, art 9(1)(d).

[124] Ibid, art 10(5).

[125] Current GSP Regulation, art 8(2). 'Vulnerable country' is cumulatively defined as: (1) one not meeting the criterion for full graduation and hence not listed in Annex I; and (2) one whose GSP-covered imports into the Community represent less than 1% in value of total GSP-covered imports into the Community. The second element of this vulnerability criterion appears most restrictive in allocating the arrangement's additional benefits among the beneficiaries of the EU GSP, as countries that have been fully graduated from the scheme (ie first element) fall outside the scope of application of the current GSP Regulation altogether.

[126] Above n 86 regarding the (estimated) 80 potential applicants of the GSP-plus, and Commission, 'Statistical notice on list of Countries considered "vulnerable" in the sense of art 8 of GSP Regulation 2009–2011' (21 September 2009).

[127] At the very best, the quantitative benchmarks identified by the EU are indicative of countries' degrees of export diversification and trade integration in terms of the EU market and hence may not (always) constitute appropriate indicators of their levels of diversification and integration with respect to the *international* trading system as a whole. Most importantly, they are not based upon any internationally recognised criterion for differentiating among developing countries on grounds of economic vulnerability, such as those used in UN circles.

[128] Regulation (EC) 980/2005, above n 59, preamble para 7, formally justifying the provisional application of the GSP-plus on the need to conform with the Appellate Body ruling in the *India-EU GSP* dispute. Whereas a substantive and procedural review of the old GSP Drugs was certainly required to comply with that WTO decision, the early introduction of the GSP-plus itself was not.

countries presumed to 'already fulfil the criteria'[129] set out for eligibility, thus de facto bypassing the general procedure for requesting 'GSP-plus' benefits. Nevertheless, on 21 December 2005, the Commission confirmed the qualification of all 14 countries provisionally included[130] and added the Republic of Moldova to the list of beneficiaries to which the 'GSP-plus' was granted from 1 January 2006 to 31 December 2008.[131] One may certainly find it surprising that the new incentive mechanism was able to attract more developing countries in just a few a months of existence than all its three predecessors taken together during a decade (that is, 12 beneficiaries for the GSP Drugs and two for the GSP Labour), even though the GSP-plus contains much more demanding eligibility conditions and has made relatively minor improvements in terms of the additional preferences accorded. It also seems suspicious that 11 out of 15 of these first beneficiaries of the GSP-plus were previously benefiting from the GSP Drugs – the arrangement under the old GSP that was found to be inconsistent with WTO law.

And yet the Commission has upheld the GSP-plus eligibility of 14 of these original beneficiaries under the current GSP Regulation and included three new countries (Armenia, Azerbaijan and Paraguay) into the GSP-plus as of 1 January 2009.[132] In June 2009, however, the EU decided to withdraw the beneficiary status of Venezuela as it had not ratified one of the listed conventions and subsequently in February 2010, that of Sri Lanka following a one-year investigation by the Commission that found 'significant shortcomings' in that country's implementation of three of the listed UN human rights conventions.[133] The GSP-plus

[129] Ibid, preamble para 8, requiring the Commission to 'confirm their qualification by 15 December 2005'; and also Annex I, column E identifying the 14 countries to which the 'GSP-plus' was provisionally granted on 15 July 2005.

[130] Namely: Bolivia, Colombia, Costa Rica, Ecuador, El Salvador, Georgia, Guatemala, Honduras, Mongolia, Nicaragua, Panama, Peru, Sri Lanka and Venezuela.

[131] Commission Decision (EC) 2005/924 on the list of the beneficiary countries which qualify for the special incentive arrangement for sustainable development and good governance, provided for by art 26(e) of Council Regulation (EC) No 980/2005 [2005] OJ L337/50.

[132] Commission Decision (EC) 2008/938 on the list of the beneficiary countries which qualify for the special incentive arrangement for sustainable development and good governance provided for in Council Regulation (EC) No 732/2008 [2008] OJ L334/90 (confirming the eligibility of Bolivia, Colombia, Costa Rica, El Salvador, Ecuador, Georgia, Guatemala, Honduras, Mongolia, Nicaragua, Peru, Sri Lanka, Venezuela; and adding Armenia, Azerbaijan and Paraguay. El Salvador and Sri Lanka were provisionally included pending the outcome of human rights investigations launched by the Commission in May 2008 and October 2008); Council Regulation (EC) 55/2008 introducing autonomous trade preferences for the Republic of Moldova [2008] OJ L020/1 (explaining Moldova's removal from the GSP-plus as it was granted more generous preferences as part of the ENP); Commission Decision (EU) 2010/318 on the beneficiary countries which qualify for the special incentive arrangement for sustainable development and good governance for the period from 1 July 2010 to 31 December 2011 as provided in Council Regulation (EC) No 732/2008 [2010] OJ L142/10 (confirming eligibility of Panama).

[133] Commission Decision (EC) 2009/454 amending Decision 2008/938/EC on the list of the beneficiary countries which qualify for the special incentive arrangement for sustainable development and good governance [2009] L149/78; Council Regulation (EU) 143/2010 temporarily withdrawing the special incentive arrangement for sustainable development and good governance provided for under Regulation (EC) No 732/2008 with respect to the Democratic Socialist Republic of Sri Lanka [2010] L45/1. Conversely, the investigation undertaken with respect to El Salvador led to the positive finding that this country was effectively implementing the ILO Convention at stake and thus it continues to benefit from the GSP plus treatment, see Commission, 'Press Release – Termination of the GSP+ investigation on El Salvador' 22 October 2009.

additional preferences are thus currently being extended to 15 countries (see table below).

Table 2. *List of Countries Qualifying for 'GSP-plus'*[134]

'GSP-plus' Beneficiary Country	*Period*	*Position old GSP*
Armenia	January 2009–present	General GSP
Azerbaijan	January 2009–present	General GSP
Bolivia	July 2005–present	GSP Drugs
Colombia	July 2005–present	GSP Drugs
Costa Rica	July 2005–present	GSP Drugs
Ecuador	July 2005–present	GSP Drugs
El Salvador	July 2005–present	GSP Drugs
Georgia	July 2005–present	General GSP
Guatemala	July 2005–present	GSP Drugs
Honduras	July 2005–present	GSP Drugs
Mongolia	July 2005–present	General GSP
Nicaragua	July 2005–present	GSP Drugs
Panama	July 2005–present	GSP Drugs
Paraguay	January 2009–present	General GSP
Peru	July 2005–present	GSP-Drugs
Republic of Moldova	December 2005–December 2008	GSP Labour
Sri Lanka	July 2005–February 2010	GSP Labour
Venezuela	July 2005–June 2009	GSP Drugs

Against this background, it can be argued that the prospects of GSP-plus benefits have been influential[135] in accelerating the ratification of the two most recent MEAs among the seven listed: the 2001 POPs Convention (by 9 countries)[136] and

[134] Elaborated on above nn 129–33, as of 1 June 2011.

[135] 1 January 2005 is taken as the date from which the GSP-plus may have begun to exert some influence in accelerating ratification rates of MEAs given that the intention of the EU to include these international agreements as part of the eligibility criteria of the GSP-plus was made public in the Commission's Communication of 7 July 2004 (above n 65). Accordingly, only ratifications that occurred between 1 January 2005 and 31 December 2008 (date of compliance with all 27 conventions, above n 90) are taken into account for the GSP-plus beneficiaries provisionally listed: Bolivia, Colombia, Costa Rica, Ecuador, El Salvador, Georgia, Guatemala, Honduras, Mongolia, Nicaragua, Panama, Peru, Moldova. For the three new countries that were granted the GSP-plus as of 1 January 2009 (Armenia, Azerbaijan and Paraguay), this period is extended only until 31 October 2008 (date of submission of requests to the Commission, above n 104). Certainly, factors other than the GSP-plus may have influenced the ratification process of MEAs by the countries concerned.

[136] Colombia (22 October 2008); Costa Rica (6 February 2007); El Salvador (27 May 2008); Georgia (4 October 2006); Guatemala (30 July 2008); Honduras (23 May 2005); Nicaragua (1 December 2005); Peru (14 September 2005); Sri Lanka (22 December 2005).

the 2000 Biosafety Protocol (by four countries).[137] Ratification of the other five listed MEAs preceded the introduction of the GSP-plus in the case of most of its beneficiaries, except for CITES (ratified by Armenia on 23 October 2008). Yet this positive influence on ratification rates does not necessarily translate into an effective implementation of the MEAs in all cases. The performance of the GSP-plus in ensuring effective implementation of the listed MEAs (as of the other 20 conventions) is still subject to discussion, particularly for the several environmental treaties that were only fairly recently adopted. Nonetheless, a recent independent evaluation of the GSP-plus (commissioned by the EU) finds that the arrangement has, overall, been more effective at ensuring de jure implementation (that is, transposition into domestic legislation and compliance with reporting/monitoring procedures) of environmental conventions than of other eligibility conditions (particularly, core labour rights). The report also points to difficulties of some GSP-plus beneficiaries in complying with the monitoring requirements of CITES and the CBD. Finally, the report argues that the GSP-plus could have also influenced the role of foreign aid, motivating donor resources to support implementation efforts of environmental conventions that would otherwise not have entered the countries concerned.[138]

4.3 Temporary withdrawal of GSP preferences

From an environmental perspective,[139] the current GSP Regulation has not introduced any new grounds for (temporarily) suspending GSP status to that existing under the old GSP,[140] namely sustainable fisheries. However, the wording of the current GSP Regulation exclusively refers to 'the serious and systematic infringement of the objectives of regional fishery organisations or arrangements of which the Community is a member concerning the conservation and management of fishery resources'.[141] The same normative arguments raised against the use of 'negative' conditionality in relation to the old GSP are thus applicable to the present GSP scheme. Nonetheless, the EU has (as yet) continued to shy away from using the 'stick' of trade sanctions under the current GSP Regulation, with only one exception on grounds of labour rights violations.[142]

[137] Azerbaijan (1 April 2005); Costa Rica (6 February 2007); Georgia (4 November 2008); and Honduras (18 November 2008).

[138] Gasiorek et al, above n 24, 154–64.

[139] Note that the grounds for (temporarily) suspending GSP preferences have been extended through the addition of 'serious and systematic violation of principles laid down in the conventions listed in Part A of Annex III [the 16 UN/ILO human rights conventions that form part of the GSP-plus eligibility criteria] on the basis of the conclusions of the relevant monitoring bodies.' (Current GSP Regulation, art 15 (1)(a)).

[140] See s 3.3 above.

[141] Current GSP Regulation, art 15 (1)(e).

[142] See the case of Belarus from which all tariff preferences were (temporarily) withdrawn in 2007 on grounds of systemic violations of the right to freedom of association: Commission, 'Press Release – The EU will withdraw GSP Preferences from Belarus over workers' rights violations' 15 June 2007. The suspension of GSP status from Belarus and Myanmar are still in force at the time of writing

5. ASSESSMENT AND CONCLUSIONS

Over the past decade, the EU has integrated environmental protection requirements into its GSP scheme in an incremental manner and as part of a broader process of rethinking the role of this trade measure within its post-Maastricht external relations. Gradually, the GSP has moved from being a trade tool primarily aimed at supporting export growth and industrialisation in least developed and developing countries to one that promotes sustainable development and good governance more broadly, in line with the emerging international consensus recognising environmental protection, human rights promotion and good governance practices as constitutive elements of the development process.[143] The EU's increasing attempt to justify its environmental integration initiatives on the basis of international normative processes on sustainable development is a particularly welcome step in the GSP context given the unilateral character of this measure. As to the modalities chosen for this integration exercise, the EU has generally favoured a positive and cooperative approach and stands out as the only GSP donor (as yet) to have devised trade incentive mechanisms that reward compliance (through additional tariff preferences) with certain environmental conditions, rather than seeking to penalise non-compliance. This mirrors the general approach of international environmental law towards compliance that is collaborative, non-confrontational and focused on assistance and problem-solving, rather than being adversarial and punitive.[144]

On its surface the current GSP-plus presents some important improvements vis-a-vis the old GSP Environment. In substantive terms, the GSP-plus adopts a much broader approach to environmental protection (now incorporating seven core MEAs), together with a stricter requirement that potential beneficiaries ratify and implement the listed MEAs. In procedural terms, the EU's decision-making on GSP-plus eligibility is tied to the assessments of competent international supervisory bodies with respect to both the substantive interpretation of the environmental standards in question and other countries' relative performance in meeting them. Such a linkage may in turn help to strengthen the persuasive action of these non-judicial and non-confrontational international bodies, particularly

(Current GSP Regulation, preamble para 23). Note that this has not necessarily halted exports from these countries to the EU market, but just reinstated MFN-based duties on the products concerned.

[143] See also Ch 1, s 4.2.3.1.

[144] Only the Kyoto Protocol and CITES compliance mechanisms may lead to sanctions: respectively, suspension of the party's eligibility to participate in the market mechanisms and trade suspensions (E Morgera, E Tsioumani, S Aguilar and H Wilkins, 'Implementation Challenges and Compliance in MEA Negotiations' in P Chasek and L Wagner (eds), *The Roads from Rio: Lessons learned from 20 years of multilateral environmental negotiations* (London, Earthscan, forthcoming 2012)). These two compliance mechanisms, however, remain essentially cooperative and targeted to facilitate compliance rather than punish non-compliance. They cannot, therefore, be considered 'dispute settlement mechanisms' in their own right, as suggested by S Switzer, 'Environmental Protection and the Generalised System of Preferences: A Legal and Appropriate Linkage?' (2008) 57(1) *International and Comparative Law Quarterly* 113, 145.

in light of the requirement for GSP-plus beneficiaries to comply fully with the relevant monitoring mechanisms under the listed MEAs. This legal nexus between EU decision-making on GSP-plus eligibility and MEA compliance mechanisms, however, exists only in relation to the initial inclusion of a country in the arrangement and the extent to which the EU continues to cooperate with, and rely on the assessments of, these supervisory bodies beyond this initial stage remains unclear.[145]

Upon closer examination a number of other caveats in the GSP-plus are noted. In particular, the EU-defined criterion of 'vulnerable country' as an additional condition for GSP-plus eligibility, coupled with some procedural obscurities observed in the granting of the arrangement's benefits to date, appears to replicate – albeit in a more disguised manner – the 'closed list' phenomenon of the old GSP Drugs. These are regrettable limitations on the GSP-plus potential to act as a meaningful instrument to encourage the observance of international environmental (and other) regimes, particularly in light of the almost universal embrace of the selected MEAs.[146] These limitations are also likely to prove more problematic from a WTO law perspective than its environmental component.[147] The ongoing review of the EU GSP thus offers an opportunity to fully unlock, both substantively and procedurally, the potential of the GSP-plus as an incentive mechanism to promote compliance with international environmental standards.

Yet, such a potential may nonetheless continue to be undermined by the proliferation of free trade agreements between the EU and some developing countries, whose conclusion is not made conditional on MEA ratification and implementation, but offers nonetheless more preferential terms of access to the EU market than the GSP-plus.[148] This is even the case of the post-Global Europe agreements, which include the ratification and effective implementation of MEAs as part of their trade and sustainable development chapter, but not as a strict condition for the granting of EU trade concessions, as does the GSP-plus. To some extent, this may be explained by the different nature of these two preferential trade measures. Certainly, the EU can more easily impose the ratification and effective implementation of MEAs as condition on the granting of GSP preferences that are unilateral and non-reciprocal. Conversely, in the context of negotiated and reciprocal FTAs, the EU may not be able to introduce (nor willing to accept for itself) the same condition.

[145] Note that some improvements in this regard have been proposed for the new GSP Regulation (see above nn 122–24).

[146] As of May 2011: Montreal Protocol (196 Contracting Parties); Basel Convention (176 Contracting Parties); POPs Convention (173 Contracting Parties); CITES (175 Contracting Parties); CBD (193 Contracting Parties); Biosafety Protocol (161 Contracting Parties); Kyoto Protocol (192 Contracting Parties).

[147] See an early assessment by these authors, G Marín Durán and E Morgera, 'Case note: WTO India-EC GSP Dispute: The Future of Unilateral Trade Incentives linked to Multilateral Environmental Agreements' (2005) 14(2) *Review of European Community and International Environmental Law* 173. For a different view, see Switzer, above n 144, 133–44. More generally, see L Bartels, 'The WTO Legality of the EU GSP+ Arrangements' (2007) 10(4) *Journal of International Economic Law* 869.

[148] See Ch 2.

Aside from the specific issue of WTO law-consistency, the legitimacy of the GSP-plus ought to be assessed from a broader international law viewpoint. The EU's proposition that the observance of core environmental standards[149] is internationally recognised as a constitutive element of the contemporary notion of sustainable development is not misled. In the 1992 Rio Declaration, for instance, world leaders clearly affirmed that 'in order to achieve sustainable development, environmental protection shall constitute an integral part of the development process and cannot be considered in isolation form it'.[150] This was further corroborated at the 2002 World Summit on Sustainable Development,[151] whose Plan of Implementation[152] explicitly refers to all seven MEAs listed as substantive criteria for GSP-plus eligibility. Thus, concerns that the GSP-plus may contribute to 'exporting the EU collective preference abroad',[153] may be alleviated by a certain degree of correspondence between the MEAs selected by the EU as part of the GSP-plus eligibility criteria and those whose ratification and implementation is periodically called for by the UN General Assembly as a contribution to more coherent and effective international environmental governance.[154] Nonetheless, it is to be stressed that there is no complete matching between the MEAs selected by the EU and those singled out by the WSSD and the General Assembly: the international legitimacy of the GSP-plus would therefore benefit from a reasoned explanation by the EU of its selection of MEAs.[155]

In any event, it does not necessarily follow that international consensus exists on the appropriateness of promoting international environmental standards through unilateral trade initiatives like the GSP-plus. Most of the listed MEAs do acknowledge, in line with the principle of common but differentiated responsibility, the 'special needs' of developing countries in honouring their commitments[156] and call upon developed countries to provide additional funding in order

[149] The observations made here are limited to the environmental component of the GSP-plus, and may not necessarily be extended to the other 20 conventions listed as eligibility criteria for the GSP-plus, particularly those identified by the EU as relating to 'good governance' given the lack of an internationally-agreed definition of this term. For an assessment, see G Marín Durán, *Development-based Differentiation in the European Community's External Trade Policy – Selected Issues under Community and International Trade Law* (EUI Doctoral Thesis, 2007), 282–89.

[150] Rio Declaration, Principle 3.

[151] WSSD Declaration, para 5.

[152] For a useful outline of relevant portions of the WSSD Plan of Implementation, see further, MC Cordonier-Segger and K Ahsfaq, *Sustainable Development Law. Principles, Practices and Prospects* (Oxford, Oxford University Press, 2004), 32–36 and tables 2.2 and 2.3.

[153] Switzer, above n 144, 141.

[154] UNGA, 'Report of the Governing Council of the United Nations Environment Programme on its Eleventh Special Session' (2010) UN Doc A/RES/65/162, para 3 where the Assembly '*[r]ecognizes* the ratification and implementation of relevant multilateral environmental agreements contribute to more effective international environmental governance . . . and, in this context, invites Member States to ratify and implement relevant multilateral environmental agreements.'

[155] To respond to the difficulty in discerning the reasons why particular MEAs were chosen and others were not, as pointed out by Switzer, above n 144, 143. The proposed new GSP could also be possibly subjected to a sustainability impact assessment (see Ch 6), as alluded to by Switzer, above n 144, 147.

[156] See Basel Convention, arts 10(3)–(4) and 14; CBD, arts 12, 17, 20(2) and (4); POPs Convention, arts 4(7), 11(2)(c), 12(5) and 13(5); Biosafety Protocol, arts 20(1)(b) and 22(2); Montreal Protocol, arts 5, 9 and 10(1)–(3).

to facilitate this endeavour.[157] Yet, none expressly foresees the use of GSP preferences as a possible means to assist developing countries' implementation efforts.[158]

In this regard, Principle 12 of the Rio Declaration specifically warns that 'trade policy measures for environmental purposes should not constitute a means of arbitrary or unjustifiable discrimination or a disguised restriction on international trade', and states that unilateral actions 'should be avoided'.[159] However, Agenda 21 also provides that 'improved market access for developing countries' exports in conjunction with sound . . . environmental policies would have a positive environmental impact and therefore make an important contribution towards sustainable development'.[160] From this angle, the GSP-plus can be accepted as an imaginative tool to assist developing countries through 'improved market access' in achieving sustainable development.

Ultimately, the extent to which the arrangement would (or would not) gain international legitimacy largely depends on whether, in practice, its functioning is firmly anchored on international standards, its implementation is open and transparent, and the legal nexus between the EU's own decisions on eligibility and the assessments of competent international monitoring bodies is upheld. The arrangement's international credibility would certainly also be enhanced by the ratification *and* effective implementation of the listed MEAs by the EU and its Member States themselves.[161]

[157] CBD, arts 21 and 39; Biosafety Protocol, art 28(2); UNFCCC art 4(3)-(4); POPs Convention, arts 13 and 14.

[158] Only some of these MEAs include trade measures among the tools for implementation, and usually in the form of trade restrictive measures rather trade liberalising ones. See, for instance, CITES, the Biosafety Protocol and the Basel Convention.

[159] This principle is reiterated in the MEAs that address the use of trade measures for environmental purposes, see, eg, art 3(5) UNFCCC.

[160] Agenda 21, para 2.5.

[161] It should be noted that some EU Member States (Italy and Malta) have not ratified the POPs Convention at the time of writing.

4

Environmental Integration in External Assistance

1. INTRODUCTION

AN IMPORTANT, LARGELY unilateral, set of tools for environmental integration in EU external relations are the financing instruments that support EU cooperation with third countries and regions. In fact, in addition to the Treaty-based requirement for environmental integration, a political commitment to mainstreaming environmental concerns into EU external cooperation is embedded in several policy documents, most notably the 2001 Environmental Integration Strategy and the later 2005 European Consensus on Development.[1] The Consensus defines the environment and sustainable management of natural resources as one of the nine areas for EU action (that is, those that can become focal sectors for support under EU funding programmes), and calls for a stronger commitment to mainstreaming environmental sustainability as a cross-cutting issue in all EU cooperation activities, particularly with a view to assisting developing countries in environmental policy-making and MEA implementation.[2] In addition, the EU has undertaken several commitments in this regard at the international level, including in relation to the achievement of MDG7 on environmental sustainability. In quantitative terms, the potential of EU external assistance as a means to support environmental integration goes largely undisputed, with the EU being the world's largest provider of aid.[3]

Against the background of Article 11 TFEU, environmental integration into EU external assistance can have several dimensions. This chapter will essentially concentrate on the *definition* element of Article 11 TFEU, namely the degree to which environmental concerns are substantively integrated into EU financing regulations. These regulations, however, can also be seen as a means to implement the environmental cooperation commitments undertaken by the EU in the

[1] Council, 'Conclusions on strategy for the integration of environmental considerations into development policy to promote sustainable development' 31 May 2001 (Environmental Integration Strategy); Council, Representatives of the Governments of the Member States meeting in the Council, European Parliament and Commission, 'Joint Statement on the European Development Policy: The European Consensus' [2006] OJ C46/1 (European Consensus on Development).

[2] European Consensus on Development, paras 75–76 and 105.

[3] That is, collectively with its Member States (see Ch 1, s 2).

framework of bilateral, inter-regional and indeed multilateral agreements. The chapter will not, however, explore the *implementation* element of Article of 11 TFEU properly speaking, which would require a detailed account of the environment-related cooperation activities that have been actually financed by the EU. It is equally beyond the scope of this book to verify environmental integration into the parallel aid programmes provided by the EU Member States individually, albeit this is certainly a critical factor in evaluating the importance of the overall EU environment-related funding.

The chapter begins by offering an overview of EU external assistance with a view to introducing the reader to key tools and actors that are peculiar to this area of EU external relations. It will then turn to an examination of financing instruments that are purposely aimed at integrating environmental concerns into EU external assistance, namely the so-called thematic programmes explicitly devoted to the environment. It will trace the evolution of EU thematic funding for the environment from the old 2000–06 measures to the current programme (2007–13) adopted after the endorsement of the European Consensus on Development, highlighting shifts in priorities, approaches and financial commitments. The chapter will finally explore environmental integration into other EU financing instruments that are not specifically targeted at environmental protection, but are important sources of EU funding to third countries and regions (so-called geographic programmes).

2. EU EXTERNAL ASSISTANCE: INSTRUMENTS AND ACTORS

The legislative framework for EU external assistance is governed by a series of financing regulations that are jointly adopted by the Council and the European Parliament (pursuant to the ordinary legislative procedure) on the basis of a proposal by the Commission.[4] As most of these external assistance instruments – with the notable exception of the European Development Fund (EDF)[5] – are sourced from the EU budget, their adoption is subject to the EU multiannual financial framework (commonly known as 'financial perspective'), which lays down maximum amounts ('ceilings') for each broad category of expenditure ('headings') for a clearly determined period of time (usually five years).[6] The current EU external assistance regulations thus follow the 2007–13 Financial Perspective,[7] and are

[4] Art 209(1) TFEU for development cooperation measures; art 212(2) TFEU for economic and technical assistance with countries other than developing countries (see Ch 1, s 5.3).

[5] See s 4.4 below.

[6] The previous financial framework, which was applicable to some of the financing regulations examined in this chapter, covered the period 2000–06, and was established by the Interinstitutional Agreement between the European Parliament, the Council and the Commission on budgetary discipline and improvement of the budgetary procedure [1999] OJ C179/1.

[7] The 2007–13 financial framework was established (without a Treaty basis) by the Interinstitutional Agreement by the European Parliament, the Council and the Commission on budgetary discipline and sound financial management [2006] OJ C139/1. The multiannual financial framework is now specifically mentioned in art 312 TFEU. On the EU budget, see further B Laffan and J Lindner, 'The Budget:

financed from resources available under Heading 4 'EU as a Global Player.'[8] Typically, these financing regulations stipulate: the general scope and objectives of cooperation;[9] the types of external assistance programmes available and the applicable eligibility criteria;[10] the general framework for programming and allocating funds;[11] and the *indicative* financial allocations (overall and per programme).[12]

Within this broader external assistance framework, EU environment-related financial and technical support to third countries or regions, as well as international bodies (such as MEA Secretariats), is provided through various channels. Of most significance for our purposes are the so-called thematic and geographic financing instruments. The latter have a defined geographic coverage and are increasingly designed to support a specific EU external policy (for example, EU enlargement), being thus the instrument for cooperation preferred by the EU.[13] Conversely, thematic instruments are not regional or country-based, but focus instead on a specific theme (including the environment) and are in principle open to all developing countries.[14] Aside from these differences in purpose and scope, another important difference between these two EU funding tools pertains to their implementation. Thematic instruments (including on the environment) are implemented on the basis of multiannual strategy papers that are elaborated by the Commission alone and that reflect the EU's priorities for the theme concerned, following an assessment of the international context,[15] but usually without direct input from third parties. These strategy papers are meant to set out the priority areas selected for financing by the EU, the specific objectives, the expected results and the performance indicators, as well as indicative financial allocations (both overall and per priority area in so-called 'multiannual indicative

Who Gets What, When and How?' in H Wallace, MA Pollack and AR Young (eds), *Policy-Making in the European Union* 6th edn (Oxford, Oxford University Press, 2010).

[8] Amounting to 5.7% of EU spending (2007–13): Commission, 'Brochure on the European Union budget at glance' (2010), 2, available at: www.ec.europa.eu/budget/biblio/publications/publications_en.cfm#glance.

[9] See eg, Regulation (EC) 1905/2006 of the European Parliament and of the Council establishing a financing instrument for development cooperation [2006] OJ L348/41 (DCI Regulation), Title I, currently in force.

[10] See eg, ibid, Title II (including both thematic and geographic programmes).

[11] See eg, ibid, Title III (including elaboration and adoption of strategy papers as well as types of financing).

[12] See eg, ibid, art 38 and Annex IV. Note that, throughout this chapter, reference is made to 'indicative financial allocations', which are resources committed by the EU (overall and per priority area) over a certain financial programming period, but which are subject to implementation and not necessarily spent by the end of that period.

[13] Commission, 'Communication on external action: thematic programme for environment and sustainable management of natural resources including energy' COM (2006) 20 final (Communication ENRTP), 3.

[14] As defined by the EU, see further s 3.2.1 below for the definition of potential beneficiaries under the current environment thematic programme.

[15] See eg, the current environment-related strategy paper: Commission, 'Environment and natural resources thematic programme – 2011–2013 strategy paper and multiannual indicative programme', 29 October 2010, (ENRTP Strategy 2011–13), section 2. All documents pertaining to EU thematic funding for the environment referred to in this chapter can be found at: http://ec.europa.eu/europeaid/what/development-policies/intervention-areas/environment/index_en.htm

programmes'). These are then implemented through annual action programmes, adopted by the Commission, which specify the operations to be undertaken.[16]

Conversely, geographic instruments are implemented on the basis of regional (RSPs) or country strategy papers (CSPs), which are drawn up by the Commission 'in principle' on the basis of a dialogue with the partner country or region, so as to ensure that the country or region concerned takes sufficient ownership of the process and to encourage support for national development strategies,[17] in line with the Paris Declaration on Aid Effectiveness.[18] These CSPs/RSPs set out priority areas for cooperation based on an assessment of each country's development agenda and political, socio-economic and (often) environmental context, are accompanied by national/regional multiannual indicative programmes (MIPs) that are subject to an agreement 'where possible' with the third country or region concerned. MIPs specify indicative financial allocations both overall and per priority area, within the margins of the indicative amounts pre-established by the EU in the relevant financing regulation.[19] These tools thus mean to provide a basis for the programming of EU aid,[20] and inject a sense of bilateralism and partnership in what is essentially a unilateral measure. In practice, however, these formally joint documents are drawn up following a standarised format laid down by the EU[21] and the whole process has been said to be largely dominated by the Commission.[22] The CSPs/RSPs and MIPs are followed up with an action programme adopted each year by the Commission to specify the objectives pursued, the fields of intervention, the expected results, the indicative amount of funding allocated for each operation and the timetable for implementation.[23] Thus, the extent to which environmental issues receive support under the geographic instruments depends on whether these are identified as a priority area in the CSPs/RSPs and follow-up documents.

Apart from these bilateral/regional financing instruments, which are the core subject of this chapter, it should be noted that the EU also supports MEAs and other international environmental processes through other channels. These include the regular contributions to the core costs of MEAs to which the EU is a party, as well as additional assistance to international environmental processes, including in terms of preparatory analytical work for negotiations, the participa-

[16] See eg, DCI Regulation, arts 20 and 22.

[17] See eg, ibid, arts 18(1) and 19(3).

[18] OECD, 'Paris Declaration on Aid Effectiveness' (2005), particularly the principles of ownership and alignment.

[19] See eg, DCI Regulation, art 19(4).

[20] The programming phase is the first in the decision-making process on EU aid delivery, during which the overall national/regional situation of the aid recipient is analysed and key decisions made regarding the EU cooperation strategy. See further, Commission, 'Environmental integration handbook for EC development co-operation' (2006) (Environmental Integration Handbook), 8 and 26.

[21] Commission, 'Communication on increasing the impact of EU aid – A common framework for drafting country strategy papers and joint multiannual programming' COM (2006) 88 final.

[22] N van der Grijp and T Etty, on 'incorporating Climate Change into EU Development Cooperation Policy' in J Gupta and N van der Grijp (eds), *Mainstreaming Climate Change in Development Cooperation* (Cambridge, Cambridge University Press, 2010), 189.

[23] DCI Regulation, art 22.

tion by developing countries in environmental meetings, and the holding of dialogues with major players on environmental issues.[24] According to the Commission, EU (collectively with Member States) funding has been crucial in putting the international environmental architecture in place, contributing to over 50 per cent of the core costs and additional work of MEAs, albeit continuing support will be needed for the functioning of governance structures and global environment assessments.[25]

A final point to be noted from an institutional perspective is that the Directorate-General for Development and Cooperation (EuropeAid) is, following the entry into force of the Lisbon Treaty, the single office responsible for the implementation of the various instruments of EU external assistance.[26] In terms of accountability, its activities are subject to external auditing by the EU's Court of Auditors, which is generally in charge of examining the accounts of all revenue and expenditure of the Union with a view to ensuring sound financial management,[27] as well as the annual budgetary control by the EU legislative authority.[28]

3. ENVIRONMENTAL INTEGRATION THROUGH THEMATIC INSTRUMENTS

This section focuses on thematic instruments that specifically target the environment as the focal area of EU financial and technical assistance, and which are complementary to aid provided under the geographic instruments. This environment-specific funding and expertise are, in principle, made available to any developing country (as defined by the EU) whose environmental activities meet the funding priorities established unilaterally by the EU. In order to trace the evolutionary nature of these EU funding priorities for the environment, this section first provides an overview of the two environment-specific financing regulations that covered the period 2000–06, namely: the Environment Regulation[29] and the Tropical Forest Regulation.[30] Following the simplification and rationalisation of the legislative framework for EU external assistance in 2006,[31] all thematic aid

[24] Communication ENRTP, 24.

[25] Ibid, 7.

[26] Until 3 January 2011, there were two separate Directorates-General (DG) within the Commission dealing with the implementation of EU aid: DG Development (mainly for ACP countries and Overseas Countries and Territories) and DG EuropeAid. Note that, since 2000, responsibilities for the management of EU aid have been progressively devolved from Headquarters to the EU Delegations based in third countries. Note also that assistance to pre-accession countries is managed by other Directorates-General of the Commission (see s 4.1 below).

[27] Arts 286–287 TFEU.

[28] Arts 318–319 TFEU.

[29] Regulation (EC) 2493/2000 of the European Parliament and of the Council on measures to promote the full integration of the environmental dimension in the development process of developing countries [2000] OJ L288/1 (Environment Regulation).

[30] Regulation 2494/2000 of the European Parliament and of the Council on measures to promote the conservation and sustainable management of tropical forests and other forests in developing countries [2000] OJ L288/6 (Tropical Forest Regulation).

[31] Communication ENRTP, 3; see also S Bartelt, 'The Institutional Interplay regarding the New Architecture for the EU's External Assistance' (2008) 14(5) *European Law Journal* 655.

programmes have been incorporated as part of one single financing instrument (Development Cooperation Instrument),[32] covering the current 2007–13 Financial Perspective. This instrument contains a thematic programme on 'environment and sustainable management of natural resources, including energy' (ENRTP) that will be analysed subsequently, together with its accompanying strategy.

3.1 Thematic instruments 2000–06

Recalling the commitments made at the 1992 Rio Summit and the principle of common but differentiated responsibility,[33] the 2000–06 Environment Regulation was adopted with a view to supporting developing countries in their efforts to integrate environmental concerns into their development process, as means to achieve 'sustainable development'.[34] To this end, the EU provided financial assistance and appropriate expertise aimed at drawing up and promoting the implementation of policies, strategies, tools and technologies in 'developing countries', with no apparent restriction on the scope of this term.[35] Among the activities eligible for such EU support, the regulation prioritised, among others: global and transboundary environmental issues (in particular those covered by MEAs, such as climate change, desertification and biodiversity); transboundary issues (air, water and soil pollution); environmental impacts of integrating developing countries into the global economy; environmental impacts of macroeconomic and sectoral policies in developing countries; and further down the line the sustainable production and use of energy as well as of chemical products (in particular hazardous and toxic substances).[36] The indicative financial allocation for implementing this regulation, covering the whole 2000–06 period, was €93 million.[37]

In addition, and similarly motivated by ongoing international processes,[38] the EU adopted a more specific Tropical Forests Regulation in 2000 to promote the conservation and sustainable management of tropical and other forests in developing countries, in order to meet the economic, social and environmental demands placed on forests at local, national, and global levels.[39] Among the activ-

[32] Above n 9, discussed in s 3.2.1 below.

[33] Environment Regulation, preamble paras 3 and 4.

[34] Ibid, preamble para 11 stating: 'Sustainable development relies on the integration of the environmental dimension into the development process'. The notion of 'sustainable development' is defined as 'the improvement of the standard of living and welfare of the relevant populations within the limits of the capacity of the ecosystems by maintaining natural assets and their biological diversity for the benefit of present and future generations' (art 2). The same definition is found in the Tropical Forests Regulation (art 2(4)).

[35] Environment Regulation, art 1(1) and (3).

[36] Ibid, art 3(1).

[37] Ibid, art 7.

[38] Tropical Forests Regulation, preamble paras 5 and 6 (referring to the principle of common but differentiated responsibility under MEAs) and para 7 (referring to the 1997 Special Session of the UN General Assembly endorsing the proposals formulated in the framework of the Intergovernmental Panel on Forests).

[39] Ibid, art 1.

ities eligible for EU financial and technical assistance, the regulation prioritised actions aimed at, amongst others: raising the status of forests in national policies; integrating forest policies in development planning, based on sustainable forest management; promoting the production and use of wood and non-wood forest products from sustainably managed resources; and contributing to the adequate valuation of forest resources and services.[40] Thus, EU support under this regulation was de facto limited to developing countries with tropical and other forests on their territories. And yet, the indicative financial allocation for implementing this regulation was considerably higher than that found in the Environment Regulation: €249 million for the same 2000–06 period.[41]

Both regulations supported environment-related activities at the global level as well as at regional and country levels. Over 35 projects were funded under the Environment Regulation between 2003 and 2006, and included at the global level:

- UNEP – Transboundary Programme for the Conservation and Management of Ecosystems in Sub-saharan Africa (€1,900,000);
- UNEP – Capacity building and technical assistance in relation to eco-labelling (€1,535,142);
- UNEP – Support to the implementation of the CBD (€1,482,948);
- UN Development Programme (UNDP) – Ecological and financial sustainable management of the Guiana Shield Eco-region (€1,676,331);
- United Nations Institute for Training and Research (UNITAR) – Climate change capacity development (€1,450,920);
- UNITAR – Advancing capacity, partnerships and knowledge to support climate change adaptation (€1,431,895); and
- a significantly large project (€2,494,000) to strengthen civil society networks to address dryland degradation and poverty issues in the context of the UNCCD.

Projects at the regional and country levels involved:

- preservation of forests and improved livelihoods of forest people in Africa and Asia (€2,400,000);
- integration of freshwater biodiversity in the development process throughout Africa (€2,054,220);
- mainstreaming the UNCCD in Africa (€1,072,570);
- conservation and sustainable use of the marine and coastal biodiversity of the Bismarck Solomon Seas, involving Indonesia, Papua New Guinea and Solomon Islands (€1,825,638); and
- strengthening national and regional capacities for implementing the globally harmonised system of classification and labelling of chemicals in ASEAN countries (€926,566).[42]

[40] Ibid, art 3.

[41] Ibid, art 8.

[42] Note that only the largest projects are indicated, the full list is available at: www.ec.europa.eu/europeaid/how/finance/dci/documents/projects_2003_2006_env_en.pdf.

During the same period, over 50 cooperation activities were financed under the Tropical Forests Regulation, and included at the global level:

- FAO – National Forest Programme Facility (€7,750,000 total);
- World Bank – Regional process for forest law enforcement and governance (€3,100,000);
- WWF – Strengthening indigenous community-based forest enterprises in eco-regions from Latin America, Asia-Pacific and Africa (€3,499,999);
- European Forest Institute – Support to the EU forest law enforcement, governance and trade (FLEGT)[43] process in developing countries (€2,500,000); and
- ITTO – Ensuring international trade in CITES-listed timber species (€2,400,000).

At the country and regional levels, the following activities can be singled out:

- several projects on improving forest governance and reducing illegal logging and associated trade in Indonesia (€7,178,408 total);
- several projects on mainstreaming market services, certification and codes of conduct in forests and fringe areas in Brazil (€5,053,594 total);
- a timber trade action plan for Latin America and Asia (€3,389,796);
- contribution to the World Bank-managed forestry trust fund for strengthening governance for natural resources in the post-conflict Democratic Republic of Congo (€3,000,000);
- WWF – project for legal and sustainable forest management in Africa and Asia (€3,485,295);
- bi-national projects on forest conservation and participation in forest management in Ecuador and Peru (€3,118,188 total); and
- a project on strengthening forest management in post-conflict Liberia (€1.833.659).[44]

3.2 Thematic programme 2007–13

3.2.1 Environment under the Development Cooperation Instrument

The Development Cooperation Instrument (DCI)[45] is one of the seven financing regulations within the current legislative framework on EU external assistance, and provides the legal basis for environment-specific funding as well as for other thematic programmes and some geographic programmes that are not covered by

[43] On FLEGT, see Ch 7, s 4.1.

[44] Note that only the largest projects are indicated, the full list can be found at: www.ec.europa.eu/europeaid/how/finance/dci/documents/projects_2003_2006_for_en.pdf. See also G Marín Durán and E Morgera, 'Towards Environmental Integration in EC External Relations: A Comparative Analysis of Selected Associations Agreements' (2006) 6 *Yearbook of European Environmental Law* 179, 202 for an overview of earlier projects funded under both regulations.

[45] Above n 9.

separate regulations.[46] The primary objective of cooperation under the DCI Regulation is the 'eradication of poverty in partner countries and regions in the context of sustainable development, including pursuit of the Millennium Development Goals.'[47] In furthering this overarching objective, cooperation must focus, inter alia, on helping to 'develop international measures to preserve and improve the quality of the environment and the sustainable management of global natural resources, in order to ensure sustainable development, including addressing climate change and biodiversity loss',[48] thus building on the language of the Treaty-based objectives for EU environmental policy.[49] Significantly, the DCI Regulation also reiterates the Treaty-based requirement that EU financial and technical assistance must comply with the commitments and objectives in the field of development cooperation approved in the context of the UN and other competent international organisations.[50]

Thematic programmes under the DCI Regulation are to complement, as a subsidiary source of funding, all EU programmes of a geographic nature, which constitute the main instruments of EU cooperation with third countries or regions, including in quantitative terms as they absorb almost 60 per cent of the total €16,897 million indicatively allocated to the DCI Regulation.[51] Each of the five thematic programmes encompasses a specific area of cooperation activity that is not geographically specific, namely: social and human development;[52] environment (ENRTP);[53] non-State actors and local authorities in development;[54] food security;[55] and migration and asylum.[56] In view of their subsidiary character, cooperation through these thematic programmes is undertaken as 'value added to' and 'consistent with' actions funded under geographic instruments, and insofar as EU cooperation objectives cannot be achieved 'in an appropriate or effective manner' through the latter, to address in particular: global initiatives supporting the MDGs, sustainable development or global public goods (implemented through an intermediary organisation); multi-regional and/or cross-cutting actions; and EU responses to an international commitment or obligation.[57] Thus, in addition to complementing geographic instruments, thematic programmes are

[46] Namely, geographic programmes pertaining to 48 countries listed in Annex I from the following regions: Latin America; Asia and Central Asia; the Middle East; a well as South Africa. On the environmental dimension of these geographic programmes, see further s 4.3 below. Note that support to the ACP Sugar Protocol countries is also provided under the DCI Regulation (art 17).

[47] DCI Regulation, art 2(1).

[48] Ibid.

[49] Art 191(1) TFEU, fourth indent (see Ch 1, s 3.2).

[50] DCI Regulation, art 2(2); Art 208(2) TFEU (see Ch 1, s 5.3).

[51] DCI Regulation, Annex IV, where the indicative financial allocation for all geographic programmes amounts to €10,057 m. See further Table 4 below, including also other geographic instruments.

[52] DCI Regulation, art 12.

[53] Ibid, art 13.

[54] Ibid, art 14.

[55] Ibid, art 15.

[56] Ibid, art 16.

[57] Ibid, art 11(2).

aimed at developing EU policies externally and ensuring sectoral consistency and visibility.[58]

In terms of scope, EU financial and technical assistance under the thematic programmes is made available to 'partner countries and regions', which are those included in the list of aid recipients drawn up by the OECD Development Assistance Committee,[59] except for candidates (or potential candidates) for EU accession that are covered by a separate geographic instrument.[60] A wide range of actors are eligible for EU assistance under the DCI Regulation, including: national, local and regional authorities; joint bodies set up by the EU and partner countries or regions; international organisations (such as MEA Secretariats); private sector organisations; and non-State actors (including NGOs).[61]

Turning to the thematic programme on 'environment and sustainable management of natural resources, including energy', its core objective is to promote international environmental governance and EU environmental and energy policies abroad,[62] thus ensuring thematic visibility for the external dimensions of the EU's internal policies.[63] In addition, the ENRTP seeks to 'integrate environmental protection requirements' into EU development and other external policies, in line with Article 11 TFEU.[64] This is further reinforced by a mainstreaming requirement of environmental sustainability as a cross-cutting issue into all (thematic and geographic) cooperation programmes, which is laid down among the general principles of the DCI Regulation.[65] It should be noted, however, that this general mainstreaming requirement equally applies to other cross-cutting issues that need to be systematically taken into account across all programmes, including the ENRTP. These are, in particular, human rights, gender equality, democracy, good governance, the rights of the child and of indigenous peoples, and combating HIV/AIDS.[66] While this multidimensional mainstreaming exercise reflects the approach enshrined in the European Consensus on Development,[67] it has been argued that it may lead to the problematic result of 'mainstreaming fatigue' and to the 'de facto delegation of policy formulation tasks and trade-offs to implementing agencies [including EU Delegations], which may not be mandated or staffed for'.[68]

The DCI Regulation further spells out key areas of activity to be supported through the ENRTP, which are closely linked to both the EU's own environmen-

[58] Ibid, preamble para 13.

[59] Ibid, art 1(1) and Annex 1.

[60] See s 4.1 below.

[61] DCI Regulation, art 24(1).

[62] Ibid, preamble para 15.

[63] Bartelt, above n 31, 661.

[64] DCI Regulation, art 13 (1).

[65] Ibid, art 3(3).

[66] Ibid.

[67] European Consensus on Development, para 101.

[68] A Persson, 'Environmental Policy Integration and Bilateral Development Assistance: Challenges and Opportunities with an Evolving Governance Framework' (2009) 9(4) *International Environmental Agreements* 409, 413.

tal priorities and international environment-related processes, namely: working upstream in assisting developing countries to achieve MDG7 on environmental sustainability through capacity building for environmental integration; promoting implementation of EU initiatives *and* agreed commitments at international and regional levels (in relation to 'current and future climate change issues, biodiversity, desertification, forests, land degradation, fisheries and marine resources, compliance with environmental standards for products and production processes, sound chemicals and waste management, fight against pollution, sustainable production and consumption, and environment-related migration'); and 'strengthening environmental governance and supporting international policy development' (including the provision of additional support to the MEA Secretariats and capacity-building to promote effective compliance and enforcement measures for multilateral environmental agreements).[69] In addition, activities financed under the ENRTP must aim at establishing a framework for the long-term protection of water resources, as well as at supporting sustainable energy options in partner countries and regions, and in particular the use of renewable energy sources, increased energy efficiency and the development of appropriate energy regulatory frameworks.[70]

Environmental components may also be detected in the thematic programme on 'non-State actors and local authorities in development', which seeks inter alia to strengthen the capacity of civil society and local authorities in partner countries to participate in the definition and implementation of sustainable development strategies.[71] This thematic programme may provide a more general avenue for environmental cooperation, in light of the internationally recognised importance of decentralisation and devolution for the sustainable and equitable management of natural resources. Environmental considerations are also important in the thematic programme on 'food security', which aims at supporting the formulation of regional agricultural policies, access to land, trade in agricultural products and natural resources management.[72]

As to resources available for implementing the ENRTP, the DCI Regulation stipulates an overall indicative financial envelope of €804 million for the period 2007–13,[73] whilst programming of specific interventions and allocation of funds is to be determined on the basis of strategy papers and annual action programmes elaborated by the Commission, as for other thematic programmes.[74] Yet, it should be highlighted that the ENRTP has the second-lowest financial allocation among the five thematic programmes,[75] accounting for just 14 per cent of the total €5,596

[69] DCI Regulation, art 13 (2)(a), (b) and (c).

[70] Ibid, art 13(2)(c) and (e).

[71] Ibid, art 14(1)(a)(ii).

[72] Ibid, art 15(2)(b)(ii) and (e).

[73] Ibid, Annex IV specifying indicative financial allocations for all programmes. Note that this indicative amount was considerably increased in the two ENRTP Strategies (see s 3.2.2 below).

[74] Ibid, arts 21 and 22 as described in s 2 above.

[75] Ibid, Annex IV, stipulates the following allocations for the other four thematic programmes: 'investing in people' (€1,060 m); 'non-State actors and local authorities in development' (€1,639 m); 'food security' (€1,709 m); 'migration and asylum' (€384 m).

million indicatively allocated to thematic programmes, and for less than 0.05 per cent of the total indicative amount (€16,897 million) available for the DCI Regulation as a whole. In addition, a certain geographic coverage of thematic programmes is required, with a fixed allocation of funds (indicative €465 million) from all thematic programmes reserved for countries covered by the European Neighbourhood and Partnership Instrument (ENPI).[76]

Aside from these quantitative considerations, it should be underscored that the DCI Regulation requires 'appropriate environmental screening' to be undertaken at the project level, including through EIAs. In addition, SEAs are required 'where relevant' in the implementation of sectoral programmes. In both cases, involvement of interested stakeholders and public access to assessment results is required.[77] This responds to the 2005 European Consensus on Development, which called for systematic environmental assessments.[78] EIAs/SEAs are considered by the Commission as important tools for ensuring environmental integration into EU cooperation programmes at the initial stages of the EU aid delivery process (identification/formulation). Their use is dependent on the type of method used for delivering EU aid, with EIAs applying to the 'project approach'[79] and SEAs to the 'sector programme approach'.[80] According to the Commission, SEAs are to assess the potential environmental impacts of implementing an envisaged sector programme with a view to mitigating negative and enhancing positive impacts, and allowing the integration of environmental considerations into the formulation of the programme.[81] Similarly, an EIA 'is an *ex-ante* environmental assessment of a project, involving a systematic evaluation of its potential environmental impacts [that is, its effects or consequences] in order to propose appropriate measures to mitigate its negative impacts and optimise its positive ones'.[82] Some shortcomings, however, have been noted in the Commission's practice in relation to EIAs/SEAs:[83] the Council thus mandated in June 2009 a stronger use of

[76] Ibid, art 38(4). These are 17 Eastern and Mediterranean neighbouring countries, see further s 4.2 below.

[77] Ibid, art 22(4).

[78] European Consensus on Development, para 102 (note 1 therein).

[79] EU aid is distributed through individual projects in particular to support initiatives outside the public sector, such as civil society and the private sector, or where conditions in the recipient country do not yet permit the adoption of sector and budget approaches.

[80] EU aid delivered through this channel targets a whole sector (eg agriculture) and, in line with the Paris Declaration on Aid Effectiveness (above n 18), it allows for greater ownership by the recipient country, as well as for coordination with other donors and involvement of stakeholders.

[81] On the role of SEAs in the sector and budget approaches, see Environmental Integration Handbook, chs 4–5.

[82] Environmental Integration Handbook, 48; see generally ch 6 on the role of EIAs in the project approach.

[83] For an early assessment of the EU practice in carrying out EIAs/SEAs, see WWF, BirdLife and FERN, 'Environmental Tools in EC Development Cooperation – Transparency and Public Availability of Documentation' (September 2007) (WWF Report 2007), 23–24 pointing to a lack of systematic approach to EIAs/SEAs on the basis of an analysis of practice at EU Delegation level from 1996–07.

these tools, particularly SEAs to ensure environmental mainstreaming in key sectoral cooperation activities.[84]

No specific sustainability guarantees are found at the level of public procurement, albeit tenderers that have been awarded contracts under the DCI Regulation are required to respect core labour rights.[85] Finally, the Commission is also to regularly monitor and review the implementation of all programmes under the DCI Regulation, and evaluate the results achieved in close association with all relevant stakeholders, including non-State actors and local authorities.[86] The Commission is then required to submit annual evaluation reports to the Parliament and the Council, paying particular attention towards progress in achieving the MDGs.[87]

3.2.2 ENRTP Strategy

As provided for in the DCI Regulation, the Commission has elaborated strategy papers to further specify the priority areas selected for financing under the ENRTP, as well as multiannual indicative programmes indicating the amount of resources available overall and per priority area. A first ENRTP Strategy Paper was adopted for the period 2007–10,[88] and following a mid-term review in 2009, a second ENRTP Strategy Paper is currently in place for the period 2011–13.[89] On the basis of these general strategy papers, cooperation activities are then implemented through annual action programmes adopted by the Commission.[90]

The 2007–10 ENRTP Strategy had an overall indicative budget of €470 million, and essentially reflected the key areas of activity stipulated in the DCI Regulation:[91] (i) supporting the integration of environmental sustainability in decision-making in developing countries through capacity-building and greater involvement of civil society stakeholders (indicatively allocated €14.2 million, three per cent of total budget); (ii) promoting implementation of EU initiatives and internationally agreed commitments (indicatively allocated €273.8 million, 58 per cent of the total budget); (iii) improving integration of environmental objectives and coherence in EU external policies (indicatively allocated €8.2 million, less than two per cent of the total budget); (iv) strengthening environmental governance and supporting international policy development (indicatively allocated €38.5 million,

[84] Council Conclusions, 'Integrating Environment in Development Cooperation' 26 June 2009 (Council Conclusions 2009), 4.

[85] DCI Regulation, art 31(11).

[86] Ibid, art 33.

[87] Ibid, art 34.

[88] Commission, 'Thematic strategy for the environment and sustainable management of natural resources, including energy', 14 May 2007 (ENRTP Strategy 2007–10).

[89] Above n 15.

[90] See eg, Commission Decision C(2010)7964 – PE/2010/7861 on approving the 2010 annual action programme (Part II) for the environment and the sustainable management of natural resources including energy, to be financed under Article 21.0401 of the general budget of the European Union, 19 November 2010.

[91] DCI Regulation, art 13(2); see s 3.2.1 above.

eight per cent of the total budget); and (v) promoting EU sustainable energy priorities abroad (indicatively allocated €115.4 million, 24 per cent of the total budget).[92]

The first area of activity of the 2007–10 ENRTP Strategy can be seen as a response to the 2005 European Consensus on Development, which stressed the need to support developing countries in mainstreaming environmental sustainability within their development processes,[93] and reflects the globally recognised cross-cutting nature of MDG7 on environmental sustainability to achieve all the other MDGs.[94] Yet, judging from the indicative allocations, this is less of a priority to the EU (three per cent of total budget) than promoting its own sustainable energy priorities abroad (24 per cent of the total budget).

The largest part of the 2007–10 ENRTP budget (58 per cent) was thus broadly allocated to promoting the implementation of EU initiatives and of international commitments. More specifically, the strategy referred to the EU Energy[95] and Water[96] Initiatives (launched on the occasion of WSSD in 2002), and a series of global environmental issues including: climate change (focusing on the implementation of the EU Action Plan on Climate Change),[97] biodiversity (including implementation of the EU Biodiversity Action Plan for economic development and cooperation and its proposed successor beyond 2010,[98] but also global governance and international trade issues); forest conservation and management (with particular emphasis placed on the implementation of the EU FLEGT Action

[92] ENRTP Strategy 2007–10, 14 and 21.

[93] European Consensus on Development, para 105; see also Commission Working Paper, 'Improving environmental integration in development cooperation' SEC (2009) 555 final (Commission WP 2009), 3 stating that 'MDG7 on environmental sustainability has not received sufficient attention and is "off-track" in many countries, with a great risk that further environmental degradation will undermine the progress made with other MDGs'.

[94] This was recognised at the 2005 UN Summit (see E Morgera, 'The 2005 UN World Summit and the Environment: The Proverbial Half-Full Glass?' (2006) 15 *Italian Yearbook of International Law* 53) and to a certain extent confirmed by the 2010 Review of the Millennium Development Goals (E Morgera, 'Environmental Dimension of the MDGs: Progress Made?' (2010) 40(6) *Environmental Policy and Law* 269, 271–72).

[95] The EU Energy Initiative for Poverty Eradication and Sustainable Development was launched as a joint commitment of the EU Member States and the Commission to support improved access to sustainable energy services in developing countries. The initiative provides a framework for policy dialogue with developing countries and other partners, and also for specific funding activities (www.euei.net/about-euei).

[96] The EU Water Initiative was also jointly launched at the WSSD with the goal of creating the conditions for mobilising all available EU resources (human and financial), and coordinating them to achieve the water-related aspects of MDG7 in partner countries. It is not a financial mechanism per se, but aims to improve coordination and cooperation through policy dialogues with partner countries, with a view to delivering more effective development assistance (www.euwi.net/).

[97] Commission, 'Communication on climate change in the context of development cooperation' COM (2003) 85 final, endorsed by the Council, 'Conclusions – Climate Change', 22 November 2004. Mention is also made of the later Commission, 'Communication on winning the battle against climate change' COM (2005) 35 final. For a discussion, see Ch 7, s 2.1.

[98] Commission, 'Communication on biodiversity action plan for economic development and cooperation' COM (2001) 162 final; Commission, 'Communication on halting the loss of biodiversity by 2010 – and beyond' COM (2006) 216 final; see further Ch 7, s 2.2.

Plan,[99] as well as on promoting community-based forest management, local and indigenous peoples' rights over forest land, and private sector investment in sustainable forest management); desertification control and sustainable land management, and chemicals (pointing to the strategic plan agreed upon under the Basel Convention, and technical assistance activities agreed under the Strategic Approach to International Chemicals Management (SAICM)[100] and the Rotterdam and POPs Conventions).[101] Notably, all these were all singled out as priority areas for action in the 2005 European Consensus on Development.[102]

According to the Commission's ex post assessment, ENRTP funding in 2007–10 was actually higher than the financial commitments made under the first ENRTP Strategy (€470 million), amounting to a total of €542.4 million.[103] Such funding was destined to:

- Global actions (€139.8 million, 25.8 per cent of total);
- Subsaharan Africa (€154.8 million, 28.5 per cent of total);
- Asia and Central Asia (€78.4 million, 14.5 per cent of total);
- Caribbean and Pacific (€69.6 million, 12.8 per cent of total);
- Latin America (€70.5 million, 13 per cent of total); and
- Eastern and Mediterranean neighbours (€29.3 million, 5.4 per cent of total).[104]

Besides this geographical breakdown, the list of the almost 120 cooperation activities that were funded under the ENRTP in 2007–08 sheds some light also on the environmental issues prioritised.[105] At the global level, by far the largest amount of resources (€45 million in total) was devoted to the Global Energy Efficiency and Renewable Energy Fund, which is a facility administered by the European Investment Bank Group (as a funds of funds) to promote private sector investments in clean energy in developing countries and emerging economies with a view to fighting climate change.[106] Other large contributions at global level included:

- World Bank – Forest Carbon Partnership Facility (€5 million);
- FAO – Support to the global forest resources assessment process (€3,100,000);
- UNEP – Strategic Approach to International Chemicals Implementation (€3 million);
- UNEP – Poverty and Environment Initiative (€2,700,000); and

[99] Commission, 'Communication on forest law enforcement, governance and trade (FLEGT): proposal for an action plan' COM (2003) 251 final; see further Ch 7, s 4.1.

[100] SAICM is a multi-stakeholder and multi-sectoral policy framework, based on a 2005 Dubai Declaration on International Chemicals Management, the Overarching Policy Strategy and the Global Plan of Action (www.saicm.org/documents/saicm%20texts/SAICM_publication_ENG.pdf), which were all endorsed by the UNEP Governing Council, Decision SS.IX/1 (2006) UN doc UNEP/GCSS.IX/11.

[101] ENRTP Strategy 2007–10, 16–20.

[102] European Consensus on Development, paras 75–76.

[103] ENRTP Strategy 2011–13, 13.

[104] Ibid.

[105] The full list is available at: www.ec.europa.eu/europeaid/how/finance/dci/documents/projects_2007_2008_enrtp_en.pdf.

[106] www.gereef.com. This is related to the EU Energy Initiative (above n 95).

- UNITAR – Capacity development for adaptation to climate change and mitigation (€2,499,520).

At the regional level, and in line with the geographic ceiling on thematic programmes established in the DCI Regulation, ENPI-covered countries benefited from support with regard to the development of Mediterranean marine and coastal protected areas (€2 million), the implementation of the CBD (€1,484,000) and climate change (€1,500,000).[107]

The 2011–13 ENRTP strategy has an overall indicative financial envelope of €517 million, corresponding to an increase of almost nine per cent compared to the previous strategy's indicative envelope, which is mainly related to new initiatives for climate change.[108] Climate change receives top priority for cooperation under the 2011–13 ENRTP strategy (indicatively allocated €237.5 million, almost 46 per cent of total budget),[109] with emphasis being placed on climate change mitigation[110] (in particular through reducing emissions from deforestation and forest degradation, low-emission development strategies, and technology transfer),[111] climate change adaptation[112] (including actions through the Global Climate Change Alliance),[113] and promoting investments in sustainable energy options.[114] The second priority area for support under the 2011–13 ENRTP strategy, entitled 'environment for development', encompasses biodiversity, forest conservation and desertification, forest governance and the green economy. In terms of biodiversity, forest conservation and desertification (indicatively allocated €73 million), emphasis is placed on the EU's post-2010 Biodiversity Strategy,[115] the global biodiversity strategy 2011–20,[116] as well as on the UNCCD.[117] As to forest governance (indicatively allocated a separate €55 million), focus is once again on the FLEGT Action Plan.[118] Also within this second priority area is the 'green economy' (indicatively allocated €26.5 million),[119] a novel theme being the subject of ongoing discussions at both EU and international levels.[120] Rather than targeting new issues, however, EU support to 'green economy' is largely limited to international processes on chemicals (that is, the strategic plan agreed upon under the Basel Convention and technical assistance

[107] Note that no list of cooperation activities funded under the ENRTP is available beyond 2008 at the time of writing.

[108] ENRTP Strategy 2011–13, 4.

[109] Ibid, 20–23 and 28.

[110] The indicative allocation for climate change mitigation is €115 m (ENRTP Strategy 2011–13, 28).

[111] On this, see further Ch 7, s 2.1.

[112] The indicative allocation for climate change adaptation is €75 million (ENRTP Strategy 2011–13, 28).

[113] A thematic dialogue launched by the Commission in 2007 to enhance climate change cooperation with SIDS and LDCs, see further Ch 5, s 4.

[114] The indicative allocation for sustainable energy is €47.5 m (ENRTP Strategy 2011–13, 28).

[115] Commission, 'Communication on our life insurance, our natural capital: an EU biodiversity strategy to 2020' COM (2011) 244 final.

[116] CBD Conference of the Parties, 'The Strategic Plan for Biodiversity 2011–2020 and the Aichi Biodiversity Targets' (2010) UN Doc UNEP/CBD/COP/10/27

[117] ENRTP Strategy 2011–13, 23 and 28. On this, see further Ch.7, ss 2 and 2.2.

[118] Ibid, 24 and 28. On this, see further Ch.7, s 4.1.

[119] ENRTP Strategy 2011–13, 24–25 and 28.

[120] See Ch 1, s 4.2.3.1.

activities agreed under SAICM and the Rotterdam and POPs Conventions), which was already part of the previous ENRTP strategy.[121]

The third and last priority area of the 2011–13 ENRTP funding is to strengthen international environmental governance (indicatively allocated €47 million),[122] and in particular climate change governance (indicatively allocated €39 million),[123] both to be '*shaped* by the external dimensions of the EU's environment and climate change policies (emphasis added)'.[124] In both cases, ENRTP funding is to be geared towards supporting: the work of MEA Secretariats (with a special focus on the chemicals/waste and biodiversity clusters, as well as the UNFCCC Secretariat), ongoing international environmental processes (including the UN Rio+20 Conference of June 2012); developing countries' participation in multilateral negotiations; and implementation of and compliance with MEAs. The third priority area also envisages more general support to mainstreaming governance and transparency in the management of natural resources (indicatively allocated €39 million); in particular, water resources management is seen as a critical issue towards achieving MDG7 on environmental sustainability.[125]

3.3 Assessment

The preceding analysis has shown that EU funding committed for the environment[126] has considerably increased in absolute terms from 2000–06 to 2007–13 (see table below), albeit remaining modest when compared to financial resources indicatively allocated to other thematic programmes under the current DCI Regulation, such as 'food security' (€1,709 million) and 'non-State actors and local authorities' (€1,639 million).[127] In terms of environmental themes, climate change, forest conservation and management, biodiversity, chemicals and desertification have been recurrent priorities for EU thematic funding in both periods. Yet climate change has clearly overtaken all other environmental challenges, being indicatively allocated almost 54 per cent of the total 2011–13 ENRTP indicative financial envelope.[128] Forest conservation and management, which already received special attention in 2000–06 through a generous individual source of funding (the Tropical Forest Regulation), have retained importance in 2007–13 with the focus of EU support being increasingly on forest governance (indicatively allocated 10 per cent of the total 2011–13 ENRTP indicative financial

[121] ENRTP Strategy 2011–13, 25 (replicating the wording of ENRTP Strategy 2007–10, 18).

[122] ENRTP Strategy 2011–13, 25 and 28.

[123] Ibid, 26 and 28.

[124] Ibid, 25.

[125] Ibid, 26–27 and 28.

[126] An indication of EU committed funding for the environment through geographic instruments is provided in Table 4 below.

[127] These are the indicative financial allocations in the DCI Regulation (Annex IV), which may have changed as implemented through strategy papers and annual action plans adopted by the Commission.

[128] Taking together the indicative financial allocations for climate change and sustainable energy (€237.5 m) and strengthening climate change governance (€39 m).

budget). Under the current ENRTP, forests are to be further supported through the additional financial indicative pool (€73 million), commonly available for forest conservation, biodiversity and desertification.

The (absolute) increase in EU thematic funding for the environment has been accompanied by more explicit linkages to supporting existing MEAs and ongoing international environmental negotiations, as seen by the increasing attention paid to mainstreaming MDG7 on environmental sustainability, as well as on strengthening environmental governance – once again, with particular attention to climate change governance – in both ENRTP Strategies. This responds to the 2005 European Consensus on Development, which called for assisting developing countries to integrate the environment into their development strategies, including through capacity-building for MEA implementation and for participating in MEA-related processes.[129]

However, the growing 'global focus' of EU thematic funding for the environment is also clearly motivated by a desire to enhance the political visibility of its external aid, and more importantly, to promote its own environmental policy interests and strengthen its own leadership within international environmental organisations and processes.[130] The most obvious example of this is the overwhelming prioritisation of climate change, and its link with sustainable energy, which was also seen in the context of bilateral and inter-regional agreements,[131] and is reflective of the 2009 EU Climate and Energy Package and EU position in ongoing climate change negotiations.[132] Similarly, the EU actively uses its external assistance as a means to build consensus on environmental issues around its own policy initiatives in the absence of dedicated multilateral negotiations, with the most notable example being the long-standing prioritisation of forests within EU funding and increased emphasis on the EU FLEGT Action Plan.[133]

Table 3. *EU Environment Thematic Funding (2000–13)*[134]

2000–06		**2007–13**	
Environment Regulation (*all developing countries*)	€93 million	ENRTP Strategy 2007–10 (*all OECD-listed aid recipients*)	€470 million
Tropical Forest Regulation (*de facto limited*)	€249 million	ENRTP Strategy 2011–13 (*all OECD-listed aid recipients*)	€517 million
TOTAL:	**€342 million**	TOTAL:	**€987 million**

[129] European Consensus on Development, paras 75 and 105.
[130] This has been explicitly recognised by the Commission in Communication ENRTP, 8–9.
[131] See Ch 2, s 8.2.
[132] See further Ch 7, s 3.1.
[133] See further Ch 7, s 4.1.
[134] Based on EU indicative financial allocations (Environment Regulation; Tropical Forest Regulation; ENRTP Strategy 2007–10 and ENRTP Strategy 2011–13).

4. ENVIRONMENTAL INTEGRATION THROUGH GEOGRAPHIC INSTRUMENTS

In light of the subsidiary character of EU thematic funding for the environment, this section explores the extent to which geographic instruments provide an additional legal basis for integrating environmental concerns into EU external assistance. The current EU legislative framework on external assistance provides for three key geographical instruments: the Instrument for Pre-Accession Assistance;[135] the European Neighbourhood and Partnership Instrument;[136] as well as several geographic programmes under the DCI Regulation. Another important geographic instrument, although not part of the EU budget, is the European Development Fund that supports cooperation with the ACP States. A separate financing instrument regulates cooperation between the EU and industrialised/high-income countries, which is not a 'geographic instrument' properly speaking, but nonetheless of relevance to some of the countries covered in this book. In what follows, an *aperçu* is offered on the weight given to the environment under each of these instruments in both legal and quantitative terms.

4.1 Instrument for Pre-Accession Assistance

Since 2007, EU financial and technical assistance to both candidates and potential candidates for EU membership has been channelled through a single financing instrument: the Instrument for Pre-Accession Assistance (IPA),[137] with an indicative financial envelope of €11.5 billion for the period 2007–13.[138] As the financial instrument of the pre-accession strategy, the IPA Regulation is managed by other Directorates-General of the Commission than Europeaid.[139] Its overarching objective is to assist these countries' progressive alignment with the standards and policies of the Union, including the *acquis*[140] that has an environmental component. The IPA thus has specific implementing modalities, consisting of a multi-annual strategy drawn on the basis of the priorities stipulated in the Stabilisation

[135] Council Regulation (EC) 1085/2006 establishing an Instrument for Pre-Accession Assistance [2006] OJ L210/82; as amended by Regulation EU 540/2010 of the European Parliament and of the Council [2010] OJ L158/7 (IPA Regulation).

[136] Regulation (EC) 1638/2006 of the European Parliament and of the Council laying down general provisions establishing a European Neighbourhood and Partnership Instrument OJ [2006] L310/1 (ENPI Regulation).

[137] Above n 135. This covers the candidate countries (Croatia, Turkey, Iceland and the Former Republic of Macedonia) and potential candidate countries (Albania, Bosnia and Herzegovina, Montenegro, Serbia including Kosovo as defined by the UN Security Council Resolution 1244/1999) listed in Annexes I and II respectively.

[138] IPA Regulation, art 26.

[139] Namely: DG Enlargement (Components I and II); DG Regional Policy (Components II and III); DG Employment, Social Affairs and Equal Opportunities (Component IV); DG Agriculture and Rural Development (Component V).

[140] IPA Regulation, art 1.

and Association Agreements with these countries,[141] as well as the conditions set out in the Commission's enlargement package,[142] which is adopted each year and accompanied by a multiannual indicative financial framework (MIFF).[143] The MIFF reflects the Commission's intentions in terms of funding allocations by country and for each of the five components contained in the IPA Regulation, namely: 'transition assistance and institution building'[144] 'cross-border cooperation';[145] 'regional development';[146] 'human resources development';[147] and 'rural development'.[148] On this basis, more specific multi-annual indicative planning documents (MIPDs) are then prepared for each country by the Commission 'in close consultation with the national authorities' and, 'where appropriate' involving civil society and other stakeholders.[149]

While the environment or sustainable development do not constitute a single component, nor are these spelled out as part of the scope of assistance,[150] sustainable development is explicitly stated as an objective in the preamble[151] and under the 'cross-border cooperation' component.[152] It can also be expected that implementation of other components (such as 'rural development' and 'regional development') has a significant environmental dimension, and most significantly that the alignment with the EU *acquis* implies also approximation to EU environmental standards and procedures. In this regard, in the multi-beneficiary MIPD 2009–11, the Commission announced the creation of a new regional cooperation mechanism, the Regional Environmental Network for Accession, with a view to improving administrative and private capacities in candidate (and potential candidate) countries to transpose and implement the environmental *acquis* in areas such as strategic planning and investment, climate change, cross-border cooperation and MEAs, and undertook to integrate environmental considerations as a cross-cutting issue in all IPA financed activities.[153] In addition, some country-specific MIPDs contain a specific environmental programme as part of the 'regional development' component.[154]

[141] Examined in Ch 2, s 3.

[142] This includes the EU Enlargement Strategy and Candidates' Progress Reports, available at: www.ec.europa.eu/enlargement/how-does-it-work/progress_reports/index_en.htm.

[143] IPA Regulation, arts 4, 7 and 14.

[144] Ibid, art 8.

[145] Ibid, art 9.

[146] Ibid, art 10.

[147] Ibid, art 11.

[148] Ibid, art 12.

[149] Ibid, art 6.

[150] Ibid, art 2.

[151] Ibid, preamble para 13.

[152] Ibid, art 9(2).

[153] Commission, Decision C(2009)4518 establishing a multi-beneficiary multi-annual indicative planning document (MIPD) 2009–2011, (16 June 2009), 30 and 37. MIPDs are available at: www.ec.europa.eu/enlargement/how-does-it-work/financial-assistance/planning-ipa_en.htm.

[154] See eg, Commission, 'Multi-annual indicative planning document 2009–2011 – Republic of Croatia' (at 54), where the environment programme is the largest of the 'regional development' component, indicatively allocated 35–40 per cent of the component's resources, and also a number of cross-border environment-related programmes are part of the 'cross-border cooperation' component (at

4.2 European Neighbourhood and Partnership Instrument

The ENPI Regulation[155] is aimed at supporting the objectives of the ENP,[156] and thus its geographic coverage corresponds to the countries that are considered by the EU as falling under the scope of that policy.[157] It constitutes the second most generous single source of EU external assistance (after the IPA) in relative terms, with an indicative financial envelope of €11.2 billion for the period 2007–13 to be distributed among (only) 17 beneficiaries.[158] In line with the ENP, the ENPI Regulation seeks to sustain the development of an area of 'prosperity and good neighbourliness' between the EU and its Mediterranean and Eastern neighbours, on the basis of 'common values', which include sustainable development.[159] It is stressed that all cooperation activities funded under the regulation must comply with the agreements concluded by the EU (and its Member States) with the countries concerned[160] – that is, the Euro-Mediterranean Association Agreements and the Partnership and Cooperation Agreements[161] – which form part of the policy framework for the programming of EU aid.[162] Assistance provided under the regulation must also respect the commitments undertaken in international conventions to which both the EU and the aid recipient(s) concerned are parties, implicitly including MEAs.[163]

The ENPI Regulation spells out a long list of cooperation areas, some of which explicitly support environmental integration into EU external assistance, namely: 'promoting sustainable development in all aspects'; 'promoting environmental protection, nature conservation and sustainable management of natural resources, including fresh water and marine resources'; 'promoting renewable energy sources, energy efficiency and clean transport'; and 'supporting cross-border cooperation through joint local initiatives to promote sustainable economic, social and environmental development in border regions'.[164] In addition, environmental integration may be implied from references to 'promoting legislative and regulatory approximation towards higher standards' (and in particular EU

28–30); see also Commission, 'Multi-annual indicative planning document 2009–2011 – The Former Yugoslav Republic of Macedonia' (at 42), where a specific environment programme is also part of the 'regional development' component (indicatively allocated 35–45 per cent of resources) and provides for integration of environmental considerations as cross-cutting issue in all IPA activities (at 46).

155 Above n 136.

156 On the ENP, see Ch 2, s 4.1.

157 These are listed in the Annex to the ENPI Regulation and are: Algeria, Armenia, Azerbaijan, Belarus, Egypt, Georgia, Israel, Jordan, Lebanon, Libya, Moldova, Morocco, Palestine, Russia, Syria, Tunisia, and Ukraine.

158 ENPI Regulation, art 29.

159 Ibid, art 1(1) and preamble para 4.

160 Ibid, art 5(1).

161 Examined in Ch 2, ss 4 and 7.2, respectively.

162 ENPI Regulation, art 3(1), together with the EU's own policy documents on the ENP.

163 Ibid, art 5(1) and preamble para 5.

164 Ibid, art 2(2)(e), (g), (o) and (y).

standards),[165] supporting the achievement of the MDGs, fostering the development of civil society and NGOs, promoting participation in EU research and innovation activities, and supporting participation of partner countries in EU programmes and agencies.[166]

As to implementation, the ENPI Regulation follows the programming process common to most EU geographic instruments, based on CSPs/RSPs and multiannual indicative programmes that are 'normally' to be elaborated 'in partnership' between the Commission and the beneficiary countries, with the involvement 'as appropriate' of regional and local authorities, civil society and other stakeholders. These are then implemented through annual action programmes adopted by the Commission.[167] Unlike the DCI Regulation,[168] the ENPI Regulation does not provide for environmental screening of financed cooperation activities, although in the specific case of cross-border cooperation programmes,[169] the Commission is required to check whether environmental impact assessments are necessary and if these have been carried out or are planned before the proposed project is implemented.[170] As for the DCI Regulation, no sustainability guarantees in public procurement are specified in the ENPI Regulation.

As an illustrative example, the Regional Strategy Paper 2007–13 for the Euro-Mediterranean partners[171] contains a specific programme on the environment, which is one of the largest within the second strategic priority entitled 'Sustainable Economic Development', indicatively allocated €33 million for 2007–10.[172] As under the Euro-Mediterranean Agreements, emphasis is placed on the implementation of the Barcelona Convention (including through collaboration with the European Environment Agency), as well as on the implementation of the roadmap for the depollution of the Mediterranean Sea (Horizon2020),[173] and the implementation of the Mediterranean component of the EU Water Initiative.[174] In addition, environmental considerations are found in the energy and transport programme, also part of the 'Sustainable Economic Development' priority area,

[165] Ibid, art 2(2)(b), stating: 'and in particular to encourage the progressive participation of partner countries in the [EU] internal market and the intensification of trade'.

[166] Ibid, art 2(2)(h), (m), (t) and (x).

[167] Ibid, arts 4(1) and 12(1). Note that special programming rules apply to cross-border cooperation programmes (art 9).

[168] See s 3.2.1 above.

[169] These cross-border cooperation programmes deal with cooperation between one or more EU Member States and one or more partner countries, taking place in regions adjacent to their shared part of the external border of the Union. They only account for 5 per cent of cooperation activities financed under the ENPI Regulation (arts 6(1)(a)(ii) and 29(b)).

[170] Commission Regulation (EC) 951/2007 laying down implementing rules for cross-border cooperation programmes financed under Regulation (EC) 1638/2006 [2007] OJ L210/10, art 5(2)(d).

[171] Commission, 'Regional strategy paper (2007–2013) and regional indicative programme (2007–2010) for the Euro-Mediterranean Partnership' (undated) (Euro-Med SP 2007–2013). All RSPs referred to in this chapter can be found at: http://ec.europa.eu/europeaid/where/index_en.htm.

[172] Euro-Med SP 2007–2013, 53.

[173] Endorsed by the Euro-Mediterranean Ministerial Conference on the Environment, 'Final Declaration', Cairo 20 November 2006, Annex I ('Horizon 2020 – Timetable for the first phase 2007–2013'). See Ch 5, s 3.3.

[174] Euro-Med SP 2007–13, 35–37. On EU Water Initiative, see above n 96.

which envisages cooperation to promote renewable energy sources and support to the 'Kyoto process'.[175] While this is just a small part of the picture, the environment does appear to have received broader support under the ENPI Regulation: in the period 2007–10, financial commitments for the environment and sustainable management of natural resources amounted to €250 million, albeit this still represents a relatively small proportion of the overall indicative financial envelope (about €5 billion for 2007–10).[176]

4.3 Development Cooperation Instrument

In addition to the various thematic programmes indicated earlier,[177] the DCI Regulation provides for EU financial and technical assistance to specific countries or regions, namely:

- Asia (covering 19 countries and indicatively allocated €5177 million for 2007–13);[178]
- Central Asia (covering five countries and indicatively allocated €719 million for 2007–13);[179]
- Middle East (covering five countries and indicatively allocated €481 million for 2007–13);[180]
- Latin America (covering 18 countries and indicatively allocated €2690 million for 2007–13);[181] and
- South Africa (indicatively allocated €980 million for 2007–13).[182]

Taken together these five geographic programmes amount to 60 per cent of the total DCI indicative budget (€16,897 million), albeit the distribution of funds among beneficiaries is rather uneven, favouring in particular Asia and South Africa in relative terms.

In exploring the legal provisions supporting environmental integration into these geographic instruments, it should first be recalled that they are all subject to the general requirement of mainstreaming environmental sustainability as a cross-cutting issue into cooperation activities financed under the DCI Regulation.[183] This requirement is given more substance in the common set of objectives for all geographic programmes, which specifically includes the 'environment and sustainable

[175] Euro-Med SP 2007–13, 30–32.

[176] Commission WP 2009, 4. See further, G Marín Durán, 'Environmental Integration in EU Development Cooperation: Responding to International Commitments or Its Own Policy Priorities' in E Morgera (ed), *The External Environmental Policy of the European Union: EU and International Law Perspectives* (Cambridge, Cambridge University Press, forthcoming 2012).

[177] See s 3.2.1 above.

[178] DCI Regulation, Annexes I and IV.

[179] Ibid.

[180] Ibid.

[181] Ibid.

[182] Ibid, Annex IV.

[183] Ibid, art 3(3), as described in s 3.2.1 above.

development of natural resources', targeting, inter alia: the protection of biodiversity and of forests (including activities for the conservation and sustainable management of forests with active participation of local communities and forest-dependent peoples);[184] ensuring respect for and supporting the implementation of international environmental agreements, such as the three Rio Conventions (UNFCCC, CBD and UNCCD) and 'their protocols and any subsequent modifications' in 'line with the EU Action Plan on Climate Change';[185] improvements in the urban environment;[186] promoting sustainable patterns of production and consumption;[187] capacity-building for emergency preparedness and prevention of natural disasters.[188]

In addition, common objectives of environmental relevance include: supporting policies aimed at achieving the MDGs (thus including MDG7 on environmental sustainability);[189] supporting sustainable integrated water resource management and sustainable and efficient use of water resources (including for agricultural and industrial purposes);[190] fostering greater use of sustainable energy technologies;[191] and supporting 'effective multilateralism' and the effective implementation of multilateral agreements relevant to the field of development (thus implicitly including environmental multilateralism beyond the three Rio Conventions).[192] In the specific provisions of each geographic instrument, protection of biodiversity and forests is also emphasised in the context of cooperation with Central Asia and Latin America,[193] while water and sustainable energy sources are underscored in the context of regional dialogue with Central Asia.[194]

In terms of implementation, the DCI Regulation follows the typical programming process of most EU geographic instruments, based on CSPs/RSPs and multi-annual indicative programmes that are drawn up by the Commission, 'in principle' on the basis of a dialogue with the third country or region concerned.[195] There is, however, an explicit requirement to include an 'MDG profile' (which includes MDG7) in these programming documents.[196] According to the Commission, a total amount of €240 million from all DCI geographic programmes was indicatively allocated to the environment in 2007–10.[197]

[184] Ibid, art 5(2)(n).
[185] Ibid, art 5(2)(q).
[186] Ibid, art 5(2)(o).
[187] Ibid, art 5(2)(p).
[188] Ibid, art 5(2)(r).
[189] Ibid, art 5(2)(a).
[190] Ibid, art 5(2)(s).
[191] Ibid, art (5)(2)(t).
[192] Ibid, art (5)(2)(j).
[193] Ibid, arts 6(e) and 7(e).
[194] Ibid, art 8(f).
[195] Ibid, arts 18–19, as described in s 3.2.1 above.
[196] Ibid, art 3(8)(e); see eg, Commission, 'Bolivia – Country Strategy Paper 2007–2013', 12 July 2007, Annex 12 (containing an MDG profile) and cf Annex 6 (containing an 'Environmental Profile' that is much more detailed in analysis).
[197] Commission WP 2009, 4. See further, G Marín Durán, above n 176, for an analysis of selected RSPs.

4.4 European Development Fund

The European Development Fund is the oldest geographic instrument of EU external assistance, first created in 1959 to provide financial and technical assistance to the African countries which were at that time still under colonial dominion or with which some EU Member States had historical links. Since then, various EDF cycles have followed the evolution of the EU relationship with the ACP States, and most recently the ninth EDF (2000–07) and tenth EDF (2008–13) have been the major instruments for cooperation with all ACP States (except South Africa) that are party to the Cotonou Partnership Agreement.[198] The current (tenth) EDF has been endowed with a total budget of almost €22.7 billion[199] – a significant increase from the ninth EDF total budget (€13.5 billion)[200] – albeit these generous figures should be viewed in the perspective of over almost 100 potential aid recipients.[201]

The EDF is also a special type of geographic instrument as it is not part of the EU budget (and thus does not follow the EU financial perspectives). It is funded through direct contributions from the EU Member States, which are not necessarily proportional to their GDP, but are rather based on ex-colonial ties with the beneficiary countries. Furthermore, as opposed to EU budget-based financing instruments, the EDF is governed and implemented within the framework of an international agreement, with detailed financing rules and financial protocols (setting the overall budget), being an integral part of the Cotonou Agreement.[202] While CSPs/RSPs and national/regional indicative programmes are also used as tools for programming EDF resources, these documents are to be jointly drawn up by the EU and the ACP State(s) concerned and 'shall be adopted by common agreement'.[203] Projects and other cooperation programmes are then implemented through joint appraisal within the EU-ACP Development Finance Cooperation Committee, and are subject to a 'financing agreement' between the Commission and the ACP State(s) concerned.[204] Given its approach to environmental cooperation as a thematic and cross-cutting issue, the Cotonou Agreement

[198] Examined in Ch 2, s 5.2. EU assistance to South Africa is channelled through the DCI Regulation (see s 4.3 above), albeit South Africa may de facto benefit from projects funded under the EDF that have a strong regional focus (eg, in the areas of infrastructure, energy and water).

[199] EU-ACP Council of Ministers, Decision 1/2006 specifying the multiannual financial framework for the period 2008 to 2013 and modifying the revised ACP-EC Partnership Agreement [2006] OJ L247/22.

[200] Cotonou Agreement, Annex I 'Financial Protocol'. Note that this amount does not include the unexpended balances from previous EDFs (total €9.9 bn) that were rolled into the ninth EDF.

[201] Note that, in addition to the 78 ACP States, a proportion of the tenth EDF resources (€430 m, around 1 per cent of total) is also allocated to cooperation with the 21 'Overseas Country and Territories' (OCTs) that depend constitutionally on four EU Member States (Denmark, France, the Netherlands, and the UK); Council Decision (EC) 2007/249 amending Decision 2001/822/EC on the association of the overseas countries and territories with the European Community [2007] L109/33.

[202] Cotonou Agreement, Part IV 'Development Finance Cooperation' and Annexes I–IV.

[203] Ibid, Annex IV, arts 2, 4(2), 8 and 10(2).

[204] Ibid, Annex IV, arts 15 and 17.

provides a solid legal basis for integrating environmental concerns into EDF funding.[205]

Looking at the Intra-ACP Strategy Paper 2008–13,[206] which lays down priorities and indicative financial allocations for cooperation activities that involve a number of (or all) ACP regions,[207] it is interesting to note that the environment figures as one of the focal areas for assistance under the tenth EDF. The environment is indicatively allocated €70 million (out of an indicative total budget of €1290 million for 'all ACP activities') over the period 2008–13, with a view to supporting ACP capacity-building in implementing the three Rio Conventions (UNFCCC, CBD and UNCCD), as well as other major MEAs (Basel Convention, Rotterdam Convention and POPs Convention) and in participating in processes related to these agreements, as well as to finance the setting of a mechanism to collect ACP environmental data.[208] An additional €40 million (out of the same 'all ACP activities' budget) is indicatively allocated to the Global Climate Change Alliance,[209] which, as previously noted, is also supported through the ENRTP.[210]

This is supplemented by the Regional Strategy Papers 2008–13 that are jointly elaborated with each of the six ACP regions individually, and where the environment also appears as a focal area for tenth EDF support in two cases, notably regions with substantial forest resources: Central Africa and the Pacific. The Central Africa RSP highlights that the forests of the Congo Basin, which contain the highest concentration of biodiversity in Africa, are under threat from increased logging, weak institutional capacity to manage these resources, and damage caused by mining and poaching. More generally, it is also noted that the energy potential of the region's considerable hydraulic resources is not yet sufficiently exploited. As a result, an indicative amount of €30 million (around 18 per cent of the total regional indicative budget of €165 million) is allocated to the management of renewable natural resources as the second focal area for tenth EDF assistance in the 2008–13 period.[211] Additional support for forest conservation and management in Congo may continue under the thematic environment programme.[212] Similarly, the Pacific RSP stresses that forest resources in the area are threatened by unsustainable land use and unregulated logging. The sustainable management of natural resources and the environment is thus set as the second

[205] See Ch 2, ss 5.2.1 and 5.2.2.

[206] EU-ACP States, 'Intra-ACP cooperation 10th EDF – Strategy paper and multiannual indicative programme 2008–2013', 13 March 2009 (Intra-ACP SP 2008–13), available at: www.ec.europa.eu/development/icenter/repository/strategy_paper_intra_acp_edf10_en.pdf.

[207] Namely: Central Africa; Eastern and Southern Africa and Indian Ocean; Southern Africa Development Community; West Africa; Pacific region; Caribbean region.

[208] Intra-ACP SP 2008–13, 26–27 and 43–44.

[209] Ibid, 41.

[210] See s 3.2.2 above.

[211] EU-Central Africa, 'Document de stratégie régionale et programme indicatif régionale pour la période 2008–2013' 30 September 2009 (Central Africa RSP 2008–13), 53–54. All RSPs for the tenth EDF are available at: www.ec.europa.eu/europeaid/where/acp/overview/rsp/rsp_10th_edf_en.htm.

[212] In 2008, two forest-related projects for a total value of almost €3 m were financed in Congo (see above n 105 for a full list of ENRTP-financed projects).

focal area for EDF support, and is indicatively allocated an amount of €40 million (40 per cent of the total regional indicative budget of €95 million) for the 2008–13 period.[213] While the environment does not figure as a focal area for EDF support under the RSPs for the other four ACP regions, it may still receive resources allocated to 'regional integration', which is the first focal area in all RSPs,[214] or from the proportion of the total regional indicative budget that is reserved for the support of 'non-focal sectors'.[215]

This regional outlook of the tenth EDF needs, of course, to be complemented by an examination of the Country Strategy Papers 2008–13 that have been jointly established with almost all 78 Cotonou partners, which is however beyond the scope of this study.[216] According to the Commission, the total amount (including, national, regional and intra-regional cooperation programmes) of tenth EDF resources indicatively allocated to the environment and sustainable management of natural resources in 2008–10 was €171 million[217] – a figure that seems very modest in light of the overall financial envelope and the high number of aid recipients involved. This figure does not include, however, activities with an environmental relevance financed under other initiatives, such as the EU-ACP Water Facility that was set up in 2004 to co-finance water and sanitation infrastructure and to improve water management and governance in the ACP countries.[218] This facility was first (indicatively) allocated around €500 million from the ninth EDF, and was followed by a reformed facility (indicatively) endowed €200 million from the tenth EDF for period 2010–13.[219] Similarly, an Energy Facility has been established with a view to promoting renewable energy sources as a means to mitigate climate change, and has been indicatively allocated €200 from the tenth EDF.[220]

It is also interesting to note that all six RSPs contain an examination of the environmental situation (with different degrees of detail) in the ACP region concerned, as required by the Cotonou Agreement,[221] while some go further and also

[213] EU-Pacific Region, 'Regional strategy paper and regional indicative programme 2008–2013' 15 November 2008 (Pacific RSP 2008–13), 67 and 69–72.

[214] See eg, EU-Region of Eastern and Southern Africa and the Indian Ocean, 'Regional strategy paper and regional indicative programme 2008–2013' 15 November 2008 (ESI RSP 2008–13), 44–45 where the environment is included as part of the first focal area 'regional economic integration.'

[215] See eg, EU-West Africa 'Regional strategy paper and regional indicative programme 2008–2013' 30 July 2008, 54 where the environment is identified as the first 'non-focal sector' for EDF support.

[216] These are available at: www.ec.europa.eu/europeaid/where/acp/overview/csp/csp_10th_edf_en.htm.

[217] Commission WP 2009, 4.

[218] EU-ACP Council of Ministers, 'Decision 1/2004 on the use of the reserve of the long-term development envelope as well as resources from the Investment Facility of the ninth European Development Fund for the establishment of an ACP-EU Water Facility' [2004] L289/68 (art 1, authorising allocation of a first tranche of €250 m to the facility); 'Decision 7/2005 concerning the use of a second allocation of EUR 250 million from the conditional EUR 1 billion under the ninth EDF to be used for the second instalment of the ACP-EU Water Facility' [2006] OJ L48/21 (art 1, authorising allocation of a second tranche of €250 m to the facility).

[219] Intra-ACP SP 2008–13, 47.

[220] Ibid, 42.

[221] Following its 2010 revision, see Ch 2, s 5.1.

incorporate 'Regional Environmental Profiles'.[222] Such environmental profiles (both at the regional and country level) are considered by the Commission (among others)[223] as an important tool for integrating environmental concerns at the initial stages of the programming of EU aid, as they serve to 'identify and avoid any harmful direct and indirect environmental impacts' of the cooperation programme envisaged, as well as 'to recognise and realise opportunities for enhancing environmental conditions' (including the advancement of environmental issues 'that are a priority for the EU').[224] These documents should therefore include a detailed analysis of the environmental situation in the country or region concerned (including its current policies, institutional capacities and environmental cooperation experience) and make clear recommendations for the integration of environmental issues during the preparation of RSPs and CSPs.[225]

4.5 Instrument for Cooperation with High-Income Countries (ICI)

For our purposes, another important EU financing instrument is the ICI Regulation,[226] which supports cooperation between the EU and a number of countries, brought together in light of their advanced level of development rather than geographic considerations. A total of 17 industrialised and other high-income countries are covered by this instrument,[227] and include countries that are considered 'strategic partners' by the EU (such as Canada and the US), other long-standing developed-country partners of the EU (such as Japan, Australia and New Zealand), as well as high-income countries from Asia (notably South Korea) and from the Gulf Cooperation Council. The ICI Regulation seeks to strengthen links with countries that 'share similar political, economic and institutional structures and values' to the Union,[228] particularly by promoting dialogue with them on bilateral and regional bases, as well as within multilateral fora, while fostering the Union's specific interests.[229]

In terms of implementation, the ICI Regulation disposes of an indicative financial envelope of €172 million for the period 2007–13,[230] and is essentially implemented through (multiannual and annual) actions plans developed by the

[222] Central Africa RSP 2008–13, Annex IV; Pacific RSP 2008–13, Annex 4d; ESI RSP 2008–13, Annex 15.

[223] Environmental profiles are also used by other donors, such as the World Bank, FAO and UNEP (see references in Environmental Integration Handbook, 27).

[224] Ibid, 26.

[225] A list of environmental profiles that have been elaborated at ACP country-level is available at: www.environment-integration.eu/content/view/166/229/lang,en/.

[226] Council Regulation (EC) 1934/2006 establishing a financial instrument for cooperation with industrialized and other high-income countries and territories [2006] OJ L405/41 (ICI Regulation). This regulation was therefore adopted on the basis of art 212 TFEU (former art 181a TEC); see Ch 1, s 5.3.

[227] ICI Regulation, Annex.

[228] Ibid, art 2(1).

[229] Ibid, arts 1 and 3(3).

[230] Ibid, art 16.

Commission, with no formal basis for dialogue with partner countries in the elaboration of these programming documents. These thus reflect primarily the Union's 'strategic priority and interests'.[231] As to the areas for cooperation, emphasis is placed on, inter alia, the promotion of cooperative projects in research, science and technology, energy, transport and environmental matters including climate change, as well as on the promotion of dialogue between political, economic and social actors and NGOs.[232] The ICI resources thus can serve to support institutionalised dialogue and environmental cooperation activities within the framework of an existing agreement between the EU and an eligible third country (for example, the 2010 Agreements with South Korea),[233] but also outside the formal framework of an agreement.[234]

4.6 Assessment

The preceding analysis has shown that all geographic instruments provide a legal basis, albeit with different degrees of strength, for environmental integration into EU external assistance as an additional venue to the ENRTP, which is significant in both policy and quantitative terms. As opposed to the environment thematic funding, the allocation of resources under most geographic instruments is determined – although to very different degrees – on the basis of a dialogue with the aid recipients concerned, which can serve to better identify their particular environmental needs and priorities and to make EU aid more responsive to them. In quantitative terms, being the instrument preferred by the EU for cooperation purposes, geographic programmes are generally endowed with indicative financial envelopes that are far more generous than those of thematic programmes, thus opening the door for complementing the comparatively more limited ENRTP resources. Yet, the extent to which the environment becomes the object of support through the geographic instruments depends on whether environmental issues or constraints are identified as a priority area in the RSPs/CSPs, and ultimately on whether these are addressed by the EU's response strategy.

Notwithstanding the legal and quantitative potential for environmental mainstreaming into geographic instruments, only a modest proportion of their indicative financial budget seems to have been allocated to the environment in 2007–10 (see Table 4 below). This raises the question as to whether environmental concerns have received sufficient attention during the programming of EU aid (that is, in the formulation of RSPs/CSPs and accompanying indicative financial programmes), as well as to whether the tools available to ensure environmental integration in the early stages of this process (for example, environmental profiles and SEAs/EIAs) were duly and systematically used. While a comprehensive

[231] Ibid, arts 5–6, and particularly 5(2).

[232] Ibid, art 4.

[233] See Ch 2, s 7.1.

[234] See further Ch 5, s 3.6, including regulatory dialogues with Japan, Canada and the US.

examination of these issues was not plausible within the context of this book, it should be noted that EU practice in this regard has received some criticism from both internal and external sources.

For instance, the European Court of Auditors (ECA) undertook an audit on the environmental aspects of the old financing instruments (2000–06),[235] to assess the progress made in light of the Treaty-based requirement for environmental integration, as well as the commitments embedded in the 2001 Environmental Integration Strategy and the 2005 European Consensus on Development to mainstream the environment into EU cooperation. It found that the Commission had only made limited progress in this regard since 2001, pointing to the need to establish a clear comprehensive strategy for the environmental aspects of EU aid, as well as to strengthen staff capacities and reporting, monitoring and evaluation systems to better perform and assess this environmental integration exercise.[236] In particular, the ECA Report highlighted that CSPs over the period 2000–06 did not take sufficient account of environmental issues: notably, in the sample of 60 CSPs reviewed, none of them mentioned MDG7 on environmental sustainability and only approximately a quarter made reference to MEAs.[237] It further unveiled the lack of a consistent system for the environmental screening of new projects, finding evidence that EIAs had not always been carried out where needed.[238]

While the ECA Report pointed to a more systematic practice by the Commission to analysing environmental issues in the preparation of CSPs/RSPs for the period 2007–13 through the elaboration of country/regional environmental profiles,[239] a later report by NGOs (April 2009) has nonetheless found significant gaps in the quality and value of the information contained in these environmental profiles. The key shortcomings identified included: lack of good environmental data; insufficient analysis of laws, policies, institutions and judiciary system in the third country or region in question; lack of depth and knowledge in dealing with critical environmental issues (such as climate change, rehabilitation and protection of biodiversity, and waste management); and failure to adequately address and analyse EU policies on fisheries, forest governance and trade.[240] Against this background, it is interesting to note that the Council endorsed a few months later, in June 2009, the Commission's proposal to update environmental profiles as a matter of 'immediate action' in the mid-term review of CSPs/RSPs 2007–13, in order to 'address environmental risks such as climate change, biodiversity loss, deforestation or desertification issues in a comprehensive way', as well as to

[235] Court of Auditors, Special Report 6/2006 concerning the environmental aspects of the Commission's development cooperation [2006] OJ C 235/1 (ECA Report 2006).

[236] Ibid, 4 and paras 18–28.

[237] Ibid, para 29.

[238] Ibid, paras 39–46.

[239] Ibid, para 33.

[240] WWF, BirdLife and FERN, 'Environmental Tools in EC Development Cooperation – An Analysis of Country and Regional Environmental Profiles' (April 2009), on the basis of an analysis of 27 environmental profiles mainly from ACP and Latin America.

prepare these profiles jointly with other international donors (such as the UNEP and UNDP), while ensuring country ownership.[241]

Table 4. *EU Environment Funding under Geographic Instruments (2007–13)*[242]

Financing Instrument	Geographical Coverage	Total Indicative Budget	Environment Funding
IPA	9	€11.5 billion	*(NA)*
ENPI	17	€11.2 billion	€250 million *(2007–10)*
DCI *(geographic programmes)*	48	€10,057 million	€240 million *(2007–10)*
10th EDF	99	€22.7 billion	€171 million *(2008–10)*
ICI	17	€172 million	*(NA)*

5. CONCLUSIONS AND FUTURE PROSPECTS

Since the 2001 Environmental Integration Strategy, the EU commitment to environmental mainstreaming in its external cooperation activities has increasingly gained importance, in both political and quantitative terms. At the political level, there has been a continuous follow-up on the approach to environmental integration in EU external assistance, including through the 2005 European Consensus on Development and 2006 Sustainable Development Strategy,[243] and a renewed strategy is due to be presented by the Commission to the Council by the end of 2011.[244] To some extent, the EU has taken stock of the shortcomings of its earlier approach and constructively responded to some criticisms raised both internally (for example, by the Court of Auditors) and externally (for example, by NGOs).[245] Yet, the overall amount of resources allocated to the environment (both through thematic and geographical instruments) remains modest, as recognised by the Commission itself: the yearly average financial commitments by the EU for the

241 Council Conclusions 2009, 4.

242 Based on EU indicative financial allocations (IPA Regulation; ENPI Regulation; DCI Regulation; 10th EDF; ICI Regulation; and Commission WP 2009). The 'environment funding' figures reflect financial commitments on the environment and sustainable management of natural resources, and do not encompass other aspects of EU funding (eg, water and sanitation, energy) that may also have an environmental dimension.

243 Commission, 'Communication on the 2005 review of the EU sustainable development strategy: initial stocktaking and future orientations' COM (2005) 37 final; European Council, 'Review of the EU sustainable development strategy – renewed strategy' Brussels 15–16 June 2006.

244 Council Conclusions 2009, 6.

245 eg, the creation of a specific website on environmental integration in cooperation policies (above n 225), which may be a response to the WWF Report 2007 pointing to shortcomings in terms of public availability of documentation in this domain.

environment over the period 2007–10 was around €295 million, representing roughly 4.3 per cent of all EU external assistance.[246]

A differentiated approach can also be observed in the environmental integration exercise in the context of EU external assistance. In the case of thematic funding for the environment, differentiation is a direct product of the EU's own determinations and, as we have seen, reflects a growing global focus with the aims of both responding to international commitments (such as supporting MDG7 and MEA-related capacity building in developing countries) and having international environmental process and regimes 'shaped' by its own policy priorities (particularly in the fields of climate change and sustainable energy). In the case of geographic instruments, differentiation may be more the result of bilateral/inter-regional dialogues underpinning the formulation of the CSPs/RSPs, and thus reflective of the different environmental needs of the various EU partners involved. However, differentiation is certainly also a reflection of the varying degrees of dependency beneficiaries have on EU aid, as well as of the EU's own environmental priorities and broader relationship with a given third country or region. In fact, differentiation in the context of geographic instruments follows the pattern seen in EU bilateral and inter-regional agreements:[247] the IPA Regulation is primarily geared to supporting an approximation to the EU *acquis* within the pre-accession strategy; the ENPI Regulation with Eastern and Mediterranean neighbours rather focuses on regional environmental issues (for example, the Barcelona Convention); and the EDF with ACP countries (as well as the DCI geographic programmes) place more emphasis on international environmental issues (particularly the three Rio Conventions).

From an international law perspective, environmental integration into EU external assistance is much less controversial than in the GSP context,[248] even though both are unilateral measures. In fact, a particularly important aspect of the principle of common but differentiated responsibility is the provision of financial and technological assistance by developed countries unilaterally to developing countries. This is recognised in most core MEAs, and the CBD in particular explicitly makes the implementation of commitments by developing countries conditional upon the effective provision by developed countries of financial assistance and technology transfer.[249] While EU thematic and other environment-related funding can thus be seen as a positive response to these international

[246] Commission WP 2009, 4 noting that, in a broader sense, when programmes that promote (environmentally) sustainable rural development, water and sanitation, natural resources and renewable energy are also included, this figure rises to around 10 per cent. See also Council Conclusions 2009, 6, inviting 'the Commission and Member States to efficiently use available and relevant instruments and, if necessary, to explore possibilities for mobilising adequate, predictable and sustainable resources' in the context of agreed ODA.

[247] Ch 2, s 8.1.

[248] Ch 3.

[249] CBD, art 20(4) stipulates: 'The extent to which developing country Parties will effectively implement their commitments under this Convention will depend on the effective implementation by developed country Parties of their commitments under this Convention related to financial resources and transfer of technology'.

commitments, there is still a risk of being perceived as using such funding as a low-hanging fruit vis-a-vis global problems, instead of taking more ambitious domestic action.[250] In addition, the ownership and partnership principles embedded in the Paris Declaration on Aid Effectiveness may be interpreted as implying that the EU should limit itself to procedural guarantees for environmental integration (SEAs, EIAs and improved follow-up, monitoring and evaluation of environmental integration),[251] leaving substantive and output-oriented environmental integration to recipient countries.[252] At the same time, the systematic and timely reliance by the EU on global consensus-based commitments to environmental integration, such as climate and biodiversity mainstreaming, is an essential normative benchmark to legitimise its unilateral funding initiatives, as well as to avoid double standards between its global commitments and those with individual third countries or regions.

In any event, increased transparency and meaningful involvement of third-country stakeholders in the policy-making, programming and delivery of EU aid appear necessary to make EU external assistance responsive to the particular needs of beneficiary countries. In this respect, it is interesting to note that the Commission has initiated a consultation process with a view to obtaining inputs from Member States and other stakeholders (including aid recipients and international organisations) on the future role and priorities of EU external funding,[253] to inform its new development policy strategy to be presented to the Council by the end of 2011.

In the Commission's Green Paper, a clear emphasis is placed on speeding progress towards the achievement of the MDGs as the EU's 'first and overriding priority', reaffirming its collective target of devoting 0.7 per cent of GNI to ODA by 2015,[254] as well as on using development policy as 'a catalyst for inclusive and sustainable growth'.[255] In addition, 'sustainable development' is defined as the 'new driver' of EU cooperation activities, showing an interest to establish close interlinkages between climate change, biodiversity and development. This represents not only an attempt to ensure a holistic approach to environmental management and effective environmental mainstreaming into all EU policies and activities, but also a pragmatic effort to make the most of high-profile climate finance[256] – both facets have been increasingly advanced by the EU at the multilat-

[250] Persson, above n 68, 417.

[251] Ibid, 442 underlining however difficulties in measuring environmental impacts.

[252] Ibid, 421.

[253] Commission, 'Green Paper on EU development policy in support of inclusive growth and sustainable development – increasing the impact of EU development policy' COM (2010) 629 final (Commission Green Paper 2010); see also Commission, 'Background document on public consultation – what funding for EU external action after 2013?' 29 November 2010, 7 setting out the strategic objectives for EU external action as a whole, including tackling global challenges such as climate change and energy security, food security, poverty, access to and sustainable use of raw materials, biodiversity and natural resources.

[254] Commission Green Paper 2010, 3–4.

[255] Ibid, 11–14, including corporate environmental accountability issues.

[256] Ibid, 17.

eral level too.[257] In this context, specific attention is also paid to facilitating 'access to sustainable energy for all citizens' as a key means to support 'climate-proof' development.[258] A final area of focus for EU development cooperation would be on enhancing food security (particularly in Africa), while ensuring environmental sustainability of agricultural and fishing practices.[259]

The extent to which the EU will engage with inputs received and provide reasoned justifications for its policy choices in light of global consensus-based environmental instruments will be a determinant factor for the legitimacy and credibility of environmental integration in future EU external assistance.

[257] E Morgera, 'Far Away, So Close: A Legal Analysis of the Increasing Interactions between the Convention on Biological Diversity and Climate Change Law' (2011) 2(1) *Climate Law* 85, 112.

[258] Commission Green Paper 2010, 17.

[259] Ibid, 18–20.

5

Environmental Integration in Institutionalised Dialogues

1. INTRODUCTION

BESIDES THE CONVENTIONAL measures analysed in previous chapters, another –less legalised– instrument used by the EU to pursue environmental integration in the implementation of its external policies is institutionalised dialogue with third countries or regions. This practice is growing and taking different forms, but has so far attracted only limited scholarly attention.[1] While it is beyond the scope of this chapter and the interest of a legal enquiry to provide a comprehensive picture of institutionalised dialogues between the EU and third parties, this chapter will instead aim to identify the legal relevance of this tool on the basis of the various types of dialogues that exist and their objectives. To that end, the chapter will differentiate between environmental integration in broader policy and regulatory dialogues, on the one hand, and the practice of setting up thematic dialogues specifically devoted to environmental issues and, more recently to climate change cooperation, on the other.

In order to gauge the relationship between these dialogues and other EU external relations tools, the chapter will distinguish dialogues with associated or partner countries or regions as a means to follow up on, and facilitate the implementation of, environmental cooperation clauses of associations and other agreements; from dialogues with regions or groups of countries that do not have a common agreement with the EU; and from dialogues that are conducted outside the formal framework of an agreement, particularly with developed countries.

Overall, the chapter aims to assess the significance of institutionalising dialogue with third parties in fostering environmental cooperation within or outside the context of a formal agreement and in contributing to environmental integration in the Union's external relations. It will conclude by identifying the opportunities and shortcomings of this tool in relation to the other external relations instruments for environmental cooperation between the EU and third countries or regions.

[1] Among the few academic contributions on this topic, see N Alecu de Flers and E Regelsberger, 'The EU and Inter-regional Cooperation' in C Hill and M Smith (eds), *International Relations and the European Union* (Oxford, Oxford University Press, 2005), 317.

2. TYPES AND OBJECTIVES OF INSTITUTIONALISED DIALOGUES

The EU has invested considerable time, efforts and resources in the creation of a multitude of highly institutionalised forms of dialogue with third countries and regions. They often include high-level meetings (summits) that serve to emphasise publicly the importance of periodic bilateral and inter-regional exchanges on joint principles and interests.[2] However, it has been acutely observed that, while dialogues have grown and diversified over time, this development has not occurred 'necessarily along precise or consistent schedules and concepts.'[3] Dialogues are generally believed to favour greater consistency in EU external action and improve the EU profile as an international actor, but they have led to an increasing number of commitments that has inevitably created its own problems of intra-EU coordination and additional strain on the EU's institutional framework.[4]

Dialogues are presented by the EU as a tool for the periodic exchange of views with third countries or regions, although they are essentially organised at the initiative of the EU. There is, therefore, an inherent tension between the bilateral/inter-regional character of these exercises and the fact that they are often dominated in practice by the EU's priorities and approaches. Dialogues have thus been criticised for their alleged basis on shared values that are, however, often identified by the EU:[5] in this respect, dialogues are seen as tools for persuasion, rather than negotiation.[6] In the particular case of dialogues with developing countries, it has been argued that dialogues allow the EU to supervise domestic implementation in third countries against the EU's own understanding of sustainable development standards and performance.[7]

With regard to the types and objectives of dialogues, in the case of countries or regions that are parties to an association or other agreement with the EU, dialogue occurs within the institutional framework set up by the agreements themselves. In these cases, dialogues are aimed in principle at following up on the areas of cooperation established by the agreements, monitoring implementation and identifying more specific priorities for the implementation of cooperation

[2] Ibid, 335.

[3] Ibid, 338.

[4] Ibid, 339.

[5] See art 21(1) TEU, making reference, inter alia, to the respect of international law and the promotion of multilateral solutions to common problems, and art 21(2)(d), (f) and (h) TEU, making reference, inter alia, to: fostering the sustainable economic, social and environmental development of developing countries, with the primary aim of eradicating poverty; and helping develop international measures to preserve and improve the quality of the environment and the sustainable management of global natural resources, in order to ensure sustainable development, and promote an international system based on stronger multilateral cooperation and good global governance.

[6] P Leino, 'The Journey Towards all that is Good and Beautiful: Human Rights and "Common Values" as Guiding Principles of EU Foreign Relations Law' in M Cremona and B De Witte (eds), *EU Foreign Relations Law* (Oxford, Hart, 2008), 268.

[7] Ibid, 273–74. See discussion of the definition of sustainable development in Regulation (EC) 2493/2000 of the European Parliament and of the Council on measures to promote the full integration of the environmental dimension in the development process of developing countries [2000] OJ L288/1 in Ch 1, section 4.2.3.1.

clauses. The latter objective seems particularly relevant in the light of the open-ended drafting of the environmental cooperation provisions in EU bilateral and inter-regional agreements, which usually include a long list of priorities for environmental cooperation.[8] Dialogues may thus serve to further prioritise the areas of environmental cooperation with a view to determining specific financial or technical assistance that could be provided by the EU (although dialogues are not always the ultimate venue for the programming and allocation of external funding).[9] In that respect, it should be noted that in the European Consensus on Development,[10] dialogue is considered a principle underpinning the EU's commitment to ensure partner countries' national ownership of development cooperation.[11] In these circumstances, dialogues may contribute to environmental integration in the *implementation* of the Union's external relations.

Dialogues have also been established through ad hoc, self-standing institutional structures. This may be the case of dialogue with countries that are not party to an agreement with the EU, such as the US and Japan.[12] These are instances in which the EU usually prefers dialogues to focus on regulatory aspects, with a view to exchanging information and enhancing mutual understanding of domestic regulation in areas that may affect trade (such as environmental regulation) and possibly discussing options for rapprochement of regulatory standards. In other instances, dialogues may be institutionalised between the EU and groups of countries that do not have a common agreement with the EU (as in the case of Asia-Europe Meetings or the EU-Africa Summits, discussed below). In these cases, the EU aims to support inter-regional cooperation and regional integration in other areas of the world, beyond the reach of its bilateral or inter-regional agreements.[13] Dialogues may also play a role in the lead-up to the conclusion of agreements,[14] as in the case of the EU-China and EU-Canada relations.[15] In these circumstances, dialogues may contribute to environmental integration in the *definition* of the Union's external relations.

[8] See Ch 2, s 8.2.

[9] Ch 4.

[10] Council, Representatives of the Governments of the Member States meeting in the Council, European Parliament and Commission, 'Joint Statement on the European Development Policy: The European Consensus' [2006] OJ C46/1: see Ch 4, s 1.

[11] N van der Grijp and T Etty, 'Incorporating Climate Change into EU Development Cooperation Policy' in J Gupta and N van der Grijp (eds), *Mainstreaming Climate Change in Development Cooperation* (Cambridge, Cambridge University Press, 2010) 172.

[12] Although note that at the 20th EU-Japan Summit held in May 2011, leaders agreed to start negotiations of an FTA/EPA and, in parallel, an agreement covering political, global and other sectoral cooperation: 20th EU-Japan Summit, 'Joint press statement' Brussels 28 May 2011.

[13] Alecu de Flers and Regelsberger, above n 1, 323 and 335.

[14] Ibid, 323.

[15] While both countries concluded an agreement with the EU (Agreement on Trade and Economic Cooperation between the European Economic Community and the People's Republic of China [1985] OJ L250/2 and Framework Agreement for commercial and economic cooperation between the European Communities and Canada [1976] OJ L260/2), both are at the time of writing involved in the negotiations of more ambitious agreements with the EU (negotiations with China were agreed in 2006, see Commission, 'Press release – EU and China to agree on opening negotiations for a new comprehensive framework agreement' (IP/06/1161) 8 September 2006; while negotiations with Canada were agreed at the 2009 EU-Canada Summit, 'Declaration' Prague 6 May 2009).

Regardless of whether dialogues occur in the framework of bilateral/inter-regional agreements or not, they may be used for the 'definition of collective principles and negotiating positions in international fora':[16] in that respect, therefore, dialogues are also used to support multilateralism.[17] In fact, the EU has increasingly manifested more clearly and programmatically the intention to use dialogues to pursue specific global environmental objectives: for instance, in the Europe 2020 Strategy for smart, sustainable and inclusive growth, the EU commits to increase its outreach at the bilateral level with a view to building mutual understanding with third countries in the search of a global solution to climate change through *regulatory dialogues* with partner countries in order to promote equivalence, mutual recognition and convergence in regulatory approaches and tools related to green growth and climate change; and the use of *high-level strategic dialogues* on energy and climate, access to raw materials and global poverty.[18] Along similar lines, in the 2020 Trade Strategy, the Commission proposed that the EU external trade policy continue to support and promote green growth (thereby including energy, resource efficiency and biodiversity protection) around the globe, based on dialogue with other countries, to ensure coherence with the development objectives of poverty eradication and good governance, specifically emphasising the role of the dialogues with the US and China, and that with civil society.[19]

The format of dialogues varies significantly from one case to another. It has been noted that the EU is increasingly seeking to engage in multi-stakeholder dialogues, with a view to supporting the participation of business, civil society organisations and national parliaments in its dialogues with third countries or regions.[20] It has been argued that this open approach, once fully realised, may contribute to create an additional layer of checks and balances in the external relations of the EU and even nurture 'collective interest in the joint management of global interdependence through common rules and mechanisms.'[21]

Before the entry info force of the Treaty of Lisbon, the EU Presidency[22] played a key role in coordinating and chairing dialogues:[23] the Member State holding the

[16] Alecu de Flers and Regelsberger, above n 1, 338.

[17] See discussion in Ch 7.

[18] Commission, 'Communication Europe 2020 – A strategy for smart, sustainable and inclusive growth' COM (2010) 2020, 21–22; which was endorsed by the European Council, 'Conclusions' Brussels 17 June 2010.

[19] Commission, 'Communication Trade, Growth and World Affairs – Trade policy as a core component of the EU's 2020 Strategy' COM (2010) 612 final (Trade, Growth and World Affairs Communication), 8, 11 and 14.

[20] Alecu de Flers and Regelsberger, above n 1, 320.

[21] Ibid, 339.

[22] Before the entry into force of the Lisbon Treaty, the Council (including its foreign affairs formation) was presided over for a period of six months by each Member State in turn, in accordance with a pre-established rota determined by a Council decision (art 203(2) TEC). Following the entry into force of the Lisbon Treaty, the Presidency of the Council is held by pre-established groups of three Member States for a period of 18 months only for certain Council configurations, including the environment, but no longer for foreign affairs (art 16(9) TEU and European Council Decision (EU) 2009/881 on the exercise of the Presidency of the Council [2009] OJ L315/50). See JC Piris, *The Lisbon Treaty. A Legal and Political Analysis* (Cambridge, Cambridge University Press, 2010), 206–09.

[23] Alecu de Flers and Regelsberger, above n 1, 320.

rotating EU Presidency represented the EU in the context of high-level dialogues, together with the European Commission and the future Presidency. Following the entry into force of the Lisbon Treaty, at annual Summits, the EU is in principle represented by the President of the European Council[24] and the President of the European Commission, assisted by the High Representative of the Union for Foreign Affairs and Security Policy.[25]

3. AN OVERVIEW OF PRACTICE

Turning to a few key examples to illustrate more practically the relevance of these initiatives from an environmental integration perspective, attention will be drawn to dialogues between the EU and: ACP countries, African countries, Mediterranean countries, Central and Latin American countries, Asian countries, and developed countries such as the US, Canada and Japan. These examples will, on the one hand, confirm the differentiated approach to environmental integration that has already been observed in previous chapters, and on the other hand allow to explore the Union's relations with countries that have not yet been discussed in this book.

3.1 The EU-ACP dialogue

In the context of the Cotonou Agreement, policy dialogue is based on the legal framework provided by the agreement and its institutional structure. Meetings of the EU-ACP Council of Ministers are held annually; meetings of the Committee of Ambassadors monthly; and meetings of the Joint Parliamentary Assembly (JPA) bi-annually.[26] Notwithstanding its consultative status, the JPA has played a visibly active role within the EU-ACP dialogue,[27] issuing a number of resolutions of environmental relevance. The EU-ACP Council is to examine and consider the JPA's resolutions and recommendations, and annually report to the JPA on the

[24] This is a new institutional figure introduced by the Treaty of Lisbon: the President of the European Council is elected for a two and a half years and, inter alia, ensures the external representation of the Union on issues concerning its common foreign and security policy (art 15(5)–(6) TEU). For a discussion, Piris, above n 22, 206–09.

[25] This is the other key institutional figure for the EU external relations introduced by the Treaty of Lisbon: the High Representative conducts the Union's common foreign and security policy, and ensures the consistency of the Union's external action policy (arts 18(2) and (4) TEU). She chairs the Foreign Relations Council and is the Vice-President of the Commission. Notably, the external role of the President of the European Council (noted above) is 'without prejudice to the powers' of the High Representative (art 15(6) TEU). Piris, above n 22, 243–49. It remains to be seen, given the plethora of dialogues, whether these two institutions will continute to rely on the rotating EU Presidency on occasions.

[26] See Ch 2, s 5.2.5.

[27] Note that the European Parliament annual reports on the activities of the JPA are easily accessible at www.europarl.europa.eu/intcoop/acp/27_01/default_en.htm. On the other hand, it is quite difficult to monitor the activity of the ACP-EU Council of Ministers, for which a similar online resource is not available.

implementation of the agreement.[28] Dialogue is also held informally, in other formats,[29] and has generally served several purposes in the EU-ACP relationship from an environmental perspective.

First, the EU-ACP dialogue sought to specify areas and activities for environmental cooperation. Emphasis was placed on climate change, for instance, as early as in the mid-1990s, with the creation of a working group on climate change by the JPA.[30] The JPA also discussed questions related to fisheries management, urging the proper level of coherence between EU fisheries and development policies.[31] Other environmental issues are also addressed rather occasionally, such as water,[32] environmental governance,[33] renewables,[34] and the social and environmental consequences of structural adjustment programmes.[35]

Second, the EU-ACP dialogue has also been used to discuss respective priorities in anticipation of multilateral environmental negotiations sessions. The Joint ACP-EU Council often addressed global environmental issues, mostly climate change: in 2006, a declaration on climate change and development pointed to the need to enhance dialogue in preparation of multilateral negotiations, including a commitment to consult regularly in the context of the meetings of the UNFCCC bodies, as well as to enhance dialogue on the integration of climate change in development and poverty reduction strategies.[36] A more recent declaration adopted in 2009 calls attention to the need to promote sustainable land management and biodiversity conservation in the international climate change regime.[37] The JPA has also served to agree on common priorities in anticipation of multilateral environmental negotiations sessions, such as reaching agreement on the inclusion of international rules on technology development and transfer,[38] a

[28] Second Revision of the Cotonou Partnership Agreement, art 15(3).

[29] For a discussion in the context of the political dialogue, see ACP-EU Joint Parliamentary Assembly, 'Resolution on ACP-EU political dialogue' (ACP-EU 3689/04/fin.) [2005] OJ C80/17, para 26; see generally, Leino, above n 6.

[30] European Parliament, 'Resolution on the outcome of the proceedings of the ACP-EU Joint Assembly in 1996' (A4-0019/1997) [1996] OJ C254/, para 10.

[31] European Parliament, 'Resolution on the results of the work of the ACP-EU Joint Assembly in 1999' (A5-0032/2000) [2000] OJ C339/263.

[32] EU-ACP Joint Parliamentary Assembly, 'Resolution on water in developing countries' [2006] OJ C330/31.

[33] EU-ACP Joint Parliamentary Assembly, 'Resolution on good governance, transparency and accountability in relation to the exploitation of natural resources in ACP countries' [2007] OJ C254/17.

[34] EU-ACP Joint Parliamentary Assembly, 'Resolution on renewable energies in ACP countries' [2002] OJ C78/35.

[35] EU-ACP Joint Parliamentary Assembly, 'Resolution on the social and environmental consequences of structural adjustment programmes' [2008] OJ C271/20.

[36] Joint EU-ACP Council, 'Joint ACP-EU Declaration on climate change and development' (ACP/84/029/06 REV1) 30 June 2006.

[37] Joint EU-ACP Council, 'Joint ACP-EU Declaration on Climate Change and Development' (CL09-130EN) Brussels 29 May 2009, para 24.

[38] EU-ACP Joint Parliamentary Assembly, 'Resolution on post-Copenhagen: technology transfer, new technologies and technical capacity building in the ACP countries' (ACP-EU/100.739/10/fin.) 2–4 December 2010, para 3.

reformed Clean Development Mechanism[39] and agriculture[40] in the post-2012 international climate change regime. The JPA further engaged in the joint evaluation of the outcomes of multilateral negotiations, as occurred after the 2002 World Summit on Sustainable Development.[41] In some instances, it served to express the intention to support the launch of new international processes, to address, for instance, gaps in the international legal framework vis-a-vis climate refugees.[42]

Third, the JPA reviewed EU 'domestic' legislative proposals with extraterritorial relevance,[43] and provided an avenue for partner countries to call upon the EU to take legislative action, for instance on binding legislation to hold European companies operating in ACP states accountable[44] or on climate change adaptation.[45]

Finally, the EU-ACP dialogue also served to discuss the need to improve transparency and public participation in the Union's external relations. The JPA called for a clearly defined role for civil society in the implementation of the Cotonou Agreement, including on the development policy objectives being pursued.[46] In some instances, these calls were directed at ACP countries in particular.[47]

3.2 EU-Africa dialogue

Aside from the EU-ACP dialogue, an institutionalised dialogue exists with the members of the AU,[48] as a means to build bridges between the different agreements that the EU has with African countries.[49] EU-Africa Summits of Heads of State and Government are convened every three years; and complemented by meetings

[39] EU-ACP Joint Parliamentary Assembly, 'Resolution on the social and environmental consequences of climate change in the ACP countries' [2009] OJ C221/31, para 8.

[40] EU-ACP Joint Parliamentary Assembly, 'Resolution on Climate Change' [2010] OJ C68/36, para 18.

[41] For instance, EU-ACP Joint Parliamentary Assembly, 'Resolution on the Johannesburg Summit' (ACP-EU3563/03/fin) [2003] OJ C231/34.

[42] EU-ACP Joint Parliamentary Assembly, 'Resolution on the social and environmental consequences of climate change in the ACP countries', above n 39, paras 25–26.

[43] EU-ACP Joint Parliamentary Assembly, 'Resolution on registration, evaluation and authorsation of chemicals' (ACP-EU 3833/05/fin.) [2006] OJ C136/31.

[44] EU-ACP Joint Parliamentary Assembly, 'Resolution on post-Copenhagen', above n 38, para 17.

[45] EU-ACP Joint Parliamentary Assembly, 'Resolution on the social and environmental consequences of climate change in the ACP countries', above n 39, para 12.

[46] European Parliament, 'Resolution on the proceedings of the EU-ACP Joint Parliamentary Assembly in 2000' (A5-0057/2001) [2001] OJ C343/289; see also EU-ACP Joint Parliamentary Assembly, 'Resolution on fisheries and their social and environmental aspects in developing countries' [2006] OJ C307/27; ACP-EU Joint Parliamentary Assembly, Resolution on small-scale fisheries' (ACP-EU3028/00/fin) [2001] OJ C64/52.

[47] EU-ACP Joint Parliamentary Assembly, 'Resolution on the social and environmental consequences of climate change in the ACP countries', above n 39, para 19, calling for participatory approaches in the drawing up and implementation of climate change adaptation strategies.

[48] Note that the second revision (2010) of the Cotonou Agreement formally recognised the AU as an actor for cooperation (art 6(1)(b)).

[49] Namely: Cotonou Agreement, Euro-Med Associations and South Africa AA (see Ch 2).

between the EU and Africa troikas,[50] EU-African ministerial meetings, as well as College-to-College meetings between the AU Commission and the European Commission.[51]

The EU-Africa dialogue has led to the adoption of a joint strategy and a first action plan at the second EU-Africa Summit in 2007, contributing to advancing environmental cooperation bilaterally on specific areas and to discuss priorities for ongoing multilateral environmental negotiations. The only environmental priority in the first action plan (2008–10)[52] was climate change, including a specific partnership on climate change to enable dialogue, cooperation and exchange on concrete actions and serve as an effective channel for holding deliberations on a shared EU-Africa vision, with a view to jointly promoting and sustaining a system of effective multilateralism.[53] Specifically, cooperation on climate change focused on: reduced rates of deforestation and better preservation of forest ecosystems, while improving the livelihoods of forest-dependent populations; increased benefits for Africa from participation in the global carbon market and enhanced capacity of African negotiators in the international market; increased energy efficiency and resilience to climate change in the African economies; and climate mainstreaming in different areas of environmental law through the elaboration and implementation of adaptation and mitigation strategies, particularly in relation to water, energy, health, environment, agricultural and food security issues. Meetings related to the strategy provided opportunities for the EU to explain its negotiating position under the UNFCCC, evaluate together with African countries the outcomes of past rounds of negotiations, and reach a common understanding for the next rounds.[54] Other environmental issues were also highlighted as key development issues accelerating progress towards the MDGs (biodiversity, toxic waste, integrated water management and sustainable use of natural resources).[55]

The most recent action plan (2011–13) was adopted at the third EU-Africa Summit in 2010, and includes a specific partnership on 'Climate Change and Environment', which contributes to a variety of environmental issues, showing the potential of climate change to act as a catalyst for coherence across the board of environmental cooperation. The new plan includes priority actions on strengthening Africa's capacity in international negotiations on climate change and biodiversity conservation,[56] as well as in the implementation of MEAs (in

[50] On the African side, the Troika consists of the current and outgoing Presidencies of the AU and the AU Commission, expanded to include chef de file countries at the expert and senior official levels.

[51] Alecu de Flers and Regelsberger, above n 1, 323–28.

[52] EU-Africa Summit, 'First Action Plan (2008–2010) for the Implementation of the Africa-EU Strategic Partnership' (undated) at www.ec.europa.eu/development/icenter/repository/EAS2007_action_plan_2008_2010_en.pdf.

[53] Ibid, para 8(iii).

[54] See, for instance, 12th Africa-EU Ministerial Troika Meeting, 'Communiqué' Luxembourg 28 April 2009, with section Ib, titled 'Climate change agenda: preparing the Copenhagen conference.'

[55] Second EU-Africa Summit, 'The Africa-EU Strategic Partnership: A Joint Africa-EU Strategy', Lisbon 9 December 2007, para 65.

[56] Third EU-Africa Summit, 'Joint Africa-EU Strategy Action Plan (2011–2013)' Tripoli 30 November 2010, 51–53.

particular of the recently concluded Nagoya Protocol on Access and Benefit-Sharing under the CBD and an unprecedented focus on integrating biodiversity in development and planning processes) and the fight against deforestation.[57] In line with the Europe 2020 Strategy, the action plan further focuses on the green economy and cooperation on climate-friendly technologies.[58] It also aims to further strengthen cooperation between the EU and the African block in the post-2012 climate change negotiations, calling for coherence between international climate change negotiations and the EU-Africa partnership among its overall objectives.[59] While the EU-Africa dialogue has therefore served to advance cooperation both for the implementation of MEAs and on multilateral environmental negotiations, the modalities of civil society involvement have varied significantly, and the private sector's participation has been limited.[60]

Among African countries, the EU established a Strategic Partnership with South Africa,[61] on the basis of which they hold high-level political Summits on an annual basis, as well as high-level ad hoc meetings on issues of common interest whenever necessary, in addition to their dialogue in the context of the EU-Africa Summits and EU-ACP meetings.[62] According to a joint action plan, South Africa and the EU agreed to establish a High-level Dialogue on the Environment to address a variety of environmental issues: *in primis* climate change, but also biodiversity, waste management, air pollution, renewable energy, and environmental governance.[63] This provided the opportunity to address questions related to sustainable production and consumption, waste minimisation and biofuels, and encouraged an examination by South Africa of the EU's arguments for the ratification of the Gaborone amendment to enable the EU to become a full member of CITES.[64] Most attention, however, has been devoted to climate change, with the EU and South Africa preparing ahead of the international climate change negotiation sessions,[65] as well as jointly reviewing the outcomes of past negotiating sessions.[66] Another development related to climate change cooperation is the creation of an Energy Dialogue Forum specifically to discuss clean coal, carbon capture and storage, energy efficiency and renewable energies.[67] Dialogue has

[57] Joint EU-Africa Strategy Action Plan (2011–13), ibid, 51 and 53.

[58] Ibid, 5.

[59] Ibid.

[60] Commission, 'Mid-term review report of the Africa-EU Strategic Partnership' (9 October 2009).

[61] Commission, 'Communication – Towards an EU-South Africa Strategic Partnership' COM (2006) 347 final, where the Commission underscored South Africa's role on the global scene as a member of the Non-Aligned Movement, WTO, Commonwealth of Nations, G-20, group of emerging donor countries, and as an important negotiator in the international climate change regime.

[62] Third EU-South Africa Summit, 'South Africa – EU Strategic Partnership Joint Communiqué' Tshwane 10 October 2007.

[63] EU-South Africa Ministerial Troika, 'The South Africa-European Union Strategic Partnership Joint Action Plan' Brussels 15 May 2007, para 6.

[64] EU-South Africa Strategic Partnership Joint Communiqué, above n 62, 6–7.

[65] Second EU-South Africa Summit, 'Joint Communiqué' Kleinmond 11 September 2009, 3–4.

[66] Third EU-South Africa Summit, 'Joint Communiqué' Brussels 28 September 2010, 3–4.

[67] EU-South Africa Summit, 'Joint Statement by President of South Africa Thabo Mbeki, President of France Nicolas Sarkozy, and President José Manuel Barroso' (12233/08 (Presse 222) 2008), 3–4.

notably intensified in the lead up to the international climate change conference in Durban in late 2011 for which South Africa held the presidency.

3.3 The Euro-Med dialogues

As opposed to the EU-ACP and EU-Africa dialogues, the Euro-Med dialogue is generally geared towards increased inter-regional cooperation in relation to the development of environmental law and policy, rather than on coordination in view of global environmental negotiations. This seems to reflect the content of the environmental cooperation clauses of the Euro-Med Association Agreements.[68] In the framework of the Euro-Mediterranean Association Agreements, dialogue is held between the EU and individual countries through the joint institutions established by each association agreement.[69] In addition, inter-regional dialogue is held, on the basis of the Barcelona process,[70] through meetings at the level of the Euro-Med Conference of Ministers, the Euro-Med Committee, and the Euro-Med Parliamentary Assembly.[71] Environmental issues are mainly discussed at regular meetings of the Euro-Med Ministers for the Environment.[72] Overall, the dialogue has resulted in a succession of programmes further prioritising and specifying the areas of environmental cooperation among the partners.

The dialogue first led to the adoption of a Short and Medium Term Environmental Action Programme (SMAP)[73] in 1997, which embodied the environmental component of the Euro-Med Partnership, laying down a framework programme of action for the protection of the Mediterranean environment. The Action Programme built upon existing inter-regional environmental cooperation, particularly in the framework of the 1976 Barcelona Convention on the Protection of the Mediterranean Sea and the Mediterranean Action Plan. SMAP provided the common basis for environmental policy and funding orientation within the region, both at the national and regional levels. It prioritised five fields of action: integrated water management, waste management, 'hot spots' (that is, a category including both polluted areas and threatened biodiversity elements), integrated coastal zone management, and combating desertification. Interestingly, the SMAP framework also provided for a follow-up, reporting and review mechanism. The mechanism was based on: a network of SMAP correspondents meeting annually; a reporting system; a review mechanism, that after two years could lead to an adjustment of the Action Programme; and consultation practices for SMAP implementation and modification.

[68] See Ch 2, s 4.3.

[69] Ch 2, s 4.6.

[70] Ch 2, s 4.1.

[71] Alecu de Flers and Regelsberberger, above n 1, 323–28. See Ch 2, s 4.6.

[72] For instance, discussion on energy and environment at the Second Euro-Mediterranean Ministerial Conference on the Environment, 'Declaration' Athens 28 March 2008 (Athens Declaration).

[73] First Euro-Mediterranean Ministerial Conference on the Environment, 'Declaration' Helsinki 28 November 1997.

In undertaking the five-year review of SMAP implementation, however, the Commission highlighted delays in processing and implementing SMAP projects and suggested improvement of procedures for proposals, training, and greater transparency in project selection procedures.[74] The Commission also noted that participation of environmental ministers in the negotiations of the Euro-Med Association Agreements had been extremely limited, and that none of the single environmental cooperation clauses in each agreement had encompassed all five SMAP priorities.[75] The Commission further recommended that the five SMAP priorities be retained with a greater emphasis on implementation, and that partners explore the possibilities of regional dialogue and cooperation on climate change effects as a cross-cutting issue.[76] It also highlighted that environmental considerations should be integrated in other Euro-Med policies, programmes and projects, at national and regional levels, with special emphasis on water, industry, transport and energy.[77]

Priorities for future action in the region were established by the 2002 Athens Ministerial Conference on the Environment, reiterating the importance of sustainable development as the 'predominant global and guiding principle' of the Euro-Med Partnership. Based on past shortcomings in implementation, the Conference recommended the consideration of ways to strengthen environmental integration in agriculture and tourism, by linking them to SMAP priorities, and encouraged national administrators to take account of SMAP in the work of the joint institutions established under the associations, in order to achieve greater environmental action at the national level.[78]

In 2006, the Horizon 2020 initiative was jointly launched for de-pollution of the Mediterranean Sea by 2020, inviting the European Commission to coordinate the partnership through the establishment of an efficient institutional steering mechanism with key representatives from the Euro-Mediterranean governments and other partners to provide overall guidance, review, monitoring and effective coordination with other related initiatives, in particular the SMAP Strategic Action Programme to address pollution from land-based activities.[79]

Further to the 2008 conclusions on strengthening the ENP,[80] the EU's bilateral

[74] Commission, 'Report on the First Five Years of Implementation (1997–2001)' (Luxembourg, Office for Official Publications of the European Communities, 2003), 25.

[75] Ibid, 27.

[76] Ibid, 31.

[77] Ibid, 36.

[78] Athens Declaration, 8.

[79] Third Euro-Mediterranean Ministerial Conference on the Environment, 'Declaration' Cairo 20 November 2006.

[80] Council Conclusions, 'European Neighbourhood Policy' 18 February 2008. Note that dialogue between the EU and its Eastern neighbours occurs in the institutional framework set up under their respective PCAs (Ch 2, s 7.2), with Armenia, Azerbaijan, Belarus, Georgia, Moldova and Ukraine being part of the ENP (Ch 2, s 4.1) and of the Eastern Partnership, that provides further opportunities for dialogue in addition to that under the PCAs (Prague Eastern Partnership Summit, 'Joint Declaration' Brussels 7 May 2009). Dialogue with the Russian Federation also occurs in the framework of its PCA: while Russia is not part of the ENP, it is a strategic partner of the EU and in 2010 a 'partnership for modernisation' was launched, including on promoting a sustainable low-carbon economy and energy

cooperation with Mediterranean countries has been revitalised on the basis of the four key principles underpinning the ENP, namely: partnership; joint ownership; differentiation and tailor-made assistance, in full compliance with a single, inclusive, balanced and coherent policy framework.[81] Euro-Mediterranean Heads of State and Government then agreed later in 2008 to establish new institutional structures with a view to achieving the political goals of the initiative, especially reinforcing inclusive co-ownership and increasing its visibility through projects such as the de-pollution of the Mediterranean Sea and a Mediterranean solar energy plan.[82]

Since the re-launch of the Barcelona process in 2008 as the Union for the Mediterranean,[83] work on the environment includes continuation of the Horizon 2020 initiative, but also new areas such as: studying the process of developing a harmonised maritime policy and promoting a foreseeable maritime strategy for the Mediterranean; and intensified cooperation on climate change through the establishment of a Euro-Mediterranean Climate Change Network in support of regional efforts to combat climate change.[84] Sustainability issues are also included in the areas of energy cooperation, transport, agriculture, urban development, water, tourism, and industrial cooperation.[85] In addition, Euro-Med partners agreed to develop a strategy for water focused on the needs of populations and future challenges.[86]

3.4 Dialogues with Latin America and the Caribbean

Several dialogues have been launched in Latin America and the Caribbean, both as inter-regional and bilateral initiatives. The geographically broadest one is the EU-LAC (Latin America and the Caribbean) Summit, that has been taking place every two years since 1999, with a Summit-level meeting devoted to the environment organised for the first time in 2008 to launch a joint initiative to promote bi-regional cooperation on climate change.[87] On alternate years to the EU-LAC Summits, there are meetings at the ministerial level between the EU and the Rio Group, which comprises 23 countries: all Latin American countries plus the

efficiency, as well as international negotiations on fighting climate change (EU-Russia Summit, 'Joint Statement on the Partnership for Modernisation' Rostov-on-Don 1 June 2010, 2; see also s 3.5 below).

[81] Council Conclusions, 'Strengthening of the European Union's bilateral relations with its Mediterranean partners' 8–9 December 2008.

[82] Paris Summit for the Mediterranean, 'Joint Declaration' Paris 13 July 2008.

[83] See Ch 2, s 4.1.

[84] Union for the Mediterranean Ministerial Conference, 'Final Declaration' Marseille 4 November 2008, 15–16.

[85] Ibid, 13–24. See follow-up on, for instance, industrial development (Conference of the Ministers for Industry of the Union for the Mediterranean, 'Conclusions' Nice 5–6 November 2008, para 6) and tourism (Euro-Med Ministerial Conference on Tourism, 'Agreed Conclusions' Fez 2–3 April 2008, para 5.)

[86] Euro-Mediterranean Ministerial Conference on Water, 'Declaration' Swaimeh 22 December 2008.

[87] Commission, 'Communication – The European Union and Latin America: Global Players in Partnership' COM (2009) 495/3, 3.

Dominican Republic, Jamaica, Belize, Guyana, Haiti and Cuba. In addition, dialogues also occur within the institutional framework set up by the agreements with the EU.[88]

The EU-LAC dialogue has placed significant emphasis on cooperation in the implementation of MEAs, as well as in the discussion on ongoing multilateral environmental negotiations, which reflects the prominent role of international environmental standards in the recent bilateral agreements with CARIFORUM, Central American and some Andean countries.[89] The 2006 EU-LAC Summit, for instance, launched a thematic political dialogue on environmental issues of comparatively significant breadth, including on climate change, desertification, energy, water, as well as biodiversity, forests, chemicals management and international environmental governance.[90] The 2008 EU-LAC Summit further contributed to discussions on environmental cooperation issues, specifically emphasising cooperation in the implementation of and multilateral negotiations related to climate change, biodiversity, energy and global environmental governance, as well as on chemicals. It also stressed cooperation in the sustainable use of various natural resources such as forests and fisheries, the importance of public participation and of sustainable consumption and production.[91] The Summit resulted in an action plan including bi-regional cooperation on climate change, identifying priority elements for discussion in the lead-up to multilateral negotiating sessions, exchange of policies on the shift towards a low-carbon economy encompassing corporate responsibility, avoidance of the impacts of climate change on biodiversity, and research.[92] It also included a wide-ranging section on fostering environmental sustainability, foreseeing cooperation in relation to specific issues under negotiations in the framework of the CBD, work on forest law enforcement and governance, as well as bi-regional policy dialogue on water and on the implementation of SAICM.[93] The Declaration explicitly provided for the EU-LAC dialogue on environmental policy to follow up on actions included in the agenda, established a timetable for its progressive fulfilment, and acknowledged the special focus on climate change with the creation of a knowledge-sharing programme on this issue.[94]

[88] Alecu de Flers and Regelsberger, above n 1, 323–28. On the agreements, see Ch 2, ss 2.1–2.2, and Inter-regional Framework Cooperation Agreement between the European Community and its Member States, of the one part, and the Southern Common Market and its Party States, of the other part [1999] OJ L112/66; Economic Partnership, Political Coordination and Cooperation Agreement between the European Community and its Member States, of the one part, and the United Mexican States, of the other part [2000] OJ L276/45. The EU and Mexico have held high-level dialogues on environment and climate change since 2008: see, Commission (DG Environment), 'Bilateral and regional cooperation – emerging economies – Mexico' at www.ec.europa.eu/environment/international_issues/relations_mexico_en.htm; Framework Agreement for Cooperation between the European Economic Community and the Federative Republic of Brazil [1995] OJ L262/54. EU-Brazil Summits have been held since 2007: see European External Action Service, 'EU-Brazil Summits' at www.eeas.europa.eu/brazil/summit/index_en.htm.

[89] See Ch 2, s 5.3 and references to COPE FTA in Ch 2, s 7.1.

[90] Fourth EU-LAC Summit, 'Declaration' Vienna 12 May 2006, para 24.

[91] Fifth EU-LAC Summit, 'Declaration: Our Peoples' Priorities Together' Lima 16 May 2008 (Lima Declaration), paras 31–37.

[92] Ibid, paras 38–40.

[93] Ibid, paras 47–50. On SAICM, see Ch 4, fn 99.

[94] Lima Declaration, paras 51–52.

In assessing the partnership in 2009, however, the Commission stressed that the full potential of the Summits' political capital had not yet been entirely unlocked, as dialogue could be made more result-focused, by concentrating attention on operational targets and the means to achieve them as the main tool to plan bi-regional cooperation. In addition, the need was noted to strengthen dialogue and coordination with other regional processes, and to involve civil society, non-State actors, cultural and financial institutions,[95] and generally stepping up dialogue on priority areas related to global challenges, such as environment, climate change, energy, and technology/innovation.[96] The Commission also emphasised the role of mid-term reviews to adapt cooperation to different needs and to mainstream climate change considerations, both on mitigation and adaptation (including the fight against deforestation) in development and cooperation programmes.[97]

The 2010 EU-LAC Summit attempted to address some of these shortcomings, by focusing dialogue on low-carbon and green technologies.[98] The Summit produced an action plan that aimed to better include biodiversity into the existing dialogue on environment, climate change and energy, as well as emphasising cooperation in science, research, innovation and technology.[99] The accompanying declaration enshrined the commitment to cooperate in ongoing negotiations on climate change and biodiversity, as well as to exchange experience, including on norms and regulations, on renewables and biofuels in particular.[100] On this occasion the EU held separate summits also with the sub-groupings in the region (MERCOSUR, Andean Community, Central America, the Caribbean), adopting declarations reviewing the state of play of multilateral negotiations on climate change,[101] and occasionally also on biodiversity and on a legally binding instrument on mercury.[102]

Coordination and cooperation related to multilateral environmental agreements and processes is also supported at the level of the EU-LAC Parliamentary Assembly, created in 2006,[103] which adopted a resolution on a coordinated strategy in the framework of the UNFCCC negotiations, proposing to create

[95] Commission, 'The European Union and Latin America: Global Players in Partnership' COM (2009) 495/3, 6.

[96] Ibid, 7.

[97] Ibid, 9.

[98] Ibid, 10.

[99] Sixth EU-LAC Summit, 'Action Plan' Madrid 18 May 2010.

[100] Sixth EU-LAC Summit, 'Declaration: Towards a new stage in the bi-regional partnership: innovation and technology for sustainable development and social inclusion' Madrid 18 May 2010 (Madrid Declaration), paras 13, 15–17 and 29.

[101] EU-CAN Summit, 'Joint Communiqué' Madrid 19 May 2010, para 3.

[102] Madrid Declaration, paras 14–18. The EU and CARIFORUM also agreed on the organisation of a high level EU-Caribbean conference on climate change ahead of the following round of climate negotiations (Fourth EU-CARIFORUM Summit, 'Joint Communiqué' Madrid 17 May 2010, para 5).

[103] Brochure, 'What is the EU-LAC Parliamentary Assembly?' (2009) at www.europarl.europa.eu/intcoop/eurolat/key_documents/flyer_eurolat_en.pdf.

mutual standards for biofuel production, and for harmonising all other multilateral and bilateral agreements with the most ambitious mitigation requirements.[104]

In this broad context, the EU-Mexico dialogue is worth singling out, as Mexico is considered by the EU a 'strategic partner' with which to exert 'significant influence on global issues.'[105] Bilateral dialogue held in the context of the institutions set up by the pre-existing bilateral agreement between the EU and Mexico was thus strengthened by the strategic partnership, by adapting the agendas of existing bodies and convening specific ad hoc meetings to coordinate their positions in international fora.[106] The strategic partnership is formalised in a joint executive plan, adopted in 2010,[107] which aims to address not only global issues of common interest at bilateral, regional and multilateral levels, but also influence the bi-regional context, as well as explore possibilities for triangular cooperation with other regions of the world, such as Africa.[108] Similarly to other dialogues, the EU and Mexico have focused on climate change,[109] with particular emphasis on the reform of the Clean Development Mechanism under the Kyoto Protocol and possible new carbon market mechanisms: this assumed particular significance at the time in which Mexico hosted the international climate change conference in 2010.[110] In addition, several other environmental 'priority issues' were identified for the strategic partnership, including: international environmental governance, the green economy, biofuels (with express reference to EU legislation on biofuels sustainability criteria),[111] biodiversity (including interactions between biodiversity and climate change measures), management of chemical substances, and sustainable fisheries management.[112]

Finally, the EU-Brazil Summits should be singled out: although they are a more recent phenomenon (being held every year since 2007), they have not only provided an avenue for exchanges on respective negotiating positions on

[104] EU-LAC Parliamentary Assembly, 'Resolution – Tackling climate change challenges together: for an EU-LAC coordinated strategy in the framework of the UNFCCC negotiations' (AP100.539v03-00) Seville 15 May 2010, paras 37–38.

[105] Commission, 'Communication – Towards an EU-Mexico Strategic Partnership', COM (2008) 447 final, 4–5.

[106] Ibid, 6.

[107] Fifth EU-Mexico Summit, 'Joint Statement' Comillas 16 May 2010, paras 3–4.

[108] Fifth EU-Mexico Summit, 'Mexico-EU Strategic Partnership Joint Executive Plan' Comillas 16 May 2010, 2.

[109] Nineth EU-Mexico Joint Committee, 'Final Joint Communiqué' Brussels 26–27 November 2009, paras 7 and 10; Sixth Joint EU-Mexico Council, ' Joint Communiqué' Prague 14 May 2009, paras 16–18; Tenth Joint EU-Mexico Committee, 'Joint Communiqué' Mexico City 27–28 October 2010, para 13.

[110] The UN Climate Change Conference was held in Cancun, Mexico, from 29 November–11 December 2010 (including the sixteenth session of the Conference of the Parties to the UNFCCC, the sixth session of Conference of the Parties serving as the Meeting of the Parties to the Kyoto Protocol, as well as meetings of subsidiary bodies). For a discussion of the importance of the Mexican presidency at the Cancun Conference, see S Aguilar, 'Outcomes of the Cancún Conference' (2011) 41(1) *Environmental Policy and Law* 10.

[111] EU-Mexico Strategic Partnership Joint Executive Plan, above n 108, 15. Directive (EC) 2009/28 of the European Parliament and of the Council on the promotion of the use of energy from renewable sources [2009] OJ L140/16 discussed in Ch 7, s 3.2.

[112] EU-Mexico Strategic Partnership Joint Executive Plan, above n 108, 19–25.

climate change and biofuels, with commitments to hold bilateral high-level meetings in the run-up to key multilateral negotiating sessions,[113] but also to discuss triangular cooperation between the EU, Brazil and other developing countries, particularly on bioenergy in Africa.[114] Already in its second session, the Summit resulted in a joint action plan including a section on enhancing the economic and environmental partnership to promote sustainable development, which provides for cooperation in preparing for multilateral negotiations on climate change, biodiversity and on sustainable forest management, as well as cooperation in the implementation of the outcomes of these international processes.[115] The plan also established, in addition to dialogue on the environmental dimension of sustainable development and climate change, a political dialogue on international environmental governance (one of the long-standing international priorities for the EU in the context of UN reforms),[116] and strengthened cooperation on water and chemicals conventions. More recently, the EU and Brazil have also used their dialogue to review the state of the multilateral discussions on biofuels.[117]

3.5 Dialogues with Asian countries

For almost 20 years the EU has held a dialogue with ASEAN including ministerial conferences every second year, meetings of the Joint Cooperation Committee, as well as an ASEAN regional forum.[118] Since 1996, a separate Asia-Europe Meeting (ASEM) has also been held every second year, as an informal and multi-dimensional dialogue and cooperation process. It encompasses political, economic and cultural cooperation with 18 Asian countries (Brunei, Burma/Myanmar, Cambodia, China, Indonesia, Japan, Laos, South Korea, Malaysia, the Philippines, Singapore, Thailand, Bulgaria, Romania, India, Mongolia, Pakistan and Vietnam) and the ASEAN Secretariat,[119] and since 2010 also the Russian Federation, New Zealand and Australia.[120] In addition, bilateral dialogues are held with individual Asian countries under their respective agreements with the EU.[121]

The EU-ASEAN dialogue has focused on cooperation for the implementation of MEAs, and in a more cautious way also on preparations before multilateral

[113] Third EU-Brazil Summit, 'Joint Statement' Stockholm 6 October 2009, paras 2–12.

[114] Fourth EU-Brazil Summit, 'Joint Statement' Brasília 14 July 2010, para 25.

[115] Second EU-Brazil Summit, 'Joint Action Plan' Rio de Janeiro 22 December 2008, 26–31 (s 2 'Promoting an environmental partnership for sustainable development').

[116] E Morgera and Marín Durán, 'The UN 2005 World Summit, the Environment and the EU: Priorities, Promises and Prospects' (2006) 15(1) *Review of European Community and International Environmental Law* 11, 16–17.

[117] Fourth EU-Brazil Summit Statement, above n 114, paras 5–8.

[118] Under the Inter-regional Cooperation Agreement cited at Ch 2, s 2.2.

[119] See European External Action Service, 'ASEM' at www.eeas.europa.eu/asem/index_en.htm.

[120] Eighth Asia-Europe Meeting, 'Chair's Statement' Brussels 4–5 October 2010, para 3. See comments by Alecu de Flers and Regelsberger, above n 1, 332.

[121] Ch 2, s 2.2.

environmental negotiating sessions, and consultations on EU internal regulatory initiatives with extraterritorial implications. The 2007 Declaration on an EU-ASEAN Enhanced Partnership, for instance, supported cooperation in the field of energy security, climate change and environment, through an EU-ASEAN policy dialogue on energy, as well as cooperation targeting concrete actions for the swift implementation of the international regime on climate change, as well as on the sustainable management of forest resources, biodiversity (particularly cooperation in promoting measures to meet the global target of significantly reducing the rate of biodiversity loss by 2010) and transboundary environmental pollution control and management.[122] The Declaration was accompanied by a plan of action to develop EU-ASEAN consultations in multilateral fora, in order to strengthen the multilateral system and, '*where appropriate*, to develop joint positions' (emphasis added)[123] The action plan also called for continuing with an existing Trans-regional EU-ASEAN Trade Initiative as a framework for promoting dialogue and cooperation on regulatory issues, such as sanitary and phytosanitary standards, product standards and technical barriers to trade, forestry and wood-based products, trade facilitation and cooperation on investment, EU economic integration, and chemicals (with specific reference to EU domestic legislation).[124]

The action plan foresees cooperation on the environment in a broad range of activities, including regular consultations, the creation of a policy dialogue focusing on the interrelated goals of climate change and air pollution, and strengthened cooperation with regional and international institutions on chemicals and waste. It also provided for closer cooperation on climate-friendly technologies, forest management, transboundary environmental pollution, desertification and illegal logging and its associated trade, and sustainable production and consumption. It further pointed to cooperation on implementing global decisions on climate change, biodiversity, forests and the marine environment;[125] and on enhancing assistance in strengthening regulatory frameworks in the mineral sector.[126] Work on energy security included close cooperation in the promotion of energy saving, energy efficiency and conservation measures, energy efficiency technology and renewable energies.[127]

The statements resulting from the EU-ASEAN ministerial meetings show that parties engage in the review of the outcomes of multilateral negotiations and dis-

[122] 16th EU-ASEAN Ministerial Meeting, 'Nuremberg Declaration on an EU-ASEAN Enhanced Partnership', Nuremberg 15 March 2007, paras 14–20.

[123] EU-ASEAN Partnership, 'Plan of Action to Implement the Nuremberg Declaration on an EU-ASEAN Enhanced Partnership' (2007) para 1.1.4, endorsed in 2007 by the EU-ASEAN Commemorative Summit, 'Joint Declaration' Singapore 22 November 2007.

[124] Ibid, paras 2.7–2.8. Namely, REACH (Regulation (EC) 1907/2006 of the European Parliament and of the Council concerning the Registration, Evaluation, Authorisation and Restriction of Chemicals [2006] OJ L396/1), discussed in Ch 7, s 3.

[125] EU-ASEAN Partnership Plan of Action, above n 123, paras 3.4–3.13.

[126] Ibid, para 3.17.

[127] Ibid, paras 3.1–3.2.

cuss to a certain extent support for their implementation, although they do not formally commit to undertake joint preparations before rounds of multilateral negotiations. Instead, they serve to highlight areas of common interest, such as general references to progress in the negotiations on a post-2012 climate change regime,[128] or to review respective regional activities.[129]

Similarly, the ASEM outcomes tend to highlight areas of common interest, calling for concrete and result-oriented dialogue on sustainable forest and water resource management.[130] ASEM produced a High-level Statement on Climate Change, encouraging continuation of dialogue on the implementation of the international climate change regime[131] and the Beijing Declaration on Sustainable Development.[132] This seems in line with the informal character of the process, which is expected to serve to stimulate and facilitate progress in other fora, in the priority areas of tackling global environmental issues, striving for sustainable development and supporting the work of the Asia-Europe Environmental Technology Centre.[133] Priorities for dialogue and cooperation are updated by Heads of State and Government at their Summit meetings, forming the basis of two-year work programmes drawn up by foreign ministers on the occasion of each Summit, and reviewed and updated at the foreign ministers' meetings between Summits.[134] The economic ministers' meetings also include an environmental component focusing on dialogue and cooperation in priority industrial sectors including agro-technology, food processing, biotechnology, information and telecommunication (including e-commerce), transport, energy, and environmental engineering.[135]

The EU-China dialogue can be singled out among the EU dialogues with Asian countries as a case of dialogue proceeding in parallel with the negotiations of a partnership and cooperation agreement. EU-China Summits have reached their thirteenth session in 2010, and have resulted in the adoption of a Joint Declaration on Climate Change,[136] the launch of an EU-China Partnership on

[128] 18th EU-ASEAN Ministerial Meeting, 'Co-chairs' Statement' Madrid 26 May 2010, para 29 supporting the Copenhagen Accord (UNFCCC COP (unadopted) Decision 2/CP.15 annex, 'Copenhagen Accord' (2010) UN Doc FCCC/CP/2009/11/Add.1); 17th EU-ASEAN Ministerial Meeting, 'Joint Co-Chairmen's Statement' Phnom Penh 28 May 2009, para 35 supporting the Bali Action Plan (UNFCCC COP Decision 1/CP.13, 'Bali Action Plan' (2008) UN Doc FCCC/CP/2007/6/Add.1); 15th EU-ASEAN Ministerial Meeting, 'Joint co-Chairmen's Statement' Jakarta 10 March 2005, para 20 welcoming the entry into force of the Kyoto Protocol.

[129] 16th EU-ASEAN Ministerial Meeting, 'Joint Co-Chairmen's Statement' Nuremberg 15 March 2007, para 15.

[130] Eighth ASEM, 'Chair's Statement' Brussels 4–5 October 2010, para 37.

[131] Sixth ASEM, 'Declaration on Climate Change' Helsinki 10–11 September 2006.

[132] Seventh ASEM, 'Declaration on Sustainable Development' Beijing 24–25 October 2008.

[133] Second ASEM, 'The Asia-Europe Cooperation Framework 2000' London 4 April 1998, paras 8 and 14.

[134] Ibid, para 20.

[135] Ibid, para 16.

[136] Eighth EU-China Summit, 'Joint Declaration on Climate Change between China and the European Union' Brussels 7 September 2005.

Climate Change,[137] and the establishment of an Environmental Dialogue and an Energy Dialogue.[138] Unusually, the declaration comprises time-bound goals for cooperation, namely developing and demonstrating carbon capture and storage technology and reducing the cost of key energy technologies by 2020, and regular follow-up at 'suitably high level . . . including in the context of the Summits.'[139] This is particularly significant in that it anticipated relevant EU internal regulation, namely the CCS Directive, which explicitly encourages technology cooperation with key countries.[140] The EU-China Summits have also served to review the outcomes and follow up on multilateral environmental processes,[141] and discuss a variety of areas for environmental cooperation (sustainable production and consumption, pollution control, natural resources management, river basin management, biodiversity conservation, international environmental governance, chemicals, illegal logging and technology transfer) with a view to encouraging the adoption of stricter environmental standards in mutual investment.[142]

3.6 Regulatory dialogues with developed countries

Generally the EU holds regulatory dialogues, rather than broader policy dialogues, with developed countries, such as the US and Japan, with which the EU has no bilateral agreement of a general nature; and with Canada, with which the 'first formal agreement of its kind between what was then the EEC and an industrialised third country was concluded in 1976.'[143]

3.6.1 EU-US dialogue

Environmental cooperation between the EU and US is based on a 1974 exchange of letters on the environment,[144] providing for annual high-level consultations to coordinate and review cooperation. In addition, the New Transatlantic Agenda and its Joint Action Plan were adopted in 1995, opening up further possibilities

[137] Commission, 'Press Release – EU and China Partnership on Climate Change' (MEMO/05/298) 2 September 2005.

[138] On the Energy Dialogue, see 13th EU-China Summit, 'Joint Press Communiqué' Brussels 6 October 2010, para 8.

[139] Ibid, paras 7 and 1.

[140] Directive 2009/31/EC of the European Parliament and of the Council on the geological storage of carbon dioxide [2009] OJ L140/114, preamble para 7. See discussion in K Kulovesi, E Morgera, and M Muñoz, 'Environmental Integration and Multi-faceted International Dimensions of EU Law: Unpacking the EU's 2009 Climate and Energy Package' (2011) 48(3) *Common Market Law Review* 829, 871–74 and in Ch 7, s 3.1.

[141] Notably the WSSD: see seventh EU-China Summit, 'Joint Statement' The Hague 8 December 2004, para 20.

[142] Tenth EU-China Summit, 'Joint Statement' Beijing 28 November 2007, para 20.

[143] European External Action Service, 'EU's relations with Canada' at www.eeas.europa.eu/canada/index_en.htm.

[144] 1974 Exchange of Letters on the Environment between the European Commission and the US government.

for dialogue by expanding EU-US cooperation to a full range of political and economic issues and at various levels, including annual EU-US Summits. The environmental dimension of the EU-US Summits generally focuses on possible cooperation on climate change and development, with cautious language on promoting agreement at the multilateral level on the post-2012 climate change regime and the creation of a global carbon market.[145] At the 2001 EU-US Summit, agreement was reached to establish a mechanism for regular dialogue on climate change (the EU-US High-level Representatives on Climate Change).[146] Following a 2005 Joint Statement stressing the link between energy policy and climate change,[147] a broader High-level Dialogue on Climate Change, Clean Energy and Sustainable Development was set up in 2006.[148] A ministerial-level EU-US Energy Council was further established in 2009,[149] and the EU and US agreed to reinvigorate their Dialogue on Development in order to ensure collaboration in terms of donors' assistance in relation to the MDGs, food security and climate change.[150]

The EU-US high-level dialogue has thus focused on the nexus between climate change, energy and environmental cooperation,[151] as well as on a broad range of environmental approaches, namely: market-based domestic policies to reduce greenhouse gas emissions, facilitating trade and investment in new clean technologies, reducing air pollution and waste, combating illegal logging, and reducing biodiversity loss.[152] The EU and US also adopted a joint Statement on Energy Security, Efficiency and Climate Change, which established as common goals the development and commercialisation of technologies related to near-zero emissions coal, renewables (particularly second-generation biofuels) and methane recovery-and-reuse projects.[153] The related action plan includes discussion of policy incentives and risk regulation, international minimum standards, as well as monitoring and remediation techniques, at the bilateral level, in cooperation with third countries and in multilateral fora.[154]

Furthermore, environmental integration is also pursued in the context of broader regulatory dialogues. At the 2005 EU-US Summit, the US and the EU issued a Roadmap for Regulatory Cooperation to promote better quality regulation, minimise unnecessary regulatory divergences to facilitate transatlantic trade and investment, and increase consumer confidence in the transatlantic market. The initiative includes exchanges on chemicals, energy efficiency and

[145] 2009 EU-US Summit, 'Declaration' Washington 3 November 2009.

[146] Commission (DG Environment), 'Bilateral Relations – US' at www.ec.europa.eu/environment/international_issues/relations_usa_en.htm.

[147] 2007 EU-US Summit, 'Statement: Energy, Security and Climate Change' Washington 30 April 2007.

[148] 2006 EU-US Summit, 'Declaration' Vienna, 21 June 2006, 10.

[149] 2009 EU-US Summit Declaration, above n 145, Annex II.

[150] 2020 EU-US Summit, 'Joint Statement' Lisbon 20 November 2010, particularly Annex I on Development Dialogue and Cooperation.

[151] 2006 EU-US Summit Declaration, above n 148, 10.

[152] 2008 EU-US Summit, 'Declaration' Brdo 10 June 2008, 14.

[153] 2007 EU-US Summit Statement, above n 147, 4.

[154] Ibid.

eco-design.[155] It is finally to be highlighted that the EU and the US have set up a series of 'transatlantic dialogues' at different levels (parliamentarians, business, consumers, and civil society).[156]

3.6.2 EU-Canada dialogue

Cooperation with Canada started off with the 1975 exchange of letters,[157] which provided for a mechanism – the periodic EU-Canada High-Level Dialogue on Environment – that is still meeting every 18 months, as well as the inclusion of environmental issues in the meetings of the Joint Cooperation Committee established under the 1976 Framework Agreement for Commercial and Economic Co-operation. In addition, environmental issues are part of the agenda of high-level political meetings (including annual Summits) under the 1996 Joint Political Declaration and the 2004 Partnership Agenda. As part of the general EU-Canada Regulatory Co-operation (led by DG Enterprise and Industry), the EU and Canada also share experiences and information on environmental regulation.[158]

Areas of dialogue on environmental cooperation included in the early 2000s fisheries management and environmental protection in the North,[159] while climate change has come to dominate discussions on domestic action and, in quite vague terms, on multilateral negotiations.[160] In 2008, it was proposed that the environmental dialogue be deepened to address biodiversity, forests, chemicals and waste, as well as encouraging the conclusion of an international agreement on the liberalisation of environmental goods and services.[161]

A High-level Dialogue on Energy was established in 2007,[162] focusing on CCS and bio-energy, while bilateral cooperation on climate change at the multilateral level has focused on the development of an international carbon market, and reducing emissions from deforestation and from maritime and avian transport.[163]

3.6.3 EU-Japan dialogue

The EU-Japan relations in the field of environment are based on a rolling action plan first adopted at the EU-Japan Summit in 2001 and periodically reviewed. A

155 2005 EU-US Summit, 'Joint Report on the Roadmap for EU-US Regulatory Cooperation', Vienna 21 June 2006.

156 European External Action Service, 'EU's relations with the USA-Transatlantic dialogues' at www.eeas.europa.eu/us/dialogues_en.htm.

157 1975 Exchange of Letters on the Environment between the European Commission and the Canadian government.

158 Commission (DG Environment),' Bilateral and regional cooperation – Emerging economies – Canada' at www.ec.europa.eu/environment/international_issues/relations_canada_en.htm.

159 EU-Canada Summit, 'EU-Canada Partnership Agenda' Ottawa 18 March 2004; EU-Canada Summit, 'Joint Declaration' Niagara-on-the-Lake 19 June 2005.

160 EU-Canada Summit, 'Statement' Berlin 4 June 2007, 3–4; EU-Canada Summit, 'Declaration' Prague 6 May 2009, 3–5; EU-Canada Summit, 'Press Statement' Brussels 5 May 2010, 2.

161 EU-Canada Summit, 'Statement' Quebec 17 October 2008, 4.

162 2007 EU-Canada Summit Statement, above n 160, 4.

163 2009 EU-Canada Summit Declaration, above n 160, 4–5.

structured dialogue exists between the European Commission and the Japanese Ministry of Environment in the form of High-level Meetings on the Environment, while concerns of a more technical nature are also addressed in the context of the annual EU-Japan Summits and EU-Japan High-level Dialogue on Regulatory Reform.[164]

The dialogue has a significant component devoted to exchanges on internal environmental regulation. The 2001 Plan for EU-Japan Cooperation, titled 'Shaping Our Common Future,'[165] includes commitments to explore possible equivalence between the EU and Japanese approaches to encourage sustainable production and consumption, and to promote cooperation on conformity assessment and mutual recognition of environmental standards. The plan also specifically mandated the Regulatory Reform Dialogue to remove obstacles and barriers to trade and investment with the aim to develop an appropriate regulatory framework, by reinforcing dialogue at a technical level to regularly review changes in the regulatory framework and their implementation in the environmental sector among others, to follow a consistent regulatory approach in the future.[166] Both proposed and existing pieces of EU environmental legislation, as well as EU negotiating positions in multilateral environmental processes are addressed in that context.[167]

The dialogue with Japan is also marked by strong commitments to collaboration in multilateral environmental negotiations that are not to be found in other dialogues with developed countries. The 2001 Plan for Cooperation, for instance, focused on the preparations for WSSD, and specifically climate change, sustainable forest management, desertification, biotechnology and mutual supportiveness between multilateral trade rules and MEAs.[168] In 2010, more explicitly, the EU and Japan welcomed 'marked convergence' in their respective negotiating positions on climate change and expressed willingness to exercise 'joint leadership', thus committing to exploring more systematically opportunities to develop and promote 'joint positions in international fora' including in the framework of the CBD.[169] This was particularly relevant as Japan was holding the presidency of the CBD Conference of the Parties, which facilitated the successful conclusion of negotiations of the Nagoya Protocol on Access and Benefit-Sharing to the CBD, as well as several other key outcomes.[170] Earlier summits also noted opportunities

[164] Commission (DG Environment), 'EU-Japan relations in the field of environment' at www.ec.europa.eu/environment/international_issues/relations_japan_en.htm.

[165] EU-Japan Summit, 'Shaping Our Common Future: An Action Plan for EU-Japan Cooperation' Brussels 2001, 16.

[166] European External Action Service, 'EU-Japan Regulatory Reform Dialogue' at www.eeas.europa.eu/japan/regulatory_reform_en.htm.

[167] See, for instance, discussion of the EU proposal to develop an international legal framework on marine biodiversity, in 'Japan's Proposal For Regulatory Reform Dialogue' December 2008, 35.

[168] EU-Japan Summit, 'Shaping Our Common Future', above n 165, 15–16.

[169] 19th EU-Japan Summit, 'Joint Press Statement' Tokyo 28 April 2010, para 12 and Annex, s 2.

[170] For a discussion of the outcomes of the CBD COP in 2010 and the role of the Japanese presidency, see E Morgera and E Tsioumani, 'Yesterday, Today and Tomorrow: Looking Afresh at the Convention on Biological Diversity' (forthcoming) 21 *Yearbook of International Environmental Law.*

for coordination in the framework of negotiations on an international legally binding instrument on mercury, implementation of the Basel Convention, and the creation of an international platform on biodiversity and ecosystem services.[171]

4. THEMATIC DIALOGUES: THE CASE OF THE GLOBAL CLIMATE CHANGE ALLIANCE

In light of the emphasis placed by the EU on climate change among its global environmental priorities, as well as in consideration of its relevance as a global security and development challenge,[172] the European Commission initiated in 2007 a Global Climate Change Alliance (GCCA), to enhance cooperation on climate change with SIDS and LDCs.[173] The Alliance principally constitutes a platform for dialogue on practical approaches to the implementation of the international climate change regime, focusing on adaptation, reducing emissions from deforestation, enhancing the participation of SIDS and LDCs in the global carbon market through the Clean Development Mechanism, promoting disaster risk reduction, and integrating climate change into poverty reduction efforts. It also aims to facilitate the provision of EU technical and financial support both for climate change response measures and for the integration of climate change into development strategies in the above-listed areas. Priorities are to be further refined during the GCCA dialogue.[174] Equally, the Alliance aims to contribute to mutual understanding and convergence of negotiating positions in the context of ongoing negotiations: the ultimate goal of the Alliance is that of promoting political dialogue on climate change at the global, regional and national levels with a view to feeding into ongoing multilateral negotiations on the post-2012 international climate change regime.

The most developed regional 'branch' of the GCCA is that with Africa, which takes place within the pre-existing framework of the EU-Africa Strategic Partnership: the Joint EU-AU Task Force in 2007 launched an EU-Africa Strategic Partnership on Climate Change for deliberations on a shared EU-Africa vision on climate change and desertification.[175] As a result, a joint EU-Africa Declaration on Climate

[171] 18th EU-Japan Summit, 'Joint Press Statement' Prague 4 May 2009, para 15.

[172] Commission, 'Climate Change in the Context of Development Cooperation' COM(2003) 85 final, 10–11; Morgera and Marín Durán, above n 116, 16.

[173] Commission, 'Press release – Commission proposes a global alliance to help developing countries most affected by climate change' (IP/07/1352) 18 September 2007; Commission, 'Communication – Building a global climate change alliance between the European Union and poor developing countries most vulnerable to climate change' COM (2007) 540 final. See also J Ayers, S Huq and A Chandani, 'Assessing EU Assistance for Adaptation to Climate Change in Developing Countries: a Southern Perspective' in S Oberthür and M Pallemaerts (eds), *The New Climate Policies of the European Union: Internal Legislation and Climate Diplomacy* (Brussels, VUB Press, 2010), 236–37.

[174] See GCCA website at www.gcca.eu/pages/1_2-Home.html. On the funding of the GCCA, see Ch 4, s 3.2.2.

[175] Ibid.

Change was adopted in 2008, which indicates that part of the EU's policy is based on the need to improve the effectiveness of MEAs and to enhance efforts to better implement, comply with and enforce their provisions, with the EU supporting Africa financially and technically to achieve these goals.[176] In addition, the Declaration served to identify priority items for enhanced regular consultations on international negotiations on climate change, as well as immediate priorities for bilateral cooperation.[177]

Similarly cooperation between the EU and the Caribbean SIDS is quite advanced and embedded in the GCCA. The EU-CARIFORUM Troika Summit adopted a Declaration on Climate Change and Energy, which identified as immediate priorities for bilateral cooperation the support for the implementation of a regional climate change strategy, as well as commitment to enhance cooperation in international negotiations. It also created a joint EU-CARIFORUM technical group at the regional level to ensure appropriate follow-up action to the Declaration.[178]

More limited progress has been achieved in Asia, where the first regional conference was held in May 2010 and a joint declaration on climate change was signed only with a small group of countries comprising Bangladesh, Cambodia and the Maldives, to enhance dialogue involving relevant stakeholders at the country and regional levels to improve the integration of climate change considerations into development and poverty reduction strategies.[179]

Overall, the GCCA is a further expression of the EU's high-level commitment to address climate change in its external action, which is so far unparalleled in other areas of environmental cooperation.

5. ASSESSMENT AND CONCLUSIONS

This chapter has illustrated the great variety in scope, modalities and objectives of the institutionalised dialogues between the EU and third countries, groups of countries or regions. Dialogues are used, first, to follow up on environmental cooperation commitments included in bilateral and inter-regional agreements: they allow for a further prioritisation of the specific areas for environmental cooperation identified in these agreements, but not for in-depth or systematic monitoring of past and ongoing cooperation activities. Dialogues are therefore opportunities to further define and specify the priorities for environmental cooperation on the basis of a bilateral exchange of views, which may lead to the elaboration of more detailed action plans. EU funding, however, is not necessarily linked to the implementation of such action plans: rather, these are generally expected to be funded through a variety of sources that may include EU aid but

[176] Second EU-Africa Ministerial Troika, 'Declaration on Climate Change' Addis Ababa 21 November 2008, para 23.

[177] Ibid, paras 27 and 29 respectively.

[178] EU-CARIFORUM Troika Summit, 'Joint Communiqué' Lima 17 May 2008, Annex II.

[179] EU, Bangladesh, Cambodia and Maldives, 'Declaration on Climate Change' Dhaka 31 May 2010.

also other sources. To give just one example, jointly agreed action plans under the ENP, including on environment and energy, are expected to contribute to realising the full potential of the Euro-Mediterranean Associations,[180] but are merely considered 'a key point of reference' for setting EU external funding priorities.[181]

Only in few instances (such as, to different extents, with Euro-Med countries, Latin American countries, and China), the action plans produced through institutionalised dialogue have provided for specific objectives and timelines for environmental cooperation, or more detailed monitoring and follow-up institutional arrangements. Monitoring is also limited by the relative lack of involvement of civil society in the dialogues.[182] This situation may, however, be bound to change, as it reflects the pre-Global Europe approach to bilateral and inter-regional cooperation, with the light-touch and ad hoc clauses on environmental cooperation in bilateral and inter-regional agreements. One may expect that more concerted efforts in monitoring and involving civil society will be undertaken in the context of the innovative institutions set up by the post-Global Europe agreements.[183]

Institutionalised dialogues bear the promise of facilitating a process of coordination of negotiating positions with third countries and groups in the context of ongoing multilateral environmental negotiations. The case of the EU-Africa, EU-Mexico and EU-Japan dialogues are glaring examples in this respect, where clear commitments are expressed to bilaterally elaborate and put forward joint positions at the multilateral level. While most attention is focused on the use of dialogues in preparations for the negotiating sessions of the post-2012 climate change regime (including through the launch of dialogue processes exclusively focused on climate change cooperation, such as the GCCA), it is clear from the overview of practice in this chapter that other areas of environmental cooperation related to multilateral processes have also, albeit less often, been discussed to the same end (such as biodiversity, chemicals and increasingly global environmental governance). Nonetheless, the special nature of the EU as an international actor may render the pursuit of such an aim unrealistic: the EU position presented to third countries through dialogues is 'already relatively final' due to the fact that it is the result of lengthy intra-EU negotiations between its 27 Member States, so that it cannot really be affected by the outcome of dialogues.[184] It therefore seems more significant to underline the use of institutionalised dialogues for the EU and third countries or regions for more pragmatic purposes: to assess jointly the outcomes of negotiating sessions or major global summits, and to better understand reciprocal negotiating priorities and proposed action for implementation.

[180] Regulation (EC) 1638/2006 laying down general provisions establishing a European Neighbourhood and Partnership Instrument [2006] OJ L310/1, preamble para 7: see discussion in Ch 4.

[181] Ibid, arts 3(1) and 4; see also Council Regulation (EC) 1934/2006 establishing a financing instrument for cooperation with industrialised and other high-income countries and territories [2006] OJ L405/41, art 3(3).

[182] Leino, above n 6, 283.

[183] See Ch 2, ss 5.3.4 and 7.1.4.

[184] Leino, above n 6, 279.

In addition, the institutionalised dialogues, particularly but not exclusively regulatory ones, are used by the EU to support the understanding beyond its borders of certain pieces of EU internal environmental legislation with extra-territorial implications. Dialogues thus support a process of mutual recognition or cooperation in the elaboration of national standards on biofuels, CCS, chemicals and sustainable forest management. While initially regulatory dialogues mostly targeted developed countries, it seems that increasingly the EU is willing to put them in place also with emerging economies (for instance in the context of EU-ASEAN relations) in particular with a view to advancing discussions on innovation and green growth.[185] Notably, regulatory dialogues focus on pieces of EU internal environmental legislation that are meant to contribute to the implementation of existing multilateral standards, or even the definition of multilateral environmental standards under negotiation.[186]

One key finding of this chapter is that the differentiated approach to environmental integration seen in the context of bilateral and inter-regional agreements, is reflected or even amplified, across the spectrum of institutionalised dialogues, and there is at present no sign that the EU may consider a more systematic approach in the latter case. Consideration is being given instead to a more uniform approach in the use of EU human rights dialogues, which identifies areas for improvement that could, in some cases, also benefit environmental dialogues.[187] For instance, the suggestion that dialogues should give priority to the signing, ratification and implementation of international instruments, as well as cooperation with international processes and mechanisms, and preparations and follow-up on international conferences and meetings of UN bodies, is equally relevant for environmental dialogues. While this is already occurring on an ad hoc basis, the agenda of environmental dialogues could be geared towards a more systematic approach to environmental multilateralism. To that end, the agenda of dialogues could be based on an assessment related to environmental performance and cooperation, based on information provided by relevant UN organisations, MEA bodies and NGOs.[188] Similarly, proposed guarantees for increased transparency in the context of the human rights dialogues could be applied to environment-related dialogues, with simultaneous interpretation in local languages and more systematic involvement of civil society, as well as the possibility for the third country or region to raise issues about the performance by the EU on a reciprocal basis.[189] Finally, the value added and progress achieved by each dialogue should be assessed regularly.[190]

Another key finding of this chapter is that institutionalised dialogues are in a circular relationship with the other tools of EU external relations. Dialogues may

[185] Trade, Growth and World Affairs Communication, 11.
[186] This aspect is explored in Ch 7.
[187] Council, 'EU Guidelines on human rights dialogues with third countries – Update' (undated) para 5, at www.consilium.europa.eu/uedocs/cmsUpload/16526.en08.pdf.
[188] Ibid, para 6.1.
[189] Ibid, para 7.
[190] Ibid, para 10.

facilitate the conclusion of formal agreements between the EU and third countries or regions, and also serve to implement environmental cooperation clauses of existing bilateral and inter-regional agreements. At the same time, dialogue is considered a principle underpinning bilateral or inter-regional agreements and a modality that is explicitly supported by the institutional structures created by EU agreements. Enhanced dialogue is, in addition, seen as an objective of the Union's external funding, as well as a means to increase the visibility of EU financial and technical assistance supporting environmental protection in partner countries.[191] Finally, dialogues may also be informed by the Sustainability Impact Assessments,[192] to which the next chapter turns, particularly as the Commission intends to carry out ex post assessments to increase the monitoring of EU bilateral or inter-regional cooperation on trade and sustainable development.[193]

[191] Commission, 'Environment and natural resources thematic programme – 2011–2013 strategy paper and multiannual indicative programme' (29 October 2010) 9 and 11.
[192] Ch 6.
[193] Trade, Growth and World Affairs Communication, 14.

6

Environmental Integration through Sustainability Impact Assessments

1. INTRODUCTION

A NON-LEGALISED INSTRUMENT for ensuring environmental integration in the definition and implementation of EU external relations is a systematic assessment of the socio-economic and environmental impacts of a proposed trade agreement (or an agreement with a trade component) between the EU and a third country or region. These so-called Sustainability Impact Assessments (SIAs) are based on a policy commitment for the fulfilment of which the European Commission has primary responsibility. In principle, SIAs are to be carried out prior to the conclusion of the agreement in question with a view to influencing the negotiating process, thus being primarily a tool for environmental integration in the *definition* of EU external relations. In practice, however, they can also be seen as a tool for environmental integration in their *implementation* for three reasons. First, at least initially, SIAs have been conducted towards the end of the negotiating process,[1] at a stage when it was too late to influence negotiations, so the Commission suggested taking their outcomes into account in the implementation phase. Second, even if more recent SIAs are carried out well in advance, the Commission still maintains that their outcomes should be taken into account both at the negotiations stage and at the implementation stage, particularly because some of the recommendations emerging from SIAs may be addressed through other EU external relations tools, such as financial and technical assistance. Third, in the context of most recent SIAs, the Commission further undertakes to carry out ex post assessments with a view to checking whether the outcomes of the SIAs were accurate and whether proposed complementary measures were adequate.

The chapter will first discuss the origins of the Union's commitment to the SIA process, its purposes and procedures, and then offer an overview of relevant prac-

[1] T Greven, A Leopold and E Molinari, 'An Analysis of the Relative Effectiveness of Social and Environmental Norms in Free Trade Agreements' (2009 Study for European Parliament), 27; D Blobel, M Knigge and B Görlach, 'Report on Trade, Environment and Sustainability Impact Assessment' (Ecologic, 2005), 7; WWF, 'Changing the Balance of Trade' WWF Briefing on Sustainability Assessment of EU Trade Policy (2002), 2–3; 'Joint NGO statement on Sustainability Impact Assessments of EU Trade Policy' (Brussels, July 2002) at www.trade.ec.europa.eu/doclib/html/122192.htm.

tice. It will conclude with an assessment of environmental integration through SIAs in relation to the other tools of EU external relations analysed in the previous chapters.

2. AN INTRODUCTION TO SIAS

As part of a larger 'Impact Assessment' process,[2] the Commission is committed to carry out 'sustainability' impact assessments of all major EU trade policy initiatives.[3] SIAs are particularly relevant to ensure environmental integration in the trade component of EU associations and other bilateral and inter-regional agreements,[4] as they aim to ensure that these agreements identify and address trade-offs between economic growth and its environmental and social impacts.[5] SIAs have both a political and technical dimension: politically, they aim to symbolise the EU's determination to 'anchor liberalization in the concept of sustainability' (notably, not to assess the desirability of further liberalisation as such); and technically, they aim to 'maximize the benefits of liberalization' by managing environmental, social and economic concerns.[6] It has been reported that a significant portion of DG Trade budget was allocated to SIAs.[7]

The first SIA was developed by DG Trade in 1999 for the Doha Development Round of multilateral trade negotiations launched in 2001. According to DG Trade, the SIA has since then developed into a policy tool for ex ante assessment of the economic, social and environmental implications of an envisaged trade agreement, which is carried out during the negotiating process with a view to integrating sustainability into EU external trade policy. SIAs are to analyse the issues covered by a trade negotiation from a sustainable development perspective; inform negotiators of the possible social, environmental and economic consequences of a trade agreement; and ultimately provide guidelines for the design of

[2] Commission, 'Communication on Impact Assessment' COM (2002) 276 final; European Council, 'Review of the EU Sustainable Development Strategy – Renewed Strategy' Brussels 15–16 June 2006, para 11. SIAs (also referred to as '*trade* sustainability impact assessments') should be distinguished from Impact Assessments (which are sometimes referred to as 'sustainability impact assessments': see Ch 1, s 4.2.2), as will be explained below; and from strategic environmental assessments (SEAs), which are connected to environmental integration into the formulation of EU external assistance programmes (discussed in Ch 4, s 3.2.1).

[3] The practice was acknowledged by the Commission, 'Communication – Mainstreaming sustainable development into EU policies: 2009 Review of the European Union Strategy for Sustainable Development' COM (2009) 400 final, 3.

[4] See Ch 2.

[5] Commission (DG Trade), 'Sustainability Impact Assessment of Trade Agreements: Making Trade Sustainable?' (Background paper prepared for DG Trade Seminar, Brussels, 6–7 February 2003) 12–13 (2003 Background Paper).

[6] C George and C Kirkpatrick, 'Sustainability Impact Assessment of the World Trade Negotiations: Current Practice and Lessons for Further Development' (New Directions in Impact Assessment for Development Conference, University of Manchester, 24–25 November 2003) 4, at www.sed.manchester.ac.uk/research/iarc/pdfs/iarc_wp02.pdf.

[7] Reportedly, 10% in the period 2005–08, according to M Knigge and A Leipprand, 'Public Participation in Sustainability Impact Assessments' (Ecologic, 2003), 3.

possible 'flanking' (complementary) measures (including internal policy, capacity building, international regulation), with a view to maximising the positive impacts and reducing any negative impacts of the trade negotiations in question. Flanking measures may either be included in the outcome of a trade negotiation, or in the design of implementation measures for the trade agreement.[8]

The SIA exercise itself is carried out by consultants contracted by the Commission. Although the Commission supervises the work of the consultant, in practice, it is the latter who bears the main workload and responsibility for the quality of the exercise.[9] A SIA Steering Committee, chaired by DG Trade and comprising representatives of other Directorates-General and Services, as well as EU negotiators, provides guidance to consultants.[10] The results of the consultant's studies are published for debate, before the Commission makes its own assessment with a view to integrating them into the EU's trade policy orientations and technical co-operation activities.[11]

SIA consultants are expected to identify the likely impacts of trade liberalisation in areas such as: income, employment, capital investment, equity and poverty; health and education; gender inequality; environmental quality of air, water and land; biodiversity; and other natural resource stocks.[12] All reports produced by the consultants are published on DG Trade website, together with the European Commission's position papers.[13] The position papers are drafted by DG Trade with a view to setting out the Commission's position on the findings of the SIA consultants, identifying points of agreement, explaining any disagreement, adding complementary analysis, flagging lessons learnt and putting forward ideas for technical assistance or monitoring. They are then endorsed by the whole Commission and discussed with the Member States, as well as being circulated to the European Parliament, EU Delegations and relevant international organizations, such as the WTO and OECD.[14]

From the outset, it is important to contrast SIAs and Impact Assessments (IAs).[15] The latter is a prior assessment to identify the economic, social and environmental impacts of EU legislative initiatives, which runs in parallel and feeds into the development of a Commission proposal.[16] IAs are conducted *before* the

[8] Commission (DG Trade), 'Sustainability Impact Assessments' at www.ec.europa.eu/trade/analysis/sustainability-impact-assessments/.

[9] Knigge and Leipprand, above n 7, 4–7.

[10] Blobel et al, above n 1, 10.

[11] See generally, 2003 Background Paper.

[12] Commission, 'SIAs', above n 8.

[13] Ibid.

[14] Commission, 'Handbook for Trade Sustainability Impact Assessment' (2006) 13 at www.trade.ec.europa.eu/doclib/docs/2006/march/tradoc_127974.pdf (SIA Handbook).

[15] For a discussion, see GC Rowe, 'Tools for the Control of Political and Administrative Agents: Impact Assessment and Administrative Governance in the European Union' in H Hoffman and A Türk (eds), *EU Administrative Governance* (Cheltenham, Edward Elgar, 2005), 452.

[16] A Alemanno, 'The Better Regulation Initiative at the Judicial Gate: A Trojan Horse within the Commission's Walls or the Way Forward?' (2009) 15(3) *European Law Journal* 382 384.

issuing of, inter alia, negotiating guidelines for international agreements:[17] IAs of guidelines for negotiating trade agreements thus precede SIAs. IAs evaluate, among other issues, the external environmental impacts of proposed measures, including the possible impacts of EU action on the environment of third countries in the light of overarching EU policies[18] (notably, environmental and development policies), as well as impacts on European companies' competitiveness, trade relations with third countries and WTO negotiations.[19] IAs rely on 'external expertise' (such as scientific committees set up by the Commission and EU agencies) and on consultation of interested parties, including those that may be affected by a new policy or who will have to implement it.[20] These consultations are expected to take place, inter alia, through policy dialogues with third countries.[21] As opposed to IAs, which are prior assessments to decide whether or not a proposed measure should be adopted, SIAs are conducted *after* a trade negotiation has been launched, that is after the Council has adopted a mandate for the Commission to conduct the trade negotiations. SIAs consequently aim at providing inputs related to the economic, social and environmental impacts into *ongoing* negotiations.[22] There may, therefore, be a transition from IA to SIA: the IA consultation group, which is made up of representatives of different Commission DGs, is expected to bear in mind the subsequent SIA phase from the outset, with a view to highlighting specific aspects on which the consultants carrying out subsequent SIAs may concentrate their research. The terms of reference for SIAs should in turn be drafted taking into account the IA results and consultations.[23]

In the spirit of the White Paper on European Governance,[24] the EU is committed to conducting SIAs in cooperation with third country partners, as well as in full consultation with all interested European stakeholders.[25] DG Trade emphasises that SIAs not only have a technical purpose as to the integration of sustainable development in trade negotiations, but also an informative purpose, being themselves tools that facilitate stakeholder involvement and constructive policy dialogue with experts within and outside the EU. Accordingly, SIAs are expected to include comprehensive consultations of stakeholders, thereby ensuring a high degree of transparency and taking account of the knowledge and concerns of relevant interest groups both in the EU and in the partner country/region.[26] In addition, SIAs are

[17] Commission, 'Impact Assessment Guidelines' SEC (2009) 92, 15 January 2009, 6 (Commission Impact Assessment Guidelines). Note, however, that C Adelle, J Hertin and A Jordan, 'Sustainable Development "Outside" the European Union: What Role for Impact Assessment' (2006) 16(2) *European Environment* 57, 62, argue that the degree of consideration of the external dimensions of proposed EU policies through Impact Assessments is 'extremely low'.

[18] Commission Impact Assessment Guidelines, 38.

[19] Ibid, 42.

[20] Ibid, 18–20.

[21] Ibid, 42. On dialogues, see Ch 5.

[22] Commission (DG Trade), 'Background paper: Towards a More Sustainable Trade Policy?' (2006) 2, at www.trade.ec.europa.eu/doclib/docs/2006/april/tradoc_127698.pdf (2006 Background paper).

[23] SIA Handbook, 11.

[24] Commission, 'White Paper on European Governance', COM (2001) 428 final.

[25] 2003 Background Paper, 17.

[26] 2006 Background paper, 1–3.

expected to provide a process through which the EU may concretely interact with relevant international organisations involved in sustainable development work in the third country or region concerned, particularly the Bretton Woods institutions and relevant UN bodies.[27] Consultation with the public at large is generally ensured through the opening of a specific website during the SIA process where civil society and the public can send their written contributions.[28] Finally, DG Trade also emphasises that SIAs may lead to a process facilitating the creation of public-private partnerships and generally supporting the EU CSR agenda.[29] To this end, SIA consultants are expected to invite the private sector to reflect its contributions to sustainable development, through fair-trade activities and other CSR tools.[30]

A stocktaking exercise of experience accrued by the EU in carrying out SIAs was undertaken in 2006. Three main shortcomings emerged that are relevant to understand the evolution of SIAs: the timing of the undertaking of SIAs; the extent of stakeholder participation; and the effective integration of SIAs' results into negotiations.[31] On the third point, it was proposed to establish consultative bodies to oversee the implementation of bilateral and inter-regional agreements and follow up on SIA results, thus offering a permanent platform for debate on sustainable development issues for governments and civil society.[32] Such a development has in effect taken place in the post-Global Europe agreements.[33]

Difficulties with the timing of the exercise have emerged in part due to the fact that initially SIAs were launched too late in the negotiating process, and in part because the timetable of the negotiations was in any event 'too tight to leave a chance for carrying out a corresponding in-depth analysis of impacts.'[34] Additional complexity in finding the appropriate timing for the SIA exercise arises from the Commission's preoccupation that the 'SIA process must be carried out without disrupting the negotiation process.'[35] Furthermore, there is a so-called 'moving target' concern, to ensure sufficient flexibility for the SIA to adapt to progress in the negotiations.[36] Proposals for enhancing the practice in this regard, which

[27] Ibid, 8.

[28] C Tébar Less and JA Kim, 'Checklist for Negotiators of Environmental Provisions in Regional Trade Agreements' (2008) *OECD Trade and Environment Working Papers*, 2008/02, 18, at www.dx.doi.org/10.1787/235708858388.

[29] 2006 Background paper, 7.

[30] 2003 Background Paper, 11. The meaning of CSR has been discussed in Ch 1, s 5.1.

[31] 'Key outcomes and work programme for follow-up action of the Trade Sustainability Impact Assessment Stocktaking Conference 21–22 March 2006' 1–2, at www.trade.ec.europa.eu/doclib/docs/2006/october/tradoc_130465.pdf (SIA Stocktaking Conference).

[32] Ibid, 2.

[33] See Ch 2, ss 5.3.4 and 7.1.4.

[34] Blobel et al, above n 1, 6.

[35] Ibid, 7.

[36] Ibid; N Lee and C Kirkpatrick, 'Methodologies for Sustainability Impact Assessments of Proposals for New Trade Agreements' (2001) 3(3) *Journal of Environmental Assessment Policy & Management* 395, 399. For a more general discussion on the timing in SIA-like processes, see A Cosbey, 'Timing and Public Participation Issues' in OECD, *Assessing the Environmental Effects of Trade Liberalization Agreements: Methodologies* (Paris, OECD, 2000); S Mahony, 'Timing and Public Participation Issues in Undertaking Environmental Assessments of Trade Liberalization Agreements' in OECD, *Assessing the Environmental Effects of Trade Liberalization Agreements: Methodologies* (Paris, OECD, 2000).

emerged from the stocktaking exercise, included to: ensure that the SIA findings are discussed in trade negotiations in real time and in any case no later than the conclusion of the trade agreement; and possibly integrate lessons learnt in the Council negotiating mandates for future FTAs.[37]

The truly participatory aspect of SIAs has been subject to debate and early exercises have incurred significant criticism in this respect.[38] In particular, it has been underlined that the European Parliament was 'largely excluded from the procedure' and that the involvement of stakeholders in the third country was variable.[39] It emerges from certain comparative analysis, however, that other countries such as Canada and the US also have a light-touch approach to public participation in SIA-like exercises, both to avoid excessive burdens and to protect the confidentiality of the negotiations.[40] Even taking into account these legitimate concerns, commentators considered that the SIA process is dominated by the EU and 'essentially centralized'.[41] The Commission reserves the right to decide about the content of the study and its possible focus, which may limit the substantive areas on which stakeholders will be able to provide inputs. In addition, the Commission generally offers the reimbursement of expenses incurred by stakeholders if they participate in the SIA process only to those participating in dialogues held in Brussels: this clearly limits the range of stakeholders that will effectively be consulted. The stocktaking exercise took into account shortcomings in stakeholder involvement and considered options to involve stakeholders earlier on in the process, such as in the drafting of the terms of reference for the various studies and generally through the convening of workshops and the creation of networks of local experts.[42] While it goes beyond the scope of this study to assess whether these options have been taken on board in the subsequent practice of the EU, the next section will analyse the SIA Handbook that was developed as a result of the stocktaking exercise, with a view to identifying improvements in the SIA methodology. Attention will be drawn to any procedures contained in the Handbook that can support environmental integration, coherence vis-a-vis other tools of the EU's external relations, and transparency.

2.1 Procedural aspects of the SIA exercise

The Handbook indicates that the SIA methodology was developed independently and originally by the EU, pointing to differences with existing approaches in

[37] Trade SIA Stocktaking Conference, 2.

[38] T Bauler, 'The Commission's Impact Assessment Process: Handling the External Dimensions of Sustainability' in M Pallemaerts and A Azmanova (eds), *The European Union and Sustainable Development* (Brussels, VUB Press, 2006), 284; Joint NGO Statement, above n 1.

[39] Blobel et al, above n 1, 10. Along the same lines, see Joint NGO Statement, above n 1.

[40] Blobel et al, above n 1, 11.

[41] Knigge and Leipprand, above n 7, 6.

[42] Trade SIA Stocktaking Conference, 2.

similar exercises.[43] On the one hand, Canada, Norway and the United States carry out national environmental reviews of trade negotiations, which however, do not cover all the pillars of sustainable development. On the other hand, guidelines developed by international organisations, such as the impact assessment methodologies developed by UNEP,[44] which cover all pillars of sustainable development based on a case-study approach, apply to policies that are already in place,[45] rather than draft agreements under negotiations.

The SIA is carried out in four phases, building upon long-standing experience in environmental impact assessment processes.[46] First, a screening exercise aims to identify which trade measures may have significant sustainability impacts within and outside the EU and thus require a SIA. The second phase (scoping) is aimed at producing terms of reference for the appraisal methods and consultation procedures, after having identified groups of potentially affected stakeholders and key issues and sectors in relation to a core set of quantitative and qualitative environmental, social and economic indicators. The result of screening and scoping is the inception report, which presents the results of a review of published information on key aspects of the negotiating agenda and their identified potential significant impacts.[47] The third phase, in turn, is an assessment of potential impacts in general and in certain key sectors; including an identification of the components of the relevant trade measures likely to be the main drivers of the predicted impacts, and to consider alternative trade liberalisation scenarios. This is based on the consideration of worst case scenarios and risk assessments,[48] and results in a mid-term report, which provides the basis for consultations.[49] The final phase consists in the drafting of recommendations including the identification of trade and non-trade-related measures that could prevent or mitigate negative impacts or enhance positive impacts. These are published in the final report, which is also subject to public comment through written submissions and meetings.[50]

The Handbook points to a series of principles that should be taken into account in conducting SIAs, including that: both impacts in the EU and in third countries should be analysed; SIAs should be carried out in cooperation with third country partners; SIAs should be based on transparency and include external consultations, so as to provide all stakeholders with an opportunity to participate in the analysis of issues and impacts; SIA results should be made public; and there should be coordination with EU Member States experts and the European Parliament.[51] In terms of environmental integration, it is notable that the

[43] SIA Handbook, 7.

[44] UNEP, *Reference Manual for the Integrated Assessment of Trade-related Policies* (Geneva, UNEP, 2001).

[45] SIA Handbook, 10.

[46] Lee and Kirkpatrick, above n 36, 396.

[47] George and Kirkpatrick, above n 6, 7.

[48] SIA Handbook, 37.

[49] George and Kirkpatrick, above n 6, 7.

[50] Ibid.

[51] SIA Handbook, 8.

Handbook indicates that the SIA should identify trade-offs specifying the principles upon which choices of proposed measures were made, including the Treaty-based environmental principles of prevention, precaution, polluter-pays and the high level of environmental protection.[52] This may play a significant role in terms of transparency and can potentially ensure a degree of accountability in complying with the environmental integration requirement, to the extent to which the use of these principles is explicitly acknowledged in the SIA process and accounted for in the Commission position papers.

The Handbook expands on the finalities and modalities of consultations, by recommending that SIA consultants: utilise emails to ensure continuous dialogue with stakeholders; create international networks of experts; create a dedicated website to publish documentation for review at various stages of the process; and use civil society dialogue meetings organised by the European Commission.[53] It further suggests involving EU Delegations to extend consultations with third-country government experts, NGOs, business representatives, academics and representatives of 'some of the local communities potentially affected,' as well as international experts and organisations (such as UNEP, for instance). The need to provide capacity building for stakeholders to better understand and effectively participate in the SIA process is highlighted to this end.[54] The Handbook, furthermore, advocates appropriate formats and length of documents adapted to the effective and constructive sharing of information also to non-specialists and the possible creation of a stakeholder observatory.[55] Notably, the Handbook includes Standard Guidelines for Consultation of Civil Society, where indicative deadlines for engaging with stakeholders are provided (including timelines for responding to comments), together with criteria to ensure inclusiveness and representativeness of consulted stakeholders, and basic requirements for the consideration and inclusion of stakeholders' inputs.[56] It has, however, been lamented that consultations should be provided for as early as the scoping phase of the SIA and be accompanied by a related commitment by the Commission to explain the choice of scenarios and indicators that were eventually chosen.[57] In effect, a similar criticism has been made with regards to the Union's internal legislation on environmental assessments.[58]

In addition, the Handbook underlines the links between the different tools of the EU external relations, notably institutionalised dialogues.[59] It suggests that SIAs improve the EU institutional and political dialogue on sustainable development

[52] Ibid, 19. See discussion in Ch 1, s 3.2.
[53] SIA Handbook, 9.
[54] Ibid, 39.
[55] Ibid.
[56] Ibid, 49–51.
[57] Knigge and Leipprand, above n 7, 7, indicate that some consultation occurs before the preparation of the inception report.
[58] M Lee, *EU Environmental Law: Challenges, Change and Decision-Making* (Oxford, Hart, 2005), 172.
[59] Ch 5.

with trading partners by offering a basis for reflecting on trade/sustainability trade-offs, particularly in relation to the MDGs; foster public-private partnerships and other CSR initiatives; help to develop policy coherence with international organisations and assist in integrating civil society views.[60] It also proposes to explicitly and systematically link SIAs with ex post monitoring measures to be put in place during the trade agreement's implementation,[61] which are then going to be taken up by the institutions set up by these agreements.[62]

The Handbook thus indicates that the SIA process should continue after the conclusion of the trade agreement, through ex post monitoring. It specifies that ex post monitoring could identify the impacts of the implementation of relevant provisions of the trade agreement (including mitigation measures) to assess whether they are having the intended environmental effect.[63] It can also compare the predictions of the SIA with the actual outcomes with a view to understanding any significant differences, proposing complementary analysis and/or recommending additional mitigation and enhancement measures to address any significant, unanticipated or unresolved sustainability impacts.[64] At the time of writing, the Commission has indicated that the first ex post impact assessment has been planned in the context of the EU-Chile Association,[65] and a more systematic practice may be expected in the future, as post-Global Europe agreements provide for a further SIA during the implementation phase of the agreement, in consultation with civil society.[66]

3. AN OVERVIEW OF SIA PRACTICE

Following the procedural examination of the SIA exercise, this section will instead look at the substantive outcomes of SIAs that have been undertaken between 2002 and mid-2011, in order to assess the extent to which the environmental integration requirement has been served by the SIA process.

The SIA of the trade provisions of the EU-Chile Association was the first to be completed among those related to bilateral and inter-regional agreements: it was launched in March 2002 (almost two years into the negotiating process),[67] with

[60] SIA Handbook, 40.

[61] Ibid, 12.

[62] Ch 2, ss 5.3.4 and 7.1.4.

[63] George and Kirkpatrick, above n 6, 22.

[64] SIA Handbook, 23.

[65] C George, 'Regional Trade Agreements and the Environment: Monitoring Implementation and Assessing Impacts: Report on the OECD Workshop' (2011) *OECD Trade and Environment Working Papers*, 2011/02, 12–13.

[66] See Ch 2, ss 7.1.3–7.1.4; and discussion in D Augenstein et al, 'Study of the Legal Framework on Human Rights and the Environment Applicable to European Union Companies Operating Outside the EU' (Edinburgh, 2010), para 118 (University of Edinburgh Report).

[67] Which were launched in September 1999, and concluded in late-2002 (see Council Decision (EC) 2002/79 of 18 November 2002 on the signature and provisional application of certain provisions of an Agreement establishing an association between the European Community and its Member States, of the one part, and the Republic of Chile, of the other part [2002] OJ L352/3, preamble paras 1–2).

the final report being delivered in December of the same year, and subsequently endorsed by DG Trade.[68] This SIA was thus completed shortly *after* the conclusion of the negotiations in November 2002.[69] The report noted that, against the background of pre-existing environmental issues in Chile, the negative environmental impacts of increased industrialisation and investment arising from the agreement would, in general, outweigh the benefits deriving from new and cleaner technologies, in a considerable number of sectors: fisheries, agriculture, mining, chemicals, electricity, transport, forestry and tourism.[70] The report, thus, suggested a series of mitigation measures, to be taken primarily by Chile, with the EU supporting ongoing national efforts and contributing to provide new resources. These measures included: support for implementing industry best practices in environmental and sanitary and phytosanitary regulations, especially for small-scale producers;[71] technology transfer;[72] and support for the analysis of different policy options for the fisheries sector and the EU-Chile dialogue on fish stock conservation, to ensure that European investment in the Chilean fishing fleet would contribute to the sustainability of Chilean fishing reserves.[73] Interestingly, such measures were explicitly expected also to rely on the voluntary contribution of the business sector, through CSR initiatives.[74]

The second SIA to be completed was that for the EPAs between the EU and various ACP regions, which was initiated in September 2002 ahead of the formal launch of negotiations and finalised in August 2007, while negotiations with all regions except CARIFORUM are still ongoing.[75] The Commission, on that occasion, stressed that the SIA served to highlight possible negative environmental impacts, which it proposed to address through cooperation (technical and financial assistance) for the implementation of environmental regulations, as well as through a permanent institutional mechanism to monitor implementation of the EPAs and their impacts on the environment, with stakeholder participation.[76] The latter was reflected in the CARIFORUM EPA.[77]

[68] PLANISTAT-Luxembourg and CESO-CI, 'Sustainability Impact Assessment of Trade Aspects of Negotiations for an Association Agreement between the EC and Chile, Final Report (revised)', November 2002 (Chile SIA Final Report). This and all other SIA final reports and Commission position papers cited in this chapter can be found at www.ec.europa.eu/trade/analysis/sustainability-impact-assessments/assessments/.

[69] G Marín Durán and E Morgera, 'Towards Environmental Integration in EC External Relations? A Comparative Analysis of Selected Association Agreements' (2006) 6 *Yearbook of European Environmental Law* 179, 207–08.

[70] Chile SIA Final Report, 111–12.

[71] Ibid, 112 and 210.

[72] Ibid, 112 and 212–13.

[73] Ibid, 126–27.

[74] Ibid, 15–16. This may be linked to the reference to the OECD Guidelines on Multinational Enterprises in the EU-Chile Association (Ch 2, s 6.4).

[75] Ch 2, s 5.2.4.

[76] Commission, 'Position Paper: Sustainability Impact Assessment of EU-ACP Economic Partnership Agreements' (November 2007) 6–9 (ACP SIA Position Paper).

[77] Ch 2, s 5.3.4.

Subsequent SIAs have been conducted following the endorsement of the 2006 Global Europe Strategy,[78] and thus the Commission was more openly advocating through SIAs the inclusion of a trade and sustainable development chapter in the new bilateral/inter-regional trade agreements. The Commission in fact consistently proposed addressing certain environmental shortcomings arising from the SIA through such an operative part of the agreement under negotiations,[79] rather than with softer measures.[80] One notable example is the SIA of the FTA with South Korea, which contains similar findings to that of the EPAs.[81] SIAs concerning other countries highlighted in the Global Europe Strategy as priority partners for the new competitiveness-driven FTAs, such as China, ASEAN, MERCOSUR, and India, also went in the same direction, as did the SIAs undertaken for the FTA with Colombia and Peru and the Association with Central America, both equally mentioned (albeit with less degree of priority) in the Global Europe Strategy.[82] At least some SIAs, however, provide evidence that not all partner countries are interested in the EU's new approach to the trade and sustainable development nexus.[83]

In this context, the Commission started emphasising the inclusion of explicit commitments on the implementation of MEAs,[84] coupled with a requirement not to use domestic environmental regulations (through relaxation or lack of enforcement) as a trade/investment incentive.[85] Both aspects can be found in post-Global Europe agreements, albeit with different degrees of legal strength.[86] This shift has not meant, however, that the EU has necessarily stopped pursuing, at least occasionally, approximation to EU standards through SIAs. In the case of EU neighbouring countries, for instance, the Commission position paper on the

[78] Ch 1, s 5.2.

[79] Commission, 'Position Paper: Trade Sustainability Impact Assessment of the Euro-Mediterranean Free Trade Agreement' June 2009, 7 (Euro-Med SIA Position Paper); Commission, 'Position Paper: Trade SIA of the Negotiations on a FTA between the EU and Ukraine' April 2009, 9 (Ukraine SIA Position Paper); Commission, 'Position Paper: Trade SIA for the FTA between the EU and the Republic of India' March 2010, 2 (India SIA Position Paper); Commission, 'Position Paper on the SIA of the EU-MERCOSUR Association Agreement' July 2010, 4 (MERCOSUR SIA Position Paper); Commission, 'Position Paper on the SIA of the EU-ASEAN FTA' June 2010, 8 (ASEAN SIA Position Paper).

[80] Such as a reference to sustainable development in the preamble, coupled with increased monitoring and policy dialogue, which was proposed in the Commission, 'Position Paper on the SIA of the EU-Cooperation Council of the Arab States of the Gulf (GCC) SIA' March 2006, 9–10 (GCC SIA Position Paper).

[81] Commission, 'Position Paper: Trade SIA of the FTA between the EU and the Republic of Korea' June 2010, 8 (South Korea SIA Position Paper).

[82] Note that in the former case, the SIA process was launched at a time when all four countries of the Community of Andean Nations (Colombia, Peru, Bolivia and Ecuador) were expected to be part of the negotiations, although in the end only Colombia and Peru concluded an FTA with the EU (the Commission position paper notes that this fact, which the Commission considered to be due to internal divergences among the Community of Andean Nations members, had no impact on the overall validity of the conclusions reached by the SIA: see Commission, 'Position Paper of the SIA of the EU-Andean Community Association Agreement' November 2010, 1 (Andean SIA Position Paper).

[83] India SIA Position Paper, 1.

[84] Commission, 'Position Paper: Trade SIA of the Negotiations of a PCA between the EU and China' February 2009, 1 (China SIA Position Paper); South Korea SIA Position Paper, 8; Ukraine SIA Position Paper, 14, where specific emphasis is placed on the Kyoto Protocol.

[85] South Korea SIA Position Paper, 7–6; Andean SIA Position Paper, 7.

[86] See Ch 2, ss 5.3.2 and 7.1.3.

EU-Ukraine SIA expands significantly on the possible content of the trade and sustainable development chapter, by pointing to the inclusion of an annex identifying a set of core EU environmental directives for the gradual convergence of Ukrainian legislation to EU standards. The Commission also proposed the inclusion of a chapter on regulatory dialogue with Ukraine, including exchange of information and experience between institutions on standardisation, accreditation and infrastructure development.[87] Another instance is found in the context of the SIA for the EU-MERCOSUR agreement concerning environmental standards for carbon dioxide emissions from cars, in which the Commission suggested cooperation with a view to mitigating possible negative environmental impacts arising from liberalisation in the automotive sector, based both on EU domestic measures and on UNECE standards.[88] The latter is particularly notable as the MERCOSUR countries are not part of the UNECE region.[89]

The analysis of SIA practice also reveals that since mid-2010, the Commission has stressed the need to address negative environmental impacts of investment and trade facilitation,[90] the role of trade liberalisation in environmental goods and services,[91] and increased technology transfer to proactively address environmental shortcomings of trade negotiations.[92] These elements have been reflected in the Post-Global Europe agreements to varying extents.[93]

Specific environmental issues identified as possibly impacted by trade through SIAs include biodiversity, and to a lesser extent chemicals, with specific reference or clear allusion to relevant pieces of EU internal legislation with extraterritorial implications (that is, with certain impacts on third countries). The Commission position paper on the SIA related to Andean countries, for instance, proposed to address specifically the production and trade of environmentally sensitive products, including forestry and fisheries products, as well as general biodiversity issues in the chapter on trade and sustainable development,[94] as is reflected in the final text of the FTA with Colombia and Peru.[95] Several other SIA reports focused on environmentally sensitive products,[96] with a view to making tariff reductions and the opening of tariff quotas for these products conditional upon compliance

[87] Ukraine SIA Position Paper, 14–15.

[88] MERCOSUR SIA Position Paper, 6; this was also suggested in ECORYS et al, 'Trade Sustainability Impact Assessment of the FTA between the EU and the Republic of India, Final Report' May 2009, 291 (India SIA Final Report).

[89] The UNECE region comprises countries of Europe, but also countries in North America (Canada and US), Central Asia and Western Asia.

[90] MERCOSUR SIA Position Paper, 4; ASEAN SIA Position Paper, 8.

[91] ASEAN SIA Position Paper, 8; South Korea SIA Position Paper, 9.

[92] China SIA Position Paper, 5; India SIA Position Paper, 11; MERCOSUR SIA Position Paper, 4; South Korea SIA Position Paper, 5 and 9, on environmental goods and services; Ukraine SIA Position Paper, 14, on technology transfer; GCC SIA Position Paper, 4, on innovation and technology transfer for environmental sustainability.

[93] Ch 2, ss 5.3.2 and 7.1.3.

[94] Andean SIA Position Paper, 7.

[95] Ch 2, s 7.1.3.

[96] Development Solutions et al, 'Final Report of the SIA EU-Libya FTA' October 2009, 72–73; Pricewaterhouse Coopers, 'SIA of the EU-ACP EPAs: Summary of Key Findings, Policy Recommendations and Lessons Learned' May 2007, 72; Ukraine SIA Position Paper, 9 (albeit more implicitly).

with a set of sustainability criteria[97] or other certification schemes for forests, ecotourism and production processes.[98] This seems in part to be inspired by the International Finance Corporation sustainability policy,[99] to which express reference is made in some other SIAs,[100] but can also be reflective of the EU's approach to biofuels and deforestation.

SIAs have, for instance, explicitly pointed to the opportunity to discuss the applicability of the EU biofuels sustainability criteria enshrined in the EU Renewable Energy Directive[101] – a notable case of the EU internal environmental legislation with extraterritorial implications – to processes carried out in third countries, as a means to prevent negative environmental and social impacts arising from the trade negotiations.[102] In recent SIAs the Commission also points to the mutual benefits of participating in the EU initiative on Forest Law Enforcement, Governance and Trade or FLEGT – another example of EU internal legislation with extraterritorial implications[103] – with regards to combating illegal logging.[104] The consultant report of the EU-ASEAN SIA, for instance, suggested exploring the possibility of granting tariff reductions for timber and timber products covered by a FLEGT voluntary partnership agreement (VPA) concluded by the EU and ASEAN countries willing to export timber into the EU to ensure verification of the legality of timber harvests.[105] While the relevant SIAs did not mention this specifically, it seems useful to recall that some of the Post-Global Europe agreements include or imply reference to FLEGT.[106]

[97] MERCOSUR SIA Position Paper, 5. See also ECORYS, 'SIA of the FTA between the EU and Central America, Final Report' July 2009, 125 (Central America SIA Final Report).

[98] ECORYS, 'SIA of the FTA between the EU and ASEAN, Final Report' June 2009, 58 (ASEAN SIA Final Report); see also Central America SIA Final Report, 91.

[99] International Finance Corporation, 'Performance Standards on Social and Environmental Sustainability' (21 February 2006), at www.ifc.org/sustainability, which expects the borrower to ensure that its management control over forests and fisheries is independently certified against internationally accepted principles and criteria for sustainable management (Performance Standard 6: Biodiversity Conservation and Sustainable Natural Resource Management, paras 16–17). For a discussion, see E Morgera, *Corporate Accountability in International Environmental Law* (Oxford, Oxford University Press, 2009), ch 7.

[100] Emerging Markets Group and Development Solutions, 'Trade Sustainability Impact Assessment of the Negotiations of a Partnership and Cooperation Agreement between the EU and China, Final Report' August 2008, 145–48 (China SIA Final Report).

[101] Directive (EC) 2009/28 of the European Parliament and of the Council on the promotion of the use of energy from renewable sources [2009] OJ L140/16; see K Kulovesi, E Morgera and M Muñoz, 'Environmental Integration and Multi-faceted International Dimensions of EU Law: Unpacking the EU's 2009 Climate and Energy Package' (2011) 48(3) *Common Market Law Review* 829, 877–87.

[102] Commission, 'Position Paper on the SIA of the EU-Central America Association Agreement' June 2010, 4 and 6 (Central America SIA Position Paper); MERCOSUR SIA Position Paper, 5; ASEAN SIA Position Paper, 9; and Andean SIA Position Paper, 6–7, which refers to biofuels and the GSP-plus (on the latter, see Ch 3).

[103] Council Regulation (EC) 2173/2005 on the establishment of a FLEGT licensing scheme for imports of timber into the European Community [2005] OJ L347/1. This is discussed in more detail in Ch 7, s 4.1.

[104] MERCOSUR SIA Position Paper, 6; Andean SIA Position Paper, 8; ASEAN SIA Position Paper, 9.

[105] ASEAN SIA Final Report, 61.

[106] Explicitly in the Central America AA, art 289, and implicitly in the COPE FTA, art 273 (see Ch 2, ss 5.3.2 and 7.1.3).

While chemicals are not directly addressed in trade negotiations, SIAs have served in a couple of instances to discuss collaboration on the basis of the EU REACH Regulation[107] – another instrument of EU internal legislation with extra-territorial implications. In that context, the Commission noted that environmental dialogue served to allow third country stakeholders both to have some input into the development of EU domestic legislation with trade implications, as well as to familiarise themselves with EU domestic requirements for imports.[108]

Fisheries are also rarely addressed in SIAs, in part due to the fact that the Commission stresses the responsibility of the Member States in monitoring and enforcing EU fisheries legislation, while the EU is committed to continue engaging with third countries in the application of rules related to regional fisheries management organisations and the fight against illegal, unreported and unregulated fishing.[109] Thus, in the case of ASEAN, the Commission proposed addressing the effective implementation of treaties related to fisheries governance in the trade and sustainable development chapter of the FTA,[110] which is reflected in some of the post-Global Europe agreements.[111]

What also emerges quite clearly from the use of SIAs in practice is that the cross-cutting approach to CSR in EU external relations has evolved in the direction of corporate environmental *accountability*.[112] In earlier SIAs, the Commission proposed encouraging the use of voluntary instruments, such as eco-labelling, eco-management and green procurement[113] – on which the EU has produced internal legislation with external relevance[114] – or leaving it to the partner country/ies to create the appropriate regulatory environment to attract environmentally responsible investment.[115] Both approaches are consistent with the EU's initial take on

[107] Regulation (EC) 1907/2006 of the European Parliament and the Council on Registration, Evaluation, Authorisation and Restriction of Chemicals [2006] OJ L396/1. For a discussion of its extra-territorial impacts, in particular on developing country partners of the EU, see F Ackerman et al, 'Implications of REACH for Developing Countries' (2008) 18(1) *European Environment* 16.

[108] China SIA Position Paper, 6; MERCOSUR SIA Position Paper, 6; this was also mentioned in India SIA Final Report, 292.

[109] China SIA Position Paper, 6–7; EU-Lybia SIA Final Report, 73.

[110] ASEAN SIA Position Paper, 8; Andean SIA Position Paper, 7.

[111] Central America AA, art 59 and COPE FTA, art 274 on global and regional international instruments respectively (see Ch 2, ss 5.3.2 and 7.1.3).

[112] As opposed to CSR (Ch 1, s 5.1), the term 'corporate [environmental] accountability', which was endorsed by the WSSD (WSSD, 'Plan of Implementation' (4 September 2002) UN Doc A/CONF.199/20, Resolution 2 Annex, para 49), can be interpreted as the the legitimate expectation that reasonable efforts will be made, according to international standards, by private companies and foreign investors for the protection of a internationally agreed environmental objectives (E Morgera, *Corporate Accountability in International Environmental Law*, above n 99, ch 2).

[113] India SIA Position Paper, 10. See also ASEAN SIA Final Report, 62; Central America SIA Final Report, 92; and Ukraine SIA Final Report, 234.

[114] Regulation (EC) 66/2010 of the European Parliament and of the Council on the EU Eco-label, [2010] OJ L27/1 (Eco-label Regulation) and Regulation (EC)1221/2009 of the European Parliament and of the Council on the voluntary participation by organisations in a Community eco-management and audit scheme [2009] OJ L342/1 (EMAS Regulation). Note also Ukraine SIA Position Paper, 16, where the Commission explicitly proposes to discuss with Ukraine the promotion of the EMAS Regulation. For a discussion of the relevance of the EMAS and Eco-label Regulations in EU external relations, see ch 7, s 4.2.

[115] Central America SIA Position Paper, 6, in relation to sustainable forest management.

CSR.[116] However, in 2010, the Commission made a bolder statement about the need to report on EU companies' compliance with initiatives for promoting CSR in the mining, oil and gas sectors. It also showed willingness to discuss with partner countries appropriate means, in accordance with international guidelines, to promote the adoption of CSR criteria by EU companies, including when investing abroad.[117] This reflects a shift in EU policy more generally, namely its support for parallel international developments such as the UN Framework on Business and Human Rights.[118]

Through SIAs the Commission has also increasingly emphasised the need to include commonly agreed monitoring mechanisms in relation to environmental integration and sustainability in its bilateral and inter-regional agreements.[119] In the context of pre-existing agreements, such as in the case of the Mediterranean neighbours, the Commission proposed using existing institutional structures for increasing monitoring of sustainability impacts.[120] Since 2010, the Commission has used the SIA position papers to express clear rejection of a sanction-based enforcement system for sustainable development,[121] which is generally the approach followed in the post-Global Europe agreements (with the notable exception of the investment and environment provisions of the CARIFORUM EPA).[122] The Commission also pointed to the need for continuous monitoring (or ex post assessment) of the overall impacts of the agreement, facilitating cooperation with international organisations, such as UNEP, FAO and WTO[123] and creating a bilateral transparent forum to ensure review of sustainability commitments[124] through the advisory participation of civil society representatives.[125] These are once again reflected in the post-Global Europe agreements.[126]

The Commission has also been increasingly emphasising that the aim of addressing possible negative environmental impacts through SIAs is not that of harmonising environmental provisions among parties to trade agreements, but rather progressing through dialogue and cooperation in making economic and trade endeavours more sustainable.[127] In that context, the Commission called for more systematic interaction between its tools for external relations, notably institutionalised dialogues and financial and technical assistance projects.[128] While

[116] Commission, 'Green Paper – Promoting a European Framework for Corporate Social Responsibility' COM (2001) 366 final.

[117] Andean SIA Position Paper, 7 and 9, making reference also to the University of Edinburgh Report.

[118] Human Rights Council, 'Protect, Respect and Remedy: a Framework for Business and Human Rights,' UN Doc A/HRC/8/7 (2007). This will be discussed in more detail in Ch 7, s 4.2.

[119] China SIA Position Paper, 1; South Korea SIA Position Paper, 8.

[120] Euro-Med SIA Position Paper, 10.

[121] South Korea SIA Position Paper, 8; Andean SIA Position Paper, 7.

[122] See Ch 2, ss 5.3.4, 7.1.4 and 8.4.

[123] ASEAN SIA Position Paper, 9.

[124] MERCOSUR SIA Position Paper, 4.

[125] Ukraine SIA Position Paper, 17.

[126] See Ch 2, ss 5.3.4, 7.1.4 and 8.4.

[127] China SIA Position Paper, 4.

[128] Ibid, 5; Euro-Med SIA Position Paper, 8; India SIA Position Paper, 11–12; Andean SIA Position Paper, 8; ASEAN SIA Position Paper, 8.

ensuring these interlinkages may appear obvious, the complexity of EU external relations tools has made coherent and synergetic use of these instruments difficult. The Commission noted, for instance, that some occasional problems with the SIAs are due to consultants' misunderstandings of the trade negotiations,[129] and of the full breadth and scope of EU external relations tools.[130] This may be partly explained by the complexity and political sensitivity of trade negotiations, and also by the opaque nature of the interactions between EU external relations tools. But it may also be due to the fact that EU negotiators were not actively involved in the SIA process so as to correct the consultants' misperceptions.[131]

4. ASSESSMENT AND CONCLUSIONS

The commitment of the Commission to undertake SIAs is commendable as an innovative instrument to ensure an informed and participatory approach to balancing non-economic interests in trade negotiations. This is certainly an essential instrument to ensure environmental integration both in the definition and implementation of EU external trade. It seeks to put in place an open and principled approach to operationalise Article 11 TFEU, as well as to monitor its application.

As with all experiments, experience has thrown up several areas for improvement and SIAs have already evolved significantly, in a relatively short period of time. Nevertheless, SIAs are inherently characterised by a significant level of uncertainty, being a complex exercise per se, that is expected to be adaptive to another complex and unpredictable process that is trade negotiation.[132] The analysis of practice shows that to a certain extent, the Commission has been responsive to criticism and has managed expectations with regard to SIAs. On the one hand, it has ensured that SIAs were carried out early enough to be completed before the end of the negotiations (as opposed to the case of Chile, Colombia and Peru, and South Korea). On the other hand, it has increasingly emphasised their role in the implementation of the agreement and the use of other external relations tools, such as institutionalised dialogues and EU financial and technical assistance. On the timing issue, however, a distinction should be drawn between SIAs being completed just before the formal end of the negotiations (as in the case of the CARIFORUM EPA), and SIAs being completed at an early stage in the negotiation process (such as ASEAN, India, China and Ukraine) so that they have an actual bearing on the negotiations outcome. For an overview of the timing of SIA exercises launched as of June 2011, see table below.

129 ACP SIA Position Paper, 3.

130 China SIA Position Paper, 5; Euro-Med SIA Position Paper, 6; GCC SIA Position Paper, 6.

131 Civil society pointed to the lack of involvement of negotiators in the SIA exercise: see WWF, 'Changing the Balance of Trade', above n 1, 3.

132 George and Kirkpatrick, above n 6, 27.

Table 4. *Timing of SIAs*

Third party	Authorization of negotiations[133]	Launch of SIA[134]	Completion of SIA[135]	Completion of negotiations
Canada	April 2009	May 2010	Ongoing (final report June 2011)	ongoing
Andean Community	April 2007 (Ecuador suspended participation in July 2009)	August 2008	November 2010	COPE: February 2010
Central America	April 2007	August 2008	June 2010	May 2011
Libya	July 2008	August 2008	Ongoing (final report October 2009)	suspended in February 2011
ASEAN	April 2007 (launch Singapore: March 2010; Malaysia: September 2010)	October 2007	June 2010	ongoing
India	April 2007	October 2007	March 2010	ongoing
Korea	April 2007	September 2007	June 2010	October 2009
Ukraine	February 2008	September 2006	April 2009	ongoing
China	December 2005[136]	July 2006	February 2009	ongoing
MERCOSUR	September 1999 (suspended in October 2004 and relaunched in May 2010)	October 2003	July 2010	ongoing

[133] Dates of authorization and conclusion of negotiations are based on European Commission (DG Trade), 'Overview of FTA and other trade negotiations' (updated 10 June 2011) at www.trade.ec.europa.eu/doclib/docs/2006/december/tradoc_118238.pdf (unless otherwise indicated).

[134] Based on the date of the terms of reference for the SIA.

[135] Based on the date of the Commission position paper (unless otherwise indicated).

[136] European External Action Service, 'EU-China Relations: Chronology' at www.eeas.europa.eu/china/docs/chronology_2010_en.pdf.

Third party	Authorization of negotiations	Launch of SIA	Completion of SIA	Completion of negotiations
Euro-Med FTA	1995[137]	April 2003	June 2009	ongoing
Arab States of the Gulf	1991	May 2002	March 2006	Suspended (informal negotiations ongoing)
ACP	2003	NA	November 2007	CARIFORUM: December 2007 (other ongoing)
Chile	September 1999	December 2001	(final report December 2002)	November 2002

Effective stakeholder participation seems to remain a challenge,[138] partly because this needs to be supported by capacity-building measures in order to familiarise stakeholders with the complex EU external relations tools and equip them to meaningfully participate in the process. Partly it is because of the multiple demands placed on stakeholders by the plethora of EU external relations tools. Attempts have been made to improve access to SIA processes for stakeholders (particularly those in third countries or regions, who suffer the most from the fact that consultations are held in Brussels or may not have access to online documentation), although such attempts have been considered insufficient. In particular, it has been lamented that the regional stakeholder meetings that are organised in third countries do not take place in the areas where the stakeholders most likely to be affected by the agreement reside and are not held in local languages.[139] In this regard, questions of translation in local languages of key SIA documents that are essential to guarantee effective public participation, do not appear to have been adequately addressed in the terms of reference of the SIA consultants.[140]

A number of commentators have suggested that the EU could consider a decentralised or partly decentralised model for SIAs, with a view to involving local consultants in third countries or combining the EU-led assessment with a third country-driven one,[141] or at least with third country-produced studies to complement that of the EU consultant.[142] Alternatively, it has also been suggested that an obligation for the SIA consultant to work in cooperation with third-country

[137] Based on the date of the Barcelona Declaration (Ch 2, s 4.1).
[138] Greven et al, above n 1, 27.
[139] Ibid.
[140] Knigge and Leipprand, above n 7, 9, reported, for instance, on the lack of Spanish translation for the final report of the SIA on EU-Chile Association Agreement negotiation.
[141] Blobel et al, above n 1, 12.
[142] Knigge and Leipprand, above n 7, 8.

research institutions be included,[143] which could also contribute to capacity development in the partner country.[144] To make it a truly bilateral instrument, NGOs have also recommended that third country representatives and civil society participate in the SIA Steering Committee.[145]

The more promising suggestion, however, is to systematically involve relevant international organisations, which may increase the legitimacy of the SIA process.[146] To some extent, this is already foreseen in the SIA Handbook. But a more systematic effort in this direction could represent a welcome move alongside the increasing opportunities for involvement of, or interaction with, international (environmental) organisations in the implementation of other EU external relations tools, such as bilateral/inter-regional agreements, external funding and the GSP.[147] Similarly, a more systematic link of SIA and ex post assessments with other monitoring mechanisms carried out by relevant international organisations could provide further opportunities for collaboration.

Furthermore, one may question whether the potential of SIAs to contribute to synergistic use of the various external relations tools of the EU has been fully realised. Increased public participation in SIAs could be achieved with limited additional costs for the EU by systematically placing SIAs and ex post assessments on the agenda of the institutionalised dialogues periodically organised by the EU with third countries or regions.[148] In addition, SIA and ex post assessment outcomes could be systematically and explicitly included in the Regional/Country Strategy Papers that are meant to determine the allocation of EU financial and technical assistance.[149] This combined course of action could effectively serve to counter the argument that a 'mismatch between high-level strategic commitments and low-level policy implementation' exists in EU external relations.[150]

Ultimately, this chapter has highlighted that SIAs' conclusions have been reflected in the text of recent bilateral and inter-regional agreements, notably the post-Global Europe ones. However, it remains quite difficult to determine whether the former has been a precondition of the latter, or whether the EU's approach to the trade and environment nexus has influenced both exercises simultaneously. Notwithstanding the crucial role of SIAs in fulfilling the environmental integration requirement, it has further been underscored that this has not 'evolved into a strict legal obligation.'[151] SIAs in effect remain a largely voluntary

143 Ibid, 4.

144 As demanded by civil society (ibid, 9).

145 WWF, Changing the Balance of Trade, above n 1, 5.

146 Greven et al, above n 1, vii.

147 Ch 2, ss 5.3.4 and 7.1.4; Ch 3, s 4.2 and Ch 4, s 4.6.

148 See Ch 5.

149 These are instruments for the planning of geographic funding (see Ch 4, s 4). Lessons learnt from all the SIAs more generally could also be reflected in the thematic strategy used for the planning of thematic funding devoted to environmental protection (Ch 4, s 3).

150 As queried in Adelle, Hertin and Jordan, above n 17, 69.

151 Tébar and Kim, above n 28, 8, where it is notable that comparable (although not exactly similar – see s 2.1 above) exercises are mandated by law in the US and Canada. See also Blobel et al, above n 1, 5 and 13.

exercise underpinned by an EU political commitment.[152] While the informality of ex ante SIAs may be considered a reflection of the EU's general approach to public participation at the level of EU institutions,[153] it should be emphasised that post-Global Europe agreements have created a legal obligation for ex post SIAs that will be jointly carried out by the EU and the third country or region concerned.[154]

152 For a recent expression of commitment, see Commission, 'Trade, Growth and World Affairs Trade Policy as a core component of the EU's 2020 strategy' COM(2010) 612, 15: 'We will step up a gear in embedding impact assessments and evaluations in trade policy making. This includes carrying out impact assessments on all new trade initiatives with a potentially significant economic, social or environmental impact on the EU and its trading partners, including developing countries. We will pay particular attention to wide consultation and involvement of civil society in the sustainability impact assessments that we carry out during trade negotiations. Once negotiations are concluded and before signature, we will prepare for the Parliament and Council an analysis of consequences of the proposed deal for the EU. Finally, to help monitor the impacts of existing EU trade agreements, we will be carrying out ex post evaluation on a more systematic basis.'

153 The Commission's standards on public participation at EU level have remained notoriously non-binding, notwithstanding the international obligations of the EU under the Aarhus Convention. For an environmental law perspective, see Lee, above n 58, 133–39; and more generally, Alemanno, above n 16, 386–87.

154 South Korea FTA, art 13.10 and COPE FTA, art 279 discussed in Ch 2, s 7.1.4.

7

Supporting Environmental Multilateralism

1. INTRODUCTION

THIS CHAPTER AIMS to shed light on the interactions between the Union's external environmental action through unilateral, bilateral and inter-regional tools (external relations tools) on the one hand, and multilateral environmental treaties and processes on the other. It reveals how the EU is increasingly using these tools to actively support the development and implementation of international environmental law in a three-fold way. First, the EU seeks to deploy its external relations tools to support politically, technically and financially the implementation of existing multilateral environmental agreements, particularly in developing countries. Second, the EU is also applying its external relations tools to build alliances with third countries, regions or groups of countries with a view to influencing ongoing international environmental negotiations. Third, the EU is further using its external relations tools to make progress on environmental issues on which the international community has been unable to officially launch negotiations towards the development of an international legally binding agreement. In the latter case, the EU wishes to pursue certain environmental goals for which it did not succeed in getting protection at the multilateral level, by addressing them with other willing countries and potentially building international consensus from the bottom up.

This typology of positive interactions between the EU external relations tools and environmental multilateralism is a dynamic one. Depending on progress in multilateral negotiations or lack thereof, the approach of the EU towards certain global environmental issues may shift from one modality to another among those outlined above: the case of climate change will be used in this chapter to illustrate this dynamic.

While this approach certainly reflects the political commitment and Treaty obligation of the EU to support multilateralism,[1] showing constructive and creative experimentation on the part of the EU, so far it has been pursued through an uneven practice. This inconsistency appears both when comparing references to multilateral environmental agreements and goals across the wide range of bilat-

[1] Art 21(2)(h) TEU.

eral and inter-regional agreements concluded by the EU,[2] and also when comparing their treatment across the spectrum of other external relations tools.[3] This chapter will also point to a significant evolution in the way in which the EU supports environmental multilateralism through an increasingly conscious and methodical interaction between its external relations tools and its internal environmental legislation. The latter appears to be increasingly drafted so as to underscore reliance on EU external action at all levels in achieving key environmental goals within and outside its borders.

This chapter will thus ultimately explore the uneven practice and evolution in the complex interactions between EU multilateral negotiating positions, external relations tools, and internal environmental legislation with extraterritorial implications in: (i) supporting the implementation of existing MEAs in developing countries; (ii) alliance-building in the context of ongoing multilateral environmental negotiations; and (iii) bottom-up consensus-building in the absence of multilateral environmental negotiations.

2. SUPPORTING THE IMPLEMENTATION OF *EXISTING* MEAS

The EU has taken a variety of steps to institutionalise and legalise its support for the implementation of existing MEAs in partner countries, by strengthening third country institutions and administrative capacity, as well as their regulation and monitoring activities.[4]

While this chapter will focus on MEAs of global coverage, it should be noted that the EU has also endeavoured to support the implementation of certain regional environmental treaties through its external relations tools. For instance, it has supported implementation of the regional environmental treaties concluded under the aegis of the UNECE[5] through its Partnership and Cooperation Agreements with CIS,[6] and the Barcelona Treaty system for the protection of the Mediterranean Sea in the context of the Euro-Med Agreements, particularly through institutionalised dialogue.[7] Both groups of regional environmental treaties have also been prioritised in the EU's thematic external funding for environmental protection.[8] In some

[2] Ch 2.

[3] Chs 3–6.

[4] Commission, 'A Sustainable Europe for a Better World. A European Union Strategy for Sustainable Development' COM (2001) 264 final, 4.

[5] UNECE membership includes countries in Europe, Central Asia and North America. UNECE has been particularly active in facilitating the conclusion of regional environmental agreements, some of which can be seen as groundbreaking from a global perspective. For a discussion in the specific context of one of the most widely-known agreements, see E Morgera, 'An Update on the Aarhus Convention and its Continued Global Relevance' (2005) 14(2) *Review of European Community and International Environmental Law* 138.

[6] All agreements cited in Ch 2, s 7.2.1 include explicit reference to the Espoo Convention.

[7] See Ch 5, s 3.3.

[8] Commission, 'Thematic strategy for the environment and sustainable management of natural resources, including energy', 14 May 2007 (ENRTP Strategy 2007–10) 8, which referred specifically to the Aarhus Convention (Ch 4, s 3.2.2).

isolated instances, the EU has also used UNECE standards in its relations with third countries that are not Parties to the UNECE region.[9] In addition, the EU has also shown support for regional environmental processes in which it is not directly implicated,[10] although this approach has met with uneven success.[11]

This section will now turn to exploring specific support for the implementation of *global* agreements through EU external relations. Attention will first be devoted to MEAs related to chemicals management and desertification, and then a more in-depth analysis will be offered in relation to the international regimes on climate change and biodiversity, with a view to illustrating varying degrees of support.

Chemicals MEAs have not been included systematically in the bilateral and inter-regional agreements concluded by the EU, with the exception of the Basel Convention.[12] This trend, however, seems to have been inverted in the post-Global Europe agreements including in their trade and sustainable development chapters a 'closed list of MEAs' that encompasses the Basel Convention, the POPs Convention, and the Rotterdam Convention.[13] This reflects the broad approach to chemicals MEAs already adopted in the context of the GSP-plus,[14] although the latter does not encompass the Rotterdam Convention. The Union's programming documents for the allocation of external thematic funding for the environment prioritised the implementation of plans and actions agreed upon under key chemicals MEAs and processes.[15] In parallel, the EU has developed internal legislation on chemicals with extraterritorial implications, namely the REACH Regulation.[16] As REACH includes obligations of information submission and registration for those importing certain substances into the EU (most industrial chemicals and minerals excluding all fuels, agricultural chemicals and pharmaceuticals), it has been discussed in the context of institutionalised dialogues,[17] as

[9] Namely when proposing cooperation on environmental standards for carbon dioxide emissions from cars, see MERCOSUR SIA Position Paper and India SIA Position Paper (cited in Ch 6, s 3).

[10] Notably, in the Association Agreements with South Africa and Chile (Ch 2, s 6.4) and Cotonou Agreement, art 32(1) (Ch 2, s 5.2).

[11] B Chaytor, 'Environmental Issues in Economic Partnership Agreements: Implications for Developing Countries' (2009) *ICTSD Issue Paper*, 35 and 8, who reports that CARIFORUM States rejected the EU proposal to use certain regional environmental standards as benchmarks out of concern that these exceeded international standards.

[12] Ch 2, ss 3.5, 4.4, 5.2.3 and 7.2.1–7.2.2 (for a direct reference, see Croatia AA, art 103; and for a reference in the context of the fight against organised crime, see Kazakhstan PCA, art 70).

[13] Namely the COPE FTA and the Central America AA (Ch 2, ss 7.1.3 and 5.3.2).

[14] Ch 3, s 4.2.

[15] ENRTP Thematic Strategy 2007–10, 18 and Commission, 'Environment and natural resources thematic programme – 2011–2013 strategy paper and multiannual indicative programme', 29 October 2010, (ENRTP Strategy 2011–13), 25 (Ch 4, s 3.2.2) make reference to the Strategic Plan of the Basel Convention, the technical assistance activities agreed upon under the Rotterdam and POPs Conventions and the Strategic Approach to International Chemicals Management (SAICM, cited in Ch 4, n 99).

[16] Regulation (EC) 1907/2006 of the European Parliament and of the Council concerning the Registration, Evaluation, Authorisation and Restriction of Chemicals [2006] OJ L396/1. J Scott, 'REACH: Combining Harmonization and Dynamism in the Regulation of Chemicals' in J Scott (ed), *Environmental Protection: European Law and Governance* (Oxford University Press, 2009) 56.

[17] eg, EU-ACP JPA resolution on REACH and EU-ASEAN Enhanced Partnership Plan of Action cited in Ch 5, ss 3.1 and 3.5.

well as in the context of Sustainability Impact Assessments.[18] The European Parliament commissioned a study on its implications for developing countries, which recommended that the EU provide assistance for a smooth transition to REACH compliance.[19] It can be anticipated that REACH will play an increasing role in EU external relations, as a 'useful source of effective standards' to allow third countries to transition to the green economy and expand their trade opportunities, as well as support corporate accountability.[20] The EU may also be expected to increasingly rely on REACH in its bid to launch multilateral negotiations on a new international framework convention on chemicals management.[21]

In comparison, the UNCCD has received scant attention in EU external relations, with the exception of the Union's external assistance.[22] This may be due to the fact that the UNCCD is considered less successful than the other two Rio Conventions (CBD and UNFCCC),[23] and is currently undergoing a reform.[24] It may also stem from the fact that the EU has not developed internal legislation on desertification.[25] In all events, EU external relations tools have substantively covered many aspects related to the fight against desertification by reference to climate change, biodiversity and forest management. Nonetheless, the Commission seems interested in continuing to examine opportunities to strengthen its internal and external action on desertification, pointing to the possible political impetus that may be generated by a global analysis of the economics of desertification, land degradation and drought to determine the costs of land degradation and of inaction in that area.[26]

These two initial examples show the complex interactions between EU external action, multilateral processes and EU domestic legislation in supporting the implementation of MEAs. Attention will now turn to EU support for the international climate change regime, which epitomises the most advanced interaction between the Union's multilateral stances, external relations tools, and its internal legislation; and the international regime on biodiversity, which has the potential to move in the same direction, but has not yet reached the same level of sophistication.

[18] Ch 6, s 3 (for instance, China SIA Position Paper, 6 and EU-MERCOSUR SIA Position Paper, 6).

[19] F Ackerman and others, 'Implications of REACH for Developing Countries' (2008) 18(1) *European Environment* 16, 27.

[20] ENRTP Strategy 2011–13, 10 and 24–25. V Heyvaert, 'Globalizing Regulation: Reaching Beyond the Borders of Chemical Safety' (2009) 36(1) *Journal of Law and Society* 110.

[21] Commission, 'Communication – Rio+20: towards the green economy and better governance' COM (2011) 363 final, 10 and 12 (Communication Rio+20).

[22] Ch 4, ss 3.1, 3.2.2, 4.3 and 4.4.

[23] Communication Rio+20, 3, where the Commission refers to the 'achieved potential' of the other two Rio Conventions. The Commission underscores, later in the Communication, the usefulness of a global economic valuation of the costs and benefits of improving land quality (ibid, 12), similar to those already undertaken for the international regimes on climate change and biodiversity, probably with a view to raising the profile and facilitating the mainstreaming of the UNCCD.

[24] ENRTP Strategy 2011–13, 8.

[25] Note that a proposed soil framework directive (Commission, 'Proposal for a Directive of the European Parliament and of the Council establishing a framework for the protection of soil' COM (2006) 232 final) has remained pending.

[26] ENRTP Strategy 2011–13, 8; and above n 23.

2.1 The international climate change regime

The international regime on climate change is undoubtedly the one that has received the highest priority and has been most systematically integrated into EU external relations. This may be explained by the ascent of climate change at the international level from an environmental issue to a development and global security challenge.[27]

At the EU level, climate change had already been singled out by the European Council as a key challenge in the late-1990s and followed up by various policy proposals.[28] This resulted in a 2004–08 action plan, including a strategy for Member States, the European Parliament, civil society and other stakeholders to contribute to the formulation and implementation of a coherent and coordinated EU climate change strategy and action plan to support third countries.[29] Several other policy initiatives followed, such as the launch in 2007 of the Global Climate Change Alliance,[30] and the issuance in 2009 of a White Paper on Adaptation encouraging the systematic inclusion of climate change adaptation into all EU external policies at the bilateral and multilateral level, particularly in the area of trade, development cooperation and security.[31] Also in 2009 the Council requested the development of a new EU-wide environmental integration strategy to be discussed in 2011, coupled with a framework for monitoring implementation by Member States and the Commission, singling out climate change among all other MEAs.[32] In parallel, EU legislation on climate change has been increasingly refined, reflecting the evolution of the international climate change regime.[33]

The treatment of the international climate change regime in the EU external relations has accordingly been characterised by a significant evolution. Initially, the inclusion of climate change in the EU external action tools was very generic[34] or specifically geared towards encouraging the ratification and implementation of

[27] F Sindico, 'Climate Change: A Security (Council) Issue?' (2007) 1(1) *Carbon and Climate Law Review* 26; E Morgera, 'The 2005 UN World Summit and the Environment: The Proverbial Half-Full Glass?' (2006) 15 *Italian Yearbook of International Law* 53.

[28] Commission, 'Communication – Climate change: Towards an EU post-Kyoto Strategy' COM (1999) 353 final, calling for, inter alia, 'strengthened dialogue' with third countries.

[29] Commission, 'Communication – Climate change in the context of development cooperation' COM (2003) 85 final and Council, 'Conclusions on Climate Change in the Context of Development Policy' 24 November 2004 (Annex 'Action Plan to accompany the EU Strategy on Climate Change in the Context of Development Cooperation').

[30] Ch 5, s 4.

[31] Commission, 'White Paper – Adapting to Climate Change: Toward a European Framework for Action' COM (2009) 147 final, 15–16.

[32] Council, 'Conclusions on Integrating Environment in Development Cooperation' Brussels 25 June 2009; see comments by N van der Grijp and T Etty, 'Incorporating Climate Change into EU Development Cooperation Policy' in J Gupta and N van der Grijp (eds), *Mainstreaming Climate Change in Development Cooperation* (Cambridge, Cambridge University Press, 2010), 181.

[33] S Oberthür and M Pallemaerts (eds), *The New Climate Policies of the European Union: Internal Legislation and Climate Diplomacy* (Brussels, VUB Press, 2010).

[34] References to climate change as an area for cooperation can be found, eg, in several PCAs with CIS (Ch 2, s 7.2.1).

the Kyoto Protocol, as reflected in certain bilateral agreements[35] and the GSP-plus.[36] This was linked to the EU international efforts to ensure the Kyoto Protocol's entry into force notwithstanding the declaration by the United States of their intention not to ratify it.[37] The EU thus put in place environmental cooperation commitments with a view to specifically supporting partner countries in the implementation of the Protocol, by raising the profile of climate change in development strategies and providing capacity development.[38] Particular emphasis was placed on supporting the implementation of the CDM – the only market-based instrument under the Kyoto Protocol that benefits developing countries – as a vehicle for technology transfer and for greening foreign direct investment.[39]

More recently, the EU has prioritised climate change through all its external relations tools, focusing in particular on the creation of a global carbon market and carbon finance. This has occurred in tandem with developments in EU environmental legislation, the implementation of which will intertwine with the Union's external action at all levels. In terms of internal legislation, the EU's 2009 Climate and Energy Package[40] contains various provisions linked to the EU's international agenda on climate change. Notably, the revised EU Emission Trading Scheme (ETS) Directive[41] aims to support the establishment of carbon trading schemes in other regions with a view to expanding the global carbon market first in countries belonging to the OECD, and later in emerging economies, including in sub-federal or regional entities.[42]

In addition, the ETS is an example of EU legislation aiming to generate climate finance for developing countries:[43] it provides, albeit in non-legally binding language, that at least 50 per cent of the revenues generated from the auctioning of allowances under the ETS or the equivalent value of these revenues should be used for, inter alia, adaptation, technology transfer, as well as afforestation and reforestation activities in developing countries.[44]

[35] eg, Bosnia AA, art 108; Montenegro AA, art 111; Serbia AA, Art 111 (Ch 2, s 3.4).

[36] Ch 3, s 4.2.

[37] K Kulovesi, 'How to Prevent Babies from Being Thrown Away with the Bathwater: Perspectives on the International Climate Regime from Buenos Aires to the Future' in E Morgera and F Francioni (eds), *The Future of Environmental Law: International and European Perspectives* (The Working Group on Environmental Law: Collected Reports 2004–05) *EUI Working Papers Law*, Law No 2006/01, 23.

[38] Council, 'Conclusions on Climate Change in the Context of Development Policy', above n 29, Annex Strategic Objectives I and IV.

[39] The Commission, for instance, proposed the development of an EU code of conduct for the use of ODA to finance CDM activities, see Commission, 'Communication – Energy cooperation with the developing countries' COM (2002) 408 final; and comments by N van der Grijp and T Etty, above n 32, 182–84.

[40] See generally K Kulovesi, E Morgera and M Muñoz, 'Environmental Integration and Multi-faceted International Dimensions of EU Law: Unpacking the EU's 2009 Climate and Energy Package' (2011) 48(3) *Common Market Law Review* 829.

[41] Directive (EC) 2009/29 of the European Parliament and the Council amending Directive (EC) 2003/87 so as to improve and extend the greenhouse gas emission allowance trading scheme of the Community [2009] OJ L140/63 (EU ETS Directive).

[42] Ibid, art 25.1(a): this went beyond an earlier formulation that limited linking the ETS only to industrialised countries having ratified the Kyoto Protocol (Kulovesi et al, above n 40, 862).

[43] Kulovesi et al, above n 40, 856.

[44] EU ETS Directive, art 10(3).

Furthermore, the Renewable Energy Directive, which is another component of the 2009 Climate and Energy Package, provides for joint projects between EU Member States and third countries.[45] This possibility may be realised on the basis of the frequent clauses in the bilateral and inter-regional agreements on cooperation concerning renewable energy,[46] utilising the framework of established institutional structures for ongoing dialogue and cooperation.[47]

This sophistication in the EU's approach to climate change has become increasingly visible in all external relations tools. Notably, post-Global Europe agreements include unprecedented cooperation clauses wholly devoted to climate change or significantly detailed language on cooperation on trade and climate change. Recent agreements therefore contain operative provisions focusing on specific aspects of climate change cooperation, such as: climate change mainstreaming, supporting both mitigation and adaptation, supporting trade measures and/or removing trade obstacles to facilitate the implementation of the international climate change regime, facilitating technology transfer and supporting the international carbon market.[48]

Climate change has also become the number one priority for EU external funding,[49] including for cooperation with industrialised countries.[50] A portion of the Union's thematic funding for the environment is reserved to specific initiatives related to climate change and renewable energy.[51] However, NGOs have lamented insufficient analysis of climate change issues in relevant programming documents for geographic funding,[52] which has been implicitly acknowledged by the Council.[53] While the EU still needs to develop its own skills to mainstream climate change in its external assistance, climate change is set to continue to take the lion's share of resources in the near future.[54]

Overall, climate change certainly represents a frontrunner area for environmental integration in EU external relations. Further evolution can be expected in this direction as the Union aims to provide sufficient visibility for the Union's pledges made at the multilateral level,[55] to ensure that climate finance is used also

[45] Ibid, art 9(1).

[46] See Ch 2, and in particular, Jordan AA, art 74; Serbia AA, arts 109 and 111; South Africa AA, art 57; South Korea FA, art 16.

[47] Kulovesi et al, above n 40, 877.

[48] Ch 2 (in particular, Cotonou Agreement – 2010 revision, arts 1, 8, 11 and 32bis; COPE FTA, art 275; South Korea FA, art 24; Central America AA, art 63).

[49] Regulation (EC) 1905/2006 of the European Parliament and of the Council establishing the financing instrument for development cooperation [2006] OJ L378/41 (DCI Regulation), art 2(2); discussed in Ch 4, s 3.2.2.

[50] Council Regulation (EC) 1934/2006 of establishing a financing instrument for cooperation with industrialised and other high-income countries and territories [2006] OJ L405/41, art 4; discussed in Ch 4, s 4.5.

[51] Such as the Global Climate Policy Alliance (ENRTP Thematic Strategy 2007–10, 3).

[52] WWF, Birdlife and FERN, 'Environmental Tools in EC Development Cooperation: An Analysis of Country and Regional Environmental Profiles' (2009) (WWF et al, 2009), 6, 8 and 17.

[53] Council, 'Conclusions on Climate Change in the context of Development Policy,' above n 29.

[54] ENRTP Strategy 2011–13, 20–23 ('Priority 1: Climate change and sustainable energy').

[55] Commission, 'Public Consultation: What Funding for EU external action after 2013?' (Background document, 2011) 9, n 13 (discussed in Ch 4, s 5).

to benefit biodiversity and sustainable development in light of other, concurrent international obligations of the EU,[56] and ultimately to keep the Union's efforts to play a constructive role on climate change credible.[57] Equally important will be for the EU to ensure, in its prioritisation of climate change, that the environmental integration requirement in its internal dimension (that is, an holistic approach within environmental policy) is respected, by putting in place sufficient guarantees in its external action and internal legislation to avoid that climate change measures undermine other environmental protection objectives.[58]

2.2 Biodiversity-related conventions

As opposed to climate change, the integration of international biodiversity-related conventions in EU external relations has had a much lower profile notwithstanding increasing international attention on the importance of biodiversity for human well being[59] and global development.[60] This may be partly related to the 'patchy' development of EU internal legislation on biodiversity, which originated in the late-1970s and 1990s[61] and focused on 'traditional' conservation measures (protected areas and species).[62]

[56] Commission, 'Green Paper – EU development policy in support of inclusive growth and sustainable development: Increasing the impact of EU development policy' COM (2010) 629 final, 17.

[57] See discussion in Kulovesi et al, above n 40, 855–58, where reference is made to EU internal struggles, unclear determination of the share of the international climate finance that the EU will shoulder, and the sheer amount of funding needed (the Commission determined that finance requirements for adaptation and mitigation in developing countries could reach roughly €100 bn euros a year by 2020: see Commission, 'Communication – Stepping up international climate finance: A European blueprint for the Copenhagen deal' COM (2009) 475/3 final).

[58] ENRTP Strategy 2011–13, 17 where there is reference to the need for external action on climate change to 'take full account of the need for sustainable resource use and conservation of biodiversity.'

[59] The global target of reducing significantly the rate of biodiversity loss by 2010 was first agreed upon by the CBD COP Decision VI/26, 'Strategic Plan for the Convention on Biological Diversity', para 11 (2002) UN Doc UNEP/CBD/COP/6/20. It was subsequently endorsed by the World Summit on Sustainable Development ('Plan of Implementation of the World Summit on Sustainable Development' (4 September 2002) UN Doc A/CONF.199/20 Resolution 2, Annex, para 44), and the UNGA ('2005 World Summit Outcome' (2005) UN Doc A/RES/60/1, para 56). A new global target has been adopted by the CBD parties in 2010: CBD COP Decision X/2, 'The Strategic Plan for Biodiversity 2011–2020 and the Aichi Biodiversity Targets' (2010) UN Doc UNEP/CBD/COP/10/27.

[60] Biodiversity loss is included in the MDGs as Target 7b.

[61] Directive (EEC) 79/409 of the European Parliament and of the Council on the conservation of wild birds as amended (codified as Directive (EC) 2009/147 of 30 November 2009 [2010] OJ L20/7); Council Directive (EEC) 92/43 on the conservation of natural habitats and of wild fauna and flora [1992] OJ L206/7; Council Regulation (EC) 338/97 on the protection of species of wild fauna and flora by regulating trade therein, as amended [2005] OJ L215/1.

[62] For a discussion, see N Sadeleer, 'EC Law and Biodiversity' in R Macrory (ed), *Reflections on 30 Years of EU Environmental Law – a High Level Protection?* (Groningen, Europa Law Publishing, 2005), 351; N Sadeleer, 'Habitat Conservation in EC Law: From Nature Sanctuaries to Ecological Networks' (2005) 5 *Yearbook of European Environmental Law* 215. Significant gaps remain in the regulatory framework on biodiversity, which are also acknowledged by the Commission itself. See Commission, 'Communication – Halting the loss of biodiversity by 2010 and beyond' COM (2006) 216 final.

As a result, it comes as no surprise that references to biodiversity-related MEAs are scattered in bilateral and inter-regional agreements, with different formulations and an apparent lack of systematic approach. While some of the agreements limit themselves to mentioning biodiversity issues in a generic way, as a specific area for environmental cooperation,[63] the post-Global Europe agreements include a 'closed list of MEAs' in their trade and sustainable development chapters referring to three global biodiversity treaties: the CBD, its Cartagena Protocol on Biosafety and CITES,[64] reflecting the approach already adopted in the context of the GSP-plus.[65]

It remains unclear, however, why other global biodiversity-related agreements, such as the Convention on Migratory Species, the ITPGR and the Ramsar Convention on Wetlands of International Importance, were not included. In particular, the Ramsar Convention and ITPGR are notable absences as they have been singled out by the World Summit on Sustainable Development as key treaties for the realisation of sustainable development.[66]

As biodiversity-related agreements cover a wide range of issues (from nature conservation and the sustainable use of natural resources, to access to genetic resources, biotechnology, and the protection of traditional knowledge of local and indigenous communities), the few, more detailed provisions related to biodiversity cooperation in bilateral treaties have addressed these issues in different ways. Three biodiversity-related *foci* can be identified in that respect.

First, all the PCAs with CIS countries feature the same, detailed article on cooperation on the conservation of biodiversity, protected areas and sustainable use and management of biological resources.[67] The only other case that has focused on biodiversity conservation and sustainable use is the FTA with Colombia and Peru,[68] which singles out both support to the creation of protected-area systems in light of international goals and the promotion of economic returns from biodiversity management.[69] The latter inclusion in an inter-regional trade agreement is quite striking, however, as these areas of cooperation are not obviously linked to trade, but rather, represent the EU's international priority in the context of the

[63] See Ch 2, in particular: Algeria AA, art 52(2); Cotonou Agreement, art 32(1); Croatia AA, art 103; Macedonia AA, art 103; South Africa AA, art 84.

[64] Ch 2: Central America AA, arts 285(2) and 287(2); COPE FTA, arts 267(2)(b) and 270(2); South Korea FA, art 23 and South Korea FTA, art 13.11.

[65] Ch 3, s 4.2.

[66] See Ch 1, s 4.2.3.1.

[67] Ch 2, s 7.2.1 (see, for instance, Armenia PCA, art 55(2)).

[68] COPE FTA, Art 272 (Ch 2, s 7.1.3).

[69] CBD, Decision X/2, above n 59, includes target 11 which provides that by 2020, at least 17% of terrestrial and inland water, and 10% of coastal and marine areas, especially areas of particular importance for biodiversity and ecosystem services, are conserved through effectively and equitably managed, ecologically representative and well-connected systems of protected areas and other effective area-based conservation measures, and integrated into the wider landscape and seascapes. An earlier international target on protected areas can be found in CBD, Decision VI/26, 'Strategic Plan for the Convention on Biological Diversity' (2002) UN Doc UNEP/CBD/COP/6/20, para 11.

CBD as a negotiating block and as a donor supporting progress on protected areas[70] and, more recently, on the economic evaluation of biodiversity.[71]

Second, more recent agreements have addressed to varying extents the interactions between the CBD and trade-related issues. The Cotonou Agreement specifically referred to the difficult relationship between the CBD and the protection of intellectual property rights, stressing the importance of adhering to the CBD in that respect and hinting at the need to cooperate in other international fora to that end.[72] The latter is further elaborated in the CARIFORUM EPA, where more explicit provisions call for a regular exchange of views and cooperation in the Word Intellectual Property Organization and WTO.[73] These concerns are mainly related to the provisions of the CBD related to genetic resources and traditional knowledge, which both the CARIFORUM EPA and the FTA with Colombia and Peru address. Both agreements include a provision[74] that basically incorporates the provisions of Article 8(j) of the CBD. This area of cooperation, that so far is circumscribed to one partner region, has the potential to become much more prominent in the near future following the adoption in late-2010 of a new international instrument under the CBD framework, the Nagoya Protocol on Access and Benefit-sharing, the prompt ratification of which is considered essential for the EU 'to continue to lead international biodiversity policy.'[75] Furthermore, SIAs have identified the likely impacts of trade liberalisation on biodiversity as another facet of the trade and biodiversity linkage.[76] In that context, the Commission suggested making tariff reductions and opening of tariff quotas for biodiversity-sensitive products conditional upon compliance with a set of sustainability criteria or certification schemes.[77]

The third focus is the need to mainstream biodiversity in other policy areas (external environmental integration), as well as in other sectoral environmental

[70] The EU has systematically supported the work of the CBD on protected areas. See, for instance, Alvarenga et al, 'Summary of the Eighth Conference of the Parties to the Convention on Biological Diversity' (2006) 9(363) *Earth Negotiations Bulletin* 2–3.

[71] The EU is one of the main proponents of the economic valuation of biodiversity and ecosystem services, and funded The Economics of Ecosystems & Biodiveristy (TEEB), 'The Economics of Ecosystems and Biodiversity: Mainstreaming the Economics of Nature: A synthesis of the approach, conclusions and recommendations of TEEB' (2010) at www.teebweb.org. The importance of the TEEB findings for the EU future external relations is highlighted in the EU 2020 Biodiversity Strategy (Commission, 'Communication – Our life insurance, our natural capital: an EU biodiversity strategy to 2020' COM (2011) 244 final (2020 Biodiversity Strategy), 2–3 and 7), where the full valuation of biodiversity is considered critical to contribute to the EU shift towards a more resource-efficient, climate-resilient and low-carbon future, in line with Europe 2020 Strategy (Commission, 'Communication – Europe 2020: A strategy for smart, sustainable and inclusive growth' COM (2010) 2020) (Europe 2020 Strategy)), as well as a contribution to the EU's position on the green economy for the Rio+20 Conference.

[72] Cotonou Agreement, art 46(2), discussed in Ch 2, s 5.2.4.

[73] CARIFORUM EPA, art 150(5), discussed in Ch 2, s 5.3.2.

[74] CARIFCORUM EPA, art 150(1); COPE FTA, art 272. The latter actually goes beyond the letter of CBD, art 8(j), by making reference to the need for 'prior informed consent' of relevant indigenous and local communities (Ch 2, ss 5.3.3 and 7.1.3).

[75] 2020 Biodiversity Strategy, 7.

[76] Ch 6, s 3.

[77] Ibid (in particular, Andean SIA Position Paper, 7 and MERCOSUR SIA Position Paper).

policies (internal environmental integration).[78] Thanks to institutionalised dialogues, several references to biodiversity mainstreaming can be found in the action plans adopted by the EU and partner countries, as well as in their joint declarations.[79] Cooperation on avoiding negative impacts of energy development and climate change response measures on biodiversity is also reflected in post-Global Europe agreements and the 2011–13 thematic funding strategy.[80] Mainstreaming biodiversity into the international climate change regime[81] is also motivated by the desire to provide additional funding for biodiversity indirectly by ensuring synergies with other relevant funding sources, notably climate finance.[82]

It should be further noted that biodiversity in EU external assistance has gradually gained more prominence. The legislation on EU thematic external funding for the environment includes among its specific objectives that of addressing biodiversity loss[83] and the programming document for 2007–12 singled out the CBD and CITES.[84] Limited attention, however, had been paid to biodiversity in the documentation for the programming of EU geographic external funding: NGOs observed limited reference to biodiversity in the country environmental profiles that contribute to the integration of environmental protection in the country strategy papers with a view to determining the allocation of the EU's external funding on a geographic basis.[85] For the period 2011–13, the Commission has increased emphasis on the protection of biodiversity and ecosystems in its thematic funding, pointing to specific challenges related to invasive alien species and access and benefit sharing from genetic resources, as well as to the role of biodiversity in the green economy and the sustainable management of traded biological resources.[86]

Overall, EU external action related to biodiversity at the unilateral, bilateral and inter-regional level has been quite inconsistent.[87] It may be anticipated, however, that with the adoption of the Nagoya Protocol on Access and Benefit-sharing, the EU's support for its implementation may provide a renewed biodi-

[78] On the external and internal dimension of environmental integration, see Ch 1, s 4.2.1.

[79] Ch 5.

[80] Central America AA, art 65(2)(c); ENRTP Strategy 2011–13, 17.

[81] As confirmed in the EU's 2020 Biodiversity Strategy, 8, where the EU is planning to promote enhanced cooperation between the CBD, UNFCCC and UNCCD to yield mutual benefits.

[82] Commission, 'Green Paper – EU development policy in support of inclusive growth and sustainable development, above n 56, 17; and 2020 Biodiversity Strategy, 10.

[83] DCI Regulation, art 2(2), discussed in Ch 4.

[84] ENRTP Thematic Strategy 2007–10, 8; see also Commission, 'Communication – Biodiversity Action Plan for Economic and Development Co-operation' COM (2001) 162 final, vol V and Commission, 'Annex to the Communication – Halting the Loss of Biodiversity by 2010 – And Beyond: Sustaining ecosystem services for human well–being' SEC (2006) 621 final.

[85] WWF et al, above n 52, 6, 8 and 17.

[86] ENRTP Strategy 2011–13, 7, 17 and 23.

[87] Commission, 'Communication – Biodiversity Action Plan for Economic and Development Co-operation', above n 84.

versity focus across EU external relations tools.[88] This may be motivated by the increased need for external funding and technical assistance in developing countries, who will face many unprecedented challenges in implementing this innovative international instrument.[89]

In any event, more concerted efforts will be needed to use the whole array of EU external relations tools to effectively support global biodiversity goals. And this is indeed the intention for the immediate future that seems to emerge from the Commission's proposed 2020 Biodiversity Strategy. Accordingly, the Commission is planning to: systematically include biodiversity as part of trade negotiations and dialogues with third countries; identify and evaluate potential impacts on biodiversity resulting from the liberalisation of trade and investment through ex ante SIAs and ex post evaluations; seek to include in all new bilateral trade agreements a chapter on sustainable development including substantial provisions concerning trade and biodiversity goals; and systematically screen the Union's development cooperation action to minimise any negative impact on biodiversity, undertaking SEAs/EIAs for actions likely to have significant effects on biodiversity.[90] It may also be anticipated that the adoption of another piece of internal legislation for the implementation of the Nagoya Protocol within the Union's own territory, which will have extraterritorial implications,[91] will contribute to a more systematic integration of biodiversity concerns in the EU external relations.

3. BUILDING ALLIANCES FOR *ONGOING* MULTILATERAL ENVIRONMENTAL NEGOTIATIONS

The EU is also actively and openly using its unilateral, bilateral and inter-regional external relations tools to build alliances with regard to ongoing multilateral environmental negotiations. This builds on a three-fold strategy, namely to: strengthen the capacity of developing countries to negotiate emerging environmental

[88] Council, 'Conclusions on Convention on Biological Diversity: follow-up to Nagoya Conference', 20 December 2010, where the Council underscored the need to reflect biodiversity priorities in the EU Financial Framework to ensure that biodiversity's contribution to green growth and human wellbeing is fully factored in.

[89] For a discussion and comparison of capacity needs in other MEAs, see E Morgera et al, 'Implementation Challenges and Compliance in MEA Negotiations' in P Chasek and L Wagner (eds), *The Roads from Rio: Lessons learned from 20 years of multilateral environmental negotiations* (London, Routledge, forthcoming 2012).

[90] EU 2020 Biodiversity Strategy, 15–16.

[91] When the Nagoya Protocol enters into force, countries using genetic resources such as the EU Member States will be mandated to ensure that genetic resources and traditional knowledge utilised within their jurisdiction have been accessed in accordance with the legislation and requirements of the third country that provided these resources. The Commission has already indicated the need to propose new EU legislation to implement the Nagoya Protocol in the EU's 2020 Biodiversity Strategy (2020 Biodiversity Strategy, 16, 'action 20'). For a discussion of the Nagoya Protocol from an EU perspective, see M Buck and C Hamilton, 'The Nagoya Protocol on Access to Genetic Resources and the Fair and Equitable Sharing of Benefits Arising from their Utilisation to the Convention on Biological Diversity' (2011) 20(1) *Review of European Community and International Environmental Law* 47.

agreements; support developing countries' efforts to participate fully in international environmental fora; and contribute to preparing their negotiating positions with like-minded groups.[92] Through these types of assistance, which are epitomised by the EU-funded multi-year programme implemented by UNEP to support ACP countries' capacity building related to MEAs,[93] as well as through all the other tools discussed in previous chapters, the EU also aims to encourage buy-in by third countries of the Union's own negotiating positions at the multilateral level.

This approach is formalised in general clauses in association and other bilateral agreements, ranging from very indeterminate references to cooperation in the context of current and *future* regional and international environmental commitments, to the promotion of cooperation on environmental matters being discussed in international fora.[94] Policy dialogues have also served to review the outcomes of ongoing multilateral negotiations sessions, to discuss and better understand respective negotiating positions, and in the case of the most cooperative partners (Africa, Mexico and Japan) commit to preparing joint negotiating positions.[95]

As to the choice of ongoing multilateral environmental negotiations for which alliance-building is pursued bilaterally, scattered references have been found in the context of the bilateral agreements and declarations emerging from institutionalised dialogues on ongoing biodiversity negotiations. The most visible cases were references to negotiations of what became the Nagoya Protocol to the CBD and the creation of an International Science-Policy Platform on Biodiversity and Ecosystem Services,[96] as well as the EU proposal to develop a new international instrument on marine biodiversity in areas beyond national jurisdiction.[97] On chemicals, few references have been identified supporting alliance-building concerning ongoing negotiations on an international instrument on mercury.[98]

[92] Commission, 'Integrating Environment and Sustainable Development into Economic and Development Cooperation Policy: Elements of a Comprehensive Strategy' COM (2000) 264, 12–13.

[93] See the description of the programme website at www.hqweb.unep.org/AfricanCaribbeanPacific/MEAs/.

[94] See Ch 2.

[95] Ch 5, s 5.

[96] Ch 5 (for instance, 18th Japan-EU Summit, 'Joint Press Statement' (9454/09 (Presse 113) 2009), para 15). The creation of the Platform has been endorsed by the UNGA, 'Report of the Governing Council of UNEP on its eleventh special session' (2010) UN Doc A/RES/65/162, para 17.

[97] Notably, the EU proposal to develop an international legal framework on marine biodiversity in areas beyond national jurisdiction, in Japan's Proposals for Regulatory Reform Dialogue (2008) 35 (Ch 5, s 3.6.3). Intergovernmental discussions on the need for such an international legal framework have been ongoing under the UNGA *Ad Hoc* Open-ended Informal Working Group to study issues relating to the conservation and sustainable use of marine biological diversity beyond areas of national jurisdiction. In 2011, the Working Group recommended that a more formal process to address these issues be initiated (see A Miller et al, 'Summary of the fourth meeting of the *Ad Hoc* Open-ended Informal Working Group to study issues relating to the conservation and sustainable use of marine biological diversity beyond areas of national jurisdiction' (2011) 25(70) *Earth Negotiations Bulletin* 1.

[98] Ch 5 (see, eg, Fifth EU-LAC Summit, 'Declaration: Our Peoples' Priorities Together' Lima 16 May 2008, paras 31–37).

There are, however, more notable cases in which the EU has been systematically pursuing alliance-building with a view to making progress on ongoing multilateral negotiations, such as climate change and the environmental sustainability of biofuel production that will be discussed in more detail in the following sub-sections.

3.1 Ongoing climate change negotiations

Immediately following the entry into force of the Kyoto Protocol, international discussions started on a successor agreement to or second phase for the Protocol because its legally binding obligations only apply from 2008–12 (the so-called first commitment period).[99] Formal negotiations on a post-2012 climate change regime were then launched in 2007[100] and continue at the time of writing.

Making progress in the post-2012 climate change negotiations has been the most prominent environmental item in the policy dialogues, as exemplified by its systematic inclusion in several declarations and work plans.[101] It has also become further institutionalised through the launch of climate-specific cooperation and dialogue initiatives: this is the case of the Global Climate Change Alliance, for instance, which aims at promoting dialogue with a view to feeding into ongoing multilateral negotiations on the post-2012 international climate change regime.[102] Some institutionalised dialogues have also served to agree on specific common priorities in anticipation of multilateral environmental negotiations sessions, such as reaching agreement on the inclusion of international rules on technology development and transfer, a reformed CDM and the role of agriculture in the post-2012 international climate change regime.[103]

In the wake of the 2009 Copenhagen Climate Change Conference, the Union's efforts toward mainstreaming climate change in its external relations have been increased to respond to the perceived failure of the EU negotiating position at the multilateral level.[104] The European Parliament adopted a resolution urging the EU to include the discussion of climate policies in every strategic partnership in order

[99] Kulovesi, 'How to prevent . . .', above n 37.

[100] See generally K Kulovesi and M Gutiérrez, 'Climate Change Negotiations Update: Process and Prospects for an Agreed Outcome in Copenhagen in December 2009' (2009) 18(3) *Review of European Community and International Environmental Law* 229.

[101] Ch 5 (see, for instance, Joint Africa-EU Action Plan 2011–2013, Partnership on Climate Change and Environment).

[102] Ch 5, s 4.

[103] Ch 5, s 3.1

[104] C Egenhofer and A Georgiev, 'The Copenhagen Accord – A First Stab at Deciphering the Implications for the EU' (2009) *Centre for European Policy Studies, CEPS Commentaries*, atwww.ceps.be/book/copenhagen-accord-first-stab-deciphering-implications-eu; N Fujiwara, 'Reinvigorating the EU's Role in the post-Copenhagen Landscape' (2010) *Climate Change, CEPS Commentaries*, at www.ceps.be/book/reinvigorating-eu%E2%80%99s-role-post-copenhagen-landscape; J Curtin, *The Copenhagen Conference: How Should the EU Respond?* (Dublin, IIEA, 2010).

to create a more coherent external climate protection strategy.[105] Thus, another emerging tool for alliance-building is the insertion of specific climate change cooperation clauses to this end in bilateral/inter-regional agreements. The FTAs with South Korea and with Colombia and Peru, for instance, contain a commitment to cooperate on trade-related aspects of the *future* international climate change regime.[106] Financial and technical assistance offered by the EU also specifically targets various issues related to ongoing multilateral negotiations, such as the reform of the CDM, adaptation, low-emission development and new carbon markets, and more generally the global governance of climate change 'to be *shaped*' by the external dimensions of the Union's climate policies.[107]

In addition, EU internal legislation with extraterritorial implications, namely the 2009 Climate and Energy Package, is directly linked to the EU role in ongoing multilateral climate change negotiations. The CCS Directive, which principally aims to ensure the environmental sustainability of carbon capture and storage[108] and is part of the 2009 Climate and Energy Package, can be seen as a pioneering example of domestic legislation that the EU is keen to discuss as a source of inspiration for the further development of the international climate change framework.[109] To support its position at the multilateral level where CCS is the subject of negotiations on its inclusion in the CDM, the EU made available to developing countries capacity-building and collaborative research and development opportunities,[110] which is explicitly reflected in the CCS Directive.[111] The latter also points to the possibility of extending the network of demonstration projects in key third countries[112] – a possibility that had already been taken through the EU-China dialogue.[113]

More systematic and creative use of external relations tools may be expected as the post-2012 climate change negotiations continue. The Europe 2020 Strategy

[105] Ch 5, s 3.1 (see in particular, European Parliament Resolution of 10 February 2010 on the Outcome of the Copenhagen Conference on Climate Change [2010] OJ C341E/25, para 7).

[106] Ch 2, s 7.1.3 (in particular COPE FTA, art 63; South Korea FTA, art 13.5(3).

[107] ENRTP Strategy 2011–13, 9, 13 and 25–6 (Ch 4, s 3.2.2).

[108] CCS is 'a process consisting of the separation of carbon dioxide from industrial and energy-related sources, transport to a storage location and long-term isolation from the atmosphere' (Intergovernmental Panel on Climate Change, 'Special Report on Carbon Capture and Storage, Summary for Policy Makers' (Report of Working Group III of the Intergovernmental Panel on Climate Change, Montreal, 22–24 September 2005). The scope of the CCS Directive relates to the capture of carbon dioxide emitted during industrial processes and power generation, and the storage of the carbon dioxide in geological formations so that it cannot contribute to climate change.

[109] See EU submission to the UNFCCC Subsidiary Body for Scientific and Technological Advice, in UNFCCC, 'Views related to carbon dioxide capture and storage in geological formations as a possible mitigation technology: Submissions from Parties' (2010) UN Doc FCCC/SBSTA/2010/MISC.2, 31–42.

[110] Ibid, 41–42; see also ENRTP Strategy 2011–13, 13.

[111] Directive (EC) 2009/31 of the European Parliament and the Council on the geological storage of carbon dioxide [2009] OJ L140/114 (CCS Directive), preambular para 7, which points to technology cooperation with key countries.

[112] J Chiavari, 'The Legal Framework for Carbon Capture and Storage in the EU (Directive 2009/31/EC)' in Oberthür and Pallemaerts (eds), above n 33, 159; art 38(2) of CCS Directive on the review of the Directive where the Commission is mandated to report, among other things, on the 'prospects for geological storage of CO2 in third countries.'

[113] In the form of time-bound goals and a follow-up mechanism: see Ch 5, s 3.5.

commits the EU to continue its efforts in the multilateral climate change negotiations, increasing its outreach on the bilateral level with a view to building mutual understanding with third countries in the search for a global solution to climate change. Emphasis is placed on the proposed use of 'regulatory dialogues' with partner countries in order to promote equivalence, mutual recognition and convergence in climate change regulatory approaches and tools; and the use of 'high-level strategic dialogues' on energy and climate.[114] While this clearly indicates that the EU wishes to pursue alliance-building with regard to the development of the post-2012 international climate change regime, in case of a stall in the multilateral negotiations, the EU is likely to continue to rely on discussions at the bilateral and inter-regional level, focusing on national or sub-national legislation with a view to building consensus on future measures on climate change from the bottom up,[115] once again relying on the Union's own internal legislation as a sounding board for these discussions.

3.2 Biofuels

Another example of the EU's efforts towards alliance-building relates to current negotiations on environmental sustainability of biofuel production and use which are underway in multiple international fora such as the CBD,[116] FAO,[117] and the Roundtable on Sustainable Biofuels.[118]

Biofuels are fuels of renewable and biological origin, including woodfuel, charcoal, livestock manure, biogas, bio-hydrogen, bio-alcohol, microbial biomass, agricultural wastes and byproducts, and energy crops. They have raised concerns among the international community for their alleged negative impacts on food security and the environment (particularly in terms of deforestation), potential negative effects on indigenous and local communities and small-hold farmers, and even the alleged lack of contribution to climate change mitigation.[119] At

114 Europe 2020 Strategy, 4.

115 As described in s 4 below.

116 Biofuel production and use has been on the agenda of the CBD COP since 2008: see CBD Decision IX/2, 'Agricultural biodiversity: biofuels and biodiversity' (2008) UN Doc UNEP/CBD/COP/9/29; and CBD Decision X/37, 'Biofuels and biodiversity' (2010) UN Doc UNEP/CBD/COP/10/27.

117 FAO hosts the Global Bioenergy Partnership (GBEP), which brings together public, private and civil society stakeholders to implement the commitments taken by the G8 in the 2005 Gleneagles Plan of Action on Bioenergy. GBEP adopted in May 2011the first global, government-level consensus set of voluntary, science-based indicators for assessing the sustainable production and use of bioenergy (see GBEP press release of 24 May 2011 at www.globalbioenergy.org/fileadmin/user_upload/gbep/docs/pdf_folder/pressreview_11/GBEP_press_release_sustainability_indicators.pdf; GBEP Sustainability Indicators for Bioenergy (May 2011).

118 This is an international initiative bringing together farmers, companies, NGOs, experts, governments, and inter-governmental agencies that has developed a third-party certification system for biofuels sustainability standards (see initiative website at www2.epfl.ch/energycenter-jahia4/page65660.html).

119 CBD Subsidiary Body on Scientific, Technical and Technological Advice, 'New and emerging issues relating to the conservation and sustainable use of biodiversity: biodiversity and liquid biofuel production' (2007) UN Doc UNEP/CBD/SBSTTA/12/9. On the international debate on biofuels, see

the multilateral level, the EU has supported the development of sustainability standards for biofuel production to ensure avoidance of negative impacts on biodiversity and relevant communities.[120]

Once again, the EU's 2009 Climate and Energy Package, and specifically the Renewable Energy Directive, provides an interesting example of EU internal legislation with extraterritorial implications that is linked to the EU's bilateral external relations tools. The Directive introduces sustainability criteria for imported biofuels to protect biodiversity and ensure substantial reductions in greenhouse gas emissions. Lack of compliance with these criteria does not lead to a ban on imports or use within the EU, but rather to a series of disincentives.[121] Expressly motivated by the concern that biofuels production in third countries might not respect minimum environmental or social requirements while promoting the production of biofuels *worldwide*,[122] the Directive indicates that the EU will endeavour to conclude bilateral or multilateral agreements with third countries containing provisions on the sustainability criteria.[123] In addition, the Directive calls upon the Commission to maintain a dialogue and exchange information with third countries and biofuels producers, consumer organisations and civil society concerning the general implementation of the Directive.[124] This is particularly significant in light of the extensive monitoring tasks assigned to the Commission with regard to the impacts of the Directive on third countries, as well as third countries' performance under relevant MEAs.[125]

The Directive has already had visible impacts in the EU's bilateral external relations: dialogues between the EU and third countries or regions have provided an avenue for the discussion of respective negotiating positions on biofuels and sometimes led to commitments to hold bilateral high-level meetings in the run-up to key negotiating sessions.[126] In addition, SIAs have addressed the issue of certification for biofuels among policy recommendations, making express reference to the Renewables Directive and its criteria as guidance for third countries.[127] SIAs have therefore provided the Commission with the opportunity to discuss the applicability of EU biofuels sustainability criteria in third countries as a means to

also E Morgera, K Kulovesi and A Gobena (eds), *Case Studies on Bioenergy Policy and Law: Options for Sustainability*, FAO Legislative Study No 102 (Rome, FAO, 2010), 15–34.

[120] A Appleton et al, 'Summary of the second meeting of the *Ad hoc* Open-ended Working Group on Protected Areas and the thirteenth meeting of the Subsidiary Body on Scientific, Technical and Technological Advice of the Convention on Biological Diversity' 9(247) *Earth Negotiations Bulletin*, 8 and 16.

[121] See detailed discussion in Kulovesi et al, above n 40, 877–82.

[122] Directive (EC) 2009/28 of the European Parliament and of the Council on the promotion of the use of energy from renewable sources [2009] OJ L 140/16 (Renewables Directive), preamble para 74.

[123] Ibid, art 18(4).

[124] Ibid, art 23(2).

[125] Ibid, art 17(7), which, among other things, mandates that the Commission monitor third countries' ratifications and implementation of the Cartagena Protocol on Biosafety and CITES.

[126] Ch 5 (for instance, Third EU-Brazil Summit, 'Joint Statement' Stockholm 6 October 2009, paras 2–12).

[127] Ch 6, s 3 (eg, MERCOSUR SIA final Report, 99; Central America SIA final report, 90–91 and ASEAN Final Report, 60–61).

prevent negative environmental and social impacts arising from the EU's bilateral trade negotiations.[128]

Similarly to the case of the CCS Directive, the EU has used a combination of internal legislation and external relations tools as a basis for building alliances to influence multilateral negotiations. The Renewable Energy Directive has been systematically referred to in the EU's negotiating position under the CBD when biofuels were discussed.[129]

4. CONSENSUS BUILDING IN THE *ABSENCE* OF MULTILATERAL ENVIRONMENTAL NEGOTIATIONS

Another interesting link between EU external action tools and environmental multilateralism concerns issues on which the international community has not reached agreement as to launching multilateral negotiations for the conclusion of a binding agreement. In these instances, when the EU's position supporting the launch of multilateral negotiations was unsuccessful, the recourse to bilateral avenues for continued cooperation with willing third countries or regions can be seen as an effort to gradually build international consensus from the bottom up with a view to returning to the multilateral negotiating table at a time when a greater number of countries are interested in going ahead with the elaboration of a legally binding multilateral agreement.

One example is the reform of international environmental governance, for which no formal negotiations have started, although intergovernmental discussions are ongoing.[130] In this area, the EU has since 2005 specifically advocated the upgrading of UNEP into a UN specialised organisation.[131] Some references to cooperation on global environmental governance can be found in the context of the declarations issued through institutionalised dialogues.[132] In one (so far isolated) case, an inter-regional agreement has also addressed this issue by committing the EU and Central American countries to promoting dialogue on global environmental issues aimed at the reform of environmental governance.[133] The EU's thematic external funding

[128] Ch 6, s 3 (eg, ASEAN SIA Position Paper, 9; Central America Commission Position Paper, 4 and 6; MERCOSUR SIA Position Paper, 5).

[129] See, for instance, A Appleton, 'Summary of the fourteenth meeting of the Subsidiary Body on Scientific, Technical and Technological Advice to the Convention on Biological Diversity' (2010) 9(514) *Earth Negotiations Bulletin* 12.

[130] See the discussion on global environmental governance in the framework of the Governing Council of the UN Environment Programme at www.unep.org/ieg.

[131] E Morgera and G Marín Durán, 'The UN 2005 World Summit, the Environment and the EU: Priorities, Promises and Prospects' (2006) 15(1) *Review of European Community and International Environmental Law* 11.

[132] Ch 5, ss 3.4 (eg, Second EU-Brazil Summit, 'Joint Action Plan' Rio de Janeiro 22 December 2008, establishes a political dialogue on international environmental governance) and 3.5.

[133] Central America AA, art 20 (Ch 2, s 5.2.1).

also supports the strengthening of environmental governance and EU leadership in that context.[134]

Two more prominent cases can also be identified: one is the quest for an international legally binding agreement on sustainable forest management and, to a lesser degree, corporate environmental accountability, which are discussed in more detail below.

4.1 Sustainable forest management

Sustainable forest management has been a long-standing international concern for the EU and as such it has been addressed at the multilateral level with support for the development of a legally binding agreement on forests[135] both at the global[136] and regional level.[137] At the unilateral and bilateral level, the EU provided early and consistent external funding for the protection of tropical forests (notably, through the Tropical Forests Regulation[138] and more recent thematic and geographic funding).[139] It also addresses this issue through generic references in earlier bilateral agreements.[140]

More recently, the idea of a global approach to deforestation has been supported by a combination of EU internal legislation with extraterritorial implications and external relations tools. Notably, the EU has been very explicit in linking these efforts to its multilateral agenda. At the internal level, the EU has first developed an action plan and then enacted a series of regulations to tackle this global problem in the immediate term, in the face of limited progress at the multilateral level.[141] The EU's approach is explicitly based on global soft-law commitments,[142]

[134] ENRTP Thematic Strategy 2007–10, 19, with explicit reference to supporting the promotion of the upgrading of UNEP; ENRTP Thematic Strategy 2011–13, 25.

[135] G Reischel, 'The EU and the UN Forest Negotiations: A Case of Failed International Environmental Governance?' (Paper presented to Marie Curie European Summer School on Earth System Governance, Vrije Universiteit, Amsterdam, 24 May–6 June 2007) at www.2007amsterdamconference.org/Downloads/07SummerSchool%20-%20Reischl.pdf.

[136] The EU advocated the development of a global, legally binding instrument on forests at the United Nations Forum on Forests (eg, A Baldwin et al, 'Summary of the fifth session of the United Nations Forum on Forests' (2005) 13(133) *Earth Negotiations Bulletin* 4).

[137] During the Forest Europe Ministerial Conference, held in Oslo, Norway, from 14–16 June 2011, ministers of European countries and representatives of the EU adopted a mandate for negotiating a legally binding agreement on forests in Europe by 2013: see Oslo Ministerial Mandate for Negotiating a Legally Binding Agreement on Forests in Europe, 16 June 2011, at www.foresteurope2011.org/pop.cfm?FuseAction=Doc&pAction=View&pDocumentId=29800.

[138] Regulation 2494/2000 of the European Parliament and of the Council on measures to promote the conservation and sustainable management of tropical forests and other forests in developing countries [2000] OJ L288/6.

[139] Ch 4, ss 3.2.2 and 4.3–4.4 (eg DCI Regulation, Arts 6(e) and 7(e)).

[140] See PCAs with CIS (Ch 2, s 7.2.1; eg, Georgia PCA, art 57(2)); as well as Croatia AA, art 103; Cotonou Agreement, art 32; and South Africa AA, art 84 (Ch 2, ss 3.4, 5.2.2 and 6.3).

[141] Commission, 'Forest Law Enforcement, Governance and Trade (FLEGT): Proposal for an Action Plan' COM (2003) 251 final, 3 (FLEGT Action Plan). The FLEGT Action Plans was endorsed by the Council, 'Conclusions – Forest Law Enforcement, Governance and Trade (FLEGT)' [2003] OJ C268/1.

[142] 'Plan of Implementation of the World Summit on Sustainable Development,' above n 59.

and is made compatible with ongoing, albeit partial, multilateral efforts.[143] It clearly emphasises the ultimate aim of leading to the development of multilateral consensual measures to address deforestation by exporter and importer countries, step by step through a multilateral instrument or the linking of regional agreements.[144]

Due to the complexity and delays in setting in motion international action, the EU has thus clearly articulated its strategy for building international consensus on sustainable forest management from the bottom up. It proposes to work with willing third countries on the *legality* of trade of timber as a neutral concept, rather than the politically charged sustainable forest management that has resisted international definition thus far.[145] The specific means chosen by the EU include increased dialogue through existing institutional structures with importing and exporting countries (notably including the US and Japan), integration of FLEGT in development cooperation programming at the stage of country strategy papers, and use of external funding.[146]

To this end, the EU first enacted in 2005 the FLEGT Regulation setting a licensing scheme for imports of timber based on a bilateral agreement, called the VPA, to be concluded between the EU and third countries exporting timber. Under the VPA, the legality of timber harvests is to be checked against compliance with the national law of the third country 'as set out in the VPA'. The main incentive for third countries to participate in the FLEGT VPA process is receiving priority assistance for the upgrading of their legal and administrative framework related to forest management.[147] Significantly, this is supported by the involvement of an independent, specialised international organisation, namely FAO, which is managing a global project funded by the EU to support ACP countries in the review of their legislation and upgrading of their forest governance and law enforcement capacities.[148]

[143] Namely, timber species listed under CITES; see FLEGT Action Plan, 20. It also points to the need to advance work in the framework of the UN Security Council to define 'conflict timber' as timber traded by armed groups and the proceeds of which are used to fund armed conflict, with a view to exploring the possible set-up of an international process similar to the Kimberly Process for diamonds (ibid, 21).

[144] FLEGT Action Plan, 9 and 11.

[145] The most recent attempt to do so, the Non-Legally Binding Instrument on All Types of Forests (UN General Assembly, 'Non-Legally Binding Instrument on All Types of Forests' (2008) UN Doc A/RES/62/98) only indicates that 'sustainable forest management, as a dynamic and evolving concept, aims to maintain and enhance the economic, social and environmental values of all types of forests, for the benefit of present and future generations' (para 3) and provides seven 'thematic elements' for global monitoring: extent of forest resources, forest biodiversity, forest health and vitality, productive functions of forest resources, protective functions of forest resources, socio-economic functions of forests, legal, policy and institutional framework (ibid, para 6(b) and related footnote). See also 'Non-legally Binding Authoritative Statement of Principles for a Global Consensus on the Management, Conservation and Sustainable Development of All Types of Forests', UN Doc A/CONF.151/26 (1992) Vol. III (Rio Forest Principles), preamble para c.

[146] FLEGT Action Plan, 8–9 and 11; and also ENRTP Thematic Strategy 2011–13, 24.

[147] eg art 15 ('Supporting measures') of the VPA between the European Community and the Republic of Ghana on FLEGT in timber products into the Community [2010] OJ L70/3.

[148] FAO, 'ACP FLEGT Support Programme' at www.fao.org/forestry/acp-flegt/en. Note that while there is no formal link between the FAO FLEGT Programme and the VPAs, FAO assistance specifically targets countries depending on 'their level of interest in the FLEGT Action Plan and in negotiating a VPA' through

The EU thus put in place a specialised parallel track of bilateral negotiations with exporter countries leading to the conclusion of VPAs. VPAs are expected to include a series of common elements, namely the commitment to developing credible legal structures that are supportive of sustainable forest management practices and procedures to licence the export of legally harvested timber.[149] A cooperative approach is therefore pursued based on the forest-related legislation of the exporting country: this arguably aims to ensure the third country's ownership of the initiative, as well as demonstrate respect for its national sovereignty over its forest resources.[150] This is then coupled with an expectation that the third country review its national legal framework when it does not support *sustainable* forest management,[151] thus potentially opening the door for a bilateral dialogue on the definition of this concept using national legislation of the third country as a departure point. An annex to the VPA includes the definition of legal harvest as agreed with local stakeholders and details standards of compliance with national forest legislation, relevant cultural norms, and occupational and health safety legislation. It also outlines areas in which national legislation should be improved.[152]

In the continued 'absence or slow pace of multilateral progress',[153] however, the EU decided to strengthen this bilateral approach by enacting another regulation to prompt broader interest in VPAs in third countries. The second regulation places an obligation of due diligence on operators placing timber and timber products on the EU market to ensure the legal origin of their timber products.[154] As an incentive for countries to conclude VPAs, the regulation establishes a presumption of compliance with its due diligence requirement for timber originating from a VPA country and licensed under the FLEGT regulation.[155]

The FLEGT approach has already made visible inroads into the external relations tools, although the negotiations of VPAs remain a separate bilateral process. EU external funding for environment explicitly emphasises the implementation of the FLEGT Action Plan at the national, regional and international policy development level; as well as promoting on the ground community-based forest management, respect for local and indigenous peoples' rights over forest land,

support for national and regional FLEGT/VPA knowledge-sharing workshops, feasibility studies on VPA-related issues, and support for the creation of national multi-stakeholder committees in charge of VPA negotiations (FAO, Improving Forest Governance in Africa, the Caribbean and the Pacific (FAO, undated) 6 and 9, at http://foris.fao.org/static/data/acpflegt/4087ForestGovernance_EN.pdf.)

[149] FLEGT Action Plan, 12–13.

[150] See Rio Forest Principles, para 1a.

[151] FLEGT Action Plan, 5, where it reads: 'Since in many countries forest legislation is based on the premise of sustainable forest management, better law enforcement will in general lead to more sustainable forest management. Where this is not the case the EU should encourage a review of the legal framework.'

[152] eg Annex II of the VPA between the EU and Ghana, above n 147.

[153] Commission, 'Proposal laying down the obligations of operators who place timber and timber products on the market' COM (2008) 644/3 final, 3.

[154] Regulation (EU) 995/2010 of the European Parliament and of the Council laying down the obligations of operators who place timber and timber products on the market [2010] OJ L295/23, art 4.

[155] Ibid, art 3.

private sector investment in sustainable forest management, and design of financial instruments for forest conservation.[156] An NGO report confirmed that FLEGT is quite well reflected in the geographic external assistance programming documents, although insufficient information was provided in the CSPs on the involvement of local communities in the VPA negotiating process or the impacts of the FLEGT initiatives on legal and institutional coherence in the partner country.[157] These issues are indeed critical for the success and perceived legitimacy of the FLEGT initiative: international debates on sustainable forest management at the UN level are tightly linked with questions related to the rights of indigenous peoples[158] and other forest-dependent communities.[159]

Institutionalised dialogues have also provided further opportunities to discuss sustainable forest management.[160] In addition, through SIAs, the Commission has pointed to the mutual benefits of participating in the FLEGT initiative with regard to combating illegal logging.[161] These efforts have been incorporated in the post-Global Europe agreements concluded by the EU: an innovative clause on sustainable trade in forest products that refers to transparency and public participation, as well as independent supervision and certification can be found in the FTA with Peru and Colombia[162] and an express reference to the EU FLEGT initiative in the Association Agreement with Central American countries.[163]

The FLEGT initiative is clearly aimed at building consensus from the bottom up in the absence of international negotiations on an international treaty on sustainable forest management through a combination of EU internal legislation and external relations tools. Deforestation issues, however, are increasingly addressed in the context of the negotiations on a post-2012 climate change regime under the so-called REDD-plus item.[164] This international development may lead the EU to

[156] ENRTP Thematic Strategy 2007–10, 18; ENRTP Thematic Strategy 2011–13, 24.

[157] WWF et al, 2009, above n 52, 19.

[158] UN Permanent Forum on Indigenous Issues, 'Report of the ninth session: 19–30 April 2010' (2010) UN Doc E/2010/43-E/C.19/2010/15.

[159] UN Forum on Forests, 'Resolution on Forests for People, Livelihoods and Poverty Eradication' (adopted by the on 4 February 2011) at www.un.org/esa/forests/pdf/session_documents/unff9/Adopted%20resolution%20at%20530PM%20%204%20Feb%202011.pdf.

[160] Ch 5 (eg, EU-Japan Summit, 'Shaping Our Common Future: An Action Plan for EU-Japan Cooperation' (2001), 15–16).

[161] Ch 6, s 3 (eg, Andean SIA Position Paper, 8; ASEAN SIA Position Paper, 9 and MERCOSUR SIA Position Paper, 6).

[162] COPE FTA, art 273 (Ch 2, s 7.1.3).

[163] Central America AA, art 289 (Ch 2, s 5.3.2).

[164] REDD-plus means 'reducing emissions from deforestation and forest degradation, conservation of forest-carbon stocks, sustainable management of forests, and enhancement of forest-carbon stocks.' This item was first officially incorporated in the agenda of the multilateral climate change negotiations in 2007 (UNFCCC COP, Decision 1/CP.13 'Bali Action Plan' (2008) UN Doc FCCC/CP/2007/6/Add.1, para 1(b)(iii); and UNFCCC COP Decision 2/CP.13, 'Reducing emissions from deforestation in developing countries: approaches to stimulate action' (2008) UN doc FCCC/CP/2007/6/Add.1, para 3, and more recently UNFCCC COP Decision 1/CP.16, 'Outcome of the work of the Ad Hoc Working Group on long-term Cooperative Action under the Convention' (2011) UN Doc FCCC/CP/2010/7/Add.1, at s III.C Policy approaches and positive incentives on issues relating to reducing emissions from deforestation and forest degradation in developing countries; and the role of conservation, sustainable management of forests and enhancement of forest carbon stocks in developing countries, and Annexes

use its external relations to influence those ongoing negotiations as part of its broader agenda on the post-2012 international climate change regime discussed above.[165] The Commission has already stressed the link between FLEGT and ongoing international negotiations for a post-2012 international climate change regime[166] and included references to REDD in recent bilateral agreements[167] and in its 2011–13 strategy for environment thematic funding.[168] Given that sustainable forest management and REDD-plus face similar questions related to participatory approaches to forestry and the role of forest-dependent communities, the EU is already considering using agreement on key concepts related to forest governance emerging from its FLEGT activities, as well as the lessons learnt in the multi-stakeholder processes leading to the conclusion of VPAs, to provide inputs into multilateral negotiations on REDD-plus.[169] This is particularly significant as it has proven particularly complex to ensure mutual supportiveness between climate change mitigation objectives, on the one hand, and biodiversity conservation and respect for the human rights of forest-dwelling communities on the other hand[170] in the multilateral negotiations on REDD-plus. NGOs seem ready to support such a course of action.[171] Should an international agreement on REDD-plus be fully developed and operationalised in the context of the climate change regime, the EU bilateral cooperation would then be likely to shift from consensus-building towards supporting the implementation of the new multilateral scheme in developing countries.[172]

I-II. For a discussion of legal issues related to REDD-plus, see H van Asselt, 'Managing the Fragmentation of International Environmental Law: Forests at the Intersection of the Climate and Biodiversity Regime' (forthcoming) *NYU Journal of International Law and Politics*; A Savaresi, 'Reducing Emissions from Deforestation in Developing Countries under the UNFCCC. Caveats and Opportunities for Biodiversity' (forthcoming) 21 *Yearbook of International Environmental Law*.

[165] See s 3.1 above.

[166] Commission, 'Proposal laying down the obligations of operators who place timber and timber products on the market', above n 153, 5.

[167] Ch 2 (Central America AA, art 20; COPE FTA, art 286; Cotonou Agreement-2010 revision, art 32bis).

[168] ENRTP Thematic Strategy 2011–13, 21–22.

[169] Ibid. For a more detailed discussion, see A Savaresi, 'The EU External Action on Forests: FLEGT and the Development of International Law' in E Morgera (ed), *The External Environmental Policy of the European Union; EU and International Law Perspectives* (Cambridge, Cambridge University Press, forthcoming 2012).

[170] This relates to the international debate on the so-called 'safeguards' for REDD-plus concerning biodiversity and forest-dependent communities. Council, 'Conclusions on the Nagoya Conference', above n 88, where Member States and the Commission are invited to 'actively contribute to the preparation of advice on the application of relevant safeguards for biodiversity in relation to REDD+, in line with the (CBD) COP 10 decision, and facilitate the development and implementation of such safeguards under REDD+.' This is already the case for the EU-Africa partnership (see Ch 5, s 3.2; Third EU-Africa Summit,'Joint Africa-EU Strategy Action Plan (2011–2013)' Tripoli 30 November 2010, 51–53).

[171] I Leal Riesco and K Opoku, 'Is REDD Undermining FLEGT?' (FERN Briefing Note 05, March 2009), the authors argue that the participatory process leading to the conclusions of VPAs can be undermined by parallel REDD pilot projects.

[172] Above s 2.

4.2 Corporate environmental accountability

As opposed to the steady support for a legally binding agreement on sustainable forest management, EU external and internal action on corporate environmental accountability[173] has been through different phases due to both the uncertain fate of multilateral efforts in this area and also changes in direction of EU policies. In parallel, integration of corporate environmental accountability in EU external relations has been subject to an evolution.

Multilateral discussions on the environmental responsibility of multinational corporations and other business entities in light of international standards have been ongoing, on and off, since the 1970s, particularly in the context of the United Nations.[174] As early as in 1999 the European Parliament called on the Commission and the Council to develop a legal basis for establishing a European multilateral framework governing companies operating worldwide.[175] EU 'domestic' regulation, however, was not enacted to that end, although, at the multilateral level, the EU presented itself as a global leader on corporate accountability issues.[176]

The EU thus appears more willing to address these issues externally than internally, as it successfully included corporate accountability clauses in a few of its earlier agreements: notably, clauses on industrial cooperation have made reference to the objective of strengthening the private sector under conditions which ensure that the environment is protected.[177] In addition, the EU has inserted clauses related to corporate accountability in the context of foreign direct investment. A joint declaration to the Association Agreement with Chile remains unique in calling upon parties to remind their enterprises to observe the OECD Guidelines for Multinational Enterprises[178] – the first intergovernmentally agreed set of corporate accountability standards.[179] No similar commitment was, however, to be found in the EU's thematic external funding, although funding for compliance with environmental standards for products and production processes made reference to eco-labelling, which is one of the voluntary tools preferred by the EU to advance the CSR agenda.[180] The new emphasis on the green economy in

[173] This term has been introduced in Ch 6, s 3 (n 112).

[174] E Morgera, *Corporate Accountability in International Environmental Law* (Oxford, Oxford University Press, 2009).

[175] European Parliament, Resolution on EU standards for European enterprises operating in developing countries: towards a European code of conduct' (A4-0508/98) [1999] OJ C104/180, particularly para 23, as discussed in D Augenstein et al, 'Study of the Legal Framework on Human Rights and the Environment Applicable to European Union Companies Operating Outside the EU' (Edinburgh, University of Edinburgh, 2010), para 12.

[176] A Gatto, 'Corporate Social Responsibility in the External Relations of the EU' (2005) 24 *Yearbook of European Law* 423, 436.

[177] Ch 2, ss 3.5, 5.2.3 and 6.4 (eg, Albania AA, art 92; Central America AA, art 64(1); South Africa AA, art 51(b)).

[178] Cited in Ch 2, s 6.4; OECD, *The OECD Guidelines for Multinational Enterprises: Text, Commentary and Clarifications*, OECD Doc DAFFE/IME/WPG(2000)15/FINAL (2001) (*OECD Guidelines*).

[179] Morgera, *Corporate Accountability*, above n 174, ch 5.

[180] ENRTP Thematic Strategy 2007–10, 17–18.

EU thematic funding may contribute in the near future to integrating corporate environmental accountability in the Union's external assistance.[181]

A change in the EU's position on this issue can, however, be detected following progress at the multilateral level, namely intergovernmental support for a UN Framework for Business and Human Rights[182] which was also supported by the EU Foreign Affairs Council.[183] The Danish and Spanish Presidencies affirmed that the UN Framework 'provides a key element for the global development of CSR practices' and 'constitutes a significant input to the corporate social responsibility work of the European Union'.[184]

This evolution in the EU's position at the multilateral level is also reflected in its external relations. The post-Global Europe bilateral agreements have more markedly included a corporate environmental accountability dimension by linking it with technical assistance[185] and trade cooperation.[186] The FTA with South Korea, in particular, includes clauses to facilitate trade and investment in environmental goods and services, including environmental technologies, sustainable renewable energy, energy efficiency, and eco-labelled products.[187] The most notable case, however, is the CARIFORUM EPA, whereby States are duty-bound to control the environmental impacts of corporate foreign investment, prevent corruption in the natural resource sector, avoid circumvention of international environmental obligations, and ensure liaison with communities in projects involving extensive natural resource-based activities 'in so far as they do not nullify or impair the benefits accruing to the other party'.[188] Policy dialogues, in turn, have effectively called attention to opportunities for cooperation on corporate environmental accountability, particularly with regard to the transition to a low-carbon economy.[189]

SIAs have clearly demonstrated the evolution of the EU approach to tackling corporate accountability abroad. In earlier ones, the Commission proposed encouraging the use of voluntary instruments, such as eco-labelling, eco-management and green procurement.[190] In parallel, recent amendments to EU legislation on eco-labelling and eco-management have emphasised the external dimension of these initiatives. The EU voluntary eco-label award scheme was

181 ENRTP Thematic Strategy 2011–13, 24–25.

182 J Ruggie, 'Report of the Special Representative of the Secretary-General on the issue of Human Rights and Transnational Corporations and Other Business Enterprises: Protect, Respect and Remedy: A Framework for Business and Human Rights' (2008) UN Doc A/HRC/8/35. Endorsed by the Human Rights Council, Resolution 8/7 'Mandate of the Special Representative of the Secretary-General on the issue of human rights and transnational corporations and other business enterprises'(2008) UN Doc A/HRC/8/52.

183 Council, 'Conclusions on Human Rights and Democratisation in third countries' 8 December 2009.

184 Swedish and Spanish Presidencies Declaration, 'Protect, Respect, Remedy – Making the European Union take a lead in promoting Corporate Social Responsibility' (November 2009) at www.se2009.eu/polopoly_fs/1.23024!menu/standard/file/Deklaration%20engelska.pdf.

185 Central America AA, art 63 (Ch 2, s 5.3.2).

186 Central America AA, art 288; COPE FTA, art 271 (Ch 2, ss 5.3.2 and 7.1.3).

187 South Korea FTA, art 13(6); see comments in Augenstein et al, above n 175, para 116.

188 EU-CARIFORUM EPA, art 72; see comments in Augenstein et al, above n 175, para 116.

189 Ch 5 (eg, Lima Declaration, above n 98, paras 38–40).

190 Ch 6, s 3 (eg, India SIA Position Paper, 10; and Ukraine SIA Position Paper, 16).

revised in late-2009. It aims to promote products with a reduced environmental impact during their entire life cycle and to provide consumers with accurate, non-deceptive, science-based information on the environmental impacts of products by allowing the placing of a logo on products that meet the standards of the scheme. The revised regulation allows EU Member States' control over business activities carried out outside the EU by entities that voluntarily join the scheme, as it is applicable to imported goods.[191] The EMAS (Environmental Management and Audit System) Regulation was also revised along similar lines. This, in turn, aims to encourage continuous improvement of the environmental management of organisations voluntarily participating in the scheme (irrespective of their public or private ownership, legal form or profit-making purposes) by allowing their registration and use of the EMAS logo for communication and advertising purposes. Similarly to the Eco-label Regulation, the EMAS Regulation allows Member States' extraterritorial control by referring to 'indirect' environmental impacts, such as environmental issues that can result from the interaction of an organisation with third parties and which can be influenced by an organisation to a reasonable degree (including the environmental performance and practice of contractors, subcontractors and suppliers in third countries, if they can be influenced to a reasonable degree by the organisation). In addition, Member States 'may' provide competent bodies with responsibility for registration of organisations located outside the EU.[192] Given the difficulty for Member States to interact and monitor companies located outside of the EU, one may conjecture that policy dialogue and the Union's external assistance may be used to this end. While it is too early to assess whether and how the extraterritorial dimensions of the two regulations will play out in the EU's bilateral external relations, it can be anticipated that the EU will explore, in the context of bilateral agreements or dialogues, how to increase the participation in EMAS and eco-labelling schemes by companies operating outside the EU.[193]

Beyond EMAS and eco-labelling, further evolution can be expected in the use of EU external action tools in relation to corporate environmental accountability: in 2010, for instance, the Commission made a bolder statement about the possibility of reporting on EU companies' compliance with initiatives for promoting corporate environmental accountability in the mining, oil and gas sectors and promoting the adoption of criteria for EU companies investing in third countries.[194]

[191] Regulation (EC) 66/2010 of the European Parliament and of the Council on the EU Eco-label, [2010] OJ L27/1, arts 2, 3(2), 6(3)(e) and 9(c).

[192] Regulation (EC)1221/2009 of the European Parliament and of the Council on the voluntary participation by organisations in a Community eco-management and audit scheme [2009] OJ L342/1, arts 2(7) and 11(1), and Annex I, paras 2(v) and 2(b)(vii).

[193] E Morgera, 'Expert Report Corporate Responsibility to Respect Human Rights in the Environmental Sphere' (May 2010), 10–13, at www.law.ed.ac.uk/euenterpriseslf/documents/files/CSREnvironment.pdf.

[194] Ch 6, s 3 (Andean SIA Position Paper, 7 and 9).

5. ASSESSMENT AND CONCLUSIONS

This chapter has looked at the EU's attempts to support and influence multilateral legal developments through its unilateral, bilateral and inter-regional external relations tools, *as well as* through its internal legislation with extraterritorial implications. Inwardly, this complex interaction is increasingly reflected in the drafting of EU internal legislation, which refers to, or reflects the Union's multilateral negotiating positions,[195] as well as its external relations tools. Outwardly, the EU relies more and more on its own legislation as well as on its external action tools in the context of its interventions in multilateral fora.

Against this proactive approach to environmental multilateralism, it should be emphasised that the EU's efforts in using its external relations tools to that end have so far been exerted in an ad hoc fashion. In backing the implementation of existing MEAs in third countries, the EU has moved from a generic reference to global environmental issues to more precise formulations related to a clear commitment to support a uniform list of key MEAs in the trade and sustainable development chapter of certain post-Global Europe agreements largely corresponding to that found in the GSP-plus. This approach seems the more promising for ensuring coherence. In addition, qualms related to the undue pressure put on third countries to ratify and implement specific MEAs through the EU external relations tools[196] could be pacified by comparing the key MEAs supported by the EU with those periodically singled out by the UN General Assembly in its consensus resolutions[197] or in the consensus outcome of the 2002 World Summit on Sustainable Development.[198] While there is significant overlap between the EU's preferred MEAs and those singled out by the international community,[199] however, there is still no perfect matching – as highlighted in the table below.

[195] See also H Vedder, 'Diplomacy by Directive: an analysis of the international context of the emissions trading directive' (2009) *SSRN Working Paper* No 1477371 at www.papers.ssrn.com/sol3/papers.cfm?abstract_id=1477371.

[196] Chaytor, above n 11, 8; S Switzer, 'Environmental Protection and the Generalized System of Preferences: A Legal and Appropriate Linkage?' (2008) 57(1) *International and Comparative Law Quarterly* 113, 141.

[197] See for instance UNGA, 'Report of the Governing Council of the United Nations Environment Programme on its Eleventh Special Session' (2010) UN Doc A/RES/65/162, para 3.

[198] See MC Cordonier-Segger and K Ahsfaq, *Sustainable Development Law. Principles, Practices and Prospects* (Oxford, Oxford University Press, 2004), 32–36, Tables 2.2 and 2.3.

[199] Particularly when compared with the closed list of MEAs included in recent bilateral trade agreements concluded by the US with developing countries: see, for instance, US-Peru Free Trade Agreement, signed on 12 April 2006, Annex 18.2, at www.ustr.gov/trade-agreements/free-trade-agreements/peru-tpa/final-text, which includes: CITES, the Ramsar Convention, and the Montreal Protocol among those singled out in the WSSD Plan of Implementation. For a discussion of the US-EU Free Trade Agreement and its relations to MEAs, see S Jinnah, 'Strategic Linkages: The Evolving Role of Trade Agreements in Global Environmental Governance' (2011) 20(2) *Journal of Environment and Development* 191.

Table 6. *MEAs and EU environmental priorities*

	EU trade measures[200]		**EU aid measures**[201]	
MEAs listed in the WSSD Plan of Implementation	**Post-Global Europe agreements (trade and sustainable development chapters)**	**GSP+**	**Thematic funding (ENRTP)**	**Geographic funding (EDF)**
UNCCD				
Basel Convention				
Rotterdam Convention				
POPs Convention				
CITES				
CBD				
Biosafety Protocol				
Ramsar Convention				
UNFCCC				
Kyoto Protocol				
Vienna Convention				
Montreal Protocol				
ITPGR				
UNCLOS and related agreements	[Note Central America AA, art 290]			

A justification of the selection of MEAs made by the EU would certainly help to increase the credibility and transparency of the EU support for environmental multilateralism through its external relations at the unilateral, bilateral and inter-regional level. In that respect, the clear articulation of the Union's approach and its links with ongoing international discussions, as in the case of the FLEGT initiative, could be replicated in other key areas of external environmental action.

With regard to building alliances and coordinating positions in multilateral fora through external relations tools, it should be stressed that the complex and time-consuming nature of the EU internal coordination over negotiating positions in multilateral fora may undermine such an aim: the EU's multilateral position presented to third countries at the bilateral or inter-regional level is 'already relatively final' due to the fact that it is the result of lengthy intra-EU

[200] Based on Ch 2, ss 5.3.2 and 7.1.3 and Ch 3, s .4.2.

[201] Based on Ch 4, ss 3 and 4.4.

negotiations and it cannot therefore really be affected by the outcome of dialogues.[202] Nonetheless, the importance of these bilateral exchanges should not be underestimated as an exercise to build trust in the EU as a fair and collaborative global negotiator and to further understanding of the EU complex policies and instruments. This is particularly the case when EU internal legislation (and its market power) are used to achieve certain extraterritorial effects and influence multilateral negotiations, in an effort that combines 'structural leadership' and 'contingent unilateralism'.[203] Cooperation with third countries on their legislation may present another avenue to draw respective negotiating positions closer at the multilateral level. This strategy, however, needs to build on actual regulatory 'success stories' at the EU level, fully taking into account the 'implementation gap' in environmental protection within the Union's borders, which affects the credibility of the EU's efforts abroad.[204]

With regard to the EU's attempt to build international consensus from the bottom up on 'multilaterally intractable' environmental issues, the importance of a truly cooperative approach cannot be underestimated. In particular, the EU's attitude in offering its own regulatory experimentations as 'useful models' to assist third countries in transitioning to the green economy and expanding trade opportunities[205] needs to be accompanied by a commitment to testing and fine-tuning the EU's positions in partnership with third countries or regions, rather than just attempting to 'sell' them on a take-it-or-leave-it basis to partners.[206] This would be necessary to ensure broad-based ownership of ideas that can then be brought back to the multilateral negotiating table. The genuine character of the EU's support for environmental multilateralism should also be openly discussed with third countries and stakeholders to effectively respond to criticism of the EU's underlying agenda of protecting competitive interests and preventing WTO challenges by exporting EU regulation[207] or of ensuring access to raw materials in third countries.[208] While to some extent the competing agendas of environmental

[202] P Leino, 'The Journey Towards all that is Good and Beautiful: Human Rights and "Common Values" as Guiding Principles of EU Foreign Relations Law' in M Cremona and B de Witte (eds), *EU Foreign Relations Law* (Oxford, Hart, 2008), 279.

[203] J Scott, 'The Multi-level Governance of Climate Change' (2011) 4(1) *Carbon and Climate Law Review* 25, 28 and 32.

[204] Generally on the implementation gap, see M Lee, *EU Environmental Law: Challenges, Change and Decision-making* (Oxford, Hart, 2005), ch 3; J Jans and H Vedder, *European Environmental Law* 3rd edn (Groningen, Europa Law, 2008), ch 4.

[205] ENRTP Strategy 2011–13, 11 and 24–25.

[206] Scott, above n 203, 33, seems to reach the same conclusion, stressing the usefulness of dialogue with third countries for the EU itself to learn about the most appropriate solutions to global environmental challenges, as well as the relevance of general principles of EU law such as 'reasons giving, proportionality and non-discrimination' in these efforts.

[207] RD Kelemen, 'Globalizing European Union Environmental Policy' (Princeton Annual Workshop on European Integration, Princeton, New Jersey, 1 May 2009) at www.princeton.edu/~smeunier/Kelemen.doc.

[208] R Hall, 'Undercutting Africa: Why EPAs Threaten the World's Forests and Forest Peoples' (2009) 8(1) *Trade Negotiations Insights* at www.ictsd.org/i/news/tni/39374/; and response by P Thompson (DG Trade), 'EPAs and Natural Resources: The European Sustainability Agenda' (2009) 8(4) *Trade Negotiations Insights* at www.ictsd.org/i/news/tni/45717.

sustainability and economic development are an inevitable characteristic of the EU and its external relations (and of any other bilateral partner), innovative approaches can be adopted more systematically to strengthen the environmental side of the equation. Channelling the Union's external funding and assistance through UN agencies, as in the above-mentioned cases of the MEA project run by UNEP or the FLEGT programme run by the FAO, and generally involving competent UN bodies across the board of external relations tools, appears the most promising avenue in that regard.[209]

Overall, it may be difficult to assess the EU's success in supporting environmental multilateralism. Several other elements play out in the successful conclusion or launch of multilateral negotiations that are clearly beyond the reach of the EU. Nevertheless, increased coherence in these efforts as a bilateral partner and as a multilateral negotiator would contribute to the Union's effectiveness and perceived legitimacy.[210] Some key substantive areas may contribute to increase such coherence, namely climate change and green growth.

The priority attached to climate change may contribute to address several global environmental threats more coherently, as long as it is pursued in full respect of the internal dimension of the environmental integration requirement so as to ensure a holistic approach avoiding negative impacts and pursuing positive synergies with other areas of environmental cooperation. The 2011–13 action plan 'Partnership on Climate Change and Environment' between the EU and Africa, for instance, shows the potential of climate change to act as a catalyst for coherence, by seeking to tackle at the same time climate change, biodiversity conservation and the fight against deforestation.[211]

The focus on green growth (one of the three pillars of the Europe 2020 Strategy that is tightly linked with the EU strategy on climate change)[212] may also contribute to step up the EU's inclusion of corporate accountability across a broad range of environmental issues tackled in its external relations. The Commission has already pointed to the need to address corporate environmental accountability by reference to the UN Global Compact,[213] the OECD Guidelines for Multinational Enterprises, sectoral arrangements under FLEGT and Fisheries Partnership

[209] The importance of involving relevant international organisations in bilateral external relations has been stressed by T Greven, A Leopold and E Molinari, 'An Analysis of the Relative Effectiveness of Social and Environmental Norms in Free Trade Agreements' (2009 Study, European Parliament), 27.

[210] For a more in-depth discussion of legitimacy in EU external environmental action, see E Morgera, 'Ambition, complexity and legitimacy of pursuing mutual supportiveness through the EU's external environmental action' in B Van Vooren, S Blockmans and J Wouters (eds), *The Legal Dimension of Global Governance: What Role for the EU?* (Oxford, Oxford University Press, forthcoming 2012).

[211] www.europafrica.files.wordpress.com/2008/07/second-final.pdf (Ch 5, s 3.2).

[212] Europe 2020 Strategy, 6 and 21–22.

[213] The Global Compact is a partnership-based global initiative on corporate accountability spearheaded by the UN Secretary General. The website of the Global Compact can be found at www.unglobalcompact.org/. United Nations, *Guide to the Global Compact: A Practical Understanding of the Vision and the Nine Principles*, 58, at http://b2b.psa-peugeot-citroen.com/fileadmin/aides/espagnol/gcguide.pdf. For a discussion, see Morgera, *Corporate Accountability*, above n 174, ch 5.

Agreements,[214] and in chemicals management.[215] This may further contribute to environmental multilateralism by feeding into parallel international discussions on the 'green economy' in the lead up to the Rio+20 Conference.[216]

[214] Commission, 'Green Paper – EU development policy in support of inclusive growth and sustainable development', above n 56, 13–14.

[215] ENRTP Strategy 2011–13, 24–25.

[216] Green growth as an impulse for certification of sustainable natural resource management is also envisaged as a new element that will increasingly be incorporated in future regional trade agreements: see C George, 'Regional Trade Agreements and the Environment: Monitoring Implementation and Assessing Impacts: Report on the OECD Workshop' (2011) *OECD Trade and Environment Working Papers 2011/02*, 17.

Conclusions

OUR ANALYSIS HAS shown that the EU political institutions have proactively responded to the environmental integration requirement stipulated in Article 11 TFEU, which has had a palpable influence on the definition and implementation of the Union's external relations through a series of legal, quasi-legal and institutional initiatives. While the practice is significant and has intensified over the years, it is by no means uniform. Differentiation exists in relation to: the relative degree of attention paid to environmental protection within the broader relationship between the EU and the third country or region concerned; the choice of standards and modalities for environmental cooperation; and the institutional mechanisms underlying such cooperation. Such a differentiated approach comes as no surprise and is, to some extent, unavoidable as it responds to both the demands of foreign policy-making and the exigencies of environmental protection. From an environmental perspective, differentiation can be reflective of the different environmental and sustainable development needs and local conditions of the EU partners involved, which vary widely from industrialised countries (such as the United States and Japan) to emerging economies (such as Chile and South Korea) and least developed countries (such as most ACP States). From a *realpolitik* perspective, differentiation is the product of the broader political and economic relations that the EU has with each country or region, and is also likely to reflect the EU's own environmental priorities and other interests towards that particular country or region.

Lack of uniform practice is not, however, necessarily to be equated with lack of coherence – understood not only as lack of contradiction but also more positively as complementarity or synergies between norms, instruments and institutional mechanisms (that is, horizontal coherence).[1] The existence or lack of horizontal coherence in EU external initiatives on environmental integration thus needs to be carefully assessed on a case-by-case basis, and is ultimately the result of political choices. Neither the Treaty provisions underpinning the EU's external action, nor Article 11 TFEU itself, establish a clear hierarchy among the environmental and other objectives that the EU is to advance in its external relations, but entrust the EU political institutions with making an integrated and balanced assessment of all these objectives in the decision-making process. In doing so, the EU political institutions are called upon to ensure coherence among broadly drafted (and at times conflicting) objectives that in practice may lead to inconsistent external

[1] On this dimension of coherence, see M Cremona, 'Coherence and EU External Policy' in E Morgera (ed), *The External Environmental Policy of the European Union: EU and International Law Perspectives* (Cambridge, Cambridge University Press, forthcoming 2012).

action once brought to a more specific level.[2] This absence of a clear priority rule among environmental and other objectives is reflected to some extent in the instruments that define and implement EU relations with third countries or regions, most notably the bilateral and inter-regional agreements whose open-ended environmental cooperation clauses equally leave the balancing exercise to be undertaken by the joint institutions thereby established. Similarly, a lack of objective-based priority rule is seen in the context of EU unilateral external measures, such as the GSP-plus and EU funding instruments, where environmental concerns are set to be promoted as a cross-cutting issue alongside other external policy objectives, and the responsibility for ensuring coherence in this context falls largely on the EU.

As we have seen, an array of instruments has been put in place and gradually refined over the years by the EU, unilaterally or together with its partners, showing a clear potential to operationalise Article 11 TFEU. In practice, however, we noticed instances in which these tools could be used in a more coherent and effective manner. For instance, in the context of bilateral/inter-regional agreements, environmental protection requirements have generally been integrated through a cooperative approach, but this has not been backed up, in all cases, by targeted institutional mechanisms to monitor and follow-up on the implementation of broadly-framed environmental commitments. It is only within the more recent post-Global Europe agreements that joint institutions have been established with a clear responsibility for these monitoring and follow-up tasks, coupled with increased opportunities for public participation. Such institutional innovations, however, have gone hand in hand with the introduction in these agreements of a trade and sustainable development chapter (tackling various dimensions of the trade and environment nexus), and it remains uncertain how they will operate in practice and affect other (non-trade-related) areas of environmental cooperation. Similarly, the full potential of prior assessments (that is, SIAs for agreements and SEAs/EIAs for funding) has not yet been fully realised in supporting a more systematic and transparent balancing between environmental and other objectives of the EU's external policies. In addition, the full spectrum of EU external relations tools have only been utilised in the context of the Union's relations with developing countries, while environmental cooperation with more advanced countries has thus far been limited to exchanges on regulatory issues without being formalised by a more comprehensive agreement, albeit some steps are being made in this direction with countries like Canada and China. With regard to institutionalised dialogues, it remains unclear whether these are seen by the EU as a constructive venue for mutual understanding and the joint definition of common environmental priorities with its partners, or mostly used to have the Union's own environmental priorities and approaches understood and accepted by its partners.

Environmental integration into the EU's external relations needs not only to be coherent, but also to be perceived as legitimate by all stakeholders involved.

[2] Ibid.

Ultimately, the international legitimacy of any such EU initiative beyond multilateral environmental processes will still be assessed against internationally recognised standards and approaches. This is all the more critical when the EU seeks to achieve environmental protection goals through unilateral tools, which do not enjoy the consent of the third party affected, and even more so when the use of such tools for environmental purposes lacks international consensus. In other words, while financial and technical assistance are explicitly recognised in MEAs as appropriate, and indeed necessary, unilateral tools to support implementation by developing countries, the use of unilateral trade measures for this purpose remains controversial, even if adopted within the framework of a bilateral/inter-regional trade agreement. In this regard, we have noticed a shift across all instruments towards an increasing reliance by the EU on international environmental standards, above all in relation to climate change but also biodiversity and chemicals. Furthermore, as far as the controversial trade and environment nexus is concerned, an approach based on mutual supportiveness and trade incentives, rather than trade sanctions, has generally been favoured in the GSP and the post-Global Europe agreements. The more systematic reliance on international environmental standards has also been accompanied by an anchoring of the EU's own decision-making processes upon the assessments and expertise of competent international organisations, most notably in the context of the GSP-plus and sustainability impact assessments. In a similar vein, post-Global Europe agreements have opened the door to the input of relevant international organisations through the innovative institutional provisions of their trade and sustainable development chapters.

However, and importantly, such growing global focus of EU environmental integration initiatives at unilateral, bilateral and inter-regional levels is not only motivated by a quest for international legitimacy, but also by a desire to see environmental multilateralism (both norms and governance structures) 'shaped' by the Union's own environmental interests and approaches. A glaring example at the cross-roads of climate change and biodiversity are the EU's sustainability criteria for biofuels, which are unilaterally set by the EU in the Renewables Directive, and which the EU seeks to have accepted by third countries at the bilateral/inter-regional level as a means to build support for these criteria within ongoing multilateral negotiations. Even in the absence of multilateral negotiations, the EU tries to influence the development of international environmental norms by gradually building consensus on its agenda at the bilateral level – the most notable example being in the area of sustainable forest management with the negotiation of specialised bilateral agreements under the EU FLEGT Initiative.

Besides relying more systematically on international standards and processes, another key element for legitimising environmental integration in the EU's external relations is internal accountability, which has only been addressed marginally in this book. As we have seen, the environmental integration requirement is very unlikely to be enforced by the Court, but it is still subject to other accountability mechanisms. First of all, it is the object of scrutiny by the European Parliament, which enjoys a power to co-decide with the Council over most instruments of the EU's external assistance, and following the Lisbon Treaty, also has increased control over the EU's external trade policy, including the conclusion of bilateral/inter-regional agreements.[3] Second, as we have also seen, environmental integration in the specific area of EU external assistance has come under the scrutiny of the European Court of Auditors. Third, the European Ombudsman may provide an avenue for individuals and NGOs to raise environmental integration failures in certain aspects of the EU's external relations as instances of maladministration.[4] This concept has been interpreted quite extensively, and could include departures by the Commission from its own guidelines on stakeholder consultations and SIAs.[5]

A final but critical point to be made on environmental integration in the EU's external relations is the credibility of the Union's actions in the eyes of third parties. In this respect, there is a certain dichotomy in the perceptions of the EU as an international actor, in the environmental and other fields. Certainly, the EU has generated high expectations abroad, as a single legal entity representing 27 countries, which has set for itself ambitious environmental and other objectives for its external action and can count on tremendous political and economic weight to achieve them. At the same time, the EU needs to be able to manage these expectations as well as its complexity as a global partner, including by ensuring coordination of positions with its Member States on the international scene – the vertical dimension of coherence that has not been addressed in this book. Finally, the credibility of the EU's environmental integration actions – at and beyond the multilateral level – rests on the Union's own environmental performance and that of its Member States.

[3] R Passos, 'Mixed Agreements from the Perspective of the European Parliament', in C Hillion and P Koutrakos (eds), *Mixed Agreements Revisited* (Oxford, Hart, 2010), 270 observes that 'for the Union external policy to be legitimate, democratic control by the European Parliament is required.'

[4] This avenue is limited to EU citizens and any natural or legal person residing or having its registered office in a Member State (art 228 TFEU and European Charter, art 44).

[5] The argument has been put forward by A Alemanno, 'The Better Regulation Initiative at the Judicial Gate: A Trojan Horse within the Commission's Walls or the Way Forward?' (2009) 15(3) *European Law Journal* 381, 388 (albeit in an internal context).

Bibliography

Abass, A, 'The Cotonou Regime and WTO Law' (2004) 10(4) *European Law Journal* 439.

Abi-Saab, G, 'Le Droit au Dévelopment' (1988) XLIV *Annuaire Suisse de Droit International* 9.

Ackerman, F, Stanton, EA, Roach, B, and Andersson A-S, 'Implications of REACH for Developing Countries' (2008) 18(1) *European Environment* 16.

Adelle, C, Hertin, J, and Jordan, A, 'Sustainable Development "Outside" the European Union: What Role for Impact Assessment' (2006) 16(2) *European Environment* 57.

Aguilar, S, 'Outcomes of the Cancún Conference' (2011) 41(1) *Environmental Policy and Law* 10.

Alecu de Flers, N, and Regelsberger, E, 'The EU and Inter-regional Cooperation' in C Hill and M Smith, *International Relations and the European Union* (Oxford, Oxford University Press, 2005).

Alemanno, A, 'The Better Regulation Initiative at the Judicial Gate: A Trojan Horse within the Commission's Walls or the Way Forward?' (2009) 15(3) *European Law Journal* 381.

Alston, P, and Robinson, M (eds), *Human Rights and Development: Towards Mutual Reinforcement* (Oxford, Oxford University Press, 2005).

Alvarenga, K, Hajjar, R, Morgera, E, Schabus, N, Tsioumani, E and Zandaryaa, S, 'Summary of the eighth Conference of the Parties to the Convention on Biological Diversity' (2006) 9(363) *Earth Negotiations Bulletin*.

Apea, Y, and Shaffer, G, 'Institutional Choice in the GSP Case: Who Decides the Conditions for Trade Preferences? The Law and Politics of Rights' (2005) 39(6) *Journal of World Trade* 977.

Appleton, A, Chiarolla, C, Johnson, T, Jonas, H, Jungcurt, S, and Moreau, MA, 'Summary of the second meeting of the *Ad hoc* Open-ended Working Group on Protected Areas and the thirteenth meeting of the Subsidiary Body on Scientific, Technical and Technological Advice of the Convention on Biological Diversity' 9(247) *Earth Negotiations Bulletin*.

Appleton, A, Gnann, J, Morgera, E, Roemer-Mahler, A, and Rosen, T, 'Summary of the fourteenth meeting of the Subsidiary Body on Scientific, Technical and Technological Advice to the Convention on Biological Diversity' (2010) 9(514) *Earth Negotiations Bulletin*.

Arts, K, and Dickson, AK (eds), *EU Development Cooperation. From Model to Symbol?* (Manchester, Manchester University Press, 2004).

Ashton, M, Cheng, Q, Kantai, T, Kohler, PM, and Templeton, J, 'Summary of the fifth meeting of the Conference of the Parties to the Stockholm Convention on Persistent Organic Pollutants' (2011) 15(182) *Earth Negotiations Bulletin*.

Augenstein, D, Boyle, A, Cabrelli, D, Harrison, J, Singh Ghaleigh, N, and Morgera, E, 'Study of the Legal Framework on Human Rights and the Environment Applicable to European Union Companies Operating Outside the EU' (Report, Edinburgh, University of Edinburgh, 2010).

Ayers, J, Huq, S, and Chandani, A, 'Assessing EU Assistance for Adaptation to Climate Change in Developing Countries: a Southern Perspective' in S Oberthür and M Pallemaerts (eds), *The New Climate Policies of the European Union: Internal Legislation and Climate Diplomacy* (Brussels, VUB Press, 2010).

Babarinde, OA, *The Lomé Conventions and Development* (Aldershot, Ashgate Publishing, 1994).

Babarinde, OA, and Faber, G, 'From Lomé to Cotonou: Business as Usual?' (2004) 9(1) *European Foreign Affairs Review* 27.

——, (eds), *The European Union and Developing Countries: the Cotonou Agreement* (Dordrecht, Martinus Nijhoff, 2005).

Baldwin, A, Davenport, D, Dimitrov, R, Hajjar, R, and Wood, P, 'Summary of the fifth session of the United Nations Forum on Forests' (2005) 13(133) *Earth Negotiations Bulletin*.

Barral, V, 'Le Développement Durable en Droit International: essai sur les incidences juridiques d'un concept évolutif' (Doctoral Thesis, European University Institute 2007).

Bartels, L, 'Art XX of the GATT and the Problem of Extraterritorial Jurisdiction' (2002) 6(2) *Journal of World Trade* 353.

——, 'The WTO Enabling Clause and Positive Conditionality in the European Community's GSP Program' (2003) 6(2) *Journal of International Economic Law* 513.

——, *Human Rights Conditionality in the EU's International Agreements* (Oxford, Oxford University Press, 2005).

——, 'The Appellate Body Ruling on EC–Tariff Preferences to Developing Countries and its Implications for Conditionality in GSP Programmes' in T Cottier, J Pauwelyn and E Bürgi (eds), *Human Rights and International Trade* (Oxford, Oxford University Press, 2005).

——, 'The Trade and Development Policy of the European Union' (2007) 18(4) *European Journal of International Law* 715.

——, 'The WTO Legality of the EU GSP+ Arrangements' (2007) 10(4) *Journal of International Economic Law* 869.

——, 'Comments on CARFORUM-EU Economic Partnership Agreement' (Comments to the European Commission, 13 February 2008).

Bartelt, S, 'The Institutional Interplay regarding the New Architecture for the EU's External Assistance' (2008) 14(5) *European Law Journal* 655.

Bauler, T, 'The Commission's Impact Assessment Process: Handling the External Dimensions of Sustainability' in M Pallemaerts and A Azmanova (eds), *The European Union and Sustainable Development* (Brussels, VUB Press, 2006).

Berdiyev, B, 'The EU and Former Soviet Central Asia: An Analysis of the Partnership and Cooperation Agreements' (2003) 22 *Yearbook of Environmental Law* 463.

Bilal, S, and Rampa, F, 'Alternative(s) EPAs. Possible Scenarios for the Future ACP Trade Relations with the EU' (2006) European Centre for Development Policy Management, Policy Management Report 11 (Maastricht, February 2006).

Biniaz, S, 'Remarks about the CITES Compliance Regime' in U Beyerlin, PT Stoll and R Wolfrum (eds), *Ensuring Compliance with Multilateral Environmental Agreements* (Dordrecht, Martinus Nijhoff, 2006).

Birnie, P, Boyle, A, and Redgwell, C, *International Law and the Environment* 3rd edn (Oxford, Oxford University Press, 2009).

Björklund, M, 'Responsibility of the EC and the Member States for Mixed Agreements – Should Non-Member Parties Care?' (2001) 70(3) *Nordic Journal of International Law* 373.

Blobel, D, Knigge, M, and Görlach, B, 'Report on Trade, Environment and Sustainability Impact Assessment' (Ecologic, 2005).

Bodansky, D, 'What is So Bad about Unilateral Actions to Protect the Environment?' (2000) 11(2) *European Journal of International Law* 339.

Boyle, A, and Freestone, D, (eds) *International Law and Sustainable Development. Past Achievements and Future Challenges* (Oxford, Oxford University Press, 1999).

Brandtner, B, and Rosas, A, 'Trade Preferences and Human Rights' in P Alston (ed), *The EU and Human Rights* (Oxford, Oxford University Press, 1999).

Bretton, P, 'Integrating the Least Developed Countries into the World Trading System: The Current Impact of the European Preferences under the "Everything But Arms Initiative"' (2003) 37(3) *Journal of World Trade* 623.

Breuss, F, Griller, S, and Vranes, E (eds), *The Banana Dispute. An Economic and Legal Analysis* (New York, Springer, 2003).

Brunnée, J, Bodansky, D, and Hey, E (eds), *The Oxford Handbook of International Environmental Law* (Oxford, Oxford University Press, 2007).

Buck, M, and Hamilton, C, 'The Nagoya Protocol on Access to Genetic Resources and the Fair and Equitable Sharing of Benefits Arising from their Utilization to the Convention on Biological Diversity' (2011) 20(1) *Review of European Community & International Environmental Law* 47.

Campling, L, 'Fisheries Aspects of the EU-ACP Interim Economic Partnership Agreements: Trade and Sustainable Development Implications' (2008) *ICTSD Issue Paper* No 6.

Chalmers, D, Davies, G, and Monti, G, *European Union Law* 2nd edn (Cambridge, Cambridge University Press, 2010).

Charnovitz, S, Bartels, L, Howse, R, Bradley, J, Pauwelyn, J, and Regan, D, 'Internet Round: The Appellate Body's Decision' (2004) 3 *World Trade Review* 239.

Chaytor, B, 'Environmental Issues in Economic Partnership Agreements: Implications for Developing Countries' (2009) *ICTSD Issue Paper.*

Chiavari, J, 'The Legal Framework for Carbon Capture and Storage in the EU (Directive 2009/31/EC)' in S Oberthür and M Pallemaerts (eds), *The New Climate Policies of the European Union: Internal Legislation and Climate Diplomacy* (Brussels, VUB Press, 2010).

Chowdhury, SR, Denters, EMG, and de Wart, P (eds), *The Right to Development in International Law* (Dordrecht, Martinus Nijhoff, 1992).

Christophe-Tchakaloff, MF (ed), *Le Concept d'Association dans les Accords passés par la Communauté: Essai de Clarification* (Brussels, Bruylant, 1999).

Coffey, C, 'Integrating Environment into the Common Fisheries Policy' (2000) Institute for European Environmental Policy.

Cole, A, 'Labour Standards in the Generalised System of Preferences: the European Communities/India GSP Dispute' (2004) 25(1) *Michigan Journal of International Law* 179.

Compa, L, and Vogt, J, 'Labor Rights in the Generalized System of Preferences: A 20-Year Review' (2001) 22(2–3) *Comparative Labor Law and Policy Journal* 199.

Cordonier-Segger, M-C, and Ahsfaq, K, *Sustainable Development Law: Principles, Practices and Prospects* (Oxford, Oxford University Press, 2004).

Cosbey, A, 'Timing and Public Participation Issues' in OECD, *Assessing the Environmental Effects of Trade Liberalization Agreements: Methodologies* (Paris, OECD, 2000).

Cosbey, A et al, 'The Rush to Regionalism: Sustainable Development and Regional/Bilateral Approaches to Trade and Investment Liberalisation' (International Institute for Sustainable Development, 2005).

Cremona, M, 'External Relations and External Competence: The Emergence of an Integrated Policy' in P Craig and G de Burca (eds), *The Evolution of EU Law* (Oxford, Oxford University Press, 1999).

Cremona, M, 'Rhetoric and Reticence: EU External Commercial Policy in a Multilateral Context' (2001) 38(2) *Common Market Law Review* 359.

——, 'Creating the New Europe: The Stability Pact for South-Eastern Europe in the Context of EU-SEE Relations' (2000) 2 *Cambridge Yearbook of European Legal Studies* 464.

——, 'A Policy of Bits and Pieces? The Common Commercial Policy after Nice' (2001) 4 *Cambridge Yearbook of European Legal Studies* 61.

——, 'The Common Commercial Policy' in C Saunders and G Triggs (eds), *Trade and Cooperation with the European Union in the New Millennium* (London, Kluwer, 2002).

——, 'The External Dimension of the Single Market. Building on Foundations' in C Barnard and J Scott (eds), *The Law of the Single European Market: Unpacking the Premises* (Oxford, Hart, 2002).

——, (ed), The *Enlargement of the European Union* (Oxford, Oxford University Press, 2003).

——, 'Enlargement: A Successful Instrument of Foreign Policy?' in T Tridimas and P Nebbia, (eds), *European Union Law for the Twenty-First Century* (Oxford, Hart, 2004).

——, 'The Union as a Global Actor: Roles, Models and Identity' (2004) 41(2) *Common Market Law Review* 556.

——, 'A Constitutional Basis for an Effective External Action' (2006) *EUI Law Working Paper* 2006/30.

——, 'Coherence and EU External Policy' in E Morgera (ed), *The External Environmental Policy of the European Union: EU and International Law Perspectives* (Cambridge, Cambridge University Press, forthcoming 2012).

Curtin, J, *The Copenhagen Conference: How Should the EU Respond?* (Dublin, IIEA, 2010).

Dashwood, A, 'Mixity in the Era of the Treaty of Lisbon' in C Hillion and P Koutrakos (eds), *Mixed Agreements Revisited: the EU and its Member States in the World* (Oxford, Hart, 2010).

Dashwood, A, and Hillion, C, *The General Law of EC External Relations* (London, Sweet & Maxwell, 2000).

Delreux, T, *The EU as an International Environmental Negotiator* (Surrey, Ashgate, 2011).

Del Sarto, R, and Schumacher, T, 'From EMP to ENP: What's at Stake with the European Neighbourhood Policy Towards the Southern Mediterranean?' (2005) 10(1) *European Foreign Affairs Review* 17.

Desta, MG, 'EC-ACP Economic Partnership Agreements and WTO Compatibility: An experiment in North-South Inter-Regional Agreements?' (2006) 43(5) *Common Market Law Review* 1343.

de Vos, AE, 'The Cotonou Agreement: A Case of Forced Regional Integration?' in G Kreijen, M Brus, J Dugard, J Duursma and AE de Vos (eds), *State, Sovereignty and International Governance* (Oxford, Oxford University Press, 2002).

de Witte, B, 'The Emergence of a European System of Public International Law: the EU and its Member States as Strange Subjects' in J Wouters, A Nollkaemper and E de Wet (eds), *The Europeanisation of International Law* (The Hague, TMC Asser Press, 2008).

——, 'Too Much Constitutional Law?' in M Cremona and B de Witte (eds), *EU Foreign Relations Law: Constitutional Fundamentals* (Oxford, Hart, 2008).

Dhondt, N, *Integration of Environmental Protection into Other EC Policies – Legal Theory and Practice* (Groningen, Europa Law Publishing, 2003)

Dickson, AK, 'The Demise of the Lomé Protocols: Revising European Development Policy' (2000) 5 *European Foreign Affairs Review* 197.

Eeckhout, P, *External Relations of the European Union: Legal and Constitutional Foundations* (Oxford, Oxford University Press 2004).

Egenhofer, C, and Georgiev, A, 'The Copenhagen Accord – A First Stab at Deciphering the Implications for the EU' (2009) Centre for European Policy Studies, *CEPS Commentaries*.

Fierro Sedano, E, *The EU's Approach to Human Rights Conditionality in Practice* (The Hague, Kluwer, 2003).

Fodella, A, 'Mechanisms for Promoting Implementation and Compliance with the 1989 Basel Convention on the Transboundary Movement of Hazardous Wastes and their Disposal' in T Treves et al (eds), *Non-compliance Procedures and Mechanisms and the Effectiveness of International Environmental Agreements* (The Hague, TMC Asser Press, 2009).

Fujiwara, N, 'Reinvigorating the EU's Role in the post-Copenhagen Landscape' (2010) Centre for European Policy Studies, *Climate Change, CEPS Commentaries*.

Gasiorek, M, et al, 'Mid-term Evaluation of the EU's Generalised System of Preferences. Final Report' (*CARIS*, 26 May 2010).

Gatto, A, 'Corporate Social Responsibility in the External Relations of the EU' (2005) 24 *Yearbook of European Law* 423

Gebhard, C, 'Coherence' in C Hill and M Smith (eds), *International Relations and the EU* 2nd edn (Oxford, Oxford University Press, 2011).

George, C, 'Regional Trade Agreements and the Environment: Monitoring Implementation and Assessing Impacts: Report on the OECD Workshop' (2011) *OECD Trade and Environment Working Papers* 2011/02.

George, C, and Kirkpatrick, C, 'Sustainability Impact Assessment of the World Trade Negotiations: Current Practice and Lessons for Further Development' (New Directions in Impact Assessment for Development Conference, University of Manchester, 24–25 November 2003).

Greven, T, Leopold, A, and Molinari, E, 'An Analysis of the Relative Effectiveness of Social and Environmental Norms in Free Trade Agreements' (2009 Study, European Parliament).

Grilli, E, *The European Community and Developing Countries* (Cambridge, Cambridge University Press, 1993).

Hakura, S, 'The Euro-Mediterranean Policy: The Implications of the Barcelona Declarations' (1997) 34(2) *Common Law* 337.

Hall, R, 'Undercutting Africa: Why EPAs Threaten the World's Forests and Forest Peoples' (2009) 8(1) *Trade Negotiations Insights*.

Hanf, D, and Dengler, P, 'Accords d'Association' (2004) 1 *College of Europe Research Paper in Law* 9.

Harrison, J, 'Incentives for Development: The EC's Generalised System of Preferences, India's WTO Challenge and Proposals for Reform' (2005) 42(6) *Common Market Law Review* 1663.

Hermann, CW, 'Common Commercial Policy after Nice: Sisyphus Would Have Done a Better Job' (2002) 39(1) *Common Market Law Review* 7.

Hession, M, and Macrory, R, 'The Legal Duty of Environmental Integration: Commitment and Obligation or Enforceable Rights?' in T O'Riordan and H Voisey (eds), *The Transition to Sustainability: The Politics of Agenda 21 in Europe* (London, Earthscan, 1998).

Heyvaert, V, 'Globalizing Regulation: Reaching Beyond the Borders of Chemical Safety' (2009) 36(1) *Journal of Law and Society* 110.

Hillion, C, 'Partnership and Cooperation Agreements between the European Union and the New Independent States of the Ex-Soviet Union' (1998) 3 *European Foreign Affairs Review* 399.

——, 'The EU's Neighbourhood Policy towards Eastern Europe' in A Dashwood and M Maresceau, *Law and Practice of EU External Relations* (Cambridge, Cambridge University Press, 2008).

——, 'Tous pour un, un pour tous! Coherence in the External Relations of the European Union' in M Cremona (ed), *Developments in EU External Relations Law* (Oxford, Oxford University Press, 2009).

——, 'Mixity and Coherence in the EU External Relations: the Significance of the Duty of Cooperation' in C Hillion and P Koutrakos (eds), *Mixed Agreements Revisited: the EU and its Member States in the World* (Oxford, Hart, 2010).

Hillion, C, and Koutrakos, P (eds), *Mixed Agreements Revisited: the EU and its Member States in the World* (Oxford, Hart, 2010).

Holder, J, and Lee, M, *Environmental Protection: Law and Policy* (Cambridge, Cambridge University Press, 2007).

Howarth, W, 'The Interpretation of "Precaution" in the European Community Common Fisheries Policy' (2008) 20 *Journal of Environmental Law* 213.

Howse, R, 'India's WTO Challenge to Drug Enforcement in the European Community Generalised System of Preferences. A Little Known Case with Major Repercussion for "Political" Conditionality in US Trade Policy' (2003) 42 *Chicago Journal of International Law* 385.

——, 'Back to the Court after Shrimp/Turtle: India's Challenge to Labour and Environmental Linkages in the EC Generalised System of Preferences' in E Benvenisti and M Hirsch (eds), *The Impact of International Law on International Cooperation. Theoretical Perspectives* (Cambridge, Cambridge University Press, 2004).

Huber, J, 'The Past, Present and Future of the ACP-EC Trade Regime and the WTO' (2000) 11(2) *European Journal of International Law* 427.

Inama, S, 'Market Access for LDCs. Issues to be Addressed' (2002) 36(1) *Journal of World Trade* 85.

——, and Vermulst, E, *Customs and Trade Law of the European Community* (London, Kluwer, 1999).

Inglis, K, 'Enlargement and the Environment Acquis' (2004) 13 *Review of European Community and International Environmental Law* 135.

Intergovernmental Panel on Climate Change, 'Special Report on Carbon Capture and Storage, Summary for Policy Makers' (Report of Working Group III of the Intergovernmental Panel on Climate Change, Montreal, 22–24 September 2005).

Jacobs, F, 'The Role of the European Court of Justice in the Protection of the Environment' (2006) 18(2) *Journal of Environmental Law* 185.

Jans, J, and Vedder, H, *European Environmental Law* 3rd edn (Groningen, Europa Law Publishing, 2008).

Jansen, B, 'The Limits of Unilateralism from an European Perspective' (2000) 11(2) *European Journal of International Law* 309.

Jinnah, S, 'Strategic Linkages: The Evolving Role of Trade Agreements in Global Environmental Governance' (2011) 20(2) *Journal of Environment and Development* 191.

Johnson, SP, and Corcelle, G, *The Environmental Policy of the European Communities* (London, Kluwer, 1995).

Kaddous, C, 'Effects of International Agreements in the EU Legal Order' in M Cremona and B de Witte (eds), *EU Foreign Relations Law: Constitutional Fundamentals* (Oxford, Hart, 2008).

Kelemen, RD, 'Globalizing European Union Environmental Policy' (Princeton Annual Workshop on European Integration, Princeton, New Jersey, 1 May 2009).

Kingston, S, 'Integrating Environmental Protection and EU Competition Law: Why Competition Isn't Special' (2010) 16(6) *European Law Journal* 780.

Klabbers, J, 'Restraints Imposed on the Treaty-Making Powers of the Member States Deriving from EU Law: A Framework for Analysis' in E Canizzaro (ed), *The European Union as an Actor in International Relations* (The Hague, Kluwer, 2002).

Knigge, M, and Leipprand, A, 'Public Participation in Sustainability Impact Assessments' (Ecologic, 2003).

Koutrakos, P, *EU International Relations Law* (Oxford, Hart, 2006).

——, 'Legal Basis and Delimitation of Competence in EU External Relations' in M Cremona and B de Witte (eds), *EU Foreign Relations Law: Constitutional Fundamentals* (Oxford, Hart, 2008).

Kramer, L, 'The Genesis of EC Environmental Principles' in R Macrory (ed), *Principles of European Environmental Law* (Groningen, Europa Law Publishing, 2004).

——, *EC Environmental Law* 6th edn (London, Sweet & Maxwell, 2006).

——, 'Regional Economic International Organizations: The European Union as an Example' in J Brunnée, D Bodansky and E Hey (eds), *The Oxford Handbook of International Environmental Law* (Oxford, Oxford University Press, 2007).

——, 'Sustainable Development in the EC' in H Bugge and C Voight (eds), *Sustainable Development in International and National Law* (Groningen, Europa Law Publishing, 2008).

——, 'Environmental Justice in the European Court of Justice' in J Ebbesson and P Okowa (eds), *Environmental Law and Justice in Context* (Cambridge, Cambridge University Press, 2009).

Kulovesi, K, 'How to Prevent Babies from Being Thrown Away with the Bathwater: Perspectives on the International Climate Regime from Buenos Aires to the Future' in E Morgera and F Francioni (eds), *The Future of Environmental Law: International and European Perspectives* (The Working Group on Environmental Law: Collected Reports 2004–2005) *EUI Working Papers Law* No 2006/01.

Kulovesi, K, and Gutiérrez, M, 'Climate Change Negotiations Update: Process and Prospects for an Agreed Outcome in Copenhagen in December 2009' (2009) 18(3) *Review of European Community and International Environmental Law* 229.

Kulovesi, K, Morgera, E, and Muñoz, M, 'Environmental Integration and Multi-faceted International Dimensions of EU Law: Unpacking the EU's 2009 Climate and Energy Package' (2011) 48(3) *Common Market Law Review* 829.

Laffan, B, and Lindner, J, 'The Budget: Who Gets What, When and How?' in H Wallace, MA Pollack and AR Young (eds), *Policy-Making in the European Union* (Oxford, Oxford University Press, 2010).

Leal Riesco, I and Opoku, K, 'Is REDD Undermining FLEGT?' (FERN Briefing Note 05, March 2009).

Lee, M, *EU Environmental Law: Challenges, Change and Decision-making* (Oxford, Hart, 2005).

——, 'The Environmental Implications of the Lisbon Treaty' (2008) 10(2) *Environmental Law Review* 131.

Lee, N, and Kirkpatrick, C, 'Methodologies for Sustainability Impact Assessments of Proposals for New Trade Agreements' (2001) 3(3) *Journal of Environmental Assessment Policy and Management* 395.

Leino, P, 'The Journey Towards all that is Good and Beautiful: Human Rights and "Common Values" as Guiding Principles of EU Foreign Relations Law' in M Cremona and B de Witte (eds), *EU Foreign Relations Law* (Oxford, Hart, 2008).

Lenschow, A, (ed), *Environmental Policy Integration – Greening Sectoral Policies in Europe* (London, Earthscan Publications, 2002).

Lyons, T, *EC Customs Law* (Oxford, Oxford University Press, 2001).

Macrory, L (ed), *Reflections on 30 Years of EU Environmental Law: A High Level of Protection?* (Groningen, Europa Law Publishing, 2005).

Mahony, S, 'Timing and Public Participation Issues in Undertaking Environmental Assessments of Trade Liberalization Agreements' in OECD, *Assessing the Environmental Effects of Trade Liberalization Agreements: Methodologies* (Paris, OECD, 2000).

Marín Durán, G, *Development-based Differentiation in the European Community's External Trade Policy – Selected Issues under Community and International Trade Law* (Doctoral thesis, European University Institute 2007).

——, 'Environmental Integration in EU Development Cooperation: Responding to International Commitments or Own Policy Priorities' in E Morgera (ed), *The External Environmental Policy of the European Union: EU and International Law Perspectives* (Cambridge, Cambridge University Press, forthcoming 2012).

——, 'The EU Role in Shaping the Trade and Environment Regulatory Nexus: Multilateral and Regional Approaches' in S Blockmans, B van Vooren and J Wouters (eds), *The Legal Dimension of Global Governance – What Role for the EU?* (forthcoming 2012).

Marín Durán, G, and Morgera, E, 'Case note. WTO India-EC GSP Dispute: The Future of Unilateral Trade Incentives linked to Multilateral Environmental Agreements' (2005) 14 *Review of European Community and International Environmental Law* 173.

——, 'Towards Environmental Integration in EC External Relations: A Comparative Analysis of Selected Association Agreements' (2006) 6 *Yearbook of European Environmental Law* 179.

Martenzuck, B, 'From Lomé to Cotonou: The ACP-EC Partnership Agreement in a Legal Perspective' (2000) 5(4) *European Foreign Affairs Review* 461.

Matambalya, F, and Wolf, S, 'The Cotonou Agreement and the Challenges of Making the EU-ACP Trade Regime WTO Compatible' (2001) 35(1) *Journal of World Trade* 123.

Mathis, JH, 'Benign Discrimination and the Generalised System of Preferences (GSP)' (2004) 31(4) *Legal Issues of Economic Integration* 289.

McGillivray, D, and Holder, J, 'Locating EC Environmental Law' (2001) 2 *Yearbook of European Environmental Law* 139.

McKenzie, M, 'Climate Change and the Generalised System of Preferences' (2008) 11(3) *Journal of International Economic Law* 679.

McMahon, JA, *The Development Cooperation of the EC* (London, Kluwer, 1998).

——, 'Negotiating at a Time of Turbulent Transition: The Future of Lomé' (1999) 36(3) *Common Market Law Review* 599.

——, 'The Long-Standing Banana Saga–Towards an Acceptable Solution' (2005) 11(6) *International Trade Law and Regulation* 181.

Miller, A, Morgera, E and Nyingi, DW, 'Summary of the fourth meeting of the *Ad Hoc* Open-ended Informal Working Group to study issues relating to the conservation and sustainable use of marine biological diversity beyond areas of national jurisdiction' (2011) 25(70) *Earth Negotiations Bulletin*.

Morgera, E, 'An Update on the Aarhus Convention and its Continued Global Relevance' (2005) 14(2) *Review of European Community and International Environmental Law* 138.

——, 'The 2005 UN World Summit and the Environment: The Proverbial Half-Full Glass?' (2006) 15 *Italian Yearbook of International Law* 53.

——, *Corporate Accountability in International Environmental Law* (Oxford, Oxford University Press, 2009).

——, 'Relevance Beyond Borders: Recent Developments in the EU' (2010) 40 *Environmental Policy and Law* 234.

——, 'Environmental Dimension of the MDGs: Progress Made?' (2010) 40(6) *Environmental Policy and Law* 269.

——, 'Expert Report Corporate Responsibility to Respect Human Rights in the Environmental Sphere' (May 2010) at www.law.ed.ac.uk/euenterpriseslf/documents/files/CSREnvironment.pdf.

——, 'Far Away, So Close: A Legal Analysis of the Increasing Interactions between the Convention on Biological Diversity and Climate Change Law' (2011) 2(1) *Climate Law* 85, 112.

——, 'Ambition, Complexity and Legitimacy of Pursuing Mutual Supportiveness through the EU's External Environmental Action' in B Van Vooren, S Blockmans and J Wouters (eds), *The Legal Dimension of Global Governance: What Role for the EU?* (Oxford, Oxford University Press, forthcoming 2012).

——, 'European Environmental Law' in S Alam et al (eds), *Routledge Handbook of International Environmental Law* (London, Routledge, forthcoming 2012).

——, (ed), *The External Environmental Policy of the European Union: EU and International Law Perspectives* (Cambridge, Cambridge University Press, forthcoming 2012).

Morgera, E, Kulovesi, K and Gobena, A (eds), *Case Studies on Bioenergy Policy and Law: Options for Sustainability*, FAO Legislative Study No 102 (Rome, FAO, 2010).

Morgera, E, and Marín Durán, G, 'Enlargement and EU Development Policy: An Environmental Perspective' (2004) 13(2) *Review of European Community and International Environmental Law* 152.

——, 'The UN 2005 World Summit, the Environment and the EU: Priorities, Promises and Prospects' (2006) 15(1) *Review of European Community and International Environmental Law* 11.

Morgera, E and Tsioumani, E, 'Yesterday, Today and Tomorrow: Looking Afresh at the Convention on Biological Diversity' (forthcoming) 21 *Yearbook of International Environmental Law*.

Morgera, E, Tsioumani, E, Aguilar, S, and Wilkins, H, 'Implementation Challenges and Compliance in MEA Negotiations' in P Chasek and L Wagner (eds), *The Roads from Rio: Lessons Learned from 20 Years of Multilateral Environmental Negotiations* (London, Routledge, forthcoming 2012).

Müller-Brandeck-Bocquet, G, 'Perspective for a New Regionalism: Relations between the EU and MERCOSUR' (2000) 5(4) *European Foreign Affairs Review* 561.

Najam, A, Halle, M, and Meléndez-Ortiz, R (eds), *Trade and Environment. A Resource Book*, (Geneva, IISD-ICSTD-The Ring, 2007).

Neuwahl, NA, 'Shared Powers or Combined Incompetence? More on Mixity' (1996) 33(4) *Common Market Law Review* 667.

——, 'The EU-Turkey Customs Union: a Balance but No Equilibrium' (1999) 4(1) *European Foreign Affairs Review* 37.

Oberthür, S, and Pallemaerts, M (eds), *The New Climate Policies of the European Union: Internal Legislation and Climate Diplomacy* (Brussels, VUB Press, 2010).

Ozden, C, and Reinhardt, E, 'The Perversity of Preferences: the Generalised System of Preferences and Developing Countries Trade Policies, 1976–2000' (2003) *World Bank Policy Research Paper Series* No 2955.

Pardo, S, and Zemer, L, 'Towards a New Euro-Mediterranean Neighbourhood Space' (2005) 10(1) *European Foreign Affairs Review* 39.

Passos, R, 'Mixed Agreements from the Perspective of the European Parliament' in C Hillion and P Koutrakos (eds), *Mixed Agreements Revisited* (Oxford, Hart, 2010).

Peers, S, 'The Reform of the European Community's General System of Preferences. A Missed Opportunity' (1995) 29(6) *Journal of World Trade* 79.

——, 'Living in Sin: Legal Integration under the EC-Turkey Customs Union' (1996) 13(3) *European Journal of International Law* 411.

——, 'EC Frameworks of International Relations: Cooperation, Partnership and Association' in A Dashwood and C Hillion, *The General Law of EC External Relations* (London, Sweet & Maxwell, 2000).

Perez, R, 'Are Economic Partnership Agreements a First-Best Option for the ACP countries?' (2006) 40(6) *Journal of World Trade* 999.

Persson, A, 'Environmental Policy Integration and Bilateral Development Assistance: Challenges and Opportunities with an evolving Governance Framework' (2009) 9(4) *International Environmental Agreements* 409.

Philippart, E, 'The Euro-Mediterranean Partnership: A Critical Evaluation of an Ambitious Scheme' (2003) 8(2) *European Foreign Affairs Review* 201.

Phinnemore, D, 'Stabilisation and Association Agreements: Europe Agreements for the Western Balkans' (2003) 8(1) *European Foreign Affairs Review* 77.

Pippan, C, 'The Rocky Road to Europe: The EU's Stabilisation and Association Process for the Western Balkans and the Principle of Conditionality' (2004) 9(2) *European Foreign Affairs Review* 219.

Piris, JC, *The Lisbon Treaty. A Legal and Political Analysis* (Cambridge, Cambridge University Press, 2010).

Psychogiopoulou, E, *The Integration of Cultural Considerations in EU Law and Policies* (Doctoral thesis, European University Institute 2006).

Ragni, C, 'Procedures and Mechanisms on Compliance under the 2000 Cartagena Protocol on Biosafety to the 1992 Convention on Biological Diversity' in Treves, T, Pineschi, L, Tanzi, A, Pitea, C, Ragni, C, and Romanin Jacur, C (eds), *Non-compliance Procedures and Mechanisms and the Effectiveness of International Environmental Agreements* (The Hague, TMC Asser Press, 2009).

Rajamani, L, *Differential Treatment in International Environmental Law* (Oxford, Oxford University Press, 2006).

Reischel, G, 'The EU and the UN Forest Negotiations: a case of failed international environmental governance?' (Paper presented to Marie Curie European Summer School on Earth System Governance, Vrije Universiteit, Amsterdam, 24 May–6 June 2007).

Rosas, A, 'The European Union and Mixed Agreements' in A Dashwood and C Hillion, *The General Law of EC External Relations* (London, Sweet & Maxwell, 2000).

——, 'The European Court of Justice and Public International Law' in J Wouters, A Nollkaemper and E De Wet (eds), *The Europeanisation of International Law* (The Hague, TMC Asser Press, 2008).

Ross-Robertson, A, 'Is the Environment Getting Squeezed out of Sustainable Development?' (2003, Sum) *Public Law* 249.

Rowe, GC, 'Tools for the Control of Political and Administrative Agents: Impact Assessment and Administrative Governance in the European Union' in H Hoffman and A Türk (eds), *EU Administrative Governance* (Cheltenham, Edward Elgar, 2005).

Sadeleer, N, 'EC Law and Biodiversity' in R Macrory (ed), *Reflections on 30 Years of EU Environmental Law – a High Level Protection?* (Groningen, Europa Law Publishing, 2005).

——, 'Habitat Conservation in EC Law: From Nature Sanctuaries to Ecological Networks' (2005) 5 *Yearbook of European Environmental Law* 215.

Sánchez Arnau, JC, *The Generalised System of Preferences and the World Trade Organisation* (London, Cameron, 2002).

Sands, P, 'Unilateralism, Values and International Law' (2000) 11(2) *European Journal of International Law* 291.

——, *Principles of International Environmental Law* 2nd edn (Cambridge, Cambridge University Press, 2003).

Santander, S, 'EU-MERCOSUR Inter-regionalism: Facing up to the South American Crisis and the Emerging Free Trade Area of the Americas' (2002) 7(4) *European Foreign Affairs Review* 491.

Savaresi, A, 'Reducing Emissions from Deforestation in Developing Countries under the UNFCCC. Caveats and Opportunities for Biodiversity' (forthcoming) 21 *Yearbook of International Environmental Law*.

——, 'The EU External Action on Forests: FLEGT and the Development of International Law' in E Morgera (ed), *The External Environmental Policy of the European Union; EU and International Law Perspectives* (Cambridge, Cambridge University Press, forthcoming 2012).

Scott, J, 'REACH: Combining Harmonization and Dynamism in the Regulation of Chemicals' in J Scott (ed), *Environmental Protection: European Law and Governance* (Oxford, Oxford University Press, 2009) 56.

——, 'The Multi-level Governance of Climate Change' (2011) 4(1) *Carbon and Climate Law Review* 25.

Shaffer, G, *Defending Interests: Public-Private Partnerships in the WTO Litigation* (Washington, DC, Brooking Institution Press, 2003).

Simmonds, KR, 'The Lomé Convention and the New International Economic Order' (1976) 13(3) *Common Market Law Review* 315.

Simmonds, KR, 'The Second Lomé Convention: the Innovative Features' (1980) 17(3) *Common Market Law Review* 99.

——, 'The Third Lomé Convention' (1985) 22(3) *Common Market Law Review* 389.

——, 'The Fourth Lomé Convention' (1991) 28(3) *Common Market Law Review* 521.

Sindico, F, 'Climate Change: A Security (Council) Issue?' (2007) 1(1) *Carbon and Climate Law Review* 26.

Smith, F, 'Renegotiating Lomé: the Impact of the World Trade Organisation on the European Community's Development Policy after the Bananas Conflict' (2000) 25(3) *European Law Review* 247.

Soveroski, M, 'EC Enlargement and the Development of European Environmental Policy: Parallel Histories, Divergent Paths?' (2004) 13(2) *Review of European Community and International Environmental Law* 127.

Spence, C, and Vavilov, A, 'Summary of the First Session of the Preparatory Committee for the 2012 United Nations Conference on Sustainable Development' (2010) 27(1) *Earth Negotiations Bulletin.*

Switzer, S, 'Environmental Protection and the Generalised System of Preferences: A Legal and Appropriate Linkage?' (2008) 57(1) *International and Comparative Law Quarterly* 113.

Sykes, AO, 'A Preference for Development: the Law and Economics of the GSP' (2005) 4 *World Trade Review* 41.

Taxil, B, *L'OMC et les Pays en Développment* (Paris, Monchrestien, 1998).

Tébar Less, C, and Kim, JA, 'Checklist for Negotiators of Environmental Provisions in Regional Trade Agreements' (2008) *OECD Trade and Environment Working Papers* 2008/02.

The Economics of Ecosystems & Biodiveristy (TEEB), 'The Economics of Ecosystems and Biodiversity: Mainstreaming the Economics of Nature: A Synthesis of the Approach, Conclusions and Recommendations of TEEB' (TEEB, 2010).

Thompson, P, 'EPAs and Natural Resources: The European Sustainability Agenda' (2009) 8(4) *Trade Negotiations Insights.*

Tietje, C, 'The Legal Status of International Law in the European Legal Order: The Case of International Treaties and Non-binding International Instruments' in J Wouters, A Nollkaemper and E de Wet (eds), *The Europeanisation of International Law* (The Hague, TMC Asser Press, 2008).

UNEP, *Reference Manual for the Integrated Assessment of Trade-related Policies* (Geneva, UNEP, 2001).

van Asselt, H, 'Managing the Fragmentation of International Environmental Law: Forests at the Intersection of the Climate and Biodiversity Regime' (forthcoming) *NYU Journal of International Law and Politics.*

van der Grijp, N, and Etty, T, 'Incorporating Climate Change into EU Development Cooperation Policy' in J Gupta and N van der Grijp (eds), *Mainstreaming Climate Change in Development Cooperation* (Cambridge, Cambridge University Press, 2010).

van Homeyer, I, 'The Evolution of EU Environmental Governance' in J Scott (ed), *Environmental Protection, European Law and Governance* (Oxford, Oxford University Press, 2009).

Vedder, H, 'The Treaty of Lisbon and European Environmental Policy' (2010) 22(2) *Journal of Environmental Law* 285.

——, 'Diplomacy by Directive: An Analysis of the International Context of the Emissions Trading Directive' (2009) *Social Science Research Network Working Paper* No 1477371.

Vogler, J, 'The European Union as an Actor in International Environmental Politics' (1999) 8(3) *Environmental Politics* 25, 32–34.

Vogler, J, and Bretherton, C, 'The European Union as a Sustainable Development Actor: the Case of External Fisheries Policy' (2008) 30(3) *Journal of European Integration* 401.

Wallace, H, Wallace, W, and Pollack, MA, *Policy-Making in the European Union* 6th edn (Oxford, Oxford University Press, 2011).

Wasmeier, M, 'The Integration of Environmental Protection as a General Rule for Interpreting Community Law' (2001) 38(1) *Common Market Law Review* 159.

Wiers, J, *Trade and Environment in the EC and the WTO – A Legal Analysis* (Groningen, Europa Law Publishing, 2002).

Winters, LA, 'Post-Lomé Trading Arrangements: the Multilateral Alternative' in J von Hagen and M Widgren (eds), *Regionalism in Europe. Geometries and Strategies after 2000* (Boston, Kluwer, 2001).

World Commission on Environment and Development, *Our Common Future* (Oxford, Oxford University Press, 1987).

WWF, 'Changing the Balance of Trade' WWF Briefing on Sustainability Assessment of EU Trade Policy (WWF, 2002).

WWF, BirdLife and FERN, 'Environmental Tools in EC Development Cooperation -Transparency and Public Availability of Documentation' (WWF, BirdLife and FERN, September 2007).

——, 'Environmental Tools in EC Development Cooperation – An Analysis of Country and Regional Environmental Profiles' (WWF, BirdLife and FERN, April 2009).

Index

African, Caribbean and Pacific Group
  see also **Cotonou Agreement**
  EU relations, 82–4, 86, 92, 97
    see also **EU-ACP dialogue**
  European Development Fund, 197–9
  exclusive economic zones, 90
  trade and economic cooperation, 92, 95, 96
Agreements with South Korea
  background, 117, 118
  biodiversity, 119, 125
  climate change, 118, 119, 120, 125
  differentiated approach, 135
  economic/political relations, 117
  energy efficiency, 119
  environmental awareness, 119
  environmental cooperation clauses, 118, 119
  environmental integration (summary), 142
  environmental integration clauses
    agriculture, 120
    best endeavours, 120
    energy, 120
    fisheries, 120
    forestry, 120
    rural development, 120
    transport, 120, 121
  environmental protection, 118
  foreign direct investment, 118
  framework agreement, 118, 127
  free trade agreement, 117, 118, 121
  hazardous waste, 119
  land management, 119
  marine environment, 119
  natural resources, 119
  sustainable development, 118, 119, 121, 125, 128
Agriculture
  Association Agreements, 137
  climate change, 267
  environmental integration clauses, 70, 79, 90, 104, 105, 112, 113, 120, 132, 137
  environmental multilateralism, 267
  external relations, 46
Association Agreements
  see also **Stabilisation and Association Agreements**
  approximation of laws, 137
  Association Council, 60, 61
  Chile
    see **Association with Chile**
  common characteristics, 60
  decision-making process, 61
  development tool, 59, 82–108
  differentiated approach, 134–6
  environmental cooperation clauses, 68, 69
  environmental impact assessments, 69
  environmental integration clauses, 69–72, 79
  environmental integration (summary), 141
  EU enlargement, 64–7
    see also **EU enlargement**
  EU Membership
    prelude, 58, 64–75, 137, 141
    substitute, 58, 59, 75–82, 141
  Euro-Mediterranean Agreements
    see **Euro-Mediterranean Agreements**
  external competence, 57, 58, 60
  financial and technical assistance, 60
  implementation, 60, 61
  institutional structure, 60
  inter-regional cooperation, 59, 60, 109–16
  legal/political aspects, 57
  legal status, 61
  policy areas, 60
  political choices, 58
  political dialogue, 60
  scope, 60
  South Africa
    see **Association with South Africa**
  strategic environmental assessments, 69
  trade, 60
  ultimate objectives, 60
Association with Central America
  aquaculture, 91
  biodiversity, 87, 91
  climate change, 87, 88, 103
  consultation-based approach, 108
  differentiated responsibility, 87
  domestic environmental performance, 100
  economic development, 91
  ecosystems, 89
  environmental issues
    cooperation, 88, 89
    governance, 87
    integration, 86, 142
    protection, 100, 101
    standards, 100
  ethnic groups, 89
  fisheries, 91, 104
  forest management, 87, 91
  free trade area, 98
  general exceptions clause, 102

Association with Central America (*cont.*):
global environmental issues, 86, 88
indigenous peoples, 89
industrial cooperation, 91
institutional aspects, 108
land use, 91
marine resources, 87
mining, 91
precautionary principle, 104
renewable energy, 87
sustainable development, 86, 103
sustainable management, 89
tourism, 92
trade/environmental cooperation, 103
transport, 92
water resources, 87
Association with Chile
Association Council, 115
cooperation areas, 109
democratic principles, 109
dispute settlement, 116
economic and social development, 109, 110, 111
economic and social progress, 110
environmental cooperation clauses, 110, 111
environmental cooperation, 110, 111
environmental integration clauses
agriculture, 112
energy, 112, 113
social cooperation, 112, 114
environmental integration (summary), 141
environmental structures, 111
exception clauses, 114, 115
financial and technical cooperation, 111
human rights, 109
institutional aspects, 115, 116
land use, 111
origins, 109
policy cooperation, 109
political relations, 109
public participation, 116
rule of law, 109
suspension of benefits, 116
trade and environment
establishment, 114
free trade area, 109, 114
services, 114
trade liberalisation, 114
trade relations, 109, 114
trade restrictions, 115
Association with South Africa
democratic principles, 110
development assistance, 110, 111
differentiated approach, 135, 136
dispute settlement, 116
economic and social development, 110
economic cooperation, 110
environmental cooperation, 112
environmental integration clauses
agriculture, 112, 113
corporate environmental accountability, 113
energy, 112, 113
rural development, 113
tourism, 112, 114
environmental integration (summary), 141
environmental management, 112
financial and technical assistance, 111
human rights, 110
institutional aspects, 115, 116
Joint Cooperation Council, 116
origins, 109
political relations, 110
public policy, 114
restrictions, 114, 115
rule of law, 110
Strategic Partnership, 110
sustainable development, 112
trade and environment
free trade area, 110, 114
global environmental problems, 112
trade liberalisation, 114
trade relations, 114
trade restrictions, 115

Bibliography, 289–301
Bilateral and Inter-regional Agreements
Association Agreements, 57–61
see also **Association Agreements**
cooperation agreements, 62–4
cooperation areas, 57, 286
differentiated approach, 57
environmental cooperation clauses, 56, 57
environmental integration
financial and technical assistance, 143
implementation, 142, 143
policy dialogue, 143
summary, 141
sustainability impact assessments, 143
verification, 142
environmental integration clauses, 56, 57
environmental protection, 2–4, 286
environmental standards, 57
evaluation, 142
external environmental competence, 18
see also **External environmental competence**
general agreements, 61, 62
implementation
procedures, 142
timeframe, 142
institutional mechanisms, 286
monitoring, 142
partnership agreements, 62–4
priority issues, 57

sustainable development, 286
trade and environment nexus, 57, 286
Biodiversity
biosafety, 44
climate change, 261
Convention on Biodiversity, 262, 263
development cooperation, 196
Environment and Sustainable Management of Natural Resources (ENTRP), 186, 188, 189
see also **Environment and Sustainable Management of Natural Resources (ENTRP)**
environmental cooperation clauses, 131
environmental multilateralism
alliance-building, 266
biodiversity conservation, 262
CARIFORUM EPA, 263
CITES, 262, 264
Convention on Migratory Species, 262
Cotonou Agreement, 263
differing formulations, 262
environmental cooperation, 262
EU external assistance, 264
EU external relations, 261, 264, 265
EU internal legislation, 261
external environmental integration, 263
FTA-Colombia and Peru, 262
internal environmental integration, 264
ITPGR, 262
mainstreaming, 263, 264
Multilateral Environmental Agreements, 256
Nagoya Protocol, 264, 265
Partnership and Cooperation Agreements with CIS countries, 262
Ramsar Convention, 262
sustainable development, 262
sustainable use, 262
trade negotiations, 265
trade-related issues, 263
genetic resources, 44
genetically modified organisms, 44
institutionalised dialogues, 212, 214, 215, 222, 223, 225–7, 229, 264
Multilateral Environmental Agreements (MEAs), 22
sustainability impact assessments, 245
see also **Sustainability impact assessments**
sustainable forests, 44
Biofuels
Climate and Energy Package, 270
climate change mitigation, 269
environmental multilateralism, 267, 269–71
environmental sustainability, 269
EU external relations, 270, 271
EU internal legislation, 271
examples, 269
institutionalised dialogues, 221, 222
multilateral negotiations, 271
negative impact, 269
Renewable Energy Directive, 270
sustainability criteria, 287
sustainability impact assessments, 246, 270
see also **Sustainability impact assessments**

CARIFORUM EPA
dispute settlement, 107, 108
environmental integration clauses
agriculture, 104, 105
biological diversity, 105
energy, 106
fisheries, 104, 105
intellectual property, 105
natural resources, 104
tourism, 105
environmental integration (summary), 142
EU-CARIFORUM Consultative Committee, 106, 107
EU-CARIFORUM Trade and Development Committee, 106
free trade area, 97
institutional aspects, 106–8, 128, 129
Joint EU-CARIFORUM Council, 106
monitoring, 106
reciprocity, 97
significance, 96
trade and environment provisions
consultation-based approach, 102, 108
due notice, 102
environmental exception clause, 102
environmental protection, 99–102
innovative approach, 98
international standards, 102
mutual supportiveness, 99
precautionary principle, 102
sanctions, 140
scientific and technical information, 102
special and differential treatment, 102
sustainable development, 97, 98
trade and environmental cooperation, 102, 103
transparency, 102
trade in services, 97
traditional knowledge, 127
Chile
see **Association with Chile**
Climate change
see also **Global Climate Change Alliance**
agriculture, 267
alliance-building, 267
biodiversity, 261
carbon finance, 258
Climate and Energy Package, 259, 260, 268

Climate change (*cont.*):
climate change negotiations
CCS Directive, 268
Copenhagen Conference, 267
EU-China dialogue, 268
financial and technical assistance, 268
FTA-Colombia and Peru, 268
FTA-South Korea, 268
international consensus, 269
Kyoto Protocol, 258, 267
post-2012 negotiations, 267, 268
regulatory dialogues, 269
strategic partnerships, 267
development cooperation, 196
energy efficiency, 44
Environment and Sustainable Management of Natural Resources (ENTRP), 186–90
see also **Environment and Sustainable Management of Natural Resources (ENTRP)**
environmental aspects
cooperation clauses, 87, 88, 131, 136, 260, 268
integration clauses, 80, 137
integration requirement, 29, 55, 261
legislation, 259
mainstreaming, 260
multilateralism, 254, 256–61, 267, 282
EU Emission Trading Scheme, 259
EU external funding, 260
EU external relations, 258–60
Europe 2020 Strategy, 44, 268, 269
global carbon market, 226, 227, 229, 259
greenhouse gas emissions, 226
GSP-plus (special incentive arrangement), 160, 161
see also **GSP-plus (special incentive arrangement)**
institutionalised dialogues, 212, 214–6, 218–28, 267
international action, 13
international regime, 258
low carbon economy, 44
Multilateral Environmental Agreements (MEAs), 21, 22
multilateral negotiations, 44
policy considerations, 44, 258
renewable energy, 44
Colombia and Peru (COPE FTA)
benefit sharing, 126
biodiversity, 126
climate change, 125, 126
cooperation activities, 125, 126
dispute settlement, 129
environmental cooperation, 125
environmental integration (summary), 142
institutional aspects, 128, 129
law enforcement, 124
level of protection, 123
renewable energy, 126
right to regulate, 122
sustainable development, 125, 126, 128
trade and environment provisions, 117, 121–5
trade restrictions, 125
traditional knowledge, 126
Commission on Sustainable Development
EU status, 7
Common Commercial Policy
customs union, 46
environmental integration, 47
European Parliament, 47
external trade policy, 46, 47
impact, 46
objectives, 46
trade agreements, 47
trade liberalisation, 46
Commonwealth of Independent States
see **Partnership and Cooperation Agreements with CIS countries**
Competence
conferral principle, 7, 8, 13
environmental competence, 6, 8, 9
external competence, 5, 7, 8
see also **External environmental competence**
necessary competence, 6
proportionality principle, 8
subsidiarity principle, 8
vertical division of powers, 8
Complementarity
external environmental competence, 20
see also **External environmental competence**
TFEU (Article 11) provisions, 20, 42
see also **Treaty on the Functioning of the European Union**
Consensus-building
continuing cooperation, 271, 282
corporate environmental liability, 277–9
economic development, 283
environmental multilateralism, 282
EU external relations, 283, 287
failed multilateral negotiations, 271
international environmental governance, 271, 272
intractable issues, 282
ownership of ideas, 282
partnerships, 282
sustainability, 283
sustainable forest management, 272–6
Corporate environmental liability
accountability, 137
CARIFORUM EPA, 278
eco-labelling, 278, 279
eco-management, 278
environmental integration clauses, 137

EU external action, 279, 283
EU external funding, 277, 278
EU external relations, 277
FTA-South Korea, 278
green growth, 283, 284
green procurement, 278
international standards, 277
mining, 279
multilateral efforts, 277
oil and gas, 279
sustainability impact assessments, 247, 278
see also **Sustainability impact assessments**
UN Framework for Business and Human Rights, 278
Corporate social responsibility
EU external relations, 45
sustainability impact assessments, 247, 248
see also **Sustainability impact assessments**
Cotonou Agreement
comprehensive nature, 83
cultural heritage, 86
development cooperation, 83, 84, 96
development finance, 85
development strategies, 87
differentiated approach, 83, 102, 134, 135, 138
dispute settlement, 95
environmental cooperation clauses
climate change, 87, 88
natural resources, 87
sustainable management, 87
environmental dimension
analysis, 84
climate change, 84, 85, 87, 88, 91
environmental sustainability, 86
general approach, 85–7
least-developed countries, 85
small island developing States, 85
sustainable development, 83, 85–8, 97
sustainable management, 87
environmental integration clauses
agriculture, 90
aquaculture, 90
best practices, 89
emergency assistance, 91
fisheries, 89, 90
humanitarian assistance, 91
marine transport, 89, 90
regeneration, 89
regional cooperation, 90
sustainability, 89, 90
environmental integration (summary), 141
European Development Fund, 197–9
financial cooperation, 84
good governance, 84
human rights, 83, 84
implementation, 213
institutional aspects, 94, 95
monitoring, 95
origins, 82, 83
participation
non-State actors, 83, 84
principle, 94
peace and security, 84
policy dialogue, 211
political dimension, 83
poverty reduction, 86, 88
regionalisation, 83
revisions, 84, 85, 87, 90, 91, 93
rule of law, 83, 84
security threats, 88
significance, 82
strategy papers, 84
trade and environment nexus, 138
trade/economic cooperation
enhanced cooperation, 93
intellectual property rights, 94
positive action, 93
protectionism, 93
sanitary/phytosanitary measures, 94
trade cooperation, 84
transitory period, 92
Criminal matters
environmental integration clauses, 72, 80
organised crime, 133

Declaration of the World Summit on Sustainable Development
EU support, 2
Desertification
Environment and Sustainable Management of Natural Resources (ENTRP), 187–9
see also **Environment and Sustainable Management of Natural Resources (ENTRP)**
environmental multilateralism, 256, 257
EU external relations, 44, 45
institutionalised dialogues, 219, 228
Multilateral Environmental Agreements (MEAs), 22
Development cooperation
see also **Development Cooperation Instrument (DCI)**
co-decision procedure, 53
developing countries, 52, 53
economic and social development, 52
environmental integration, 52–4
financial aid 54
geographical scope, 52
Lisbon Treaty, 52
Maastricht Treaty, 52
sustainability, 52, 53
technology transfer, 54
Development Cooperation Instrument (DCI)
biodiversity, 196
capacity-building, 183, 185, 196
climate change, 196

Development Cooperation Instrument (DCI) (*cont.*):
effective multilateralism, 196
Environment and Sustainable Management of Natural Resources (ENRTP), 178, 181–3
see also **Environment and Sustainable Management of Natural Resources (ENRTP)**
environmental issues
governance, 183, 185
impact assessments, 184
screening, 184
sustainability, 182, 183, 185, 186, 196
environment-specific funding, 180
eradication of poverty, 181
evaluation reports, 185
financial and technical assistance, 181, 182, 195
food security, 181, 183, 189
forest management, 196
geographic programmes, 195
implementation, 183, 185, 186, 196
international policy development, 183, 185
mainstreaming requirement, 182
migration/asylum, 181
monitoring, 185
multidimensional mainstreaming, 182
natural resources, 178, 181, 196
non-State actors, 181, 183, 189
public procurement, 185
resources, 183, 185
social and human development, 181
strategic environmental assessments, 184, 185
sustainable development, 181, 196
sustainable energy, 196
sustainable management, 178, 181
thematic programmes, 181–3
water resources, 196
Differentiated approach
cooperation priorities
bargaining powers, 136
climate change, 136
degree of differentiation, 136
dependency, 136
environmental cooperation clauses, 136
emphasis on environment
Agreement with South Africa, 135, 136
Agreements with South Korea, 134
Cotonou Agreement, 134, 135
degree of differentiation, 134
economic/political relationship, 134
environmental standards, 135, 136, 285
Euro-Mediterranean Associations, 134–6
Partnership and Cooperation Agreements with CIS countries, 134, 135
relative emphasis, 134
Stabilisation and Association Agreements, 134
environmental integration clauses
agriculture, 137
climate change, 137
corporate environmental accountability, 137
energy, 137
fisheries, 137
industrial development, 137
mining, 137
tourism 137
transport, 137
environmental protection, 285
external assistance, 204
institutional differentiation
dispute settlement, 139, 140
institutional mechanisms, 285
institutional provisions, 139
monitoring, 139
public participation, 140
sanctions, 139, 140
local conditions, 285
trade and environment nexus
best endeavours clauses, 138
Cotonou Agreement, 138
domestic environmental performance, 139
environmental protection, 138
environmental standards, 139
general exception clause, 138
mutual supportiveness, 138, 139
sustainable development, 139, 140
trade and investment, 138
trade restrictions, 138
Doha Ministerial Conference
external trade policy, 48, 49

Energy
bioenergy, 227
clean energy, 187
energy efficiency, 27, 44
environmental integration clauses, 71, 72, 80, 106, 112, 113, 120, 132, 133, 137
institutionalised dialogues, 219, 220, 225, 226
renewable energy, 27, 44
solar energy, 76
sustainable energy, 186, 188, 190, 196, 205
Environment and Sustainable Management of Natural Resources (ENTRP)
biodiversity, 186, 188, 189
capacity-building, 185
cooperation activities, 186–9
development cooperation, 178, 181–3
effect, 181
energy
clean energy, 187
sustainable energy, 186, 188
environmental issues
climate change, 186–90
desertification, 187–9

forestry, 186–90
global dimension, 186
governance, 185, 189
green economy, 188
integration, 185
priorities, 187
protection, 182, 183
sustainability, 185, 186
implementation, 183, 185–7
policy development, 185
priority areas, 185
resources, 183, 201
Strategy Paper (2007–10), 185–8
Strategy Paper (2011–13), 185, 188, 189
water resources, 183, 186, 189
Environmental cooperation
environmental cooperation clauses
administrative structures, 68
alliance-building, 132
approximation of laws, 131
best-endeavours, 78
biodiversity, 131
climate change, 87, 88, 131, 136
environmental degradation, 68, 69
environmental impact assessments, 69, 78, 131
environmental information systems, 78
function, 56
implementation, 77
inclusion, 57
natural resources, 87
pollution control, 131
priorities, 78
regional cooperation, 78
specific priorities, 69
strategic environmental assessments, 69
sustainable development, 68
sustainable management, 87
variations, 77
institutionalised dialogues, 4
see also **Institutionalised dialogues**
Environmental impact assessments (EIAs)
development cooperation, 184
environmental cooperation clauses, 69, 78
environmental integration requirement, 34
Environmental integration
see also **Environmental integration requirement**
compliance, 3
credibility, 4
development cooperation, 52–4
differentiation, 134
see also **Differentiated approach**
environmental integration clauses
agricultural sector, 70, 79, 90, 112, 132, 137
best practices, 89
climate change, 80, 137
construction, 133
corporate environmental accountability, 137
criminal matters, 72, 80
ecological balance, 79
economic cooperation, 79
economic/social development, 69, 70, 79
energy, 71, 72, 80, 106, 112, 113, 132, 133, 137
fisheries, 70, 79, 89, 90, 104, 105, 137
forestry, 79, 120
function, 56
implementation, 77
inclusion, 57
industrial development, 133
industrial waste, 80
mining, 133, 137
natural resources, 104
sustainability, 89, 90
tourism, 80, 105, 112, 114, 137
transport, 70, 71, 112, 114, 120, 121, 137
variations, 77
Environmental Integration Strategy (2001), 203
environmental mainstreaming, 182, 201–3, 205
environmental multilateralism, 3
see also **Environmental multilateralism**
EU credibility, 288
EU external relations, 5, 285, 286
EU initiatives, 3
EU policy objectives, 286
EU political institutions, 285
external assistance, 201, 203–6, 288
legal and policy issues, 3
legal scholarship, 1, 2
legitimacy, 4, 287
non-legalised instruments, 4
political science, 1
unilateral measures, 286
Environmental integration requirement
Cardiff process, 33, 34
climate change, 29, 261
duty of sincere cooperation, 31
emergence
Amsterdam Treaty, 26
animal welfare, 27
Community environmental policy, 25, 26
energy policy, 27
First Environmental Action Programme, 25, 26
Fifth Environmental Action Programme, 26
Lisbon Treaty, 26, 27
Maastricht Treaty, 26
Rio Conference, 26
Single European Act, 25, 26
Third Environmental Action Programme, 26
environmental impact assessments, 34

Environmental integration requirement (*cont.*):
EU institutions, 30, 31
executive discretion, 55
implementation, 30, 31
joint action, 33
judicial involvement, 55
transposition of national laws, 31
Treaty on the Functioning of the European Union (Article 11), 1, 5, 13, 25, 27, 28, 285–7
see also **Treaty on the Functioning of the European Union (TFEU)**
legal significance, 25
policy coherence, 25
policy-making, 33, 34
policy objectives, 28–31, 33
policy rationale, 28
precautionary principle, 29
prevention principle, 26
procedural aspect, 28, 33
substantive integration, 28
sustainable development, 25
sustainability impact assessments, 234, 235, 239, 240, 242, 252
see also **Sustainability impact assessments**
Environmental law
polluter pays principle, 15–7, 38
precautionary principle, 38
sustainable development, 38
see also **Sustainable development**
Environmental multilateralism
alliance-building
developing countries, 265, 266
environmental commitments, 266
environmental negotiations, 265–7, 281, 282
external assistance, 266
policy dialogues, 266
third countries, 254, 255
biodiversity, 256, 257, 261–6
biofuels, 267, 269–71
chemicals, 256, 257
climate change, 254, 256–61, 282
see also **Climate change**
consensus-building, 254, 255, 271–9, 282, 283, 287
see also **Consensus-building**
desertification, 256, 257
EU environmental interests, 287
EU external relations, 254, 280
EU internal legislation, 2821
EU support, 281
evolution, 255
forestry, 257
green growth, 283
implementation, 254
legal developments, 280
Multilateral Environmental Agreements, 255–7, 280, 281
political commitment, 254
positive interactions, 254, 255
regional treaties, 255, 256
Environmental policy integration
EU commitment, 2
EU sectoral policies, 1
internal policies, 2
Member State practice, 1
Environmental protection
bilateral and inter-regional agreements, 2–4
see also **Bilateral and Inter-regional Agreements**
EU external policies, 2
EU internal policies, 2
geographic perspective, 3
global environmental governance, 2
historic perspective, 3
legal appraisal, 3
multilateral processes, 2
third country relationships, 3
unilateral action, 4
Environmental Regulation (EC/2493/2000)
adoption, 178
environmental impacts, 178
environmental integration, 177
projects, 179
scope, 179
sustainable development, 178
trans-boundary issues, 178
EU as international actor
Bilateral and Inter-regional Agreements, 6
see also **Bilateral and Inter-regional Agreements**
competence, 6–9
see also **Competence; External environmental competence**
constitutional order, 7
development aid, 6
emergence, 6
environmental policy, 5, 6
EU constitutional law, 5
global environmental actor, 5
international commitments, 8, 9
international environmental processes, 6
international law, 5, 6
international legal personality, 6, 7
judicialisation, 8
legalisation, 8
Multilateral Environmental Agreements, 6
see also **Multilateral Environmental Agreements**
negotiating partner, 6
treaty-making powers, 9
EU enlargement
accession
Accession Treaty, 65

applications, 64
assent, 65
decisions, 64
negotiations, 65
partnership, 65, 66
pre-accession period, 65, 66
bilateral association agreement, 65
common values, 64
Copenhagen criteria, 65, 67, 68
enlargement policies, 4
environmental dimension, 64, 66
financial and technical assistance, 66
screening, 65
EU environmental policy
see also **Environmental policy integration**
constitutional dimension, 3, 5
external dimension, 6
EU external relations
see also **EU as international actor**
consensus-building, 283, 287, 282
see also **Consensus-building**
consultation, 134
definition, 133
developing countries, 286
development policies, 4
differentiation, 134
see also **Differentiated approach**
enlargement policies, 4
see also **EU enlargement**
environmental issues
cooperation, 134, 286
integration, 5, 55, 134, 286
multilateralism, 254, 280
policy, 6
priorities, 44, 45
protection, 2, 287
standards, 287
environmental themes
biodiversity, 44, 261, 264, 265
climate change, 44, 258–60
corporate social responsibility, 45
desertification, 44, 45
disclosure of information, 45
forestry, 276
health issues, 44
human rights, 45
natural resources, 44
sustainable use, 44
waste management, 44
external assistance
see **External assistance**
extra-territoriality, 135
financial and technical assistance, 4
financing instruments, 173
horizontal coherence, 55
institutional mechanisms, 134
international legitimacy, 287
natural resources, 2
neo-colonialism, 135
policy documents, 43
policy instruments, 55
policy tools
agriculture, 46
development cooperation, 45
energy, 46
fisheries, 46
industrial policies, 46
trade policy, 45, 46
transport, 46
priorities, 134
sustainable development, 2
third countries, 2–4
trade and environment nexus, 134
trade policy, 45–50
see also **EU external trade policy**
EU external trade policy
common commercial policy, 46, 47
see also **Common commercial policy**
cooperation measures, 49, 50
developing countries, 4
development cooperation
see **Development cooperation**
Doha Ministerial Conference, 48, 49
environmental standards, 49, 50
free trade agreements, 51
Generalised System of Preferences, 4
see also **Generalised System of Preferences**
Global Europe Strategy, 50, 51
international competitiveness, 49–51
international discussions, 47, 48
Lisbon Treaty, 47
market access, 49
product requirements, 49
sustainability impact assessments, 235
see also **Sustainability impact assessments**
trade and environment nexus, 49–51
trade measures
domestic support measures, 48
import/export bans, 48
non-discrimination principle, 49
procurement measures, 48
quantitative restrictions, 49
trade liberalisation, 49, 50
unfair competitive advantage, 49
WTO Committee on Trade and Environment, 47, 48
EU-ACP dialogue
biodiversity, 212
climate change, 212
Council of Ministers, 211
domestic legislative proposals, 213
environmental cooperation, 212
environmental governance, 212
EU external relations, 213
fisheries, 212
informal dialogue, 212

EU-ACP dialogue (*cont.*):
  Joint Parliamentary Assembly, 211–3
  land management, 212
  meetings, 211
  multilateral negotiations, 212, 213
  poverty reduction, 212
  renewables, 212
  structural adjustment programmes, 212
  technology transfer, 212
  water resources, 212
EU-Africa dialogue
  action plan, 214
  biodiversity, 214, 215
  climate change, 214–6
  Energy Dialogue Forum, 215
  environmental cooperation, 214
  forestry, 214, 215
  joint strategy, 214
  meetings, 213, 214
  Millennium Development Goals, 214
  Multilateral Environmental Agreements, 214, 215
  Strategic Partnership with South Africa, 215
  Summits of Heads of State and Government, 213
EU-Asian dialogue
  air pollution, 223
  ASEA regional forum, 222
  Asia-Europe Meeting, 222, 224
  biodiversity, 223
  climate change, 223, 224
  common interests, 224
  energy, 223
  EU-ASEAN Enhanced Partnership, 223
  forestry, 223
  marine environment, 223
  Multilateral Environmental Agreements, 222
  product standards, 223
  sanitary and phytosanitary standards, 223
  sustainable development, 224
  technical barriers to trade, 223
EU-Brazil dialogue
  biodiversity, 222
  biofuel, 222
  climate change, 222
  forest management, 222
  joint action plan, 222
  sustainable development, 222
EU-Canada dialogue
  biodiversity, 227
  bioenergy, 227
  climate change, 227
  exchange of letters, 227
  fisheries, 227
  forestry, 227
  global carbon market, 227
  liberalisation of goods and services, 227
EU-China dialogue
  biodiversity, 225
  climate change, 224, 225
  energy, 225
  environmental cooperation, 225
  environmental governance, 225
  environmental standards, 225
  partnership and cooperation agreement, 224
  pollution control, 225
EU-Japan dialogue
  action plan, 227
  biodiversity, 229
  biotechnology, 226
  climate change, 228
  desertification, 228
  environmental cooperation, 228
  environmental standards, 228
  forestry, 228
  internal environmental regulation, 228
  sustainable consumption/production, 228
  trade barriers, 228
EU-LAC dialogue
  biodiversity, 219, 220
  biofuel, 221
  climate change, 219,220
  desertification, 219
  energy, 219, 220
  environmental governance, 219
  environmental standards, 219
  fisheries, 219
  green technology, 220
  institutional framework, 219
  meetings, 218, 219
  mid-term reviews, 220
  Multilateral Environmental Agreements, 219, 220
  operational targets, 220
  sustainable consumption/production, 219
  water resources, 219
EU-Mexico dialogue
  biofuel, 221
  climate change, 221
  environmental governance, 221
  priority issues, 221
  strategic partnership, 221
Euro-Med dialogues
  Athens Ministerial Conference, 217
  Barcelona process, 216, 218
  climate change, 218
  Environmental Action Programme
    adoption, 216
    areas of action, 216, 217
  environmental law/policy, 216
  European Neighbourhood Policy, 217, 218
  Horizon 2020, 217, 218
  inter-regional cooperation, 216
  joint institutions, 216
  pollution control, 217

priorities, 217
sustainability issues, 218
water resources, 218
Euro-Mediterranean Agreements
approximation of laws, 77
Association Council, 81
Barcelona Declaration, 75, 80
Barcelona process, 75, 76, 78
best-endeavours provisions, 77
bilateral agreements, 75
differentiated approach, 134–6
dispute settlement, 81
environmental cooperation clauses, 77, 78
environmental integration clauses, 77, 79, 80
environmental integration (summary), 141
Euro-Mediterranean Partnership, 75–7
see also **Euro-Mediterranean Partnership**
European Neighbourhood Policy, 76
see also **European Neighbourhood Policy**
exception clauses, 81
institutional aspects, 81
Mediterranean and North African Partners, 75, 76
monitoring, 81
regulatory convergence, 77
trade liberalisation, 80
unilateral measures, 81
Euro-Mediterranean Partnership (EMP)
civil protection, 75, 76
cooperation matters, 76
cultural initiatives, 75
democratic principles, 77
economic cooperation, 77
free trade area, 75, 77
goals, 75
human rights, 75, 77
political ties, 77
pollution control, 75
reform, 75
regional integration, 77
regional/international cooperation, 77
rule of law, 75
security issues, 77
solar energy, 76
sustainable development, 75
trade liberalisation, 77
Union for the Mediterranean, 75
Europe Aid
accountability, 177
function, 177
European Development Fund
African, Caribbean and Pacific Group, 197–9
Cotonou Agreement, 197–9
country strategy papers, 197, 199
financial allocations, 198
financial and technical assistance, 197
funding, 197
implementation, 197
natural resources, 198
regional environmental profiles, 200
regional strategy papers, 197–9
sustainable management, 198
European Neighbourhood and Partnership Instrument (ENPI)
common values, 193
cooperation areas, 193, 194
cross-border cooperation, 194, 195
European Neighbourhood Policy (ENP), 193
see also **European Neighbourhood Policy (ENP)**
implementation, 194
objective, 193
public procurement, 194
sustainable development, 193, 194
European Neighbourhood Policy (ENP)
enhanced cooperation, 76
Lisbon Treaty, 76
privileged relationships, 76
EU-US dialogue
air pollution, 226
biodiversity, 226
climate change, 226
energy, 226
environmental cooperation, 226
environmental integration, 226
exchange of letters, 225
global carbon market, 226
greenhouse gas emissions, 226
New Transatlantic Agenda, 225
Roadmap for Regulatory Cooperation, 226
External assistance
alliance-building, 266
capacity-building, 204
differentiated approach, 204
environmental issues
governance, 190
integration, 201, 203–6
mainstreaming, 203, 205
management, 205, 206
meetings, 177
multilateralism, 266
sustainability, 173, 190
Europe Aid, 177
financial aspect
allocation of funds, 175
ceilings, 174
cooperation, 175
eligibility criteria, 175
financing instruments, 173, 174
framework for programming, 175
headings, 174
indicative financial allocations, 175, 176
multiannual indicative programmes, 175, 176
performance indicators, 175
priority areas, 175, 176

External assistance (*cont.*):
food security, 206
future role, 205, 206
geographic programmes, 174–6
see also **Geographic instruments**
international law, 204
legislative framework, 174, 177, 191
Millennium Development Goals, 205
Multinational Environmental Agreements, 176, 177
parallel aid, 174
policy documents, 173
policy priorities, 204
political commitment, 173
political visibility, 190
preparatory analytical work, 176
procedural guarantees, 205
provision of aid, 173
sustainable development, 205, 206
sustainable energy, 190, 205
thematic funding, 174, 175, 189, 190
see also **Thematic instruments**

External environmental competence
Association Agreements, 57, 58, 60
see also **Association Agreements**
benefits/costs of action, 17
Bilateral and Inter-regional Agreements, 18
see also **Bilateral and Inter-regional Agreements**
climate change, 13
co-decision procedure, 12
conferral principle, 13
decision-making
autonomous measures, 20
conclusion of agreements, 20, 21
Member State control, 20
mixed agreements, 21
national sovereignty, 20, 21
ordinary legislative procedure, 20
unanimity, 20
development cooperation, 52
economic and social development, 17
emergence
active cooperation, 10
Amsterdam Treaty, 12
approximation of laws, 10
First Environmental Action Programme, 10
flexibility clause, 10
international agreements, 9
Lisbon Treaty, 12, 13, 52
Maastricht Treaty, 11–3, 52
Stockholm Conference, 9
treaty-making powers, 10, 11
Treaty of Rome, 9, 11
environmental conditions, 17
environmental protection, 15
explicit competence, 11, 13
flexible approach, 14
historical perspective, 5
implied external competences, 10, 11
margin of appreciation, 13, 14
Multilateral Environmental Agreements (MEAs), 18, 21, 22
see also **Multilateral Environmental Agreements (MEAs)**
ordinary legislative procedure, 12
polluter pays principle, 15–7
precautionary principle, 12, 15, 17
prevention principle, 15, 16
proportionality principle, 14
rectification at source, 15, 16
regional conventions, 23, 24
scientific and technical data, 17
shared nature
complementarity, 20
duty of cooperation, 17, 19
joint participation, 18
mixed agreements, 18, 19
negotiation process, 21
pre-emption doctrine, 17, 18
third parties, 19
treaty-making powers, 18
vertical coherence, 19
subsidiarity principle, 14, 15
substantive scope, 5, 7, 8, 13–7
sustainable development, 12, 13
territorial scope, 14
TFEU provisions, 13–20, 29
see also **Treaty on the Functioning of the European Union (TFEU)**
UN Economic Commission for Europe (UNECE), 23, 24

External relations
see **EU external relations**

External trade policy
see **EU external trade policy**

Fisheries
environmental integration clauses, 70, 79, 89, 90, 104, 105, 120, 137
EU external policy, 46
institutionalised dialogues, 212, 219, 227
Multilateral Environmental Agreements (MEAs), 22
sustainability impact assessments, 245, 247
see also **Sustainability impact assessments**

Food and Agriculture Organisation
EU membership, 7
forest management, 273
REIO clauses, 7

Forestry
see also **Tropical Forest Regulation (EC/2494/2000)**
climate change, 259
deforestation, 275
development cooperation, 196

due diligence, 274
Environment and Sustainable Management of Natural Resources (ENTRP), 186–90
see also **Environment and Sustainable Management of Natural Resources (ENTRP)**
environmental integration clauses, 79, 120
environmental multilateralism, 257
EU action plan, 272
EU external funding, 272
EU external relations, 276
EU internal legislation, 272
FLEGT Regulations, 273–6, 281, 283, 287
Food and Agriculture Organisation, 273
forest governance, 273
global approach, 272
indigenous peoples, 274
institutionalised dialogues, 214, 215, 222, 223, 227–9, 275
international consensus, 273, 275
law enforcement, 273
multilateral consensual measures, 273
REDD-plus, 275, 276
soft law commitments, 272
sustainability impact assessments, 245, 246
see also **Sustainability impact assessments**
sustainable management, 44, 87, 178, 179, 189, 196, 272, 274, 275
tropical timber products, 151–4, 161
Voluntary Partnership Agreements, 273–5

General Agreement on Trade and Tariffs (GATT)
Enabling Clause, 146, 157
EU status, 7
most-favoured nation treatment, 146
tariff treatment
effectiveness, 157
non-discrimination, 157
objectiveness, 157
specific intent, 157
Generalised System of Preferences
beneficiary countries, 144, 148, 152, 155, 157
common commercial policy, 144
developing countries, 145, 148, 152, 169
development policy, 147, 148
differential treatment, 145
differentiation requirement, 157
environmental protection, 147, 148, 169
evolutionary process, 145, 148
good governance, 155, 159, 160, 169
GSP scheme (2001–5)
additional tariff preferences, 149–51, 154
conditionality, 151,153, 155, 156
environmental integration, 150, 151, 170
everything but arms (EBA) initiative, 149
General GSP, 148, 152
general structure, 148
GSP Drugs, 150, 152, 155, 156, 157
GSP Environment, 149–55
GSP Labour, 149, 150, 152, 155
legislative background, 148, 150
MFN-based duties, 148, 151
most favourable GSP treatment, 149
nominal beneficiaries, 148, 152
product coverage, 148, 149
special incentive mechanisms, 149, 150, 155
tariff margins, 148
trade liberalisation, 151
trade restrictions, 153
tropical timber products, 151–4, 161
withdrawal of preferences, 151, 153–5
GSP scheme (2005–11)
duration, 156
everything but arms (EBA) initiative, 156, 159
general guidelines, 156
good governance, 155, 159, 160
special incentive arrangements, 159–68
sustainable development, 155, 158, 159
withdrawal of preferences, 168
historical/legal context, 144
human rights, 169
implementation, 145
India-EU GSP case, 156–8
least-developed countries, 145, 149, 169
market access, 144, 145
origins
GATT/WTO law, 146
North/South trade relations, 146
UNCTAD, 145, 147, 148
unilateral changes, 147
positive trade conditionality, 147
preference tariff treatment, 145, 146
reforms, 155–7
special incentive mechanisms, 147, 149, 150, 157, 159–68
see also **GSP-plus (special incentive arrangement)**
sustainable development, 148, 169
trade and environment nexus, 144
trade sanctions, 158
Genetically modified organisms
biosafety, 44
Geographic instruments
allocation of resources, 201
country strategy papers, 176, 196, 201, 202
development cooperation, 195
differentiation, 204
environmental issues
integration, 191, 201, 202
mainstreaming, 201, 202
profiles, 201–3
sustainability, 202
financing aspect, 175, 176, 203
regional strategy papers, 176t, 196, 201, 202

Global Climate Change Alliance
see also **Climate change**
Africa, 229, 230
Asia, 230
Caribbean, 230
disaster risk reduction, 229
environmental multilateralism, 258, 267
global carbon market, 229
international climate change regime, 229, 230
least-developed countries, 229
objective, 229
reduction in emissions, 229
response measures, 229
small island developing states, 229, 230
Global Europe Strategy
environmental protection, 51
free trade agreements, 50, 51, 98
implementation, 117
international competitiveness, 51
labour standards, 51
trade and investment policies, 51
GSP-plus (special incentive arrangement)
additional tariff preferences, 159, 165, 166
beneficiary countries, 159, 161, 164–7
climate change, 160, 161
eligibility criteria, 159–61, 169–71
good governance, 155, 159, 160
hazardous waste, 160
international agreements, 159–65, 167–9
international standards, 161
least-developed countries, 159
legitimacy, 170–2
limitations, 170
margin of discretion, 161
measure of discretion, 165
monitoring performance, 164, 168–70
procedure for inclusion, 162–4
reporting requirements, 165, 168
scope, 160, 169
sensitive products, 159
suspension, 164
sustainable development, 155, 158, 159
vulnerable countries, 159, 162, 165, 170

Institutionalised dialogues
action plans, 230, 231
ad hoc institutional structures, 209
benefits, 208
collective principles, 210
conclusion of agreements, 209
cooperation clauses, 207, 208
coordination, 210, 211
countries with no common agreement, 207, 209
different forms, 207, 210
differentiated approach, 232
enhanced dialogue, 233
environmental cooperation, 209, 230, 232, 233
environmental priorities, 286
EU external relations
definition, 209
implementation, 209
EU initiative, 208
EU Presidency, 210, 211
EU representation, 210, 211
following up areas of cooperation, 207, 208
high-level meetings, 208, 210, 211
human rights issues, 232
internal environmental legislation, 232
legal relevance, 207
limitations, 207
monitoring, 231
multilateral environmental negotiations, 231
multilateralism, 210, 232
mutual understanding, 286
negotiating positions, 210
opportunities, 207
outside framework of agreement, 207
parties to an association, 207, 208
persuasion/negotiation, 208
policy/regulatory dialogues, 207, 210
significance, 207
sustainability impact assessments, 233, 241
see also **Sustainability impact assessments**
sustainable development, 208
thematic dialogues, 207
third countries/regions, 207, 208
Instrument for Cooperation with High-Income Countries
advanced level of development, 200
areas of cooperation, 201
high-income countries, 200
implementation, 200
resources, 201
strategic partners, 200
Instrument for Pre-Accession Assistance (IPA)
cross-border cooperation, 192
financial framework, 192
human resources development, 192
institution-building, 192
management, 191
multiannual indicative planning documents, 192
multinational strategy, 191
objective, 191
regional development, 192
rural development, 192
sustainable development, 192
transition assistance, 192

Lisbon Treaty
development cooperation, 52
environmental integration requirement, 26, 27
European Neighbourhood Policy, 76
external competence, 12, 13, 52

external trade policy, 47
significance, 2
sustainable development, 2

Millennium Development Goals
commitment, 84–6, 88
environmental sustainability, 54
external assistance, 205
Official Development Assistance, 54
Mining
corporate environmental liability, 279
environmental integration clauses, 133, 137
seabed mining, 22
Multinational Environmental Agreements (MEAs)
biodiversity, 22, 256, 257, 261–5
chemicals, 256, 257
climate change, 21, 22, 256–61
desertification, 22, 256, 257
external assistance, 176, 177
external environmental competence, 18, 21, 22
see also **External environmental competence**
external relations, 255, 256
EU participation, 6, 7, 255–7
financial and technical assistance, 287
fisheries, 22
forestry, 257
hazardous substances, 22
implementation, 4, 53, 214, 215, 219, 220, 244, 255–7, 280, 281, 287
law of the sea, 22, 25
legal status, 21, 24, 25
ozone layer, 22
seabed mining, 22
sustainable development, 41, 42
see also **Sustainable development**
trade-related measures, 48–50

Partnership and Cooperation Agreements
democratic principles, 130
environmental cooperation, 130
Generalised System of Preferences, 130
see also **Generalised System of Preferences**
human rights, 130
institutional structure, 130
market access, 130
political relations, 130
Partnership and Cooperation Agreements with CIS countries
differentiated approach, 134, 135
environmental clause, 117
environmental cooperation, 130
environmental cooperation clauses
alliance-building, 132
approximation of laws, 131
biodiversity, 131
climate change, 131
environmental assessment, 131
pollution control, 131
environmental integration clauses
agriculture, 132
construction, 133
energy, 132, 133
industrial development, 133
mining, 133
organised crime, 133
social cooperation, 132
institutional structure, 130
political/economic relations, 130
trade and investment, 130
Peru
see **Colombia and Peru (COPE FTA)**
Policy integration
see **Environmental policy integration**
Pollution control
air pollution, 223, 226
environmental cooperation clauses, 131
Euro-Mediterranean Partnership, 75
institutionalised dialogues, 217, 223, 225, 226
polluter pays principle, 15–7, 38
Precautionary principle
effect, 15
environmental integration requirement, 29
environmental law, 38
EU external competence, 12, 15, 17
Pre-emption doctrine
external environmental competence, 18
see also **External environmental competence**
substantial harmonisation, 18
Prevention principle
effect, 15
EU external competence, 15, 16
Proportionality principle
EU competence, 8, 14
meaning, 14

Rectification at source
effect, 16
Regional Economic Integration Organisation (REIO)
REIO clauses, 7
Rio Declaration
EU support, 2
influence, 26
sustainable development, 40

South Africa
see **Association with South Africa**
South Korea
see **Agreements with South Korea**
Stabilisation and Association Agreements
approximation of laws, 68, 70, 71, 74
bilateral political relations, 67
Copenhagen criteria, 67, 68

Stabilisation and Association Agreements (*cont.*):
differentiated approach, 134
dispute settlement, 74
economic cooperation, 67
economic integration, 72
environmental commitments, 73
environmental cooperation clauses, 68, 69
environmental integration clauses, 68–70
environmental integration (summary), 141
exception clauses, 73
free movement provisions, 72, 73
free trade, 67, 68, 72, 73
fundamental freedoms, 72
institutional aspects, 73, 74
interpretation, 74
liberalisation of services, 68
monitoring, 73, 74
pre-accession strategy, 67
regional cooperation, 67, 68
regulatory competition, 73
sustainable development, 68
transition to market economy, 67
unilateral measures, 74
Stabilisation and Association Council
composition, 74
powers, 74
role, 73
Stabilisation Association Committee
function, 74
Strategic environmental assessments
development cooperation, 184, 185
environmental cooperation clauses, 69
Subsidiarity principle
EU competence, 8, 14, 15
meaning, 14, 15
Sustainability impact assessments
assessment stage, 240
background, 235
consultants, 236, 249, 251
consultations, 237, 238, 240, 241
decentralised model, 251
development, 235
environmental integration requirement, 234, 235, 239, 240, 242, 252
EU external trade policy, 235
EU practice, 4
ex post assessment outcomes, 252
flanking measures, 236
impact assessments, contrasted, 236, 237
implementation, 234
improvements, 249
information sharing, 241
institutionalised dialogues, 241, 248, 249
integration of results, 238
international organisations, 252
legitimacy, 252
methodology, 239
monitoring measures, 242, 248, 252
national environmental reviews, 240
policy commitment, 234, 235, 237, 249, 253
policy dialogue, 237
political/technical dimension, 235
predictions/outcomes, 242
principles, 240
procedural aspects, 239–42
public participation, 252, 253
public-private partnerships, 238, 242
recommendations, 240
results made public, 240
scoping, 240
screening, 240
SIA Handbook, 239–42
socio-economic/environmental impacts, 234, 235
stakeholder participation, 238–40, 251
substantive outcomes
Association with Central America, 244
biodiversity, 245
biofuels, 246
CARIFORUM-EPA, 243, 248, 249
chemicals, 247
corporate environmental accountability, 247
corporate social responsibility, 247, 248
ecotourism, 246
EU-ACP Group, 243
EU-ASEAN, 244, 246, 249
EU-Chile Association, 242, 243
EU-China, 249
EU-MERCOSUR, 244, 245
EU-Ukraine, 245, 249
financial and technical assistance, 248
fisheries, 245, 247
forestry, 245, 246
FTA-Colombia and Peru, 244, 245
FTA-South Korea, 244
Global Europe Strategy, 244
India, 244, 249
investment/trade facilitation, 245
Multilateral Environmental Agreements, 244
tariff quotas, 245
tariff reductions, 245
trade liberalisation, 245
trade negotiations, 249
sustainable development, 241, 242
timing, 234, 238, 239, 249–51
trade agreements, 234, 235
trade liberalisation, 236, 245
trade-offs, 241, 242
transparency, 237, 240, 241
voluntary nature, 252, 253
Sustainable development
balance of interests, 36, 40
Commission on Sustainable Development, 7

concept, 34, 35
continuous improvement, 38
cooperation agreements, 38
definition, 35–8, 40
development cooperation, 36
different contexts, 36
differentiated approach, 139, 140
economic activity, 35
economic development, 40, 41
economic priorities, 36
environmental cooperation clauses, 68
environmental integration requirement, 25, 40, 41
environmental law, 38
environmental protection, 41
external assistance, 205, 206
flexible approach, 39
fundamental rights, 38
globalisation, 38
good governance, 41
green economy/growth, 39
guidance, 36, 37
inflationary use, 39
institutionalised dialogues, 208
inter-generational equity, 38, 41
international law, 40
intra-generational equity, 38, 41
Johannesburg Plan of Implementation, 41
jurisprudential approach, 35, 36
multidimensional aspect, 41
Multinational Environmental Agreements (MEAs), 41, 42
see also **Multinational Environmental Agreements (MEAs)**
natural resources, 52
policy formation, 36
policy integration, 38
Principles for Sustainable Development, 37, 38
Rio + 20, 39
Rio Declaration, 40
social development, 41
stimulus for debate, 39
Sustainable Development Strategy, 37–9, 44, 45
sustainable use, 41
sustainability impact assessments, 241, 242
see also **Sustainability impact assessments**
trade and environment nexus, 139, 140
treaty-based provisions, 35, 42
UN Conference, 2
World Summit on Sustainable Development, 36, 37

Thematic instruments
differentiation, 204
financing aspect, 175, 177
funding priorities, 177

Tourism
environmental integration clauses, 80, 105, 112, 114, 137
Trade policy
see EU trade policy
Transport
environmental integration clauses, 70, 71, 112, 114, 120, 121, 137
Treaties
environmental dimension, 3
foreign policy-making, 3
treaty-making powers, 9, 18
Treaty on the Functioning of the European Union (TFEU)
Article 11
analysis, 3, 5, 28–31
common objectives, 42, 43
complementarity, 20, 42
consistency provisions, 42, 43
cooperation policies, 43
decision-making process, 55
definition element, 173
enforceability, 32, 33
environmental integration requirement, 1, 5, 13, 25, 28, 34, 42, 54–6, 285–7
environmental policy, 29–32
environmental protection, 54–6
financing regulations, 173
horizontal coherence, 42, 43, 285
implementation element, 174
implications, 32, 33
interpretation, 5, 30–2
judicial approach, 32, 33
legal relevance, 5
legal strength, 29, 30, 32
legislative/policy implementation, 30, 31
mandatory terms, 29
objectives, 28, 29, 31
policy coherence, 42
procedural dimension, 28, 30
scope, 28, 30, 32
significance, 3, 28
substantive integration, 28, 30
sustainable development, 34, 35
external competence
Article 191, 13–20, 29, 31, 33
Article 192, 20
Article 218, 20
objectives
human health, 13
quality of the environment, 13
utilisation of natural resources, 13
Tropical Forest Regulation (EC/2494/2000)
adoption, 178
development planning, 178
environmental integration, 177
projects, 180
scope, 179

Tropical Forest Regulation (EC/2494/2000) (*cont.*):
status of forests, 178
sustainable management, 178, 179, 189

United Nations General Assembly
EU status, 7

Waste disposal
environmental integration clauses, 80
hazardous waste, 160
radioactive materials, 80
Water resources
development cooperation, 196
sustainable management, 183, 186, 189
World Intellectual Property Organisation (WIPO)
folklore, 105
intellectual property, 105
traditional knowledge, 105
World Trade Organisation
Committee on Trade and Environment, 47, 48
eco-labelling, 50
environmental measures, 49–51
EU membership, 7
India-EU GSP case, 156–8
protectionism, 49
WTO law, 146